D1736626

THE BUSINESS MEETINGS SOURCEBOOK

THE BUSINESS MEETINGS SOURCEBOOK

A Practical Guide to Better Meetings and Shared Decision Making

Eli Mina

AMACOM
American Management Association
New York • Atlanta • Brussels • Buenos Aires • Chicago • London • Mexico City
San Francisco • Shanghai • Tokyo • Toronto • Washington, D.C.

Special discounts on bulk quantities of AMACOM books are available to corporations, professional associations, and other organizations. For details, contact Special Sales Department, AMACOM, a division of American Management Association, 1601 Broadway, New York, NY 10019.
Tel.: 212-903-8316. Fax: 212-903-8083.
Web site: www.amanet.org

Library of Congress Cataloging-in-Publication Data

Mina, Eli.
The business meetings sourcebook : a practical guide to better meetings and shared decision making / Eli Mina.
p. cm.
Includes bibliographical references and index.
ISBN 0-8144-0670-X
1. Business meetings. 2. Group decision making. 3. Teams in the workplace. I. Title.
HF5734.5 .B87 2002
658.4'56—dc21 *2002001079*

Printing number

10 9 8 7 6 5 4 3 2 1

Contents

PREFACE

I began serving as a professional meeting facilitator and management consultant in 1984, and have been fascinated by the complexities of this work ever since. As my practice evolved, my clients and seminar participants presented me with a seemingly never-ending set of questions and challenges to address. This process has been enlightening and has forced me to continually develop my thinking.

My purpose in this book is to pass on to you the practical lessons I've learned and the tools I've developed through my facilitation, consulting, and training assignments. The tools I present should be immediately usable by the corporate or civic leader who facilitates or participates in meetings and who leads shared decision-making processes.

So what will this book do for you? Naturally, the first set of tools you might expect from a book on meetings relates to planning and managing meetings, and, yes, this book gives you plenty of them. However, if this were all I gave you, my advice would be of limited use, and would address only a part of your task.

To consider your leadership challenge more holistically, we must first consider the tools required to build a healthy foundation for shared decision making. Without this foundation, truly meaningful meetings would be impossible to achieve.

Just what do I mean by "a foundation for shared decision making" and why is it important? Here are four examples of well-run meetings, where the outcomes are undermined by a flawed foundation:

First, let's consider strategic planning workshops. Such sessions are invariably very exciting and invigorating. Participants leave optimistic and confident and ready to make changes in their organizations. But how long does this enthusiasm last? I make it my habit to contact past clients to check how much of a difference a workshop made. Often the answer is enthusiastic: "Yes, we are putting the ideas to work, and the workshop has been a real benefit." But other times the answer is: "Yes, it was a great session. But when we tried to persuade our CEO to implement the ideas, he would have none of it." This raises an important question: What tools do you need to "manage upwards," to ensure that your meetings and decisions are taken seriously?

Second, let's consider a management team that meets and agrees on policy changes that profoundly affect employees. Upon attempting to implement the changes, managers encounter resistance from the staff. Some of them indeed follow their leaders obediently. But many follow reluctantly. Others undermine the changes, and others leave. That situation leads to this question: What tools do you need to manage "downwards," so those who will implement the decisions made in your meetings will do so willingly and enthusiastically, because they want to and not because you tell them to?

Third, let's consider a government agency that decides to consult community stakeholders about a proposed project. Community consultation meetings are productive, but part of the consensus cannot be responsibly implemented and is therefore rejected. Upon learning about this, stakeholders get angry and go to the media with allegations of tokenism and dishonesty. They thought that their input was binding, and were never told of it being only advisory. Yes, the meetings were productive, but the overall result was negative. This creates another question to answer: What tools do you need to ensure that expectations of external stakeholders are consistent with yours?

And finally, let's consider a committee that is given a loosely defined assignment. It then holds productive meetings, conducts research, makes commitments, and spends money. It comes back a few months later with what it believes to be sound recommendations, only to be criticized for acting irresponsibly, spending money recklessly, and exceeding its authority. The question that arises from this situation is: What tools do you need to make sure your committee's mandate is sound, accountability is maintained, disputes do not develop, and time and resources are not squandered?

By providing answers to the questions raised in the above four examples, this book gives you tools to build a solid foundation for shared decision making. These tools will help you manage "upwards," "downwards," and "sidewards," and make your group's consensus-building efforts more meaningful.

After giving you the tools to build a healthy foundation for shared decision making, my next step is to give you practical tools with which to plan and run good meetings. The challenges you may face are domination by outspoken members, an inappropriate focus, an adversarial climate, and more. Let me elaborate on some of the meeting management tools that this book offers.

A frequent frustration with meetings is that "the playing field is uneven." Talented but unassertive individuals just won't speak up. On the other hand, experienced and outspoken members dominate and take up most of the time. As a result, people leave a meeting frustrated and dissatisfied, and, in the absence of their input at the meeting, narrow-sighted decisions are made. What tools do you need to "even the playing field," "rein in" dominant members, and capitalize on the talents of quieter ones? How do you convert passive spectators into active and empowered contributors?

Another serious meeting ailment is squandered time: 90 percent of a meeting's time is often spent on minutiae and only 10 percent on significant and relevant issues. Items that have little or no relevance to the group's mandate often appear on the agenda. What tools do you need to focus a meeting on the things that are significant and make the meeting truly beneficial? How do you ensure that meeting time is properly allocated and spent?

Sometimes you find a meeting becoming a war zone, with members entrenched in adversarial positions, attacking, accusing, and blaming one another, being verbally abusive, trying to figure out how they can overpower others, and all but forgetting to pay attention to the group's mandate. What tools do you need to turn your contentious meeting from a war zone into a construction zone, and convert it from a problem into an opportunity? What tools will help you motivate the members to listen to one another and build win-win solutions that will work for the organization as a whole?

The list goes on: What tools do you need to deal effectively with a complex issue? How do you balance the need for creative and free-flowing discussions with the need to move forward on the agenda? How do you make your meetings more interesting, engaging, and even fun? How do you encourage creative thinking and innovative solutions, unconstrained by past traditions?

This book contains practical and proven tools to answer these questions, and to address these challenges and many more. I hope your organization will benefit from it. No one deserves the pain and agony of confusing and monotonous meetings, nor the acrimony that comes from dysfunctional relationships and communication breakdowns. Given your expenditure of time, money, and other resources in meetings and consensus-building efforts, you, your group, and your organization deserve substantial returns on this investment. Insist on them.

Dedication

I dedicate this book to my parents for instilling in me the values of hard work and loyalty and for inspiring me to demand excellence of myself and others; to my in-laws for being the most enthusiastic supporters of my work; and to my wife Michelle, who always manages to find infinite amounts of patience to listen to my progress reports and give me feedback on my work. I have been blessed with a great family that has helped me shape and refine my ideas.

Acknowledgment

It would have been impossible to write this book without the many unique assignments that my clients have given me. I am grateful to them for their trust and respect and for the confidence they have placed in me. I thank them for being prepared to learn from me and to teach me many valuable lessons, and for helping me turn my work from an occupation into a passion and a mission.

THE BUSINESS MEETINGS SOURCEBOOK

INTRODUCTION

This book is intended to assist corporate and civic leaders in planning and facilitating meetings and consensus-building efforts. It is much more than a meetings book. A major portion of it shows you how to create a healthy foundation for your group's consensus-building efforts. Once the foundation is set, the book gives you tools to respond to the many challenges of planning and running meetings.

This book is highly practical. In writing it I assumed that you are a busy manager or executive who needs practical and proven tools for immediate use, without spending much time analyzing theoretical concepts. The book is based on many years of hands-on experience of planning and facilitating meetings and consensus-building efforts, ranging from peaceful and harmonious settings to ones that are complex, controversial, and dysfunctional. I am sharing the lessons learned from both the successes and failures I've had as a professional meeting facilitator and procedural adviser.

The need for this book arises from the increasing appetite of organizations to shift from "telling people what to do" to empowering and involving them in corporate decision making. The idea of including individuals in participatory decision making is not new and is great in theory, but it often fails miserably on the ground. There is growing cynicism towards "pretend democracies," where managers claim to be inclusive, but use their clout to impose the decisions that really count. The other extreme is when corporate democracy becomes a free-for-all, with all accountability lost and with vocal minorities getting their way, leaving the manager and others wondering what went wrong.

Is there a place for meaningful but responsible democracy in your meetings and corporate decision making? Is corporate democracy desirable and, if so, is your management team truly ready to embrace it? Are you ready to manage the risks of letting go of control and empowering staff to make or influence decisions? Conversely, are your staff members ready to operate more proactively? Are they willing to let go of the dependency on others for leadership? Will they take more initiative? Will they pay the price of the greater accountability that comes with higher levels of empowerment?

And if you already have a degree of democracy in your organization, how meaningful is it? Do you have an accurate reading of the pulse of the majority, or are you governed by the most vocal and outspoken individuals? Are participants in your meetings speaking up, and is their input genuinely making a difference? Are their collective recommendations taken seriously? How often and to what degree is their consensus embraced and implemented?

And just what does corporate democracy mean in your organization? Does it mean you do everything that staff wants you to do, making it a free-for-all? What can you do to balance the need to benefit from the talents and expertise of staff and stakeholders with the need to maintain accountability and make responsible and profitable decisions?

The above questions must be addressed at the highest levels of your organization and at each decision-making level. The answers to these questions will determine which of the tools offered in this book should be used and the degree to which they will apply.

In my view, there is a need and a place for responsible democracy in corporations, even though chief executive officers are not elected by their subordinates, and even though managers often have the full power to act without consultation. If well managed, corporate democracy can help you boost the quality of your decisions by capitalizing on the knowledge and expertise of individuals. It can also increase staff loyalty and commitment to the organization and its mandate. But to truly gain from corporate democracy you need tools to reap its benefits while managing the risks associated with it.

This book offers tools to help you establish a healthy, meaningful, and responsible democracy in your own team and your entire organization. Using these tools, you should be able to engage your staff and stakeholders in discussions and decision making, while maintaining accountability and ensuring that responsible, credible, and durable corporate decisions are made.

The types of tools you'll find in this book include:

- ▲ Proven ideas and tips to turn problems into opportunities
- ▲ Scripts for managing meetings
- ▲ Scripts to deal with difficult people and challenging situations
- ▲ Tables and checklists
- ▲ Assessment tools
- ▲ Case studies

Some of the tools in this book are accompanied by an explanation of the suggested approach and its effects. In other instances, such as the many scripts offered, my approach is implied in the tool itself and no detailed explanation or analysis is given.

This book is not meant to be read cover to cover in one stretch and then filed away on your shelf. It is meant to be used as a reference on an ongoing basis. I suggest you experiment with some tools and ideas, and then come back for more. Some of the ideas will be useful in the immediate term, some you'll need to modify, some will be useful later, and some will not apply to your meetings in their present form. Improving your meetings should be an evolutionary, not a revolutionary, process.

Here are some of the things this book will not give you:

- ▲ This book does not cover rules of order for formal meetings, in which motions, amendments, points of order, and other formal procedures are used. If you need ideas on how to simplify, demystify, and humanize the rules of order and parliamentary procedure, you may want to review Chapter 7 in *The Complete Handbook of Business Meetings* (AMACOM, 2000).
- ▲ Although this book addresses sensitive issues like personal conflict of interest, confidentiality, and "in-camera" meetings, it does not offer legal advice. I am not a lawyer, and I therefore focus only on the practical impacts of these sensitive issues on meetings and consensus building.
- ▲ As tempting as it may be, I cannot claim this book is an all-inclusive encyclopedia of ideas and tools to improve your meetings and consensus-building efforts. I fully anticipate that, by the time the book is published, I will have chaired many more meetings and will have led many more training programs, which will undoubtedly expand my inventory of tools and ideas. However, I expect the fundamentals and the principles behind my approach to remain the same.

The book is structured as follows:

- ▲ Part 1 (Chapters 1 to 7) includes tools to build a healthy foundation for consensus building and shared decision making.
- ▲ Part 2 (Chapters 8 to 18) includes tools with which to plan and manage meetings.
- ▲ The two appendixes include case studies that show you how the approach given in this book can be used to deal with challenging and complex situations.

Eli Mina's Guiding Principles for Meetings and Consensus Building

- ▲ A healthy meeting may be impossible to achieve if the organization itself is not healthy.
- ▲ The success of a meeting is ultimately measured by the quality of the decisions made in it.
- ▲ The process of reaching a collective decision is just as important as the decision itself.
- ▲ In a good meeting everyone arrives at the same destination at the same time, as proactive and enthusiastic partners, not as reluctant neighbors.
- ▲ Your challenge in a meeting is to create the right balance between inclusiveness and efficiency.
- ▲ Never attribute to malice what can be attributed to a misunderstanding or systemic problem.
- ▲ To truly gain control, a leader must know how to share control and build partnerships.
- ▲ It is much easier to be a critic and oppose something than to be a creator and propose a better alternative.
- ▲ We were given two ears and one mouth, so we could listen at least twice as much as we speak.
- ▲ Diversity of opinions is something to celebrate. An opposing view or a piece of criticism should not be seen as a threat, but as another piece of the bigger truth.

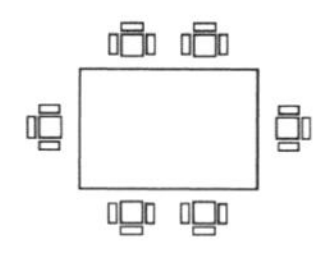

Part One:

Building the Foundation for Shared Decision Making

Healthy meetings are impossible unless you have a healthy organization and a solid foundation for shared decision making. Without such a foundation, problems and disputes can plague your team and make your meetings dysfunctional.

When people look for the causes of difficulties in meetings, they are often tempted to point a finger of blame at individuals. But this is likely to be a mistake. Even the most capable individuals will flounder in an environment that brings out the worst in them. Before you point the finger at individuals, it is imperative to examine the foundation for decision making and see if difficulties can be attributed to systemic flaws.

Part 1 of this book describes the various building blocks that must be in place if your team is to work effectively on its given mandate. If all building blocks are in place, you will have a solid foundation for your consensus building efforts. Here are some of the benefits of having such a foundation in place:

- With a clear and compelling mandate, your team will be better focused on its core issues and less likely to be distracted by side issues.
- A well-developed workplan will make it easier for you to measure progress. With it, your team will be better positioned to make a difference, and its work will be more meaningful.
- With your team well selected, oriented, and supported, everyone will work cohesively towards achieving your mandate. You will be less likely to have "bad apples" and "loose cannons" on it, and you will be less vulnerable when key individuals leave.
- With clearly defined roles and responsibilities, the likelihood of interpersonal tensions and disputes will be reduced.
- With harmonious relationships with internal and external stakeholders, your work will be taken seriously. Your team will be more likely to be supported and less likely to be undermined by outside parties affected by its work.

Building the foundation for shared decision making is a complex and time-consuming task. It is like knitting a quilt. You build each piece first. You then assemble all the pieces, create a new entity, and ensure the final product will endure the rigorous tests and pressures of challenging realities.

For your foundation and relationship-building efforts to succeed in both the short and long terms, two conditions should be met:

1. Your team members should be involved in constructing the foundation for shared decision making. They should want "to live in this building" and not be forced to do so ("because it's their job"). You can involve them in developing your mandate and workplan (Chapter 3), rules of engagement (Chapter 5), and code of ethics (Chapter 6). You may even want to involve them in selecting new team members (Chapter 4).
2. Once set, the foundation for shared decision making will require maintenance, upgrades, and renovations. Like a building, it will be put through tests (such as disputes and controversies). These tests may point to systemic weaknesses, such as unrealistic mandates and schedules, and confusing roles and responsibilities. You will need to keep an eye out for such weaknesses and make appropriate changes to the foundation.

Part 1 gives you tools to assemble the following building blocks of your team's shared decision-making process:

▲ Chapter 1 explains the goals and parameters of shared decision making and gives you tools to assess your team's consensus-building efforts.

▲ Chapter 2 describes the team's leader as a critical building block for the consensus-building efforts. It describes the many hats a facilitator may be required to wear. It offers tools and principles that will help you lead your team to quality decision making. It shows how you can address the various challenges you may encounter along the way.

▲ Chapter 3 explains how to negotiate your team's mandate with your boss and make it clear, realistic, and compelling. It outlines the steps to establish your workplan and the resources needed for your team's efforts.

▲ Chapter 4 includes the criteria and tools for selecting, orienting, and nurturing your team and each one of its members.

▲ Chapter 5 describes the rules of engagement your team might need. It explains how to establish and maintain accountability, conflict of interest and confidentiality guidelines, and the various parameters of formal voting.

▲ Chapter 6 includes sets of affirmations, reflecting your group's values, ethics, and culture. You can customize the affirmations to your group's needs. Once you've done this, each team member should confirm that she or he is prepared to live by these affirmations.

▲ Chapter 7 gives you tools to build and maintain relationships with internal and external stakeholders. It explains how to manage "upwards" and build the relationship with your boss. It then discusses how to build relationships with other stakeholders.

With a strong, tested, and well-maintained foundation for shared decision making, and having this foundation endorsed by each team member, you will be ready for the tools to plan and manage your meetings. These tools are given in Part 2 of this book (Chapters 8 to 18).

ONE

Goals and Parameters of Shared Decision Making

Shared decision making (SDM) takes place when a corporate decision is made or at least influenced by more than one individual or group. SDM is a form of corporate democracy.

SDM should be applied in a measured and responsible manner. It is not practical nor is it desirable to have every corporate decision made democratically, since not every decision can or should wait for the deliberate and measured involvement of all those who might be affected. Many decisions must be made by the manager who will be held accountable for them, and delegating such decisions to a team would be irresponsible. SDM should not become a free-for-all in which everyone gets what they want and accountability is lost.

If applied responsibly, SDM can boost the quality of corporate decisions and increase the understanding, acceptance, and support of those decisions. If staff and stakeholders are engaged in the decision-making process in some way, they are less likely to resist change and are more likely to embrace it as active and enthusiastic partners and not as reluctant followers. SDM can save time, money, and other resources, and can advance the organization towards its goals.

This chapter covers the following topics:

- Defining the goals of corporate decision making
- Defining your vision of shared decision making
- Choosing among four decision-making models
- Using SDM parameters to make collective decisions

DEFINING THE GOALS OF CORPORATE DECISION MAKING

Whether you make a corporate decision unilaterally or facilitate shared decision making, you should be attempting to achieve the same *substantive* and *process-related* goals.

Substantive Goals

First, you need to consider the decision itself. Substantively, a corporate decision should be:

- *Mandate- and Service-Driven.* The decision advances the organization's mandate and serves its stakeholders in the most substantial and effective manner.
- *Proactive, Visionary, and Durable.* The decision addresses not only short-term crises, but also focuses on long-term needs and emerging trends and on what must be done to make the organization viable and thriving for years to come.
- *Balanced, Holistic, and Credible.* The decision is based on complete information and balances as many legitimate needs and interests as possible. As many "pieces of the truth" as possible are taken into account before the decision is finalized.
- *Creative and Thoughtful.* The decision reflects creative thinking, unconstrained by past traditions and precedents. The quality of the decision earns the respect of all internal and external parties who are affected by the decision.
- *Affirmative.* The decision is focused not only on what is to be prevented but also on what needs to be accomplished.
- *Logical and Responsible.* The decision is realistic and can be implemented by using available or attainable resources (fiscal, human, and other resources).

Process-Related Goals

Looking beyond the decision itself, you need to consider the manner in which the decision is made. Your corporate decision-making process should be:

- *Measured, Deliberate, and Gradual.* The decision is not rushed through, especially if it has significant impacts or if the issues are complex or controversial. Sufficient time and efforts are allocated to scrutinizing the decision and its impacts, and enhancing the quality of the decision. It is sometimes wise to "test-run" the decision before finalizing it.
- *Efficient.* The decision is reached in a reasonably efficient manner, conserving time, money, and other corporate resources and maximizing the return on investment (ROI) in meetings and other consensus-building activities.
- *Inclusive.* Parties that will be affected by the decision are kept informed and, where appropriate, involved in shaping the decision in some way. This increases the likelihood that everyone will reach the same destination together, as willing and enthusiastic partners, and not as reluctant and acquiescent followers.

Assignment: Assessing Your Corporate Decisions

Consider a significant corporate decision that you recently made or facilitated. Use the following questions to help evaluate the extent to which the substantive and process-related goals were met. Use your answers to determine what has worked and which areas require improvement.

- How responsible, credible, and durable was the decision?
- Did you take into account all significant data?
- To what extent did the decision advance your organization's mandate?
- Did you only try to prevent something from happening, or did your decision also make an affirmative difference?
- Did you consider long-term needs and emerging trends in making the decision?
- Does the decision reflect creativity and visionary thinking outside the box?
- How measured was the decision-making process? Did you allow enough time to explore all relevant information, or was the process rushed?
- Did you take into account impacts on stakeholders?
- Did you keep all stakeholders "in the loop"? Did you give them early warnings of the decision?

- Did you actively look for stakeholder feedback before the decision was finalized? Did you leave anyone out of the process?
- How many affected people and parties understood and embraced the decision?
- How many parties resisted the decision? Did this resistance have a negative impact on implementation?
- How much of the resistance can be attributed to the quality of the decision?
- How much of the resistance can be attributed to the manner in which the decision was made (in a hurry, with no advance warning, with inadequate consultation, behind closed doors)?
- In the end, was the decision fully implemented, or was it derailed by authority figures or by assertive stakeholders?

DEFINING YOUR VISION OF SHARED DECISION MAKING

Some corporate decisions need to be made unilaterally and some democratically. This section assumes that stakeholders are engaged in some form of shared decision making. Examples of this type of decision making include:

- A CEO consults with the senior management team about cost-cutting measures.
- Management forms a staff committee to recommend computer security measures.
- Management initiates a staff consultation program on improving customer service.
- A municipality forms a stakeholder committee to give it advice on a rezoning proposal.

There is an old adage: "If you don't know where you are going, any road will take you there." If you engage others in shared decision making, you need a vision of how the process will unfold and what characteristics it will have. You need to know what to avoid and what to create. The following subsections cover the characteristics of the overall SDM process as well as the traits of an effective SDM leader and participant.

Characteristics of the Overall Shared Decision-Making Process

A shared decision-making process should be:

- *Clear.* Participants in the process understand its mandate and long-term agenda. They are also aware of the limitations on their authority and decision-making powers, and are unlikely to develop unfounded expectations.
- *Logical.* The process engages only participants who have knowledge, expertise, talents, and skills that can enhance the decisions, and who will also be affected by the decisions and be involved in implementation duties.
- *Appropriate.* Only issues that stand to benefit from collective input are referred to the group. Decisions in which the participants have no interest or have no useful input to offer are made unilaterally.
- *Meaningful.* Participants are involved at an early stage. They receive advance warnings of proposed changes, well before they are finalized, so they can truly be a part of defining the problem and forming the solution. There are no predetermined outcomes.
- *Majority-Directed.* Decisions are based on broad input. Domination by outspoken members or assertive minorities is avoided. Silence is not seen as approval. Deliberate efforts are made to integrate the views of the "silent majority" into the decisions.
- *Diverse.* A variety of methods are used to build group consensus, including team meetings, virtual meetings (see Chapter 16), customer interviews, meetings with community groups, focus groups, and other techniques as appropriate.

Traits of an Effective Shared Decision-Making Leader

Having described your vision of the overall SDM process, you need to consider the traits of an effective SDM leader. An SDM leader should be:

- *Diverse.* Able to wear the many hats of a team facilitator (see Chapter 2).
- *Confident and Firm.* Knows the group's mandate and is firmly entrenched in it. Confidently and calmly leads the group. Knows the members, brings out the best in them, capitalizes on their skills, knowledge, and expertise, and guides them to deliver the greatest value for the organization.

- *Able to Delegate and Share Control.* Is prepared to let go of control and delegate important leadership tasks to others (a good succession planner). Facilitates shared decision making, instead of imposing decisions on the group without any input.
- *Creative.* Able to both consider and conceive unconventional and innovative solutions and encourage others to do the same.
- *Proactive and Visionary.* Identifies not only what should be prevented but also what should be created. Takes initiative and makes things happen, instead of waiting for them to happen. Deals proactively with emerging disputes instead of ignoring them and hoping that they will take care of themselves.
- *A Mentor, Coach, and Team Builder.* Challenges each individual to excel, overcome self-imposed limitations, and contribute as a member of a cohesive team. Is a reliable and dependable source of personal support for each team member.
- *Humble and Eager to Learn.* Is a superb listener who is genuinely interested in hearing what others have to offer and in helping to integrate it into the consensus-building process. Invites and welcomes feedback and, regardless of how harsh it may seem; takes it as a gift and an opportunity to learn.
- *Courageous.* Able to say "no" respectfully but firmly. Capable of soft but confident assertion with a subordinate and also with an authority figure. Shows sensitivity and respect to individuals, but stands firm on objective principles.
- *Majority-Driven.* Balances the rights of individuals to be heard with the right of the group to make progress, thereby avoiding domination by stubborn individuals or aggressive minorities.
- *Objective.* Maintains a broad perspective on issues.
- *Articulate.* Communicates clearly, concisely, and convincingly.
- *Lighthearted and Ego-Free*: Is not driven by his or her ego and has a healthy but appropriate sense of humor: "Take yourself lightly, but take your work seriously."

Assignment: Rate Yourself as a Shared Decision-Making Leader

With the above description in mind, consider the questions in the following table. Rate your satisfaction level on a scale of 0 (could not be worse) to 10 (could not be better) for each of the groups of questions. Use the results to determine your strengths and the areas that require improvement.

Questions about you as an SDM leader:	The ratings (0 to 10): 0 = Could not be worse 10 = Could not be better
How confident and firm are you?	
Are you able to keep meetings on track and on time?	
Are you able to stick to your group's mandate?	
Do you get distracted by members bickering over side issues?	
How well do you know the strengths and weaknesses of each member? Are you able to bring out the best in them?	
Do you tend to want absolute control over everything?	
Do you share the credit for good things or do you keep it to yourself?	
Do you impose decisions or do you facilitate decision making?	
Have you ever been accused of not knowing how to delegate?	
Do you save the interesting tasks for yourself, or do you teach others how to do them?	
How creative and open-minded are you to fresh and new ideas?	
Do you often find obstacles to new or "off the wall" ideas?	
Which do you try to do more of: prevent bad things from happening or make good things happen?	
Do you tend to ignore rumors and signs of conflict, or do you address them proactively?	
Do you find yourself making things happen, watching things happen, or having no idea what happened?	

Questions about you as an SDM leader:	The ratings (0 to 10): 0 = Could not be worse 10 = Could not be better
Are you sensitive to the needs of your members to develop their skills?	
Do you challenge your members to perform their best or even better?	
Are you able to get your members to work as members of a cohesive team?	
Are you able to deal effectively with renegade members and "loose cannons"?	
How well do you listen?	
Do you find yourself talking a lot in meeting and lecturing to people?	
Do you find yourself saying "yes, but" often? Have you been accused of pretending to listen, and then ignoring what was said?	
Do you take feedback defensively and instinctively deny its validity?	
Do you make it easy for subordinates and bosses alike to give you feedback?	
Can you assert yourself without getting angry?	
Are you a super-nice person and do you find it hard to say no?	
Are you easy to manipulate?	
Are you able to rein in dominant members and engage "the silent majority"?	
Are you able to introduce objectivity and broader perspectives to discussions?	
Do you get threatened easily?	

Do you enjoy your work?	
Have you ever been told that you're too serious and should lighten up?	
Total Score	

Use the following key to interpret your score on the team leader rating worksheet:

If your overall score as a team leader is:	Consider this:
0 to 50	You've got some work to do. If you are passive and hesitant and always try to be "nice," you need to "toughen your backbone," learn to say no graciously but firmly, give honest and constructive feedback, and be more decisive. On the other hand, if you are too aggressive, dominant, and controlling, learn to let go of the need for absolute control, and empower those who follow your lead to perform their best.
51 to 70	This is where most leaders find themselves. You probably show some leadership, but are not "in touch and in tune" with your team members to the degree they and the organization need you to be. Identify your specific strengths and work to reinforce your weak spots.
71 to 85	You are doing well. You know how to balance the need for control with the need to let go and make room for others to shine. You need to go beyond just "getting the job done." Become a visionary and strive for excellent (not just adequate) results. Build a team of individuals who will be there because they want to, not only because it's their job.
86 to 100	You are a rare breed. There aren't many people who can honestly claim such a high leadership standard. You bring out the best in others and lead to solid and long-lasting collective

If your overall score as a team leader is:	Consider this:
	decisions. You are probably in the enviable position of having good people clamoring to join your team. Your greatest enemy is likely to be boredom or frustration that others don't always display your level of excellence, so you need to be patient and allow for changes to happen at their own pace. It's likely you work well with your own team members, but you may need to work to building relationships with outside stakeholders (see Chapter 7).

Traits of an Effective Team Member

Having defined your vision of the SDM process and the traits of an effective SDM leader, you need to consider the traits of an SDM team member. An SDM team member should be:

- ▲ *A Team Player*. Works together with others and helps to bring out the best in them. Avoids domination and helps to make room for others to shine.
- ▲ *Conscientious, Reliable, and Consistent*. Attends meetings regularly and participates fully in them and in other consensus-building activities. Keeps promises and delivers quality work and documents every time.
- ▲ *A Good Listener*. Is open-minded and is prepared to listen and learn from others. Invites feedback, takes it nondefensively, and treats it as a gift and an opportunity to learn, even if it is given in a harsh tone.
- ▲ *Courageous and Prepared to Question Conventional Wisdom*. Is able to offer fresh ideas, despite potential resistance to them. Is prepared to share feedback and raise critical questions about issues and proposals, regardless of how unpopular this may be. Gives feedback in a manner that makes it easy for others to receive.
- ▲ *Proactive*. Shows independent initiative but works within the context of a team. Is prepared to step into leadership positions or to let go of them when needed.

See Chapter 4 for ideas on selecting, orienting, and nurturing your team.

Assignment: Rate Your Shared Decision-Making Team Members

With the above description in mind, consider the questions in the following table to evaluate each member of your SDM team. Rate your satisfaction level on a scale of 0 (could not be worse) to 10 (could not be better). Use the results to determine the strengths of your team members and the areas that require improvement.

Questions about a team member:	The ratings (0 to 10): 0 = Could not be worse 10 = Could not be better
A team player or a "loose cannon"? Supportive of others and sensitive to them?	
Does not dominate meetings, and creates room for others to participate?	
Does not take unauthorized action without consulting the leader or the team first?	
Avoids building cliques?	
Is not possessive of the spotlight?	
Shares the credit for achievements?	
Delivers quality results and documents every time?	
Attends meetings, arrives early, and stays for the full duration?	
Keeps promises to perform follow-up duties and meets specified schedules?	
Listens to others?	
Is open-minded to other ideas, as opposed to having many "yes, but" arguments?	
Is always eager to learn and improve his or her performance?	
Takes feedback nondefensively, regardless of how harsh it is?	

Questions about a team member:	The ratings (0 to 10): 0 = Could not be worse 10 = Could not be better
Treats feedback as a gift and an opportunity to learn?	
Is not afraid to share an "off the wall" idea?	
Is not afraid to raise unpopular questions about proposals?	
Is prepared to raise a concern about the way a meeting is run?	
Shares feedback regularly, and does it in a way which makes it easy to receive it?	
Is like a breath of fresh air?	
Steps in when needed, or waits for someone else to take the initiative?	
Is prepared to take on leadership positions?	
Total Score	

The following key will help you interpret the score you gave your team member in the above evaluation.

If your team member's overall score is:	Consider this:
0 to 25	You've got some work to do with this member. The individual is either too timid or too aggressive. Either way, the group's decision-making process is not benefiting from the insights and expertise of all members (due to nonparticipation or, conversely, domination and

	intimidation). Work with this person to optimize his or her participation. Don't assume that entrenched behavior patterns cannot be changed, and don't be intimidated by the member's personality or tenure with the organization. Focus on objective issues, such as counterproductive behaviors and the overall needs of the organization.
26 to 40	This is where most team members will be. This member probably does an acceptable job, but is not motivated or positioned to advance the decision-making process in an excellent manner. You need to work with this member to boost his or her motivation. Give him or her assignments that will test and expand his or her skills, and call on him or her to speak in meetings (even if he or she is not asking to do this). Remember to celebrate successes, too.
41 to 50	You are truly lucky to have this individual on your team, but don't take her or him for granted. Stay in touch, find out what will continue to bring the best in this person, express appreciation for jobs well done, give opportunities to represent the team and shine publicly, and delegate leadership opportunities (make her or him a part of your succession planning). Remember to recognize such individuals and reward them for special contributions.

Choosing Among Four Decision-Making Models

Having considered the goals of corporate decision making, and having defined your vision of a shared decision-making process, you need to decide which decision-making model to use in which situations. Corporate decisions are typically made using one of four models:

1. *Autocratic Decision Making*. One person makes the decision unilaterally and without consultation with affected parties.

2. *General Agreement (Consensus)*. The decision is made by the group after discussions of the relevant facts. If someone objects to the decision or to an element of it, efforts are made to address the concerns before the decision is finalized. The overall goal is unanimous support, or preparedness to accept the decision without substantial opposition to it.

3. *Majority-Based.* The decision is made by a formal vote, usually on the basis of "one-person-one-vote." If a majority is obtained (more votes are cast in favor of the proposal than against it), the proposal is approved. If not, the proposal is defeated. Tie votes mean that a majority was not obtained and the proposal was defeated. Abstentions are usually not counted unless your group has a rule or governing document that states or implies otherwise.

4. *A Combination Democratic-Autocratic Model.* Your team's consensus is seen as advisory, and a higher authority (like your boss or your board of directors) reserves the right to follow your team's recommendations (with or without amendments) or ignore them altogether.

The following table compares the four decision-making models.

	Autocratic	General Agreement (Consensus)	Majority-Based	Combination
Definition	You or your boss make the decision, without consultation	Decisions are made by the group, after discussions of issues. Efforts are made to reach unanimity, or at least members are ready to live with the outcome and accept it as an imperfect but necessary compromise (knowing that their views were heard).	Decisions are made by the group, by a vote. A majority (more than half of the votes cast) means that a decision is approved.	An individual or group makes the final decision, after receiving advice and input from other interested parties.
Advantages	Efficient, simple. Keeps control in the hands of the ultimate decision maker and establishes clear accountability.	More "pieces of the truth" are considered. The talents and expertise of team members enhance the quality of the decision. Affected parties are involved in shaping decisions, and are therefore more likely to embrace them. Members are more likely to take responsibility and show initiative	Similar to "general agreement," but provides a fair and logical way of resolving disputes (instead of succumbing to dominant members or stubborn minorities). This model has the potential of being more efficient and more truly representative than general agreement (consensus).	Balances the need for inclusion and for holistic decision making, with the need to retain overall accountability. If the process is managed well and if expectations are clearly established (i.e., that the outcome is advisory and not binding), affected parties are likely to understand and embrace the decision. ("We don't agree,

		(good succession planning). Affected parties know they were heard and are therefore less likely to undermine the implementation of the decision.		but at least we've been heard.")
Disadvantages	Not inclusive, could leave some stakeholders disenfranchised. Risk of acting without significant facts that affected parties could have presented. People may become lazy and defer too many decisions to the leader (not much of a succession plan). Disenfranchised parties may resent not being heard or paid attention to and could undermine the implementation of the decisions.	Can be slow and time-consuming. Can become "the minority rules," when vocal members hijack the process, and when stubborn individuals refuse to listen and make adjustments. The requirement of unanimity can either stall the decision or force the group to make concessions to a minority, which can dilute the strength of the decision. Members may not be ready for empowered participation yet. Management may not be ready to truly let go of control. Team members can develop unreasonable expectations about the impact of their input.	If not monitored carefully, it can be used by an aggressive majority to push through a bad decision. This can create a disgruntled minority, which, in turn, may end up undermining the decision at the implementation stage.	If expectations are not clearly communicated and subscribed to by all players, unrealistic expectations can develop (i.e.: advisory bodies think that they are making the decision, and not just a recommendation). If recommendations are ignored, accusations of tokenism and dishonesty could be made. Alternatively, the parties offering the advice that was ignored could become demoralized and skeptical and lose their motivation and enthusiasm.
Appropriate for	Routine or administrative decisions. Decisions that have little or no impact on stakeholders. Decisions for which the decision maker is	Decisions that affect parties in a significant way, and which can wait for the time that it takes for the consensus to emerge. Complex decisions that will	Decisions that require input from members, but cannot wait for everyone to agree 100% on everything.	Significant decisions that could benefit from outside input and advice, but which cannot be delegated (the advisory body is not held accountable for the decision).

	Autocratic	General Agreement (Consensus)	Majority-Based	Combination
	solely accountable and that cannot be responsibly delegated to a group; e.g., hiring or firing decisions. Decisions on issues that are too emotional to have a rational discussion on, or when the group prefers to leave them in the hands of one person.	be enhanced by diverse input and a broad perspective. Settings where people are empowered but don't expect unlimited clout and control ("responsible democracy"). Settings where management is genuinely interested in listening and is prepared to let go of control, at least to a degree.		Condition: Make sure the terms of reference of the advisory body are abundantly clear at the start of the process and as it continues: "Our mandate is to give advice. We do not make binding decisions here."

Example: De Facto Dictatorship

A CEO convenes a meeting of senior managers that is presumed to operate in a democratic fashion (consensus- or majority-based). He leaves the meeting for half an hour. He returns late in the discussion of an issue and raises a few questions, indicating that he missed some important information that was brought up during his absence. The managers are too intimidated to respond, and a bad decision is made. The CEO in this case is a de facto dictator, even though he claims to be an inclusive leader. This is a "pretend democracy." The dynamics have a negative impact on the managers (who allowed themselves to be ignored) and on the quality of the decisions.

Assignment: Assess Your Corporate Decision-Making Style

Given the above four decision-making models, consider your own decision-making style, as well as the overall decision-making culture within your organization by thinking about the following questions:

- Does your style lean towards autocratic or democratic?
- Are you too autocratic (making too many decisions) when you should be taking a more facilitative style? If so, do you find subordinates hesitating to take the initiative and depending on you too much?
- Have you thought of who might take over in your absence? Do you have a succession plan, and, if not, does your organization need you to have one?
- Are you too "democratic," trying to appease and accommodate every individual, sometimes with the result of slowing things down needlessly, and sometimes appeasing one person at the expense of the rest of your team?
- Do you avoid making decisions for which you are accountable and do you defer too many of them to the group, even if they have no interest in getting involved in making them, or are not qualified or comfortable offering advice? Do you use democracy as a way of avoiding tough decisions?
- Is the "playing field" in your meetings truly even? Who really makes the decisions: The group collectively, or the most outspoken and knowledgeable members? In other words, is it a meaningful democracy or is it "the rule of the minority"?
- Do you facilitate democratic decision making because you truly believe it can work, or because someone said you should, or because it is trendy? Do you "kind of listen" but then ignore what you heard? If so, what effect has it had on relationships with your team members and with other affected parties?
- What is your boss's decision-making style? Does she or he consistently override the decisions made by you or your team? Do you do anything to "manage upwards" and increase the likelihood that your team's decisions will be taken seriously?
- Have any limitations on your team's decision-making power been fully clarified? If limitations on powers have indeed been established, do team members fully understand them? Do you make it abundantly clear whether your team's consensus is advisory or binding?
- Is your corporate culture truly democratic, or is it a "tokenism democracy"? Are your bosses genuinely interested in hearing what you and your team have to say? Are they committed to addressing legitimate concerns? If not, have you done anything to address it?

Using Shared Decision-Making Parameters for Making Collective Decisions

Having defined the goals of corporate decision making, your vision of a successful SDM process, and the decision-making models that you can use, you need to consider a few parameters of shared decision making and manage them for profitable decisions.

The SDM parameters to consider are:

- Lateral movement versus forward movement
- Problem-mode versus solution-mode
- A six-step problem-solving model
- The natural evolution of an issue
- Formality versus informality

Lateral Movement vs. Forward Movement

As you facilitate a meeting or other consensus-building activity, you will likely need to alternate between "lateral movement" and "forward movement." Lateral movement (LM) means that an open discussion of an issue or a proposal takes place. Forward movement (FM) means that, at the end of an open discussion (LM), a forward movement (FM) statement is made that consists of two parts:

1. "What we've just done": An interim summary of progress is articulated and recorded.
2. "What's up next": An indication of what the next topic or subtopic is.

There are two common difficulties in meetings. First, members are often not decisive in reaching closure on issues, and don't know when and how to stop an open discussion (LM) and shift to closure and forward movement (FM). The result is that no consensus is articulated and the meeting lacks focus and direction. Second, the group proceeds to the next issue without properly closing off the current one, i.e., lateral movement on one issue is followed by lateral movement on another issue, omitting the much-needed full forward movement statement. This leaves loose ends and unfinished business. The following is an illustration of alternating between forward movement and lateral movement.

Example: Alternating Between Forward and Lateral Movement

Facilitator: "The next item on our agenda is the hiring of new support staff. We'll start with the receptionist position. Are there any comments about our interviewing process?" *(Forward)*

Discussion of the receptionist's position and the qualifications of applicants ensues. *(Lateral)*

Facilitator: "Let me summarize our consensus so far: We seem to agree that the receptionist's job is needed and that Rebecca Moore is the most suitable candidate for the job. Am I right? If so, let's have this decision recorded in the minutes and move on to the next issue, which is the hiring of a part-time project assistant. Tracy, can you please give us the background on this issue? [Tracy speaks.] Is there any discussion on the position of project assistant?" *(Forward)*

Discussion of the part-time project assistant ensues. *(Lateral)*

Facilitator: "Let me summarize our consensus. It seems like there isn't enough work to justify hiring a full-time project assistant now. Would it be reasonable for us to revisit this issue in six months? Thank you. We'll move on to the next issue, which is ____." *(Forward)*

Note that both of the above FM statements contain two parts:

▲ Closure on the current issue ("what we've just done")

▲ Announcement of the next issue ("what's next")

Assignment: Balancing Forward Movement with Lateral Movement

Consider how effective you are at bringing closure to issues by thinking about these questions:

▲ How effectively do you balance the need for open discussion and problem solving (LM) with the need to articulate consensus and move forward (FM)?

▲ How much discussion do you allow before a decision is made? Is there too much of it, with repetition and rambling? Is there too little of it, meaning that you rush to making decisions and risk making bad ones?

Problem-Mode vs. Solution-Mode

In addition to lateral and forward movements, you need to consider another set of parameters of your consensus-building process: problem-mode versus solution-mode.

In our mad rush to get things done, we often end up discussing solutions ("solution-mode") before the nature and scope of a problem has been fully explored ("problem-mode"). This practice is risky, especially when the issues are complex or controversial. Entering solution-mode prematurely may constrain creativity and cause your group "to solve the wrong problem."

To avoid such an outcome, you need to slow things down and resist the temptation to discuss solutions prematurely. Here is a sample script that could help you achieve this goal:

> *"Thank you, David, for this idea. Can I suggest that we put it on our "parking lot" flip chart for now? We can look at it again once we've identified the full scope of the problem, which we haven't done yet." (Use a "parking lot" flip chart to record all suggestions to address later at the meeting.)*

A Six-Step Problem-Solving Model

As your group prepares to solve a problem, consider this: The more complex the issue, the more important it is that the problem-solving process be measured, gradual, and deliberate.

Here is a six-step problem-solving model that will help your group give detailed and deliberate attention to a complex or controversial issue (thereby increasing the likelihood that logical and smart consensus will emerge):

1. Identify the problem. Make sure that the real issues are explored, and don't be distracted by surface issues. By fully exploring the problem, you will be more likely to address its root causes and not just the symptoms. This will help you clarify the key questions that must be answered to achieve a holistic solution.
2. Establish the criteria that the chosen solution must meet. Such criteria may include:
   - ▲ Cost-effectiveness
   - ▲ Time-effectiveness
   - ▲ Fairness and equal treatment of affected parties
   - ▲ Responsiveness to as many legitimate needs as possible
   - ▲ Ease of implementation with available resources
   - ▲ Customer-friendliness
   - ▲ A fresh and creative touch
   - ▲ Leading the group to work smarter and not harder
3. Brainstorm for solutions and use flip charts or "sticky notes" to record all suggestions. At this stage all ideas are welcome, including those that, on first look,

seem to be unworkable, and no ideas are evaluated. Discourage "Yes, but," or "This would never work," or "We tried it before" responses by saying: "I need to remind everyone that right now we are only collecting and listing ideas. This is not the time to evaluate ideas, so can you please hold your evaluation for now? Thank you. Are there any more ideas on ____? Any idea is welcome, regardless of how unusual it may appear to be."

4. Facilitate an evaluation of each of the options generated under step 3 against the criteria which were agreed upon (step 2). Does it meet these criteria and, if so, to what degree?
5. Facilitate a selection of the best option, which may be one of those generated in step 3 or may be a different one altogether. Prevent your group from being constrained by past traditions or perceived obstacles to new ideas. Instead, be guided by present realities, the organization's mandate, and what will be the best decision in both the short and long terms.
6. Facilitate decisions on implementation duties. Avoid asking: "Who would like to volunteer for this?" (You may always end up with the same volunteers, and the less assertive members will have no incentive to be proactive and make a difference). Instead, have duties assigned to those who are the best suited for them, and try to engage quieter members: "Rob, can you help us out with this assignment? We need to spread the work around. What do you think?"

Assignment: How Deliberate and Measured Is Your Decision Making?

In light of the above six-step problem-solving model, consider your group's decision making by thinking about these questions:

- Are you or some members of your group impatient? Do you tend to solve problems quickly? Did any decisions that your group rushed through come back to haunt you some time later?
- Do you allow members to dismiss or trivialize an idea because "We've never done it this way," or "The CEO will never agree to this"? Do you have too many critics and too few creators in your group?
- Are there some members who always volunteer (and end up "burning out," not delivering quality results, or complaining that no one else does anything)?

Example: Looking Beyond Customer Complaints

You are leading a management committee in a discussion of customer complaints about having to wait a long time on the phone and about being treated as a nuisance. Someone who works in the department immediately suggests a solution: "We've got to hire more staff to man the phones. Our call volume has gone up by 50 percent, so we need to add three people to the six who work there now."

What will you say or do? How should problem solving and consensus building proceed? It would be unwise to leap to solution-mode until the nature and scope of the problem and its causes have been fully explored. The complaints about long waits on the phone could be only one symptom of the problem. Another symptom may be that customers are poorly treated, and there may yet be other symptoms. You need to look beyond the symptoms and take the time to find the underlying causes of the problem. Otherwise, you may end up solving the wrong problem, with the real one coming back to haunt you later.

What causes for the department's ineffectiveness might you discover? You might find out that, indeed, demand for services has increased. But you might also discover that the department has been operating inefficiently and has been able to get away with it under low pressures. You might also discover that staff members have not received training in customer service etiquette. Finally, low morale and poor leadership may have contributed to inefficiencies.

To make a responsible, credible, and durable decision, you need to slow down the mad rush to solution-mode: "Thank you, Trevor, for your suggestion. We will record it for later. For now, I suggest that we start by finding out what is happening in the department and what exactly our customers are complaining about. When the problem is clear, we will explore solutions for it."

Slowing your group down and taking the time to examine the real problem may mean that the solution will be delayed. The efforts to find a solution for the real problem (and not the symptom) may consume more time, money, and other resources. However, this extra investment should pay for itself by saving the money that would have been wasted on the wrong solution.

The Natural Evolution of an Issue

Using the problem-solving approach as indicated in the previous section implies that the problem is ready for discussion. But often it isn't. This typically happens when a member adds his or her own pet issue to the agenda, and no one asks the question: Is this issue ripe for discussion and decision making at this point?

Complex and controversial issues should be allowed to evolve. Your group should assess the evolutionary stage of an issue before placing it on a meeting agenda.

Here are the various stages in the evolution of an issue:

- ▲ *Conception*. The issue is brand-new and has just emerged as a result of discussing another issue. If a "conception stage" issue is easy to deal with or is urgent, the group can deal with it at the same meeting in which it is conceived. However, conception stage issues should generally not preempt items that have already been scheduled on the agenda. On the other hand, if a "conception stage" issue is not urgent and it is complex or controversial, it should be placed on the group's "idea list" or "parking lot" for later consideration. When planning agendas for future meetings, you will need to review the idea list and see if any issue is ready for its next evolutionary stage: birth.

- ▲ *Birth*. The issue was just taken from the "parking lot" and added to this meeting's agenda. The issue should only be opened for general discussion and preliminary exploration. The group should resist the temptation to rush decisions on issues still in the birth stage, which have not been sufficiently explored, and are therefore not mature for decision making.

- ▲ *Adolescence*. The issue has now become contentious, and members are fighting over it and acting to protect their own turfs. Under these conditions, the group should not force closure on the issue, or else its decisions could be made by narrow majorities and divide the group. A decision in an adversarial setting is likely to lack maturity and durability and may be undermined. Your group should recognize an adolescent issue and postpone decision making until maturity.

- ▲ *Maturity*. The issue has been fully explored and it is now ready for mature exploration and decision making. With the full understanding of the issues and with the right timing, the decisions will be responsible, credible, and durable.

- ▲ *Old Age*. The issue is no longer in the forefront, but it is used by the group as a case study and a source of learning when approaching other complex or controversial issues in the future.

- ▲ *Reincarnation*. If your decision-making process was flawed, the issue may be reincarnated. You may have thought it was dead, but it is alive and well and has come back in full force to haunt you. What went wrong? One reason could be that you made your decisions at the conception, birth, or adolescent stages of the evolution of the issue.

Example: Office Renovation

Here is an example of addressing an office space problem proactively, using an evolutionary process:

- *Conception Stage (Meeting 1)*. The group identifies office space as an emerging issue. The division's premises are getting crowded and, given your company's anticipated growth, things could only get worse. But right now there are more pressing issues to deal with, and the office space topic is placed on your group's "parking lot," waiting to be added to a meeting agenda.
- *Birth Stage (Meeting 2, Sometime Later)*. The issue is taken from the group's parking lot and is placed on a meeting agenda. The following questions are addressed in the discussion:
  - What is the office space problem and how bad is it?
  - How is the problem affecting staff and customers?
  - How is the problem affecting productivity and profit levels?
  - What is the real problem? Is it too little space, or is it too many people?
  - How soon must this problem be addressed?
  - What would be a reasonable process to address this problem?

As a result of this meeting, a committee, which includes an outside consultant, is appointed to research the issue and analyze the problem further. The committee makes several observations and recommendations, and some of them are likely to be controversial.

- *Adolescent Stage (Meeting 3)*. The report of the committee is scheduled for discussion at the next meeting. The agenda designer structures the discussion as follows:
  - Presentation of report (three parts, no more than 10 minutes each).
  - After each of the three parts, members are invited to ask

questions and comment on the report (10 minutes per Q & A segment).

During this adolescent stage discussion members seem to be very protective of their own office spaces. Some of them are defensive when the committee's analysis points to inefficiencies in their areas. This is not the right time to finalize any decisions. Instead, each member is asked to review the proposed changes and contact the consultant after the meeting with his or her suggestions.

With the team's feedback, the consultant prepares a second report for presentation at the next meeting.

- *Maturity Stage (Meetings 4, 5, and 6)*: Given that member concerns have been integrated into the report, the members are ready for mature and broad-based discussion and decision making. The agenda unfolds as follows:
  - Consultant presents report.
  - Questions and discussion.
  - Approve the criteria for decision making.
  - Evaluate four options:
    - Renovations and reallocation of office space
    - Move to new premises
    - Office sharing and shift work
    - Tele-commuting
  - Choose an option, which may be a combination of the above.
  - Establish an implementation plan.
- *Old Age*. The solution has been implemented smoothly and with only a few small difficulties. The problem-solving process is documented and is used by other divisions in the same company. It is also presented as a success story in conferences of professional associations.
- *Death*. Office space is not an issue. It's history.
- *Reincarnation.* Hopefully not, unless the company experiences phenomenal growth and again runs into office space problems. But if you had paid attention to details and were able to anticipate emerging trends, your plan would have taken this eventuality into account.

Assignment: Examining the Evolution of Your Group's Issues

The issues that your group deals with should evolve naturally, from conception to old age, avoiding reincarnation. If this is the case, your decision-making process will be measured and deliberate and you will be able to minimize nasty surprises. Your agendas will be more proactive and less reactive. Consider how your group deals with issues by answering the following questions:

- ▲ Do your issues evolve naturally? Is your agenda design process governed by long-term and proactive thinking? Or is it random and reactive?
- ▲ How often do you rush a decision through despite significant concerns and strong opposition (an adolescent issue), possibly using a narrow majority to force the decision? Are there any consequences to this?
- ▲ How often do you find a persistent minority trying to revisit a decision (reincarnating an issue that was closed off prematurely)?
- ▲ How often do you find yourself surprised by a major issue that you knew little or nothing about, or one that grew to be a monster issue because you ignored it or hoped that it would go away? (It was born some time ago, but you didn't know, or you ignored the warning signs.)
- ▲ If so, how effective are your early warning systems? How proactive are your efforts to anticipate issues and study emerging trends, so that issues come to your attention on a timely basis?

Formal vs. Informal Discussions

Formality is another parameter that could affect the quality of your discussions and collective decisions.

Some formality and protocol are always needed to facilitate civilized and orderly discussions and to ensure that members have equal opportunities to speak and influence the decision making. However, too much formality may constrain and stifle creativity and may have a negative impact on the quality of the consensus reached by the group.

Here are two examples of problems caused by too much formality in meetings:

1. A speakers' lineup is established to ensure fairness and equality at a meeting. Members add their names to the list, speak when their turns come, and speak a second time only after those who wish to speak for the first time have done so.

A speakers' lineup can be helpful. However, it can also be too rigid and constraining and may prevent the natural flow of discussions during meetings. For example:

- ▲ The comments to be made by the fifth speaker on the list have already been made by previous speakers. Recognizing this member to speak would lead to unneeded repetition. You may want to say: "Given our busy agenda, would you please consider skipping your turn to speak if your comments have been made by a previous speaker?"
- ▲ By the time a speaker's turn has come, the group is on to a different topic or subtopic and his or her comments would amount to backtracking. You may need to say: "When your turn to speak comes, please pay attention to where we are in the discussion and consider whether your comments are still relevant."

2. Formality also occurs in a large meeting, when people can speak only from a microphone. This procedure helps to establish order and decorum and ensure that speakers can be heard. However, one common consequence is that discussions are dominated by members who are comfortable speaking in public, while others are excluded. You can depart from this formality by having some discussions in small breakout groups, with the groups reporting back to the full group later. This will involve everyone in the discussions.

Choosing the Level of Formality for Your Group

What do you do if some members of your group believe that something terribly wrong will happen if formal rules are not followed with scientific accuracy in your meetings? For example, they may insist that, in a board of directors meeting, a proposal is not valid unless it is "moved and seconded." Or they assert (incorrectly) that no discussion can take place "until there is a motion on the floor."

You need to deal with this dilemma fairly and squarely. The best way to avoid being subjected to the wishes of strong individuals and minorities is to put the majority back in charge. You need to facilitate a decision by your group as to the level of formality that it finds appropriate for its needs. Your group can decide to opt for formality level 1, 2, or 3, as follows:

- ▲ *Informal (Level 1)*. No formal rules of order are used. Members introduce proposals (instead of moving and seconding motions), suggest that issues be postponed or referred to another group for study, or withdrawn altogether (instead of "moving to table"). The facilitator balances the need for progress with the need for flexibility and free flowing discussions. Basic protocol and etiquette are observed (see Chapter 8).

- *Semiformal (Level 2).* The same principles stated for level 1 are observed (clarity of proposals, scrutiny and discussion, participation protocol, and efficiency), but greater formality is maintained. Members make and second motions, and speak more formally ("Mr. President" instead of "Joe"; "I move to postpone this motion" instead of "I suggest that we delay this decision"). An example of when such formality would be appropriate is a publicly held meeting of a municipal council.
- *Formal (Level 3).* Meetings are very formal, and members are highly sophisticated in parliamentary procedure and are thoroughly fascinated by the procedural intricacies of the rules of order. The formality is a kind of religion, and the rules are sometimes used for strategic purposes (to win and defeat the opposition) instead of working together to build win-win solutions. An example of a place where this level of formality may be desirable is a meeting of a legislative body.

So how does the above discussion help you combat procedural nonsense in meetings? Let's suppose your group considered the three options and chose level 1 (informal). Each new member, prior to starting his or her work with your group, should receive an orientation, part of which would be this important piece of information: "We work informally around here. Here are some of the principles and parameters by which we run our meetings: _____. Here are some of the things we don't do: _____."

If someone resorts to old habits, or has just completed a course on rules of order and begins to raise points of order, remind him or her of what the group decided: "John, as you may remember, our group opted for formality level 1. The level that you are introducing does not fit here."

Even if your group chose formality level 2 or 3, it should be clear to the members that the rules of order are intended to help facilitate progress and protect majority and minority rights. The purpose is not to confuse, frustrate, and intimidate people or needlessly slow things down.

The remainder of this book assumes that your group chose formality level 1.

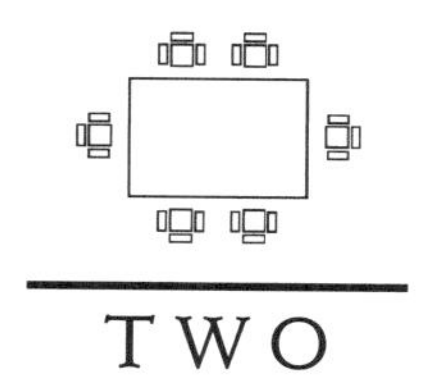

TWO

The Many Hats of a Facilitator

Having established the goals and parameters of shared decision making (Chapter 1), you need to have an effective team facilitator. If a team is cohesive, the work of a facilitator is limited to the management and coordination of team and meeting-related activities. However, in many settings, the ideal of a cohesive team and empowered members is far from a reality. Therefore, the facilitator is often required to assume many roles and "wear many hats."

This chapter describes the many hats that the facilitator may need to wear. The focus of this chapter is primarily on the facilitator's work outside of meetings. (For more on the facilitator's roles in planning and chairing meetings, see Chapters 9 to 14). For ease of reference, the various hats are arranged in alphabetic order. Specifically, this chapter describes the facilitator as a(n):

- Advocate
- Balancer
- Battery needing a boost

- ▲ Breath of fresh air
- ▲ Confidant
- ▲ Consultative leader
- ▲ Coordinator
- ▲ Delegator
- ▲ Diplomat
- ▲ Eternal optimist
- ▲ External facilitator
- ▲ Healer
- ▲ Inventory keeper
- ▲ Island of sanity
- ▲ Mediator
- ▲ Mistake maker
- ▲ Motivator
- ▲ Negotiator
- ▲ Quitter
- ▲ Realistic visionary
- ▲ Sheepherder
- ▲ Spokesperson
- ▲ Succession planner
- ▲ Voting member
- ▲ Vulnerable human being

The facilitator should also consider sections in other chapters in this book. For example, the facilitator needs to be a:

- ▲ Communicator (see Chapter 13 about communicating in a meeting)
- ▲ Listener (see Chapter 13 about listening in a meeting)
- ▲ Presenter and public speaker (see Chapters 9 and 10 for a presenter's checklists)
- ▲ Team builder (see Chapter 4)

- ▲ Team player (see Chapters 6 and 13; the same person may be a leader of one team, and a follower on another team)
- ▲ Relationship builder (see Chapter 7)

Advocate

Some people will tell you that, as a facilitator, you are not allowed to speak in the discussion unless you allow someone else to chair the meeting. This notion is probably borrowed from some rulebooks on formal meetings. Such rules may place restrictions on the chairperson in large meetings and require him or her to focus primarily on the facilitation task.

The above notion makes no sense in typical corporate meetings. Why would one want to muzzle one of the most knowledgeable individuals within the group? Doing so could lead to poor decisions being made. Forcing you to stop chairing a meeting every time you want to speak would be unnecessarily disruptive and formal. Therefore, as a facilitator you should be allowed to speak and add your "piece of the truth" to the discussion.

At the same time, you should be careful not to dominate the discussions and not to give an unfair advantage to your view, especially when the issues are divisive. The facilitator position can give you an advantage over others, and you should be careful not to bias the consensus-building efforts against one view or another. Here are a few tips for you to consider.

When you speak, it should be on the same basis as everyone else. If there is a speakers' lineup, add your name to the lineup. Try these scripts:

> *"I want to speak about this issue, so I will add my name to the speakers' lineup. We have Jill and Lyle ahead of me. Jill, go ahead."*
>
> *"I have something to add here, but I've already spoken and Cleo, you haven't spoken yet, so you get priority. Go ahead, Cleo."*

When other people speak, take notes of any points that you may want to make in response. Save these points as you listen to a few speakers. Your points may be brought up by others, and you may not need to raise them. When your turn comes to speak, share only the comments that were not already made. This will help you balance your need to speak with the need to manage the discussion fairly.

When you speak, make your comments concise and to the point and avoid lecturing to the members. If you expect others to be focused and avoid rambling, it's only fair that you do the same. Try the sandwich approach: Tell them what you'll them, then tell them, and then tell them what you told them. For example:

> *"I have two issues to raise here: economics and ethics. The economic issue is ____ (elaborate briefly or give an example). The ethical issue is ____ (elaborate briefly or give an example). Therefore, I think we should ____."*

Resist the temptation to answer all questions, even if they are directed at you. See if you can get members to give their own answers. (It's the accountable way to go.) Try one of these approaches:

> *"I have a sense that you have your own answer to this question. Do you? What do you think the answer should be?"*
>
> *"I have a sense that other people may have a better answer than I do. Connie, what do you think about this question?"*
>
> *"I am wondering why you are asking me this question. It sounds like there is a concern underneath this question, and it would help everyone to know what it is."*

Balancer

You will have individuals on your team and in your meetings who are influential, vocal, and possibly intimidating. In the absence of your moderating influence, such individuals could dominate discussions, and quieter individuals may be too afraid to say anything about it. As a facilitator, one of your key tasks will be to create balance by moderating the influence of vocal members and bringing the quieter members into the decision-making process.

Sample Script: Premeeting Discussion with Your Boss

Your boss is planning to attend your next meeting, and you are concerned that he might dominate the discussions or that his presence might intimidate some members.

"Ian, I am really glad you are coming to our meeting. I think you will get to know our team better and have a better appreciation of what we do. This should help you explain our work and represent us well at senior management meetings.

"I have one favor to ask of you: In our group we keep a speakers' lineup, to give members equal opportunities to speak and to avoid domination of the discussion by a few members. Would it be OK for you to participate in our meeting on the same basis? Thank you. This will mean a lot to everyone."

Note: If Ian is amenable, you could suggest that he make an introductory statement to the group, encouraging them to participate fully even though he is present (or even emphasizing that he insists that they do this).

Sample Script: Premeeting Discussion with a Dominant Member

"Monique, I have a request for you for the next meeting. I am going to try to get some of our newer members to take on leadership roles and establish the direction for discussions. You can help me achieve this by holding back a bit and letting other people be the first to speak on issues. What do you think? Will you help me out?"

Sample Script: How to Establish the Direction Collectively

One difficulty in meetings occurs when a dominant member is the first to speak, and the discussion continues in the direction of that first statement. Here is a script that will allow the group, collectively, to establish how the discussion will go:

"In the past, some of our discussions were not as organized as needed, and we ended up not covering important points. Can we try a different approach for the next topic, which is ________? Here is my suggestion: Please take a couple of minutes to jot down the key questions that you think we should focus on. I will then ask each one of you for a quick comment and will list your suggestions on the flip chart. We will then prioritize the ideas and deal with them in a logical order. Does this sound reasonable? OK, two minutes for thinking: What key questions should we address?"

The Affinity Diagram

Here is a technique to use to build consensus on an important issue:

- ▲ Ask members to jot down on sticky notes the most important thoughts they have on addressing an important issue, one thought per sticky.
- ▲ Ask everyone to place their stickies on a big board, in complete silence.
- ▲ Then, have everyone work together, *in complete silence*, to organize the various stickies into several categories.

Like magic, thirty minutes later, the collective thought process becomes apparent, and certain clear directions and trends emerge. The outcome includes input from everyone, including the quiet members. The vocal members don't get to dominate, and true balance is established.

BATTERY NEEDING A BOOST

As a leader you are often in a position to give. But a fact that goes unnoticed by many facilitators is that they also need to receive and "recharge" their batteries. Here are a few sources of energy for your batteries:

1. Have a mentor or an executive coach. Find an individual that you respect, in your organization or outside of it, and ask whether they would serve as your personal mentor. Choose a person that you would feel comfortable confiding in. Take advice and guidance from this person, especially when the going gets tough. And don't consider it an imposition; most people are honored to serve as mentors.
2. Look for advice and support from the members of your team. "Stan, I need some advice on ____. Can you help me out?" By asking for advice you will be honoring them. And asking for advice from subordinates will not diminish your stature and authority as a leader; instead, it is likely to boost respect and loyalty for you.

3. Look for support from your boss and from external stakeholders.
4. Create your succession plan (see the section on the facilitator as a succession planner) and make the group less dependent on you, so you can take time out when needed.
5. Treat yourself as an important person and feel free to take time out when needed. If you need private time for thinking, make an appointment with yourself and treat it like a meeting with an important person. Close the door to your office and post a sign: "In a meeting with an important client. Not to be disturbed until 4 P.M."
6. Vacations are also a way to recharge. Don't worry, the world will not collapse in your absence. Feel free to leave your cell phone behind, and don't call the office for messages or check your e-mails while you're away. You deserve a break.
7. Value your family and personal relationships and don't compromise them for the sake of your work. Look for a win-win balance between work and private life. If you are working too much, you could probably learn to delegate more responsibility (see section on the facilitator as a delegator).

Breath of Fresh Air

To entice the group to follow your lead, you should always stay fresh:

- ▲ Be genuinely enthusiastic about the group's work and have fun with it.
- ▲ Challenge yourself to be creative and fresh, without being constrained by past traditions.
- ▲ Be a few steps ahead of the group in your understanding of the issues.
- ▲ Make it your goal to bring smiles to people's faces.
- ▲ Find fresh ways of dealing with conflict (see example below).
- ▲ Challenge your "traditional thinkers" by questioning the status quo and past traditions.
- ▲ Keep an inventory of short fun stories to tell when downtime is needed in a meeting.
- ▲ Keep an inventory of inspiring examples on how individuals overcame adversity, learned from mistakes, or came up with exceptionally creative solutions to major problems.

- Have a few words of wisdom and quotes to use at opportune moments.
- Have a few fun games and puzzles to stimulate creative thinking.
- If your members lose sight of the broad perspective and are bogged down, keep the meeting fresh by sharing new perspectives that will expand the discussion. For example:

> *"Would it be useful to look at this from a completely different perspective? How about looking at this through the eyes of an elementary school student? How would this solution work for them?"*
>
> *"I think we are stuck because we are only looking at one part of the picture. How about if we looked at some of the stakeholders that we typically forget, like ____?"*

Example: A Walk Around the Park

Lyle was not looking forward to a meeting with Rick, one of his team members, to resolve some serious disputes. Previous interactions were in face-to-face meetings in the office across a desk and were very confrontational. Lyle thought that a change of venue might bring a fresh attitude and new solutions. He suggested a walk in the park. Removed from the constraints of the office and immersed in nature, fresh air, and light drizzle, they discovered the fresh outlook and creative solutions that they needed.

The Closet Entertainer

Part of staying fresh is taking yourself lightly and your work seriously. There may be times in a meeting when you inadvertently say or do something really goofy that makes everyone laugh. If so, don't fight the success by getting embarrassed and blushing. You may have discovered a talent that you didn't know about. Just say: "Wow. I didn't know I could be this funny," or "Did I say something funny?" Remember: You've got to leave your ego at home. One of your strengths is the ability to bring smiles to people's faces and help them take themselves more lightly.

Confidant

Your relationship-building efforts may lead people to trust and confide in you. This in itself is not a bad thing, but it could place you in awkward positions. For example:

- What will you do if the law or your code of ethics compel you to reveal this information?
- What if the organization will be at risk if the information is not revealed or acted upon?
- What if the fact that this person has this information points to a leak of confidential data?

The above examples pose a serious question: What should come first? Your informal commitment to keep things private, or the higher interests: the law, your code of ethics, and the organization as a whole? Here are a few tips to reduce the likelihood of being stuck in such awkward situations.

In general, it is best to not promise confidentiality until you know what you are getting yourself into. Of course, it is difficult to know what you are getting yourself into until you know what the information is, and a person may not want to tell you what it is until you promise confidentiality. It's like the chicken and the egg. Do your preventive work by explaining a few things to your group:

- Reassure them that you would be glad to discuss things in confidence if it helps them resolve issues or if it helps the group make progress.
- Explain that, in some cases, you may not be able to keep the information confidential. Give them a few examples (see above).

The problem is that people will not always ask you in advance to keep the discussion confidential. But they may end their comments by saying: "Would you promise to keep it between us?" In such a case, there are three possibilities:

1. If you are able to keep it confidential, you can give the promise that you'll do so.
2. If it would be very helpful for you to use this information, say something like this: "Ken, I understand that you want to stay out of the spotlight. But this issue is really important. Can I bring it up on my own without mentioning that you passed it on to me? I'll do everything to not identify you. Is that OK?"
3. If you are compelled to reveal the information, say something like this: "Christine, I can see how uncomfortable this is for you. At the same time, I hope you

can appreciate that I cannot keep the information confidential because of ____. How about if we work out a way to make it known to the individuals who need to have it, without making it uncomfortable for you."

If someone begins to reveal something to you in confidence and you sense that you may not be able to keep it confidential, say something like this: "Dawn, before you go any further with this issue, I need to caution you: Based on what I think you are about to tell me, I may not be able to keep it confidential, because of ____. I will be glad to hear the full story and see if I can help you, but I don't want to give a promise that I may not be able to keep. Are you sure you want to continue to talk about this issue? If you do, I promise to deal with it as discreetly as I can."

CONSULTATIVE LEADER

What is the facilitator's greatest enemy? It is a one-letter word: "I." "I make the decisions" is the assumption that many facilitators often operate under. Delaying a decision until the affected individuals or parties have been consulted is often seen as a sign of weakness and poor leadership.

The "I" approach is the lazy way to go. Yes, it is simpler if only one person makes the decisions. However, if decisions are made without any consideration of your group's input, you may encounter the following problems:

- You may end up making a narrow and shortsighted decision.
- You may find yourself at the destination alone, with no real followers.
- Members of your group may follow you because they feel they have to (it's their job . . .) and not because they really want to.

The "I" focus makes organizations dependent on leaders for initiative. Followers are expected to do what they are told and to be grateful that they have paying jobs. The result of the "I" focus is that employees are reactive and always wait for someone to tell them what to do.

As an effective facilitator, you should use the word "I" less and the word "we" more. It is especially important to consult your members if the issue is complex and could benefit from their wisdom, or when they will be significantly affected by the decision. You need to make it your habit to ask questions instead of giving orders. This will make them feel more valued. The organization will be more likely to capitalize on their knowledge and insights.

Using Questions to Develop a Consultative Style

Here are a few examples of how questioning can be used to develop a more consultative style, build consensus, and engage the group in shared decision making:

Instead of giving this order:	*Try asking this question:*
"I will allow five more minutes and then we'll move on."	"I am looking at my watch and at the remainder of our agenda. Is it OK to end this discussion in five minutes?" Or: "Does anyone have anything new to add, and—if not—shall we move on?"
"I don't think it's a good idea. It's a nonstarter. Let's move on."	"I'm not sure about this idea. Here are a couple of concerns. How do other people feel about it?"
"George and Rebecca will prepare the report."	"Are we in agreement that George and Rebecca should prepare the report?"
"Philip, please call Purchasing and find out what's holding up the supplies. Pauline, you will contact customers who are waiting and let them know that we'll take another week to deliver their orders."	"We need someone to contact purchasing and find out what is holding up the supplies. Philip, would you do it? Thanks. We also need someone to contact customers who are waiting. Pauline, would you do it? Thank you."
"Let's postpone this issue to the next meeting."	"We seem to be making very little progress on this issue and time is running out. What shall we do with it? Shall we postpone it to the next meeting?"
"This is so frustrating. We seem so close. We agree on just about everything, except one silly and insignificant detail. This is really a shame. There is	"Great news. We have agreement on 90 percent of the document. Let me suggest this: We could record that we agree on the following items: ____. We

no hope for us. I quit!" (This is said while throwing the paper on the table and leaving the room in frustration.)	could refer the remaining items to Rose and Kimberly to work on and suggest a solution by the next meeting. Does this sound reasonable to everyone? Great, let's move on."
"Option A looks best. Let's move on to the next subject on the agenda."	"Based on what you're saying, option A seems to be the best. Am I right? Shall we go with it then? Thanks. Shall we move on to the next subject or are you ready for a break?"
"It's time for a break."	"We've been working hard for a while. How about a ten-minute break?"
"The discussion will go like this: _____."	"Here is a suggestion on how the discussion could unfold: We could start by _____, then we could do _____, and then we could _____. Does this sequence make sense to you?"
"Ethel, I can't let you add this item to the agenda. There was no study done on it" (the "I" approach).	"Ethel, can we go through the normal process and bring this issue to the next meeting? It seems to need some study."
Or, conversely: "OK, Ethel. You obviously feel very strongly that we should discuss it. I'll let you do it this time, but it's the last time. I won't allow it again" (capitulation to the minority).	If Ethel persists: "What does the group want to do? Do you want to add this item to the agenda?" If needed, you could take a show of hands on whether the item will be added to the agenda.

What to Do When You Have Unilateral Decision-Making Power

Even in cases when you are solely accountable for a decision and cannot delegate it, you should look for ways to involve members in the process. Here are the things that you could do to involve the members without actually giving them decision-making power:

- ▲ *Keep them informed.* In the case of a routine decision that has little or no impact on them, you should just go ahead and make the decision and let the members know. There is no need to slow down decision making.
- ▲ *Give them early warnings.* If a decision has significant impacts on members but you are solely accountable for it, you should, whenever possible, give the group early warnings. You may also need to explain why consensus building is not appropriate in this case. Examples of decisions that should be made unilaterally by the manager are staff hiring, firing, or disciplinary actions. Keep in mind that it will be easier for members to accept unilateral decisions if many other decisions are reached by consensus.
- ▲ *Ask for nonbinding advice.* In many cases, you could ask for nonbinding advice before finalizing a unilateral decision. Before asking for input, clarify that it is advisory and nonbinding, and that you need this input to make the decision more balanced and responsive to the group's needs.

Sample Script: Asking for Nonbinding Advice

"There is a decision that I need to make soon and I need your advice. It's about how to resolve the tensions between our department and the Accounts Payable department. As a manager, it's a decision that I will need to make. However, I welcome your input because the situation is challenging. Do you want to help me out? Thank you. Here is the situation: ____. Here are some of the options that I am thinking about: ____. What do you think? Do you have any advice for me?"

Coordinator

As a facilitator, one of your duties is to coordinate team activities. As a coordinator you will:

1. Oversee the efforts of building the foundation for your team's work.
   - ▲ Negotiate the team's mandate, workplan, and required resources (Chapter 3).
   - ▲ Select, orient, and nurture your team (Chapter 4).
   - ▲ Establish the rules of engagement and your team's culture (Chapters 5 and 6).
   - ▲ Build relationships with stakeholders (Chapter 7).
2. Always be aware of your group's broad and long-term mandate and what stakeholders it is intended to serve. By doing this you will ensure that the day-to-day activities are geared towards advancing the broad mandate and that time and efforts are well spent.
3. Learn from the past; assess how far the group has progressed along its mandate, what successes it has had, and what obstacles it has encountered.
4. Plan for the future. Assess how much work remains to be done on your group's mandate and plan future activities accordingly.
5. Be aware of the ten key ingredients of a successful meeting and work to include as many of them as possible in your meetings (see Chapter 8).
6. Determine what needs to be achieved at a meeting and coordinate all planning activities to maximize its success (see Chapter 9).
7. Ensure that a meeting is smoothly launched, steered, and landed, with everyone pulling their weight while the meeting is in progress (see Chapters 10 to 14).
8. Monitor the implementation of follow-up tasks and the postmortem analysis of a meeting (see Chapter 15).

DELEGATOR

Your overall style as a facilitator should be to delegate work with clear instructions and then monitor its execution. While delegating work, you may also need to become a mentor and coach for your members. Here are a few tips for the facilitator as a delegator:

1. Delegate tasks, small and large, and encourage members to excel while performing them.
2. Don't be possessive. Even if you really enjoy the task, let go of it. Even if the task will make you highly visible and boost your personal profile and credibility,

give it away. Be prepared to share the spotlight and the credit for successes. Your goal should not be personal gratification, prestige, and recognition (which you are bound to get anyway if you learn to let go), but to get the job done well.

3. Never underestimate people. They are often capable of doing much more than you expect and even more than they might initially think. With the right amount of coaching, they could exceed their own expectations and operate beyond their comfort levels. Helping them stretch their skills will boost their confidence, satisfaction, motivation, and loyalty.
4. Delegate duties responsibly and with clear instructions, and build accountability into the process, i.e., the person to whom the work is delegated will report on progress, and you will reserve the right to monitor the work from time to time.
5. If you give inexperienced individuals certain jobs for the first time:
   - ▲ Assess your risk level and determine whether it is acceptable, i.e., what will be the consequences if the job does not get done right? Is it OK to allow mistakes on this task? If not, delegate the task to a more experienced person. On the other hand, if the risk is acceptable, let the person know that you do not expect perfection and that it is OK to make small mistakes and learn from them.
   - ▲ Give the job with some guidance, while leaving enough room for the person's own style, creativity, and initiative to show.
   - ▲ Ask the person to contact you if she or he needs support or help with the task.
   - ▲ Check with the person from time to time about progress.
   - ▲ When the person completes the task, close the learning cycle by giving him or her honest feedback. Feedback should always consist of two parts: commendations (what they did well) and recommendations (what they could do better next time).
6. Resist the temptation to micromanage people. Let them do their jobs with as little interference and monitoring as needed. Don't let yourself be targeted as not being able to let go. If you delegated a task to an experienced member or an external expert, remember this: "If you hire a chef, stay out of the kitchen."
7. If you are teaching someone how to do something, be patient and let them get their feet wet, and resist the temptation to jump in, take over and show them "how it's done." They need to develop their own confidence by doing things themselves, and your expert way of doing things may only intimidate and frus-

trate them. If they ask you, "What's next?" say, "Think about it. What do you think should be next?" If they express frustration, don't solve their problem, but say: "That's OK. Frustration is a natural part of the learning process. I went through a lot of it myself. Just keep on going."

8. There may be times when a certain task must be completed immediately and no one is available to delegate it to. In such instances, you may just need to get the job done yourself. Do the required work willingly and enthusiastically and without any resentment, regardless of how trivial it appears to be. Examples may include the following:

   - ▲ You detect a significant error in a document that must be e-mailed right away, and the secretary who typed it has gone home. Go ahead and edit the document and send it. Don't get angry with your secretary, but ask him to proofread more carefully next time.
   - ▲ You arrive at a meeting location and discover the room has been set up incorrectly. You may be able to summon the hotel staff to address the problem, but sometimes the most expeditious and least stressful thing to do will be to roll up your sleeves and move some chairs and tables (possibly with help from your members).

Sample Script: Delegating a Facilitation Task

You: "Kim, can I give you a job to do at the next meeting? As you know, we will be discussing a new telemarketing initiative. I need someone to take a leadership role in the discussion. I know you have some experience in this area.

"What I need you to do is to review the discussion document, prepare a five-minute presentation to the group, and then lead a thirty-minute discussion on two questions: First, whether this new initiative is a good idea, and second, if the answer is yes, what should be the next steps. What do you think? Will you do it?"

Kim says: "But I'm not a very good public speaker. I really get nervous in front of groups. I don't know if I can do it."

You respond: "Kim, I understand completely. Speaking before a group can be scary and unnerving. I get nervous too, especially at the start of a presentation, even if I may not show it. But once I get going, it becomes easier. In fact, I even enjoy the experience. I know you can do it, Kim, and I will give you any help you need.

We need more people like you to move into leadership positions. Would you do it? Can I count on you?"

With very minimal coaching, Kim gives a surprisingly effective presentation and follows by leading an interactive discussion. She exceeds everyone's expectations. At the end of the meeting you close the loop with an acknowledgment:

"I would like to acknowledge an individual who made a special effort at this meeting. Kim prepared and delivered a great presentation for us and facilitated a very productive discussion. She did it despite some nervousness and she showed us that we can do better than we think we can. For that effort, Kim, you earned 'the spark of the meeting' award." (Follow with a round of applause.)

Sample Script: Allowing Them to Complain

As a facilitator, you need to give people permission to complain about your leadership style. Why not go a step beyond that, and offer them a sample script that they could use? Here is a script that will enable them to complain if you are coming across as micromanaging them:

Member to facilitator: "Jim, I am having a hard time. You gave me this job and that's great. But now you're telling me how to do it and checking on my progress every day. I know you're doing it because you want to make sure things get done right. But, as a professional, I need room to maneuver. I need to use my own judgment and put my own expertise to work. I promise I will do the job and will do it well. How about if we meet next Wednesday at 10 and I will show you what I have done?"

Diplomat

As a facilitator, you may have a great deal of influence and personal clout. As a result, you may become the object of manipulation, with individual members trying to enlist you to help them achieve their goals. At times it will be best to ignore such attempts and move on. Other times it will be appropriate and necessary to confront such attempts honestly and directly.

Sample Script: Being a Juggler

Greg is pressing you to make a commitment. You have no objection to it, but you know that Joan and Shelly will be affected by your decision. You prefer to consult them before finalizing your commitment, so they are not surprised by it. You say this to Greg:

You: "Greg, I understand what you want. Before I say yes to it, I need to check with Joan and Shelly, because this decision will have an impact on them."

Greg persists: "Why the delay? You have the power to make this decision. It would really mean a lot to me if you just allowed me to get on with things right away. I really need to get this initiative going now. Joan and Shelly will probably want to delay it."

You respond: "Greg, I can see how important this is to you. At the same time, can you see why I need to check with Joan and Shelly? You wouldn't want me to make important decisions that affect you before consulting you first, would you? I promise to be sensitive to your schedules when I talk to them. If they give me reasons to delay this project, they will have to give me legitimate reasons to justify such a delay."

Sample Script: You Are Being Manipulated

You are invited to chair a contentious meeting as an impartial facilitator. Brian, one of the "combatants," approaches you before the meeting and tells you how pleased he is that you will be there and how impressed he is with your credentials and reputation. Now that he complimented you, he thinks he has you on his good side and gets to his real agenda. He tries to persuade you that his position is right. You need to resist his attempt to manipulate you by flattery. Here is a sample script for you:

"Thank you, Brian. First, I want to say how much I appreciate your vote of confidence. I need all the help I can get to make this meeting focused and productive. There are several tough issues for us to address, and it's great that you are prepared to work as a constructive participant. As to your point of view, I understand how strongly you feel about it. At the same time, I need to clarify that my job is not to agree or disagree with you, but only to structure the discussion so that all sides, including yours, can be heard and understood. Why don't you come to the meeting ready to state your opinions? And by the way, can I suggest that you also come ready to listen to other points of view? The differences between you and Bill may not be that great after all."

Sample Script: An Attempt to Make You a Mouthpiece

Phyllis: "Can you please explain to them how important this point is? You have such an effective way of saying things."

You respond: "Thank you, Phyllis. I am flattered. At the same time, my job is to run the meeting and not to represent one opinion or another. You'll need to present your ideas yourself."

Example: Your Boss Is Trying to Coerce You

Alex, your company's president, asks you to serve as an impartial facilitator at a contentious meeting. He says: "If things don't turn out this way, I will have to fire somebody. We just have to make the right decision, and it's got to be option A."

Your possible response: "Alex, can I make an observation? I can see that this meeting is a difficult one for you, as I am sure it will be for other people. I hope you will accept that my role as an impartial facilitator is to lead the discussion in a fair manner, and that I cannot guarantee you or anyone a certain outcome. Can you accept that?

"I should add this, Alex: I am confident that, with all the facts on the table, the committee will make the right decision, whatever it may be. Of course, I don't know what the decision will be. You think it should be A, and others think it's B. Perhaps there is a decision C out there that is better than both A and B, and if everyone listens we will find it. It doesn't have to be a win-lose outcome. It can be win-win."

Note: No effort is made in the above script to respond to the threat of firing someone, or to the fact that Alex may have been trying to influence you to bias the meeting in favor of option A.

These are not your immediate problems, and they are probably not for you to solve. They should not become factors in planning and running the meeting.

And what if Alex persists and even makes suggestions on how you might structure the discussion to steer the meeting towards option A? Try this:

"Alex, I am having a problem. You asked me to run the meeting, and I am glad to help. At the same time, you seem to want me to lead it to a certain outcome, and, in fairness to other committee members, I cannot do that. I need the freedom to use my skills as a facilitator and create a fair and equal process for the committee. Are you comfortable with this? If not, I would have no difficulty walking away and making room for someone else to run the meeting. What would you like me to do?"

And do feel free to walk away if your position is severely compromised.

Example: The Pitfalls of Personal Recognition

You are running a tough meeting and have been successful at "reining in" a dominant and outspoken member whom many people apparently dislike. As a result of this, you notice one or more of the following things:

- ▲ Someone who seems to be appreciating your success is winking at you or cheering you on: "Keep up the good work!!"
- ▲ Someone else seems ready to applaud you for your effective stewardship.
- ▲ Someone else congratulates you during the break: "That was fantastic!! You are handling these people really well. Keep it up. Sean was being a total nuisance. What he said was completely unfair to you!!" You may not be aware, but Sean is close by and may be sensitive to your facial expression and to what you say.

Your response? As difficult as it may be, you must stay on the high road, keep a straight face, and resist the temptation to respond enthusiastically to the flattery. Don't smile, and don't say:

"Thank you so much. It's so wonderful to hear you say that. It feels great to be appreciated. Very few people know how to give a compliment."

As good as the approval by others may feel, it can be intoxicating and deceptive, and it can impair your judgment as a leader. Responding enthusiastically to it may create resentment towards you by those who do not share the enthusiasm for what you did. It may also give the impression that you do your work to get approval and that you are dependent on it. This dependency on approval can be used to manipulate you, by giving it or by withholding it in order to get you to do something.

Here is a situation for you to consider. You say no, firmly but graciously, to a persistent member. The group seems very impressed with what you did, since no one had been able to manage this member until you came to town. . . . One member even begins to applaud you. But you know the risk. You say: "Please do not applaud. This is not a contest, and we need to be careful not to create winners and losers. Why don't we just work together, focus on the issues that are before us today, and create win-win solutions for the organization."

There are several benefits to this approach:

- ▲ You will earn the group's respect.
- ▲ Members will learn to be more mature and sensitive to others. They will find better ways of dealing with conflict than by overpowering their opponents or by celebrating their defeat.
- ▲ The disruptive member could turn from a foe to a supporter and become a constructive team member.

Example: Are Strings Attached to This Gift?

From time to time you will be in a position to receive something tangible from a team member, a consultant, or someone else. This could include an invitation to a lavish lunch or dinner; the offer of a special assignment or a promotional opportunity; or gifts such as flowers, chocolates, a bottle of wine, or free tickets to a play, concert, or sporting events.

On the surface there is nothing wrong with such gifts. However, there is the possibility that the giver might expect something in return, such as preferential treatment, a lucrative contract, or getting away with shortcuts and inferior work. Here are a few tips:

- ▲ Use your judgment. If there is only a low risk that the gift will impair your ability to say no to this person in the future, you can go ahead and accept it. But pledge to yourself that the gesture will not cloud your judgment and will not cause you to give the person preferential treatment under any conditions.
- ▲ Even if the risk associated with accepting the gift is low, it may still be safer to say something like: "Thank you very much for this gift. Just so you know, our company does have a policy on accepting gifts. It says gifts like this are OK to accept, as long as they do not affect our decision making on contracts. I appreciate the gesture very much. I know my staff will enjoy the chocolates." The message is simple yet subtle: No strings attached.
- ▲ If it appears that the gift has strings attached to it, or it poses a risk that it will affect your ability to say no to this person in the future, say thanks but no thanks: "I appreciate the gesture very much, but, in fairness to other people who might be bidding on our projects in the future, it's best if I say no. I hope you'll understand. But I do appreciate the gesture."
- ▲ If it becomes apparent after the fact that a gift was not unconditional and the person indeed had an expectation of a return, you can return it (if it's not too late) or you can clarify: "Mr. Smith, I did appreciate the complimentary theater tickets, but I didn't realize that there was an expectation that I do something in return. This is an expectation that I cannot meet without compromising the integrity of my work. I wish I could return the tickets to you, but it's too late. I will gladly refund the cost of the tickets if you want me to."

Example: Should You Say It in Person or in Writing?

A diplomat knows when to communicate in person, when to use written communication, and when to combine the two:

- When dealing with contentious issues, it may be advantageous to delay the face-to-face discussions until key concerns have been documented. This process slows people down and gets them to think before they speak (see example below).
- At times it may be appropriate to build consensus through the exchange of e-mails.
- Other times, you may need to stop the exchange of e-mails and call a face-to-face meeting, because too much is missed in the written communication.

Here is an example. You have a difficult message for Leo, and he tends to be very defensive. He is impatient, interrupts people, and jumps to conclusions before hearing them out. You know that if you approach him "cold," it will be an uphill battle to create openness to your hard message and ensure that you are fully heard and understood. You need to communicate your full message and have him absorb it before responding to it. To achieve this, it may be best to start with a memo:

Dear Leo,

I need to discuss with you a difficulty that I have with the way we work together. I thought to start by explaining my concerns in writing, so you can review them in full, think about your response, and get ready for a face-to-face discussion with me. The reason I am doing it this way is that in the past we've had a tendency to become argumentative and jump to conclusions before hearing each other out.

Here is my difficulty: (explain the difficulty).

Leo, can you please read this memo once or twice in its entirely, and think about it for a few days? Call me when you are ready and we can meet to discuss these issues.

Eternal Optimist

If your group or organization has a history of suspicion and distrust, it will be hard to fault its members for being skeptical about your fresh and optimistic approach.

As you speak about "teamwork" and "working together," the cynics will respond with statements like:

- "You don't know who you're dealing with here."
- "Wait a few months. You'll see what I mean."
- "We've already tried that. What makes you think you can do any better?"
- "Good luck when you talk to him. He'll be fine to your face, but you'd better not turn your back to him."

The cynics may have their reasons to be skeptical. But don't let them extinguish your fire. You must keep believing in people and in the power of a principled approach to conflict resolution and consensus building.

Naiveté and innocence are not such bad traits to have, even for grown adults. Yes, you may get burned as a result of it, but, if you are persistent and consistent, you will withstand the heat, outlast the personal attacks, and come out unscathed. You may also find yourself earning the trust and respect of people that everyone is afraid of and who managed to alienate many others. So keep that naiveté and optimism. The world needs more leaders like you.

EXTERNAL FACILITATOR

There may be times for you to consider inviting an external facilitator to lead one meeting or a series of meetings. Here are the advantages and disadvantages of doing this:

Potential advantages of an external facilitator	Potential disadvantages of an external facilitator
Objectivity and distance from the issues and the history of the group.	Lacks in-depth knowledge of the organization and may take a long time to get up to speed.
The ability to see things that inside people can't, because they are too close to the issues and too entrenched in the status quo or past traditions.	Is an unknown entity. You don't really know what you're getting and whether this person's style is compatible with your group.

The ability to introduce a fresh approach to dispute resolution and consensus building.	May be too passive or too weak for the strong personalities that you have. Conversely, he or she may be too aggressive and controlling and may thereby constrain the discussions.
The ability to level with people and raise tough questions with them, including questions that an internal facilitator may find difficult to raise, or may not be listened to or taken seriously when raising them.	May be too expensive for what you'll get. It's often hard to gauge the return on your investment in an external facilitator until a few meetings have passed. May end up hurting the process instead of helping it.

What to Look for in an External Facilitator

- ▲ Versatile, i.e., able to wear as many of the hats explained in this chapter as possible
- ▲ Superb articulation, listening, thinking, and presentation skills
- ▲ Objective and independent
- ▲ A strong sense of fairness, equality, and common sense
- ▲ Facilitates decision making, instead of imposing decisions
- ▲ Balances the needs of individuals with the needs of the organization
- ▲ A creative and fresh outlook on issues
- ▲ Inspires creativity and innovative and nontraditional thinking
- ▲ Naturally curious with a strong desire to learn
- ▲ Approachable and humble
- ▲ Genuinely caring and compassionate
- ▲ Turns conflicts and failures into opportunities
- ▲ Treats people as reasonable and principled, even when they misbehave
- ▲ Leads a group to a destination and keeps everyone on board, as enthusiastic and active partners, being there because they truly want to be and not because they have to be

▲ Steers a group from problems and complaints into affirmative directions

▲ High commitment level to the group and its work

▲ Good sense of timing

▲ Healthy and appropriate sense of humor

▲ Can say no, graciously and gently but firmly

▲ Engages every member in the decision-making process in some way

▲ Can be direct and blunt without appearing to threaten anyone

▲ Can manage strong personalities and maintain an even playing field

▲ Can let go of control and let the group determine its own direction

▲ Forms and articulates consensus

▲ Separates the "wheat" from the "chaff," i.e., keeps the focus on the things that matter (core issues and real problems) and avoids wasting time on surface or side issues

▲ Confident and inspires confidence in others

▲ Happy to pass on his or her skills and tools of the trade to others

Sounds like a super human being? Maybe. If you find such facilitators, hold on to them for a while and learn the tools of the trade from them.

Tips for Hiring an External Facilitator

1. Check the facilitator's references. Ask probing questions to give you an idea about his or her strengths and weaknesses.
2. Interview several facilitators before making your choice. There is too much at stake and your organization cannot afford to be casual about the selection process.
3. Before making your choice, explain your expectations and the dynamics of the group and get a sense of whether the prospective facilitator is confident about the assignment.
4. Tell the external facilitator what you want done and what should be avoided. Explain what did not work with previous facilitators. For example, you may have had facilitators who:

- ▲ Talked more than they listened
- ▲ Were too passive when the group needed firm leadership
- ▲ Were too proactive when the group needed to establish its own direction
- ▲ Were too casual, sloppy, and unprofessional
- ▲ Interrupted people too often
- ▲ Were too passionate about their views and thereby stifled the group
- ▲ Were ineffective in maintaining a clear focus in the discussions
- ▲ Were ineffective in articulating consensus
- ▲ Were ineffective at managing disruptive or dominant members

5. Tell the facilitator what needs to be done (the issues to be addressed and the decisions to be made), but not how to do it (how to plan meetings and what discussion techniques to use). Give room for the external facilitator to put his or her expertise and skill set to work.
6. Avoid compromising the facilitator's role by trying to influence the outcome ("I really hope you can get them to realize that _____").

Cautions for the External Facilitator

As an external facilitator, you have a unique advantage of being removed from the problem. Therefore it will be easy for you to earn the trust and respect of the members of the group. If the issues to be resolved are controversial, you may find members doing the following:

- ▲ Trying to form alliances with you.
- ▲ Trying to persuade you that they are right and that someone else is all wrong.
- ▲ Quoting you to other people, sometimes incorrectly, to validate their point: "Even Linda thinks so, and she is our outside facilitator, you know."
- ▲ If they don't get their way, blaming you for it.
- ▲ Accusing you of bias.

Whatever your clients do, be patient and humble and learn from it. Be a super-diplomat (see earlier section on the facilitator as a diplomat), and learn to deal with attempts to manipulate you. Leave your ego at home. The moment you begin to develop personal animosities is probably the moment that you should make room for someone else to fill the leadership void (see the later section in this chapter about the facilitator as a quitter).

Example: Your Words Could Come Back to Haunt You

An external facilitator was speaking to a key member (member A) of a group, and expressed frustration with member B. Member A was delighted because he didn't like member B very much. He called member C, complained about member B, and told him that even the external facilitator didn't like him. It turned out that member C liked member B, and told him about what the facilitator said. Needless to say, the facilitator's impartiality was called into question. The lessons?

- ▲ Ideally, you should communicate your frustration directly to the individual (member B in this case), and not complain behind his or her back.
- ▲ If you don't want to be quoted, say so: "Sam, can we keep what we talk about private for now? I haven't spoken to Roger about it yet, and I want to make sure he hears my criticism directly from me, and not through a third party."
- ▲ Regardless of any precautions you may take, you should operate under the assumption that any word you utter will eventually become public knowledge. In the end, there is no guarantee that anything will stay off the record. To put it more dramatically: Nothing should leave your mouth unless you are prepared for it to be shown on the six o'clock news.

HEALER

If the group or one of its members is hurting, they may need a soft touch and some support and comfort from their leader. This is especially true if your group suffered a setback or if one of its members is upset.

Sample Script: Dealing with Failure

After several months of hard work, your sales team prepared a winning proposal for a large contract with a major client. But alas, the proposal was rejected. Your members are demoralized and need some comforting. Here is a sample script for you:

"Before we move on, I need to say something about the ____ proposal. The fact that the client chose another vendor is very hurtful and disappointing to me, and I know that every one of you shares this feeling. I know how hard each one of you worked on this proposal and it's a major letdown to have it rejected.

"We still need to analyze what happened, what we missed, why things went the way they did, and what we can learn for future proposals. But before we do any of that, there is something else that we must do, and that is to recognize what an outstanding effort we managed to put together. The fact that we were able to compete against such formidable competitors and come so close to winning this project is truly amazing.

"Yes, we did not win the contract, but I don't think we should allow this setback to erase our achievements and make us any less proud of what we did together. We worked as a cohesive team and did the best we could with what we had. No one could expect any more than that. I think each one of us deserves a pat on the back for a job well done. So why don't you raise your right hand and give your neighbor a gentle pat on the back for a job well done.

"In recognition of what we did, all of you are invited to a team dinner, on the company, at the Cannery seafood restaurant. Is everyone free next Monday night?"

Sample Script: An Unfair Accusation

In the course of a heated discussion, Mac makes a condescending generalization about women. You intervene decisively and make it clear that this is not acceptable, but the damage has already been done, and Fiona seems close to tears. What do you do? Here are a few suggestions:

Call a break, and speak privately to Mac and see if he will apologize. "Mac, did you see how Fiona reacted to what you said? I am assuming you were not using these words maliciously, but as you can see they were very hurtful. I need your help to get us back on track. I need you to say 'I'm sorry' and promise that you will try to be more sensitive in the future. Can I have you do this?"

If Mac doesn't want to apologize, you may have a disciplinary issue at hand (see the subsection in Chapter 4 on disciplining a team member).

Speak to Fiona, comfort her, and assure her that statements like Mac's will not be tolerated: "Fiona, can I talk to you? I can see that Mac's comment was very hurtful, and I am really sorry about this. When we reopen the meeting I will talk about using appropriate language and about being sensitive to other people. I need you to let me know when you are ready for us to restart the meeting. Take your time, please. Do you need a glass of water or anything else?"

Is physical touching OK to comfort an individual? The answer depends on you and the individual and the rapport that you have. You should definitely proceed with caution. A light pat on the back may come across as a supportive and caring gesture and may be well taken. But a hug is likely going too far.

When everyone is ready, reconvene the meeting and have a discussion of the issue: "Before we continue, we need to discuss etiquette and decorum in our meetings. Mac, is there something you want to say?" (Mac apologizes, hopefully.) "Thank you, Mac. Can I ask everyone to be thoughtful about the language that we use and to be more sensitive to other people? Thank you. Do we need to talk about this anymore? OK, let's move on."

Sample Script: The Presentation Went Very Badly—or Did It?

People tend to be their own worst critics. Suppose a team member seems visibly upset and disappointed with a presentation that he just made. He needs some comforting at the meeting or after the meeting:

Team feedback at the meeting: "Jim, you look unhappy. Does it have anything to do with the fact that the overhead projector broke down in the middle of your presentation? Well, you can't be blamed for a malfunctioning projector. OK, it's time for feedback from the team on Jim's presentation. How about if we went around the room and gave Jim feedback, starting with what he did well, and then suggesting what he could do better next time? How about commendations first? Rick?"

If it is awkward to give this feedback at the meeting, add it to your IOUs, or follow-up list, and speak to Jim after the meeting: "Jim, can we talk about your presentation at the last meeting? I had a sense that you might not have been happy with it, and I thought it might be useful to debrief about it. Would you like that? OK. First, I should say that, from my perspective, I saw an amazing improvement in this presentation compared to the one you made last month. You were organized, included relevant facts, spoke clearly, and had great slides. Did you sense any of this? Well, I just thought I'd tell you, because I know people can sometimes be their own worst critics."

Sample Script: A Key Member Is Ready to Quit

You are chairing a committee and progress appears to be elusive. One of the key members becomes very discouraged. She tells you: "If you don't see me at the next meeting, the reason is I decided to quit." Here is what you might say:

"Donna, first I want to thank you for talking to me. I have a few things to say in response. Do you have a moment for me now? Thanks. The first thing I want to say is that I understand your frustration completely. I know how much work you've been putting into this project and how hard it's been for you to have your ideas turned down several times. I can see that it is getting to be tiring and frustrating. If you choose to leave because of it, I will understand and respect your decision.

"At the same time, I want to say this: We really need you now, more than ever. You bring insights, knowledge, and a sense of vision and purpose, and you have been a real asset to the group. Yes, some people might say that no one is indispensable, but I think that if you leave now, there will be quite a disruption in our work. So, as much as I would respect your decision to leave, I would really prefer it if you stay.

"I want to promise you one thing: If you choose to stay, I will work hard to help you and the group to move forward. We need to talk about the pace of progress. I have a sense that other members have the same frustration as you do, and this discussion should help. I'll leave it to you to think about it. Can I call you next week and talk about this decision again?"

Assuming that Donna chooses to stay, it would help if, at some point, you recognize her efforts in front of the group. Better yet, arrange with a member of the group to do so. For example, "Before we continue with the meeting, I would ask Chris to make a special award presentation to one of our members. Chris, go ahead."

Inventory Keeper

The group facilitator should keep several inventories. First, you should maintain an inventory of ideas that could be pursued to advance the group's mandate. Some of these ideas will be useful in the short term and some in the longer term. The contributors of such ideas should be acknowledged privately or publicly, to offer an incentive to keep those ideas coming and keep the group fresh. Ideas can come from:

- Your members, who can share them during and between meetings
- Your internal stakeholders, e.g.: your boss, customers, support staff, or even someone you met at an elevator on the way to your office
- Research on the Internet or other resources
- Conferences of professional associations

Second, you should maintain an inventory of what each team member can give: his or her knowledge, skills, and expertise, along with an inventory of what each team member needs to perform his or her best, including the following:

- Preferred types of assignments
- Assignments that will challenge the individual to develop new skills and facilitate personal growth, e.g.: presentation skills, writing skills, negotiation and conflict resolution skills, etc.
- Areas in which the individual needs training: time and priority management, etc.
- Things that make the member happy and bring out the best in him or her
- Things that should be avoided, because they make a member angry and bring out the worst in him or her

Here are a few ways in which the above inventories can be used:

- ▲ Review the idea inventory file before each meeting and see if you can add fresh agenda items that will advance the group's mandate and make the meeting interesting.
- ▲ Review the skills and knowledge inventories when planning a meeting, and determine who should prepare reports or presentations and who should lead the discussion on major issues.
- ▲ Use the matrix below or a variation thereof at a meeting, to ensure that you capitalize on everyone's skills and knowledge, including the quieter members. It will help you balance the meeting and avoid domination by vocal members.
- ▲ Review the matrix before bringing closure to an issue, and determine who still needs to be heard. This will help you improve the quality of the decisions. Here is a sample script:

> *"Before we make a decision, I need to make sure that we covered all grounds and that we are making a decision that will work. Let me see, from whom do we still need to hear? How about you, Phil, do you have anything to add? How does this decision look from a purchasing department perspective? Will it work? Any concerns?"*

	Jack	**Bonnie**	**Ruth**	**Derek**	**Steve**	**Ron**	**Phyllis**
Agenda item 1	S	M	O	M	S	S	P
Agenda item 2	M	S	M	O	S	M	S
Agenda item 3	O	P	S	S	O	M	S
Agenda item 4	S	O	S	S	P	S	O

- ▲ *S* means *substantial knowledge and expertise*. You must hear from this member.
- ▲ *M* means *marginal knowledge*. This member has very little to contribute on this issue.
- ▲ *P* means *potential interest* in this topic. It may be productive to delegate a low-risk assignment to this person, to "get their feet wet."
- ▲ *O* signifies an *out of the box* thinker. This member is a potential source of fresh ideas on this issue.

Island of Sanity

When a group faces divisive issues and chaotic meetings, when things seem like they are beyond hope, and when everyone else is panicking or crying "doom and gloom," it is great to have a facilitator who is like an oasis, or an island of sanity; who:

- Is calm, calming, peaceful, and reassuring.
- Is always there for you when needed.
- Is approachable and easy to talk to.
- Transcends the personal nature of controversies and focuses on issues instead.
- Treats differences of opinions as something to celebrate and benefit and learn from.
- Inspires confidence that, as tough as things may be right now, there is hope.
- Can be counted on to be a source of wisdom and proper perspective.
- Smiles in the face of adversity without minimizing the importance of tough issues.
- Does not panic easily, if at all.

MEDIATOR

Tensions and conflict among members of your group are only natural. If handled poorly they can divide the group, create underlying strain in meetings, and compromise the quality of your group's work. On the other hand, if conflict is well handled, it can become an opportunity to learn and improve the working climate of the group.

The facilitator should monitor the relationships among members, look for spots of stress or breakdown, and intervene when necessary. It's like an electrician inspecting the wiring in a complex system on a regular basis, and doing whatever repair work is required (i.e., replacing overheated or broken wires).

This section includes tips on mediating disputes among members of your group. It assumes that a dispute involves only two members of your group and that it should be resolved outside a meeting. Here are a few ideas for mediating disputes:

- Before offering mediation, suggest that the two individuals try to resolve the dispute themselves, and set a time when they will report back to you on progress. You can offer each one of them an opportunity to use you as an impartial sounding board before the two of them meet.
- If attempts by the two individuals to resolve the dispute themselves are unsuccessful, you can offer yourself or another impartial individual to mediate the

dispute. If the impact of the dispute is significant, it may be worthwhile engaging a paid professional mediator.

▲ The goal of mediation should be to reach a specific agreement between the two parties, preferably in writing. For them to say "OK, let's forgive and forget" will only work as a stopgap measure. Without a specific commitment to change behaviors, the dispute will likely flare up again.

▲ Keep in mind that although disputes are often caused by individuals, they are made worse by systemic problems, such as a lack of clearly defined roles and responsibilities, or a lack of rules of engagement, or a poor organizational culture (see Chapters 5 and 6). You need to work on the foundation for shared decision making to reduce the likelihood of disputes.

A Step-by-Step Mediation Process

The following describes a process that you could use to mediate a dispute between, say, Peter and Jim. Please note that the process is elaborate. You could skip a step if it seems unnecessary. Here is the progression of steps for the mediation meeting:

First, you explain the process:

> *"Thank you, Peter and Jim, for coming to this meeting. Our purpose in the next two hours is to address tensions between the two of you and see what can be done to have you work together in a more reasonable and collaborative manner.*
>
> *"My job as your mediator is to make sure that both of you are heard and understood. I am here to help you reach your own agreement, not to tell you what to do. I may interject by asking questions and summarizing the discussion from time to time. I may also interject if we go off track.*
>
> *"Before we start, we need to discuss a few ground rules. First, I would ask you to keep your comments to the issues and avoid personal criticisms. I realize that things have been difficult between the two of you. To get the issues resolved, you will need to listen, give each other the benefit of the doubt, and really try to understand the other person's perspective. We need to get away from the adversarial mode: 'You against me,' and we need to shift into the collaborative mode 'It's you and me against the problem.' Are you prepared to work with me on this basis? Thank you.*

"Let me now explain how I plan our discussion to unfold:

"Each of you will have an opportunity to explain your view of the situation. When you finish explaining, the other person and I will ask clarifying questions. I will record key points on the flip chart. In the process, you may discover that the differences between the two of you are not that large, and that you have a lot by way of common interest.

"Once both of you have spoken and once it is clear that you have been heard and understood, I will summarize the issues. We will then begin to discuss potential ways of resolving the dispute.

"Our goal is to reach a win-win agreement on how to develop a more collaborative working relationship between the two of you. The agreement should be specific and tangible, and leaving with a good feeling will not be enough. We cannot afford to have a stopgap solution that will not address the real problems.

"Does this process sound reasonable to you?"

Ask Peter to explain his view of the problem. Allow him to speak without interruption, except if he becomes verbally abusive. If so, say this: "Peter, can you please focus on the issues? We agreed to be hard on the issues but soft on the people." When Peter is through, you and Jim can ask probing questions. Questions should be of a purely clarifying nature and should get the other person to elaborate on confusing, vague, or incomplete statements. Probing questions should not be adversarial arguments (e.g., "How can you say such a thing?" or "Can't you see how wrong that is?"). They should be neutral and open. Questions should generally start with "what" and "how":

- What do you mean when you say ____?
- Tell me more about ____.
- Can you elaborate on ____?
- Can you be more specific about ____?
- Can you give any examples?
- What do I do that gives you the impression that ____?
- How does this affect you?

Record key points on the flip chart in front of both of them. Your flip chart should use objective, affirmative, and nonblaming language, e.g., convert "You keep on ignoring me" into "I need you to hear me out"; or "Pay attention to what I'm saying or doing."

When Peter has finished, it may be useful to ask Jim to summarize how he thinks things look from Peter's perspective, but without any editorial comment (like: "You are saying that I do _____, and of course you've got it all wrong"). Jim's summary should be objective and help him develop understanding and empathy for Peter's position. It should indicate to Peter that he has been fully heard and understood. Here is a sample summary statement:

> *"Peter, here are the main issues that I heard you raise. You need me to hear you out before interpreting what you mean. You need to be reassured that I respect your position and decision-making power. Some of the things that I do that give you the impression that I ignore you are _____. Is this an accurate summary of what the problem is from your perspective?"*

After the summary statement, you or Peter can give Jim feedback on what he got right and what he missed. Here is a sample response:

> *Peter: "Jim, here is what you captured correctly: _____. Here are a few subtle points that I may not have explained as well as I should have and you missed: _____."*

Note: Instead of talking about "points that you did not get," Peter talks about "points that I may not have explained well." This language is more accountable and nonblaming. This approach is softer and easier to take. Encourage both parties to use it.

Next, ask Jim to explain his view of the problem. You and Peter will then ask probing questions. You will record key points raised. When Jim has finished, it may be useful to ask Peter to summarize what he heard Jim say in an objective form and without editorial comments (see above). After the summary statement, you or Jim can give Peter feedback on what he got right and what he missed.

When the problem has been fully explored, you should be able give a summary statement that captures the areas of agreement and disagreement in a concise point format:

> *"Let me see if I can summarize our discussion. Both of you seem to agree that _____. Where you disagree is _____. Peter, you think _____ (solution A) should be done, and Jim, you think _____ (solution B) should be done. Is this an accurate sum-*

mary of what we discussed?" (Make corrections to the summary based on what they tell you.)

With the above summary statement, Jim and Peter will need to develop a win-win solution that will address their two sets of needs, and which will be better than the solutions each one of them had in mind. Here are a few tips for building the agreement:

- ▲ Get them to be specific.
- ▲ Set realistic targets and schedules for implementing the agreement.
- ▲ Establish how progress on implementing the agreement will be monitored.
- ▲ Establish how feedback will be exchanged if progress is less than satisfactory, or if the agreement is breached.
- ▲ Question them when they rush to make promises that they may not be able to keep. If they still want to pursue such promises, suggest that they try these ideas for a specified period before finalizing the commitments: "Before you agree to this, may I make a suggestion? Would it be better to try this for a week and see how it works before finalizing the commitments?"
- ▲ Question them when they make large commitments on behalf of other people. For example, if each of them represents a department and the decisions will affect many people, it may be better for them to go back and consult their departments before finalizing the agreement. "Before you agree to do this, it seems to me that it would be a good idea to delay it until you go back to your departments and get some feedback on it. This may slow things down, but it's probably better to make an agreement that your stakeholders can live with. Do you agree or not?"
- ▲ Put things down in writing, or prepare a follow-up memo and send it to them for signature. "Feel good" verbal agreements are only good as long as the good feeling persists, and that may not be very long. A signed written agreement serves as an objective frame of reference for both parties.

Example: Conflict Resolution Through Mediation

The complaints in this conflict are:

- ▲ *Peter's Complaint.* Jim interrupts him when he speaks to customers and corrects the information that he is giving. This embarrasses Peter in front of customers. In his view, the corrections amount to nit-picking and do not have significant impacts.

- ▲ *Jim's Complaint.* Peter is too casual and doesn't take the time to read his e-mails, which contain important new information. He plays computer games during work hours and speaks loudly on the phone. Sometimes he makes personal calls that are very distracting. However, Jim acknowledges that Peter puts in a full day by working during lunchtime and by staying late.

It's a real art to convert complaints into legitimate affirmative needs. Here is what Peter's and Jim's needs may be:

- ▲ *Peter's Needs.* To be treated with respect, especially when speaking to customers.
- ▲ *Jim's Needs.* To have a professional work environment maintained, to be allowed to give feedback, and to be able to concentrate on his work without being distracted.

The mediation could lead to this agreement:

- ▲ Peter will only play computer games during lunchtime or after hours.
- ▲ Peter will make his private phone calls from another office and will lower his voice so he does not distract other people.
- ▲ Peter and Jim will meet once a week and discuss updates that are relevant to customers. This will minimize or eliminate the need for embarrassing interruptions of conversations with customers.
- ▲ Jim will not interrupt Peter in the middle of a phone call. The only exception will be if there is a major problem with what Peter is saying. Even then, the interruption will be nonverbal, by passing a red alert note. If the problem with what Peter is saying is minor, Jim will offer his comments after Peter hangs up or save it for next week's meeting.
- ▲ When giving feedback, Peter will be constructive and respectful.

Mistake Maker

It's inevitable. As experienced as you may be as a leader and as a facilitator, you will make mistakes. Small mistakes should be easy to recover from, but the big ones can be painful, especially when you embarrass yourself in front of a group. Here are a few general tips. First, accept the fact that you are a human being and that you are capable of making mistakes. Don't be so self-conscious in front of a group. Take yourself lightly (and your work seriously). Next, reduce the likelihood of mistakes by doing the following:

- ▲ Pay attention to information that is available to you through various sources, such as your incoming mail basket, your e-mails, and the newspaper. Stay aware of industry trends, and attend professional association meetings.
- ▲ Pay attention to rumors and disputes that are simmering under the surface. Find out what's behind them. You don't want nasty surprises at the meeting.
- ▲ Pay attention to nonverbal messages and feedback that others give you. Find out whether they point to a problem that may have an impact on your group's work.
- ▲ Encourage feedback by welcoming it, listening to it with an open mind, taking corrective action, and thanking the giver for it. With feedback, you are less prone to making mistakes.
- ▲ Listen to all internal and external stakeholders, including your boss, customers, suppliers, and others. See Chapter 7 on building relationships with stakeholders.
- ▲ Give others early warnings and alert them to events that might affect them. They will likely return the favor by giving you "heads-up" warnings that will help you avoid making mistakes or encountering nasty surprises.

If you made a mistake, acknowledge it and do what you can to repair the damage. If the damage is beyond repair, apologize for it. Promise to not repeat it and keep your promise. Keep in mind that some people will insist on staying angry with you, and your apology for your mistake will not satisfy them. You need to make it OK for them to remain angry with you for a while, and see if you can reconcile with them when they are ready. The more desperate you are for their forgiveness, the more likely you are to lose your personal power to them. You could end up making substantial and unjustifiable concessions to them.

Learn from your mistakes and work to avoid them in the future, but don't dwell on them. Forgive yourself, and move on. There is no sense beating yourself up forever (unless you really enjoy doing it . . .). If you insist on being driven by guilt, your effectiveness as a leader will be diminished.

Here are examples of unnerving mistakes and how you might recover from them:

The mistake	The recovery
You worked very hard and planned what you thought was an amazingly clever consensus-building activity, to be done in small subgroups. However, your brilliant efforts fall flat. The group just won't go for what you suggested. They just want something simple, like talking without breaking into small groups.	"It seems that my approach is not working. How do you prefer to deal with this issue? Do you want to talk about it in the full group? OK, let's do it and see how the discussion unfolds." Hopefully you left your ego at home. If you get mad and defensive about the group's response, or if you feel guilty and beat yourself up "for being a failure," you will lose your effectiveness as a facilitator and may indeed become a failure.
You make a comment that seems to offend Paula (you can tell by her facial expression).	If you know what the problem is, say: "Oops, I'm sorry, Paula. I think I offended you by using these words. I should have said: _____." If you don't know what the problem is, say: "Is there a problem with what I said? Paula?" If Paula does not respond, try speaking to her privately during a break or after the meeting. Find out what caused the irritation. If it was a misunderstanding, clarify it. If an apology is called for, give it without hesitation.
You notice a distracting side conversation that does not subside. You interject: "Can we have only one meeting at a time?" During the break, Roberta approaches you and says: "It was very rude and insensitive of you to interject. Clarence is handicapped and was having a serious physical discomfort. All I was doing was trying to help him out, and I did it as quietly as I could."	First, apologize to both Rebecca and Clarence for the inappropriate interjection. You acted to stop a distraction, without finding the cause for it. Second, thank Roberta for giving you her feedback. Third, open the meeting by acknowledging your error, thanking Roberta, and asking members to give you such feedback anytime: For example: "Before the break I made the mistake of being overzealous about

The mistake	The recovery
	keeping the meeting focused. This is what I did: ____. I want to thank Roberta for giving me feedback on how I came across, and I want to apologize to both her and Clarence. I welcome feedback from any of you about a mistake that I may make in the future."
Dan accuses you of biasing the outcome of the meeting and running it in an unfair manner.	"Dan, can you tell me what I did that gave you the impression of bias? I need specific feedback from you so I can do something about it." Dan may tell you that you ignored members with a certain point of view or interrupted them too often, or that you nodded and smiled enthusiastically when someone with a certain point of view was speaking, but frowned when someone with an opposing view spoke. Thank Dan for his feedback and take corrective action, as needed.
Without realizing it, you take a long time to explain your point of view on a contentious issue. The silence in the room is deafening. During the break Ian tells you: "I know what you were trying to do, but that did not go over too well. I think the group wants to make its own decision."	After the break, say this: "I received some feedback and I thank Ian for giving it to me. It appears like I took too much time to speak on the issue of ____. In hindsight, I should not have done it. Let's go back to the issue now. We can start from scratch if you want."
You interrupt an emotional speech by a member because he was missing the point and digressing for too long. He gets mad and starts yelling at you: "Why do you always interrupt me, you ____ (using foul language)?"	Being practical, it may be best to apologize and let him finish. Sometimes you need to accept that members just need some time to vent. Your interjection could have come at the end of the speech: "Thank you, Roger. Before we continue, can I ask everyone to please focus on the issue at hand, which is ____? The issue of ____ may

	be significant to some of you, but we are not dealing with it right now. We have a busy agenda and we need to stay on track." Note that, in the above intervention, you ask members to stay on track, rather than telling Roger that he was digressing. This approach is softer and less confrontational.
You try to lighten things up by telling a short anecdote. Some people are chuckling politely, but apparently you offended a few. You can tell by their frowns and sighs of frustration.	"I really blew it, didn't I? I am sorry. I'll try to choose more appropriate jokes next time." Another option: Stop telling jokes in a meeting, especially when issues are sensitive. Leave it to other people to do it. You have more important things to do.
You have finished recognizing members who helped you. You realize later that you forgot to acknowledge a very important contributor.	It may be awkward to find another opportunity to recognize the individual. If you find one, say something like this: "I omitted one very important person from my recognition list. It's an individual who made a substantial contribution in the area of _____. Please help me recognize _____." To avoid this mistake next time, do your homework. You could also conclude your recognition remarks by saying: "Did I miss anyone?" One of your team members may remind you of someone you missed.

Example: A Peace Offering

Under the pressures of a meeting, a facilitator inadvertently made a comment that offended one of the members. The facilitator apologized for this as soon as he realized that he made a mistake. But then he went a step further. He sent the member a card and a box of chocolates as a peace offering. The facilitator did not have to do this, but he took the extra step to heal the wound and repair the relationship. The member receiving the peace offering appreciated both the gesture and the treat.

MOTIVATOR

As your group's leader, you need to "motivate" people to take actions and follow your lead. The question is: Why will they follow you? Will they follow you because:

- ▲ You are their boss and they accept your authority?
- ▲ They are afraid they'll lose their jobs if they don't follow you?
- ▲ They have nothing better to do?
- ▲ Everyone else follows you?

Or will they follow you because:

- ▲ They truly want to do it?
- ▲ You make it natural and easy for them to do so?
- ▲ They respect you and your leadership style?

If your answers are yes to the former set of questions, there is some serious work for you to do in adjusting your leadership style, empowering your team and raising its levels of motivation and commitment to the job.

On the other hand, if your answers are yes to the latter set of questions, give yourself a pat on the back. But don't rest on your laurels. Keep on doing the work that has gotten you and your team to this place.

Motivating your members is best achieved through relationship building, which includes doing the following:

- ▲ Be a compelling role model and show excellence in your work.
- ▲ Keep your promises and demand that others do the same.
- ▲ Give members jobs that they enjoy.
- ▲ Demand that they excel in their work.
- ▲ Challenge them to overcome self-imposed limitations and do better than they think they can.

- ▲ Cheer them on when they succeed.
- ▲ Compliment them privately and publicly.
- ▲ Thank them for helping you or others.
- ▲ Share the spotlight and the credit with them.
- ▲ Comfort them when they fail.
- ▲ Be there for them when they need your support.
- ▲ Listen to them and learn about what brings the best and the worst in them.
- ▲ Keep them informed and involved.
- ▲ Ask them for advice.
- ▲ Give them honest and direct feedback.
- ▲ Welcome their feedback and treat it as a gift.
- ▲ Show interest in them as human beings, while keeping professional distance.

Many of the facilitator's relationship-building efforts have been described in this chapter. Look further in Chapter 4 for tips on how to select, orient, and nurture your team.

Negotiator

As a facilitator, you may need to negotiate with internal or external stakeholders, including your boss, suppliers, consultants, guest speakers, and others. This section is not meant to replace your book on negotiations skills, but only to make a few practical suggestions.

To negotiate effectively on behalf of your group, you need to:

- ▲ Know your group's needs and be able to articulate them clearly.
- ▲ Understand the needs of the party with whom you are negotiating.
- ▲ Work together with the other party to define an outcome that will address both sets of needs (win-win).

Sample Script: Negotiating with an External Consultant

"Thank you for coming in to see me. My group was very pleased to hire you to assist us with this project. You come highly recommended and I am confident that we can work together to get the greatest benefit from your skills and expertise.

"My purpose in calling this meeting is to discuss the parameters of our working relationship. I prepared a written list of the key questions that we need to discuss, which include:

- ▲ The areas we need you to help us with
- ▲ The areas we're OK with on our own
- ▲ The time commitment we need from you
- ▲ How we need you to participate in meetings
- ▲ How we can ensure that you operate within the established budgets for your work
- ▲ What you need from us so you can perform most effectively
- ▲ How we can share feedback on performance as the project progresses

"This is the agenda I've thought of. I believe an hour and a half will be enough for us to cover it. Is there anything that you want to add to this agenda?"

As part of the ensuing discussion, you may want to emphasize a few points, some of which are often ignored when groups hire consultants:

- ▲ You expect the consultant to give you the best professional advice, even if it includes things that you or some members of your group may resist hearing.
- ▲ As a client, you retain the right to follow the consultant's advice, ignore it, or modify the proposed approach. The consultant should be prepared to accept and respect any of those eventualities.
- ▲ The consultant must give you clear and complete advice, but do so in a dispassionate and nonimposing manner, making it comfortable for the group to make its own choices on accepting or ignoring the advice.
- ▲ You expect the consultant to be accountable, give you progress reports, and comply with established deadlines and budgets.
- ▲ The consultant should give sufficient notice of any need to revisit schedules and budgets, so you can decide whether the activities that require additional expenses will be pursued.
- ▲ You expect the consultant to keep things confidential, unless specified otherwise.

The consultant's legitimate expectations may include:

- ▲ Having access to documents needed to offer professional advice
- ▲ Having access to key people in the course of the assignment
- ▲ Being paid on a timely basis, and possibly receiving a retainer deposit
- ▲ If the advice is not followed, being given an explanation (if possible)

As a result of the above meeting, your mutual expectations should be documented, and an agreement should be signed. Keep in mind that having a nice feeling about each other is great, but it's not enough. To protect all sides (both you and the consultant), you need to define and agree in writing on the parameters of your working relationship.

Quitter

A quitter? No way, you say. It's not in my blood to quit. Quitters are losers. When the going gets tough, the tough get going. Right? Well, maybe, but not necessarily.

There may be legitimate reasons for you to want to quit as the group's facilitator. This section offers tools to address some serious challenges that you may face. If, after trying to address them, you determine that indeed your best option is to quit, don't finalize your decision before reading the tips at the end of this section.

If this is reason why you want to quit:	**Try asking or doing this instead:**
You are bored. The group's members are stuck. They don't want to let go of the past and embrace new ideas. They always want to revisit past consensus. Or: The group is adversarial, with members too busy fighting each other. You worked on it for years, but progress eludes you.	Determine if the entire group is stuck or just a few dominant members. Have you done enough to bring quieter members into the process? Try leveling with the group: "I have been with you for two years now and our progress seems to be very slow. The thought occurred to me that I might have lost my effectiveness with you. Perhaps you

If this is reason why you want to quit:	Try asking or doing this instead:
	need a new facilitator and I should move on to other things. Do you have any feedback for me? You can give it to me now or after the meeting, but do give it to me. I need it." Note: In this script the finger of blame is not pointing at them, but at you. (Your message is: "I may have become ineffective" and not "You are beyond hope.") Humility and accountability are precious commodities in today's society.
Your group makes great progress and does impressive work, but management does not take this work seriously. Members are getting demoralized, and so are you. Or: The group's mandate is outdated and it should be dissolved.	It's time to talk to your boss or make a presentation to senior management: "My team has been working hard to achieve its mandate, but none of our recommendations have been accepted. We need to ask a simple question: Is our mandate still relevant? Are we missing something? I'll be frank with you. I personally cannot see the point of leading a group to do meaningless work, even if you are happy to pay me for it. Can you help me out?"
You are being harshly criticized by the group. The feedback is vicious. You say to yourself: "I don't need this."	If you have become the issue, perhaps the group could indeed benefit from a fresh approach. But don't give up yet. Again, the negativity may come from a small number of individuals. Try sending this memo to everyone: "Recently several members criticized me for ____. I would like to explain why I did it and then ask for your feedback. Let me put it to you clearly: If I am the issue and I don't have your support, I will gladly step aside and let someone else take over."

Your boss demands that you force a decision without consulting your group, but you promised your team that you would consult them before making decisions of such magnitude.	Talk to your boss: "Bonnie, I understand what you want, and I have a concern about it. I have made a commitment to my team to consult them and not force decisions of this magnitude on them without advance warning. Can you see the impact on me and on them if I break this promise? Would you let me think about it and suggest a way to meet your goals and at the same time preserve the relationship that I've been building with them?"
You are asked to do something unethical or immoral.	Talk to your boss: "Richard, I want to make sure I understand. Are you asking me to _____? Well, do you realize that I would be violating company policy and my code of ethics by doing that? If you insist on it being done this way, you will need to find someone else to do it for you, because I can't work this way."

What should you do if your efforts to address the problem are unsuccessful? If your valiant efforts to address the challenges stated above proved fruitless, your best option may indeed be to leave. If you are coming to this conclusion, here are a few tips.

Think one last time: Am I making the right decision by leaving? Have I done all I could to change things? Is there still hope for this group and this organization? Do they deserve to have me stay, and do I want to stay? Then, if your decision to quit is final:

- Have your succession plan in place. Give the company and the new players plenty of notice and time to learn the facilitator's tools of the trade.
- Quit with grace, humility, and confidence.
- Bear no grudges, bitterness, or anger against yourself or anyone else.
- Don't burn any bridges behind you; who knows, your services may still be required as a highly paid consultant.

Learn from the circumstances that led you to quit. It may have been a combination of the things that you did or did not do, the way the organization and the group that you led are set up, or the chemistry between you and the group. Or it may just be that this is the perfect time to move on to bigger and better things.

Consider the notion that in life there is no such thing as a failure, except the failure to learn from the past, forgive yourself, and move on. Time is a great healer. Some of the lessons from this experience will become clearer with the passage of a few years. Turn the perceived failure in leading this team into a learning opportunity.

REALISTIC VISIONARY

As a facilitator, you need to combine your group's sense of vision with a sense of realism. You need to ensure that your members have their "heads in the sky," but their feet firmly "on the ground." Being a realistic visionary, you may need to intervene in two types of situations:

1. *The Steamroller*. A seemingly great idea lands before your group. Members appear enthusiastic and excited, and the idea takes on a life of its own. However, you are aware of information that points to significant flaws in this idea. You must introduce your sense of realism, stop the steamroller, and not be afraid of being unpopular by "raining on their parade."
2. *Tunnel Vision*. Your team seems bogged down in small details and minutiae. Each individual is focused on the narrow interests of his or her department, instead of the interests of the organization as a whole. You need to elevate the level of the discussion. A touch of vision is desperately needed.

Tips for Introducing Realism

It is probably best to prevent the steamroller from even starting to move. You can achieve this by sharing your knowledge with members regularly and giving them frequent updates. This will reduce the likelihood of the flawed idea even coming up. You will not be the only one to recognize the problem. With a few knowledgeable members in the room, it will be much easier to stop the steamroller from starting to move.

If the steamroller has begun to move, it is easier to stop it before it builds up speed. The earlier you break bad news to the members, the easier it will be for them to accept it. If you delay your intervention, members will be justified in resenting you: "Why did you let us get all excited about it? Why didn't you tell us about this problem sooner?"

To stop a steamroller that is already moving, you need to overcome your anxiety and present the touch of realism nonetheless. As terrifying as it may be to stand in the way of an out-of-control steamroller, someone must do it. As the team's facilitator, it is up to you to be the first roadblock.

Sample Script: Introducing a Missing Piece of Information

"Can we slow down a bit? I hate to rain on your parade, but there is an important piece of information that makes this idea problematic. As some of you may know, our board of directors has been looking at ____ recently. The latest development is ____. The idea that Ruth came up with sounds great, but it is premature for us to explore it until the board study is completed. Shall we park this idea on our idea list until then?"

Or:

"There is this little question that nags me. I feel I wouldn't be doing my job if I didn't at least raise it. You can ignore me if you want, but at least I know I asked it. Here it is: ____. Is this a legitimate question to ask? Am I being a total nuisance by asking it?"

Note: The humility and the soft approach shown in the above scripts can be very effective. It makes it easier for members to hear you out. It can slow them down and entice them to look at a piece of information they did not consider.

Introducing a Broad Perspective (Radio Station WIIFT)

To broaden the group's focus and avoid tunnel vision, you need to remind the members of the group's mandate. You need to shift its attention away from side issues and into long-term priorities and bottom-line issues. For example:

"Can I make an observation here? I think there is one difficulty with what we're doing right now. We seem to be tuned in to radio station WIIFM: What's in it for me (and for my department), and we should tune in to radio station WIIFT: What's in it for them? We need to think about the company as a whole and about our customers and stakeholders and see how we can best serve them. They should come first."

More Tips on Being a Realistic Visionary

As a realistic visionary, you need to keep several things in mind. First, never celebrate your successes or mourn your losses too quickly. Things are not necessarily what they seem to be. For example:

▲ *Don't rest on your laurels.* Under your guidance, two members quickly resolve their differences and agree on how they will work together. They now seem like best friends, and you congratulate yourself on a job well done. A few days go by. Everything falls apart, and the two are back to their old habits. Of course each one blames the other for the difficulties. The lesson? If something happens too quickly and it seems too good to be true, it probably is. As the old adage says: "The proof of the pudding is in the eating." Wait for enduring success before you pop the champagne cork.

▲ *Don't give up too soon.* You are really having a tough time giving feedback to a team member. He seems defensive and refuses to accept your feedback. You leave with a sense of loss. Two days later he calls you, apologizes for the defensive reaction, and tells you how much he appreciated your honesty. You clearly underestimated the difference that you made.

▲ *Don't succumb to threats.* Keep a vision of what is right and act on it. For example, someone may express a strong but unreasonable position, like: "This is non-negotiable. If you insist on discussing it, we'll walk away from the table." You can indeed give in, or you can say this:

> *"Did I miss something here? I thought we said we were going to discuss all issues with an open mind and see what decision would work for everyone. How will we get there if some important things are non-negotiable? Even if this is an important area for you, at the very least we should be able to discuss it. Can you help me out?"*

Sheepherder

As your group approaches a crucial decision point, some members may conveniently want to stray from the path, sidestep the central question and instead deal with side issues. In such instances, you need to be the aggressive and persistent sheep-herder, reining them in and steering them towards the core question that they must address.

One way to force an issue is to write down the core question that everyone is avoiding on a flip chart in front of the group, and repeatedly say (forcefully and assertively if you need to):

> *"Can we pause for a moment? How is this discussion dealing with the core question of ____, which is on the flip chart?"*

Or

> *"I hate to nag you, but you have yet to address this very direct and very difficult question: How should Tom deal with a situation like the following: ____? He needs a simple answer from you today so he can do his job and deal with this situation. I know it's a tough question, but we cannot avoid it. We have to deal with it today."*

Spokesperson

As your group's facilitator, you will often be its official spokesperson to outside parties, such as your boss, the senior management committee, the general public, the media, and others. Here are a few tips:

1. Represent your group proudly and stand up for it and its work.
2. Represent your group accurately and fairly. There is no need to exaggerate accomplishments or hide unpleasant facts.
3. Share the spotlight with group members. If you are asked to make a presentation to your senior management team or board of directors, consider making it a team presentation, followed by a panel discussion. This approach of sharing the spotlight will:

   ▲ Be more fun.

   ▲ Be more interesting for the listeners.

   ▲ Challenge team members to excel.

   ▲ Boost your team members' skills and confidence.

- ▲ Develop pride, ownership, and commitment among your team members.
- ▲ Build cohesion and unity.

SUCCESSION PLANNER

As a facilitator, you should be transferring your knowledge and leadership skills to others. Succession planning is essential and will achieve the following outcomes:

- ▲ It provides leadership continuity in the event that you are absent or leave your position.
- ▲ It allows you to take a vacation, knowing that things will be just fine without you.
- ▲ It expands the leadership base and makes team members more empowered and accountable.
- ▲ It reduces the pressure and anxiety about "dropping the ball." With an empowered team, someone else will catch it.

Here are a few tips for the facilitator as a succession planner:

- ▲ Don't be possessive and protective of your position of authority.
- ▲ Don't guard your knowledge and expertise. Give it all away.
- ▲ Don't create a dependency on yourself as your group's sole leader. If your group is heavily dependent on you, then it is vulnerable to the possibility that you might be unavailable to lead it for any reason. No one person should be made indispensable.
- ▲ Plan for succession by delegating leadership roles to team members. One example is to assign the task of planning and chairing a meeting to a different member every time.

Sample Script: Transferring Skills

Suppose you are an external facilitator. Your group has become too reliant on you as its leader and is not thinking about developing its own facilitation strength. You can address this issue by saying something like this:

"We need to talk about succession planning, specifically for me as your facilitator. I know that you and I have had a good working relationship. I am proud of the fact that we have been able to work together and build a cohesive and highly effective team. At the same time, I think the organization needs to build some of its own leadership talents. I need volunteers to work with me, so I can train and coach you and transfer some of the skills that I have been using. It is very flattering that you want to keep me working with you, but you have several good leaders internally."

Voting Member

Some people will tell you that, as a meeting facilitator, you should never vote. Others might say that you should only vote if the result of a vote is inconclusive, like when there is a tie. Both of these notions and the assumptions behind them may not be correct.

In fact, if formal voting is to take place and you are a voting member of the group, there is no reason why you should not vote like everyone else, unless a governing document or policy prevents you from doing this. Why should you be punished for being the group's facilitator?

Having said that, in most corporate settings there is no binding voting structure. In other words, the group's preference is taken into account, but the manager reserves the right of a final say. In such settings, it makes sense to leave it to the manager to cast a deciding vote if the group is deadlocked or the result is too close for comfort. Here are two examples:

Sample Script: Choosing Between Two Options

"There are four of you who prefer consultant A and four who prefer consultant B. We have to make a decision today and we cannot wait for unanimous support. I am inclined to go with consultant B. Can the four who prefer consultant A live with the choice of consultant B? Thank you."

Sample Script: Choosing None of the Options

"Three of you are in support of option A and four are in support of option B. I think we need to work harder and find an option C, which will be better than both A and B. Given that we are running out of time, I'll ask everyone to do this: Please see if you can come up with a solution C that will have as many of the advantages of both A and B and eliminate as many of the disadvantages of both, and bring it to the next meeting."

Vulnerable Human Being

Your leadership position may make you the target of unwarranted and sometimes vicious attacks. People may criticize your facilitation style, the decisions you make, and the initiatives you undertake. A previous section in this chapter discusses the facilitator as a mistake maker. But having learned from your mistake, you still need to address the personal impact and the wear and tear that unfair attacks inflict on you as a human being.

Here are a few things that make a personal attack especially hurtful:

- ▲ The animosity, ferocity, and the emotional and hostile tone of the attack
- ▲ The inference that you are incompetent, uncaring, or malicious
- ▲ The fact that the criticism is leveled at you at a meeting, potentially embarrassing and humiliating you in front of your colleagues and subordinates

Your instinctive reaction to such an attack may be to:

- ▲ *Attack back*. You may get angry, accuse the person of being cruel and unfair and then look for opportunities to take your revenge.
- ▲ *Retreat*. You may keep quiet for a while, "lick your wounds," and possibly retaliate by not talking to or working with the attacker, or by communicating to him or her only by e-mail or by memo. Tensions, suspicion, and mistrust among you are bound to grow.

Here are a few better alternatives for dealing with the verbal abuse:

- ▲ Review the section in Chapter 13 on recognizing and managing your "hot buttons."
- ▲ Review the section in Chapter 13 about asserting yourself in a meeting without getting angry.

- ▲ Be a "self-cleaning oven." In other words, get over it and get busy doing other things. Your self-esteem and confidence will recover quickly, and time will heal the wound.
- ▲ Phone the attacker and say: "How about lunch? You owe me one." Try to learn more about this person. You may find some redeeming features about him or her.
- ▲ If this is a recurring problem, you may want to address it directly. Here are two sample scripts for you to consider.

Sample Script: Discussion with the Attacker

"Wayne, can I have a minute with you? Thank you. The first thing that I need to do is thank you for your feedback. I now realize how much the way I ran the meeting offended you. I understand the problem much better now than I did at the meeting, and I have taken steps to address it. You'll notice a difference at the next meeting, and I would welcome your feedback on it, positive or negative.

"Having said that, I want to say that I found it hard to take the tone of your comments and the words that you used. They could suggest that I am a malicious person and that I did what I did deliberately to offend you. It was particularly embarrassing for me to have this outburst in front of people who report to me. Could we look at ways of softening how we communicate with each other, while continuing to give each other direct and honest feedback? Do you have any suggestions?"

Sample Script: Discussion with Your Group

"Before we carry on with the meeting, we need to discuss how we communicate and how we treat one another, especially when the going gets tough, like it did in the last meeting. Can we spend a few minutes talking about it? Thank you.

"My observation is that all of us seem to be very passionate about our ideas and views, and that's just great. We need everyone's enthusiasm and commitment. There is no doubt about that.

"At the same time, in the heat of our discussions we sometimes forget to pay attention to the fact that the people we are working with are human beings who are sensitive, have feelings, and can be hurt by what we say and how we say it.

"It seems to me that all of us should learn to slow down and think about what we say, how we say it and how it may affect other people. I'm not suggesting we should tiptoe around issues. Certainly not. In fact we can be quite passionate about issues, and I would never want to lose that. But I think we need to be sensitive to people, because the emotional outbursts tend to hurt and take a toll on us. I believe we need to be hard on the issues, but soft on the people.

"Am I making any sense? Does anyone want to comment on this?"

THREE

Negotiating Your Mandate, Workplan, and Resources

As indicated in Chapter 1, shared decision making has substantive and process-related goals:

- *Substantive.* To make responsible, credible, and durable decisions that will serve the organization and its stakeholders well.
- *Process-Related.* To have your group and its stakeholders arrive at the same destination together, as willing and enthusiastic partners.

With an effective team facilitator (Chapter 2), the next building blocks for your shared decision-making process are your group's mandate, workplan, and required resources. This chapter covers the following steps:

- Negotiating your group's mandate
- Preparing your group's workplan
- Establishing your required resources

NEGOTIATING YOUR GROUP'S MANDATE

If you don't know where you are going, any road will take you there. Without a clear, meaningful, and compelling mandate, your group is likely to wander aimlessly and waste the organization's resources. A confusing, unclear, and irrelevant mandate can be demoralizing and frustrating for highly motivated individuals. How can they make a difference if they don't know what difference they are supposed to be making?

Conversely, a clear, meaningful, and compelling mandate offers the following benefits:

- Your group is more likely to work as a coherent and cohesive team, moving forward with confidence and a sense of purpose and direction.
- With well-established short- and long-term goals, you will be able to select the members of your team logically (see Chapter 4), so you can capitalize on each member's skills, knowledge, and expertise throughout the life of your mandate.
- A clear mandate will help you ensure that your meetings are well focused, and that you spend most of your time on the things that make a difference.
- A specific mandate will enable your group to measure progress against interim and long term goals, and will help your team develop a sense of pride and accomplishment.
- With your group's mandate understood and accepted by its stakeholders (see Chapter 7), your group's decisions are more likely to be respected and accepted by outside parties.

To define your group's mandate, ask questions like these:

- What exactly are you and your team expected to achieve?
- What difference will your team's efforts make to your organization?
- What will you be able to point to as your group's proud achievements when its work ends?
- Which stakeholders will be served by your group's mandate and how?
- How does your mandate fit within the overall organizational mandate?
- Do you personally understand and embrace this mandate as defined?
- Can you and your group get excited about this mandate?
- Can you and your group fulfill this mandate in the given time frame?
- Is your boss or senior management team fully supportive of this mandate?
- Do outside stakeholders, such as customers, suppliers, and the community, understand and support this mandate?

- Does another group within the same organization have a mandate that overlaps, competes, or conflicts with yours?

With the above questions in mind, your group's mandate should be:

- Clear, concise, and free of ambiguities
- Easy to understand and appreciate
- Sufficiently broad to allow your group to respond to changing circumstances
- Specific, tangible, and attainable within a finite period
- Supportive of your organization's mission and objectives
- Relevant, current, and responsive to emerging trends
- Affirmative, i.e., states what is to be achieved, not just what is to be avoided
- Meaningful, credible, and compelling
- Distinct from mandates of other groups within the same organization, and not in conflict with those mandates
- Fully understood, accepted, and supported by your group and its stakeholders

Here are a few examples of mandate statements:

- The mandate of the safety committee is to increase employee safety in the mine by developing safety standards, coordinating safety awareness and education programs, monitoring safety performance, and integrating emerging trends and technologies into mine safety standards and programs.
- The mandate of the stakeholder involvement committee is to engage the company's external stakeholders (customers, suppliers, and other affected parties) in discussions of company initiatives and practices that affect them, so that stakeholder insights and ideas can assist the executive committee and the board of directors in making better corporate decisions.
- The mandate of the relocation committee is to investigate options for relocating the company's premises and, once approved by the board of directors, to coordinate the relocation and have it completed by May 31, 2007.
- The mandate of the board of directors is to formulate broad policies and establish directions, priorities, and principles by which the company will be run and by which its mission will be fulfilled.

Note: Displaying the board's mandate prominently and reading it at the start of every board meeting can serve as a useful reminder that the board's focus is broad, and that its members should resist the temptation to micromanage the operations of the company, which are the mandate of the chief executive officer and the management team.

Additional Tips for Fulfilling Your Mandate

Reinforce your mandate by explaining it to your team members and securing their commitment for it. Keep the mandate in mind as you design meeting agendas, and remind your team members of it when you open your meetings, and when you bring them back on track, as shown in the following examples:

- "Teri, our mandate is ____. How does this issue relate to our mandate? If it doesn't, I cannot include it on the agenda."
- "As a reminder, our team's mandate is ____. We are making good progress. The things that we have achieved so far are ____. What's left for us to do is ____."
- "Sandy, just a reminder that the board's mandate is to focus on broadly based policies and not on the day-to-day operations of the company."

Periodically, you will need to review how your team is progressing in relation to its mandate. As time progresses, there may be a need to review the parameters of your mandate and renegotiate them with your boss. At some point your mandate will be completed or may become outdated or irrelevant. It will then be necessary to end your group's work and dissolve it. There is no point continuing (as some groups do) if the mandate has become outdated or is no longer relevant.

Example: Is This Mandate Meaningful?

Your municipal council is required by law to consult the community before it approves rezoning bylaws. You are asked to plan the public consultation process on a proposed new bylaw. The proposed rezoning from residential to commercial is very controversial. Your boss gives you and your consultation team the following mandate:

- ▲ Ensure that our regulatory requirements are met
- ▲ Demonstrate that we are willing to listen
- ▲ Avoid embarrassing and chaotic public events

Is this mandate appropriate, and, if not, what should it be? Here are a few problems with this mandate:

- ▲ The first part suggests that your council may be engaging the public only because it has to meet regulatory requirements, and not because it expects to benefit from the process. This is a reactive approach. It may create cynicism and cause people to view it as a gesture of tokenism: "All the decisions have already been made, so why bother participating?"
- ▲ The second part of the mandate is anything but compelling. You might wonder why your council needs to demonstrate anything to anyone. Needing to prove something implies that there are reasons to doubt it. If the council truly listens to the community, its actions will make it abundantly evident that it listens, and it will not need to prove it.
- ▲ The third part of the mandate states what the municipality wants to avoid, not what it wants to achieve. In the absence of an affirmative direction for your efforts, focusing exclusively on what you want to avoid may make it a self-fulfilling prophecy, which could mean that you'll have those chaotic meetings after all.

Given that this mandate seems inappropriate, what can you do? One solution is to approach your boss and say something like this:

"Kevin, thank you for asking me to plan and lead this public consultation process. I am looking forward to it. If you don't mind, I would like to make our mandate statement more credible and compelling for the community. I suggest something like this: 'The purpose of this public consultation process is to engage the community in discussions on the proposed rezoning bylaw, so that the council can take into account legitimate concerns and useful ideas, and so that the council can make better decisions on the proposed bylaw.' What do you think? Can I make the change? Do you need to get it approved by the council?"

Example: Potential Duplication and Interference

Your committee's mandate is to develop programs to make all employees nationwide more Internet-literate. However, you are aware that five branch office managers hired consultants to examine exactly the same issue with their own staff. You are also aware that one vice president, who is your boss's boss, considers himself very knowledgeable, and has some very definitive ideas on how Internet literacy can be achieved. He has an appetite to get involved and micromanage, and he might end up interfering in your group's work or even undermining it.

This mandate is problematic. There is a duplication of efforts and the potential for interference and conflict when it comes to implementation. What might you do? Being proactive, you could approach your boss, state the problem, and look for guidance:

"Warren, I want to thank you for asking me to lead the Internet-literacy initiative. It's an interesting project, and I'm very flattered to be asked to lead it.

"I would like to discuss two main concerns about our mandate. First is the fact that five branch offices are already doing work in this area. Can I negotiate with them on coordinating our efforts, to make sure that all of us read from the same page and avoid duplication and wasted time and money?

My second concern is this: I have a sense that your boss has a very strong interest in this area, and he may be eager to get involved. We need to find a way to benefit from his ideas while making sure that our group's mandate is respected. Do you have any ideas about how we might achieve this? Can I speak to him directly, or do you want to be the one to do it? Or should both of us meet him together? What do you think?"

With your boss's permission, you could approach branch office managers and discuss coordination of your efforts. Try sending an e-mail message like this:

Dear Janet,

By way of introduction, my name is Joseph Chan. I am the leader of a team that was recently appointed to develop programs to increase Internet literacy across the company. Our mandate is to work with all branch offices and see how our efforts can be coordinated.

I understand that your branch has already started to do something in exactly the same area. This is very positive. I would like to find out more about what you've done, so we don't have to reinvent the wheel and so we can coordinate our efforts.

Here are a few questions for you: ____, ____, and ____. Can we speak on the phone next Wednesday? My schedule is open between 2 and 5 P.M. I will need about thirty minutes of your time. Please let me know what time would work for you, and I will give you a call then.

Thank you, Janet. I am looking forward to speaking to you.

Example: A Predetermined Outcome

Your CEO invites you to his office and says: "I prepared this new organizational structure and I want your HR team to sell it for me. I want you to organize information meetings throughout the company, tell everyone about this new structure, coordinate a team to implement the changes, and deal decisively with any resistance to change."

"Yes, sir," you might say, and follow the orders that you were given to the letter. After all, you don't want to risk losing your job for insubordination. Right? Well, hopefully you can do better than that, because there are some serious flaws with this mandate:

- First, the outcome has been preconceived and predetermined in one man's head, and input by affected parties does not appear to be a part of the equation.
- Second, this approach is autocratic. It tells people what to do and forces outcomes on them.
- Third, the CEO told you not only what needs to be done, but also how to do it.
- Fourth, do you really want to be the mouthpiece for your CEO and sell his message?

Instead of the proverbial "Yes, sir," you can say something like this:

"Thank you, Mr. Lion King. Before taking on this assignment, may I make a suggestion? Thank you. First, I want to make it very clear that I respect what you've done here and that you have the authority to tell me to get it done. Having said that, I have to also say that I believe we stand a much better chance of making a smooth transition if we use a more inclusive approach. Based on my past HR experience, I believe that it would work better if people get to a destination because they really want to, and not because they are told to.

"I need two things from you: First, would you allow me to start the process by defining the problem that we want to solve first, before locking into one solution? Second, would you be prepared to give me the latitude to manage this process using my professional judgment?"

PREPARING YOUR GROUP'S WORKPLAN

Having negotiated your group's mandate (the *why*), you need to develop your workplan, or the *what* and the *how*. Your workplan will guide your group's consensus-building activities and help you in preparing meeting agendas. In preparing your workplan you need to consider the following questions:

- What exactly needs to be done and what "products" (e.g., a new staff orientation manual and a plan to implement it in various departments) are expected?
- What process-related results (e.g., all affected departments must be consulted before the manual is finalized) need to be achieved?
- What deadlines must be met?
- What is the logical series of events for the mandate to unfold?
- What results should come first and which ones can wait for later?
- What research should be done?

Your workplan should be:

- Geared to fulfill your group's mandate
- Designed to achieve certain outcomes and meet specific deadlines
- Measured and deliberate, delivering expeditious results on immediate priorities and allowing more time for long-term priorities

- Flexible, to allow for the natural evolution of consensus within the available time frame and to respond to changing circumstances
- Cost-effective and in compliance with established budgets

Example: Building a Consensus Among Stakeholders

A university is facing increasing costs and is considering revenue generation and cost-cutting options to address the problem. The obvious options are to:

- Raise tuition and fees.
- Eliminate poorly subscribed programs.
- Reduce faculty and support staff levels.
- Attract more students and increase enrollment.
- Increase class sizes.

You are appointed to organize a stakeholder committee and facilitate consensus building on what should be done to overcome this financial crisis. The committee's consensus will be advisory in nature and will be presented to the university's board of governors for approval. You are given three months to complete your assignment.

Here is an example of what your workplan might include:

- *Step 1: Personal Interviews*. First, you will conduct personal interviews with key stakeholders:
    - Chief financial officer
    - Student leaders
    - Faculty leaders
    - Support staff leaders
    - Community leaders
    - Experts from other universities
    - Consultants and others, as needed

As a result of this process, a few creative options will begin to emerge for addressing the financial difficulties. You will have also built rapport with the various stakeholders.

- *Step 2: Discussion Paper*. Based on step 1, you will write a report, explaining the problem and outlining a few proposed solutions. Avoid the impression of a predetermined outcome by labeling the report "discussion paper, for preliminary discussions only." Send the report to the management team. When given the green light to continue, make the report public.

- *Step 3: Stakeholder Committee.* A stakeholder committee will be established, with a balanced representation from management, students, faculty, and support staff. All stakeholders will be advised that their input will be taken seriously, but that it will be advisory and nonbinding. The university's board of governors will make the final decisions for which it is accountable.
- *Step 4: Committee Meetings.* Stakeholder committee meetings will be held. Options will be discussed and consensus will be developed on the options to be recommended to the board of governors. You will encourage creativity and innovative solutions.
- *Step 5: Progress Report.* The consensus that emerges from the stakeholder consultation process will be summarized. The report will be presented to the stakeholder committee for confirmation of its accuracy. After corrections are made, the report will be presented to the board of governors.
- *Step 6: Decisions.* The board of governors will make its decisions. It will approve some recommendations and amend or ignore others. You will communicate the board's decisions to all stakeholders and thank them for their participation in the process.
- *Step 7: Implementation.* The board's decisions will be implemented. Given that stakeholder input has been considered, support for changes will increase and resistance to them will be minimal.
- *Step 8: Evaluation.* You will conduct a postmortem evaluation of your assignment and learn lessons for future consultation projects. You may present this process as a case study in conferences of professional associations.
- *Step 9: Celebration.* You will celebrate the success of the process.

Example: Implementing a Strategic Plan

A board of directors considers its vision for a company. It develops a strategic plan for the next five years. The plan lists initiatives on which immediate progress must be made, and initiatives that are long-term priorities.

To facilitate measured progress and to ensure that the plan does not just sit on the shelf and gather dust, a detailed year-by-year workplan (a "macro-agenda") is prepared. For example, assume that five important priorities have been identified in the strategic plan for the first year:

- State-of-the-art information technology
- Highly motivated staff
- Excellence in customer service
- Market competitiveness and innovation
- Harmonious relationships with internal and external stakeholders

Your board's workplan for the first year may be as follows:

- Ten face-to-face board meetings will be scheduled per year.
- Teleconferences, videoconferences, electronic meetings, or consultations by e-mail or fax will be held between face-to-face meetings, to sustain momentum and continue to build consensus on the implementation of the strategic plan.
- Five advisory committees will be created to address the main segments of the strategic plan. Each committee will be given specific assignments and clear limitations on its power and budget. The committees will generally be expected to facilitate research and present reports at board meetings. Their consensus will constitute advice to the board.
- Each face-to-face meeting agenda will include a segment from the strategic plan, scheduled according to established priorities. Only issues that are ready for discussion and decision making will be scheduled on face-to-face meeting agendas.
- Every meeting will include a "progress assessment segment," during which the progress on the strategic plan will be assessed. Having such a segment will ensure that the strategic plan is always in the forefront, and does not gather dust on the shelf (as it does in many organizations).
- At the end of the first year, the overall progress on the strategic plan will be assessed and priorities for the second year will be established.

Example: A Parking Lot of Issues

A strategic plan helps you make your group's work and meeting agendas proactive. However, your workplan should be flexible and allow your group to respond to emerging new issues (reactive agenda).

If an emerging issue is easy to deal with, it can be addressed immediately. However, if it is complex and requires more time, it should be added to your "parking lot" or "idea list" and dealt with through a more deliberate process.

Here are a few tips for managing parking lot issues:

- ▲ Parking lot issues should be prioritized.
- ▲ A parking lot issue should be pursued immediately if it is urgent and cannot wait.
- ▲ A parking lot issue that is not urgent should stay in the parking lot until the resources needed to research it are available.
- ▲ A parking lot issue that becomes irrelevant should be deleted from the parking lot.
- ▲ A parking lot issue that is ready for discussion can be added to the next meeting agenda.
- ▲ The introduction of a contentious or complex parking lot issue should be measured and gradual. See Chapter 1 for more details on the natural evolution of issues.

ESTABLISHING YOUR REQUIRED RESOURCES

In order to fulfill your mandate and complete your workplan, you must ensure that you have the needed resources for them. If the project is large and complex, you may need to use project management methodologies to determine your required resources, which may include:

- ▲ Team members with the right combination of knowledge, expertise, skills, connections, and clout (see Chapter 4 on selecting, orienting, and nurturing your team)
- ▲ Consultants, experts, and contractors, to help your group on an as-needed basis
- ▲ Stakeholder representatives who will give feedback on your group's work on behalf of their departments or organizations

- ▲ Office space, furniture, phones, computer equipment, Internet access
- ▲ Meeting rooms, audiovisual aids
- ▲ Financial resources, i.e., a budget that will allow you to pay for staff salaries, consultant and contractor fees, office/meeting space, and supplies

Here are a few tips for establishing your required resources:

- ▲ Plan carefully and anticipate everything that might be needed.
- ▲ Look for advice from experienced colleagues, team members, and possibly accountants and budget experts. Ask them to review your proposed resource requirements and give you feedback. Encourage them to nitpick and be devil's advocates and welcome their tough questions. Chances are you missed a few things, and it's better to find out now.
- ▲ Add a certain percentage to your budgets for contingencies and unanticipated expenses. It would not be unreasonable to add 25 percent to your budget estimates for a complex project. It's better to have extra resources to start with than to find yourself short and beg for more later.
- ▲ Always ask: Is this the most effective and efficient way of doing things? Are there any fresh ideas that could help us achieve the same results with fewer resources, by working smarter, and not harder?
- ▲ If the money is not available from the expected sources, be creative and look at other sources, e.g., outside sponsorships, stakeholder contributions, etc.

If your estimates are clearly beyond reach, you may need to do one of two things: scale down the scope of your group's activities, or determine whether this mandate is truly a high priority and whether it addresses the most pressing problems in the most effective manner. If not, the organization's resources may be better spent in other areas. You can explain this to your superiors and suggest that this mandate be revisited or abandoned altogether.

If the resources for this mandate are within reach, prepare a detailed cost proposal for your superiors to approve. To increase the likelihood of acceptance, do the following:

- ▲ Schedule a formal presentation of your proposal at a meeting.
- ▲ Prepare a workplan and cost proposal and include a cost-benefit analysis. Cover tangible and intangible benefits, and consider both short- and long-term benefits.
- ▲ Make your proposal "reader-friendly," circulate it in advance, and anticipate the questions that might be raised (see presenter's checklists in Chapters 9 and 10).
- ▲ Listen to any questions and concerns raised by your superiors and determine what changes are needed to make your proposal more palatable.

FOUR

Selecting, Orienting, and Nurturing Your Team

Having negotiated your team's mandate, workplan, and required resources with your boss (see Chapter 3), you need to select the people who will work with you to fulfill your given mandate. The quality of your team is an essential building block of your shared decision-making process.

In this chapter, the following topics are discussed:

- ▲ Determining the desired makeup of your team
- ▲ Determining the desired size of your team
- ▲ Attracting good talent to your team
- ▲ Selecting your team members
- ▲ Orienting your team members
- ▲ Learning about your team members
- ▲ Nurturing your team

- Assessing your team
- What to do if you inherit an imperfect team
- Starting a quiet corporate revolution
- Working with external consultants

Determining the Desired Makeup of Your Team

Your team will likely consist of the following:

- Full-time and part-time staff
- Volunteers (as in the case of an unpaid board of directors)
- Contact persons in other departments and stakeholder organizations
- Outside contractors and consultants

In an ideal setting, you will be able to build your team to achieve the best combination of skills, knowledge, expertise, connections, influence, and attitudes. This section offers you tools to determine the desired makeup of your team. It covers four areas:

1. Specific strengths needed for your team
2. Core competencies of every team member
3. Attitude and commitment expected of every team member
4. Red flags to watch for when selecting team members

Specific Strengths Needed for Your Team

Your team may need the specific strengths offered by the following types of individuals:

1. *Key Decision Makers.* Individuals such as your boss and other key stakeholders, who have the power to make decisions that will have an impact on your team's mandate and work.
2. *Influencers.* Individuals with connections and clout outside your team, who can help increase the respect for your team's work among other groups or organiza-

tions. Examples could include a *team sponsor* who also sits on the senior management team, or a respected *community leader* who can help you make inroads with the municipal council and community organizations that you need as supporters.

3. *Stakeholder Representatives*. Individuals representing departments, groups, or geographic regions that will be affected by your team's decisions, and whose input will be essential to making responsible, credible, and durable decisions.
4. *Visionaries*. Individuals with problem-solving and conceptualization skills who will add creativity, innovation, and vision to the consensus-building process.
5. *Researchers*. Individuals who have the patience to research what other organizations have done in certain areas, browse the Internet, and learn about emerging technologies and trends that are relevant to your group's work. Researchers will help you save time and avoid reinventing the wheel by capitalizing on what others have already done.
6. *The Voice of Experience*. Individuals who know the history of the organization and the dynamics within departments and between them. Keep in mind that the voice of experience can be a double-edged sword. Yes, it can help your team avoid nasty surprises, but it can also deter you from taking necessary risks and breaking new ground. Watch for experienced members who say emphatically: "We've tried it and didn't work," or "Tom will never agree to this. It just won't happen and we'd be fooling ourselves if we thought otherwise."
7. *Tutors*. Recent high school or college graduates who can tutor your "old-timers" in technology or computer skills. In turn, the tutors can benefit from the maturity, depth of knowledge, and industry experience that the "old-timers" can teach them. It can be a win-win relationship.
8. *Reliable Workers*. People who can be relied on to get things done for your team, with the turnaround time that you need.
9. *Nitpickers and Devil's Advocates*. Individuals with an eye for detail and with plenty of "what if" questions. Their involvement may slow down the decision-making process, but it will likely protect your group from missing important points or making significant errors in its decisions. Put their nit-picking to good use by:

   ▲ Asking them to review important documents before a meeting

   ▲ Asking them to draft decision-making options or analyze them

   ▲ Turning to them for input during the meeting; ask them, "Have we missed anything?"

10. *Specialists*. Individuals who specialize or excel in certain areas and have limited interest in others; for example, computer programmers, accountants, human resources specialists, public relations practitioners, etc.
11. *Generalists*. Individuals who enjoy variety, excel in a range of areas, and learn new skills easily.

If applicable in your situation, you may need to be sure you have an appropriate mix of genders, races, and ethnic backgrounds. You may also need the following outsiders on your team:

- *Subject Matter Experts*. These are usually outside consultants who specialize in an area that affects your mandate, and whom your team will probably need on a part-time or one-time basis. Examples include lawyers, information technology experts, futurists, accountants, public opinion polling firms, environmental consultants, etc. See the later section in this chapter on dealing with external consultants.
- *Professional Facilitators*. If your mandate covers contentious or complex issues, your group may benefit from the involvement of an impartial team facilitator. For selection tips, see the section on the external facilitator in Chapter 2.

Assignment: Assess Your Own Team

- Is the makeup of your team appropriate?
- Does your team have the right combination of knowledge, expertise, skills, and connections?
- Do you have too many critics and too few creators?
- If your team's composition is not appropriate, what needs to be done about it?

Core Competencies of Every Team Member

Each member should be required to have certain core competencies (in addition to the unique strength that she or he brings). Team members who don't have these competencies should be on your list of members slated for professional development or private coaching. Every team member should be able to:

- Communicate clearly, concisely, and coherently
- Listen actively
- Read effectively
- Write clear memos and reports
- Manage their time and priorities
- Use a keyboard (this is essential if a member is to participate effectively in electronic meetings; see Chapter 16)
- Send e-mail and browse/search the Internet
- Assert himself and disagree with others without getting angry
- Give feedback that is clear and easy to receive
- Receive feedback constructively and make it easy for others to give it

Assignment: Assess Your Own Team

- Does every team member have the above core competencies?
- If not, how do the deficiencies affect the quality of your team's work?
- What coaching or training programs are needed to strengthen your team in these areas?

Attitude and Commitment Expected of Every Team Member

In addition to core competencies, it is fair and reasonable for you to expect a certain attitude and commitment levels from your team members. They should demonstrate the following characteristics:

- An open mind and eagerness to learn. This may compensate for a lack of experience. With some training and private coaching any individual will become effective in a new field.
- An understanding and appreciation of your team's mandate ("the bigger picture") and what goals it is intended to achieve.

- ▲ Enthusiasm and a firm commitment to your team's work.
- ▲ Reliability, dependability, and consistency.
- ▲ Availability for your team's work without being compromised by other priorities.
- ▲ Accountability; being prepared to work within established parameters and budgets and be accountable for progress or lack thereof.
- ▲ A realization that blaming and pointing fingers at others is a waste of energy, and that the same energy could instead be channeled towards getting things done.
- ▲ A commitment to work as a team member and to be sensitive and respectful of others.
- ▲ Willingness to take the initiative to do what needs to be done, even when the individual is not specifically instructed to do so. This means going beyond the call of duty when needed.
- ▲ Compassion and humility.
- ▲ Commitment to stand up and fight for a principle in a gracious but firm manner.

Assignment: Assess Your Own Team

- ▲ Do your team members have the right commitment levels for your work?
- ▲ Does each team member have the right attitude? (see above questions)
- ▲ If not, what should be done about it? (see later section on inheriting an imperfect team)

Red Flags When Choosing Team Members

Here are some types of individuals you might want to think twice about before putting on your team:

- ▲ An individual who is well qualified but is also in great demand and has many other commitments

- A "lone operator" or a "loose cannon" who may not work well in a team environment
- An "eternal critic" who always looks for problems and misses opportunities
- A person who has good skills and knowledge, but also has a reputation for being one or more of the following: unreliable, inconsistent, dishonest, deceptive, lacking integrity, and placing self-interest before any other interests

DETERMINING THE DESIRED SIZE OF YOUR TEAM

The desired size of your team will depend on the scope of its work and the range of skills, knowledge, and expertise required to complete its mandate. The size of your team will also depend on what your payroll and consulting budgets will allow. Here are a few general considerations.

A smaller group is usually easier to manage and build consensus with. A committee to examine a noncontentious issue and develop recommendations should generally not have more than five to eight members, while a board of directors that meets regularly and forms policies for governing an organization should generally have no more than about a dozen members.

With a larger group you can have a broader representation of skills, knowledge, and expertise, and you can also include more stakeholders in the decision-making process. However, large meetings are more challenging to manage. In most cases you can keep your core team small and augment it as needed, by adding consultants and experts, or by adding individuals with certain strengths to your team for a limited time or on a part-time basis.

Don't assume that the team will have to stay the same for the life of its mandate. Your team's composition and size may need to change as your mandate evolves. Certain skills may no longer be needed, and new skills may be required. For example, at the start of the mandate you may need problem solving and conceptualization strength. As the mandate progresses, you may need more implementation and customer training expertise.

ATTRACTING GOOD TALENT TO YOUR TEAM

It's one thing to want effective members on your team. It's quite another thing to get them. Good talent is in demand. To attract effective members to your team you need to be competitive, and you must make your team and its mandate compelling, exciting, and attractive. If you don't, you may only get average performance and mediocrity. Here are a few tips for making your team attractive:

- Negotiate a meaningful and exciting mandate with your boss, and don't settle for less than that. (See Chapter 3 for tips on negotiating your team's mandate.)
- Project enthusiasm about your team's work to everyone. Once people find out about the fact that you are leading this project, your phone should start ringing and your e-mails should start coming, and you may not need an expensive and time-consuming search campaign.
- Establish your group's ethics and culture (see Chapter 6) and make it known. When people find out about your work ethics and the high standards that you expect of your team, they will want to join it and help you achieve your mandate.
- Establish a track record and reputation for being an effective facilitator who empowers people, is an effective consensus builder, and knows how to make meetings productive, engaging, and fun. Read Chapter 2 on the various hats of a facilitator and Chapter 12 on steering a meeting to its destination.
- Be selective when recruiting team members (see next section). Demand high standards and give them the support they need to perform to their best ability. This will help you build cohesion and loyalty among your members. It will develop your team's reputation, and make it very attractive to join. Wouldn't it be nice to have people with good talent lining up at your door, eager to join and work with you?
- Negotiate your budgets so you can pay highly skilled individuals the salaries or fees that they expect and deserve. An exciting work environment is a great asset, but it alone may not be enough to attract talented individuals and keep them for long. A substantially better compensation package elsewhere may be too seductive for your members to resist.

Selecting Your Own Team Members

Having made your team attractive to join and being flooded with interest, you need to select the right members for it. Here are a few things to consider:

- Establish your selection criteria. Use the previous sections to establish the desired blend of knowledge, expertise, skills, connections, and attitudes needed for your team's assignment.

▲ Create a general checklist that every team member will be evaluated against.

▲ Create specific checklists for the various positions on your team.

You should then establish an interviewing process to ensure that you get the most effective candidates. The process should include the following steps:

▲ Explain your group's mandate, workplan, rules of engagement, and culture (see Chapters 3, 5, and 6) to each candidate and find out whether he or she is comfortable with these parameters.

▲ Check references and avoid getting caught up in the enthusiasm of the moment. Have a list of pointed questions to ask the individuals giving references. Avoid asking questions that will naturally lead to positive answers, like: "He learns fast, doesn't he?"

▲ Have a colleague or two join you for the interviews, to get additional perspectives and make the selection process more balanced and objective.

▲ When considering new members for an existing team, you may want to have the team interview them. Take the team's input into account before making the selection.

For more on the selection processes, talk to your HR practitioner.

INFLUENCING THE SELECTION OF TEAM MEMBERS BY OTHERS

Following are three examples of factors that come into play when your control over the selection of your team is limited, and some suggestions on how to handle those situations.

Example: Stakeholder Committee

There are occasions when the members of your groups are appointed by other organizations and you have little say in their selection. For example:

▲ You are chairing an interdepartmental committee to develop new corporate standards. Members are appointed by their department managers. You have no say.

▲ You are leading a committee of community stakeholders, to give your company feedback on a proposed new development that could affect the local environment rivers, parks, air quality, noise, etc. Committee members are appointed by their stakeholder organizations.

In both of the above situations, you have no control over the selection process, but you should attempt to influence it. If not, you could be stuck in the following situations:

▲ Representatives who are chosen because they are the only ones available.

▲ Individuals who have very low commitment levels to the assignment, and would much rather go back to their respective departments or groups.

▲ Individuals who have very little knowledge or talent that is relevant to the task at hand.

▲ Individuals who are not truly representative of the department or group that sent them.

▲ Individuals who have very little influence in their departments or organizations.

▲ A "revolving door" participation, whereby represented departments or organizations send different people to each meeting. This offers no continuity and requires your committee to bring new members up to speed every time.

What can you do to ensure you get the right representatives for your committee? Although you cannot tell the departments whom to send, you can tell them what you want, i.e.,

▲ Representatives who are well versed in the sending department or organization's history, philosophy, needs, and interests.

▲ Individuals who are well connected within their sending organizations and can represent them well.

▲ Representatives with credibility and influence within the sending department or organization.

▲ Individuals who have a genuine interest in your committee's work and want to make a difference.

▲ Individuals who will stay with you for the duration of the assignment and provide continuity. Revolving doors (sending alternates to different meetings) will not be acceptable.

- ▲ Team players who will be prepared to listen to what other organizations have to say.
- ▲ Individuals who are authorized to negotiate and make commitments on behalf of the sending organizations or departments.

Example: The Office Space Committee

Imagine this scenario: As a respected facilitator, you are asked to chair a staff committee dealing with office space problems. Things are getting too crowded for some departments and too spacious for others. Traffic flow between offices is poor.

The building manager who asked you to lead this effort also chose the committee members for you. (You wish he hadn't done this without asking you first, but it's too late to change it now.) The members are the most vociferous critics of any change. They were successful at aborting previous attempts to rearrange office space. The reason for including them on the committee was to move them from working on the outside (being the problem) to working on the inside (creating the solution). Sound like a bright idea? Maybe, but you encounter a few problems:

- ▲ These committee members are accustomed to being critics, but not to being creators. They will likely have difficulties examining or inventing fresh and unusual solutions to problems.
- ▲ Members are not experts on office space. They know what they don't want, but do not have the professional expertise to conceptualize new solutions. This significant deficiency in expertise must be addressed before you agree to take on this assignment.

Here is what you may need to say to the building manager before starting your assignment:

"Thank you, Erin, for asking me to chair this committee. Before I start my work, we need to discuss the makeup of the team. It's great that you included all the critics, and I will work hard to convert them into creators.

"I need your permission to facilitate a decision by the committee to retain an interior designer for some professional input. I know that in the past people resented outside advice, but I think that if they are involved in making the decision and in choosing the consultant, they will be more open to their input. Going this route may cost the company more money, but I think it will be a good investment. Does this sound OK to you?"

Assuming that Erin gives you the green light on your request, it would probably be wise to delay your suggestion that a consultant be hired for now, especially if some members are suspicious of outsiders. Let them carry on with the discussions and be open to the possibility that they will come up with a good solution for the problem on their own. After all, being a professional interior designer does not mean having a monopoly on good ideas.

However, if after one or two meetings it becomes clear that you were right, look for the appropriate opening to share an observation with the committee:

"Can I make an observation? Our progress has been slow, and part of the problem seems to be that we don't have professional expertise in office space design. I am wondering whether we might benefit from an outside assessment by a professional person. I know that outside advice was not always well received by some of you. Therefore I think it would be for you to decide whether you could use outside advice and to be involved in choosing the consultant and in specifying exactly what you need done. What do you think?"

For more on working with external consultants, see the later section in this chapter.

Example: Influencing the Selection of a Board of Directors

Boards of directors are important decision-making bodies that govern organizations and establish policies for them. Yet often boards are fragmented and dysfunctional. A part of the problem is that many people join boards for the prestige, perceived power, and connections, and not with the motivation of serving the organization and making a difference.

What complicates things is the fact that a board of directors is typically elected by a larger body of members or shareholders, and the organization's leadership has limited control over who will join the board. Many people dread the prospect of receiving unexpected nominations during the annual meeting or having a hostile takeover of the board attempted by dissident factions.

To increase the likelihood of effective members being elected to your board, while ensuring that the nomination process is open (i.e., nominations are made both by a nominating committee and by members), you may wish to follow this approach:

- ▲ Send a letter to the voting members or shareholders well in advance of the election and announce the board positions that need to be filled. Then explain the board's mandate, the required time commitment, the roles and responsibilities and the code of conduct for board members. Having done that, invite nominations to be sent in by a specified deadline.
- ▲ In parallel with this open process, approach qualified individuals and encourage them to run in the election. Try to include some incumbents, for continuity, and some newcomers, for a fresh perspective. Look for individuals with leadership potential who could take over if an incumbent officer is unable to serve. Look for team players and for visionaries.
- ▲ When the nominations deadline passes, compile a list of nominees and send it to the voting members. Your letter should include candidate statements, indicating their backgrounds and qualifications and how they intend to serve the organization if elected. You can indicate who was nominated by the nominating committee and who was nominated by members at large.
- ▲ If there is a competition for board positions (i.e., more candidates than available positions), ensure that the voting members have as much information about the candidates as they need to make an informed selection.
- ▲ To avoid nasty surprises at the annual general meeting, your governing document (the bylaws or the articles of incorporation) should establish a nomination deadline and preclude last-minute nominations at the annual general meeting.
- ▲ The above steps will make the election process more objective, measured, and performance-driven. This process will likely remove much of the hype and emotion that often come with contested elections. It will likely provide the responsible and

visionary leadership needed at your organization's most senior level of governance.

Orienting Your Team Members

Before an individual starts working on your team, he or she should be aware of the following:

- ▲ The team's mandate, workplan, and resources (see Chapter 3)
- ▲ The team's rules of engagement (see Chapter 5)
- ▲ The team's ethics and culture (see Chapter 6)
- ▲ Roles and responsibilities of each member between meetings and during meetings (see Chapter 9 on planning a meeting and Chapter 13 on pulling your weight in a meeting)

For a new member to gain an appreciation of the group's work and its expectations, an orientation program should be in place. Here are a few tips for orienting new members:

- ▲ *An Orientation Manual.* It is good practice to have the parameters relating to the team and its work documented in an orientation manual.
- ▲ *A Personal Orientation.* A prospective new member should be asked to review the orientation package and decide whether he or she is prepared to give the commitment that your team expects. This should be done before a decision is made on adding this member to the team.
- ▲ *A Team Orientation.* Once your team is assembled, dedicate one meeting to discussing your mandate, rules of engagement, team culture, and ethics. Take feedback on the orientation manual and make adjustments to it as needed.
- ▲ *A Formal Commitment.* Some organizations or boards of directors go as far as requiring a new member to formally affirm that he or she will comply with a code of ethics and with conflict of interest and confidentiality guidelines (orally and, in some cases, in writing).
- ▲ *Refresher and Assessment Programs.* Have a refresher program at least once a year, to remind members of the parameters and standards that apply to the team and to assess how closely they performed to these standards.

▲ *A Mentoring Program.* Start a mentoring or "buddy" system, whereby a new member receives guidance and support from an experienced member. A mentor should discuss with the new member the amount of help needed and in what areas. The mentor should then stay in touch on a regular basis and offer the member support and feedback.

LEARNING ABOUT YOUR TEAM MEMBERS

In addition to establishing your expectations of new members, you also need to learn about each one of them and determine what they need to perform to their best ability. First, try to find out if this person is likely to be a "low-maintenance" member, who needs very little direction and operates best with only minimal supervision, or a "high-maintenance member," who needs more monitoring, support, guidance, and feedback. Then ask yourself, what will bring the best in this individual and capitalize on his or her skills, knowledge, expertise, and potential? This would include determining the:

▲ Types of assignments that will interest and engage the member

▲ Skills that this member would like to develop

▲ Assignments that will challenge this member, stretch his or her skills to the limit (and beyond), and boost his or her confidence

▲ Activities that this person does very well

▲ Things that make this individual happy, e.g., recognition, regular feedback on performance, social interaction or lack thereof (a person for whom work is strictly business, who prefers to leave the social part for family and friends)

Finally, what brings out the worst in this person? Some of those factors could be the following:

▲ Too much supervision and guidance

▲ Too little feedback ("If I don't tell you anything it means everything is fine.")

▲ Talking behind people's backs instead of direct communication

NURTURING YOUR TEAM

It is not enough to attract good members and establish expectations at the start of your team's work. Just as an engine needs periodic maintenance, so does your team. Here are a few activities to consider for nurturing your team:

▲ Challenging your team to achieve excellence

▲ Celebrating successes and special events

▲ Celebrating failures

▲ Educating your team members

▲ Keeping your team members "in the loop"

▲ "Taking the pulse" of your group

▲ Giving feedback to team members

▲ Receiving feedback from team members

▲ Disciplining team members

Challenging the Team to Achieve Excellence

A key goal of shared decision making is to benefit from the skills, knowledge, and expertise of your members. Yet often teams and individuals operate at only a fraction of their potential, settle into a mundane routine, and deliver mediocre results. You need to challenge your team as a whole to be much better than ordinary. You also need to challenge individuals to excel and go beyond their comfort levels.

Here are a few examples of how to challenge your team and its members to operate outside their proverbial boxes and comfort levels:

▲ Ask a shy member to do some research on an emerging issue and make a presentation at your next meeting. Offer any help that she or he needs in preparing the presentation. Remember that public speaking is one of humanity's greatest fears, and be as reassuring and supportive as possible. Tell the member frequently, "I know you can do it."

▲ If you are making a presentation to a high-profile group (such as the senior management committee or board of directors), share the spotlight and invite a few team members to join you. Make it a panel presentation instead of a solitary one.

▲ Ask an "eternal talker" to only listen for an entire meeting and present periodic progress summaries in concise-point format.

▲ Invite advocates of certain views to speak passionately in support of positions that they oppose.

▲ Prevent the formation of cliques and narrow alliances, where subgroups of members always socialize and work together, and where others are excluded and isolated. Mix the group and challenge the members to work with people that they don't know.

Celebrating Successes and Special Events

To perpetuate successes, you need to recognize members for special achievements and showcase and celebrate their successes:

1. Publicly acknowledge a member who made a special effort (e.g.: wrote an excellent report).
2. Acknowledge consistent attendance at meetings.
3. Recognize unique and creative ideas that made a difference.
4. Give members a treat (a special lunch) every time they meet or beat a significant deadline.
5. Thank individuals privately between meetings, by using statements like the following:
   - "I really appreciated the way you explained this technical issue. Many people were confused, and your explanation really helped."
   - "Thank you for that piece of advice. It really helped."
   - "Thank you for bringing to my attention that I was ____. I had no idea I was doing it."
   - "The way you spoke about the budget cutbacks was very strong on the issues, yet you managed to avoid all the personal accusations. That was just great!!"

You can also celebrate other successes or special events:

- Have a cake to celebrate a team member's birthday.
- Acknowledge a member's special event, such as a special anniversary or a new offspring.

However, keep this caution in mind. Some people prefer to keep personal events private and would be uncomfortable or even annoyed by having them celebrated in front of the group. Get to know your members and use their feedback to determine what is appropriate and what isn't.

Celebrating Failures

Does it sound odd to want to celebrate failures? It shouldn't. Naturally, you will want to cultivate successes and achievements and avoid failures. But the odd failure is inevitable. The question is not whether you will encounter failures, but how you and your team will deal with them. Here are some of the counterproductive ways of dealing with failure:

- Trying to determine who is to blame for the failure
- Allowing the failure to overshadow or erase the pride in impressive achievements
- Becoming discouraged, demoralized, and losing confidence
- Becoming afraid to take risks
- Holding on to the sense of guilt for too long
- Allowing your preoccupation with the failure to distract you from giving upcoming tasks the full and undivided attention that they need and deserve

Here are some of the more effective ways of dealing with failure:

- Remember what Richard Bach said in his book *Illusions* (Delacorte Press, 1977): "There is no such thing as a problem without a gift for you in its hands."
- Establish that failures are opportunities to learn and do better next time. The premise should be that "the only permanent failure is when you don't learn and move on."
- Stop the search for guilty people, and look instead for systemic problems that allowed this failure to occur, e.g., communication gaps, vague or loosely enforced policies, confusing definitions of roles and responsibilities, a lack of channels to share feedback, etc.
- Learn from the failure and bridge the systemic gaps that caused it to occur.
- Count your blessings, i.e., be thankful that the failure occurred, since things could have been much worse. It was good to catch the systemic problem that caused the problem and fix it before it caused a much greater failure.

Educating Your Team Members

Each team member is likely to have skills and knowledge in some areas and need reinforcement in other areas. As a team leader you should ensure that:

▲ Each member has the skills and knowledge needed to contribute to the team's efforts.

▲ The team is not so dependent on one person for a certain type of work that it becomes dysfunctional when this person is absent or leaves. No one should be made indispensable, and members should be enthusiastic about sharing their knowledge and skills with others.

Your team members may require training and private coaching in order to be more effective. You'll need to determine what can be done to reinforce their knowledge and skills in important areas. For example:

▲ A member who has unique knowledge or skills in a specialized area should be asked to teach some of it to other team members.

▲ A member who has trouble meeting deadlines may need time and priority management training, or may benefit from private coaching by a mentor.

▲ A team member who is preparing to make an important presentation may need writing and presentation skills training or private coaching.

▲ If the entire team needs to understand a particular subject—such as the budgeting process, or e-commerce, or a legal matter—you may need to invite an internal or external expert to speak on it to your group. But make sure the expert speaks in plain language and responds effectively to questions.

▲ If a conference of a professional association is held, consider sending one or more members to it. The advantage of sending more than one member is that each one can attend different concurrent sessions and bring the information back to the group.

▲ If members want to join a professional or business association that will provide good education and networking opportunities, see if you can help them by having the organization pay part or all of the membership dues or fees for local events. To maximize the benefits of this investment, ask the members to report back to the group on what they learned.

Education should be ongoing, especially if your team is continually challenged to break new grounds and do visionary and creative work. Here are a few principles to make sure your education efforts are the most effective:

1. Don't just look for training options outside the organization. It may well be that expertise is available at your fingertips, without costing anything. For example:

- Internal reports or documents in your department or in other departments
- In-house experts
- Staff members who attended similar training
- Colleagues in other organizations
- Valuable information that can be found on the Internet
- Internet-based and computer-based training programs

2. Don't always select the cheapest training option available. The cost of the program is not the only factor to consider. You need to consider issues like these:
   - What is the direct relevance of the content to the needs of the individual and the team?
   - Will the training program solve the identified problem?
   - Is the program a pure lecture or a hands-on training session? Keep in mind that people learn best by doing and receiving direct feedback on what they do. You may pay more for hands-on training, but the investment may be worth it.
   - What is the reputation of the training provider and the facilitator (check references)?
3. Don't send people on a training program only to make them feel good. "Feeling good" is not a good enough return on investment.

Keeping Your Team Members "in the Loop"

A key goal in your consensus-building process is inclusion, i.e., ensuring that all members arrive at the same destination together, as enthusiastic and active partners. To achieve this goal you need to keep your members informed and involved, and avoid surprises. Here are a few tips:

- Give early warnings of upcoming events that will affect the team and individual members.
- Break both good and bad news early, so that they get it from you with the proper explanation, rather than through "the rumor mill." For example, "Tony, I wanted to let you know that I chose Judy to make the presentation on our behalf at the management committee meeting. I know that you wanted this assignment, so let me explain to you why I chose her and not you."

Here are a few guidelines to follow to keep your team in the loop:

1. Avoid telling members more than they need to know and giving them information that has no direct or significant impact on their work. There is a risk in communicating too much; don't inundate members with e-mails, faxes, and voice messages that they don't need.
2. Don't withhold significant information for fear that it will hurt or frighten people. Even if it does hurt them, you should have faith in their ability to withstand the pain. In addition, the disappointment will be much greater if they will learn about this development from an outsider. They will feel betrayed, and ask: "Why did I have to find out about this from someone else?"

Taking the Pulse of Your Group

Implement "management by walking around" (MBWA), and always seek to be "in-touch and in tune" with team members. Make it your business to find out how your group is doing. Schedule a private chat with each member at least once every month or two, and don't wait for the annual appraisal to do it. Ask questions like:

- "How are things going?"
- "Are things working out as you expected?"
- "Any problems or difficulties? Any pet peeves about our team?"
- "Are we doing all we can to bring out the best in you?"
- "Have we managed to push any hot buttons and annoy you yet?"
- "How about your concern about _____? Has it been addressed or do we need to do more about it?"
- "Do you have any advice on how we should run our meetings?"
- "Can you give me advice on a couple of difficult decisions that I need to make?"

Always be on the lookout for things that may be happening with your team. Err on the side of caution and check things out instead of ignoring them. Never trivialize tensions and unrest by saying: "It's always the same member complaining."

Always gather "field intelligence" and seek to integrate it into future meeting agendas. For example, if someone raises a concern privately but is afraid to raise it publicly, introduce it in a way that does not identify the source. For example, "We seem to have missed an important point," or "Here is something that came up during the break."

Here are a few more guidelines on how to keep in touch with your group:

1. Be careful not to press individuals to talk about something when they don't appear ready to do it. Instead, make it abundantly clear that you maintain "an open door policy" and that when the individual is ready, she or he should feel safe to discuss the issue with you.
2. You don't have to accommodate everyone every time, especially by including their personal requests ("pet projects") when their relevance to the group's mandate is marginal. Being in touch and in tune with members should not equal trying to be popular and should not become a "free-for-all."
3. Avoid focusing too much of your attention on problematic members, at the expense of other members who need your positive support and leadership. Yes, you need to combat problems, but you also need to nurture and guide the rest of your team. Don't let your energy be completely sapped by negativity.

Giving Feedback to Team Members

As your team progresses through its work, it will become necessary to give your members feedback. Feedback can be corrective and it can also be positive (see previous section on celebrating successes). Feedback is the lifeblood of a well-functioning team. Its absence breeds tensions and mistrust and can place your group's efforts in jeopardy.

Give feedback in a way that makes it easy to receive it. Here are a few tips:

- ▲ Give feedback regularly. Don't wait until the problem is acute or things are unbearable, and don't wait until the annual performance appraisal to give it. By then things may be beyond repair.
- ▲ Treat the exchange of feedback as a problem-solving discussion, whereby both you and the recipient work together to address an ineffective behavior and decide together what needs to be done to solve it.
- ▲ Deliver the feedback in a sensitive, respectful, and caring manner. At the same time, be honest, confident, direct, and unapologetic.
- ▲ Make your feedback specific, precise, and clear.
- ▲ Make the feedback principled and objective. Be hard on the issues but soft on the person. Focus on behaviors, and not on emotions and personalities.

- Make the feedback balanced. State positive observations (commendations) and follow by suggested changes (recommendations).
- Give the feedback only after you have established that the person is ready to hear you: "Randy, I need a few minutes to discuss some feedback on your work with suppliers. Is this a good time to talk about it?"
- Make the feedback constructive and solution-oriented. Instead of just saying, "You are doing this all wrong," say, "Here is how you could do it differently, and here is the difference that I think it would make."
- Make the feedback interactive and consultative. Avoid lecturing. Punctuate your comments by asking questions, like "Am I making any sense?" or "Does this ring a bell for you?" or "I need some ideas on how we might work better to avoid situations like this one. Can you help me out?"
- Make the feedback purposeful. The feedback should lead to an agreement on what changes need to occur and establish deadlines for implementing them: "We've come up with some great ideas to reduce the tensions between you and other team members. How can we follow up on this and make sure we build on the progress that we made today? Shall we schedule another meeting in two weeks to assess how things are going?"
- When giving the feedback, create a balance between organizational and individual needs: "Your idea on working better with customers sounds great. At the same time, we need to follow an evaluation and approval process for new ideas, so that the team is involved and so that we can achieve consistency in this area."
- Avoid giving long preambles and excessive apologies, making it difficult for the listener to figure out what you are trying to do and leaving him or her wondering: "Just where are you going with this?" Also be sure to avoid using a harsh, accusatory, or condescending tone.

Example: Observation-Impact-Suggestion Approach

Here is an example of a three-stage feedback statement:

- Start with an observation of a problem.
- Continue by stating the impact of what you observe.
- Make a suggestion for a different behavior and outcome.

"Ken, I need to give you some feedback. It's about your participation in meetings. Is it OK to speak to you now? Thank you. Here it is: What I observe is that sometimes you interrupt people in midsentence. It's probably because you have a lot to say and you don't want to forget your point. The problem that this is creating is that other people get annoyed with you. It also makes the discussion repetitive because we don't hear each other out.

"I have a suggestion. It's a technique that I learned to slow my brain down and force me to listen. What I do is keep a pen and paper handy. When people talk and I have a response, I put a word or two on paper to remind me of what I wanted to say. When they finish, I go back to my list and see if there is anything that I still need to say. This forces me to listen and helps me remember my points. What do you think? Is this a helpful idea for you?"

Examples: Problem-Solving Approaches

"Rita, I have a concern, and I need you to help me with it. The issue is that we have missed you in the last two meetings. I know you are busy with other assignments, but we need your input and expertise. Can you help us with this problem?"

"Joe, I need to discuss a concern with you. My dilemma is that, on the one hand, you are amazingly effective at what you do, and everyone values your contribution to our success. On the other hand, some customers and employees have complained about habits they find irritating. Can we discuss their specific feedback?"

Receiving Feedback from Team Members

When you receive feedback, you need to welcome it and make it easy for the other individual to give it. You need to assess whether you can benefit and learn from this feedback. The person giving feedback should be seen as generous and courageous, even if she or he follows none of the tips given in the previous section on how to give feedback, and may be using a harsh, accusatory, and aggressive tone.

Here are a few tips for making it easy for others to give you feedback:

1. Treat it as a gift. Welcome the complaint with the same enthusiasm that you would greet a compliment. You may even want to go as far as rewarding or publicly recognizing those who gave feedback or suggestions that improved relationships or enhanced productivity.

2. Create opportunities for members to give you feedback. For example, at the end of every meeting say: "Does anyone have feedback on the way the meeting went?" or "Does anyone have a concern about how we work together? You can give me your comments now or you can see me or phone me after the meeting." You can also contact individuals directly and ask for their observations and suggestions. Keep the feedback channels open.
3. When someone is giving you feedback, be curiosity driven. Look for clarification and elaboration and ask open questions, such as:
   - "Tell me more. What do you mean when you say ____?"
   - "I am wondering what I did that gave you this impression."
   - "Can you explain how this affects you?"
   - "I need you to elaborate for me. Why is this important?"
   - "I am not sure I understand. Can you elaborate?"
4. Treat the feedback exchange as a problem-solving discussion and look for constructive suggestions:
   - "Do you have any suggestions for me on how I could make our meetings more focused and productive in the future?"
   - "What do you think we should do to satisfy this customer? You know him much better than I do."
5. Offer suggestions to avoid the difficulty in the future:
   - "Here is one thing I could do to alleviate this problem: I could ____. Does it sound like it would solve the problem? Maybe I can try it and you can give me feedback on whether this works."
   - "Thanks for giving me your feedback. I know that giving feedback is not exactly an easy thing to do, and so I appreciate the fact that you did it. Here is one thing I promise to do ____. What do you think? Would it solve the problem?"
6. Follow up and take corrective action on feedback, and let the giver know of the outcome. If you don't follow up, the giver of the feedback will likely become cynical and won't bother giving it to you again.
7. Let the feedback giver know if you chose not to follow their advice and explain why. Again, if you don't follow up, your invitation to give feedback will be seen as a meaningless and insincere gesture.
8. Don't hesitate to apologize if warranted. No one is perfect, and your apology will make it clear that you did not act with malice: "I really apologize for not

seeing that you raised your hand to speak. I will work hard to pay more attention and be fairer in the future."

9. If the person continues to use verbal abuse, even after you acknowledged his or her point and apologized, there will come a time to be firmer and bring the tone of the discussion to a more rational level. For example:

   ▲ "Jack, with all due respect, I prefer that we focus on the issues. I am the first to acknowledge that I am not perfect and that I do make mistakes. But I don't deserve to be called names. It makes your comments very hard to take. I need to work with you on a mature and respectful level. Can you help me out here?"

   ▲ "Can we slow down for a minute? (pause until you have space to speak without interruption). Peter, can we turn down the volume please? I appreciate the fact that you are annoyed with me, and I already apologized for _____. I think we are at a stage where we can keep the discussion at a more respectful level, so we can look at how to avoid this situation in the future. Is this something you want to do?"

   ▲ "I think I heard you, and this is what I think I heard _____. Now, do you want to hear me?" If the person says no, feel free to end the conversation. You need to know when to disengage. Given some space, the individual may realize that he or she went too far and may even come back and apologize.

10. If the feedback is positive, be gracious and appreciative, rather than being dismissive: "I don't deserve it" or "You don't have to thank me. It's my job." Say something like: "Thank you. What you said is humbling and heartwarming. It feels great to be appreciated and acknowledged like this."

When receiving feedback, avoid the following:

▲ Becoming defensive, taking the feedback as a personal attack, and fighting back: "You've got it all wrong" or "I find this offensive. You have done many things wrong yourself. You're not so perfect" or "You have no right to accuse me of _____."

▲ Interrupting, arguing, and denying the validity of the feedback through "Yes, but" statements. ("Yes, but" works as a verbal eraser. The "but" is so loud, that it erases the "yes.")

▲ Pretending to listen and even thanking the giver, but trivializing the feedback by thinking: "Everyone else is telling me what a great job I'm doing. This is only a complainer." What you may be forgetting is this: For every person who complains there may be ten others who have the same comment but don't bother to state it.

Disciplining Members of Your Team

From time to time you will need to deal with performance issues or with breaches of your team's rules of engagement (see Chapter 5), such as:

- Absence from meetings
- Failure to complete an assigned task
- Acting unilaterally and without consulting you or the team
- Breaching conflict of interest guidelines
- Revealing confidential information to outsiders
- Unacceptable behaviors during or between meetings

Anticipating the possibility of such occurrences, you need to establish how they will be handled. Depending on the breach and its impact, there may be three types of interventions:

- Soft interventions
- Hard interventions
- An examination of the violated rule itself: Does it work, or should it be changed?

Cautions About Disciplining Your Members

If the behavior or performance of one of your members is unsatisfactory, avoid the following mistakes:

- Don't delay your intervention, or you could be seen as hesitant and indecisive, and the issue may become worse. Some members who sense hesitancy may try to test your patience.
- Don't wait until things are unbearable and you lose your temper. It's better to intervene early.
- Start with soft interventions (they're much easier and less stressful for both you and the member). If needed, move on to harder interventions.

▲ Don't let the poorly performing member sap your energy and get you to become preoccupied with him or her, at the expense of everyone else. The well-performing members of your team need your attention and positive energy. Don't neglect them.

Soft Interventions

A soft intervention means that, before taking disciplinary action, you give a member the benefit of the doubt and see if, with some feedback, the problem will be addressed. The fundamental assumption is that the individual who violated the rules of engagement did not act with malice and that he or she is a reasonable person (or is capable of acting as one).

The results of a soft intervention may be as follows:

▲ It may become evident that the member was not aware of the rule or of the fact that he or she had violated it. In this case, the clarification of the rule and its intended effect will be sufficient and no further action will be needed.

▲ The member may apologize and promise to respect the group's guidelines and become a constructive team player.

▲ The individual may realize that your team is not right for him or her, in which case he or she may make the choice to leave (without any hard intervention needed).

Here is an example of a soft intervention:

> *"Libby, can we talk? It's about attending team meetings. We've really missed you for the past few meetings. I know that you had good reasons to be absent, such as commitments to other projects and to your family. At the same time, our team needs your skills and expertise to make good decisions. I need to know whether you are interested in continuing to be on our team. If so, is there something that can be done to make it easier for you to attend? Is there possibly a problem with the way we run our meetings that makes you not want to be there? I need your feedback."*

The above conversation could lead you to one the following actions:

If Libby's feedback suggests this:	*You may need to do this:*
Your meetings are held at very inconvenient times.	Consult the group and facilitate a decision on an adjustment to your

If Libby's feedback suggests this:	*You may need to do this:*
	meeting time (assuming you really want Libby on your team and that this is the only impediment to her attendance).
Your meetings are dominated by a few vocal members and Libby is given very few opportunities to speak, or the agendas may be unclear and unfocused.	Improve how you plan and run your meetings (see Chapters 8 to 14). Thank Libby for her feedback and promise that you will ask for it more regularly. Confirm that she will attend the next meeting and that she will give you advance notice if she has difficulty doing so.
Libby's boss is putting a great deal of pressure on her. This makes it extremely difficult to come to your meetings (which are not a priority for her boss).	It is time to talk to Libby's boss. He agreed to assign her to your project, with the clear understanding that he would fully support her involvement in it.
Libby has trouble managing her time and priorities.	Coach her, or assign a mentor to her, or send her on a time and priority management course.
Libby is really not that interested in your project. Her heart is just not in it.	If she is not prepared to give a full commitment to the project, it's time for her to go.

Hard Interventions

A hard intervention is needed when a soft one does not work. For example:

- ▲ An individual refuses to acknowledge that the breach of a rule of engagement is significant and is very defensive to your feedback.
- ▲ An individual apologizes and makes promises to be a constructive team player, but then goes ahead and breaches your group's guidelines again.

A hard intervention means that you need to punish a member. Hard interventions can be risky, and you should proceed with caution. Start by developing policies on disciplinary actions and including them in your rules of engagement (see Chapter 5). Hopefully you won't have to use them, but you do need them, at least as a deterrent. Discipline policies should specify the types of breaches that could occur and the penalties that they may attract. The policy should also provide for a gradual progression, starting with a warning for a first offense to a harsher penalty for subsequent ones, such as:

- A formal reprimand
- A probationary period, during which the individual's conduct will be closely monitored
- A reduction in clout, powers, and responsibilities
- Suspension or removal from the group

Your organization's policy on "due process" needs to be considered as well. You may be required to document the offenses, and then follow a detailed disciplinary process whereby the individual is given an opportunity of defense.

The following are sample scripts for repeat offenses or for serious violations of the group's rules of engagement, when there is not much room left for accommodation and leniency.

The performance issue:	*Your intervention:*
Failure to complete an assigned task	"Sam, I am having a hard time. On several occasions you promised to prepare a report or do some research for us, and you did not do it. In the past I ended up doing your jobs myself or delegating them to other people. This is not fair. Each one of us needs to pull his or her weight. Given that I gave you several warnings, I don't see the point of keeping you on our team."
Breaching conflict of interest guidelines	"Connie, it has come to my attention that your husband is the owner of a company that is bidding on one of our major projects. You did not disclose

The performance issue:	*Your intervention:*
	your conflict of interest, and you actively promoted his bid. Each one of us agreed to follow conflict of interest guidelines. This is an unacceptable violation, and I cannot have you continue on our team."
Revealing confidential information	"Moe, did we not clarify that this report is confidential and that it is not to be discussed with the media or the general public? I see your name being quoted in the newspaper, and as much as I want to, I can't give you the benefit of the doubt. This project has been seriously compromised because of this leak."
Unacceptable behaviors during meetings or between meetings	"Ben, I have to ask you to stop swearing and stop interrupting people in midsentence during meetings. We need to have some decorum. It's fine to be passionate about the issues, but we need to be gentle with the people. I have spoken to you about this several times, and I haven't seen any evidence of change. I'll give you one more chance, and if this doesn't work, I'll need to remove you from our team."

Note: The above scripts will apply in corporate settings where the manager has the authority to fire an employee. However, reality may be more complicated than that. For example, if the problem occurs on a board of directors or a stakeholder committee, you may not have the authority to remove the individual in question. In this case, you will need to go through the process articulated in the organization's governing documents (bylaws or policies), or a committee's terms of reference. For example:

▲ If the person is an elected member of a board of directors, the organization's governing documents may require a vote during a board meeting or a meeting of shareholders or members to remove him or her from office.

▲ If the person was appointed by an outside body (as in a stakeholder committee with various organizations or departments appointing the representatives), you may need to negotiate the replacement of the individual with the appointing body. For example:

> *"Mr. Smith. I have to talk to you about your department's representative on our committee, Brad. He is ignoring our guidelines and I cannot get him to work as a team member. The committee is having serious difficulties making progress as a result of his behavior.*
>
> *"As you know, I have no power to replace Brad as a member of the committee, since he is appointed by you. We need a representative from your department on our committee, but Brad is not working out. What should we do about this?"*

Examining the Violated Rule Itself

If a rule of engagement is repeatedly violated, you need to ask why this is happening. To get the answer, you may need to examine the rule itself and then examine how the rule is communicated.

First, examine the rule itself, possibly in consultation with your members:

▲ Is this rule realistic?

▲ Is it in line with the group's needs?

▲ Is it a help or is it a hindrance?

▲ Is it too rigid and constraining?

▲ Is the cost of having this rule greater than the benefit that it provides?

▲ What is this rule designed to protect against?

▲ Is this rule depriving the group from some opportunities?

The answers to the above questions may lead you to one of the following conclusions:

▲ Recognize that the rule is legitimate and valid and keep it the way it is.

▲ Modify the rule to address current circumstances.

▲ Cancel the rule.

For example, suppose one of your rules states that members of your team can authorize expenses not exceeding $100 per month, and that anything exceeding this amount must come to you or the group for approval. This restriction may prevent the group from benefiting from real opportunities when you are not there to approve the extra expenses. The rule should be amended to make the spending authority more realistic.

In addition to examining the rule itself, frequent breaches may lead you to examine how this rule is communicated. Here are a few questions to ask:

- Are the rules of engagement documented?
- Is the document reader-friendly?
- It the document widely available?
- Has enough been done to explain the rule and what it is intended to accomplish?

Assessing Your Team

Without a clear vision of an effective team and periodic assessments of its performance, it can become dysfunctional. This can occur despite your members' good intentions and initial enthusiasm for the job.

The worksheet below describes where teams often are (left column) and where they should be (right column). Use this worksheet to assess your team, as follows.

- When you first form your team, show this table to your members and facilitate a discussion on how everyone can work together to move away from 0 (could not be worse) and come closer to 10 (could not be better) in each category.
- Periodically (e.g., every six months), facilitate an assessment of the team.
- Ask each member to rate the team and its effectiveness on a scale of 0 to 10.
- Ask them to add up the scores, to a total of between 0 and 100.
- Ask them to share their grand totals and compare notes.
- Get down to specifics and ask: On which factor did we score well, and why?
- Then ask: On which factor did we score poorly, why, and what can we do to improve our performance?
- After each periodic assessment, the team should take concrete steps to improve its effectiveness in identified areas.
- Acknowledge progress and celebrate successes that occurred since the last assessment.

Ineffective team (0)	*Effective team (up to 10 points for each row)*	*Score*
Bogged down in small details, micromanagement.	Maintains broad focus and perspective.	
Fragmented, driven by narrow interests, and dominated by "personal agendas."	Cohesive and driven by its mandate and the interests of the organization as a whole.	
Powerless, reactive, crisis driven.	Empowered, visionary, proactive.	
Win-lose culture: "you against me." Decisions are often forced by narrow majorities.	Win-win culture, "You and me against the problem." Decisions are broadly supported and are reached by much more than narrow majorities.	
Members advocate for their own positions and don't listen to others.	Members listen much more than they speak: "We were given two ears and one mouth, and we should use them in that proportion."	
Slow pace, monotony, boredom. Routine, predictable, and menial work.	Dynamic and engaging pace. Exciting progress made. Freshness maintained. Excellence and high-quality work.	
Low commitment levels. Members often have plenty of reasons, excuses, and apologies for not completing their assignments.	High commitment levels. Members keep their promises and deliver quality work. Reasons and excuses are replaced by results.	
Embraces the status quo and always plays "devil's advocate." The critics (opponents) outnumber the creators (proponents).	Questions the status quo and examines new and unusual ideas with an open mind. More creators than critics.	
A sense of duty and obligation. Members are there because they "have to" be there.	A genuine enthusiasm and commitment for the job. Members are there because they truly "want to" be there.	
Members dread meetings and see them as "suffering and pain."	Meetings are varied and engaging and are rarely missed. "Suffering is optional."	
	Total: Add up the numbers in the right column. Minimum = 0. Maximum = 100.	

What to Do if You Inherit an Imperfect Team

Suppose you read Chapters 1 and 2 and took steps to become a democratic facilitator. You also read this chapter and are ready to put together a dynamic and exciting team. But then your boss asks you to take on the leadership of an existing dysfunctional team, consisting of individuals that could be compared to either sheep or deer.

The *sheep* are individuals who:

- ▲ Always wait for someone else to tell them what to do.
- ▲ Feel that the following concepts are in a foreign language: being proactive and self-driven, going beyond the call of duty, taking charge, and sharing responsibility.
- ▲ Are not used to being asked for their opinion.
- ▲ Think that the words "empowerment" and "corporate democracy" are a threat.
- ▲ Have been told in a previous job or under an autocratic leader: "Just sit down, be quiet, and be thankful that you have a job. Speaking up in a meeting is a career-limiting move."

The *deer* are individuals who:

- ▲ Have big egos and have never had to work in a team environment
- ▲ Are bright and creative, but tend to go off in all kinds of directions, forgetting about their team's mandate and any organizational rules or structures
- ▲ Are impulsive and do not pause to consider the impact of their actions on other people
- ▲ Become defensive if someone tries to impose any restrictions on them or establish certain structures or guidelines to which they must conform

What could you do? You could choose to accept this as the reality you have to live with, forget your ideals, and change your style to accommodate the dynamics of this group. You could then act in one of two roles:

- ▲ A shepherd's dog, barking at the sheep and ordering them to go in a certain direction
- ▲ A turtle, watching the deer racing past you and doing whatever they want

The above approaches may work to a degree. Many corporate leaders indeed operate as shepherd's dogs or turtles, and they even get promoted. But, recognizing that you can create a much more exciting and fulfilling reality for this imperfect team, you would probably prefer to reshape this team, by reining in the deer and empowering and propelling the sheep to action. Here are a few tips for dealing with a dysfunctional team that you inherit:

1. Assess the composition and size of your team (see previous sections in this chapter) and make adjustments, such as:
   - ▲ Remove the members who should not be there.
   - ▲ Add members who should be there.
   - ▲ Change the roles of the members you keep so their work is better focused and delivers more value.
2. Interview members in person and learn about what they can contribute and what they need to perform to their best ability. Determine who tends to be a deer, who tends to be a sheep, and who is ready to participate as an empowered and proactive team member.
3. Give your proposed rules of engagement and team ethics and culture (Chapters 5 and 6) to all members, ask them to review them, and schedule a meeting to discuss these documents.
4. At the meeting, discuss your team's mandate, proposed rules of engagement, team ethics, and culture. The purpose of the meeting should be to reach consensus on how you will work together, as a cohesive team, to serve the organization and fulfill your mandate. The outcomes of the meeting should be to:
   - ▲ Establish a team commitment to making quality decisions, achieving excellence, and advancing the team's mandate.
   - ▲ Establish the expectation of more proactive participation.
   - ▲ Establish the expectation of accountability and compliance to established guidelines.
   - ▲ Begin to empower group members by allowing them to propose changes to the proposed guidelines. Ask them to state concerns or offer suggestions.
5. Follow up on this first step by nurturing, supporting, monitoring, and giving feedback to your new team (see previous sections in this chapter). It's a tough road, but you'll need to persist. People may have accepted your message intellectually, but old habits are hard to break and they may put obstacles in your way and in their own way.

Sample Script: A System Development Team

Below is a sample script to start your first meeting with your imperfect team. The team is made up of computer programmers and systems analysts, who are involved in designing and testing a complex system for a demanding offshore customer.

There are several deer (programmers who spend plenty of time developing concepts that have no foundation in the customer's needs) and several sheep (quiet followers who are afraid to speak up) on the team. A few important deadlines have been missed because of the team's ineffectiveness. Management is getting impatient and wants you to take a hard line with the team. But you want to try a different approach: "Good morning everyone and welcome to this meeting. As your new team leader, I am looking forward to working with you to develop a computer system that our customers will appreciate and benefit from, and that every one of us will be proud of. I know that we have the best talent and expertise that money can buy in this room, and that our customers will be well served by the system that we'll develop for them.

"We have two hours for this meeting. Our purpose today is to establish how we will work together to achieve our goals. We have a tough challenge of delivering an excellent system on budget and within a tight schedule. I know a few deadlines have been missed, but I want to reassure you that I am not here to point fingers at individuals. That would be counterproductive.

"Instead of pointing at individuals, we need to learn from past mistakes and find ways to be more efficient and better focused on the client's needs. I need your help so all of us can work more effectively together, as a cohesive team. We need to catch up and deliver the excellent system that our customer deserves. We need to be able to combine creativity with a strong sense of purpose.

"Over the last week I met each one of you and discussed my proposed rules of engagement and team ethics. I appreciated the feedback that you gave me privately. Today we will discuss the document and see if there is anything that needs to be changed to make them more realistic and comfortable, without weakening them.

"Just so you know, one of my first rules for meetings is that there is no such thing as a stupid comment or question. The only stupid comment is the one you keep to yourself. Also, if you are used to sitting back and watching, be forewarned that I may call on you to speak. And if you are used to speaking up a lot, I may ask you to make room for others to speak. You should also know that I

> don't hold back my constructive feedback, but I will also be the first one to cheer you on if you do well. I feel like I've lectured you for a while, so let me pause and ask whether anyone has any questions or concerns about what I said. Anyone? Your silence speaks volumes. Well, can I count on your support? How many of you are in? Is anyone out by chance? You're out, Fred? No? You just have a question? Go ahead. (Answer a few questions.)
>
> "Let's discuss the proposed rules of engagement and team ethics document, starting on page 1. The main points on page 1 are ____. Are there any questions or comments on page 1? Is there anything that seems inappropriate or unworkable? (Take comments and make changes to the document where needed.) Any more comments on page 1? Can you live with it? Can you be enthusiastic about it? It seems like I'm asking too much. OK, shall we move on to page 2?"

A Challenge to Ponder: The Merger

Company A and Company B decide to merge. The corporate culture of Company A is one of inclusion and empowerment. Teams are included in decision making and member input is valued and taken into account before corporate and team decisions are made. The culture could be described as "responsible corporate democracy," whereby empowerment and accountability are maintained.

On the other hand, the culture of Company B is autocratic, and staff are used to being told what to do. There is little value placed on staff input, and managers are expected to "show leadership and make tough decisions" on their own. For the staff, the thought of "corporate democracy" is scary and uncomfortable. It would take quite an effort to get them to let go of the security and comfort of being "sheep." They are very far from genuinely embracing the notion of being proactive participants in shared decision making.

The joint management of the merged company recognizes the value of staff empowerment, and decides that the predominant culture to move towards is that of company A. You are asked to offer creative ideas on how to merge the vastly different cultures. What would be your approach, and what transition will you plan? Here are a few ideas that you might consider:

- Mix the autocratic leaders from company B with the empowered team members of company A, so the latter could teach the former to become more inclusive and let go of the need for absolute control of outcomes.

- Mix the democratic leaders from Company A with the reluctant followers from Company B, to show them the benefits of taking more initiative and not relying on others for leadership and guidance. It is like showing someone that a gourmet meal is healthier, tastier, and more satisfying than depending exclusively on French fries. The trick is you have to let go of the French fries to make room for the gourmet meal. It is not always an easy sacrifice to make.

Can you come up with any other ideas on merging the two corporate cultures?

STARTING A QUIET CORPORATE REVOLUTION

Suppose you empower your team and run it in an inclusive manner. You allow members to make some decisions and you ask for their input before making other decisions unilaterally. You know and appreciate the benefits of responsible democracy.

But you have a problem: The rest of the company, including your senior management team, does not operate this way. Most managers are used to telling their staff what to do, and most staff are not used to taking risks and showing initiative. This reality is bound to have an impact on your group's work. For example:

- What do you do if your boss has absolutely no clout and cannot stand up for your team in senior management meetings, because the CEO runs them like a tyrant?
- What do you do when your colleagues in other departments think of you as a naïve optimist, and validate their thinking by undermining your team and not taking your decisions seriously?
- What do you do if your team members approach other departments for help and encounter very slow responses, because the staff are not free to make even simple decisions on their own, and always look for guidance from their managers before they do anything?

The question is: Can you start a quiet corporate revolution, to gradually convert the rest of your organization from pure "top-down" to more "bottom-up"? If so, how might you do it? Here are a few ideas on starting a quiet corporate revolution:

1. Start by ensuring that your team does excellent work, largely thanks to member empowerment. Make your team's work so impressive that even the cynics will be compelled to take notice of it. Once your track record has been established over an extended period, you'll be in a good position to influence change.

2. Be humble about your team's success. Arrogance and conceit will turn people off.
3. Build relationships with other leaders and stakeholders within the same organization (see Chapter 7), by doing some or all of the following:
   - ▲ Make your group a team player in the overall corporate scene.
   - ▲ Keep other leaders and departments informed on decisions that affect them.
   - ▲ Look for opportunities to build partnerships and work collaboratively with them on joint initiatives and on issues that affect both them and your group.
   - ▲ Consult them before finalizing decisions that affect them.
   - ▲ Give them advance warnings on potential problems.
   - ▲ Ask for their advice.
   - ▲ Share feedback with them.
   - ▲ Show appreciation for any help they gave you. The odd "thank you" card, flowers, or other small tokens of appreciation will help.
   - ▲ Make yourself and your team such a pleasure to work with that other executives and managers will want to follow your lead and emulate what you do.
4. Build your group's credibility with customers and other external stakeholders (see Chapter 7), but never do this at the expense of anyone within your organization. For example, if a customer expresses frustration with another department, don't say: "Yes, I know exactly what you mean," but look for ways to address the problem with the manager: "Gordon, do you have a moment? I was speaking to a customer the other day, and there is a problem that you should know about."
5. Having established a successful track record and having built your relationships with internal and external stakeholders, you can offer yourself and your team members as resource people and advisers for other teams who are intrigued by your success. Be prepared for invitations to be a guest presenter in meetings of other groups. But don't be too aggressive with these efforts. Give people lots of room to say no to you.

Having earned respect from your boss and other executives and managers, you can offer to make a presentation at the organization's most senior management level. You can initiate such a process by saying this to your boss:

> *"I have an idea that I would like to discuss with you over lunch. It's about looking at some of our successes and seeing if other*

parts of the organization can benefit from the lessons we learned. Will Tuesday be OK to have lunch together?"

At lunch say this:

"I believe one of the main reasons for my team's success has been the inclusion of individuals in consensus building and decision making, and our ability to capitalize on their knowledge, skills, and talents. Lately people from other departments have been speaking to me about this. Some of them want to move in this direction but are having trouble letting go of old traditions and management styles.

"I believe old habits are hard to break, but not impossible. I have quite a few ideas on how management can break corporate silos and change our culture to be a responsible democracy, without losing control and accountability. I am thinking it would be a good idea for me to make a presentation about this at a senior management meeting. What do you think? Would it work? If so, how can we make it happen?"

If you encounter resistance to your efforts at starting this revolution, don't give up too fast. You may need to switch from a revolutionary mode to an evolutionary mode. Change can be difficult to accept and may present a threat to some people. They may look for ways to justify the status quo and protect their own turfs. Suspicion and resistance to change are only natural.

If you hear the voice of doubt nagging at you ("You can never make this much change happen. Not in this organization."), remember what Richard Bach wrote in his book *Illusions* (Delacorte Press, 1977): "Argue in favor of your limitations, and sure enough, they are yours." Your predictions of failure may well become self-fulfilling prophecies. Instead, be patient, have your vision clear, and continue to lead your team to excellence. Have the confidence that if the change is right for the organization, it will happen, if not today, then some other day.

WORKING WITH EXTERNAL CONSULTANTS

From time to time, your team will need to rely on external consultants to supplement its knowledge and expertise. Typically you will hire an external consultant on a part-time basis or for a limited time. Hourly consulting fees will likely be substantially higher than your own hourly wages.

If a consulting assignment is not substantial in duration or scope, it may be hard to justify the costs of an elaborate selection process. In such cases, it may be best to simplify the consultant selection process. Here is an example of a simplified selection process:

- ▲ Establish the expertise that your team needs from the consultant.
- ▲ Establish the required time commitment, deliverable products, and deadlines.
- ▲ Establish the available budget for the consulting assignment.
- ▲ Delegate the decision to hire the consultant to a subgroup (or the team leader could do it).
- ▲ The decision maker starts an informal search for qualified consultants, often by asking professional colleagues for leads.
- ▲ The decision maker contacts prospective consultants, asks them to send resumes, interviews them in person or by phone, and checks references.
- ▲ The decision maker then selects the consultant, in conformance with the parameters that the group established.
- ▲ The decision maker sends a letter to the consultant, confirming the details and terms of the assignment, and asks the consultant to sign it before embarking on the project.

On the other hand, if the consulting assignment is substantial, it will be prudent (or required by policy) to go through a more formal and extensive selection process. Here is an example of such a process:

- ▲ Prepare a request for proposal (RFP), outlining the scope of the assignment, the required expertise and other consultant attributes, the required time commitment, the deliverable products, and the deadline by which the proposal must be submitted.
- ▲ Make the RFP detailed enough, but not excessive. The RFP should be simple and it should be easy to respond to it. If not, you may lose the interest of the better (and usually busier) consultants. They may not want to invest precious time to virtually write a book for you, when they could use the same time for paying work, and when they are not assured of any compensation.
- ▲ Send the RFP to a range of established consulting firms as well as new ones.
- ▲ You may want to advertise the consulting contract in newspapers and in publications and on Web sites of professional associations. You may also want to "put

feelers out" by contacting your colleagues inside and outside your organization. Advertising by word of mouth costs nothing and often delivers impressive results.

- ▲ Designate a subcommittee to review and assess the proposals.
- ▲ The subcommittee may interview prospective consultants by phone and/or in person.
- ▲ The subcommittee then makes recommendations to the full group.
- ▲ The full group chooses the consultant based on established criteria.

A dilemma to consider is this: Should you reveal your consulting budget to the consultant? In some instances it may work well to "keep them guessing." In other cases it may be best to just let them know what your budget is and see whether they can live with it. In any event, make sure to clearly state your expectations of the consultant, which may include:

- ▲ Specific deliverable results and deadlines. For example, "A search of information technology options to meet our needs, and a report on three options by May 31, 2002."
- ▲ How the consultant will be held accountable. How often will he or she report on progress, how will budgets be managed, and how will the quality of his or her work be measured?
- ▲ How the consultant will work with your members, and what he or she will or will not do.
- ▲ How the contract will be terminated if things don't work out.
- ▲ If the issues on which you are looking for advice are controversial, you may need to emphasize that the consultant must not hold back and must give full and objective advice, regardless of whether it may offend some people, including yourself. A truly professional consultant will never hesitate to tell you things you may not expect or want to hear. That's value for consulting dollars.

Here are additional guidelines for working successfully with consultants:

- ▲ Tell the consultant "what to do" but not "how to do it." For example, avoid saying, "Here are the people that I want you to contact, and here are the questions you should ask." Give the consultant the latitude that he or she needs to put his or her expertise and best judgment to work.

- ▲ Don't try to become the consultant's best friend and thereby undermine your capacity to complain about poor performance. It's helpful to have an amicable and supportive relationship, but you also need to keep your professional distance.
- ▲ Don't wait until the end of the assignment (when all the money has been spent) to measure performance and demand necessary adjustments. You need to assess your returns on investment at regular intervals, when you can still take corrective action.
- ▲ Never ask the consultant to adjust his or her report or advice because it might offend or embarrass certain people.
- ▲ Don't become angry and attack the consultant's credibility because you don't like the advice that he or she has given.
- ▲ The consultant should not dominate your group and its agenda. The consultant's job is to offer dispassionate professional advice, not strong advocacy statements that give you no room to maneuver. Feel free to say, "Judy, we appreciate your advice and the work you've put into this report. At the same time, we need you to present it to us in a way that allows us to question you and scrutinize the options that you are presenting. We are the client, and as such we are the ones who will spend the money on the equipment."

FIVE

Defining Your Team's Rules of Engagement

A masterful facilitator (Chapter 2), a clear and compelling mandate (Chapter 3), and a cohesive and empowered team (Chapter 4) are not enough on their own. Another important building block in your shared decision-making process is your team's "rules of engagement."

This chapter addresses various aspects of the rules of engagement. The first two sections address the following questions:

- What are the rules of engagement and why are they important?
- How can the rules of engagement be entrenched?

The remaining five sections in this chapter outline the various sets of rules of engagement:

- Establishing accountability in decision making
- Establishing the supremacy of collective interests
- Conflict of interest (COI) guidelines

▲ Confidentiality guidelines

▲ Parameters of formal voting

Please note that that the information in this chapter does not constitute legal advice and should not be viewed as such. It only addresses the practical considerations for some difficult and sensitive "process" issues that teams often struggle with. If you need legal advice, consult a trained professional, qualified to practice in your jurisdiction.

What Are the Rules of Engagement and Why Are They Important?

Rules of engagement are formal guidelines on how a team works together. They can be seen as the "bones" in the foundation for your group's work. They are different from the ethics and culture of the group (see Chapter 6), which are the informal understanding of how it operates.

Rules of engagement are intended to establish clarity and define the structures within which your team operates. They are also intended to protect the integrity of the decision-making process. If they are absent or poorly defined, even the best of teams with the most exciting mandate can become dysfunctional and paralyzed by tensions and conflicts.

Rules of engagement cover parameters such as the following:

▲ Lines of authority and accountability ("solid lines")

▲ Who is authorized to make what type of decision

▲ How the integrity of the decision-making process can be protected.

Below is an example that illustrates why rules of engagement are important and what can happen if they are not in place.

CASE STUDY:

The Loose Cannon

A company's executive committee asks an information technology (IT) committee to solicit proposals for new IT equipment, examine them, and recommend the best one.

The IT committee is loosely established and no formal guidelines on confidentiality and conflict of interest are in place. Working relationships are built on trust. Accountability is not defined nor is it carefully monitored.

The chair of the committee becomes very enthusiastic about one IT vendor (who happens to be his close friend) and promises him that he will be the vendor of choice. In his enthusiasm, he also reveals to the vendor significant details of proposals already sent in by other vendors, and also discloses the upper limit of the budget for this project.

The committee chair's unilateral actions compromised the process in various ways:

- The chair's capacity to make an objective decision has been impaired by his close friendship with the vendor.
- The chair acted unilaterally and bypassed the committee's mandate to evaluate vendors. He undermined its ability to make a balanced and informed recommendation.
- The chair breached confidentiality and gave an unfair advantage to one vendor over others. As a result of this breach, the organization could end up spending more money than needed and receive inferior outcomes.
- The chair made a promise that was neither his nor the committee's to make. The committee was only asked to make a recommendation. The final commitment to a vendor was to be made by the executive committee.
- The company was made vulnerable to adversarial actions by disenfranchised vendors if they found out they were treated unfairly. In addition, not many of them would want to submit bids in the future when the company did not act in good faith and the integrity of the selection process was in doubt.
- The company's credibility and image could be harmed if this violation of the selection process became public knowledge.

How Rules of Engagement Can Be Entrenched

The previous example illustrates what can happen when rules of engagement are not established or respected. In order to prevent such problems and preserve the integrity of a team's decision-making process, it is essential to have rules of engagement in place that are:

▲ Clearly defined

▲ Understood, endorsed, and respected

▲ Closely monitored and reinforced

Here are the steps necessary to achieve these goals:

1. Have the rules of engagement defined and documented. Avoid operating on informal verbal commitments and on trust and good faith. See later sections in this chapter on the areas that should be covered by written rules of engagement.
2. Review your proposed rules of engagement with your team and find out whether the members are comfortable with them. Make changes to address legitimate concerns without diluting the rules, and facilitate a commitment by everyone to abide by them.
3. Make the rules of engagement a part of your orientation program for new team members. Ask prospective new members to review them, invite any questions, and then ask for their commitment to abide by them. Some organizations even have new members formally affirm (verbally or in writing) that they will abide by certain rules of engagement.
4. As your team's work progresses, you'll need to remind the members from time to time of an applicable rule of engagement. For example:

   ▲ A reminder about confidentiality: "Before we start this discussion, here is an important reminder: Our policy is that personnel matters are confidential. Therefore we need to keep the discussions on the next item between us. The purpose of confidentiality is to protect the privacy of individuals. Does everyone understand that? Any questions?"

   ▲ A reminder not to make unauthorized promises: "The next item is the selection of a contractor for the IT project. I need to remind everyone that, when you speak to potential contractors, you are not to make any promises or even suggest that they may have an advantage. We need to do our assessment among ourselves, and we must be fair and objective. In addition, the final decision to hire a contractor is not ours to make. We only make the recommendation. The executive committee makes the decision. Does everyone understand that? Does anyone have any questions about this?"

   ▲ A reminder of who is accountable and who makes the final decision: "Before we start this discussion, I need to clarify that your input will be advisory. As your manager, I am accountable for this decision, and I will have the final say. Of course, I value your input, and will take it seriously."

- If the committee chair violates a rule, a conscientious team member could say: "Brad, I need to raise a concern with you about our selection process. It's very delicate, but it's important. I know that in the past you have had a close friendship with XYZ company president, which is one of our bidders on this project. Will you be able to remain objective and respect our conflict of interest guidelines? I am sure you thought about this, but I thought it would be safer to bring it up anyway, so we're all comfortable."

Having established what the rules of engagement are, why they are important, and how they can be entrenched, the next five sections outline the following categories of rules of engagement to consider:

- Establishing accountability in decision making
- Establishing the supremacy of collective interests
- Conflict of interest guidelines
- Confidentiality guidelines
- Parameters of formal voting

Establishing Accountability in Decision Making

Decision-making power comes with a price: The group or person who makes the decision is held accountable for it. Therefore it is important that your rules of engagement clarify the following:

- The authority and accountability of the leader
- The authority and accountability of the group
- The authority delegated to subgroups or individuals
- Solid lines versus dotted lines

The Authority and Accountability of the Leader

The rules of engagement should clarify:

- What types of decisions are made unilaterally by the group's leader
- How much discretion this person has
- How she or he remains accountable to a higher authority (i.e., by reporting and receiving directions on a regular basis, and by not exceeding the scope of the given authority without prior consultation)

In most corporate settings, managers have the authority to act unilaterally within the powers that are delegated to them. They reserve the right of a final say on any decision that relates to their groups and their collective assignments. In such cases, the leader may make some decisions without input, and other decisions with input from the group.

Here are the types of decisions that should be made by the leader unilaterally without input from the group:

- Decisions on routine, administrative, or operational matters
- Decisions that are not appropriate for the group (e.g., disciplinary actions)
- Decisions that do not affect the group or its work in a substantial way
- Decisions on which the group cannot offer useful input
- Decisions that the group expects the leader to make, or is not interested in, or prefers not to get involved in, or would be uncomfortable making

Remember, a leader can be seen to be shirking responsibility and avoiding making tough decisions by consulting the team too frequently.

The types of decisions that should be made with input from the group include:

- Decisions that have substantial impacts on the group and its work
- Decisions that will benefit from the knowledge and expertise available within the group

The Authority and Accountability of the Group

When your team is given decision-making powers, the rules of engagement should clarify the following parameters:

- The scope of authority and the types of decisions that are made collectively by the group
- To whom the team is accountable, such as a manager, an executive committee, or a board of directors

The rules should also specify how the team remains accountable:

- The team works within its given mandate, budgets, and schedules and does not exceed them without prior authorization

- The team is required to make periodic progress reports
- The team takes and follows directions from the higher authority
- There are consequences if the group goes outside its mandate without prior authorization, and who decides on any "collective punishment"(such as disbanding the group or curtailing its powers)
- Whether the group's collective decisions are of a binding nature or of an advisory nature, such as when an outside party (a CEO or board of directors) retains the final say on whether or not to ratify the group's decision, with or without changes

The Authority Delegated to Subgroups or Individuals

It is not practical to have every decision brought to the group for consideration. Many day-to-day decisions that relate to the implementation of your group's work have to be made by subgroups or individual members.

If subgroups or individuals are delegated a task, the parameters of their work should be clearly and fully defined, including:

- Their authority and decision-making powers
- Their base budgets and leeway
- What process they should follow if they need to exceed their given mandates and budgets
- Their schedules and deadlines
- Whether they have the authority to hire staff and consultants
- What promises they are authorized to make to outside parties
- How often they will report on progress and keep their higher authority in the loop

Example: Delegation of Duties to a Subcommittee

A management committee appoints three staff members to identify a suitable location for a management retreat and make all logistical arrangements for it. The management committee defines the following parameters of authority and accountability, as part of the subcommittee's rules of engagement:

- The subcommittee is authorized to spend up to $10,000 and may finalize commitments to vendors, as long as they meet management's requirements.
- The subcommittee will report back at the next management committee meeting.
- If the subcommittee encounters any problems or needs to exceed its budget, it must consult a designated manager, who has the authority to make decisions on this task on behalf of the management committee.

Example: Unspecified Parameters and Accountability

What should you do if your authority and accountability have not been clearly established by your higher authority? Don't make it a problem. It is your golden opportunity to be proactive, define a mandate, and get back to your boss and negotiate. For example:

"Pat, do you have a moment? Thanks. First, I want to thank you for asking me to do this research and prepare a report for you. Before I go ahead with it, I think we should agree on how much time I can put into it, what budgets I will need, what deadlines I should meet, and how I should be accountable to you. I thought about these issues, and here is my proposal: _____. What do you think? Will it work for you? Thank you. I will send you an e-mail to confirm these parameters in writing, and will wait for your confirmation before I carry on."

Example: Authority of the Board of Directors vs. the Chief Executive Officer

Many organizations encounter problems when their boards of directors get involved in the day-to-day operation of the organization and try to micromanage it. To prevent such problems, rules of engagement should be established, to govern the relationship between the board and the chief executive officer (CEO) and the division of duties among them. Here are a few tips to consider:

- The rules of engagement should state that the role of the board is to establish policies, goals, priorities, and principles by which the organization should be operated.
- The board's outlook should be broad and visionary. The board should resist the temptation to micromanage and get involved in the day-to-day decisions that the CEO should be free to make, such as who should be hired for a certain position, how the office space should be allocated, etc. The board should focus on the *whys* (the values, principles, and purposes) and the *whats* (the end results) and leave it to the chief executive officer to establish the *hows* (how to implement the board's policies).

In addition to the division of powers between the board and the CEO, the rules of engagement should establish accountability, ensuring that:

- The CEO reports to the board on policy implementation at every board meeting.
- The CEO works within the delegated authority and discretionary powers, unless authorized to exceed them by the board.
- Concrete "checks and balances" are in place to measure the CEO's performance.
- The CEO's performance is assessed and feedback is exchanged on a regular basis between the board and the CEO.
- The board may want to depend on more than just the CEO's word that things are progressing well. There should be mechanisms in place to verify independently that standards are met and that problems are resolved in a timely and professional manner. A CEO may be a perfectly charming and believable individual, but he or she may not be aware of problems caused by his or her management style.

With the above lines of authority and accountability established and respected by all, typical jurisdictional difficulties will be avoided. For example:

- Individual directors should not approach the CEO or individual staff members with their personal demands: "I am an elected director, so you'd better listen to me and do what I tell you." It should be understood that the board is the only body that gives directions to the CEO, and it does so by a majority vote. It is OK for board members to communicate with individual staff members, but not to tell them what to do. If everyone told everyone else what to do, it would be a confusing organization, with staff members left wondering: "Just who is my boss? My manager, or each of the directors?"

- The CEO should resist the temptation to dominate board meetings or take strong advocacy positions. Such positions may lead to complaints that the CEO is meddling with the board's business. This does not mean that the CEO sits silently during a board meeting and watches the board make a stupid decision, but that she or he should intervene "softly," and introduce missing pieces of information: "Can I offer a piece of information that may help in making this decision?"

Solid Lines vs. Dotted Lines

As indicated earlier in this section, it is important to establish the authority and accountability of the leader, the team, and each one of its members and subgroups. Lines of authority and accountability are the "solid lines" of the organization. These lines are essential in enabling the group and each of its members to work responsibly and within established limits on their powers. Clearly defined solid lines are likely to reduce the tensions, risks, and potential anarchy that could grow without them.

Conversely, it is important to note that an obsessive focus on solid reporting lines may lead to a military style hierarchy-driven organization, where the only thing that matters is "who is my boss." In addition to solid reporting lines, you need to also pay attention to informal relationship building, which cannot be documented in rules of engagement. Here are a few points to consider:

- It may be abundantly clear who is the boss, but if the boss spends most of his or her time in the office, drawing organizational charts, he or she may be out of touch and out of tune with the realities in the field. His or her decisions will be limited in scope and relevance, may not earn the respect of subordinates, and are likely to be met with resistance.
- The existence of formal lines of reporting and accountability does not automatically mean that people will indeed respect them. You have probably seen organizations with fancy hierarchical charts, but with plenty of insubordination and other dysfunction. How does management typically respond? It restructures the organization, not realizing that the problem is not the structure, but the internal relationships.

- Similarly, you have probably seen very effective organizations without clearly documented lines of authority and accountability, but with very solid and harmonious internal relationships and with very compelling organizational vision, ethics, and culture. No organizational chart can force people to work as enthusiastic team members. Some things cannot be legislated by formal rules of engagement, and are much more likely to be achieved through informal relationship building.

You also need to consider that in every organization there are "solid lines" (reporting and accountability) and "dotted lines" (informal communication). Examples of dotted lines are as follows:

- Members of the same team do not report to each other, but they do need to communicate and help each other in performing their jobs.
- Staff in other departments may not report directly to you, but you do need access to the information they have. Your members need to work with them on joint projects.
- Outside stakeholder organizations do not report to you, but their support may be crucial to the success of a project that you are leading. You must maintain informal communications and build relationships with them.

Establishing the Supremacy of Collective Interests

Each member of your team is likely to bring his or her own biases, concerns, and issues to the table. This in itself does not have to be a problem, as long as the individual is able to act in the best interests of the full organization, and as long as broad interests supersede narrow interests.

The above statement may sound logical, but in reality there are circumstances that may put it in jeopardy. Here are a few challenging situations to consider:

- A corporate committee consists of representatives from various departments. In the absence of rules of engagement to the contrary, some members spend most of their energies fighting for their respective departments and not for a collective interest. This fragments the group and makes it adversarial and dysfunctional. Instead of working together for the good of the whole, members work hard to protect their own turfs and power bases.
- A national board of directors consists of twelve representatives from the various regions in the country. In the absence of clear rules of engagement, board mem-

bers may act exclusively in favor of their own regions, instead of making decisions in the broader national interest. Conversely, if an issue does not affect a certain region, the member representing it might say, "That's not my issue," and leave the room or begin to daydream.

Noting the above potential difficulties, it is crucial to establish the following premises as part of your group's written rules of engagement:

1. A member's first obligation is to act in favor of the broad interest, in preference to any other interests that the member may have or represent
2. Once a decision is made, it is a collective decision and everyone must accept it as such, even if she or he voted against it

Obligation to Put the Broad Interest Ahead

A member's first obligation is to act in the best interests of the entire organization, even if they are contrary to other interests that the member may have. Specifically, in the previous examples, a person representing a department or a region must always act in the broad interest, even if this works against his or her own department or region.

This raises an interesting question: Where do the departmental or regional interests fit in? Here is how the process should work:

- ▲ Each member must be familiar with and fully apprised of the interests and legitimate concerns of the group that she or he represents. She or he must have the support of the represented group to present its views, but then be guided by the broader interest.
- ▲ Before a collective decision is made, the various representatives give departmental or regional input. In essence, different people contribute their "pieces of the truth" and help in building the broader perspective that the group needs.
- ▲ Once all distinct "pieces of the truth" are on the table, each member is duty-bound to examine the "full truth" and make the best decision for the organization as a whole.
- ▲ Each member should maintain accountability to the represented group by informing it of the decisions made at the broader level. They should explain to the represented group which of the concerns were accommodated and which ones were not, and why.

Obligation to Respect Collective Decisions

Many group decisions are made by consensus, after careful consideration of all viewpoints and issues. If all relevant concerns are taken into account before a collective decision is made, the likelihood of decisions being made by narrow majorities is slim, and it is easy for each member to embrace the group's decisions.

However, there are times when achieving unanimity is not possible, and a formal vote may be needed to bring an issue to closure. In such instances, there will indeed be a winning side (a majority) and a losing side (a minority). See the section later in this chapter on the parameters of formal voting.

Your group's rules of engagement should make it clear that once a decision is made, it is not a majority decision anymore. It is a decision of the group as a whole. The minority is duty bound to accept it as a collective decision and move on. Yes, at a later time it may prove productive to revisit the decision (if it has not been fully implemented), but until the group reverses the decision, it stands as a collective decision and must be accepted and respected as such.

Here are two dilemmas that your group's members may encounter:

1. What should a dissenting member who voted against a decision do if asked by an outside party or a media reporter: "How do you feel about this decision?" Here is a suggested approach: "We've had a full discussion of all sides of the issue, and after this discussion a decision was made. Yes, I spoke against the proposal, but I fully accept that we had a healthy process and a full discussion of all options. In a democracy, the minority must be heard, but, in the end, the majority governs."
2. Suppose you represent a department on a corporate committee, and, after hearing the discussion on an issue, you realize that the right decision is opposite to the one that your department asked you to support. You go ahead and make the correct and principled (and brave) decision to support the proposal. But what can you do now to deal with the potential fallout from your department? Here are two suggestions:
   - ▲ To reduce the potential fallout from such a situation, you should have clarified your role to your department manager: "I need to clarify how I see my role as a member of this committee. Essentially I will be wearing two hats, one representing our department, and the other working for the company as a whole. Wearing the first hat, I will bring our concerns forward fully. Wearing the second hat, I will listen to what other people are saying. In the end, though, I will be duty-bound to put my corporate hat on and support what seems to be good for the company as a whole, even if it goes against some

of the things that we say we want. It's a tough position to be in, and I need your support. Can I count on it?"

- After supporting the broad corporate interest, report back to your department: "You asked me to present our concerns about the proposed restructuring and to indicate that we opposed it. I did this. I also listened to what other people had to say. At the end of the discussion, the proposal was modified, as follows: ____. I was convinced that this modified proposal addressed some of our concerns. I also thought it was a good compromise and that it would work well for the company as a whole, and I voted in favor of it. As I told you, I had to put on the corporate hat and not the departmental hat when voting, and I did just that. Do you have any questions for me?"

Conflict of Interest (COI) Guidelines

The previous section discussed the need for the rules of engagement to clarify that the broad interests must take precedence over the interests of groups or departments that your members represent.

This section deals with a different challenge: What happens when a member of your group (or his or her close relative, close friend, or associate) encounters an opportunity for personal gain from your group's decision making?

The member in question may then have a direct or indirect conflict of interest (COI). His or her ability to make an independent and principle-based decision for the organization may be impaired by this COI.

This section addresses the following topics that should be covered in your rules of engagement:

- Definition of a personal COI
- Examples of what a personal COI is
- Examples of what a personal COI is not
- Purposes of COI guidelines
- What a member with a personal COI should do
- What members should do if they are unsure whether they have a personal COI
- What a member who believes someone else has a personal COI should do
- What should happen if a COI is discovered after a decision was made

- Penalties for breaching personal COI guidelines
- Reinforcing personal COI guidelines

Definition of a Personal COI

A personal COI occurs when a group member (or his or her close relative or possibly a close friend or associate) has the opportunity to gain personally from a decision that the group is about to make. This becomes a personal COI if:

- This member stands to gain in a way that is unique to him or her, and no other member stands to gain in the same way.
- This potential gain has the potential of clouding the member's judgment and reducing his or her capacity to exercise due diligence and scrutinize ideas.

Examples of What a Personal COI Is

- The spouse of a member of your team owns a management consulting firm, which is currently bidding on one of your team's projects. The affected member stands to receive an indirect monetary gain from this project, and therefore should not be in the meeting room when it is discussed.
- A member of your group is an independent consultant. His contract is about to expire, and your group is discussing whether to hire a new consultant or extend the existing contract.
- Downsizing a department is under discussion, and one of your members is the head of that department. It will be extremely challenging for such a member to let go of the personal interest of turf protection. After all, her own position and compensation could be at stake. If she is fully open to the possibility of "working herself out of a job," she can be included in the discussions, but the others should monitor her participation and keep her honest. On the other hand, if she is too attached to her current position, her capacity to participate openly in discussions may be impaired, and she should not be a part of the decision-making process.

Examples of What a Personal COI Is Not

- Speaking on behalf of your own department at a management committee meeting or representing your own region at a national board of directors meeting is not a personal COI. You are not the only person who stands to gain from the decision. You should be allowed to stay at the meeting and speak and vote. However, you should also remember the supremacy of the broader interest (see earlier section).

- Having a strong opinion on an issue is not a COI. Yes, members should come to a meeting with open minds, but they are not required to come with empty minds.
- A personal COI does not occur when the opportunity of personal gain is shared by other members of the group. For example, if a decision is being made about holding a special event, to which all are invited at the company's expense, the opportunity to benefit is not unique to one member, and therefore no personal COI exists.

The Purposes of COI Guidelines

Personal COI guidelines are intended to:

- Preserve the integrity of the group's decision-making process by excluding members whose judgment and ability to act objectively may be impaired by personal interest
- Increase the capacity of members to make independent and principled decisions
- Increase the likelihood that collective decisions will be driven by the group's broad interests and mandate
- Ensure that members who do not have a personal COI can speak and participate freely and comfortably and without worrying about the negative reactions of a member who has an opportunity to personally gain from the decision

Caution: The topic of conflict of interest is extremely sensitive and complex. Your group should consider carefully what situations should be considered a personal COI and document them in its rules of engagement. But don't overdo it, or you may end up excluding too many members from too many decisions. The purpose of COI guidelines is to ensure that individuals are able to show due diligence and act with as much objectivity as possible and with the best interests of the organization in mind. COI guidelines should not be so strict that they paralyze your group or deprive it of the knowledge and talent of its most capable members. COI guidelines need to be reasonable, realistic, and enforceable.

What a Member Who Has a Personal COI Should Do

A member who believes that he or she is in a personal COI position (i.e., he or she or a close relative or possibly a close friend or associate has an opportunity to personally gain or lose from a decision that the group is about to make) should explain the COI to the group immediately upon becoming aware of it. The member should then leave the meeting when the issue is discussed, in order to avoid risking even a perception of influencing the other members, and to avoid the possibility of making other members uncomfortable making an honest decision or expressing themselves in a way that is not favorable to this member's personal interest.

It is good practice to record in the minutes of the meeting the fact that a member declared a personal COI on an issue and was absent from the meeting while the issue was discussed.

What Members Should Do if They Are Unsure Whether They Have a Personal COI

A member who believes she or he may be in a COI position, but is not sure, should disclose this fact to the leader or to the group and ask for feedback. The manager or the group may determine that:

- ▲ A personal COI exists and it is substantial, and therefore requires the member to be absent from the meeting while the issue is being discussed.
- ▲ A personal COI exists, but it is minor and is unlikely to impair the member's judgment or ability to make an independent decision, and it is unlikely to compromise the integrity of the decision-making process. In this case, the group can decide that the member can stay.
- ▲ A personal COI does not exist, and the group is comfortable with the member staying at the meeting.

What a Member Who Believes Someone Else Has a Personal COI Should Do

A member who believes someone else is in a COI position, and becomes aware of the problem while a meeting is in progress, should pass a note to the meeting facilitator expressing concern, or ask for a break to confer privately with the facilitator, or just interject and explain the concern: "Ron, I was just wondering, doesn't your wife own shares of XYZ software, which is one of our bidders today? Doesn't this place you in a conflict of interest position?" The member with the alleged COI will then respond to the question, and may need to leave or stay, depending on the outcome of the discussion.

If the member becomes aware of the other person's potential COI between meetings, she or he should check if the meeting facilitator has been advised of it and whether any private discussion with the other member is necessary.

Disagreements on whether a member is in a COI position or not should be resolved by the group's leader or by the group. For example:

> *"I'm not sure that there is a personal COI here and, even if there is one, I am not sure how significant it is. Let's find out how other members see it. Brian, do you mind leaving the room while we discuss this? Thank you." (Wait for him to leave, then take comments). "Shall we take a show of hands? Please raise your hands if you believe this is a personal COI and that it is significant enough to ask Brian to leave the room while this contract is discussed. Thank you. Put your hands down. Please raise your hands if you believe there isn't a personal COI here or that it is not significant, and that Brian can stay. Thank you. Would someone go outside and ask Brian to come back?"*

What Should Happen if a COI Is Discovered After a Decision Was Made

If an important decision is made, and it is later discovered that a member was in a COI position and participated in the discussions, the following may need to be done:

- The group's leader or the group can decide whether the personal COI was significant, whether the decision would have been different had this COI been known, and whether the interests of the organization were indeed compromised.
- If the answer is yes, the group may need to check whether the decision can be revisited and act according to the answer, i.e., was the decision fully implemented? Is it possible to reverse it? Would it be too disruptive to reverse or change it, and, if so, should it be left unchanged and used as something to learn from?

- If the member knew of the COI and did not disclose it, it may be necessary to initiate disciplinary action against him or her (see next subsection).

Penalties for Breaching Personal COI Guidelines

Your group's rules of engagement should specify the penalties for conscious or deliberate breaches of COI guidelines. The penalties should be proportionate to the severity and impact of the violation. The rules of engagement should clarify who is authorized to impose the penalty and what process must be followed. The disciplinary process must be fair and must offer the individual the opportunity of being fully heard before any penalty is imposed.

Examples of penalties may include:

- A warning or a reprimand
- A reduction in clout and scope of duties
- A suspension or removal from the group or from the entire organization

Reinforcing Personal COI Guidelines

Like other rules of engagement, COI guidelines should be reinforced, as follows:

- At the inception of your group's work the COI guidelines can be introduced as part of your rules of engagement (see Chapter 5) and orientation program (see Chapter 4).
- COI guidelines should be discussed by your group, adjusted to be consistent with its needs, and then agreed to by the group.
- Compliance with COI guidelines should be monitored by the leader and each member.
- Members may need to be reminded of COI guidelines from time to time.
- Some boards of directors and other formal groups require new members to affirm orally or in writing that they will comply with COI guidelines.

CONFIDENTIALITY GUIDELINES

Your rules of engagement should include confidentiality guidelines. Such guidelines should address the following issues:

- ▲ Purposes for keeping things confidential
- ▲ What topics should be kept confidential
- ▲ Who decides that confidentiality is required
- ▲ What should be included in minutes of in-camera (private) meetings
- ▲ Impacts of freedom of information and protection of privacy legislation
- ▲ How confidential information should be handled
- ▲ Declassifying confidential documents
- ▲ Penalties for violations of confidentiality guidelines
- ▲ Reinforcing the confidentiality guidelines

Purposes for Keeping Things Confidential

Typically, confidentiality is intended to achieve one of two purposes:

1. To protect the organization, its operations, economic interests, and delivery of its mandate from the harm that could result from the release of certain information
2. To protect individuals, when the release of certain information would be an unreasonable invasion of their personal privacy

Caution: There is a risk in keeping too much information confidential and being overly protective of it. Most documents should not be considered confidential. There should generally be transparency and easy access to information, except when there is a legitimate interest to protect and a valid reason for keeping them confidential.

What Topics Should Be Kept Confidential

There are certain subject areas that justify keeping documents and decisions relating to them confidential. Among them:

- ▲ The security of the property of the organization
- ▲ The disclosure of intimate, personal, or financial information in respect to a person

- The acquisition or disposition of property
- Decisions with respect to negotiations with employees
- Litigation affecting the organization
- Other issues as defined in your rules of engagement

Who Decides That Confidentiality Is Required

In corporate settings, the decision that an issue requires confidentiality is typically made by the group's leader, possibly with input from the group. In the case of a board of directors or a more formal group, the decision to designate an item as confidential can be made by the group itself, or it can be delegated by the group to its leader.

The decision to designate an item as confidential should be made in the planning stages of the meeting, so it can be scheduled on the agenda of an "in-camera" (private) meeting. If it becomes apparent during an open meeting that an agenda item requires confidentiality, the agenda item should be moved from the open meeting to the agenda of a closed meeting.

Only the voting members of the group and invited parties (e.g., lawyers, consultants, confidential secretary, key staff members) are entitled to attend an in-camera meeting.

Note: In principle, there is no reason a group cannot make decisions during an in-camera meeting. Unless the group's governing documents (statute, bylaws) require otherwise, members should not be required to return to an open meeting to finalize decisions, as this would defeat the purpose of keeping things confidential.

What Should Be Included in Minutes of In-Camera (Private) Meetings

Minutes of in-camera meetings should be kept confidential. They should:

- Focus on the consensus and the decisions that were made by the group. They should not record what each individual said.
- Summarize the discussions in a concise point-format, without attributing remarks to individuals. For example, "The main points in favor of the organizational restructuring plan were: 1, 2, 3. The main concerns were: 1, 2, 3. The

decision was to proceed with an amended plan, as follows: ____." (See Chapter 15 for more details on minutes.)

- Omit off-topic discussions and off-the-record remarks.

Impacts of Freedom of Information and Protection of Privacy Legislation

Your group may be subject to freedom of information (FOI) and protection of privacy (POP) legislation. If this is the case, you must take into account legislative requirements when determining whether something can justifiably be kept confidential and when access to documents can be legitimately denied. FOI and POP legislation may also articulate a procedure by which outside parties (the general public, the media, etc.) can obtain access to information or appeal a decision by the organization to deny access to a certain document.

How Confidential Documents Should Be Handled

Confidential documents should be filed separately from documents that are available for general access and are open for inspection.

Minutes of in-camera meetings and related documents should be stamped "confidential" on every page, or you may choose to have a running header that includes the word "confidential." Such minutes should be verified for accuracy in a future in-camera meeting and not in an open meeting, so as to preserve the confidentiality.

Declassifying Confidential Documents

If there is no longer a need to protect the organization or an individual by keeping minutes or other documents confidential, the leader or the group can agree to declassify the document and make it available to those who request it.

Penalties for Violations of Confidentiality Guidelines

Leaks of confidential documents pose several serious risks for the organization:

- The organization's economic interests and legal position, which the confidentiality is designed to protect, are threatened or compromised.

- ▲ Personal privacy is invaded.
- ▲ Confidence in the decision-making process is undermined.
- ▲ Trust among members is eroded.

Penalties for breaches of confidentiality should be proportionate to the severity and impact of the violation. The rules of engagement should clarify who is authorized to impose the penalty and what process should be followed.

Reinforcing the Confidentiality Guidelines

The obligation of confidentiality should be clarified at the start of an "in-camera" meeting or at the start of the discussion of a confidential agenda item. Some formal groups require members, staff, and consultants who attend such a meeting to affirm (orally or in writing) that they will comply with confidentiality guidelines.

PARAMETERS OF FORMAL VOTING

In most corporate settings team members have some influence over decisions, but have no true voting power. Typically the group's manager, who is ultimately accountable for a decision, makes it, with or without input from the group. Input from members is advisory and nonbinding.

This section deals with settings where formal voting powers are established. Formal voting applies when the accountability for a decision is collective (shared among the members of the group, and not assumed by one person). For example, a board of directors bears collective responsibility for governing an organization. Each member has actual voting power. Board decisions are made by the board, as a collective decision-making body (usually by a majority vote), and not by the leader or one of its members.

Although this section applies to formally structured decision-making bodies, parts of it can also be useful for teams or corporate committees that operate more democratically and give their members real and binding clout in some areas.

If binding voting structures are desirable, it is best to have them documented in the group's rules of engagement, or in your governing documents (such as bylaws). If this is not done, confusion and tensions are likely to develop.

Here are the some of the questions that may need to be addressed when defining the parameters of formal voting:

- How much voting power does each person have?
- Can members who are not present in a meeting vote?
- What majority is required to approve a proposal?
- When is a "super-majority" required to approve a proposal?
- What is the effect of a tie vote?
- What is the effect of an abstention?
- Can the chair vote and speak in discussions?
- Does an ex-officio member have a vote?
- How many members must be present in order to make a binding decision?
- Is voting power really significant?
- How can you reduce the number of win-lose votes?

How Much Voting Power Does Each Person Have?

The voting power of each member of the group should be specified in the group's governing documents (terms of reference, bylaws, or rules of engagement). Here are a few examples of the allocation of voting powers:

- *One Person, One Vote.* On a board of directors or a committee, each member typically has one vote. No one has more than one vote and no one has veto power.
- *Weighted Voting.* The bylaws of a group with representatives on it from different organizations may give those who represent larger organizations greater voting clout. For example, the number of votes that a person carries may be proportionate to the size of the affiliated organization's membership, staff, geographic jurisdiction, annual budgets, or other factors. Weighted voting can be confusing and difficult to track and count.

Can Members Who Are Not Present in a Meeting Vote?

There are two ways of voting without being present in a face-to-face meeting:

1. By giving a proxy to another member acting on your behalf (if proxies are allowed).

2. By using virtual meetings to facilitate decision making.

Proxy Voting

Some governing documents allow voting by proxy, whereby a member can assign his or her vote to another person for a certain meeting.

Sometimes a proxy giver instructs the proxy holder to vote a certain way on a precirculated proposal. This practice can present two dilemmas for the proxy holder at the meeting:

- How should the proxy holder vote if new information surfaces at the meeting that could have caused the proxy giver to vote differently?
- How should the proxy holder vote if the proposal is modified at the meeting?

In light of the above, proxy voting is unlikely to be useful or desirable in an informal corporate setting, since the member who is absent does not hear the discussion, and does not make an informed decision on how his or her proxy will be exercised. It is recommended that your rules of engagement do not allow proxy voting, unless there is a strong argument in favor of it. Proxies would generally be more appropriate and relevant in shareholder meetings.

Virtual Meetings

As a replacement to proxy voting, there are other mechanisms that allow members to vote without being present at a face-to-face meeting. To introduce such mechanisms, you need to establish the following parameters in your group's rules of engagement:

- Whether members can vote in a virtual meeting, such as a teleconference, videoconference, or electronic meeting, or by mail, e-mail, or fax.
- Who is authorized to initiate a virtual meeting as a form of shared decision making (typically the group's leader or a specified minimum number of members can do so). See Chapter 16 for more on virtual meetings.

What Majority Is Required to Approve a Proposal?

Unless the governing documents of the group have a different requirement, the standard practice is that a simple majority is needed to approval a proposal. A simple majority means that more than half of the votes cast are in favor of the proposal, e.g., five in favor and three against means the proposal is approved; three in favor and eight against means that the proposal is rejected.

When Is a Super-Majority Required to Approve a Proposal?

A super-majority is more than a simple majority. An example is when a two-thirds or 75 percent vote or even unanimity is required for an important proposal. A super-majority should only be required if the group's governing documents indicate that it is.

As an example, the bylaws of an organization may require a two-thirds or 75 percent vote to amend the bylaws, to remove a member from a board of directors, or to approve an unusually high expenditure. Going to the extreme, some groups even require unanimity on certain decisions (not realizing the paralyzing impact of such a requirement; see below).

Here are simple ways to calculate what type of voting result has been achieved.

1. A *two-thirds vote* means that for every person who voted against a proposal, two or more voted in favor of it. To figure out whether a proposal is successful, you need to multiply the negative votes by two, and if the total is equal to or less than those who voted in favor, the proposal is approved. Otherwise the proposal is defeated. For example:
   - ▲ 8 in favor and 4 against means that the proposal is approved (4 times 2 equals 8).
   - ▲ 9 in favor and 5 against means that the proposal is defeated (5 times 2 equals 10, which is more than 9).
   - ▲ 13 in favor and 6 against means that the proposal is approved (6 times 2 equals 12,which is less than 13).
2. Similarly, a *75 percent vote* means that for every person voting against a proposal there must be three or more voting in favor of it. To figure out whether a proposal is successful, you need to multiply the negative votes by three, and if the total is equal to or less than those who voted in favor, the proposal is approved. Otherwise the proposal is defeated. For example:
   - ▲ 9 in favor and 3 against means that the proposal is approved (3 times 3 equals 9).
   - ▲ 7 in favor and 2 against means that the proposal is approved (2 times 3 equals 6, which is less than 7 positive votes).

- ▲ 11 in favor and 4 against means that the proposal is defeated (4 times 3 equals 12, which is more than the 11 positive votes).

3. Finally, *unanimity* requires that no negative vote be cast. This means that one member has the power to stop progress. This amounts to veto power and can be very problematic (see note below).

Caution About Imposing a Super-Majority Requirement

Leaders sometimes decide that a certain proposal is so significant that it should require a super-majority, even though there is no such stipulation in the group's governing documents.

Although a super-majority is typically imposed with the intention of establishing broad support for an important proposal, it also presents a risk: What the leaders may not realize is that they have just turned the decision making into "the tyranny of the minority." In other words, to defeat a proposal that requires a two-thirds vote, the opponents will need to mobilize just over one-third of the votes. If a simple majority was achieved (e.g., 62 percent, but not quite two-thirds), this majority would be correct in claiming that it was disenfranchised of its right to govern.

Insisting on unanimity on certain decisions is even worse, since one stubborn person would have veto power and would be able to paralyze the group and stop it from making progress. Yes, it is desirable to have an all-inclusive debate, covering the issues in a holistic and collaborative manner, which would preclude winning majorities and losing minorities. But there are times when progress must be made, and a simple majority should suffice to do so.

To address the above issues, your rules of engagement could specify that:

- ▲ All proposals that require a group decision need a simple majority vote to be approved.
- ▲ Narrow majorities should be the exception and not the norm. If about half the group wants solution A, and about half wants solution B, it may mean that the group has not worked hard enough to find solution C, which would be better than both A and B. Forcing a decision in such a case by a narrow majority may prove to be shortsighted and counterproductive.

What Is the Effect of a Tie Vote?

A tie vote means that the votes in favor and against a proposal are equal. Assuming that a simple majority is required to approve a proposal (more members vote in favor than against), the effect of a tie vote is that a majority was not achieved and that the proposal is defeated. In other words: a vote of five in favor and five against a proposal produces the same outcome as three votes in favor and seven against. The proposal is defeated in both cases.

Some people assume that the chair of a meeting automatically gets to vote a second time and break the tie. There are a few things to consider regarding this assumption:

1. As explained earlier, a tie vote does not mean a deadlock. All it means is that a proposal was defeated. There is no need to give the chair a second vote.
2. Under the principle of equality the chair should only get one vote (unless the governing documents state otherwise), and should generally be allowed to vote at the same time as everyone else.
3. In some team settings, the leader indeed has the authority to break ties or have the ultimate say when the group is divided on an issue. For example, if a consultant is to be chosen and the votes for the various candidates are close or tied, the leader can be given the power to make the decision. Your team's rules of engagement should state when the group makes the decisions and when it delegates unilateral decision-making power to the leader.

Your group's rules of engagement should clarify the impact of a tie vote and the role of the chair.

What Is the Effect of an Abstention?

An abstention means that a voting member who is present does not vote in favor and does not vote against a proposal. The impact of an abstention depends on stipulations in your governing documents. There are three possibilities:

1. If the governing documents stipulate or imply nothing about how abstentions are counted, they should not be counted, and only the votes cast in favor and against should be used to determine the outcome. For example, if four vote in favor, three against, and two abstain, the two abstentions are ignored and the proposal is approved by four to three votes.

   In principle, a member should be allowed to take a neutral position ("sit on the fence") and not be forced to vote in favor or against a proposal. It is unfair to force a member to vote yes or no when neither one would be an honest choice.

2. Some governing documents (statutes or bylaws) stipulate that an abstention counts as a vote in favor of a proposal. If this is the case, the two abstentions in the example above would be added to the four affirmative votes. The result would be six votes in favor and three against, and the proposal would be approved.

   A stipulation that an abstention is counted as a vote in the affirmative is unfair, since it takes away the member's right to make an honest decision to sit on the fence. It also means that those who daydream may unintentionally vote in favor of a proposal that they oppose.

3. Other governing documents stipulate that "an affirmative vote of a majority of those present is needed to approve a proposal." Taking the above example, with only four out of nine members present voting in favor, a majority of those present (five out of nine) was not achieved and the proposal was defeated. Strange, isn't it?

A Note About Abstentions

Yes, it is important for your rules of engagement to clarify how abstentions are counted. However, far too often people are too busy trying to figure out how to count an abstention, when they should be asking more important questions about abstentions, such as:

- ▲ Why are people abstaining?
- ▲ Is it a good idea to force a vote when there are many abstentions?
- ▲ What work can be done to reduce abstentions?

Most times people abstain for other reasons than just wanting to take a neutral position, as shown in this list:

If this is the reason for wanting to abstain:	Do this:
The proposal is a last-minute addition to the agenda. You don't have enough details on the issue to make an informed decision.	Propose that the group refer the proposal to a smaller group or to an expert for study and advice, so it can be presented a later meeting.

You need more time to think about the proposal (it's late in the evening and you are tired).	Propose that the group postpone the vote to a future meeting.
The proposal is confusing and poorly written.	Work to improve or clarify the wording of the proposal, or suggest that it be referred to a smaller group to develop a clearer proposal.
The proposal is of no interest to the group and seems to be a waste of time.	Suggest that the proposal be withdrawn altogether (suffering is optional . . .).

In any of the above four cases, the group should be asked whether it agrees with the proposed option in the right-hand column. For example:

- "In light of what just came up, is it OK to have this proposal withdrawn? Any objection to this? Thank you, the proposal has been withdrawn. The next item is. . . ."
- "Given the lateness of the hour, do you want to deal with this issue tonight, or can it wait for next week? Wait until next week? Any objection? OK, we'll postpone this issue until next week."
- "Some of you seem to want to make the decision today and some want to wait for analysis from the finance committee. Let me take a show of hands. Raise your hand if you want the finance committee to do more work on this proposal between now and the next meeting. Thank you. Raise your hand if you prefer to deal with the issue tonight. Thank you. The proposal has been referred to the finance committee. Next on the agenda we have _____."

Can the Chair Vote and Speak in Discussions?

There are many myths and misconceptions about the role of the chair in a meeting, and whether she or he is entitled to speak or vote. These misconceptions are borrowed from ball games, where the only objective is to win, and the only way to do this is if the other side loses. In such games there is a need for a referee, who remains neutral and whose only role is to ensure that the rules of the game are followed.

Not so in most meetings.

Although there are still many meetings where the objective is to win at the expense of the other party, this is not the case in most corporate settings and boards. People are generally there to work together and make the best decisions for the organization. Yes, they do disagree from time to time, and, if it is impossible to reach common ground, a formal vote can be taken to settle an issue. But in healthy organizations such situations are the exception and not the norm.

The leader of a group in most corporate settings (a chairperson of a board of directors or a committee, or a team leader) is often one of its most knowledgeable and experienced members. Your group's rules of engagement should clarify that the leader has the same rights (to vote and to speak) as other members, as long as he or she does not dominate the discussion or bias it against certain views or members. This means that the chair will follow the same protocol as members do, by lining up to speak, and by observing other relevant guidelines.

See earlier section on the role of a chair when there is a tie vote.

Does an Ex-Officio Member Have a Vote?

In many organizations certain individuals are designated to serve as ex-officio members of a board or a committee. Ex-officio means "by virtue of office." For example, the president or the CEO may be designated in the governing documents as an ex-officio member of the board of directors or an ex-officio member of committees. This means that the individual holds the position only as long as she or he holds the office that entitles them to it. When the person stops holding the position, she or he no longer sits on all committees as an ex-officio member.

Though many people believe that ex-officio members do not have a vote, several rule books stipulate the exact opposite, i.e., that an "ex-officio" member has all the rights and privileges of other members, including the right to vote, but none of the obligations and responsibilities.

If it is desirable to give the ex-officio member no voting rights, this should be specified in the group's governing documents. For example:

- A bylaw may state that the CEO is a nonvoting ex-officio member of the board.
- The rules of engagement may clarify that the president is a nonvoting ex-officio member of all committees.

How Many Members Must Be Present to Make a Decision?

A quorum is typically specified in order to protect the group from unrepresentative decisions being made by minorities. A quorum is the minimum number of voting members who must be present in order to make valid decisions.

A quorum should not be too high (impossible to achieve) nor should it be too small and unrepresentative. For boards and committees a quorum is usually specified as a majority of the voting members holding office.

A quorum should be present for the full duration of a meeting (or at least as long as collective decisions are made). If important decisions must be made when there is no quorum, they should be communicated to absent members and be brought back for ratification at a later meeting during which a quorum is present.

Groups that are not formally organized and have no governing documents should follow these principles:

- ▲ Meetings should not be scheduled at a time when too many members will likely be absent.
- ▲ A meeting should only start when a majority of the members of the group are there.
- ▲ Members who will miss a meeting should be contacted prior to a meeting, to ensure that their concerns and insights are taken into account before decisions are made.
- ▲ Absent members should be informed of outcomes and of decisions made at a meeting.

Here is a typical question that people ask about a quorum: What do we do if we consistently have difficulties meeting our quorum requirement? There are two possible answers to this question:

1. The quorum requirement might be too high and is therefore unrealistic to achieve. In this case you need to have your governing document amended to make the quorum more realistic.
2. You may need to ask another question first: Why are you having trouble getting a quorum at your meetings? Why are members missing them? The answer may be that your meetings are too dull, long, dominated by a few vocal members, or not clearly focused on the organization's mandate. If this is the case, you need to address the real problem and make your meetings more interesting, engaging, productive, balanced, relevant, and enticing to attend. Try scheduling controversial topics or interesting guest speakers.

Is Voting Power Really Significant?

Formal groups often agonize over voting entitlements and about the parameters of formal voting. They sometimes go to great lengths to answer the questions that this section addresses. There is a limit to the usefulness of such efforts, and they can distract the group from focusing on its mandate and solving real problems.

In fact, after the questions about the parameters of formal voting have been fully and satisfactorily addressed, people often discover that the significance of a vote has been overplayed and that it receives far more attention than it truly deserves.

An excessive focus on formal voting often leads people to think about majorities overpowering minorities, and about one interest winning over another. There are two problems with this focus:

1. The adversarial approach can distract members from what they should be focusing their energies on: working collaboratively, as a cohesive team, and making responsible, credible, and durable decisions for the organization.
2. In reality, certain individuals exercise far more power and influence than their voting powers, with their clout being proportionate to their knowledge, skills, experience, connections, passion, persistence, and the ability to exert control during meetings.

Here are a few examples that illustrate how insignificant formal voting powers can be:

- ▲ In a poorly managed meeting, a few outspoken members dominate the discussions, and through sheer persistence, dictate the outcome. The fact that they only have a few votes is insignificant. The majority, by its silence and acquiescence, helps in making it "the tyranny of the minority." Having a vote is really not all that significant in this setting.
- ▲ In many boards of directors, the chief executive director (typically a nonvoting member) has far more clout than voting members of the board, due to his or her influence, credibility, and extensive knowledge and experience. The fact that he or she does not have a vote does not diminish his or her actual clout.

How Can You Reduce the Number of Win-Lose Votes?

Win-lose votes, whereby a majority flexes its muscle and forces the outcome, are sometimes the way to go. This is typically the case when, after an exhaustive examination of an issue, no common ground can be found, no more time is available, and the group needs to reach closure. The general principle that is followed in these cases is that the majority rules, provided that the minority has been given a fair opportunity to be heard.

Notwithstanding the fact that "majority rule" is correct procedurally, having too many close votes typically indicates an unhealthy organization and a poor foundation for shared decision making. The risks of having too many close votes and narrow majorities are:

- Losers may feel powerless and demoralized. They may end up acquiescing and following the majority's wishes, bitterly and reluctantly. Yes, it is possible to impose a decision, but it would be ludicrous to order everyone to be enthusiastic and genuinely committed to it. Positive attitudes cannot be forced or legislated.
- Disenfranchised minorities may become "eternal critics" and may undermine the group's decisions. The fact that a decision was made will not necessarily mean that it will be successfully implemented. The majority's sense of victory may be short-lived.
- Some individuals may feel strongly enough against a decision that they will look for ways to challenge the decision-making process. They may take adversarial actions or even pursue costly lawsuits against the organization or against some of its members.

Given the risks of too many close votes, a group should work hard to reach a greater degree of support than a simple majority for most decisions. This means more work, but it's an investment well made. The result of it will be not only better decisions, but many more members will be on board when the group reaches its destination, as active and enthusiastic partners.

Here are a few ideas to replace the majority-versus-minority decision making on complex or controversial issues by a softer, more inclusive and more holistic model.

- Resist the temptation to enter "solution mode" prematurely. Premature proposals for closure can constrain discussions and reduce the opportunity to be creative. Instead of leaping to solutions, encourage the members to explore the problem first. Ask questions like these:
  - What exactly is the problem that we are trying to solve?
  - Is this a real problem or only a perceived problem?
  - Who is affected by this problem and how?
  - What is significant about this issue and what isn't?
- Conduct informal surveys (written or oral) before the meeting, asking members and stakeholders about their perspectives and views. Look for areas on which

people agree (you may be surprised how many of those there are) and areas on which they need to work. This way you will be able to turn the meeting from a "war zone" to a "construction zone."

The above suggestions should make it clear that formal rules of engagement are not enough for your shared decision-making process. Rules of engagement can be seen as the skeleton foundation for your group. You need to add the "soft tissue" to make things really work. This "soft tissue" is the subject of Chapter 6, on the ethics and the culture of your team, and Chapter 7, on building relationships with stakeholders.

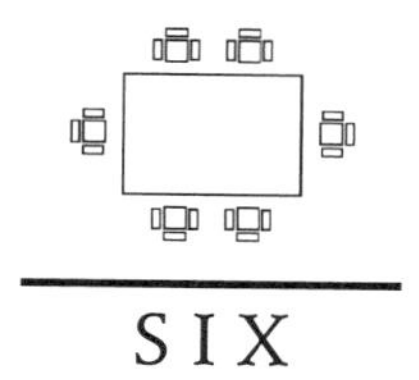

SIX

Establishing Your Team's Ethics and Culture

Looking beyond your group's rules of engagement (Chapter 5), you need to consider the ethics and the culture of your group. Unlike the rules of engagement, which can be seen as the hard foundation for your group's work (like the body's skeleton and bones), the group's ethics and culture can be seen as the soft foundation (like the flesh and the muscles).

The various segments in this chapter are phrased as a team's affirmations of what it values and how its members prefer to work together. Feel free to change or delete some of them. Don't hesitate to add new segments that you believe will add to the quality your group's work and to its work climate and ethics. Use this chapter as your starting point, not as the final outcome.

To make the affirmations work, I suggest that you present them to your team when its work begins. Allow the group to modify these affirmations, or delete some and add others to reflect its needs. Introduce the affirmations even though they do not reflect the group's current reality or appear like pipe dreams. Use them as the ideal to move towards, and then reintroduce them periodically and ask: "How are we doing in relation to this goal? Are we making progress?"

It is also suggested that you include the affirmations of your group's ethics and culture in your new member orientation program and manual. Give the affirmations to each candidate to join your team and to each new member. Ask them to review the affirmations and answer their questions. Then confirm whether they can live by these affirmations. It is best to talk about ethics when a person joins your group, to clarify expectations up front and avoid conflict later on.

Please note that the affirmations given in this chapter repeat and consolidate points that are made in other chapters in this book.

The sets of affirmations are organized in alphabetic order, starting with accountability and ending with transparency and access to information, as follows:

- Accountability
- Being in the forefront
- Communicating
- Conflict resolution
- Due diligence
- Empowerment of individuals
- Enjoying work and having fun
- Fairness and equality
- Honesty
- Integrity
- Listening
- Objectivity
- Respect and sensitivity
- Risk taking
- Teamwork
- Transparency and access to information

ACCOUNTABILITY

- We operate responsibly and within our given authority and jurisdiction.
- We operate within our allocated budgets and resources.
- If our authority and resource allocations are unclear, we establish what we need and look for approval from the party to whom we are accountable.

- ▲ If we need additional resources, we look for permission to extend our mandates before making any extra commitments.
- ▲ We report regularly on progress to the person or the group to which we are accountable.
- ▲ When we disagree with an instruction from a higher authority, we seek to renegotiate it.
- ▲ We avoid insubordination, turf protection, and blaming or accusing a higher authority for our lack of progress. Instead, we approach the party and try to address the issue directly.

Being in the Forefront

- ▲ We always study current and emerging trends and integrate them into our decision making.
- ▲ We find opportunities (such as conferences and other networking opportunities) to learn and exchange ideas with other professionals.
- ▲ We share our new ideas and success stories in public and professional forums.
- ▲ We research the Internet and other sources for the latest information, while watching for unreliable information.
- ▲ We subscribe to trade magazines and other publications and we take the time to read them.
- ▲ We encourage creativity and visionary thinking: "Heads in the sky, but feet on the ground."
- ▲ When fresh and creative ideas emerge, we refuse to be constrained by statements like: "We've already tried it and it didn't work," or "There is too much opposition to it."

Communicating

- ▲ We communicate with the listener in mind.
- ▲ We give the listeners the information they need, nothing more and nothing less.
- ▲ We communicate to be heard and understood.
- ▲ We communicate to inform, educate, or advocate.
- ▲ We communicate with clarity, simplicity, brevity, and purpose.
- ▲ We keep our comments well organized and easy to follow and digest.
- ▲ We avoid rambling, repetitions, and digressions, believing that "It is best to quit while we're ahead."

- We keep our words simple and use plain language whenever possible.
- We explain technical jargon and abbreviations before we use them.
- We avoid annoying and tired clichés, like: "You've got to go the extra mile."
- We keep our language clean, business-like, and respectful.

Conflict Resolution

- We believe that differences of opinions are not a cause for panic but a cause for celebration.
- We believe that each conflict brings with it opportunities to learn and strengthen the group, its decision making, and the organization as a whole.
- We believe that the negative impacts of disputes can be minimized through preventive measures and through early detection and intervention when a conflict first emerges.
- We avoid ignoring signs of emerging disputes and hoping that they will just disappear.
- If disputes occur, we deal with them in a direct, principled, and timely manner. We do not let them fester and grow beyond control.
- We expect members to prevent tensions by knowing their individual roles and responsibilities and the lines of reporting and accountability, and by following our rules of engagement.

Due Diligence

- We maintain fiscal responsibility and we consciously look for returns on the investment in our team's work and its meetings.
- We make decisions that make the optimal use of the organization's resources. We look to work smarter, not harder, and to conserve resources.
- We ensure that our decisions respond to the organization's needs, solve the problems at hand, and are reasonable and realistic to implement.
- We consider the impacts of our decisions on all affected parties (internal stakeholders, such as other staff and departments, and external stakeholders, such as customers and suppliers).

- We examine issues and proposals carefully against objective criteria.
- We do not hesitate to scrutinize and question an expert's proposal, regardless of how respected, trustworthy, and likable the individual may be.
- We make sure that a problem has been fully explored before identifying solutions for it. We recognize that doing otherwise is equivalent to placing the cart before the horse.
- We make every effort to attend all meetings, and be there, from start to finish, in body and in spirit. We discourage daydreaming and allowing cell phones to disrupt a meeting.
- We prepare for meetings by reading reports and documents and by asking for needed clarifications prior to a meeting.
- When we write documents, we make them easy to read and understand, and thereby more conducive to informed and responsible decision making.
- Conversely, we state our concerns if a report is confusing or not "reader-friendly."
- We state our concerns if other team members did not prepare adequately for a meeting.

Empowerment of Individuals

- We encourage and challenge members to excel and perform to their best ability or better.
- We encourage members to take measured risks, learn from their mistakes and successes, and boost their skills and confidence levels.
- We value, recognize, celebrate, and reward individual achievement.
- We consider everything a success. Though we try to avoid mistakes and failures, we treat them as something to learn from. We then forgive ourselves and others and move on.
- We give individuals the latitude they need to perform to their best ability. We avoid constraining them with rigid lines of reporting, or by monitoring them too closely.
- We offer members private coaching and encourage them to take practical training to boost their effectiveness.

- We encourage members to share diverse views, as unusual or unpopular as they may be. There is no such thing as a stupid question, except, perhaps, the one you don't ask.
- We subscribe to the motto, "Suffering is optional." We make it OK for members to question the quality of a proposal or complain about the integrity of our decision-making process.

Enjoying Work and Having Fun

- We take ourselves lightly, and we take our work seriously.
- We make our meetings inclusive, efficient, dynamic, engaging, varied, and fun.
- When we don't enjoy meetings we find out why and do something about it.
- We introduce variety and creative and fun touches to our meetings.
- We only have meetings when there is a clear purpose for them.
- We encourage individuals to lead a healthy and balanced life. We believe that work should not be the only focus, and that it should fit in the broader context of private and family life.

Fairness and Equality

- We give every person the same opportunity to influence the group's decisions.
- We avoid domination of our meetings and decision making by experienced, outspoken, dominant, or persistent members. We make deliberate efforts to benefit from and capitalize on the knowledge, skills, and insights of each team member, including quiet ones.
- We know when to speak up, but we also know when to sit back, make room for others to participate, and listen to them with an open mind.
- We treat each member's opinion as having equal weight, regardless of the individual's position, stature, clout, length of service in the organization, passion, or experience.

Honesty

- We tell the truth like it is, as unpleasant as it may be.
- We expect others to tell the truth, and we do not hesitate to ask questions to get it

- We recognize that it may be difficult for others to be frank and open. We do our best to make it easy for them to be honest and direct.
- We realize that the truth may hurt, but this short-term pain is a small price to pay for long-term gain.
- Our first attempt is to communicate concerns directly to the affected individual. We generally avoid speaking behind people's backs. If we do it at all, it is only if our attempts of direct communications were not successful, and we do this only with the intention of finding a way to have a problem addressed.
- We hold no grudges and seek no retribution against someone for speaking the truth. We have no "sacred cows" and no sensitive spots that we should talk about but don't.
- We say what needs to be said when it can make a difference.
- We make room for the possibility that our version of the truth may be limited in scope.
- We avoid misrepresenting the views of others to advance our positions.

Integrity

- Our actions match our words.
- We act selflessly and follow a principled approach.
- We act with the broader interest in mind, even if it means our personal interests may suffer.
- We keep the commitments that we make.
- We are guided by the desire to make a difference and serve the organization and its stakeholders.
- We know that if we act with integrity, we will be able to look back at any given time and be proud of our achievements and track record.
- We avoid making promises that we know we cannot keep or have no intention of keeping, and then looking for excuses to backtrack.
- We avoid game playing with the intent of protecting our own power bases.
- We avoid getting what we want through manipulation or deception.
- We avoid using slogans and fancy concepts to support unjustifiable actions or positions.

- We avoid being driven exclusively by a desire for personal recognition, wealth, prestige, and power.
- We happily share the credit for efforts and we help other people shine. We refuse to accept credit when it is not ours to take.

LISTENING

- We listen more than we speak.
- We listen with a genuine desire to learn.
- We make it a habit to ask questions before we form an opinion.
- We avoid and discourage selective listening (listening only to the part of the message that validates and confirms our position, while ignoring the rest) and combative listening (looking for problems with the speaker's logic, to build a "Yes, but" rebuttal). We recognize that "Yes, but" is a verbal eraser.

OBJECTIVITY

- Our approach to decision making is based on objective goals and principles.
- We are always guided by the organization's broad mandate and mission.
- We are guided by a desire to serve the organization's internal and external stakeholders.
- We act with the best interests of the full organization in mind, in preference to the interests of any component part.
- We do not allow personal interests or other interests to cloud our judgment.
- We do not allow anger or emotions to interfere with our duty to make impartial decisions.
- We step aside if our capacity to make objective decisions and act in the best interests of the organization is impaired.
- We always focus on issues, principles, and systemic structures, and not on individuals or personalities.

Respect and Sensitivity

- We treat each person with respect and decency.
- We check with people before taking actions that could affect them.
- We give each person the benefit of the doubt.
- When we witness a counterproductive or disruptive behavior, we try to understand what caused it before pointing the finger at the individual. We resist making swift judgments and reading malice or hidden intentions into individual actions.
- We avoid judging people based on past actions and assuming that they will never change.
- We avoid allowing our personal dislike for someone get in the way of hearing them out.
- We recognize that it is possible to disagree passionately with someone's views while showing deep respect for the individual.
- We recognize that the tone of our voices, our facial expressions and our word choices do not have to be harsh or aggressive to convey a tough message.
- We generally avoid interruptions or forming rebuttals when someone else is speaking.
- We recognize that the timing of a tough message is just as important as the message itself. We look for times when the other person is receptive for such a message, and avoid giving it when the person is under pressure, or, conversely, rejoicing and celebrating an achievement.
- We avoid giving individuals condescending lectures. Instead, we look to engage them in a meaningful dialogue. We make fewer statements and ask more questions.

Risk Taking

- We dare to make the unpopular statement or to question the status quo.
- We dare to ask tough questions about a decision or how it is made or how a meeting is run.
- We dare to question flawed arguments, regardless of the position of the person who makes them.

- We soften our comments by focusing on the issues and the principles, not the people.
- We dare to bite the bullet and make the right decision, regardless of any criticism that it may attract. We know that the right decision will survive the wrath of the critics and the cynics.
- We dare to let go of our own power bases and of our need for control over others.
- We dare to assume the best about others and to be naïve optimists, even when people give us many reasons not to do so.
- We dare to give feedback, even if it is not pleasant, but we work to make it easy to receive.
- We dare to listen to feedback openly and learn from it. We treat it as a gift, even when it is highly critical of us or when it is delivered in a harsh and abusive manner.
- We are prepared to admit mistakes or failures and be subject to scrutiny for them.

TEAMWORK

- We remain sensitive to others and keep them informed and consulted, especially on issues that affect them or when they could offer information to enhance the quality of our decisions.
- We replace adversity (you against me) with collaboration (you and me against the problem).
- We genuinely listen to one another and seek to make better collective decisions together.
- We participate on the team as proactive partners, not as passive or reluctant spectators.
- We give others advance warnings of events and developments that might affect them.
- We help others out if needed. We do what's needed to get the team's job done, even when it is not within our job description. We go beyond the call of duty.
- Conversely, we resist the temptation to do things for other people when we should only offer coaching and advice. We recognize that it is more effective to "teach someone how to fish" than to "catch the fish and cook it for them."

- We avoid being "loose cannons," pursuing new ideas on our own and without consultation.
- We avoid splitting the group by forming strategic alliances and cliques and by lobbying and recruiting others to form a majority in favor of our causes.
- We are driven by a desire to serve and to help the team succeed and make better decisions.
- When our ideas lose, we accept the majority's decision and avoid undermining it.
- When our ideas win, we avoid gloating at the expense of those whose ideas lost.
- We share our knowledge, expertise, and skills freely and willingly with others. We do not hesitate to cultivate successors.

Transparency and Access to Information

- We avoid hiding information just because it is unpleasant or potentially embarrassing.
- We generally make information and documents accessible. We have nothing to hide.
- We have clear guidelines on when to keep information confidential, and we always have legitimate reasons for doing so.
- We accept our obligation to keep confidentiality on certain issues.

SEVEN

Building Relationships with Stakeholders

Making good substantive decisions is only one goal of your meetings and shared decision-making process. A goal that is equally important is having everyone arrive at the same destination together, as willing and enthusiastic partners. "Everyone" should include not only your team members, but also your team's internal and external stakeholders.

A stakeholder is an individual or a group:

- ▲ Who is affected by your team's mandate and decisions in some way
- ▲ Whose support is needed for the successful implementation of your team's decisions
- ▲ Who can offer useful ideas and insights to enhance the quality of your team's decisions

Some stakeholders are internal, i.e., from within your organization, and others are external. Some are affected more substantially by your group's decisions, and others are only affected marginally.

All stakeholders should be engaged in some way in your group's decision making. Some, like your boss, should be engaged in a more substantial way. Others, like customers and suppliers, can be engaged by being given advance warnings on initiatives that affect them and by being asked for feedback and advice.

This chapter gives you tools for building relationships with your stakeholders. It covers the following topics:

- ▲ Identifying your stakeholders
- ▲ Identifying the risks of poor stakeholder relationships
- ▲ Establishing the benefits of good stakeholder relationships
- ▲ Cautions about stakeholder consultation
- ▲ Building the relationship with your boss
- ▲ Building relationships with other stakeholders
- ▲ Evaluating relationships with stakeholders
- ▲ Repairing a dysfunctional relationship with a stakeholder

Identifying Your Stakeholders

Having decided to build relationships with stakeholders, you need to address these questions:

- ▲ Who are your stakeholders?
- ▲ What levels of relationship building do you need to consider?

To identify your stakeholders, you need to ask questions like the following:

- ▲ To whom are you and your team accountable?
- ▲ Who will need to ratify the recommendations that you make?
- ▲ Who could offer useful advice to enhance and enrich the quality of the consensus?
- ▲ Who will be affected by your team's decisions, and to what degree?
- ▲ Who might benefit or lose as a result of your group's decisions?

- Whose power base might be threatened by the group's potential decisions?
- Who should be aware of your progress, even if they are only marginally affected by it?
- Whose support would be nice to have, to increase the legitimacy of your group's work and elevate its stature?
- Who will implement your group's decisions, and what advance warning do they need? To what extent should their input be considered before decisions are finalized?

Internal Stakeholders

Your internal stakeholders start with parties to whom you are directly or indirectly accountable. They may include:

- Your boss
- Your boss's boss
- Your organization's executive committee
- Your organization's board of directors

Other internal stakeholders will include parties to whom you are not accountable, but still need as partners and supporters, such as:

- Your peers and colleagues, including managers of other departments that are affected by your mandate
- Regional and branch offices
- Your support staff and any other staff with whom you interact
- Your company's investors and shareholders, or your organization's members

External Stakeholders

External stakeholders include parties from outside the organization who will be affected by your mandate. They may include some or all of the following parties, and possibly others:

- Your customers
- The community within which you operate
- Influential individuals and organizations within the community
- Government agencies, e.g., municipal government, regulators, funding agencies
- Parent or sibling organizations, e.g., counterparts in other states, or national or international umbrella organizations
- Your suppliers (yes, them too)
- Your professional colleagues in other organizations
- Media reporters

Identifying the Risks of Poor Stakeholder Relationships

Poor stakeholder relationships can lead to the following outcomes:

- Your group may end up making bad decisions, because it worked in isolation and depended only on the knowledge and expertise of its own members.
- Your group's decisions may be theoretically and technically sound, but may fail to address the realities in the field.
- Your group's decisions on contentious issues may be undermined by influential stakeholders who resent not being consulted.
- You may encounter resistance to change by those who will be affected by the decisions.
- Stakeholders may follow your lead reluctantly, making the end results less than satisfactory.

Example: Torpedoed by an Outspoken Board Member

A proposal for a significant real estate acquisition is researched by a committee. When the proposed purchase is brought to the board of directors for approval, it is "shot down" by a vociferous board member, who is also a professed expert on the real estate market.

The lesson? To prevent its consensus from meeting such a fate, the committee should have invited the director to give his input at the start of the assignment. The committee might have also invited him to comment on its emerging consensus from time to time. To manage the expectations of this director, the committee chair might have said this to him:

"Trevor, can I talk to you about the real estate research assignment? I understand that you are very interested in this project and that you've had some experience in the real estate market. Your ideas can help us out. If you want to give the committee some input, there are two ways for you to get involved: You can either come to committee meetings, or I can consult you informally from time to time. Which would you prefer?" (Get his feedback.)

If Trevor opted to come to committee meetings, the chair could have said this:

"I need to address one concern: I want to make sure that committee members feel free to speak their minds and raise tough questions about any idea or proposal, including any ideas that you may bring to the table. Given your position on the board of directors, they may be hesitant to criticize your ideas. What do you think we can do to prevent this from happening?"

Example: Community Not Consulted

A private company proposed a development of a ski resort. It applied for and received all government permits and approvals for the project. Based on this, the company went ahead and purchased construction equipment and made commitments to contractors. There had been warning signs about community opposition to the project for environmental and other reasons, but the company did not consider this opposition important or significant.

When the work on the project was about to begin, there were human blockades in front of the construction equipment, put in place by community activists and members of the local Indian tribe. The matter went to the courts and the project was delayed. Eventually the company won in court, but as result of the delay went bankrupt. Ironically, it was later learned that there was not much opposition to the project itself, but there was plenty of resentment of the company's perceived arrogance and insensitivity. The lessons?

- ▲ The company should not have ignored or trivialized the warning signs.
- ▲ It was not enough to have a financially viable project that could attract many tourists and revive the local economy, and to obtain all the required government permits and approvals. The company needed to go beyond the mandatory approval process and get the moral approval and support at the community level.
- ▲ The fact that some community stakeholders did not have legal clout did not mean that they did not have actual clout, and plenty of it.
- ▲ The company should have been more sensitive to the communities in the vicinity of the proposed ski resort. It should have initiated a stakeholder consultation program, to hear the concerns of the various affected parties and integrate them into the project plan. It should have pursued such a process even though government agencies did not require it.

Example: Members and Union Not Consulted

As a cost-saving measure, the board of directors of a credit union decided to reduce its opening hours. However, members of the credit union were not consulted before the decision was made nor was the union representing the staff. The change was made on very short notice, and several patrons, including many senior citizens, were surprised to find their financial institution closed when they came in to do their banking.

Resentful patrons vented their anger at their first target: the frontline unionized staff. This added to the frustration of the union and the staff, who believed that the change in opening hours placed jobs at risk. A media reporter got wind of the story, and interviewed angry members and staff. The matter became an organizational nightmare and an expensive public relations fiasco, wiping out any cost savings that the change was supposed to generate.

Why did this happen? The difficulties were the result of an ivory-tower mentality and a top-down approach to decision making, with no respect or sensitivity shown to affected parties. The negative outcomes could have been prevented by taking a softer and more inclusive approach.

As an alternative, the process could have started with a letter sent to all affected parties (staff, patrons) including:

▲ An explanation of the problem to be solved (competitive and financial pressures)

▲ An explanation of the various options being considered, as well as the solution that the board was leaning towards

▲ A reassurance that every effort would be made to minimize job losses and reduce the disruptive effect of the change on staff and patrons of the credit union

▲ An invitation to offer feedback, ask questions, and share concerns by a given deadline

Here is a sample letter that could have been sent to the members of the credit union:

Dear Members of the Pooling-Our-Assets Credit Union:

As you may know, our credit union has faced increased competition from banks and other financial institutions in the community. As a result of these pressures, your board of directors is considering several options to make us more competitive and viable, so we can continue to give you, our members, the excellent service that you expect and deserve, and so we can continue to provide our staff with a supportive and stimulating work environment.

Change is not easy to accept, especially when it affects you personally. However, the reality is that the status quo is not an option. Your board has some tough decisions to make. We believe the quality of our decisions will be improved if we take your input into account. We therefore invite you to help us shape the future of our credit union.

Our financial analysts tell us that we must start implementing change to improve our financial performance within six months. This gives all of us an opportunity to pool our ideas, just like we pool our assets, and come up with the best solutions. Our goal should be to make us more competitive, while minimizing the negative impact of any changes on our members and our staff.

Here are your opportunities to offer input:

▲ First, we ask you to review the enclosed analysis of the challenges that we face and some of the options that are being considered.

▲ Second, we ask you to fill out the enclosed member questionnaire entitled "Pooling Our Ideas." Please send it by February 15 to the address below or drop it off at your branch. There will be a drawing and you may win a small prize. But more importantly, your ideas will help us make better decisions for the credit union.

After the questionnaires are analyzed, we will have focus group discussions in March. Please let us know if you want to participate.

Please call Rick Thomson at 555-555-5555 if you have any questions or concerns, or send him an e-mail at rick@poolingour resources.com. We are looking forward to hearing back from you and, with your help, keeping our credit union successful.

Establishing the Benefits of Good Stakeholder Relationships

Building relationships with stakeholders requires a deliberate and sustained investment of time, effort, and money. Relationship building can be a tedious and sometimes treacherous road. But if your efforts are genuine, sincere, sustained, and consistent, and if they are carried out with care and professionalism, the payoffs can be substantial.

Good relationships with stakeholders will:

▲ Enable you to benefit from stakeholders' insights, ideas, knowledge, and expertise.

▲ Gain allies and supporters for your group's consensus-building efforts.

▲ Convert some of your potential critics and skeptics into active and enthusiastic partners.

- ▲ Increase stakeholder appreciation of what your group is working towards.
- ▲ Establish good will and "credit" to draw on with stakeholders. If they know that your decisions are responsive to their needs and concerns, they will be more forgiving of your mistakes, and will be more readily accepting of changes that affect them.
- ▲ Provide you with an early detection system. Stakeholders who appreciate the way you treat them will give you "heads-up" warnings of potential problems, and you will be able to address them proactively.

Example: A New Building

A church congregation was considering a move to new premises. One proposal was to lease a building. The other was to purchase a new one. The latter proposal was clearly the better option in the long run, but would have meant a more substantial financial commitment by each member. The proposed move proved to be an emotional and contentious issue. The risk of forcing a vote was that the congregation could lose many of the members who would vote on the losing side.

Over a period of six months, the church board conducted a member consultation program. As part of the program, the church president made a point of contacting each member in person at least once. This way the president "took the real pulse" of the congregation. Beyond that, each member felt that she or he was respected, heard, and understood.

The consultation process culminated in a general meeting and a vote on a proposal to purchase a new building. As a result of the consultation program, there was a significant majority in favor of the proposal. The members who voted against it accepted the outcome as a democratically made decision. They remained loyal supporters and active members of the church. Their sentiment was, "Yes, we did not win the argument. But we were fully heard, and the process was open and inclusive. This is the kind of congregation we want to belong to."

Example: Advice from the Janitor

You are managing a project that has company-wide impacts. One day you are riding an elevator with the janitor. You tell him about your project (which affects him also) and how exciting it is. While you're at it, you tell him about a problem you're having and you wonder aloud whether he might have a piece of advice for you. To your surprise, he has a profound insight that helps you in your next meeting. Next time you see him, he shares another idea or alerts you to a problem that you have not been aware of.

The results?

- ▲ You have gathered "field intelligence," and learned a few things that will help you and your group make better decisions. Does it matter that the idea came from a janitor? Clearly, the answer should be no.
- ▲ You gained an ally and a partner, who will be aware of your work and will share ideas and alert you to problems.
- ▲ By asking for the janitor's advice, you gave him a compliment and added meaning to his work life, and it did not cost you anything. This is very different from the prevailing corporate attitude in some organizations: "You should be grateful that you have a job." Perhaps they should be grateful, but you should also be grateful for them and their talents.

Cautions About Stakeholder Consultation

As you engage stakeholders in discussions and consultations on issues that affect them, consider the following cautions:

- ▲ Manage stakeholder expectations, i.e., avoid giving (or appearing to give) promises that you cannot keep. If their input is advisory, make this abundantly clear at the outset. Explain that your team will consider their advice in the context of other data (technical and financial data and expert advice) and make the appropriate decision. Stakeholder input is only "one piece of the truth," and it is therefore of an advisory and nonbinding nature.
- ▲ Avoid consultation overload, i.e., don't attempt to engage stakeholders on issues in which they have no interest or have very little advice to offer. Involve them in addressing questions that they can easily understand and "sink their teeth into." Too many consultation programs fail because of confusion or because the issues draw no stakeholder interest. After all, they are busy people. You need to make it easy and logical for them to give you helpful advice.

It's not enough to have a one-time interaction with the stakeholder. You need to maintain the relationship as long as your team's efforts are ongoing. Here are a few activities to consider:

- ▲ Send stakeholders periodic newsletter containing updates on progress. Always include a feedback and advice sheet, so they can keep those precious ideas coming.
- ▲ Maintain an "open door policy," whereby feedback and questions are welcome anytime, and are given expeditious and appropriate acknowledgment and attention.
- ▲ Always thank stakeholders for their advice and let them know what was done with it, i.e., how it was used, or why it could not be used.
- ▲ Written communication is fine, but it sure is nice for a stakeholder to receive an occasional personal phone call and hear a real human voice on the other side.

Too often stakeholder consultation programs are dominated by outspoken individuals, to the exclusion of others, who are just as wise (or wiser) but tend to be less assertive. You need to ensure that stakeholder feedback is balanced and truly representative. Look for ways of engaging members of the "silent majority" and making it easy for them to share their views. For example, if you are inviting the community to a public meeting, you will likely hear only from those who enjoy public speaking. You may need to engage "silent members" by:

- ▲ Having an "open house" prior to the meeting, whereby stakeholders get to review charts and maps and speak to you and your team members in person.
- ▲ Having discussions in small breakout groups, with clearly defined questions, and with the guideline that everyone gets to speak at least once.
- ▲ Inviting them to give their feedback in writing. Have a suggestion box out and remind them of it from time to time.
- ▲ Conducting random surveys, interviews, and focus groups, possibly by professional polling firms.

If you engage community groups in consultation and ask representatives to participate in meetings, keep in mind that volunteer organizations may not be well funded. As a result, there may be an expectation that, as a corporate sponsor, your organization will pay:

▲ Travel expenses for the stakeholder representative

▲ Salary replacement for volunteers (given that they give up a working day and offer your organization the benefit of their knowledge, expertise, and insights)

Always keep in mind your group's overall two purposes:

1. To make the best decisions for the organization and its stakeholders. Your group's decisions will be diluted if you make your consultation process a free-for-all, and try to accommodate and please everyone (see examples below).
2. To make sure that as many parties as possible reach the same destination together, as willing and supportive partners.

Example: Saying No to a Stakeholder

"Good morning, Mr. Richards. This is Tracy from Copper Explorations Company. I am calling to follow up on your suggestions that we change our project plans to reduce environmental impacts. Is now a good time to talk? Thank you.

"First, I want you to know that everyone on the committee appreciated the time you took to prepare your summary. Your document was concise and clear, and it was easy to follow and understand. Everyone thought you were an effective advocate for your group.

"We looked at your concerns at our committee meeting. We also considered comments and suggestions made by other individuals and organizations. Some of your ideas are very helpful and they will be used. Others won't. As you can appreciate, we are working very hard to balance all the interests.

"Later today I will send you an e-mail with a more detailed response to the suggestions that you made. I welcome your feedback on it. Do you have any questions for me now, or do you want to save them for after you receive the e-mail?

"In any event, thank you for your help, Mr. Richards. Have a great day."

Building the Relationship with Your Boss

Your boss is a "must have" ally if your consensus building efforts are to truly work and make a difference. She is your bridge to higher management levels. You need to do all you can to ensure that your boss is:

- ▲ Always kept in the loop and is given progress reports on a regular basis.
- ▲ Given advance notices of important developments.
- ▲ Given early warnings of potential problems that may affect her or his work.
- ▲ Given reassurances that your team continues to be accountable and operate within its mandate, workplan, and budgets.

The benefits of building the relationship with your boss are that he will be more likely to:

- ▲ Remain sensitive and responsive to your group's needs
- ▲ Appreciate your group's difficulties and challenges
- ▲ Stand up for your group in management meetings and ensure that your work is understood, appreciated, and taken seriously by other managers
- ▲ Listen to management concerns about your team's work and convey them to you
- ▲ Give you advance warnings of developments that might affect your group's work
- ▲ Serve as your personal mentor and adviser

Here are a few suggested steps to kick-start the relationship with your boss. First, establish your team's mandate, workplan, budget, and required resources with absolute clarity at the outset. Since your boss is likely to be too busy to define the details, it is probably best to be proactive by defining them yourself and asking for your boss's approval. If your given mandate is unrealistic or confusing, you'll need to renegotiate it.

Second, establish how you will remain accountable (even if your boss is inclined to "trust you"), by discussing:

- ▲ The frequency of reporting
- ▲ The matters on which you will report
- ▲ The level of detail that is significant to your boss
- ▲ The process to follow if you need to exceed your given mandate and budgets

Establish how your boss will support you and your team, such as by:

- ▲ Representing your progress and consensus well at the senior management meeting or at the board of directors

▲ Possibly scheduling you to make a presentation to them from time to time.

Having kick-started the relationship with your boss, here are a few things to do to maintain it as your group's consensus-building efforts evolve:

▲ Remain accountable and keep your boss in the loop, so she can avoid surprises.

▲ Inform your boss of progress and of any difficulties. Give your boss advance warnings of deadlines that may be missed or budgets that may need to be exceeded. Look for his direction and advice when needed.

▲ Be proactive and alert your boss as soon as you know of potential problems, so that she gets the news directly from you first: For example:

> *"Rebecca, I thought I'd let you know that one of our customers was annoyed with the way he was treated, and is threatening to complain to the CEO directly. We are trying to address his concerns right now, but I thought I'd give you a "heads up" warning that this might happen, so you're not caught off guard. Do you need me to explain to you what happened?"*

▲ Avoid boring your boss with small details. Instead concentrate on general performance and overall results. For example, your boss will not need to know the gossip about every team member, but he may be interested in knowing how well they are working together.

▲ Ask your boss to support you and your team at higher management levels. For example:

> *"Sam, I really need you to stand up for us at the next board meeting. I have a feeling that the board may be under pressure to make decisions that may be politically correct but will undermine what we are doing and be bad for the company. I need our perspective to be well represented and explained. I am even prepared to join you at the meeting, make a presentation, and answer any questions that the board may have. If it's not appropriate for me to be there, I can prepare briefing notes for you. What do you think?"*

▲ Ask your boss to give you advance warnings of developments that could affect your mandate.

"Glenda, I have a feeling that some significant decisions will be made at the next management meeting. Is it fair for me to assume that you will give me an advance warning of any developments that could affect my team?"

- Ask your boss for feedback and advice on key issues.

"Brent, do you have a minute? I need your advice on something."

- Resist your boss's inclination to micromanage your group or interfere with your decision-making process. For example:

"Doris, thank you for suggesting that I add Jim Jones to my committee. I just wanted to clarify with you that I have the authority to make the final decision on this, and that you will accept and respect whatever choice I make. Do I have your support?"

- Express appreciation, verbally or in writing, for your boss's support of your group's efforts:

"Rudy, I wanted to tell you how much I appreciated the fact that you allowed me to make the adjustments to our project schedule. I know that you have many priorities, and it was great that you were able to take the time to hear me and that you were prepared to say yes to most of my requests."

Building Relationships with Other Stakeholders

When building relationships with stakeholders other than your boss, you need to establish:

- The impact that your mandate has on them
- What they need from you and your team
- What you and your team need from them

You may opt for one of the following relationship levels:

- Information exchange
- Consultation
- Collaboration

Information Exchange

If a relationship with a stakeholder is at the information-exchange level, you need to:

- Keep the stakeholder informed.
- Ask them to keep you informed of anything that could affect your decisions.
- Welcome any ideas that could enhance the quality of your group's decisions.

The information-exchange level would be appropriate if the direct impact of your mandate on the stakeholder is not substantial, but there are still some benefits from keeping them informed. Examples of such stakeholders may include peers and colleagues, managers of other departments, support staff, and some outside stakeholders (suppliers, community groups).

Example: Kick-Starting Town Hall Meetings with Staff

Here is an example of a letter to kick-start your relationship-building efforts with your company's staff at the information-exchange level:

To: All staff members, ABC company

From: Theresa Moore, manager, customer service standards

As you may know, I am heading a team to look at making our company more responsive to customers. This is a good news story, and we would love to tell you about our mandate and the types of operational changes we are considering.

Consider yourself personally invited to our first town hall meeting, being held on Tuesday July 17th, at noon, in the conference room adjacent to the cafeteria. In this meeting we will report on the project and ask for your feedback and advice. Bring your lunch with you.

Consultation

If a relationship with a stakeholder is at the consultation level, you need to engage them in active dialogue and exchange of views. The consultation level is appropriate if the impact of your group's work on a stakeholder is substantial. In such cases it is smart and prudent to consult the stakeholder and ask for his or her input before any decisions are finalized. Consult them even if you are not required to do so.

Stakeholder consultation can take various forms. For example:

- ▲ Private consultations and interviews with key stakeholders
- ▲ Large public meetings or forums (see Appendix 2 for an example)
- ▲ Open houses, whereby project plans are displayed and stakeholders can discuss them with agency representatives
- ▲ Small stakeholder committees, with key stakeholders represented on them

Example: A Proposed New Government Policy

Your government agency is preparing a new policy on forestry practices. In order to develop a credible and well-respected policy, you will need to consult stakeholders and integrate their input into the policy. Those stakeholders may include:

- ▲ Forest company management
- ▲ Forest company unions
- ▲ Environmental and community activists
- ▲ Municipal government leaders
- ▲ Forestry faculty professors
- ▲ Business experts

Collaboration

Engaging stakeholders on the collaboration level means that an organization delegates a degree of control and decision making to its stakeholders. This level gives stakeholders a definitive say in designated areas. Their collective decisions are binding, not advisory. Here are a few tips for the collaboration level:

▲ Protect your organization's interests by appointing members of your own staff or volunteers to the stakeholder committee.

▲ Ensure that the parameters of the assignment (mandate, deliverable results, schedules, budgets, spending authority, etc.) are abundantly clear and that the committee agrees to them before its work begins.

▲ Establish the rules of engagement for the committee (see Chapter 5) and have them discussed and agreed on by the committee.

▲ Ensure that the stakeholder committee is held accountable for the results of the assignment by being required to report on its activities.

Here are two examples of the collaboration level:

1. A municipal council establishes the annual block funding for community arts projects. It then appoints a stakeholder committee and delegates to it the authority to allocate the funds to specific arts projects. The committee has representatives from the municipal council and arts organizations. The committee's decisions are final and it does not have to go back to the council to have them ratified. It maintains accountability by periodically reporting to the council on its activities. The council reserves the right to disband the committee.
2. A mining company decides to fund an independent research on how the environmental impact of a proposed new mine can be minimized. It establishes a stakeholder committee to select the consulting firm to conduct the research and to establish what questions will be addressed. The committee has members from affected municipalities, environmental groups, local native groups, and the mining company. The committee's decisions on managing the research are final.

Note: Influencing the Selection of a Stakeholder Representative

On both the consultation and collaboration levels, you will likely work with representatives of stakeholder organizations. Each of those individuals will be appointed by their respective organizations. Although you won't be making the selection, you should look for opportunities to influence it. You don't want to have individuals on your stakeholder committee who:

- ▲ Are there because no one else from the stakeholder organization was available
- ▲ Have no influence within their organizations
- ▲ Have no authority to negotiate or make commitments on behalf of their organizations (meaning that any decision made by your committee will have to go back to their groups for ratification, making your consensus-building process useless and wasteful)
- ▲ Have no long-term commitment to your assignment
- ▲ May be replaced by an alternate at a later meeting, disrupting the continuity of your work.

To prevent the above problems, you need to let stakeholder organizations know what you expect of their representatives and why. Tell them you want a representative who:

- ▲ Knows the stakeholder organization's history, philosophy, needs, and interests.
- ▲ Is well connected within the stakeholder organization and can represent it well.
- ▲ Has credibility and influence within the stakeholder organization.
- ▲ Is authorized to negotiate and make commitments on behalf of the stakeholder organization.
- ▲ Will stay with you for the duration of the assignment and provide continuity. Avoid revolving doors, with alternates coming to different meetings.
- ▲ Is a team player who will listen to what other stakeholders have to say.
- ▲ Will go back to his or her group and ensure that its members are advised on progress on the stakeholder committee and agree to continue to support its work.

Note: Dealing with Dysfunctional Stakeholder Organizations

When you look to involve stakeholder organizations on the consultation or collaboration levels, you need to be careful *not* to make the automatic assumptions that these organizations:

- Are harmonious and collaborative
- Speak with one voice on the issues that affect your committee's work
- Are united in their support of your committee and its work
- Share your interest in bringing closure to tough issues

As tempting and as convenient as it may be to make the above assumptions, they are risky. If you check more closely, you may discover that:

- Community groups are rarely homogeneous and harmonious bodies.
- Often nonprofit organizations are only vehicles of convenience to increase clout and advance a certain cause. It does not mean people get along with one another.
- Opinions on contentious issues may be quite diverse within the same organization.
- Many boards of directors are fractious and conflict-ridden.
- Decisions made by democratically elected boards are often ignored or undermined by influential individuals.
- It may be difficult or impossible for the group's representative to go back and convince its members to implement or support the committee's consensus, especially when members are volunteer activists and have a difficulty establishing proper accountability
- You may be dealing with a principled person today, only to discover the next day that a mini-revolution took place: the president and board of directors were removed and a brand-new, inexperienced, and much more adversarial administration has taken over. You end up having to rebuild the relationship with the stakeholder organization from ground zero.

To reduce the likelihood of the above difficulties, you need to do your research and find out more about the stakeholder organization before engaging it in consultation. You need to learn about the organization's mandate, history, philosophy, governance structure, how decisions are made, and the dynamics among people. As a result of your research, you may decide to:

- Go ahead and involve the stakeholder organization in consultation.

- Involve it after certain conditions have been met to your satisfaction, e.g., after it is clear that you will have collaborative and principled participation for the life of the assignment.
- Choose to not involve the organization in consultation.
- If it is really important to involve this stakeholder organization on your committee, you may on some occasions be in a position to offer assistance in:
  - Mediating internal disputes within the stakeholder organization.
  - Helping the organization strengthen its governance structures.
  - Helping the organization develop its approach to consensus building.

EVALUATING RELATIONSHIPS WITH STAKEHOLDERS

Here is a sample script that shows how your team can evaluate its relationships with internal and external stakeholders. Feel free to modify the diagram, shown in Figure 7-1, and the script to suit your circumstances.

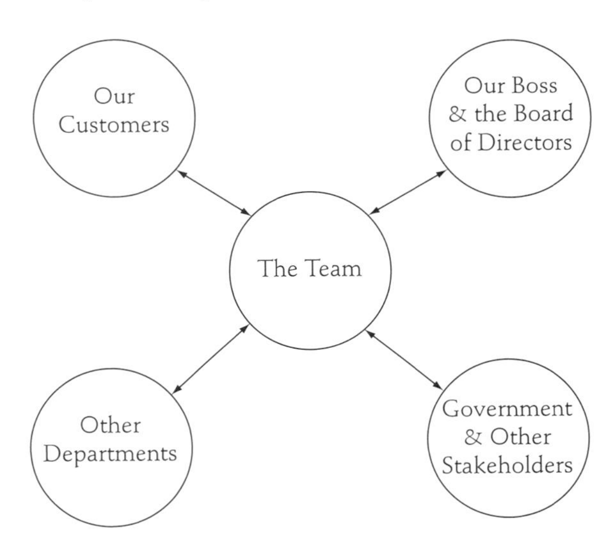

Figure 7-1: Relationships with stakeholders 360° management.

Script: Evaluating Stakeholder Relationships

"The purpose of this meeting is to evaluate our team's relationships with our internal and external stakeholders.

"Here is a diagram that illustrates how our team works with internal and external stakeholders (show Figure 7-1). We need to look at the relationships, or the arrows going in both directions.

"First, you'll see the lines of communications and accountability between us and our boss and the board of directors. We need to consider questions like these:

▲ How well do we work with our boss? Any strengths in this relationship? Weaknesses?

▲ How good is our relationship with the board of directors?

▲ How well do we keep our boss and the board of directors informed?

▲ How well do they keep us informed?

▲ Do they understand and support our mandate?

▲ Do we understand and support what they do?

▲ What can be done to improve these relationships?

"Second, let's look at our relationship with customers. Here are some questions to consider:

▲ Do we give our customers enough of an advance warning of new developments?

▲ Do we let them know about new products and features?

▲ Do we keep them informed about new procedures?

▲ Do we listen to our customers?

▲ Do we respond to their questions and concerns as professionally and as expeditiously as we should? Do we do as well as our competition in this area?

▲ Do we take our customers' concerns seriously, or do we dismiss and trivialize them?

▲ What can we do to build better relationships with our customers?

"Third, we need to consider relationships between our team and other departments, especially those that we work with on a regular basis. Here are the questions to consider:

- How good are we at keeping them in the loop?
- How well do we understand them and what they do?
- How well do they understand us and what we do?
- Do we consult them enough before making decisions that affect them?
- Do they consult us enough before making decisions that affect our department?
- What can we do to build and maintain these relationships?

"Finally, let's look at a few other stakeholders (government agencies, community leaders, important organizations, etc.).

"Now, why don't we split into four discussion groups of three members each, with each group looking at each stakeholder group and addressing the relationship-building questions that I raised. I suggest that we set aside twenty minutes for the small-group work, then report back to the full group and discuss it further. Does this sound reasonable? Any questions?"

REPAIRING A DYSFUNCTIONAL RELATIONSHIP WITH A STAKEHOLDER

At times you will need to repair a dysfunctional relationship with a stakeholder. For example:

- You are asked to take over the leadership of a team that has never heard the term "stakeholder relationships" and is used to working in isolation. Stakeholder trust and respect for the group are nonexistent.
- Tensions with a stakeholder have been left to build over time and, having read this chapter, you want to do something to repair the damage.

Example: Discussion with a Community Leader

The president of an important community organization has been like a thorn in the side of your government agency. He has been speaking to the media and describing your agency as being incompetent and out of touch with the community. Your predecessor was angry with him and refused to speak to him until he would apologize for his public statements.

Now that you've taken over, you want to start with a fresh approach:

"Good morning Ms. Jones. My name is Shirley Smith and I am the new CEO of the agricultural land reserve agency. I was wondering if we could meet sometime in the next few days.

"I know that in the past the relationship between your group and our agency was not all that positive. Nonetheless, my view is that we need to work together to change that. I believe your group can give our agency valuable input and help us make better decisions for the community. So what do you say? Shall we meet? Would next Tuesday at 10 A.M. be OK with you? Shall we meet in your office or mine or somewhere else?"

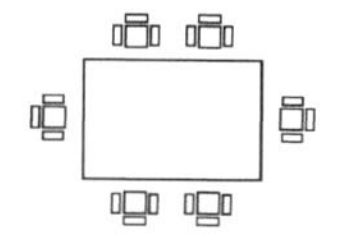

Part Two:

Making Meetings Work

Having built the foundation for shared decision making (Part 1, Chapters 1 to 7), you are ready for meeting-related tools. Part 2 (Chapters 8 to 18) offers you tools, tips, and ideas to make your meetings better focused, more productive, inclusive, engaging, and even fun.

Specifically, Part 2 covers the following topics:

- Chapter 8 describes a vision of a successful meeting. It presents the ten essential ingredients of a good meeting and gives you tools to ensure they are in place.
- Chapter 9 offers you tools for planning a meeting. It contemplates a team process for planning, and describes the planning roles of various meeting masters.
- Chapter 10 outlines the prelaunching activities that take place just before a meeting begins.
- Chapter 11 describes the steps of a smooth launch for a meeting.
- Chapter 12 describes how to steer a meeting to its destination. It shows a logical progression for a meeting, and gives you tools to manage time, issues, and people in a meeting.
- Chapter 13 explains how each individual can pull his or her weight and help make the meeting successful.
- Chapter 14 shows you how to bring the meeting to a smooth landing.
- Chapter 15 describes activities that should take place after a meeting. It gives you tips on how to create good summaries (minutes), how to ensure follow-up on decisions made in a meeting, and how to assess the meeting and learn lessons from it for the next one.
- Chapter 16 describes consensus-building activities between face-to-face meetings. It covers consensus building by correspondence, teleconferences, videoconferences, and electronic meetings.
- Chapter 17 gives you survival tools for contentious meetings and shows you how such meetings can be converted from problems into opportunities.
- Chapter 18 is your troubleshooting guide for meetings. It includes condensed and easy-to-use tables on how to cure common meeting ailments. It gives you options to address meeting ailments at the meeting itself, and explains how they can be prevented in future meetings.

EIGHT

The Ten Key Ingredients of a Successful Meeting

People have no difficulty identifying what they dislike about meetings, but they often have trouble describing the characteristics of a good meeting. Without a clear affirmative vision of a successful meeting and in the absence of good examples to emulate, you are likely to repeat what you are familiar with. To break this cycle, you must articulate what you want to achieve in a meeting, and not just what you want to avoid. You need a set of affirmative principles and performance indicators with which to measure the success of a meeting.

This chapter lists ten key ingredients of a successful meeting and how to use them to measure the success of a meeting. The key ingredients are:

- Clarity of mandate, purpose, issues, and process
- Participation protocol and etiquette
- Productivity and forward movement
- Flexibility and creative thinking

- ▲ Quality discussions and decision making
- ▲ Openness, listening, and collaboration
- ▲ Balance, inclusion, and equality
- ▲ Shared responsibility
- ▲ Variety and a light touch
- ▲ Logistical support

For each of these ten ingredients this chapter gives you:

- ▲ An explanation of what to look for
- ▲ Symptoms that indicate that this ingredient is absent in a meeting
- ▲ Premeeting steps to help ensure that the ingredient will be present at the meeting
- ▲ Interventions in the meeting to help restore the ingredient

CLARITY OF MANDATE, PURPOSE, ISSUES, AND PROCESS

Clarity will help your group discuss issues and make decisions in a deliberate and confident manner. For a meeting to succeed, there must be clarity of:

- ▲ Mandate
- ▲ Purpose
- ▲ Issues
- ▲ Process

To assess whether there is clarity in your meetings, try asking members the questions below and see if they can answer them with confidence.

Clarity of Mandate

- ▲ Why was the group formed and what is it mandated to achieve?
- ▲ Who is the group intended to serve?
- ▲ Who are the group's internal and external stakeholders (see Chapter 7)?
- ▲ What decisions is the group authorized to make?

See Chapter 3 for ideas on how to establish a clear, compelling, and realistic mandate, and how to ensure that it is understood and embraced by your members.

Clarity of Purpose

- Why was this meeting called and what benefits is it intended to deliver?
- How closely are the desired outcomes tied to your mandate?
- To what degree will the outcomes of this meeting enhance relationships with stakeholders?
- Does each member know why she or he was invited to the meeting and how her or his participation is expected to make a difference?
- Do the desired outcomes of the meeting truly require interaction and face-to-face discussions, or can they be achieved equally well without a meeting?

Clarity of Issues

- Is it clear at the outset of a discussion what problem needs to be solved?
- Is each decision-making option articulated clearly?
- Do members know the precise impacts of the various proposals?
- Is it clear which agenda items are for information only and which are for decision making?

Clarity of Process

- What decisions can be made unilaterally by the facilitator or the group's leader, and what decisions are for the group to make, collectively?
- What types of decisions should be made informally, by consensus?
- When should a formal vote be taken, by a show of hands?
- When is it acceptable to make a decision by a narrow majority, and when should the group work harder to achieve a better and broader win-win solution?
- What options do members have if they want to modify, delay, delegate, drop, or park an agenda item?
- What conditions justify revisiting a previous decision?

Indicators of a Lack of Clarity

- There are issues on the agenda that have little or nothing to do with your group's mandate.

- You are not sure why a meeting was called or why you were invited to be there.
- You are not sure why an item is on the agenda and how it will be handled.
- Members digress from the agenda.
- You find yourself confused by technical terms and abbreviations.
- Members argue about the detailed wording of a proposal, instead of its substance.

Premeeting Steps to Increase Clarity

- Conduct member orientation programs, to discuss the group's mandate, members' roles and responsibilities, lines of communications and accountability, and how meetings are run.
- Emphasize the group's mandate in premeeting documents and communications.
- Screen and prioritize proposed agenda items, and place only those that relate to your mandate on the agenda. It's OK to say "no" to other items. The agenda should not be a "free-for-all."
- Have all necessary research done, summarized in clearly laid out reports, and communicated to the members in advance, so they can review it and get ready for the meeting.
- Make all premeeting documents clear, concise, and reader-friendly. Encourage report writers to use plain language and explain all technical terms and abbreviations.
- Clarify each agenda item: Is it for information? For discussion? For decision making?

Interventions at the Meeting to Ensure Clarity

- Articulate the group's mandate and the purpose of the meeting at the start of the meeting, and reinforce them as the meeting progresses.
- Let members know it's OK to question the relevance of an agenda item to the group's mandate and how much time it should consume at the meeting.
- Let members know it's OK to insist that proposals be clarified before decisions on them are made.

- Ensure that technical jargon and abbreviations are explained.
- Respond to facial expressions of confusion and uncertainty.

Participation Protocol and Etiquette

The more contentious and the larger the meeting gets, the more important it is to establish participation protocol and etiquette. This will help you ensure fairness and will give members equal opportunities to participate and influence the group's decisions. Here are a few principles to follow:

- Only one person speaks at a time. The exception may be an electronic meeting, where everyone can share ideas and read everyone else's thoughts at the same time (see Chapter 16 on virtual meetings).
- Members line up to speak (by raising hands or waiting at a microphone) instead of "barging in" with their voices.
- Interruptions are generally discouraged, except when they are absolutely necessary, e.g., when a member strays off the topic or takes too long to make a point.
- Side conversations are generally discouraged, except when there is a valid reason for them and their negative impact on the meeting is minimal. Another exception is electronic meetings, where a "whisper" can be used for private discussions without disrupting the meeting.
- Members are courteous and use appropriate language.
- Members keep their comments to the issues and avoid personal criticisms.
- Members are generally expected to arrive on time and stay for the full duration of the meeting, in body and in spirit.
- In informal or small meetings, the need for strict enforcement of participation protocol is small. Under such conditions, members can be asked to "police themselves" and ensure that everyone is treated fairly and that everyone has equal opportunities to participate.

Indicators of a Lack of Protocol and Etiquette

- There are distracting side conversations.
- Everyone speaks at the same time.
- Interruptions are rampant, especially when issues are controversial.
- Members who raise their voices get to speak first, and those who raise their hands and wait patiently are left behind. Chaos reigns.

- ▲ Some members are verbally abusive. Others stoop to personal accusations, name calling, and emotional arguments. Foul language is not far behind.
- ▲ Cell phones and beepers go off.
- ▲ Members arrive late and leave early, or come in and out. There is no continuity in the meeting.

Premeeting Steps to Establish Protocol and Etiquette

1. Notify members in advance that the meeting will start on time. Ask them to arrive on time and make arrangements for others to take care of any commitments or take messages. Ask them to plan to be there for the full duration of the meeting, from start to finish, in body and in spirit.
2. Prepare an opening script to communicate participation guidelines at the start of the meeting: "Here is a reminder of our participation guidelines. Please raise your hand, not your voice, if you want to line up to speak. Please hear people out and give them the respect and attention you want when you are speaking. You may want to jot down notes while listening to other members, so you are less tempted to interrupt."
3. If the issues are difficult, add the following sentence: "Recognizing that we have tough issues to deal with at this meeting, let's remember to be hard on the issues, but be soft on the people."
4. If members have cell phones, say this at the start: "Just in case you forgot, would you please raise your hand, reach over to your cell phone, and turn it off? Thank you."
5. Have private discussions with "frequent offenders" (those who speak without waiting for their turn, interrupt others, have side conversations, arrive late, or leave early). Offer them direct feedback. For example:
   - ▲ "Ben and Tracy, can I ask you to deal with any business you have before the meeting begins? The side conversations are distracting. We need your full and undivided attention at the meeting. Is this a reasonable request?"
   - ▲ "Dan, can I give you some feedback? Thank you. I can't help but notice during our meetings that you often ask the person sitting next to you questions, when it seems like this person is trying to concentrate, but is having trouble saying no to you. Can I ask you to be more sensitive to other people?"

- "Romeo, is there a reason why you've been coming late to meetings? We need you here at the start. Also, we recently changed our agenda and put some interesting items at the very beginning. Can we count on you to arrive on time at the next meeting?"

Interventions at the Meeting to Reinforce Protocol and Etiquette

The facilitator or any member should feel free to intervene to reinforce participation protocol and etiquette. For example:

- "Can we please speak by raising hands, not voices? Albert has been raising his hand and waiting to speak for a while. Go ahead, Albert."
- "Can we please have one meeting at a time? Thank you."
- "Can we please comment on the issues, not the people?"
- "Can we please let people finish speaking?"
- "Can we hear people out?"
- "Can we give other people the respect and attention we want when we are speaking?"

Productivity and Forward Movement

A good meeting moves forward at an appropriate pace (not too fast and not too slow), allowing members to make timely progress along a predefined agenda. At the conclusion of such a meeting, members leave with a sense of accomplishment and renewed enthusiasm and commitment.

When considering productivity, your departure point should be that meetings are expensive. Given that a great deal of time, money, and effort are invested in them, they should be planned and run to maximize the return-on-investment (ROI).

Indicators of Low Productivity

- The agenda is not completed within the available time.
- Significant items are scheduled at the end of the agenda and are rushed through, because members run out of time (the "rush-hour syndrome").

- Meetings habitually run late, making it difficult for members to keep subsequent commitments.
- Discussions are aimless and no decisions are made.
- Decisions are made but follow-up duties are not assigned.
- Much time is spent on side issues at the expense of substantive issues.
- The discussions are repetitive, rambling, and unfocused.

Premeeting Steps to Increase Productivity

- Send members to training programs to help them communicate clearly, concisely, and logically.
- Establish a realistic scope and time frame for the meeting. Avoid unfinishable agendas.
- Estimate how much time main agenda segments will require and prepare timed agendas.
- Schedule high-priority items early in the meeting.
- Prepare action-oriented documents and reports, with clearly laid out decision-making options.
- Offer private feedback to members who consistently ramble and repeat themselves: "Stan, can I give you some feedback? Thanks. I sometimes have trouble focusing on what you say and following your logic. What will help me understand you is if you could speak more precisely and to the point. If you like, I have a few specific suggestions for you. Do you want them?"
- Delete agenda items that are not "ripe" for productive discussion.
- Analyze time consumption at a meeting on a "per issue" and on a "per member" basis and share the results with the members. (Do you spend 90 percent of the time achieving 10 percent of the results? Do 10 percent of the members consume 90 percent of the available time?)
- Establish time limits with guest speakers. Let them know before the meeting how they will be alerted when their time is about to run out.
- In large or controversial meetings, you may need to establish limits on comments by members, e.g., they may comment up to two times per issue, each time no longer than three minutes.

Interventions at the Meeting to Increase Productivity

- ▲ At the start of the meeting reach agreement on the agenda and the time frame for the meeting.
- ▲ Establish that it is OK for the facilitator or any member to intervene to ensure productivity, e.g., "Have we covered this issue sufficiently? Are we ready to move on?" or "Are we spending too much time on side issues at the expense of important ones?"
- ▲ Give timing alerts: "We have fifteen minutes left before we move on to the next issue."
- ▲ Give concise progress summaries: "The points we appear to agree on so far are: first _____, second _____, and third _____. The unresolved issues are: first _____, etc. Did I get it right? Did I miss anything? OK, let's move on."
- ▲ Use creative methods to encourage members to speak more concisely: an hourglass, a cowbell, a train whistle, timing lights, cue cards ("Focus," "Circle the field," "Time to land," etc.), or prizes for clear and concise communications.
- ▲ Deal creatively with time-consuming deadlocks. For example, ask each member to go for a walk with someone who holds an opposing view, and try to passionately advocate the opposite opinion. The other person would then confirm whether she or he was heard and understood. This should show how much listening has been taking place.

Flexibility and Creative Thinking

In a successful meeting a good balance is created between *structure* and *flexibility*. Establishing the structures for a meeting (agenda, time limits, participation protocol, and etiquette) is important. At the same time, departures from a preestablished plan may be needed when a group is bogged down and is not making progress. For example:

- ▲ If an approved agenda is proving unworkable, the group should be allowed to change it.
- ▲ If formal participation protocol (e.g., a speakers' lineup) is proving too restrictive, the group should give itself permission to have informal and unstructured discussion.
- ▲ If a document or proposal needs to be approved, but it proves to be too cumbersome, and amending it is difficult, the group should be free to discard it and create a brand-new one.

Indicators of a Lack of Flexibility or Creative Thinking

- ▲ Members are intimidated by the formalities and therefore hesitate to speak.
- ▲ Time limits are enforced too rigidly and discussions end abruptly and prematurely.
- ▲ A solution to a problem is introduced prematurely (before the problem has been fully explored). This constrains the group and limits its ability to be creative and consider other options.
- ▲ The meeting is dominated by "negaholics" who always argue against fresh and creative ideas, such as "We already tried it," or "Our CEO will never go for it."
- ▲ Discussions and decisions are predictable, uninspiring, and lacking creative touches.

Premeeting Steps to Increase Flexibility and Creative Thinking

- ▲ Indicate in premeeting communications that the timed agenda and participation protocol will be used in a flexible manner. Make it clear that the group can make the discussions less formal if it helps members become more creative and make better decisions together.
- ▲ Plan diverse discussion activities, to stimulate creativity, innovation, and fresh ideas. Try discussions in small breakout groups, case studies, etc.

Interventions at the Meeting to Increase Flexibility and Creative Thinking

- ▲ Expand the range of possible solutions when complex or contentious issues are discussed.
- ▲ Discourage members from locking into the first and most obvious solution. Challenge them to explore more options.
- ▲ Check whether a meeting is ready for closure when the time for an agenda item has ended. If needed, facilitate a decision to extend the time for it (assuming that the extension will not take too much time away from subsequent issues).
- ▲ Keep a broad perspective on issues and discourage nit-picking.
- ▲ Protect members whose unpopular or unusual ideas are criticized or trivialized too quickly.

Quality Discussions and Decision Making

The success of a meeting is ultimately measured by the quality of the decisions made in it. It is important to ensure that the group's consensus and decisions:

- Support the organization's best interests and the attainment of its mandate
- Are logical, responsible, credible, durable, and compelling
- Take into account the needs of your internal and external stakeholders
- Are made after showing due diligence and consideration of all known data
- Are made after an analysis of short- and long-term impacts of solutions
- Reflect courage, creativity, and visionary thinking
- Solve the real problems, and not just the symptoms and the surface issues

What Reduces the Quality of Discussions and Decisions?

- Important reports are circulated late, sometimes at the meeting itself.
- Members don't prepare for the meeting.
- Members open precirculated envelopes (containing important reports) just before the meeting begins.
- Too much time is spent on clarifying technical terms and small details, and less time is spent on the larger perspective and the real issues.
- Too much time is spent on far-fetched theories and speculating on unlikely eventualities, instead of discussing fundamental principles and likely impacts.
- Members routinely "rubber stamp" committee recommendations without questioning them. They operate on trust and fail to scrutinize proposed solutions, even if the solutions don't feel right.
- Members are guided by past precedents and hesitate to question the status quo or conventional wisdom.
- Significant decisions are rushed through by a dominant facilitator or aggressive members, and quieter members hesitate to interject.

Premeeting Steps to Add Quality

- ▲ Let everyone know how important it is to prepare for meetings.
- ▲ Emphasize the need to review documents in advance of a meeting.
- ▲ Contact members who habitually do not prepare for meetings and remind them to do so.
- ▲ If issues are significant, complex, or contentious, arrange for a full analysis of the problem and the proposed solutions.
- ▲ Allocate the appropriate amount of time to substantive issues, so they are not rushed through.

Interventions at the Meeting to Add Quality

- ▲ Encourage questioning and scrutiny of proposals: "There is no such thing as a stupid question or comment," or "The only stupid question is the one you don't ask."
- ▲ Make it OK to question past traditions, conventional wisdom, and the status quo.
- ▲ Focus the discussion on real problems and away from surface issues.
- ▲ Question the validity of options that don't feel right.
- ▲ Caution members against making hasty decisions.

OPENNESS, LISTENING, AND COLLABORATION

Frequently members come to meetings with their minds made up on key issues. If this is the case, why have a meeting? Why invest time and money if the meeting will not change anyone's mind?

If meeting time is to be spent in a meaningful way, members must come with an open mind. They should be prepared to learn from others, regardless of how new to the organization they are, and regardless of how objectionable their views may be. Everyone must work as a cohesive team, to advance the mandate of the entire organization. The broad interests must take precedence over any single interest that a member may represent or believe in.

Indicators of a Lack of Openness, Listening, or Collaboration

- ▲ Frequent interruptions are made starting with the proverbial "Yes, but . . ." (which is known as "a verbal eraser").
- ▲ Members fight for narrow interests, instead of advancing the broad interests of the organization.
- ▲ Each side is too busy fighting for their own views to listen and consider the views of others.
- ▲ Open-minded members are intimidated by the adversarial tone of the discussion and hesitate to participate. They keep their comments to themselves.
- ▲ Intimidation, manipulation, and strategic alliances develop before the meeting, with efforts to build a majority to approve or defeat a proposal. The real meetings take place outside the meeting. A win-lose group culture develops.

Premeeting Steps to Increase Openness, Listening, and Collaboration

- ▲ Have private discussions with subgroups or members and see what can be done to boost collaboration at the meeting.
- ▲ Establish that everyone must place the broad interests of the organization ahead of the interests of respective departments or other groups that members represent.
- ▲ Involve members in premeeting assignments, thereby turning them from critics and opponents to active and constructive contributors. Instead of fighting against one another, they will fight for a common goal.

Interventions at the Meeting to Increase Openness, Listening, and Collaboration

- ▲ Intervene firmly but courteously to keep members listening and working collaboratively to serve the broad interests of the organization.
- ▲ Encourage critics to become creators, e.g., "I understand your concern, Dawn. Do you have an idea on how it might be addressed?"

- ▲ Establish the following principles:
- ▲ *On Listening.* "We were given two ears and one mouth. This means we should listen at least twice as much as we speak," or "The fact that your lips are not moving does not mean you are listening."
- ▲ *On Collaboration.* "Instead of working against each other, we should work together against the problem. Collective decision making is not about one side winning and another side losing, but about making win-win decisions for the entire organization."
- ▲ *On Divisive Issues.* "Debate can be hard on the issues, but must be soft on the people," and "Diversity of opinions is what makes us a strong organization. A seemingly opposing opinion should not be seen as a threat, but as a different piece of the truth. If we listen carefully, we will be able to make intelligent decisions based on the bigger truth."

BALANCE, INCLUSION, AND EQUALITY

It is troubling to see bright and insightful individuals sit through a meeting without uttering a single word, while outspoken members dominate the discussions (usually not out of malice, but because no one has ever given them feedback). Many facilitators express the wish and hope that they could overcome this and engage quieter members in discussions, but don't quite know how.

Balance in meetings means that an "even playing field" is created, whereby each member has the same opportunity to speak, share insights, and influence the decisions. It means you must make it easy, comfortable, and safe for as many members as possible to participate. It does not mean everyone will speak, but those who have a new piece of information or a fresh perspective to share will find an opening to do so.

The benefits of balanced participation are:

- ▲ People are included in discussions and are more likely to support the decisions.
- ▲ Discussions are more broadly based and holistic.
- ▲ With more pieces of the truth shared, the quality of the decisions is boosted, and the likelihood of making bad decisions is reduced.
- ▲ With more diverse participation, meetings are more interesting and stimulating.

Indicators of Unbalanced Participation

- Dominant members establish the direction of discussions every time.
- Ninety percent of the time is consumed by 10 percent of the people.
- Discussions and decisions are predictable.
- Follow-up assignments are usually given to the same volunteers. No efforts are made to delegate them to newer or less outspoken members.
- The wishes of the majority of the group are ignored (or never checked), and passionate and persistent members always get their way (which amounts to "the tyranny of the minority").

Premeeting Steps to Ensure Balanced Participation

Contact the quieter members between meetings, and:

- Solicit their input and views and use them when planning the meeting.
- Remind them it's OK to raise questions and concerns at the meeting.
- Alert them that you might call on them for input, even if they don't raise their hands.
- Give them lead roles at the meeting, like preparing a report and making a presentation, or facilitating a discussion on an agenda item.

Also contact the dominant members before the meeting, and:

- Ask them to make room for others to participate.
- Alert them that you will might intervene to ensure balanced participation.

For example:

> *"Dick, can I give you some feedback? Thank you. It's about your participation in meetings. You always seem to have a lot to say, and that's great. At the same time, we need to work together to give our newer members equal opportunities to speak and make a difference. Can I count on you to help me make room for them to participate? Will you support me if I shift the discussion from you to people who have not spoken, if needed?"*

Interventions at the Meeting to Ensure Balanced Participation

Make a statement about balanced participation at the start of the meeting:

> *"As we carry on with the meeting, we will need to give people equal opportunities to speak. If I notice that some of you are quicker to speak than others, I may do something to bring other people into the discussion. Are you comfortable with this? Thank you."*

When needed, solicit responses from members who are quieter but are knowledgeable and are likely to have insights to share, even if they don't ask to speak. For example:

> *"What about you, Frank? How do things look from accounting's perspective?"*

Vary the discussion activities to engage more members in the meeting. For example:

- ▲ Give everyone a few minutes of quiet time, to think and jot down their responses to a key question. Then invite quieter members to share what they came up with.
- ▲ Have well-focused discussions in small breakout groups. Such discussions will engage quieter members, who may hesitate to speak in the larger group.

When assigning follow-up duties, avoid asking, "Who would like to do this?" since you will likely get the usual volunteers. Instead say something like this:

> *"Rose, can you help us out with this assignment? We need to spread the work around and get more people involved. Would you do it? Thanks. Let me know if you need any help."*

You can estimate the percentage of meeting time consumed by each member and then share the statistics. If you think this would be too cruel, try sharing a simple observation instead:

> *"I need to share an observation about our meetings. It seems like some of you have no trouble speaking, while others stay rela-*

tively quiet. This means that we don't hear new and possibly relevant pieces of information from quieter members. Can we do something to change the dynamics and make it easier for everyone to participate?"

Shared Responsibility

Who is responsible for the success or failure of a meeting? Typically, if anything goes wrong, the finger of blame points in one direction: the facilitator. Why is she or he so disorganized and so hesitant to manage the meeting, or, conversely, why is the facilitator so dictatorial and impatient?

Other times, the finger of blame points at a dominant or disruptive member: Why is he so stubborn and inflexible? Why won't she listen? Why is he such a nitpicker?

Here is a metaphor to consider: Every time you point the finger of blame at someone else, you fail to consider the three fingers pointing back in your direction. Blaming others means that you trivialize the difference that your participation can make in a meeting and in the success of your organization. Finger pointing and blaming are a waste of good energy and work as excuses for not getting things done. You, your colleagues, and your organization deserve better.

Shared responsibility means that each member is proactive and empowered and knows when to speak up or take action, and when to sit back and allow things to unfold. It also means that each member maintains high commitment levels to the organization and contributes willingly, actively, and enthusiastically towards achieving its mandate, without having to be asked to do it.

Shared responsibility also means that "suffering is optional." If a meeting is not going well and the facilitator is doing nothing about it (or may even be worsening the situation), members should not suffer quietly. Instead, they should raise concerns about the issues and the decision-making process. For example:

- "I am confused. How are these comments related to the question of ____, which is supposed to be the focus of our discussion?"
- "Excuse me, I'm having trouble concentrating when everyone speaks at once. Can we have a speakers' lineup and let people finish what they're saying?"
- "I was wondering how this looks from an information technology perspective. Tony, can you help me out on this one?"

- "Aren't we getting bogged down in small details right now, at the expense of the bigger issues? Can we get back to the core question of ____?"

Note: You may find it uncomfortable to state a concern about the way a meeting is going. You may hold back and think that "it is not the polite or nice thing to do." However, if you dare to interject, you may discover that you are not alone. Other members who share your concerns will likely thank you, and they may even be motivated to follow your lead and do the same in future meetings.

Indicators of a Lack of Shared Responsibility

- Members suffer quietly and don't complain when the meeting is run poorly.
- There is silence when a decision is made. However, during the coffee break, the real discussion takes place and major concerns are raised about the decision that was made. Why were these comments not made before the decision was made?
- Members have excuses for not keeping their promises, and they deliver very few results.
- Members blame others and are quick to criticize, but offer no constructive suggestions.
- There is little or no interest in assuming leadership positions or taking on follow-up duties.
- Members are at the meeting, but are busy doing something else. They are there in body, but not in spirit.

Premeeting Steps to Increase Shared Responsibility

- Establish the need for shared responsibility in your premeeting communications.
- Have private discussions with members who refuse to take on follow-up duties, do not keep their promises, miss meetings, or come late and leave early.
- Develop a recognition program to celebrate and reward successes, and showcase special efforts and unique contributions. This will perpetuate constructive and proactive participation.
- Solicit feedback from members between meetings.

Interventions at the Meeting to Increase Shared Responsibility

- At the start of the meeting remind members that suffering is optional, and that it's OK to raise concerns about the quality of the discussions or the way the meeting is run.

- ▲ Take member feedback humbly and nondefensively. Examine the merits of this feedback with an open mind, and take appropriate action.
- ▲ Thank members for expressing a concern, especially when it helped to improve the quality of the discussions and the decisions made at the meeting.
- ▲ Give members token rewards for proactive participation.

Variety and a Light Touch

Are your meetings boring and monotonous? Does every member sit in the same spot, talk to the same people, drink the same coffee, and say almost the same thing at every meeting? Do you sometimes wonder if you've been to the exact same meeting before? Does this monotony and predictability make you want to avoid meetings altogether?

It doesn't have to be this way. Meetings can be varied, dynamic, engaging, and invigorating. They can even be fun. Variety can and should be introduced to help make a meeting an event to look forward to, not something to dread or want to avoid.

To be varied, a meeting needs to engage people in as many of the following ways as possible:

- ▲ Intellectually
- ▲ Emotionally
- ▲ Through the five senses (sound, sight, touch, taste, and smell)

Engaging the Members Intellectually

Introduce variety to your meetings by making them intellectually stimulating. Here are a few ideas on how to achieve this goal:

- ▲ Focus the discussions on interesting core issues and avoid boring side issues.
- ▲ Invite thought-provoking guest speakers with timely and relevant material.
- ▲ Always have one or more proactive agenda items, discussing a new issue or an emerging trend that the members would find interesting and relevant. This way you avoid the sense of: "We only do the things we have to do, and none of the things we want to do."
- ▲ Induce creative thinking by not being a slave to established traditions. For example, try changing the standard sequence of items on the agenda. One group even

tried a "backward-meeting," with the closing being the first item, and a review of the minutes being the last item.

- Have members work on "mind-bending" case studies in small groups and report the results to the full group. The case studies should be relevant to issues that the group is trying to address.

Engaging the Members Emotionally

Introduce variety to your meetings by engaging the members on an emotional level. But don't overdo it, and keep it appropriate. Here are a few examples of how to achieve this goal:

- Look beyond the theories and the statistics and focus the discussions on people and real-life examples that members can relate to. Include heartwarming and inspiring stories of success and overcoming adversity and recovering from failure. You may not need to look very far for such stories. Start by asking your members if they have any.
- Build relationships and create emotional links with members by challenging them to excel and take on tasks that will stretch their skills to the limit, e.g., leading a panel discussion at the next meeting.
- Share the leadership and the spotlight by "rotating the chair," i.e., a different member organizes and chairs the meeting every time. In addition to variety, this approach increases shared responsibility. It can also be your succession plan, whereby you develop future leaders and make the team less dependent on you for guidance.
- Recognize members for special contributions or unique ideas. Start a token award program for "the most innovative member at this meeting," as well as other fun awards. You can intersperse special recognition and awards between major agenda items, to provide for some downtime.
- Schedule networking events before the meeting and possibly immediately after it, to give members opportunities to build a social rapport. But don't make such events compulsory. Members should participate because they want to, and not because it's expected.
- Celebrate special personal events at the meeting. For example, if someone has a birthday, "press the pause button" after a major agenda item, bring in a cake, and sing Happy Birthday in the member's native language. This is time well invested, yielding benefits like a morale boost and lightening things up at the

meeting. You can celebrate other special personal events: a tenth wedding anniversary, a new offspring, fifteen years with the company.

- Have short fun stories and anecdotes to lighten things up when needed. But keep them appropriate.
- You can ask members to take turns at being the "levity master" at meetings.
- Avoid touchy-feely games and exercises. They are generally inappropriate in a business environment.

Engaging the Sense of Sound

Make the sounds of the meeting varied and engaging. For example:

- Encourage speakers and members to avoid monotony and be more vocally animated.
- Encourage members to take presentation skills and public speaking training. You could even start a corporate speakers' bureau or your own public speaking club.
- Consider appropriate uses of music and other audio effects, to vary the pace of the meeting and to make it more appealing to the ear.
- Make sure there are no distractions that disrupt the continuity of the meeting, like piped-in music, a loud fan, or a disco next door.
- If the meeting room is large, arrange for microphones, so members won't have to suffer as they try to hear others, and so speakers won't have to scream (and lose their voices) to be heard.

Engaging the Sense of Sight

Make the meeting visually varied and engaging. For example:

- Consider sending members to workshops on presentation skills, so that they can become aware of and avoid distracting body language, and use eye contact, facial expression, and body language to better connect to the listeners.
- Encourage presenters to use visual aids to enhance presentations and discussions: flip charts, computer-based presentations (like PowerPoint), slide shows, props and demonstration aids, etc. But don't overdo it to the extent that the interactive aspects of the meeting are lost. Some groups have come to dislike PowerPoint so much that they ban it from their meetings.

- Try holding the meeting at different locations every time. How about an off-site location to avoid distractions? How about branch offices or even field locations instead of the head office, with local members designated to organize the logistics for each meeting?
- Try varying the seating arrangement, so that members will sit next to someone new every time. Prepare name tents (with names on both sides, so people walking behind a person will know his or her name), and then designate a different member at each meeting to "shuffle the decks" and decide who will sit where.
- When possible, select a meeting room that is visually appealing (perhaps one with paintings or flowers), or at least not unappealing (with depressing colors).

Engaging the Sense of Touch

People learn by hearing and seeing (vocal and visual senses), but they learn much more by doing things. In many of today's meetings people just talk, but don't do anything. Here are a few things you can do to engage their sense of touch:

- Have members work together on puzzles and games that relate directly to the group's work.
- Give members pens and paper and ask them to jot down their thoughts as the meeting goes on. This will give them something to do and help them listen. A fun exercise would be to convert a rambling statement by a member into a point-format summary: "Here are the three main points that you are making: first ____, second ____, and third ____."
- Here is an activity used by a facilitator to get members moving instead of sitting around a table. In trying to prioritize eight tasks for the coming year, she listed them on separate flip charts and placed them on the walls around the room. Members were given four small stickers each, and were asked to place one sticker on each of the four charts with the issues they considered most important. They were also asked to discuss the issues with other members as they were walking around the room. After fifteen minutes, it was very clear which issues were more significant (those with the most stickers). Quieter members were involved (balance and inclusion), and everyone returned to the table excited and rejuvenated. They did more than just plain talking.
- If you have an aerobic exercise instructor among your members, see if he or she would lead mild aerobic exercise during a break. This would be particularly useful to break the tedium of a long meeting. But do give members the option of not partaking in this if they're not comfortable.

▲ Put clay, crayons, or small toys in front of members. This will keep their hands busy and may get them to focus better on the discussion (as long as they don't start throwing things at each other).

▲ To get members moving, try a stand-up meeting from time to time, with no chairs, no tables, and no sitting on the floor. You may find the meeting time reduced by 40–50 percent.

Engaging the Sense of Taste

Do what is needed and appropriate to make the meeting appeal to the members' sense of taste. Here are a few examples:

▲ Try different refreshments every time. Surprise them.

▲ Food and beverages should be fresh and tasty.

▲ Arrange to put ice and lemon in the water.

▲ The coffee and tea should be fresh and hot (not too hot).

▲ The soft drinks should be cold (but not frozen).

▲ You can try for a taste of the exotic (international desserts), but don't overdo it. The members are here to work, and the food should not become a distraction.

▲ You can try a potluck, with different members being designated to take care of refreshments each time. Keep in mind that if the meeting is held in a hotel, you may encounter objections to bringing in outside supplies.

▲ To facilitate a timely start for meetings, try scheduling a premeeting meal, with different ethnic foods served each time. The meals should end just in time for the meeting to start.

Engaging the Sense of Smell

Do what is appropriate to make the meeting appeal to the members' sense of smell. For example:

▲ You can try flowers, but don't overdo it. This is a business environment.

▲ Avoid scent sticks. They are a bad idea for people with allergies.

▲ Avoid rooms that are stuffy and smelly and with no air circulation.

▲ Avoid rooms that are adjacent to a kitchen. The food may smell delicious, but the smell is also likely to be distracting.

A Word of Caution About Variety

Make sure your ideas for variety are appropriate for your group and do not offend members. In fact, the best ideas for variety will come from your members. To solicit their ideas, try this approach:

> *"It's been suggested that we could benefit from spicing up our meetings and putting some variety in them. Here are a few ideas that other companies have tried: ____. What do you think? Do any of these ideas sound interesting? Do any of you have any other ideas to add variety to our meetings and lighten things up, without reducing our productivity? If you come up with ideas after the meeting, would you please contact me?"*

LOGISTICAL SUPPORT

Nothing is worse than wasting precious meeting time fighting logistical battles. Members do not deserve to be kept waiting while a speaker figures out how the overhead projector works, or how to strangle the microphone's high-pitched sound. You need to consider logistical support with Murphy's Law in mind: "If anything can go wrong it will, at the worst possible time."

In a good meeting, no one notices the logistical details. Everything is there when and where you need it. The room setup is appropriate. The temperature is comfortable, the lighting level is just right, and the ventilation works. The room offers a private and distraction-free environment. Audiovisual aids (overhead projector, flip chart, apparatus for computer-based presentations, and microphones) function like clockwork. Refreshments and meals are tasty, healthy, and sufficient (not excessive), and are served unobtrusively, exactly when needed.

Indicators of Poor Logistical Support

- ▲ The room is too dark, too cold, or too hot, and no one knows how to adjust the levels.
- ▲ The overhead projector's light bulb is burned out, and there is no backup.
- ▲ A noisy swimming pool or a disco next door has just opened for business.
- ▲ The chairs are too hard, or, conversely, you just sink in them.
- ▲ The coffee is old and cold, and the soft drinks and juices are warm.
- ▲ Meals arrive late, and sandwiches have plenty of butter and very little meat.

- ▲ Corky the vegetarian was served a platter with a huge steak and no vegetables.
- ▲ And the list goes on.

Premeeting Interventions for Smooth Logistical Support

Logistical requirements must be fully considered and all details must be addressed before the meeting. See Chapter 9 on planning a meeting for the logistics master's checklist.

Using the Ten Key Ingredients as Assessment Tools

The ten key ingredients of a successful meeting are based on simple common-sense principles. They have the potential of making your meetings more productive, inclusive, engaging, and fun. They can help you ensure substantial returns on the time, money, and effort invested in your meetings.

In order to make your vision of a successful meeting a reality, several things need to happen:

- ▲ Visionary (and proactive) and preventive planning (see Chapter 9)
- ▲ Smooth launching, steering, and landing of a meeting (see Chapters 10 to 14).
- ▲ Follow-up and postmortem on a meeting (see Chapter 15)

It will be difficult or impossible to make your vision of a successful meeting a reality without the support of your members. To gain their support, you need to share the vision and its underlying principles. Explain to them the ten key ingredients, and look for their ideas and suggestions on using these ingredients to create a recipe for a successful meeting.

You can use the ten key ingredients as assessment tools. Use the evaluation form (see below), or a modified version of it, to rate your meetings on a scale of 0 to 10, 0 being "as bad as it can get," and 10 being "could not be better." Do some soul searching on your own to determine what is working and what needs improvement. Send the same evaluation form to your members along with an explanatory covering memo. Ask them to assess your meetings:

▲ What is working well?

▲ What could be working better?

▲ What are their ideas for improvement?

Compare notes about the results of the evaluation at your next meeting. You can also invite members to give you informal feedback after the meeting, by phone, memo, or e-mail.

Facilitate a discussion on which of the ten key ingredients are present in your meetings and which ones are missing. Ask your members to prioritize their ideas for improvement and then implement a few at a time. This way, progress would be gradual, ongoing, and sustained, and your meetings will always have something fresh and new to look forward to. Repeat this evaluation process periodically (e.g.: every six months), to determine where you have made progress and what other improvements the group is ready for.

As an alternative, you can also schedule a fifteen-minute segment at the end of every meeting, for members to comment on what went well at that meeting, what did not go well, and what should be improved next time.

Sample Evaluation Form for a Meeting

On a scale of 0 (as bad as it gets) to 10 (could not be better), rate your meetings on the ten key ingredients represented by the ten subheadings below. Then add the numbers up. The total should be between 0 (hopefully it's not *that* bad) and 100 (if you're at this level, you should start teaching other groups about meetings).

Key ingredients for a meeting	*Rating (0 to 10)*
Clarity of mandate, purpose, issues, and process ▲ Is the purpose of the meeting clear? ▲ Do members know why they are there? ▲ Are technical terms and abbreviations explained? ▲ Are options for decision making clearly outlined?	
Participation protocol and etiquette ▲ Do members take turns to speak, on a first-come-first-served basis? ▲ Do members let others finish speaking? ▲ Do members focus on issues and avoid personal criticisms and verbal abuse? ▲ Do members keep their language clean?	
Productivity and forward movement ▲ Is time carefully allocated and well spent? ▲ Is enough time spent on significant issues?	

▲ Is progress measured and deliberate, avoiding the "rush hour syndrome"? ▲ Do members leave the meeting with a sense of accomplishment?	
Flexibility and creative thinking ▲ Is the agenda used flexibly, responding to circumstances that arise? ▲ Does the meeting protocol allow creative thinking or is it too constraining? ▲ Are members free to bring forward "off the wall" ideas without fear? ▲ Is the group prepared to experiment with fresh and unusual ideas?	
Quality decision making ▲ Are the group's decisions responsible, credible, and durable? ▲ Do members show due diligence and do they scrutinize proposals? ▲ Do members read meeting documents prior to the meeting? ▲ Are late additions to the agenda the exception and not the norm?	
Openness, listening, and collaboration ▲ Do members come to a meeting with open minds and no hidden agendas? ▲ Do members work together or do they fight and argue with each other? ▲ Do members go for win-lose (narrow majority) or for win-win solutions?	
Balance, equality, and inclusion ▲ Does each member have the same opportunity to speak? ▲ Are quieter members encouraged to share their ideas and insights? ▲ Is domination by outspoken members avoided? ▲ Is time evenly divided, or do 10 percent of the people consume 90 percent of the time?	
Shared responsibility ▲ Do members keep their promises? ▲ Do members state concerns constructively or do they hold back? ▲ Do members avoid deferring to someone else for leadership? ▲ Do members shift from the weak position of opponent to proponent?	
Variety and a light touch ▲ Is the meeting varied and fun? ▲ Does the meeting engage the members intellectually and emotionally? ▲ Does the meeting engage the members through the five senses?	
Logistical support ▲ Are logistical arrangements (room, a/v aids, etc.) professionally managed? ▲ Is Murphy's law taken into account to prevent logistical problems? ▲ Do members have contingency plans in case of logistical difficulties?	
Grand total	

CASE STUDY:

A Dream or a Working Reality

Two managers attended a seminar on running effective meetings, based on the material in this book. Six months after the seminar, I had an opportunity to speak to each of them. Naturally, I asked whether the seminar made a difference in their meetings.

The first manager suggested that the material he learned at the seminar was great in theory, but his members were too tough and resisted change. He had tried to pursue some of the ideas, but gave up when he faced resistance.

The second manager reported substantial progress. How did she do it? After the seminar, she made a list of ideas to use in her meetings. She implemented one or two new ideas in each meeting and made sure her members (who were also "tough") understood why she was trying these ideas and what they were intended to achieve. Six months later, she was still introducing new ideas and keeping her meetings fresh. Moreover, her members liked her approach so much that they began to introduce their own new ideas to improve meetings.

The difference? One manager had a vision only. The other manager had a vision *and* a plan.

NINE

Planning a Meeting

Having identified the ten key ingredients of a successful meeting (Chapter 8), you know what a good meeting should look, sound, and feel like. You now need tools to plan your next meeting, to ensure that as many key ingredients as possible are in place to maximize the meeting's success.

It is astonishing how casual managers can be about planning meetings. A meeting is sometimes held with no notice and with only a vague explanation of its purpose. Attendees have no idea why they were invited to attend and what difference they are expected to make at the meeting. It is no wonder that many people treat meetings with cynicism and contempt, and say things like, "There is no such thing as a 'productive meeting,'" or "The best meeting is the one that gets canceled."

Here are a few things to note about this chapter:

- ▲ It introduces a deliberate, proactive, and visionary approach to planning meetings.
- ▲ It gives you sample planning checklists, which should be customized to your circumstances. Some activities may not be needed, some may need to be modified, and new ones may need to be added.

- It suggests a team approach to planning meetings, by designating planning duties to certain taskmasters. This approach supports the principles of inclusion, teamwork, and shared responsibility. It suggests that every member should have a role in planning the meeting. This approach will likely convert more members from passive spectators to active contributors in your meetings.
- The designation of duties to certain taskmasters does not preclude one individual from taking on more than one set of duties. A meeting participant may be a presenter and may also serve as the variety master. A meeting facilitator may also be the overall planning coordinator.

The topics covered in this chapter are:

- General planning principles
- Every participant's checklist
- Meeting facilitator's checklist
- Planning coordinator's checklist
- Return on investment (ROI) master's checklist
- Timing master's checklist
- Agenda master's checklist
- Logistics master's checklist
- Invitation master's checklist
- Report writer's checklist
- Presenter's checklist
- Script master's checklist
- Minute taker's checklist
- Variety master's checklist
- Boss's checklist
- Mentor's checklist
- External consultant's checklist
- Guest or observer's checklist

General Planning Principles

Your meeting planning efforts should be:

1. *Preventive*, intended to stop some things from happening
2. *Proactive*, intended to make certain things happen

Here are some of the things that preventive planning can help you avoid:

- ▲ Bad decisions being made or being rushed through
- ▲ Slow progress
- ▲ No closure on issues
- ▲ Waste of time and resources
- ▲ Confusion about issues
- ▲ Uncertainty about the meaning of proposals
- ▲ Members arriving late, leaving early, or missing the meeting altogether
- ▲ Members disengaged from the process, daydreaming, or even falling asleep
- ▲ Members working against one another
- ▲ Domination, digressions, and interruptions
- ▲ Nasty and disruptive logistical surprises
- ▲ Suffering and pain
- ▲ Members leaving stressed, confused, and frustrated
- ▲ Members looking for excuses to avoid the next meeting

Here are some of the things that proactive planning can help you achieve:

- ▲ Meeting time well spent
- ▲ Steady and substantial progress made
- ▲ Good decisions made, advancing the group's mandate and serving its stakeholders
- ▲ A sense of inclusion, teamwork, and joint ownership of the process and the decisions made
- ▲ Engaging all participants in the meeting and giving them opportunities to make a difference

- A sense of pride in the group's accomplishments
- A sense of purpose, clarity, and confidence
- Members leaving satisfied, energized, and rejuvenated
- Members genuinely looking forward to the next meeting (won't miss it for the world)

EVERY PARTICIPANT'S CHECKLIST

As a participant in a meeting, it is incumbent on you to be fully prepared for it. Think about your role as that of a rower on a canoe, and not as a passive passenger on a train. You need to pull your weight and do your part in preparing for the journey.

This section lists the planning duties that are common to all meeting participants, above and beyond any specific planning roles that you may have as a meeting facilitator (see later sections in this chapter):

1. Review the purpose of the meeting. Feel free to contact the planning coordinator to question the need for the meeting if the potential benefits seem to be minimal or nonexistent.
2. Keep any commitments you made (e.g., preparing a report or a presentation for the meeting) and deliver quality results every time.
3. Review the planning checklists that apply to you and complete them (see the discussions later in this chapter).
4. Establish how you can best make a difference at the meeting, and how the group can benefit from your knowledge, expertise, skills, insights, and ideas.
5. If your role or potential contribution at the meeting seems unclear or marginal, contact the planning coordinator and question whether you should be at the meeting. You probably have better things to do than to be at a meeting in which your presence will make no difference.
6. Feel free to speak to the agenda master or planning coordinator and propose that an important item be added to the agenda.
7. Also feel free to question why a certain item is on the agenda, e.g., an item that:

- ▲ Is outside your group's mandate
- ▲ Offers limited value
- ▲ You believe is not ready for discussion and decision making

8. Ask whether supporting documents were prepared. (You and your group deserve better than to receive reports on the day of the meeting.)
9. If you believe that an agenda item requires confidentiality, suggest that it be moved to the agenda of an in-camera meeting (see Chapter 5 for confidentiality guidelines).
10. When making the above agenda suggestions:
    - ▲ Be sensitive to the needs of the group as a whole.
    - ▲ Respect the agenda master's task to prioritize issues and decide which should be included on the agenda. He or she will face requests from you and others and may need to decline your suggestions. An agenda should not be a free-for-all.
    - ▲ If you disagree with the agenda master's decision to refuse your request to add or delete an agenda item, you can bring it to the group for a final decision on whether it should be included on the agenda.
11. Review carefully the premeeting package, including all reports and documents, and clarify with a document's author any technical concepts, terms, and abbreviations, so that such clarifications will not consume time at the meeting.
12. Share your concerns about a report or a document that is poorly written, and make suggestions on how to improve it, e.g., include lists of terms and abbreviations, have an executive summary or "a snapshot" of the report, and make the document more "reader-friendly," so it requires less time for members to read and comprehend
13. Let the planning coordinator know if you:
    - ▲ Are having trouble meeting a deadline and could use some help.
    - ▲ Are feeling discouraged and need some moral support.
    - ▲ Might be late or miss the meeting. If this is the case, you'll need to ensure that your tasks are taken care of.
    - ▲ Believe you or someone else have a personal conflict of interest on an agenda item and will need to be excused the meeting while it is discussed (see Chapter 5 for conflict of interest guidelines).

14. Consider any feedback that people gave you in the past, and establish what changes you need to make and how you need to participate constructively at the meeting:

    ▲ Speak clearly, briefly, and concisely.

    ▲ Listen actively and show genuine interest in what others are saying.

    ▲ Keep an open mind to new ideas.

    ▲ Let go of any preconceived notions and ideas.

    ▲ Avoid domination, digressions, backtracking, interruptions, and other bad habits.

15. Alert the planning coordinator or another team member of a problem or a dispute that could negatively affect the meeting and that should be addressed before it begins: "Ian, there is a problem you should know about. Susan and Doug just had a nasty argument, and they are not talking to each other. This could have a very negative impact on the meeting. I thought you might want to know."

16. See if you can resolve disputes between you and others before the meeting, so you can focus on the meeting and listen to everyone, without being burdened and distracted by any animosity, resentment, or tensions. Your first attempt should be to resolve a dispute directly with the other party. If you need help, ask the group leader or another individual to mediate the dispute.

17. If you are opposed to a proposal that is scheduled for discussion (or you are puzzled about it):

    ▲ First try to understand its benefits and the problem that the proposal is intended to solve. Talk to the proponent, ask a few questions, and suggest a few changes that will address your concerns. If your concerns are addressed, there is no need to pursue them further.

    ▲ If your concerns are not addressed, shift from the weak position of opponent to proponent. Be prepared to suggest some changes at the meeting. Better yet, try to create an alternative proposal that will address the same problem, but will do so more effectively, and will have none of the drawbacks of the current proposal.

18. Offer to help with specific tasks, especially if you have not been given any. Look for new duties that will take you beyond your comfort level and enable you to develop new skills, especially ones you've been putting off.

19. Question or turn down a task that is being assigned to you if:

    ▲ The value of the task seems marginal.

    ▲ There are others who are more suitable for it.

    ▲ Your other commitments will not permit you to do quality work on it: "Thank you, Robin, for asking. It is best if I say no. Given my workload, I can't see how I can do a quality job for the group. I am wondering if this would be a good task for one of our newer members, like Pauline, to get her feet wet with."

20. Plan to be there for the full meeting, in body and in spirit:

    ▲ Plan to arrive before the scheduled opening time.

    ▲ Plan to be there because you genuinely want to, and not because you have to.

    ▲ Plan to turn your cell phone or beeper off for the full duration of the meeting.

    ▲ Avoid scheduling back-to-back meetings or overlapping meetings, where you have no time to wind down from one meeting and get properly organized for the next, or have to leave one meeting midway to go to the next. Instead, insist on sufficient intervals between meetings. Doing otherwise would be unfair to you and to the members in both meetings.

    ▲ Advise your staff or message service of the time frame for the meeting and tell them that you are not to be disturbed, except in absolute emergencies. Specify what emergency will justify an interruption, e.g., a call from the President of the United States.

21. Plan to avoid the following:

    ▲ Arriving late, leaving early, or missing the meeting altogether

    ▲ Forming rigid opinions about issues and closing your mind off to input from other people

    ▲ Coming to the meeting ready to fight for personal views or narrow interests, instead of working together with others to advance the mandate of the full organization

    ▲ Reading hidden motives behind other people's actions

    ▲ Skimming through meeting documents too quickly

    ▲ Conspiring, lobbying, and building strategic alliances to overpower other viewpoints

A Success Story: To Oppose or to Propose

Ann, a member of a board of directors, was alarmed by a proposal that was to be considered at the next meeting. The proposal was to move the headquarters to new premises, at a substantial cost. She saw the following difficulties in the proposed move:

- ▲ First, the need for the move was questionable. It appeared to have been proposed to take advantage of the depressed real estate market. The idea was in part due to the persistence of an aggressive real estate agent.
- ▲ Second, the board was not well focused on advancing the organization's mandate and serving its stakeholders, and too much money was being spent on side issues (a wrongful dismissal lawsuit, this proposed move, etc.).
- ▲ Third, Ann could identify at least ten mandate-related initiatives that could have been launched for the cost of the move to the new premises.

After trying in vain to obtain clarifications from the executive committee about the proposal, Ann considered how to fight this proposal. In the end she opted for a more constructive and proactive route. She did the following:

- ▲ Prepared a written analysis of the move proposal, indicating its various flaws.
- ▲ Prepared a proposal to pursue the ten mandate-driven initiatives.
- ▲ Spoke to the board chairperson, who agreed to circulate her report to all board members and schedule time for her to present it at the next meeting.

Ann's conviction paid off. The proposed move was shelved, and the organization got back on track. The lessons?

- ▲ Ann was able to make a difference even though she was not the chairperson or another officer of the board, but a regular member and meeting participant.
- ▲ She was proactive and placed the organization's needs in the forefront.
- ▲ She was able to assert her position and make a difference by doing her homework and planning for the meeting.

▲ Ann achieved more by proposing than by opposing.

Because it is easier to oppose than to propose, there are far more critics than creators in most meetings. If you want to boost your effectiveness as a meeting participant and help lead your group to higher achievements, you need to leave behind the weaker position of an opponent, or a critic. Instead, embrace the stronger and much more effective position of a proponent, or a creator.

Meeting Facilitator's Checklist

In typical corporate settings a meeting facilitator does most of the work of planning a meeting. She or he may serve as planning coordinator, agenda master, logistics master, presenter, report writer, and more. A facilitator may end up doing too much. The risk is that she or he may become a "jack of all trades, but a master of none."

An effective meeting facilitator delegates as many planning duties as possible to various meeting participants. This is why this chapter separates planning duties into distinct categories and refers to meeting masters who perform these duties.

Acting in a purely facilitative role, a meeting facilitator has the primary responsibility of planning for the following outcomes:

- ▲ Ensuring quality discussions
- ▲ Leading the group in its consensus-building activities
- ▲ Creating opportunities for all members to contribute their "pieces of the truth"
- ▲ Benefiting from the knowledge, expertise, skills, ideas, and insights available at the meeting
- ▲ Managing people and resolving disputes that arise at the meeting
- ▲ Ensuring that decisions are reached through an inclusive process, whereby as many people as possible arrive at the same destination together, as willing and enthusiastic partners

Here are several planning tips for the meeting facilitator

- ▲ Review Chapter 2 on the many hats of a meeting facilitator.
- ▲ Review Chapters 10, 11, 12, and 14 on launching, steering, and landing a meeting.
- ▲ Become familiar with the core issues and know what side issues should be avoided.

- ▲ Get to know the group's dynamics, the people, their strengths, and weaknesses.
- ▲ Become familiar with the group's mandate and the stakeholders that it is intended to serve.
- ▲ Plan the overall flow for the meeting and prepare a script or a checklist of things to do (see Chapters 11 and 14 for scripts for launching and landing the meeting, and Chapter 12 on steering a meeting to its destination).
- ▲ Plan discussion activities that will stimulate creativity, innovation, collaboration, and consensus building.

PLANNING COORDINATOR'S CHECKLIST

This section includes a list of overall meeting planning and coordination tasks. It should be noted that, in most settings, the planning coordinator also serves as:

- ▲ The meeting facilitator (see previous section)
- ▲ The ROI master (see next section)
- ▲ Timing master and agenda master (see the two sections after the next)

Specifically, as a planning coordinator you should do the following:

As an overall goal, plan to ensure that issues, people, and time are well managed at the meeting:

1. *Issue Management*. The success of the meeting will be measured by the quality of the discussions and the consensus reached. Plan with the goal of quality decisions in mind.
2. *People Management*. See what can be done to engage the members in the meeting intellectually, emotionally, and through their five senses.
3. *Time Management*. Meeting time should be treated as a precious resource. Good planning will ensure that it is well invested and is not squandered (see ROI master's and timing master's checklists further in this chapter).
4. Determine whether the meeting is worth holding:
   - ▲ If not, cancel it (see eight reasons for canceling a meeting under ROI master).
   - ▲ If the meeting is worth holding, see what can be done to maximize its value to the organization.
5. Address timing issues, i.e., plan appropriate opening and closing times and allocate time to agenda items (see timing master's checklist).

6. Engage members in planning the meeting by delegating duties to them and designating them as meeting masters. Delegate planning duties based on the following principles:

   ▲ *Expediency*. Give critical tasks to "low-maintenance" members who are consistent and reliable and have the most appropriate combination of skills and experience. Give less critical tasks to newer members.

   ▲ *Variety*. Give each member different types of assignments for different meetings, to keep his or her interest levels high.

   ▲ *Challenge*. Offer members tasks that will interest them, take them beyond their comfort levels, or get them to test newly acquired skills or knowledge. But make these tasks realistic to achieve and offer support and coaching. This approach will keep them learning while boosting their confidence and skill levels.

7. Serve as the agenda master or delegate this task to someone else (see later in this chapter).

8. Stay in touch with members and stakeholders and keep them informed and consulted prior to the meeting. Positive relationships with them will make them want to return the favor and keep you in the loop. They will likely alert you to potential problems and help you reduce the likelihood of nasty surprises at the meeting.

9. Monitor progress on planning activities with the different meeting masters and take corrective action when needed.

10. Never assume anything, and don't rely on vague promises. If in doubt, check it out. For example:

    ▲ To a team member: "Thank you, Gordon, for agreeing to coordinate things with the hotel. Since this is the first time for you to do this, I need to be sure that all small details will be taken care of. Would you please prepare a to-do list and run it by me, to be on the safe side?"

    ▲ To a hotel catering manager: "We had a few problems with catering last time. Thank you for reassuring me that everything will be fine. For my own peace of mind, I need to know what you have done to prevent these problems from happening again. I need you to be specific. There is too much happening at this meeting and I cannot afford to worry about these details on the day of the meeting."

11. *Dress Rehearsal*. If the meeting is large or a great deal is at stake, consider having one or more "dress rehearsals" with the planning team, to review the agenda, the flow of the meeting, the facilitator's script, key presentations, the logistical

arrangements for the meeting, and other details. Dress rehearsals can be a very valuable tool in ensuring that a meeting is not only trouble-free, but that it also achieves substantial benefits.

12. Be sensitive to rumors and other indicators of problems or disputes. Avoid the instinctive inclination to dismiss or trivialize them and pretend all is well. Instead, be proactive and make it your business to find out what's behind such problem indicators. Determine whether any preventive action needs to be taken to avoid difficulties at the meeting. For example:

    ▲ To a team member: "Stella, I am sensing that there is some tension between you and Dan. I may be reading too much into it, but I thought to check. Is there something all three of us should talk about before the next meeting? There is too much at stake at that meeting, and I need to have all of us working together. Can you help me out? Am I justified in being worried?" As a result of the ensuing conversation, you may need to schedule a meeting between the three of you. See Chapter 2 on the facilitator as a mediator.

    ▲ To a representative of a stakeholder group: "I understand that you're having some concerns about how the stakeholder committee meeting will be run. Can we talk about it? I cannot influence the outcomes, but I want to hear if you have any questions or concerns about the agenda and the flow of the meeting." See Chapter 7 and Appendix 2 on building relationships with stakeholders.

Example: Premeeting Dispute Resolution

A meeting coordinator became aware that two angry members were plotting to disrupt a meeting and frustrate progress. Instead of developing strategies on stifling and controlling the "troublesome" members, the meeting coordinator arranged to meet with them and find out about the nature of their concerns.

At their private meeting, the coordinator discovered that the dissenters had some legitimate issues that could be integrated into the meeting agenda. He also recognized that if these concerns had not been presented, a bad decision would have been made. He then:

▲ Thanked the two members for meeting with him.

▲ Suggested that they prepare proposals to address their concerns in the context of the broad goals of the organization.

▲ Informed all members that the agenda was changed to address these concerns.

By intervening in this manner, the meeting coordinator converted a problem into an opportunity. Due to his intervention before the meeting:

- ▲ The two individuals abandoned their goal of coming to the meeting as aggressive combatants and disrupting it. Instead they were ready to work as constructive members.
- ▲ Everyone's anxiety about the meeting was relieved. Members were able to focus on the issues at hand without fear of disruption.
- ▲ The group was able to capitalize on the insights of the two individuals and converted them from vociferous critics into proactive visionaries and creators.
- ▲ The tone and quality of the discussions at the meeting was enhanced substantially.

Return on Investment Master's Checklist

The larger the meeting is, the more expensive it can get. To heighten awareness of the costs of meetings, it makes sense to calculate the investment in a meeting and anticipate the return on this investment. A return on investment (ROI) analysis can be used to assess the meeting as a whole and each agenda item:

- ▲ The meeting as a whole: Is it worth having?
- ▲ Each agenda item: Is it ready for beneficial discussion?

This section gives checklists for the ROI master (who is typically the overall planning coordinator, see previous section). Use these checklists with caution. Yes, calculating ROI can be a useful exercise. However, there is a risk in making it strictly a numeric exercise. Stay with the overall concept, but don't get bogged down in the numbers.

An ROI analysis consists of three steps:

1. Examining the investment in a meeting
2. Examining the potential returns on investment
3. Making decisions based on the ROI analysis

Examining the Investment in a Meeting

The costs of a meeting can be *tangible* (hard) costs and *intangible* (soft) costs, which can lead to hard costs in the long term. As a first step in considering the costs of a meeting, you need to examine the tangible (hard) and immediately apparent costs. The following is a sample list of tangible costs:

- ▲ Salaries and wages of members preparing for and attending the meeting
- ▲ Salaries and wages of support staff and contractors
- ▲ Consultant fees
- ▲ Costs of travel, accommodation, and meals
- ▲ Meeting room and equipment rental
- ▲ Paper production (reports, proposals)
- ▲ Tasks that follow the meeting: preparation of minutes, research, and reports

As a second step in considering the costs of a meeting, you need to examine the intangible (soft) costs, which may lead to hard costs in the long term. For example:

- ▲ Meetings disrupt schedules and routines of attendees. The continuity of their working days is disrupted and they are not available for other beneficial and profitable duties.
- ▲ Unproductive meetings cause stress, frustration, and anxiety.
- ▲ Unproductive meetings can sap individual energy and enthusiasm and make attendees unproductive for the rest of the working day, which means there is an indirect hard cost to this.
- ▲ A poorly run meeting may lead to bad decisions being pushed through. Resources may be wasted on implementing them, only to discover later that important factors were overlooked because of the way the meeting was run, e.g., quiet members who had concerns were stifled or felt too intimidated to participate.
- ▲ Valued members can become frustrated by bad meetings and leave the organization. Recruiting and training new individuals to replace them can be time-consuming and costly.

Examining the Potential Returns on Investment

Your meeting may yield a hard ROI (direct benefits that can be measured in financial terms) or a soft ROI (intangible benefits that cannot be measured in financial terms, at least not immediately).

Examples of the ROI that you can expect from holding a good meeting include:

- Creating a sense of teamwork, unity, cohesion, purpose, and commitment
- Boosting commitment and loyalty to the organization
- Generating ideas to boost revenues
- Generating ideas to save money and make the organization more efficient
- Generating ideas to reduce duplication and redundancies
- Generating ideas to work smarter, not harder
- Resolving divisive and costly disputes without adversarial actions
- Clearing up costly misunderstandings that lead to inefficiencies and tensions

You can use the ROI analysis for assessing the meeting as a whole and for assessing each agenda item.

Assessing the Meeting as a Whole

With the lists of costs and potential benefits, you can assess the meeting as a whole. This analysis may lead you to one of the following conclusions:

- The potential benefits from this meeting are indeed worth the investment. In this case, go ahead and hold the meeting, but make sure that it is well run, so you receive the potential ROI or more.
- The meeting has potential benefits, but it is not planned well enough to realize them. In this case, make the necessary adjustments to increase your ROI.
- The same or even better results can be achieved without a face-to-face meeting. In this case, give yourself permission to cancel the meeting, possibly after consultation with the members. You may opt for a virtual meeting instead (teleconference, videoconference, electronic meeting, or consultations by e-mail or fax; see Chapter 16 on virtual meetings).

Eight Reasons for Canceling a Face-to-Face Meeting

1. The meeting is too costly and the potential ROI is too small.
2. The issues to be discussed are minor and have no significant impact on members, and decisions can be made without consulting the members. There is no

need to tire and bore them with an unneeded meeting. Take charge, make the decisions yourself, and let them know what you did.

3. All issues can be easily addressed by informal consultation by phone, fax, or e-mail.

4. Everyone is very busy and productive and a meeting would be too disruptive.

5. The meeting is purely for information sharing with no consensus building or decision making. The same result can be achieved by sending memos to everyone and asking them to contact designated individuals if they have any questions.

6. The issues are far too divisive, the organizational climate is too adversarial, and the parties are not ready for face-to-face discussions. In such cases, more harm could be done by holding the meeting than by waiting. In the absence of collaborative discussions, people will just blame, attack, defend, and deny. Holding a meeting only for venting may not be worth the costs.

7. The meeting is a "last-minute" emergency, with no time to study the issues or plan the meeting properly. Discussions are bound to be unfocused and unproductive, and members will resent the imposition on their schedules. Holding such a meeting is setting it up for failure. It will build cynicism and contempt towards meetings, and rightly so.

8. Many people, especially key decision makers, are not available for the meeting. Attendees will get frustrated by the inability to reach closure.

Assessing Each Agenda Item

You can use the ROI analysis to screen, prioritize, and allocate time to agenda items:

- ▲ Allocate more time to beneficial agenda items. Plan to spend 90 percent of the time on the things that are important, instead of the opposite.
- ▲ Allocate less time to agenda items that provide low value
- ▲ Refuse to include agenda items that offer no value, or delegate them to an individual or to another group.

For more information on how to use the ROI analysis, see timing master and agenda master checklists below.

Timing Master's Checklist

The timing master's role is to set the time frame for the meeting. The timing master's tasks are typically performed by the planning coordinator (see earlier in this chapter), but can be delegated to another member. Specific tasks include setting the starting and closing times for the meeting.

Setting the Starting Time

The starting time of the meeting should be set after consulting the members. Every effort should be made to make this time as convenient for as many members as possible. Here are a few mistakes to avoid when setting the starting time for the meeting:

- ▲ Avoid starting too early (when people are barely awake).
- ▲ Avoid starting too late (when people are ready to go home).
- ▲ Avoid scheduling a meeting to start when another meeting (that several of your members will attend) will still be in progress or will have just barely ended.
- ▲ Avoid starting just before lunch or suppertime, unless catering is provided or you ask people to bring a brown bag.
- ▲ Avoid starting in the middle of rush hour if people have to drive to get to the meeting location.
- ▲ Avoid starting just before an important event that people are looking forward to, such as a much-anticipated ball game. They may come and be there in body, but their spirits will be elsewhere, and they may resent you for taking them away from their favorite pastime.

To increase the likelihood that members will be there on time, consider these ideas:

- ▲ Tell the members in advance that the meeting will start on time.
- ▲ Plan to keep your promise and start on time, which means arriving early and getting organized (see Chapter 10 about preparing to launch a meeting).
- ▲ Try scheduling a premeeting social gathering, networking opportunity, a meal, or a fun event. Everyone will be there and it will be easy to start the meeting on time.

- If a member or a guest presenter needs to set up audiovisual aids, ask them to be there well before the meeting, so the meeting can start on time and proceed without disruption.
- Put a fun activity that no one would want to miss right at the start of the meeting.
- Alternatively, schedule issues that do not require full attendance at the start of the meeting.
- Talk to habitual latecomers outside the meeting and see what can be done to have them come on time. For example, "Fred, is there a reason why you cannot make it on time? In fairness to those who make the effort to be here on time, we really need to arrive before the starting time and get organized for the meeting. Is there a problem I should be aware of?"

Example: A Creative Way to Ensure a Timely Start

A group recognized the consequences of tardiness and decided to deal with it in a creative way: Members decided to institute a fine system, whereby each individual would pay $2 for coming late, $2 for leaving early, and $5 for missing the meeting altogether. The only exceptions were illness or family emergencies. At the end of the year they held a pizza party and publicly recognized the reliable and consistent attendees.

Setting the Closing Time

The closing time for the meeting will depend on the scope of the agenda. For example:

- A regular staff or team meeting, usually held for information sharing, progress reports, updates, and a few decisions, is likely to require between one and two hours.
- A consensus- or team-building workshop, addressing a broad range of subjects, may require a full day or even longer.

- ▲ If people have traveled long distances to get to a meeting, it may be hard to justify a short one.
- ▲ An evening meeting should end no later than 10 P.M.

The ending time of a meeting should be scheduled in consultation with the members. Meetings should not be scheduled back to back. The ending time of one meeting should allow each member enough time to:

- ▲ Do any minor follow-up on the meeting that ended.
- ▲ Make their way to their next location without having to risk a speeding ticket.
- ▲ Unwind, freshen up, and get ready for the next meeting or other commitment.
- ▲ Arrive at the next commitment relaxed and ready to work.

Here are a few ideas to ensure a timely closing for the meeting:

- ▲ Print the projected closing time on the agenda.
- ▲ The facilitator should state the proposed closing time when the meeting begins: "Our target closing time is 4 P.M. Some of you need to go other meetings, so we'll need to work together to ensure that your schedules are respected."
- ▲ The facilitator or a timing master should monitor the clock, remind the members how much time is left for an agenda item, and ensure that each item receives close to its allocated time. This approach will prevent the "rush hour syndrome," i.e., when very little time is left and less than half the agenda has been concluded. Here is an example of a timing alert: "It is 2:45 and we have 15 minutes left for this issue. We need to think about closure."
- ▲ The facilitator or the timing master should alert the members when the closing time is near: For example, "It is now 4:10. We have 20 minutes left before the meeting ends, and we have three items to cover. They are: _____."
- ▲ For more on managing time in meetings see Chapter 12.

Agenda Master's Checklist

A meeting is like a journey. An agenda is like a timed road map for this journey, telling you:

- ▲ When your journey is scheduled to begin
- ▲ What the various segments (agenda items) of your route are
- ▲ What stops you will have and what time you are scheduled to arrive at each of them
- ▲ What your final destination is and when you are scheduled to reach it

The agenda master, who is typically also the meeting planning coordinator, is responsible for planning the agenda, with input from the various meeting participants. This section addresses the following topics:

- ▲ Recognizing a poor agenda
- ▲ Reactive agenda items
- ▲ Proactive agenda items
- ▲ Assessing an agenda item
- ▲ Using the 4 Ds to prioritize agenda items
- ▲ Allocating time to agenda items
- ▲ Communicating with proponents of agenda items
- ▲ Dealing with late additions to the agenda
- ▲ Establishing the sequence of agenda items
- ▲ Indicating the nature of agenda items
- ▲ Sample agenda

Recognizing a Poor Agenda

You need to avoid an agenda that:

- ▲ Is nonexistent, e.g., a last-minute meeting with no set agenda. No one knows why they're there or what they are supposed to be doing or talking about. As the old adage goes, "If you don't know where you're going, any road will take you there."
- ▲ Has little or nothing to do with the group's mandate.
- ▲ Is dull, uninspiring, and contains too many meaningless items.
- ▲ Has too many presentations ("lecture mode") and not enough time for interactive discussion.

- Is confusing and vague as to the nature of each item. Is it for information? For decision making?
- Includes too many items for the available time. As a result, you may be unable to conclude the agenda; you may end up rushing the agenda, taking a few short-cuts, compromising the quality of your decisions, and annoying your members; or the meeting may run past its scheduled closing time.
- Includes too few items for the available time. As a result, work may expand to fill the available time, and the meeting may become aimless, slow, and uninspiring.
- Is disjointed, fragmented, and poorly sequenced, e.g., the most important item is scheduled last.
- Is poorly timed. Very little time is allocated to significant issues, too much time is allocated to insignificant issues, or no time is allocated at all.
- Does not integrate team members' concerns and suggestions.

Reactive Agenda Items

Agendas are typically reactive in nature. They include all the items that *must* be dealt with. There is nothing inherently wrong with being reactive, as long as there is also room to be proactive and visionary and talk about things that the group finds exciting and interesting (see next section).

Your reactive agenda may include issues that:

- Are regularly scheduled on each meeting agenda (progress reports)
- Were not completed in previous meetings
- Are brought forward as a result of a crisis
- Are raised by external parties, like senior management, or customer complaints

Proactive Agenda Items

To make meetings more interesting, meaningful, fun, and enticing to attend, you need to look beyond the things that your group *has* to do. You need to add things to the agenda that members would *want* to do and enjoy talking about. Proactive agenda items may include:

- ▲ Discussions of emerging trends related to the group's mandate
- ▲ Strategies to place the organization on the leading edge, well ahead of competing organizations
- ▲ Discussions that will make your members visionaries and creators
- ▲ Presentations by speakers with unusual messages, success stories, or stories of how they learned from failure and benefited from it
- ▲ Presentations by spokespersons for controversial causes
- ▲ Discussions that will force the group to be creative and consider unusual ideas
- ▲ Discussions on how to improve relationships with customers and suppliers
- ▲ Ideas and issues that came up during previous meetings and were placed in the group's idea list (or "parking lot")

Assessing an Agenda Item

Placing every conceivable item on the agenda will make the scope of the meeting too large. This may make the agenda impossible to complete and frustrate the members. Therefore the agenda master should assess each item before placing it on the agenda. Here are some questions to ask when assessing a potential agenda item:

1. Is it within the mandate of this group and, if not, which group or individual should deal with it? For example, a board of directors should not be micromanaging the organization by deciding how the phones will be answered. This level of decision making should be delegated to management and should not be allowed on the board's agenda.
2. To what extent does this item fit within the overall purpose of this meeting?
3. How ripe is this item for productive discussions and decision making? Has all necessary research been carried out? Have the needs of all stakeholders been considered before proposals were prepared?
4. What is the developmental stage of this issue? (See the subsection in Chapter 1 on the natural evolution of issues.)
   - ▲ Is it a "baby issue," suitable for preliminary discussion and exploration only?
   - ▲ Is the issue at the adolescent stage, with members fighting over it? This means that they are not ready to make mature and rational decisions on it. More discussion on this issue is needed, but don't plan to force a final deci-

sion on it by a narrow majority. Doing so may come back to haunt your group later (the issue may end up being reincarnated).

- ▲ Is the issue at the adult stage? ("We talked about it enough, we know all the facts and have done all the research, and we are now ready to make some decisions in a calm, mature, principled, and objective manner.")

5. How much time will this issue consume, and will the return on investment on this agenda item be proportionate to the value of the time invested in it? (See ROI master's checklist earlier in this chapter.)
6. Is this an issue that requires confidentiality? If so, it should be scheduled for an in-camera (closed) meeting and not for an open meeting (see Chapter 5 for confidentiality guidelines).
7. Does any member have a conflict of interest with this issue? If so, the member should be required to leave the meeting while the item is discussed (see Chapter 5 for COI guidelines).

Using the 4 Ds to Prioritize Agenda Items

Having assessed all potential agenda items, the agenda master needs to make one of the following four decisions (4 Ds) about each item:

1. *Deal with it.* Schedule it on the agenda and allocate the appropriate amount of time for it.
2. *Delay it.* If the item is not urgent, or not ripe for discussion and decision making, or there isn't enough time to deal with it effectively, postpone it to a future meeting.
3. *Delegate it.* If the item should be dealt with by another group or person, or should be studied more by a subcommittee, delegate it to the appropriate person or group.
4. *Drop it.* If the item's relevance to the group's mandate is marginal, or it will not advance the purpose of the meeting, or there is no benefit in having interactive discussion of it, feel free to drop it from the agenda altogether.

Allocating Time to Agenda Items

The agenda master should estimate how much time each major agenda item will require and create a timed agenda. Here are a few ideas on allocating time to agenda items:

- Time should be allocated to an issue based on its significance and the anticipated benefits of the discussion. Avoid the common mistake of allocating 90 percent of the time to the issues that make little or no difference.
- Estimate realistically. Avoid allocating time too tightly (you may need leeway) or too generously (to avoid work expanding to fill the available time).
- Ask discussion leaders how much time their items will require.
- Ask presenters how much time they will need for their presentations. If they are asking for too much time, negotiate a more realistic limit: "Bert, we have a busy agenda. Can you tighten things up? Can you live with fifteen minutes?" or "Professor Jones, can you keep the lecture part of your presentation to thirty minutes and spend more time on the question period?"
- "Pad the agenda." Here is an example with an extra five-minute padding between major items, providing the group with some leeway:
  9:00–9:25: System management issues
  9:30–9:55: Selection of human resources consultant
  10:00–10:25: New customer service ideas (brainstorming session)
  10:30–10:45: Refreshment break
- Avoid indicating the number of minutes that each item will take; for example, "first item: 15 minutes; second item: 25 minutes; third item: 35 minutes." With this method it is difficult to figure out whether a meeting is on time, i.e., the meeting facilitator will need a pocket calculator to add up the allocated times to determine whether the meeting is on schedule.
- Avoid a minute-by-minute allocation of time; for example, "7:00 P.M.: Review of minutes; 7:01: Chair's report; 7:02: Vice chair's report." Such allocations are unrealistic to enforce, and are likely to be ignored or not taken seriously.
- Integrate the lessons learned in previous meetings. If your estimates were too tight, make them more generous. If they were too generous, tighten things up.

Communicating with Proponents of Agenda Items

If the agenda master is uncertain about an agenda item and is not quite ready to choose one of the 4 D's for it, she or he may need to contact the proponent of an agenda item, to ask questions about the nature of the item, how it is related to the group's mandate, the expected benefits from it, and how much time it will likely require. The discussion with the member may lead to one of these outcomes:

1. The member may adjust the item to address any concerns, e.g.: address it more directly to the group's mandate.

2. The member may agree that the item should be delayed, delegated, or dropped. This will prevent the perception of a "top-down" autocratic decision by the agenda master.

3. The agenda master and the proponent may end up disagreeing on whether the item is appropriate for the meeting. In such cases, one of three things could happen: (1) the agenda master's decision will be respected; (2) the group's leader will make a decision; or (3) the decision on whether the item will be on the agenda will be made by the group at the start of the meeting. Some groups take a show of hands to resolve such disagreements (see section in Chapter 11 on establishing support for the meeting agenda).

Dealing with Late Additions to the Agenda

A chronic problem in meetings occurs when members introduce last-minute agenda items. Sometimes they do it at the start of the meeting, and sometimes at the very end, under an obscure category called "New Business." Common difficulties with late additions to the agenda are:

- ▲ Last-minute items are typically not well researched. It may be difficult to make measured, informed, and responsible decisions on them.
- ▲ Last-minute items are often pursued because of a crisis. This may mean that the group has a reactive approach to meetings, doing more "firefighting" and less preventive and visionary work. A more proactive approach is needed.
- ▲ Last-minute items may extend the meeting beyond its stated closing time. Members may end up discussing significant issues halfheartedly, when they would rather leave. The risk of making bad decisions is substantial.
- ▲ The chair and the proponent may end up arguing about the inclusion of the item, and this argument may consume precious time, at the expense of prescheduled agenda items.

To prevent or reduce the likelihood of late additions to the agenda and to minimize their impact on other issues, the group should adopt a policy that:

- ▲ Late agenda items are only allowed in emergencies. They are the exception, and not the norm.
- ▲ The proponent of a late addition to the agenda may be required to explain why the item should be considered and why it needs to bypass the usual process,

whereby issues are studied, reports are prepared, and members are notified of them in advance.

▲ The group may refuse to deal with a late item and may choose to delay, delegate, or drop it instead, or the meeting facilitator may be empowered to make such decisions.

▲ As a general rule, if a late agenda item is accepted for discussion, it should be scheduled after all prescheduled items have been dealt with. Exceptions may be emergencies and other reasons that compel the group to rearrange the agenda and schedule the late item earlier on.

Establishing the Sequence of Agenda Items

The agenda should be planned so that items flow logically. Here are a few ideas to consider:

1. Agenda items that have an impact on one another should be grouped together and should be placed in a logical sequence. Decisions that need to be made first should be scheduled earlier. The items at the start of the meeting should include:

   ▲ Opening remarks, to set the tone for the meeting.

   ▲ Mapping out the agenda and establishing support for it.

   ▲ Explaining the participation protocol, if needed.

   ▲ See Chapter 11 for a sample script to launch a meeting.

2. Next, establish an interactive tone with an "icebreaker." For example, each member can be invited to make a brief comment, expressing his or her expectation of the meeting.

3. Schedule a few short routine items at the beginning of the meeting, to build momentum and synergy and get the group ready for the more substantive issues. Such routine items often include a review of previous minutes and progress reports.

4. Significant decisions that require time and concentration should be placed early in the meeting when members are fresh and alert, and not late in the meeting, when they may be tired and unfocused. Note that creativity and alertness may not be abundant after a heavy meal.

5. Agenda items that involve "lecture mode" (e.g., reports, guest presentations) should be alternated with items that require interaction. This mix will vary

the pace of the meeting and reduce the risk of sleep-inducing boredom and monotony.

6. Light agenda items should be interspersed between those that require focus and concentration. Light items will provide some "downtime" that will give members an opportunity to reenergize and get ready for the next heavy issue. Light items may include:

   - Fun items, like a special award, a happy birthday song, or a short funny story
   - Routine and noncontroversial items that require simple decisions
   - Items that are purely informative and require no discussion or decision making
   - See Chapter 12 for more ideas on providing downtime in a meeting

7. Feel free to introduce variety and experiment with the sequence of agenda items. Avoid locking into one routine unless it works really well for your group.

8. Schedule breaks (unless the meeting is shorter than two hours). Breaks will enable members to rest, chat informally, and have some "downtime." The rule of thumb is that they should not be seated for more than 1.5 to 2 hours in one stretch. Remember, "The human mind will absorb only as much as the human seat will endure." Breaks can also be a way of disengaging from intense and deadlocked discussions. After the break people may come back with fresh ideas, especially if you sent them for a brisk walk around the block or had them do stretching exercises.

9. It may be useful to group noncontroversial items together, as a "consent agenda." This means that all items under the "consent agenda" are dealt with at once, unless there are requests to pull certain items from the package and deal with them separately.

Indicating the Nature of an Agenda Item

To increase clarity, the agenda master should indicate the nature of each item:

- Is it for information only, requiring no action, but allowing questions?
- Is it for discussion and decision making?
- If it is for decision making, what are the decision-making options? If known, these options should be clearly indicated (possibly bolded or underlined) in an attachment to the agenda.

- ▲ Has any background documentation been provided with the agenda?
- ▲ If the item is substantial, how much time has been allocated to it?
- ▲ Who is responsible for this item, i.e., who will make a presentation or lead the discussion on it?

Sample Agenda

INFORMATION TECHNOLOGY DEPARTMENT MEETING (April 4, 2001)

Date: Wednesday, April 4, 2001
12:45 P.M.: Networking and refreshments.
1:00 P.M. SHARP: Meeting begins.
4:00 P.M. (or sooner): Closing.
Location: Committee room 1, head office

1:00 PM:

1. Opening remarks — Libby Smith
2. Review of agenda
3. Review of minutes and action items
4. Progress reports — Everyone
5. Financial report (for information only) — Derek Ng
6. Personnel report (hiring proposal, see attachment) — Joan McCarthy

2:30: Refreshment break

2:40:

7. Computer upgrade (for discussion only, see report) — Norm Sutton

3:30:

8. Staff recognition program (brainstorming session) — Everyone
9. Announcements
10. Closing (no later than 4 P.M.)

Note: Allocated times are only estimates. They will be used as flexible guidelines.

LOGISTICS MASTER'S CHECKLIST

The logistics master's role is to ensure that all logistical details are addressed. The logistics master should keep in mind Murphy's Law: "If anything can go wrong, it will, at the worst possible time." This section covers the many details that a logistics master may need to attend to. You can treat this section as a collection of tips and ideas, to be used if and when needed.

Logistics planning should be both *proactive* (creating smooth logistical support for the meeting) and *preventive* (stopping minor logistical details from becoming major distractions). The logistical aspects to attend to may include some or all of the following:

- Meeting room selection
- Room setup, seating, and name tags
- Audiovisual aids
- Catering arrangements

Meeting Room Selection

This section discusses the advantages and disadvantages of on-site and off-site meeting rooms. In addition, it gives you a list of questions you should ask about each of the following aspects of room selection:

- Room size
- Room shape
- Room temperature and ventilation
- Lighting
- Curtains
- Furniture
- External distractions
- Access to the facility and room

Advantages and Disadvantages of On-Site and Off-Site Meeting Rooms

You may choose to hold the meeting in an on-site room. You may also opt to rent a meeting room in a hotel or conference facility. The following lists show the advantages and disadvantages of both options.

Advantages of an on-site room	Disadvantages of an on-site room
Familiarity. You have held meetings in the room before and know how to make things work, e.g.: how to turn the air-conditioning on or off. *Control.* You are working with in-house staff and don't have the uncertainty of working with outside parties, who may or may not be reliable or responsive to your group's needs. *Comfort.* Members know the room and are comfortable working in it. *Proximity.* The room is within reach and does not require driving or struggling to find parking. *Cost.* The meeting room is likely to be less expensive than an off-site rented facility. You are also likely to have more flexibility and leeway, e.g., you can arrange your own catering.	*Routine.* The on-site room and environment may be too predictable, boring, and unexciting. *Bad memories.* In adversarial climates, the on-site room may be too reminiscent of past infighting, and there may be a need for a fresh and neutral venue to "turn a new page." *Inadequate.* The room may not be large enough or may have other unacceptable constraints.

Advantages of an off-site room	Disadvantages of an off-site room
Outside the norm. An off-site meeting room provides variety and a departure from the status quo. The different setting may make members more comfortable exploring fresh and unusual ideas and questioning conventional wisdom. *Neutrality.* If issues are controversial, an off-site location may provide a degree of objectivity and distance from the suspicion and distrust that may exist among the various parties. *A sense of adventure.* Meeting in a new place can introduce a sense of excitement and adventure and can also	*Lack of certainty and predictability.* Being unfamiliar with the facility, you don't know what could go wrong and disrupt the meeting. *Too many details to look after.* You may not have the time or resources to negotiate with banquet staff and coordinate logistical details. *Inconvenience.* Members may need to drive through heavy traffic, add travel time to their commitment to the meeting, and struggle to find parking. The disruptive effect of the meeting is likely to be greater than one held on-site.

be seen as a form of recognition and reward for the group.

Versatility and better facilities. An off-site facility may offer meeting rooms that are larger, better laid out, and better equipped. They may also offer better catering and may relieve you of mundane logistical duties (done by hotel staff).

Cost. Added costs include meeting room rental, hiring a meeting planner to look after logistical details, being locked into hotel catering (which is typically more expensive than private catering), and possibly other hidden costs.

Room Size Questions

- ▲ Is the room large enough to hold the expected group size?
- ▲ Conversely, is the room too large, losing the sense of closeness and privacy?
- ▲ What will happen if an unexpectedly large crowd shows up?

Typical Mistakes

- ▲ Renting a huge ballroom for a meeting of fifteen people
- ▲ Renting a small room for a community meeting to discuss a contentious issue
- ▲ Failing to ask what the maximum capacity of the room is, and then being surprised when the fire marshal breaks the news to you (halfway through the meeting) that you are violating fire safety regulations by having so many people in the room

A Success Story

A mining company was holding a community meeting and anticipated a large audience. It rented an extra meeting room to accommodate potential overflows, which indeed materialized. Here are a few of the details that the planners attended to:

- ▲ The discussions in the main meeting room were televised and displayed on a large screen in the second room.
- ▲ A public address system was used so people in the overflow room could hear what was said in the main room.

▲ Microphones were set up in the overflow room with a connection to the public address system in the main room. This enabled people in the overflow room to address the presenters in the main room.

Room Shape Questions

▲ Is the room too narrow?

▲ Is the room oddly shaped or does it have large pillars in the middle, making it difficult for people to see one another? If so, is there a better alternative? If not, what can be done to minimize the effect of the odd room shape?

▲ Are the entry or exit doors located in a place that will allow latecomers to enter the room without distracting the meeting?

Room Temperature and Ventilation Questions

▲ In the winter: Is the room warm enough? Conversely, is it too warm?

▲ In the summer: Is the room air-conditioned? Is it too cold?

▲ Are there windows or doors that can be opened to provide fresh air and prevent a sense of being enclosed?

▲ Where are the heat, ventilation, and air conditioning controls?

▲ Is it easy to make adjustments to the heat and ventilation? If not, who knows how to make adjustments? Will this person be available on short notice if there is a problem?

▲ How noisy are the ventilation fans? Is this noise level acceptable? If not, should you look for another room or ask for complimentary microphones?

▲ Do the fans turn on automatically or can you control them manually (to avoid the noise they make or to prevent the room from getting too hot or too cold)?

Lighting Questions

▲ Are the lights bright enough? Are they too bright? Do they shine in people's faces?

- ▲ Do you need the option of adjusting the lighting level, e.g., dimming lights for a video or slide presentation, without turning them off altogether?
- ▲ Do you know where the lighting controls are and how they work? If not, who does? Will this person be readily available if there is a problem?
- ▲ Are there any flickering neon lights that could distract the group?
- ▲ Who can replace burned-out light bulbs if needed? How quickly?

Curtains Questions

- ▲ Does the room have curtains?
- ▲ Is it easy to open and close the curtains? Will they collapse if you try?
- ▲ Is it desirable to have the curtains closed or open, i.e., is privacy desired? Would the view or the events outside the room be distracting?
- ▲ What can be done if the sun shines in people's faces, the curtains don't close, and the members don't want a tan? Note: It may be difficult to anticipate this problem. Your first visit to the room may be on a cloudy day, and the day of the meeting may be sunny.

Furniture Questions

- ▲ Are there enough chairs and tables to accommodate the group?
- ▲ Are any chairs or tables broken, squeaky, or wobbly? You may need to actually test all of them. The last thing you need is a member getting hurt just when a meeting is about to begin.
- ▲ Are the chairs comfortable? Too hard? Too soft? Too high? Too low? Would you sink into them or would you be able to lean forward and remain alert?

External Distractions Questions

- ▲ Is a noisy function scheduled to be held next door, e.g., a choir rehearsal, a revival meeting?
- ▲ Is there separation between the public address system in the adjacent room and your room, so you won't have to listen to the speech and the applause next door?

- Is there a bar or restaurant with live entertainment or loud music next door? If so, when is it scheduled to open? (Obviously, when you visit the hotel in the middle of a business day, these facilities will be closed and you will not even be aware of a potential problem.)
- Is there a swimming pool with lots of users next door, scheduled to open in the middle of your meeting?
- Is there a public address (PA) system with announcements made or with music that could be distracting? If so, how can it be turned off?
- Is there a fire hall or a hospital emergency room next door, with sirens going off from time to time or doctors being paged on the PA system?

Facility and Room Access Questions

- Is the building easy to find? If not, should you include a map and detailed instructions in the meeting package?
- Is the meeting room itself easy to find within the building? Will the name of your group and function be posted on a bulletin board? Should you have signs directing the members to the room or have greeters waiting for people and directing them to it?
- Is parking readily available? Where? Is there a fee for it? Does it have to be exact change or will credit card payment work? Should you let everyone know? Can you negotiate with the hotel to waive the fee in light of the fact that you are paying for a meeting room?
- Is there public transit to the meeting location? If so, what are the routes, the schedules, and the fares?
- Is the building handicapped-accessible? If not, what can be done if a member needs help?
- Will you have access to the meeting room at least half an hour before the meeting begins (longer if your logistical and audiovisual requirements are complex)? Is another event held in the same room and scheduled to end exactly when your meeting is set to begin, leaving you no time to set up and get organized? If so, should you look for an alternative, like postponing the start time, or looking for a room that will be available sooner?
- Will you be able to inspect the meeting room before you actually reserve it, to ensure suitability?

Note: The above questions may sound trivial, but they are important. You would not want members to arrive late and angry because they could not find parking, or have them resent you for not telling them that the bus to the location leaves only once an hour.

Room Setup, Seating, and Name Tags

It is essential that the setup of tables and chairs, seating, and name tags be suitable to your group's needs. This section covers the following topics:

1. Square, circle, u-shape, or boardroom-shape tables
2. Round tables
3. Theater-style seating
4. Random seating versus prearranged seating
5. Use of name tags
6. Use of name tents
7. "Suffering is optional" tools
8. Seating in a very small meeting

A Square, Circle, U-Shape, or Boardroom Shape

In small groups (up to twenty people), the suitable room setup is a square, circle, or u-shape of tables and chairs, or members can be seated around a boardroom table. The advantages of these types of seating arrangements are:

- ▲ Everyone sees everyone else and no one looks at anyone's back.
- ▲ It is easier to hear people's voices and watch their facial expressions.
- ▲ The opportunities for full and meaningful interactions increase.
- ▲ The tables make it easy for members to write and work on.

Here are two common mistakes with this room setup:

- ▲ The boardroom table is too narrow and too long, making it difficult for those seated at one end to see and hear those seated on the other end.

- ▲ The square is too large and therefore more formal and less conducive for teamwork.

Example: The Wrong Setup

The staff in a classy hotel sets up a square large enough for twenty people when you told them that there will only be only ten. They space the chairs far apart, because they believe customers want space and privacy. What can you do?

- ▲ To prevent this from happening, you need to map out the desired room setup to the hotel staff well in advance of the meeting.
- ▲ If you find yourself stuck with such an arrangement on the day of the meeting, don't accept it. Ask hotel staff to make an immediate adjustment, such as pulling a few tables away and making the square smaller. Of course, this means that you should have come to the meeting location early, and not two minutes before it is set to begin (see Chapter 10 about preparing to launch a meeting).
- ▲ If the hotel staff are nowhere to be found or are not available to make the adjustment, feel free to do it yourself, possibly with assistance from your members.

Round Tables

An alternative setup is several round tables, with up to ten chairs per table. This room setup is suitable for:

- ▲ Medium groups (e.g., twenty-five, with five tables of five)
- ▲ Large groups (e.g., 100, with ten tables of ten)

The advantages of round tables are that the setup:

- ▲ Creates a sense of community and allows for social interaction
- ▲ Is conducive to structured discussions in small breakout groups

Common mistakes of using round tables are:

- ▲ Spreading the tables too far apart, and thereby causing physical fragmentation. The ability to have interactive discussion at the full group level can be reduced or lost.
- ▲ Leaving virtually no space between round tables. It becomes awkward to move around. It can also be dangerous, as people can trip over chairs.

Theater Style

A third type of room setup is parallel rows of chairs (with or without tables, depending on available space), with a head table and a podium set up in the front of the room.

This room setup is suitable for medium or large groups (thirty and more). There may be times when you have no option but to go with theater style, e.g., when chairs are bolted to the floor in a theater-style configuration.

The main advantage is that this room setup can accommodate a larger group. Common mistakes are:

- ▲ Using a large theater for a small group, and thereby making it very challenging to have fully interactive discussions and consensus building.
- ▲ Using theater style when a circle or a round table configuration would be possible. Typically the problem is that the meeting facilitator accepts an inappropriate room setup and does not even consider changing it.

Example: The Impact of a Switch from Theater Style to Round Tables

A credit union's board of directors surveyed the members about the effectiveness of its annual meetings. Many members said they did not like those meetings for two reasons:

- ▲ Members were seated in theater-style room setup, positioned against their board of directors (whose members were seated at a head table). This setting was adversarial and made it a natural forum for attacking and criticizing the performance of the board.

- Meetings were dominated by the same vocal members every year. Others just sat and observed. This made meetings predictable and meaningless.

In response to this feedback, the board changed its next annual meeting in the following ways:

- Instead of theater style, members were seated at round tables, thereby building more social interaction and a sense of community.
- The only person at the front of the room was the president, who chaired the meeting. There was also a podium set up for report presenters and guest speakers.
- Each member of the board was asked to join one of the round tables, moving physically closer to the members and becoming a part of the community.
- At the end of the formal part of the meeting, each director facilitated a twenty-minute discussion with the members who were seated at his or her table on how the credit union's relationship with its customers (the members) could improve. These discussions engaged everyone, and not only the vocal members who enjoyed speaking in public and dominated past meetings.

The meeting went well and the feedback on it from members was very positive this time. Moreover, the small group discussions offered a crop of creative and practical ideas for the board of directors' consideration.

Random Seating vs. Prearranged Seating

In most meetings members sit where they want. In other meetings seats are preassigned (e.g., by preparing name tents and placing them on the tables). Here are the advantages and disadvantages of both options:

Random seating		Prearranged seating	
Advantages	**Disadvantages**	**Advantages**	**Disadvantages**
Members are free to choose where they sit, and are	Members "gravitate" to the same spot and interact	By preassigning seats, you can mix the group to	Members may complain about "being con-

less likely to complain.	with the same people. This can lead to the formation of cliques and the fragmentation of the group.	achieve a better interaction, e.g., have opponents sit next to each other. Side talkers sit apart from each other.	trolled." You'll probably need to explain what the prearranged seating is intended to accomplish and get the group to support this approach.

There is a third "middle of the road" option: You can ask members informally to mix and sit next to people they haven't met or worked with before:

> *"I've noticed that in our meetings several of you go to the same corner and work and talk with the same people. I have a suggestion: Next time, would you consider sitting next to someone you haven't met or worked with? This way you can get to know more about other members and learn about different perspectives on the issues that we're discussing."*

Name Tags

If the group is meeting for the first time and members don't know one another, you will need name tags or name tents to identify them to the people they meet and to enable the meeting facilitator to manage the meeting by referring to people by name. Here are a few tips for preparing name tags or name tents:

- ▲ Adhesive name tags are an inexpensive option, but they fall off easily and can ruin good clothes.
- ▲ Pinned name tags stay on but can also damage garments.
- ▲ Clipped name tags don't damage garments. However, some garments don't have pockets or lapels to clip them on to.
- ▲ The best compromise is name tags with adjustable thin ropes that can be worn around the neck. However, they are more costly.
- ▲ You can ask people to return pinned, clipped, or roped name tags for recycling.
- ▲ Suggest that name tags be worn on the right hand side, since people typically shake the right hand and look in the direction of the name tag.
- ▲ If you prepare the name tags, make sure the printing is large and clear and that names are spelled correctly. You may choose to have people write the name tags themselves, but ask them to write clearly and in large print.

- If there is space on the name tag, include the member's organization or occupation. Another variation is to type the first name in large letters, and the remaining information in small letters.
- For guest speakers or members who have unique roles, you can prepare special color name tags or attach a ribbon to the bottom of the tags, stating their titles: "Guest speaker," "Director," etc.

Name Tents

Having name tags on each person may not suffice during the meeting, since they are too small and difficult to read from a distance. It also helps to have "name tents" placed on the tables, in front of members. Name tents can also help you preassign seats to members and thereby remove the anxiety of "Where will I sit today?"

If you don't have premade name tents, here is a crude and simple way of preparing them:

- Cut 8.5″ by 11″ sheets into two 8.5″ by 5.5″ sheets.
- Fold each half (8.5″ by 5.5″) into two. The dimensions of the folded name tent will be 8.5″ (horizontal) by 2.75″ (vertical).
- Give members fresh felt pens to prepare their name tents. (If they use their own pens or pencils, the name tents may not be readable from a distance). Make sure that the felt pens are not dry.
- Ask them to print their names in large and legible letters.
- You may ask them to write at the bottom of the name tent the department or the organization they represent (if there is room).
- Ask them to print their names on both sides of the name tent. The inevitable question will be, "Why is that? So I remember who I am?" Very funny. But there is an explanation: It is so that those who sit next to an individual will know who their neighbor is. This will also make it clear to those who walk outside the U-shape configuration which seats are taken and by whom.
- Avoid toxic-smelling felt pens, and use those with pleasant fruit smells or no smell.
- Consider different-colored pens for different people, for variety.
- You can encourage members to use creative touches as they prepare their name tents.

- To avoid name signs falling off the tables during the meeting, you may want to use Scotch tape or masking tape to attach them to the tables in front of individuals.

"Suffering Is Optional" Tools

A motto used throughout this book is "Suffering is optional." Meeting participants should be free to complain if a meeting is not going well, e.g., digressions, domination, wasted time, too much sitting without a break, etc.

Many participants find it difficult to interject and complain verbally. A creative way to make it easy for them to express concerns is by giving them tools to complain without speaking. Tools that have been tried by some groups include:

- Squeaky toy animals
- Small red flags
- Cue cards with words stating typical concerns: "Focus, please!!," "Circle the field," "Time to land," "Off the rails," "Volume, please," "Repeat the proposal," etc.
- Cue cards with pictures showing typical concerns: an hourglass, a train going off the rails, a plane getting ready to land, etc.

When considering room setup, plan to do one of the following:

- Place the tool of choice in front of each meeting participant, or
- Place one tool for every three or four members, or one for every round table (if there aren't enough of them, or if you want to avoid an overuse of these tools).

Seating in a Very Small Meeting

When you are meeting with only one or two people, assess whether it's best to sit across a table or on the same side:

- If you are trying to solve a problem together, it generally works better to sit next to each other or in a small semicircle, so you're all facing in the same direction and not against one another.

▲ If you are discussing a disciplinary matter or a performance issue with a person reporting to you, it may be preferable to maintain the distance and formality and sit on opposite sides of the table.

Audiovisual Aids

Audiovisual (AV) aids are valuable tools that can enhance formal presentations and can help facilitate interactive discussions. However, logistical difficulties may make audiovisual aids more of a problem than a source of help. This section covers the following topics:

▲ General planning tips for audiovisual aids

▲ Comparisons of the most commonly used visual aids

▲ Typical difficulties with equipment of various types

General Planning Tips for Audiovisual Aids

Contact all presenters and discussion leaders in advance of the meeting to determine:

▲ What, if any, audiovisual equipment they will use. But don't make them feel guilty about not using such equipment. Some speakers do just fine or even better without it.

▲ Whether they will bring their own equipment or will need you to reserve it for them.

▲ Whether they need support when getting ready to use AV equipment, e.g., preparing slides or computer files, coaching on how to operate the apparatus for computer-based presentations (like PowerPoint), etc.

You may need to negotiate the AV requirements with speakers if the following occurs:

▲ You don't have the equipment they're used to.

▲ The equipment is too expensive to rent and you cannot justify the cost.

▲ The AV presentation is not appropriate for your group. For example, some groups find PowerPoint presentations too formal. They may prefer simpler and more interactive presentations to fancy lectures with many "bells and whistles."

Having done the above, you will have a list of the various AV aids that presenters and discussion leaders will need. Depending on the type and size of the meeting, this list may include:

- A PowerPoint apparatus: projector, screen, and laptop computer
- An overhead projector and screen
- One or more flip charts (reliable and stable, with blank paper and fresh felt pens)
- A white board
- A slide projector
- One or more microphones (lapel, cordless, or podium microphone). For example, one microphone for the meeting facilitator, one for presenters, and one or more "floor microphones" or cordless microphones for comments or questions from members.
- Video equipment and a TV monitor

Establish (possibly in consultation with the presenter) where in the room the AV equipment should be positioned for best visibility and effectiveness. Pretest the equipment and ensure it works properly. This may include a dress rehearsal on or before the day of the meeting (see Chapter 10 on preparing to launch a meeting). For example:

- You may need to go to different corners of the room and check whether the overhead screen can be seen, whether the projector is properly focused, and whether the print on slides is large enough.
- If you are using microphones, you will need to test each one of them and check whether they can be heard clearly in the different corners of the room. Ask team members to assist you by giving feedback while you test the equipment.

Have spare parts ready, or establish who can get them fast. This may include:

- Extra light bulbs for an overhead projector
- Fresh batteries for cordless microphones
- Extension cords for equipment that needs to be plugged in (find out where the outlets are located in advance of the meeting and whether they are 'live')
- Extra blank paper pads for flip charts
- Fresh felt pens of different colors, in case the ones you have dry up

Never assume anything. If a hotel's manager tells you, "Everything will be fine," you should say, "Thank you for the reassurance. I have a few questions to ask for my own peace of mind." If they say, "The acoustics are perfect. You won't need a microphone," get one anyway, for soft-spoken speakers or those who want to "save their voices," and for members who have hearing difficulties.

If you are renting AV equipment, ensure that you are working with a reliable supplier. Tell them exactly what you need and when you need it (set up and ready to go at least half an hour before the meeting starts). Be there when they test the equipment on the day of the meeting. You may also want a technician available to help you with any equipment difficulties at the meeting.

Comparisons of the Most Commonly Used Visual Aids

Below are three lists comparing the advantages and disadvantages of the most commonly used visual aids:

- PowerPoint apparatus (computer-based presentations)
- Overhead projector and screen
- Flip chart

PowerPoint apparatus

Advantages	Disadvantages
▲ Suitable for both large or small groups. ▲ Provides versatility and many presentation options. ▲ Special effects can add visual appeal, clarity, variety, and fun. ▲ Does not require you to darken the room.	▲ Requires PowerPoint knowledge and skill. ▲ Requires special equipment. ▲ Requires space and setup work. ▲ Can formalize a presentation and turn it into an extended lecture, at the expense of interactive discussions. ▲ Can shift the attention from the people at the meeting to the "bells and whistles" of the presentation. ▲ Can become an obsession, especially if the presenter gets fascinated with the special effects and focuses on them more than on the message. Speakers can become competitive on

	how many features they'll use, and others may become discouraged about not using as many special effects.

Overhead projector	
Advantages	**Disadvantages**
▲ Suitable for both large or small groups. ▲ Flexible and relatively easy to set up. ▲ Requires less equipment than a PowerPoint presentation. ▲ Preparing transparencies and working with the equipment is relatively easy. ▲ It is possible to record emerging consensus on blank transparencies. ▲ Transparencies last longer than flip chart paper.	▲ Visually less interesting than a PowerPoint presentation. ▲ Can formalize the presentation and turn it into a lecture. ▲ Requires space and setup work.

Flip chart	
Advantages	**Disadvantages**
▲ Suitable for small groups (up to 25) ▲ Less formal and structured than a PowerPoint presentation ▲ Conducive to facilitating interactive discussions, where key points and consensus are recorded on a flip chart ▲ Flexible and easy to move around ▲ Requires little space and minimum setup work ▲ Simple and easy to use	▲ Not suitable for larger groups ▲ Can be unstable or collapse as you work with it ▲ Not as elaborate or impressive-looking as PowerPoint presentations

Typical Difficulties with Overhead or Computer-Based Equipment

- There are no power outlets where you need them.
- There is no electricity in the outlet. (People assume there will be, but this is not always the case).
- No one knows how to set up the apparatus or make it work.
- The projector is poorly aligned or poorly focused.
- There are blown fuses or burned-out light bulbs with no spare ones available. No person who can remedy the situation is available, and the presenter has no contingency plan.
- The overhead screen cannot be seen from all corners of the room.
- The colors used on slides are too light and the print size is too small to read from a distance.

Typical Difficulties with Flip Charts

- The easel's legs are shaky, causing it to collapse and possibly hurt someone.
- The easel's legs are too short. It is designed to stand on top of a table, not as a stand-alone.
- The flip chart paper is mounted on the swiveling door that covers a white board, making it awkward to flip the sheets over. You should have asked for a freestanding flip chart instead.
- There is no blank paper or not enough of it.
- There is no metal strip to hold the paper. When you flip a sheet over, the entire pad falls over and the structure collapses (in the middle of a presentation . . .).
- There are no felt pens, or not enough colors, or the felt pens are dry.
- Flip chart paper with valuable information is left overnight and the diligent cleaning staff throws it in the garbage. (This is obviously not an equipment problem, but a communication problem.)

Note: Flip charts are relatively inexpensive and are a highly effective tool for presentations and for facilitating interactive discussions. Why not just buy a good one for use in your meetings?

Typical Difficulties with White Boards

- ▲ No erasable felt pens are available.
- ▲ The felt pens are dry.
- ▲ No eraser is available.
- ▲ Someone left information on the board that seems important and you are not sure whether it's OK to erase it.
- ▲ Someone wrote on the board with tough-to-erase ink.

Typical Difficulties with Video Players

- ▲ No one knows how to operate the equipment.
- ▲ The hookup to the TV monitor does not work.
- ▲ The channel on the TV monitor keeps flipping and it is impossible to lock on to channel 3.
- ▲ The tape is not rewound or fast-forwarded to the right spot.
- ▲ The presenter has brought an 8-mm tape, but you have a VHS video player.

Typical Difficulties with Microphones

- ▲ The microphones do not work, or are intermittent, or produce deafening squeaky feedback.
- ▲ A microphone is attached to a podium when presenters need lapel or cordless microphones.
- ▲ A speaker tries to speak without a microphone, but doesn't have a strong enough voice. Members have trouble hearing and hesitate to complain.
- ▲ A speaker speaks too close to the microphone (deafening sound), or speaks too far from it, or moves back and forth so that his or her voice projects intermittently.
- ▲ There are no microphones available. Perhaps someone reassured you of good acoustics, but they did not count on the noisy fan turning itself on halfway through the meeting, with no one knowing how to turn it off permanently.

Catering Arrangements

When people are asked to describe a bad meeting, they often complain about the quality and quantity of the food and beverages. Since you don't want such complaints to ruin an otherwise perfect meeting, you need to arrange for catering that will make your members comfortable and satisfied. With the culinary discomforts out of the way, members will be better able to focus on the issues at hand. Yes, catering will cost you some money, but treat it as a good investment. This section covers the following topics:

- ▲ Typical complaints about catering
- ▲ General tips for catering arrangements
- ▲ Who should provide the catering
- ▲ How to work with outside caterers

Typical Complaints About Catering

- ▲ No muffins (or doughnuts, or yogurt, or whatever).
- ▲ Cold or old or weak coffee, no decaffeinated coffee or tea, and no herbal varieties.
- ▲ Warm soda or juices.
- ▲ Dietary needs of members are not accommodated.
- ▲ The same boring menu every time.
- ▲ The food arrives late.
- ▲ The service is too slow (in case of a sit-down meal).
- ▲ There is only one buffet lineup and only half an hour for lunch (more lineups would have helped).
- ▲ Catering staff is rude; they appear to be under stress or just do not care about your meeting.
- ▲ The hot and heavy food is delicious, but puts members to sleep in the afternoon.
- ▲ A meeting is scheduled for 5:30 to 8:00 P.M., and only coffee and cookies are served.

General Tips for Catering Arrangements

- ▲ The amount of catering will depend on the length of the meeting, the expectations of the members, and your budgetary constraints.
- ▲ Don't overdo the catering by being too lavish. People are coming for a meeting, not a gastronomical experience. Keep it simple, light, fresh, nutritious, balanced, tasty, and appealing.
- ▲ See if you can introduce variety and creativity to your menu selection, e.g., ethnic meals, international desserts, or a potluck arrangement.
- ▲ Find out about special dietary needs of members and see what can be done to accommodate them. If you can't, let them know in advance, so they can make their own arrangements.
- ▲ Avoid (or ask your caterer to avoid) the following:
  - ▲ Extra spicy food (unless you provide non-spicy alternatives)
  - ▲ Very fatty food or condiments, e.g., creamy sauce, heavy pastas, sandwiches with excessive amounts of butter and mayonnaise, six types of rich cakes that everyone will want to sample (one of each), etc. You want them to stay awake and alert.
  - ▲ Food with lots of garlic, raw onions, and other ingredients that leave a strong aftertaste and overpowering breath.
  - ▲ Food that looks like it's been sitting outside for a day or longer. If it does look this way, remove it. It is better to be safe than sorry.
- ▲ It is best to avoid serving alcohol before a meeting, since it tends to reduce alertness and focus.
- ▲ If you serve alcohol at all, do so after the meeting, but limit the amount served, and make sure there are designated drivers and that no one drives away impaired. You want them to arrive home safe and sound, and you also want to avoid any question about liability for injuries suffered as a result of on-the-job drinking.
- ▲ It generally works better to have buffet-style meals, since they provide more flexibility and less concern about speed of service by catering staff. Sit-down meals are more appropriate for large gatherings, when lining up would be too time consuming.
- ▲ If you choose buffet style and want to shorten your meal break, ask the catering manager to set up more than one lineup. This will enable people to move more

quickly, and will help you shorten the break and increase the likelihood of re-starting the meeting on time.

Who Should Provide the Catering

Here are a few options on who should provide the catering for your meeting:

- Each member may bring their own food and beverages. This would apply if the meeting is held over lunch or dinner and you cannot afford to pay for outside catering. Advise members in advance to bring a brown bag.
- Members can take turns bringing refreshments or finger food to share, or they can bring potluck.
- You can provide the beverages only and ask members to handle the food themselves.
- You can order food and beverages through an outside caterer.

How to Work with Outside Caterers

If you hire an outside caterer, here are a few things that you should consider:

- Choose a caterer who is known for reliability and quality. Check references if needed.
- Specify exactly what you need and at what time, and allow a "buffer" to be on the safe side, e.g., if your lunch break is at noon, ask for the food to be set up by no later than 11:50 A.M.
- Never assume anything. Ask the caterer to confirm your instructions. It may also be advisable to document your requirements in a written contract.
- Let the caterer know it's OK to enter the room even if the meeting is in progress, but to do so quietly. Ask him or her to subtly signal to you when the food is ready.
- Give the caterer feedback after the meeting. Acknowledge good service and suggest improvements when needed. They deserve and would likely prefer to receive the feedback directly from you, rather than hearing from someone else that you complained about them.
- Don't forget the small details, like asking for plates, cups, cutlery, napkins, sugar, cream (and possibly low-fat milk), and water jugs (or bottled water if the tap water is highly chlorinated or unsafe to drink).

Example: A Caterer's Predicament

In one meeting lunchtime arrived, but lunch did not. Members assumed that the caterer was delayed and continued with the meeting. At 12:45 someone went outside to make a phone call, only to see the caterer waiting anxiously with all the food. He apparently was waiting for an hour and did not think it was OK to enter and interrupt the meeting. By then the food was cold.

Invitation Master's Checklist

The invitation master's tasks are to establish who should be invited to a meeting and communicate with all invitees. Some planning coordinators perform these tasks themselves, but they can easily be delegated to another member. This section covers the following topics:

- Who may need to be invited to a meeting
- Potential reasons for excluding someone from a meeting
- Dealing with absences
- Communicating with group members
- Communicating with external speakers and advisers
- Preparing a guest speaker's introduction
- Preparing to formally thank a guest speaker
- Communicating with observers and visitors

Who May Need to Be Invited to a Meeting

- Members of the group.
- Individuals with unique knowledge or expertise that can help the group make good decisions.
- Individuals who are known for their creativity and visionary approach, and who are bound to enrich the discussions and boost the quality of the decisions.
- Representatives of groups who will be significantly affected by the outcomes of the meeting (internal or external stakeholders).

- ▲ Individuals who are likely to be involved in implementing the group's decisions. They can offer practical input and prevent unrealistic decisions from being made.
- ▲ Decision makers or individuals with clout and connections that are essential to the group and the decisions made at this meeting.
- ▲ Stakeholders who could block or undermine the decisions if not included at the meeting.

Potential Reasons for Excluding Someone from a Meeting

- ▲ The person's potential contribution to the meeting is marginal or nonexistent.
- ▲ The person has no interest or commitment to the group's work.
- ▲ The person is preoccupied with other priorities and is unlikely to give the issues the full and focused attention they need.
- ▲ The person is on the invitation list for no reason except that he or she has always been at meetings, or he or she would be offended if not invited.
- ▲ The person's presence will intimidate people and stifle discussions (e.g., an authority figure or an outspoken or intimidating person).
- ▲ The person has a personal conflict of interest (COI) and stands to personally gain from the group's decisions (see Chapter 5 for personal COI guidelines). This individual may need to be excluded from part of the meeting.

Sample Script: "You Don't Need to Be There"

"Robin, as you know, we've been reorganizing our meetings and making sure that we only invite people who have a direct contribution to make. The next meeting does not involve you in any way, so you don't need to attend. I will send you the minutes of the meeting so you know what we did."

Sample Scripts: "It's Best if You Don't Come"

There are times when a member should not come to a meeting, even if she or he has an important contribution to make. For example, this member is ill or has a family emergency. Here are sample scripts for such members:

"Heather, it's wonderful that you are so dedicated and still want to come to the meeting, but it's best if you don't. You don't want to take a chance on passing your cold to other people. You'd better take care of yourself and give your body a rest. So why don't you stay home and have lots of chicken soup and orange juice. We'll use the report that you prepared, and we'll send you updates on any progress. Take care of yourself."

Or:

"Jeremy, it's very nice that you are so conscientious, but no one in their right mind would expect you to come to a meeting when your wife just had a new baby today. Why don't you take the day off and pass your report on to Dan to present to us. Come back as soon as you're ready. Congratulations !!"

Dealing with Absences

If someone is unable to attend a meeting, the invitation master should notify the planning coordinator, who will do one of the following things:

- ▲ See what can be done to bring the absent member's input to the meeting, so the decision-making process could still benefit from his knowledge, skills, and insights.
- ▲ Contact the member after the meeting and update her about progress and about anything that she needs to do.
- ▲ If the absence is chronic, contact the member and check about his or her commitment level to the group and its work.

Communicating with Group Members

Having established who should be at the meeting, the invitation master should do the following:

- Prepare the notice of the meeting.
- Assemble the meeting package.
- Send the notice and the package to the meeting participants.

Preparing the Notice of the Meeting

The notice of the meeting is a cover letter, inviting every participant to the meeting. The notice may include some or all of the following:

- A welcoming note.
- The purpose and nature of the meeting.
- The time, date, and place of the meeting.
- Dress code (e.g., casual, informal, formal).
- Information about the meeting location, e.g., a map or directions on how to get there; where to park (and alternatives if the parking lot is full); parking fees and accepted method of payment (cash, coins, or charge cards); public transit lines, schedules, and fares.
- Where in the building the meeting room is located.
- An indication of catering arrangements, e.g., lunch provided, or bring a brown bag, etc.
- A request to confirm any special dietary requirements with the logistics master.
- A request to confirm attendance (RSVP) or absence (regrets) by a certain deadline.
- A request to presenters to confirm any required audiovisual aids with the logistics master.
- A reminder to arrive on time and to be there for the full duration of the meeting.
- A request to switch cellular phones off and to arrange for someone to take messages. Members should only be alerted in the event of an emergency.

Example of a Meeting Notice

To: The members of the human resources committee
From: Dave Rowland, Committee Chair

Date: November 4, 2002

RE: November 18th meeting

Dear members,

I am pleased to invite you to our next committee meeting. We have several policy issues to address, as shown in the enclosed agenda and package. Some of the issues are challenging and may be contentious, but I am confident that, as we did in the past, we will be able to work together, as a cohesive team, to achieve the best results for the company.

Here are some essential details about the meeting:

Date: Monday, November 18, 2002

Time: 8:45 A.M.: Networking and refreshments
9:00 A.M. sharp: Meeting begins.
Estimated closing time: no later than 3 P.M.
(leaving plenty of time for those who want to go to the hockey game)

Dress code: Casual

Beverages and refreshments and a light lunch will be provided.

If you're unable to attend, contact Rick Smith ASAP (contact information enclosed).

Place: As a departure from past traditions, the meeting will be held at the Ramada Hotel at 444 Seventh Avenue West, in the Explorers Room. Driving and parking instructions, as well as public transit information, are attached. Please plan to be there for networking and refreshments at 8:45 A.M., so we can start the meeting at 9:00 A.M. sharp.

As a reminder, we need everyone to participate actively and fully, without any distractions. In light of this, please do the following:

- Plan to turn off your cell phone while the meeting is in progress.
- Let your secretary or message center know that there will be a refreshment break from 10:15 to 10:30 and a lunch break from noon to 12:45.

Please contact Jim Jones about any audiovisual aids that you need and about special dietary requirements. Please contact our meeting facilitator, Leslie Smith, if you have any questions or concerns about the meeting. Jim and Leslie's contact information is enclosed.

I am looking forward to working with you on November 18th.

Preparing the Meeting Package

A package of reports and other documents is essential to quality decision making. Here are the documents that you may need to send to each meeting participant:

- ▲ The notice of the meeting (see previous section).
- ▲ The meeting agenda.
- ▲ Minutes of the last meeting, as a reminder of what was done and what follow-up actions each member agreed to take.
- ▲ Progress reports.
- ▲ Reports that relate to specific agenda items, and which specify research and analysis that was done on the issues at hand.
- ▲ Decisions that need to be made at the meeting.
- ▲ Options for decision making, possibly with a pro-con analysis of each option.

Here are a few tips to consider when preparing the meeting package:

1. The package should not be excessive. It should contain only the documents that are essential to the meeting. If low-priority documents are to be included, they should be at the end of the package and should be flagged as optional reading.
2. The package should be well organized. Here are a few tips to consider:
   - ▲ Include a cover sheet that lists the documents included in the package. The order of documents in the package should match the sequence on the agenda, to make it possible to follow the reports and the agenda at the same time.
   - ▲ Consider color coding the various documents. If you do so, explain the color code in the cover sheet. For example, use blue paper for financial issues, green for environmental, etc.
   - ▲ Consider packaging the documents in a binder (rather than having them loose or wrapped with a rubber band), with colored tabs at the start of each document.

3. The documents in the package should be reader-friendly, so members can find relevant information quickly and easily (see report writer's checklist in this chapter).

Sending the Meeting Package

1. The meeting package should be sent to all members in sufficient time before the meeting, allowing them to:
   - ▲ Review and comprehend the documents.
   - ▲ Contact the author of a document for clarification.
   - ▲ Raise concerns about the meeting with those who can address them. For example, is the agenda too ambitious for the available time? Is a certain agenda item truly relevant to the group's mandate and worthy of meeting time? Is a certain agenda item of high priority? Is a certain item ripe for decision making?
2. The package can be sent by courier, mail, fax, interoffice mail, or as an e-mail attachment.
3. It may be advisable to contact some or all of the members before the meeting:
   - ▲ To check whether they received and reviewed the meeting package
   - ▲ To check if they have any questions about the meeting
   - ▲ To check if they have any suggestions to improve the productivity of the meeting
4. Confidential documents should be separated from nonconfidential documents and should be considered in an "in-camera" (closed) meeting and not in an open one. A confidential document should have a clear indication of the requirement to keep the information within the group (see Chapter 5 for confidentiality guidelines). This requirement should be printed on every page, to address the possibility that pages might get separated.

Communicating with External Speakers and Advisors

As the invitation master, you may be required to communicate with external speakers or advisers. To ensure that your group gets the most value out of an external speaker's presentation, you need to convey some information to him or her in advance of the meeting. You may also need to negotiate how the presentation would be customized to your group's needs. Here is some specific information that you may need to convey:

- ▲ Background about your organization and its mission statement.
- ▲ Background about the group, its mandate, and culture (see Chapters 3 and 6).
- ▲ The dynamics of your group, the individuals involved, their work and interests.
- ▲ Why the group is looking forward to hearing from the speaker.
- ▲ Why the topic is relevant to the group and what impact it has on its work.
- ▲ The problem your group is facing and the advice members expect from the speaker.
- ▲ The issues that should be addressed and the questions that should be answered.
- ▲ The presentation style and content preferences of your group, e.g., the group may prefer a straight lecture or it may prefer a fully interactive discussion or it may want something in between. The group may like certain types of examples and case studies (e.g., industry-related) and may find others irrelevant.
- ▲ The things your group appreciated about past guest speakers.
- ▲ The things members did not appreciate about some experts in the past. For example, pushing their views without paying attention to the group's unique circumstances, lecturing for too long, taking too much time to answer a question, trying to appease every questioner, etc. But don't overdo it, or the speaker may feel so uptight that it will affect the quality of his or her presentation.
- ▲ Emphasize again that the group is looking forward to the presentation.

If you are sensing that the speaker is not confident that she or he can meet your group's expectations, ask why. You may need to offer help or reassurance. Conversely, if it becomes clear that this is the wrong speaker for your group, you may need to look for another speaker.

You may need to negotiate the speaker's fee. Will it be a flat fee or will she charge by the hour? If it is the latter, establish whether you will be billed only for presentation time or also for preparation and travel time. You may want to invite her to come for only a part of the meeting, to avoid extra costs. You may also need to establish whether there are any additional costs, such as travel and incidental expenses.

If you agree on the speaker coming to your meeting, you will need to ask him a few questions:

- Find out about his background, so you can properly introduce him to your group (see below for a sample speaker's introduction).
- Find out about any audiovisual aids required for the presentation, and put the speaker in touch with the logistics master.
- If the speaker is invited to join your group for a meal and has agreed to do so, find out whether he has any special dietary needs.

Finally, you need to give the speaker information about the meeting:

- The meeting notice, agenda, and the documents that are relevant to the speaker
- Instructions on how to get to the meeting location, how to park, and how to find the meeting room
- What time the speaker is scheduled to speak and for how long, and whether this includes the time for questions and interactive discussion following the presentation
- How the speaker's presentation will be kept within the allotted time (e.g., alerted that ten minutes are left, etc.)

Preparing a Guest Presenter's Introduction

To properly introduce the speaker to your group, you will need the following information:

- The speaker's unique qualifications, skills, and expertise relating to the topic
- Any noteworthy achievements, especially those that relate to the topic at hand
- Any books or articles published by the speaker on the topic
- Interesting and intriguing facts about the speaker
- How the speaker pronounces his or her name

With the above information, you can prepare to introduce the speaker to your group. Here is a sample speaker's introduction:

> *"I am pleased to introduce to you our guest speaker. Fred Speer will address emerging trends in telecommuting, a subject that we have been considering for a while. Fred's presentation is about twenty minutes long, and afterwards there will be ten*

minutes for questions. [Note: This is a subtle reminder to the speaker and the audience about time constraints.]

"Fred is well qualified to speak on this topic. He is ____. He has ____ (list his qualifications and achievements). Based on my discussion with Fred before the meeting, I believe you can look forward to an intriguing and thought-provoking presentation. Please welcome Fred . . ."

Here are a few mistakes to avoid when introducing a guest speaker:

▲ Don't make the introduction too long. The presentation is for the speaker to make, not for you. A speaker's introduction should be brief and to the point, no more than about a minute.

▲ Avoid arguing in favor of or against the speaker's points before he or she has made them.

▲ Avoid describing the speaker in unusually flattering language, making it sound as though an angel has just descended upon the meeting. Flowery introductions make speakers uneasy.

▲ Avoid mispronouncing the speaker's name or including incorrect information in your introduction.

Preparing to Formally Thank a Guest Presenter

One of the fine touches often missed in meetings is a thank-you comment to the speaker. Here are a few of the things that you could say and do in your thank-you remarks:

▲ Acknowledge the speaker for the information and advice offered.

▲ State what you have personally learned from the presentation.

▲ State how you believe the group has benefited from the presentation.

▲ State the potential impact of the presentation on the group's work in general.

▲ Possibly give the speaker a token of appreciation.

Here is a sample thank-you comment:

"Thank you, Fred, for this presentation. I believe I can speak on behalf of everyone here by saying that the material you gave us

is highly relevant to our group's work. I personally learned a few things, such as: ____ (highlight key points, but make it brief). You certainly left us with some food for thought today, and we appreciate you coming to speak to us. On behalf of our group, here is a token of our appreciation. Thank you very much."

Make your thank-you comments sincere. Don't dwell on about the presentation if it was less than satisfactory. If the presentation did not go well:

▲ Be courteous and keep your thank-you comments to the essential minimum (or omit them altogether).

▲ After the meeting, see if you can find the right opening to give the speaker some feedback. The speaker will likely appreciate hearing the feedback directly from you than being given the cold shoulder.

▲ It will be essential to give feedback to the speaker if the individual is to do any follow-up work for your group. For example:

"Fred, can I see you privately for a moment? I need to give you some feedback on your presentation, especially since our group may want to consider hiring you again in the future. There are some things about your presentation that worked well and there are some things that didn't. The things that worked are ____. The things that did not work so well are:

"We asked you to cover the subject of ____ specifically, and it somehow got missed.

"When people asked you questions about the subject of ____, it came across as though you were getting a bit impatient with them. In my view, this reaction detracted from the quality of the presentation and the discussions. It would have worked better to hear them out before answering their questions.

"Is my feedback helpful?"

Communicating with Observers and Visitors

In some meetings observers and visitors are allowed to attend. For example, a municipal council may be required to allow citizens to observe meetings. Often visitors don't know what is expected of them, whether they can participate, and, if so, under what protocol.

The invitation master should address this problem by compiling a welcome package for observers and visitors. This observer's package should be sent to them in advance of the meeting, or be given to observers as they come in. The observer welcome package may include the following:

- A welcoming letter.
- An explanation of the meeting's agenda and how it is set to unfold
- Some background on the issues to be discussed by the group
- Where guests are to be seated
- When and under what protocol guests may participate in the meeting

Example: Observer Guidelines

The following is an example of observer guidelines for a municipality whose meetings are open to the general public. It can be changed to suit the needs of your group:

Dear Attendee:

Thank you for coming to this meeting. We welcome members of the community who are interested in the work of their elected officials. We appreciate and value any input that you may have for us. Here are a few things to keep in mind:

- Guests and observers are seated in the public gallery and are not allowed to approach elected officials in person while the meeting is in progress.
- We need quiet surroundings to focus on the business of the community. Please assist us by avoiding side conversations and spontaneous vocal responses, such as rounds of applause or negative responses to our discussions.
- We welcome your comments during the twenty-minute "Public Comments" segment on the agenda, from 8:00 to 8:20. If you want to speak, we ask that you let the person wearing the "Greeter" badge know in advance, so your name can be added to the speakers' list.

▲ To accommodate as many people as possible in the twenty-minute segment, we ask speakers to keep their comments to no more than two minutes each. The mayor will let you know when your speaking time is about to run out. We generally allow a maximum of one comment per person.

▲ If you have a comment but prefer not to speak in public, or if there isn't enough time to accommodate you, we invite you to submit a written comment and deposit it in the green "written comments" box. The greeter has response forms for you.

We value and appreciate your attendance and participation in our meetings. You are helping us in remaining accountable to the community. Your feedback, verbal or written, will help us make better decisions on your behalf.

Report Writer's Checklist

As suggested in various sections in this chapter, planning a meeting should be a team effort, and as many members as possible should be given lead roles in meetings. This approach will likely convert more members from passive spectators to engaged and active contributors at the meeting.

One type of assignment is for a member to perform some research and analysis and prepare a report on a selected topic. Reports should generally be in writing. They should be circulated to the members in advance of the meeting and not at the meeting itself. Last-minute reports should be the exception and not the norm. Under this approach, each member can read and understand the reports, and is able to contact the author for factual or technical clarifications, if needed.

The report writer should consider the fact that other members are busy individuals, with full-time jobs, volunteer work, and a personal life. With this in mind, the writer should make the report easy to read and comprehend. The key points in a report should be easy to capture.

Here are a few typical mistakes to avoid when writing reports:

▲ Too much information, some of it being marginal to the decisions that need to be made.

▲ Unexplained technical terms and abbreviations.

- Long and aimless sentences and paragraphs.
- Boring and uninspiring content.
- Confusing flow and a fragmented structure.
- Decision-making options hidden in a mountain of information, virtually requiring detective work to find them. Is it any wonder that busy people just ignore such reports?

Here are a few ideas to make your report more reader-friendly and compelling to read:

- Make it simple, brief, concise, and to the point.
- Focus on the data that is most relevant to the group's mandate and to the decisions that need to be made. The goal should be relevance and quality and not comprehensiveness of data.
- Include a page numbering system.
- Include headers and footers to establish the context of the report. If a page is separated from the report, it will be easy to place it back.
- For a longer report (five pages or longer), consider including a cover page, a table of contents, and a brief executive summary, with a synopsis of the report and a concise point-format summary of the recommendations it contains.
- Highlight recommendations and decision-making options. Make them easy to capture by bolding, underlining, or boxing, using different font size and style and other techniques.

If the report addresses a highly technical topic, consider the following tips:

- Write the report to the reader's level of knowledge and experience.
- Wherever possible, replace technical jargon with plain language.
- Include a glossary of terms and abbreviations.
- Include examples and illustrations, to make the report more interesting and compelling.
- Some charts, tables, and graphic illustrations would be helpful.
- Convert long paragraphs into concise point-format summaries.

▲ You may want to take training in technical or business writing. Alternatively, you can ask for feedback on your writing style and suggestions from colleagues.

Here is an exercise for you to consider: Take a really bad report, and ask:

1. What are the key points made here?
2. What are the apparent recommendations?

Then rewrite the report in reader-friendly format.

Sample Format for a Report

Report of the new premises task force

To be presented at the April 18, 2001, meeting of the senior management committee

Task force members:

▲ Tom Gingrich, chair

▲ Inga Schmidt

▲ Derek Chow

Task force mandate:

1. To interview internal stakeholders and find out about their office space needs.
2. To compile a summary of office space needs across the company.
3. To prepare a space requirements document, with input from a real estate adviser.
4. To request bids from real estate companies on a search for appropriate premises.

This is an interim report about the task force's progress:

▲ To date we have completed stages 1 and 2. Attached is a progress summary.

▲ We have begun to search for a real estate expert to help us in preparing a space requirement document. It is becoming apparent that our proposed budget of $5,000 for the expert is inadequate and should be increased to $6,500.

Suggested discussion at the senior management April 18, 2001, meeting:

- ▲ Review the progress summary and give the task force feedback on it.
- ▲ Vote on a recommendation that the budget for the real estate expert be increased from $5,000 to $6,500.

PRESENTER'S CHECKLIST

This section includes checklists and ideas for an individual who is planning to make a presentation at a meeting. The ideas in this section would be relevant to presenters from within your group and to outside presenters.

Involving members in making presentations in meetings has the following advantages:

- ▲ It engages them in the work of the group and makes them more proactive.
- ▲ It forces them to develop essential skills: thinking, analysis, writing, public speaking, and leadership skills.
- ▲ It allows the group to benefit from a presenter's unique insights, skills, and expertise.
- ▲ It allows the group to get to know its members better.
- ▲ It builds leaders for the group and helps in succession planning.
- ▲ It introduces variety to meetings.

In addition to your members, you can draw on external talent to make presentations to your group:

- ▲ Invite managers of other departments to explain how their departments operate and relate to your group or department. This approach can help break down internal "silos" and barriers to effective communications. It can encourage departments to work more collaboratively.
- ▲ Invite a representative of an external stakeholder group to speak to your group, e.g., a member of a customer group, your municipal council, an environmental group, a community group that has been critical of your company, etc.

- Invite an expert to speak to your group about a timely subject.

Here are a few typical mistakes for presenters to avoid:

- Making the presentation too long, monotonous, and dull
- Giving information that is not relevant to the audience
- Relying too heavily on written notes
- Relying too heavily on audiovisual aids, at the expense of interaction with the listeners
- Running out of time and skipping the question period

When preparing a presentation, you will need to consider:

- The content, or what you will say
- The delivery, or how you say it

If a great deal is at stake (e.g., you are making a presentation to your senior management team or your board of directors), you may want to rehearse your presentation and get feedback on it. You could do one of a few things:

- Rehearse the presentation in front of your colleagues, and ask for specific feedback on what works and what needs improvement.
- Videotape your presentation and view it privately or together with your colleagues.
- Take hands-on training courses on presentation skills.
- Hire a professional speech coach to give you personal feedback on your presentation.

The remainder of this section gives you planning ideas for the content and delivery of your presentation.

The Content of Your Presentation

When planning the content of your presentation, you will need to consider five factors:

1. Purpose and overall key messages
2. The material used
3. Scope
4. Structure and flow
5. Word selection

Purpose and Overall Key Messages

Establish the purpose and focus of your presentation by answering questions like these:

- Who will be present at the meeting, and why are they interested in this topic?
- What difference should my presentation make to the listeners individually?
- What difference should my presentation make to the group as a whole?
- If I could condense my presentation into a few one-sentence messages, what would they be?
- If the group were to remember just one thing about what I say, what would I like it to be?
- How can I make my messages relevant to their circumstances?

Example: Presentation on Employee Safety

Ron, a safety supervisor in a lumber mill, is preparing a presentation on employee safety for office staff. The purpose and key messages of his presentation are as follows:

Purposes:

- To present information on new safety procedures for office staff.
- To boost employee commitment to their own safety and the safety of others.

Key messages:

- Safety applies to everyone, including nonunionized staff members who do not work in the mill. This includes individuals who work in an office environment.

- ▲ Never take anything for granted.
- ▲ Never look for shortcuts that could compromise your safety and the safety of others.
- ▲ When in doubt, ask a question. There is no such thing as a stupid question, especially when it comes to safety. It is better to be safe than sorry.

The Material Used

In selecting material for your presentation, you may need to include:

- ▲ Simple plain-language explanations of important concepts.
- ▲ Research and statistical data to support the points you are planning to make.
- ▲ Insights and ideas that will engage the listeners and stimulate critical and creative thinking.
- ▲ Fresh ideas and new information, e.g., emerging industry and society trends.
- ▲ Interesting and relevant examples, success stories, and failure stories.
- ▲ Appropriate humor to lighten things up and introduce variety. Avoid ethnic, sexist, and religious jokes. Yes, some listeners may laugh, but others may be offended, stop listening, and miss your serious message. When it comes to humor, remember this: If in doubt, leave it out.

Common mistakes to avoid with the material you choose for the presentation:

- ▲ Too much theory and too few practical examples
- ▲ Material that is too dry and too technical

Example: Building a Presentation on the Group's Questions

Bill, an e-commerce expert who was invited to speak at a meeting, decided to replace his standard presentation with a different one. He interviewed the group's leader and some of its members in advance and asked, "What are your main questions about my area of expertise?" He then planned his presentation to address the questions, and opened it with this script:

"As you know, the subject of e-commerce is large, and I could talk to you about it for a long time, much longer than you have for me today. What I chose to do instead is this:

"Based on my interviews with some of you, I made a list of questions that seem to be the most relevant to your group. I will tell you what the questions are up front. Then I will address them one by one. When I finish, I will ask if there are any more questions.

"To cover what we may not be able to address today, I prepared a complete handout package for you, for follow-up and reference.

"Here are the five main questions that you asked me: ____."

Note: The above technique is even more useful when you are about to address an angry audience on a controversial topic. Consider the difference:

- ▲ If you give them your stump speech, they may be polite and pretend to listen to you, but your presentation will go "over their heads."
- ▲ If, on the other hand, you list their most significant concerns up front, and then address them one by one, you will have shown them that you understand their anger, and they will likely listen to you with interest.

The Scope

When planning your presentation for the meeting, you need to establish how much material would be reasonable to cover within the available time. You should aim to have quality, not quantity. Your goal should be to have a meaningful interaction with the listeners, not a full coverage of every detail. A good slogan to keep in mind is, "Quit while you're ahead." Here are a few tips:

- ▲ Find out how much time will be available for your presentation.
- ▲ Determine whether the time for your presentation includes a question period, or whether extra time will be available for questions and interactive discussion.
- ▲ If the allotted time is too tight for what you're asked to cover, see if you can negotiate more.

- If more time is not available, cut the lecture time down and keep the interaction time intact.
- Conversely, if you are given more time than you need, plan to have more time for questions and discussion. Another option is to advise the meeting coordinator of this, so the extra time can be made available for something else.
- Prepare a handout package or a written report. If you are unable to complete your presentation, the listeners will have backup material, or "a doggy bag to take home."
- Get to know your speaking pace (120 to 150 words per minute is probably a good pace). With this in mind, estimate how much information can be contained in the available time. Reading a double-spaced page should take about a minute and a half (unless you make the mistake of editorializing as you read through it).
- Avoid rambling. Just give a point, explain it briefly, then move on to the next. With a dynamic pace, you will avoid running out of time and "hitting rush hour," with five minutes left and half your presentation unfinished.
- If you end up in rush hour, don't attempt to rush the remaining twenty overhead transparencies. Stop the formal presentation part and move decisively to the question period. Plan to say, "I have more material to present, and all of it is covered in the handout material. Since we only have ten minutes left, it would be more productive for me to respond to your questions. Are there any questions about my presentation?"
- Plan your presentation so you can easily pull segments of it out if time runs out.
- Again, always plan to have a question and discussion period.
- If your presentation is long, you may want to pause every fifteen minutes or at the end of major segments for questions. But do observe the clock and move on from the question period to the next segment when needed.

Here are a few typical mistakes to avoid with the planned scope of your presentation:

- Trying to give too much information, at the expense of interaction with listeners.
- Assuming that you have plenty of time, then rambling and editorializing, then being surprised by the fact that you ran out of time and were unable to finish your presentation. Your listeners will be right to feel cheated.

- Going overtime and overstaying your welcome. Some facilitators may find the courage to interrupt you, but many will find this difficult to do. Remember the old adage, "It is better to leave your audience before they leave you." Some of them may actually leave the meeting. Others may become restless or get busy doing something else and stop paying attention to you. What's the sense of continuing to speak under these conditions?
- Locking into an argument or a string of follow-up questions with one individual and leaving everyone else impatient: "Get going, already!!" Don't hesitate to say, "We need to move on." This is not a popularity contest, whereby you try to please everyone. By pleasing one person you may be alienating everyone else. You need to learn to say no, graciously but firmly.

Example: The Rambling Professor

A group invited a university professor to its meeting. He lectured to them at length. With no time limit established, he spoke for a full hour. No one knew how to stop him. How would you suggest this be handled?

Here are the proposed solutions:

- Preventively, the planning coordinator should have agreed with the professor on a time frame before the meeting began. The planning coordinator should have also established how the professor would be notified if time was running out.
- Given that this preventive work was not done, the meeting facilitator should have gently interjected and indicated that time was running out. For example, "Professor Higgins, I have to interject. How much time do you need to conclude? We have other agenda items to address. Would ten minutes be enough? Thank you."

Example: Robbed of Your Time Allotment

You were given a time frame of thirty minutes to speak at a meeting and prepared your presentation accordingly. However, because of the way the meeting was run, the facilitator says you only have fifteen minutes. How would you address this situation?

The possible solutions:

- ▲ Having observed that the time for your presentation was approaching, you should have gently reminded the facilitator of this and asked whether it was realistic to expect to start on time.
- ▲ Anticipating this situation, you should have planned your presentation to be flexible, so you could deliver its essential parts in less than the full time allotment. In other words, your presentation would consist of a prioritized list of topics. The first priority are topics that you must address, and the second priority are topics that you will address if you have time.
- ▲ You could always skip the planned presentation, give them the handout package, state your key points briefly, and facilitate a fifteen-minute question period.

The Structure and Flow of Your Presentation

Your presentation should flow logically and be well organized.

- ▲ Divide the presentation into distinct segments, so listeners will only need to focus on one of them at a time. For example, "There are three parts in my presentation: Economics, people, and systems. I will speak about each one of them for five minutes, and will then have a ten-minute question period. Let me start with the economics."
- ▲ Each segment could include an argument, and then an example or a success or failure story to substantiate it.
- ▲ Build clear transitions between segments, letting the listeners know one segment is over and the next one is about to begin. For example, "So far I have covered the ethical issues. Next I will address the economic issues."
- ▲ A good overall formula to consider for structured presentations is the sandwich approach: Tell them what you'll tell them, then tell them, and then tell them what you told them.

Here is an example of the structure for a three-segment presentation that is twenty-five minutes long, including transition statements between the segments:

- ▲ Introduction: "The main points that I'll cover in my presentation are the impacts of this proposal on finances, operations, and staff.

- First segment: "Let me start with the impact on finances." (Address it for five minutes, and give an example.)
- Transition to second segment: "I've covered the impact on finances. Let me move on to the impact on operations." (Address it for five minutes.)
- Transition to third segment: "Having covered the impacts on finances and operations, we need to consider the impact on the staff." (Address it for five minutes.)
- A recap and transition to question period: "I've covered the impacts of this proposal on finances, operations, and staff. Are there any questions?" (ten minutes)

If the segments of your presentation are long (e.g., thirty minutes each), break them into subsegments, and invite questions before proceeding from one to the next one. For example, "I've covered the impact on finances. Before we move on to operations, are there any questions so far?"

Make the sequence of segments logical. Here are a few options to consider:

- Start with the easiest or simplest segment and continue to the more complicated.
- Start with the past, move to the present, and then to the future.
- Start with the less controversial and continue to the most controversial, or try the other way around.
- Start with one extreme view, then discuss the opposite extreme view, and then discuss a reasonable middle of the road solution.
- Using PowerPoint or flip charts to list the main segments and subsegments is a great way to pace your presentation and reduce your dependency on notes. But the lack of notes can also lead you to ramble and editorialize and lose track of time. You'll need to be disciplined.

Here are a few common mistakes to avoid when structuring your presentation:

- Avoid leaving the most important segment for the very end, and then giving it very little time. Your listeners will be frustrated and disappointed with you, and rightly so.
- Avoid making some segments too long and others too short.
- Avoid having segments run into each other, without a clear transition between them.

Word Selection

In considering the words you use in your presentation, choose words that are:

- ▲ Simple and easy to understand. Use plain language whenever possible.
- ▲ Business-like, courteous, and respectful.
- ▲ Appropriate to the occasion.

Here are a few common mistakes to avoid with word selection:

- ▲ Avoid excessive use of technical jargon and abbreviations, unless you (1) explain them when you use them for the first time; or (2) treat the listeners to a list of definitions of technical terms and abbreviations you'll use in your presentation, and remind them of it when you begin to speak; (3) or are positively sure every person present understands these terms and abbreviations.
- ▲ Be sensitive to newcomers and guests and people for whom English is a second language. They may be too embarrassed to ask you to explain. Encourage them to interrupt you if they don't understand a technical term or abbreviation, and make it clear that "The only stupid question is the one you don't ask." Pay attention to facial expressions indicating confusion about what you are saying.
- ▲ Avoid repeated use of old clichés, like "going the extra mile." A speaker was once given feedback on the use of this cliché, and she modified it the next time to "going the extra 1,700 yards."
- ▲ Avoid using more words than necessary to convey a message; for example, instead of "at the present time" try "now."
- ▲ Avoid accusatory or condescending language. Instead of "You are failing to understand the following facts: _____", try "It looks like I may not have explained a few things well enough. Let me try again." The finger is pointing at you, and not at the listener. You come across as confident and accountable.
- ▲ Avoid street language or inappropriate words in a business environment.
- ▲ Avoid casual words that could be seen to trivialize a serious situation. Consider the following example of how the use of casual language can cause problems. After a major mine accident, the mine manager had a meeting with media reporters. He didn't know the number of fatalities yet, so when the reporters pressed on, he said, "It's too early in the game to have this data for you." The use of the words "the game" in the context where people's lives were at stake appeared to trivialize the serious event. You can imagine the next day's headline: "Mine managers play a deadly game."

The Delivery of Your Presentation

Having planned the content of your presentation to address the five content aspects in the previous section, you need to consider how you will deliver it. Your delivery should make the presentation appealing to the various senses. You need to keep in mind that people learn mainly:

1. *By Hearing*: Your presentation needs to have vocal appeal (sense of sound).
2. *By Seeing*: Your presentation needs to have visual appeal (sense of sight).
3. *By Doing*: Your presentation needs to be interactive (sense of touch).

In some instances, your presentation could engage the listeners through the remaining two senses:

- The sense of taste (if you're a chef and are describing a delicious meal, or have goodies to reward those who ask especially relevant questions)
- The sense of smell (if you are a scent expert or a florist)

Adding Vocal Appeal to Your Presentation

You need to project your voice, so the listeners in your meeting can hear you. If you have a soft voice or have any doubt that you will be heard (a noisy fan, poor acoustics, large room), there are various options:

- Ask the logistics master to arrange a microphone.
- Plan to ask people who have difficulty hearing you to move to the front of the room.
- Learn to project your voice and control your volume by breathing properly and by speaking through your diaphragm instead of your throat. Take voice training.

Speaking pace is another factor to consider:

- If you tend to speak too slowly, learn to pick up the pace.
- If you tend to speak too fast, practice slowing down and pausing after each point. Pauses will give you time to breathe. They will also enable your listeners to absorb what you've given them and get ready for your next idea.

You need to avoid speaking in a monotone and develop an animated vocal delivery. If you don't, you could put the listeners to sleep, regardless of how interesting your material is.

- Record yourself on audiotape recorder, listen to the tape, and determine whether your voice will keep the listeners interested or cure their insomnia. If the latter is indeed your goal, fine. If not, you need to add vocal expression to your voice. Record it again and work with the feedback.
- To develop an animated voice, try reading an interesting children's book aloud into an audiotape recorder and work with the feedback.

Try varying your volume, pace, and tone to emphasize key points. For example, instead of saying "Another point to consider is the fact that ____," try "The next key point to consider is this: (pause for separation, and then continue)."

You can also add vocal appeal by playing a video or music that relates to your presentation. You can try other creative touches, but don't overdo it.

Adding Visual Appeal to Your Presentation

Plan to dress to the occasion, e.g., if you are speaking at a senior management meeting, formal or semiformal attire will likely be required. On the other hand, if you are speaking to a meeting of community activists, you will come across better if you dress more casually (but not too casually).

Consider also the color of your attire. In one case, a female surgeon was describing a surgical procedure and did not understand why she was losing the audience's attention. It turned out that she was wearing a red dress, the color of blood. The association was too much.

Practice smiling when you express enthusiasm, but keep a straight face when you are discussing sensitive issues. Practice maintaining meaningful eye contact with listeners (but avoid staring at any one individual for an extended time. It will make the individual uncomfortable, and others will feel left behind). Evenly directed eye contact will help you achieve two things:

1. It will engage the listeners in your presentation.
2. It will alert you to signals of confusion or other feedback from your listeners, i.e., if someone appears confused, you may need to pause and say, "Did I miss anything?" or "Did I leave anyone behind?" or "Tom, do you have a question?"

Prepare visual aids if they will enhance the presentation, but do it in moderation. Here are a few tips that apply to all visual aids:

- ▲ Review the logistics master's checklist in this chapter for tips and for the advantages and disadvantages of using PowerPoint, an overhead projector, or a flip chart as presentation aids.
- ▲ Be mindful of technical pitfalls and vulnerabilities of the equipment you use. Communicate your requirements in precise detail to the logistics master and plan to come early to test the equipment. You don't want to waste precious meeting time figuring out how to operate your PowerPoint equipment (especially after you receive a glowing introduction and everyone is waiting with bated breath for your profound message).
- ▲ Always have a contingency plan, especially if you depend on power supplies and complex apparatus, in case of insurmountable technical glitches.
- ▲ Keep in mind that the visual aid is just an aid. It should not be the primary focus and should not overshadow you as a presenter.

Here are a few typical mistakes that presenters make with visual aids:

- ▲ An excessive use of PowerPoint, video, and overhead equipment, turning a presentation into a show-and-tell one-sided lecture, at the expense of interactive and free-flowing discussions.
- ▲ Using visual aids as toys and making them a goal in itself. The moment you find yourself doing this is probably the moment you should stop and ask yourself: Am I trying to impress them, or am I trying to serve their needs by giving them useful information?
- ▲ Using overhead transparencies with small and unreadable print, or too much print, and then daring to say, "I hope you can read this," knowing very well that there is no hope.
- ▲ Reading transparencies aloud, word for word, when they should be used only as aids, and when lengthy paragraphs should be replaced by a concise point-format presentation.
- ▲ When using slide presentations, mounting some slides upside down or sideways, or in the wrong sequence.
- ▲ Turning the lights down (and risking putting people to sleep), when the overhead screen is perfectly readable in a fully lit room. Listeners may resent the fact that the room is dark and they cannot read the handout package or jot down comments.

▲ Some audiovisual presentations have high entertainment value but are very low on substantive value.

▲ Turning away from the audience and speaking to the screen or the flip chart.

Planning Your Presentation to Be Interactive

Your listeners learn by hearing and seeing, but they learn even more by doing, or being engaged in the presentation. With this in mind, you need to make your presentation more interactive.

Here are a few ideas for making your presentation more interactive:

▲ Plan interesting case studies for the audience to analyze as part of your presentation.

▲ Prepare puzzles, trick questions, and fun exercises that relate to the issues at hand, to challenge them to think creatively and examine their beliefs and attitudes.

▲ Include stories and examples that the listeners can easily relate to, especially success and failure stories.

▲ Use a conversational style, as though you are speaking to each one of them, e.g., instead of saying, "A relatively unknown fact is that ____," use the second person (you) and say, "One thing you may not know about the issue of ____ is ____," or "You may find it interesting to know that ____," or "You can imagine how you might feel if ____."

▲ Plan to ask rhetorical questions: "Who would have thought that ____?" or "You can't help but wonder: Does it make any sense to ____?"

▲ Plan to give question-answer combinations "You may ask: Is it feasible that ____ would happen? Well, here is my answer: ____."

▲ Plan to ask survey questions, like "How many of you have ever ____? Please raise your hands if you have. Thank you. I see that I am among friends here." But don't overdo it, and don't get upset if they don't respond. Just move on.

▲ Plan to invite their questions and comments when you finish speaking, or after completing each major segment of your presentation, or throughout the presentation. Note: This option will present a time management challenge if you have a substantial amount of material to present. You'll need to learn to say no: "We need to move on. We have plenty more to cover. Please save your other questions for later or see me during the break."

A Speaker's Predicament: The Hanging Hand

A speaker was in the first five minutes of his presentation when he saw someone raise his hand and keep it hanging. He turned to the person and asked what the problem was. The individual asked a question about the presentation, and then engaged the speaker in a ten-minute dialogue. This continued, breaking the continuity of the presentation, and frustrating the other listeners. No one knew how to intervene and rescue the group from this overly enthusiastic member.

What could have been done?

- ▲ The speaker should have asked the individual why he was raising his hand. If it became apparent that the individual had a question, the speaker should have said, "Can you please wait with your question for another ten minutes? It may well be answered by then."
- ▲ Observing that the speaker was trapped in this dialogue and was too polite to say no, the meeting facilitator or any member could have interjected: "Can we please continue with the presentation and save the questions for later? I really want to hear the full presentation first."

SCRIPT MASTER'S CHECKLIST

In a small meeting with a reasonably skilled meeting facilitator the need for planned scripts is minimal. However, scripts can be helpful under the following conditions:

- ▲ The meeting is large.
- ▲ The issues are complex or controversial.
- ▲ The meeting facilitator is new at this task.

Planned scripts will help you address the noninteractive portions of the meeting:

- ▲ Launching the meeting (see Chapter 11 for a sample)
- ▲ Mapping out agenda items (see Chapter 12 under managing issues in meetings)
- ▲ Landing the meeting (see Chapter 14 for a sample)

Depending on the facilitator's needs, the following script styles can be used:

- Word-for-word format
- A point-format
- A combination, where some portions of the script are in word-for-word format and others are in point-format

This section covers the following topics:

- General tips for a scriptwriter to consider
- A sample word-for-word script
- A sample point-format script

General Tips for a Scriptwriter to Consider

In most corporate meetings the facilitator writes his or her own script. However, in some settings, scriptwriters or speechwriters are designated to assist leaders by writing their scripts for them.

Here are a few tips for the scriptwriter:

- Make the paragraphs short, i.e., no more than six or seven lines each.
- Use a large font size, to make the script readable. Try 14 point or even larger.
- Double space between the lines and don't overcrowd the pages. This will make it easy for the facilitator to make last-minute changes on the printed script.
- Make sure each paragraph begins and ends on the same page.
- Avoid long and awkward sentences that can make the facilitator excessively focused on the notes and less attentive to the audience.
- Insert bolded or underlined titles to separate agenda items.
- Use running headers or footers, to identify the group, meeting, and date on every page.
- Use a page numbering system, to help the facilitator deal with anxious moments, such as when the script gets mixed with other documents, or when the pages are out of sequence.

- Print the script on one side of the page only.
- If you staple the pages, do so in two places on the left side of the page: one staple about two inches from the top of the page, and one about two inches from the bottom of the page. This will enable the facilitator to turn the pages over like a book.
- The facilitator should review the script and make any adjustments to it. This should be done even if the scriptwriter has done it many times.
- If the meeting is large and potentially controversial, it may be useful to have a dress rehearsal, using the script as a guide. From time to time, you can "push the pause button" and discuss any concerns about the flow of the meeting. The script should be adjusted after the dress rehearsal to address any concerns.
- Avoid making the script so rigid that it makes the facilitator dependent on it and leaves no room to be spontaneous and interactive.

Sample Word-for-Word Script

Below is a sample script to launch a meeting. For a more elaborate script, see Chapter 11.

12:57 P.M.: Can everyone get their coffee and take their seats? We will start the meeting in three minutes.

1:00 P.M.: Good afternoon, everyone, and welcome to this meeting. It's a pleasure to be back with you after the summer break to continue our work on the corporate training initiatives. The agenda was sent to you a week ago. It starts with progress reports, followed by decisions on three new initiatives. We are scheduled to end this meeting by 4 P.M., with a fifteen-minute coffee break at 2:30.

We have a busy agenda. To keep us on track and on time, we'll need to participate by raising hands, not voices, stay focused on the issues, and keep our comments concise and to the point. Am I correct in assuming that all of you have turned off your cell phones and asked your secretaries to take messages for you? Thank you. Are there any questions or concerns about the meeting?

Sample Point-Format Script

Here is how the above script might look like in point-format:

12:57 P.M.: Three-minute alert

1:00 P.M.: Welcoming remarks

Purpose of meeting

Review of agenda

Projected closing time: 4 P.M.

Coffee break: 2:30 P.M.

Participation guidelines

- Raising hands
- Staying on track
- Speaking concisely
- Cell phones off?

Questions or concerns?

Minute Taker's Checklist

Many people dread the prospect of taking minutes of meetings. However, this task should not be as onerous as it is made out to be. In fact, it can be an opportunity to develop listening, summary, and writing skills. Instead of having the minutes always taken by the same person (the secretary), you may want to have various individuals develop skills in this area.

As the minute taker, you need to prepare for the meeting in some or all of the following ways:

- Review the section on minutes in Chapter 15 of this book.
- Review your group's previous minutes as well as any policies on minute taking. Feel free to suggest improvements to the way minutes are recorded.
- Review the meeting's agenda and all precirculated documents.
- Become familiar with the issues at hand and with any technical terms and abbreviations.
- Contact presenters and report writers and ask them to clarify points about which you are not certain. This will improve your ability to record key points and decisions made.

▲ Prepare a template of minutes with blanks to fill in during the meeting. Here is a sample, which you can customize to your needs:

Agenda item	*Discussion points*	*Decisions*	*Action items*
1. Minutes of April 11 meeting.			
2. Progress reports			
3. IT equipment			
4. Presentation by Dr. Shirley Jones			
5. Celebrating successes			
6. Next meeting date			

Talk to the meeting facilitator and establish how the two of you can work together to ensure that good minutes can be taken. For example, you can ask the facilitator to do the following:

▲ Ensure that only one issue is discussed at a time.

▲ Repeat and clarify proposals and decisions made before moving to the next item.

▲ Check whether you captured the consensus before forging ahead to the next issue.

▲ Let you know what is the best way for you to communicate any concerns or requests while the meeting is in progress, i.e., by interjecting, passing a note to the facilitator, or raising a cue card saying "Slow down, please."

Plan to be seated close to the meeting facilitator, so you can readily ask for help, and prepare an SOS list and share it with the meeting facilitator. For example:

If this happens at the meeting:	I need you to help me by saying:
There is chaos. Everyone is talking at once. Interruptions are rampant.	"Can we slow down? Dan is trying to take minutes. Can we have only one person speaking at a time, please?"
Members start with one issue and then move on to the next, leaving several loose ends.	"Before we rush to the next issue, Dan needs to record what we decided about _____."
A member says: "Let's do it." Everyone agrees, but it is not clear what IT is.	"Judy, when you say 'let's do IT,' what exactly do you mean by 'IT'? We need to record the precise decision in the minutes."
A member uses technical terms and makes assumptions on the level of knowledge and expertise of others.	"Phil, is there a plain language explanation of this idea? We need to make sure everyone follows the discussion, and that we can record simple minutes."
A member articulates an important proposal very fast.	"Toni, slow down, please. Our secretary does not have shorthand training. In addition, everyone should hear every word of this important proposal."

Variety Master's Checklist

The variety master's assignment is to find ways to vary the meeting and make it more engaging, interesting, and fun. Each meeting a different person can be appointed as the variety master. Here are a few planning tips for the variety master:

- ▲ Survey members for ideas on making meetings engaging, fresh, and fun to attend.
- ▲ Borrow ideas that have worked well in meetings of other groups or organizations.
- ▲ Review the section on variety and a light touch in Chapter 8.
- ▲ Coordinate with the meeting facilitator when and how your variety ideas will be used.

BOSS'S CHECKLIST

If a boss or another authority figure is invited to a meeting, his presence can be disconcerting and intimidating for some members, and may prevent or impede spontaneous and free participation. Worse yet, a strong-minded authority figure can dominate the discussions, making it awkward for the meeting facilitator to "rein her in" (after all, it's the boss . . .).

This section includes a checklist for a boss attending a meeting chaired by a person who reports to him. It also includes tips for the meeting facilitator in such cases.

First, here is what you, as a boss, need to do before the meeting:

- ▲ Get familiar with the group's work and mandate.
- ▲ Review the meeting's purpose, agenda, and materials.
- ▲ Speak to the facilitator before the meeting and clarify that he or she has your full support.
- ▲ Insist on being treated like any other member, despite your higher position.
- ▲ Plan to restrain yourself and listen more than you speak.
- ▲ Prepare a brief statement to make at the start of the meeting, asking members to speak freely, and emphasizing that your presence should not intimidate or constrain them.

Here is an example of a statement by the boss attending a meeting:

> *"Thank you for having me at this meeting. My purpose in being here is to listen to your discussions and get to know more about what you do. You have been doing important work and I can tell you that your management team is impressed. I should say I was a bit concerned that my presence here might make some of you less than spontaneous at this meeting. I want you to know that I've asked Trudy, your facilitator, to treat me exactly like any of you. I will speak only when needed, and I will take turns, like you do. So please be as creative and as spontaneous as you always are in your meetings. Pretend I'm not even here. . . ."*

Conversely, a planning coordinator or meeting facilitator who knows the boss will attend a meeting should contact him or her for an informal discussion of the benefits of the boss attending the meeting, such as:

- Gaining an appreciation of the group's work, needs, and concerns
- Being able to better represent the group at higher management meetings
- Offering information on the broad corporate perspective
- Building the relationship with the group

The facilitator should also discuss the following with the boss:

- What is the boss's role at the meeting? Will she just observe? Make a presentation? Take questions and feedback to management?
- What can be done to ensure that the boss's presence adds value?
- How can the facilitator and boss work together to ensure that the boss does not become the dominant focus for the meeting?

Here is an example of a statement from the planning coordinator or meeting facilitator to the boss:

> *"Dwight, can I talk to you about the next team meeting? Thank you. First I want to thank you for planning to attend. It's great you can make it. I see several benefits to you and the team in having you join us. I think it will help you get to know us better. It will also help us get some pointers from you about the broader corporate perspective.*
>
> *"I need to discuss one point with you before the meeting. As you can appreciate, with your position in the company, some team members may feel a bit shy about speaking up when you're there. We need to make it comfortable and safe for everyone to speak up and be as creative and spontaneous as they always are. Do you have any suggestions on how to achieve this?"*

Mentor's Checklist

If you were appointed as a mentor or coach for a relatively new member of your group, your preparation for the meeting may include the following steps:

- Contact your buddy and check whether he or she understands the issues scheduled for the meeting, and whether he or she needs any information or clarifications.

▲ Check if your buddy has any concerns about the issues or the decision-making process. If you can address the concerns, do so. If not, send the member to the person who can.

▲ If your buddy has a challenging assignment, give him or her the advice and support needed to conclude it effectively and confidently. The individual may need advice on report writing, making presentations, or facilitating interactive discussions.

▲ Avoid being overzealous about your role as a mentor. Your role is to assist and support the person on an as-needed basis. Your role is not to pester, lecture, judge, or impose your style on him or her. Don't make yourself a nuisance or hamper the person from developing confidence and self-reliance.

EXTERNAL CONSULTANT'S CHECKLIST

To make good decisions, a group may require the expertise and knowledge of an outside adviser, uniquely qualified to address a certain issue. As an external consultant, your planning for the meeting should include asking the following questions to help you learn about the group:

▲ Who are the members of the group? What are their areas of expertise?

▲ How knowledgeable are the members in your area of expertise?

▲ What is the "chemistry" and culture of the group?

▲ What caused the group to look for outside advice?

▲ How can you customize your advice to the circumstances of the group?

▲ How was the decision to hire you made? Was the group involved in making it, or was it made unilaterally by the group's leader?

▲ How receptive and open are the members to your advice?

Having learned about the group, prepare your advice and get ready to present it at the meeting:

▲ Prepare the best professional advice suitable for the group's needs and circumstances. Your objective is not to please people or tell them what they want or expect to hear. Your goal is to give them your professional perspective.

▲ Prepare to offer professional advice in a dispassionate manner, but fully respect the group's prerogative to follow or ignore it. Plan to avoid being judgmental, defensive, or too forceful when giving your advice. Here is an example of a script you could use:

> *"Before I present my analysis and advice, I need to acknowledge a few things.*
>
> *"First, the areas I'll be discussing appear to be sensitive and controversial. My job is to give you my best professional advice, based on my experience and a careful assessment of the facts that you gave me. Some of the things I have to say may be difficult for some of you to hear. But it would be irresponsible and unprofessional of me to not say things for fear of how you might react to them.*
>
> *"Another thing to acknowledge is that my role is only to give you advice. It is your job to decide whether or not to follow this advice. I want to reassure you that I left my ego at home and that I will not be offended by anything that you choose to do.*
>
> *"With this in mind, let me proceed with my analysis and observations."*

CASE STUDY:

A Unilateral Hiring Decision Made by the Group's Leader

A group's leader believed his group did not have enough expertise to address a complex issue. He decided to hire Rita, an outside expert, to help out, but did so without consulting the group. Several members of the group were surprised to see Rita scheduled on the agenda. Some were insulted by the fact the leader thought they needed her advice. Their frustration ended up being directed at Rita, who was never notified of the problem. She felt like she had just walked into an ambush.

The lessons?

1. Given the group's sensitivity, the decision to hire Rita should have been made with plenty of advance warning and only after receiving input from the group. In an ideal setting, the group would have identified the areas in which it needed additional expertise, and would have had a say in how this need would be met.
2. Rita should have made it her business to find out whether the group knew she was coming and how it felt about her being on the agenda. She could have also asked to interview several of the members before the meeting, so her advice

would be based on a broader set of questions than the group's leader had given her. Such interviews might have defused the anger and suspicion towards her and might have made the group more open to his advice.

3. Faced with resistance to her advice and realizing the problem was the group's internal dynamics, Rita could have said something like this:

   "I can see that these issues are sensitive. Let me clarify a few things. First, if you don't want my advice I am perfectly OK to leave and come back at a time when you want it. On the other hand, I want to reassure you that, if you choose to have me stay, I will give you objective and professional advice. If you want, I can leave the room and give you time to decide whether or not you want to hear me today. What do you think?"

   The above statement would have likely defused the anger towards Rita and made it easier for the members to invite her to stay.

4. Rita should have given the leader her advice after the meeting:

   "Rudy, can I give you some feedback? It was quite a challenge for me to speak to your group, and I had a few obstacles to overcome before they were prepared to listen to me. I believe a part of the problem may have been the fact that the group was not consulted about inviting me. My suggestion for the future is that you ask for their input before bringing in experts. This would make it easier for the members and for any outside experts you invite."

Guest or Observer's Checklist

As a guest or observer invited to a meeting, you should prepare in the following ways:

- ▲ Learn about the group and its mandate (see invitation master's checklist in this chapter).
- ▲ Find out about the purpose of the meeting and get familiar with the agenda.
- ▲ Find out what is expected of a guest and what are your do's and don'ts.
- ▲ Find out whether it's acceptable for you to offer any comment or ask questions at the meeting, and, if so, what is the protocol for doing this. See earlier section on communicating with observers and visitors (under "Initiative Master's" checklist).

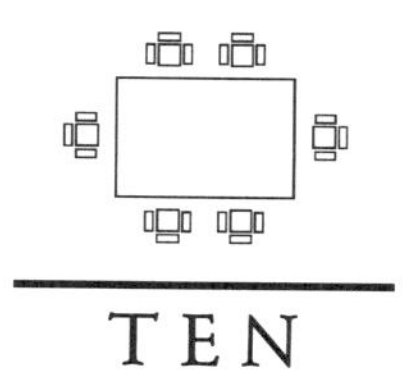

TEN

Preparing to Launch a Meeting

Now that you have defined what a good meeting looks, sounds, and feels like (Chapter 8), and planned it (Chapter 9), the day of the meeting has finally arrived, and it is time to reap the fruit of your labor.

Before launching your meeting, you need to make sure your engines are revved up, you have the fuel and supplies needed for the journey, and all crew members are positioned and ready to pull their weight (see Chapter 13) and help you steer the meeting to its destination (Chapter 12). Prelaunch activities are necessary even if you planned the meeting well, and even if you went as far as having an on-site dress rehearsal. You never know what unanticipated eventualities and nasty surprises might greet you on the day of the meeting.

This chapter covers the roles of key meeting masters in ensuring that the meeting can be launched without a hitch. Keep in mind that in many meetings one person may assume the roles of various meeting masters. The meeting facilitator may also be the logistics master and may also be the one greeting people as they arrive.

Specifically, this chapter includes the following checklists:

- Every participant's checklist
- Meeting facilitator's checklist

- Logistics master's checklist
- Presenter's checklist
- Greeting master's checklist
- Minute taker's checklist

EVERY PARTICIPANT'S CHECKLIST

As a meeting participant, you should act as a crew member, getting ready to pull your weight and contribute to the success of the meeting. Here are a few things for you to do on the day of the meeting:

1. Leave the previous events of the day or upcoming events that you may be anxious or excited about behind you. Focus only on your group and its mandate. The group deserves to have you at the meeting in body and in spirit, ready to give your full and undivided attention.
2. Make arrangements with your support staff or message center to free you to be at the meeting for its full duration, without being interrupted by messages (on cell phones or delivered by people walking into the meeting), except in absolute emergencies.
3. Turn off your cell phone, pager, mobile Internet access device, and other sources of distractions before the meeting begins.
4. Come to the meeting prepared, having reviewed the agenda and meeting materials and having followed up on any assignments that were given to you.
5. Avoid scheduling meetings back to back. Allow a buffer of at least fifteen minutes between this meeting and the next, to allow you enough time to tie up any loose ends at this meeting, and get organized and make your way to the next meeting. You want to arrive at the next meeting as fresh, relaxed, and ready to work as you did at this meeting.
6. Do what is needed to arrive at the meeting early (at least fifteen minutes before the scheduled start time). Consider the following:
   - If you are driving, allow extra time for heavier than normal traffic.
   - If you are driving, allow enough time to find a parking spot. Find out where to park, how much the parking costs, and what methods of payment are accepted by the parking meter or attendant. Bring enough change for parking, just in case the parking meter does not take a credit card. You don't

want to have to rush in and look for change, while being anxious about the possibility of getting a parking ticket or having your car towed away. It's not a good way to start a meeting.

- ▲ If you are taking public transit, allow for delays in published schedules or take an earlier bus, to be on the safe side.
- ▲ If you are giving a ride to other members, let them know when you will leave and make it clear that you will not wait for them if they are late.
- ▲ If you are car pooling with another member, be fair to your driver and don't keep him or her waiting for you.
- ▲ Conversely, don't look for a ride from someone who is notoriously late for meetings. If you have no option, let the individual know what time you must be at the meeting, and ask whether she or he can be depended on to get you there on time. If this is not workable, consider taking a taxi or public transit instead.
- ▲ Don't take an important phone call two minutes before you need to leave for the meeting.
- ▲ Just before you leave for the meeting, go through your briefcase and make sure you did not leave any important document behind.

7. If, due to unavoidable circumstances, you know you'll be late to a meeting or need to leave it early:
   - ▲ Let the facilitator know in advance of the meeting.
   - ▲ Ask someone to do any equipment setup for you before you arrive.
   - ▲ Ensure that your duties at the meeting are taken care of in your absence.
8. When you arrive at the meeting location, you will need to:
   - ▲ Find the meeting room. (This is not a trivial step. The risk of getting lost and finding yourself at the wrong meeting is real.)
   - ▲ Find a place to sit. Consider sitting in a different place every time, next to someone you don't know or haven't worked with.
9. Do what's needed to be comfortable at the meeting:
   - ▲ Dress appropriately and comfortably.
   - ▲ Eat something prior to the meeting, unless catering is provided (in which case, you should have told the logistics master about any special dietary needs).

- ▲ If the meeting is long and you prefer your own chair, bring it along with you.
- ▲ Go to the washroom.
- ▲ Have a glass of water in front of you. Have anything you might need at the meeting handy (e.g., medications, snack or other refreshment).
- ▲ Network with others.
- ▲ Get your documents organized in front of you.
- ▲ Make sure you have a functioning pen and blank notepaper, so you can jot down your thoughts as the meeting progresses. This will make it easier for you to listen without being distracted by your thoughts, and make it less tempting for you to interrupt those who speak. It will also enable you to prepare well-structured responses to the discussion ("I've been listening and taking notes, and I have four main points to make in response to what's been said. First, _____," etc.).

10. Attend to last-minute details that relate to your specific role at the meeting.
11. Talk to the facilitator if you have a question or concern about the agenda, and let the facilitator know if you are aware of potential trouble.
12. Lend a hand to the logistics master or others, as needed.
13. Be set, comfortable, and ready to go when the meeting begins. Find your place "on the canoe" and be there "with your paddle," ready to row.

MEETING FACILITATOR'S CHECKLIST

If you successfully delegated duties to the various meeting masters, your tasks as a meeting facilitator on the day of the meeting will be as follows:

1. Arrive early and position yourself in a good place to facilitate the meeting. Take a seat on the opposite side to the entry or exit door, so members will not be distracted by latecomers or those who leave early.
2. Work with the logistics master to ensure you have what you need:
    - ▲ Your own table with plenty of room for documents
    - ▲ A full water pitcher and water glasses
    - ▲ A good view of all participants

3. Ensure you have the facilitator's tools of the trade handy. For example:

   ▲ A few pads of paper and some pens (some of which you may need to lend to members who forget to bring their own).

   ▲ A flip chart, to help you record consensus in front of the group.

   ▲ Your own fresh felt pens, just in case the ones you prefer are not available or the pens provided by the facility are dry.

   ▲ Something to get everyone's attention with if several of them speak at once, interrupt each other, or ramble. You can try a soft-sounding train whistle or another unique noisemaker, something to tap a water glass (without breaking it), or a gavel (suitable for a formal group).

   ▲ Something to help you keep the meeting on time. For example, take off your wristwatch and put it in front of you. (If you keep it on your wrist and look at it in the middle of the meeting, other people will look at their own watches and be distracted.) You can also place a freestanding clock in front of you, or use an hourglass. If precise time limits are customary, try a stopwatch and possibly timing lights, e.g., green (one minute left), amber (thirty seconds left), and red (time's up).

   ▲ Tools to make it easy for members to complain if they are suffering; for example, squeaky toy animals, one for every few members. Red flags can be given out to allow members to visually signify their discomfort. Cue cards, such as: "Let get going," "Off the rails," "Need a break," etc., are another way to allow for complaints.

4. Be in touch with the logistics master, greeting master, and other members and see whether they need support from you or someone else. In large meetings, some groups designate a "runner," to run small errands for the meeting facilitator and other leaders before and during the meeting.

5. Obtain information from guest speakers and consultants, so you can properly introduce them (see Chapter 9 for a sample speaker introduction, under invitation master's checklist).

6. Talk to members as they arrive, to become aware of their mood and to find out whether:

   ▲ They are prepared for their designated assignments at the meeting.

   ▲ They are nervous about making a presentation and need a boost.

   ▲ There is a logistical problem or another challenge they need help with.

- ▲ They are aware of any development that may make it necessary to revisit the agenda or the approach for the meeting.
- ▲ There are any tensions or potential for trouble you should be aware of. If so, solve the problem or establish how it will be addressed at the meeting.

7. Confirm your expectations of speakers and report presenters, i.e.:
   - ▲ When they will speak and for how long
   - ▲ How much time will be available for questions
   - ▲ How you will notify them that their time is running out
   - ▲ Whether there are any topics they should pay special attention to or avoid
8. Close to the start of the meeting, check if those responsible for the first few agenda items are there. If not, you may need to make a phone call to find out where the member is. You should also be prepared to change the order of agenda items if needed, to avoid having everyone wait for the late member.
9. If you are anxious about running the meeting (i.e., you've never done it before, or the issues are contentious), here are a few tips for dealing with nervousness:
   - ▲ Minimize any uncertainties or potential for surprises by being as prepared as you can be.
   - ▲ Drink water, and go to the washroom if you need to. Do whatever else is needed to make yourself physically comfortable. Don't drink alcohol and don't overeat before the meeting.
   - ▲ Socialize before the meeting begins. This will boost your confidence and give you a feeling that you are not alone in facing this challenge. Interact with pleasant, supportive, and energetic individuals, and avoid people that make you nervous or sap your energy.
   - ▲ Think of meeting participants as people who truly want you to succeed. After all, a well-run meeting, under your capable stewardship, will benefit everyone.
   - ▲ Remind yourself of the group's mandate and the purpose of the meeting. Envision a productive and positive outcome. The more confident you are, the more compelling your leadership will be.
   - ▲ Keep in mind that you are not alone. If you are nervous about a controversial issue, chances are that others are feeling the same way. Acknowledging this shared sentiment at the start of the meeting can relieve tensions. It can also establish a common bond and a joint sense of purpose.

- ▲ Smile and remind yourself of your proudest achievements.
- ▲ Remember that things could be a lot worse.

10. Gear up for an on-time launch (see Chapter 11 for details on facilitating an on-time start for a meeting).

Logistics Master's Checklist

The more complex the logistical details of the meeting, the more important it is for the logistics master to arrive early (at least thirty minutes before the meeting begins). The greatest mistake is assuming everything will be as you expect and relying on someone else's word: "Everything will be just fine. Don't you worry about a thing. . . ." Always be cautious: "Thank you for the reassurance. At the same time, for my own peace of mind, there are a few things I have to check."

Specifically, this section covers the following topics for the logistics master:

- ▲ General tips for the day of the meeting
- ▲ Access to the room
- ▲ Reception area
- ▲ Meeting room condition
- ▲ Furniture
- ▲ Room setup
- ▲ Audiovisual aids
- ▲ Catering arrangements

General Tips for the Day of the Meeting

Here are a few general tips for the logistics master on the day of the meeting:

- ▲ Have a checklist of logistical details that need to be inspected or attended to.
- ▲ Arrive at least half an hour prior to anyone else, and even earlier if the logistical details for the meeting are complex. This means that if your meeting is set to start at 2 P.M., you should book the meeting room from 1 P.M. to make sure that you have access to it in advance of the start time.

- Go through your checklist and confirm everything is in place for the meeting.
- If there is a problem, arrange for someone else to make the adjustment. However, in some instances it may be simpler to make the adjustment yourself. Waiting anxiously for a hotel staff member to arrive may be just too stressful and upsetting. Save your energy for other things.
- Avoid getting so caught up in one small detail that you are ignoring other important tasks. If a logistical problem cannot be addressed immediately, put it on hold or delegate it to someone else, and carry on with the remainder of your checklist.
- If a logistical obstacle seems insurmountable, assess how essential it really is and whether the meeting can do without it or with an alternative approach, e.g., perhaps a flip chart can be prepared quickly to replace a nonfunctioning overhead projector or PowerPoint apparatus.
- Keep in mind that the substantive parts of the meeting are more important than achieving absolute logistical perfection (which is an impossibility anyway). You may need to prioritize. What is more important: the bells and the whistles (e.g., fancy graphics), or the interactive discussion?
- Remember that your task as logistics master is not over until the meeting is over. As prepared and as organized as you may have been, things do have a way of falling apart, e.g., members suddenly discover that the room is too hot and expect you to do something about it.

Access to the Meeting Room

For the meeting to be launched smoothly, members should be able to arrive at the building, park, and find the meeting room easily. Here are a few questions to consider on the day of the meeting regarding access to the meeting room:

- Was it easy for you to park? If not, you may need to alert the meeting facilitator of the difficulty and let him or her know it may be a challenge to start the meeting on time. You should also ask the facility's manager about parking alternatives.
- Is the door to the building unlocked at the time scheduled for your meeting? If it is locked (e.g., an office building after hours), you will need to have someone at the door to let people in or to alert security staff. You will also need someone at the door to let the catering staff in when they arrive.

- Is there easy handicapped-access to the room? If not, you will need to arrange help for handicapped members in getting to the room.
- Are there stairs but no elevator? If so, you will need to arrange help for elderly members.
- Is your meeting listed on the bulletin board? If so, is the listing correct?
- Was the meeting room easy to locate? If not, should you post signs?
- Should you have a sign outside the room directing latecomers to enter through the back door or to enter quietly, to avoid distracting everyone else?
- Does the door to the room open from the outside? (A latecomer or a member who goes to the washroom should be able to get back in without having to knock and distract everyone.)

Reception Area

In a larger meeting, you may need to have a reception area, where meeting participants can be greeted and registered. Items that you may require at the reception area include:

- A list of meeting attendees.
- Name tags or name tents (preprinted, but also blank ones in case names are spelled incorrectly, or in case unexpected people arrive).
- If there is a fee for attending your meeting, your list should indicate who paid and who needs to pay the full fee or part of it. You may also need a cash box, credit card machine and slips, change, and receipts.
- Meeting packages (agenda, meeting documents), in case they were not precirculated, and extra packages for members who misplaced their own copies or forgot to bring them. (Remind them to bring the packages next time.)
- New material that was not circulated to the members before the meeting.
- Printouts of PowerPoint slides or other presentations that will be made at the meeting.

Condition of the Meeting Room

Having arrived early, you will need to inspect the room and ask:

- Is the room clean and tidy? Were dirty dishes left over from a previous meeting?
- Is the room temperature warm enough? Too warm? Too cold? Is the room stuffy?

- Do the air conditioning, heating, and ventilation work?
- Where are the temperature and ventilation controls? Can you adjust them easily if needed?
- How noisy are the fans? Are these noise levels acceptable? If not, what are the alternatives?
- Can any windows or doors be opened to provide fresh air when needed? Conversely, can they be closed easily, to shield the group from outside noise?
- Does the room have curtains? If so, can they be closed easily (e.g., if the group needs privacy, or if the sun might be shining over their faces and they are not interested in a tan)?
- Are the lights bright enough? Are they too bright? Can adjustments be made? By whom?
- Can you dim the lights if speakers require it for certain presentations?
- Are there any flickering lights that would distract the group? How quickly can they be replaced?
- If a public address system is audible in the room, can it be turned off or, at least, can the volume be turned down? Is there any "piped-in" music that could be distracting?
- If a microphone is turned on in the room next door, does it project into your room?
- Is the room next to the kitchen with the overpowering smells of garlic and other scents? If so, is this acceptable, or should you be looking for remedial action or another room now?

The Furniture

- Are there enough chairs and tables for the group? If not, where can you get extra ones?
- Are any chairs or tables broken, squeaky, or wobbly? (You may need to test each one of them.) If so, can you find replacements? Where should faulty furniture be put, so no one uses it by mistake and gets hurt?
- Are the chairs comfortable? Too hard? Too soft? Too low? Too high?

7. The Room Setup

- Is the room set up to your specifications? If not, who can make the adjustments? (It may end up being you, hopefully assisted by your colleagues.)

- Is the room setup conducive to an interactive meeting, and, if not, what changes must be made now? You may need to place yourself in various parts of the room and ask: Is it easy to see and hear everyone else from where I am?
- Are there enough water glasses and full water pitchers with ice on each table? (Lemon slices in the water would be nice.)
- Is there bottled water in case the tap water is highly chlorinated?
- Have name tents been set up in case of prearranged seating?
- If you chose a U-shape setup: Is the U large enough to accommodate everyone? Conversely, is it too spread out, making the meeting physically fragmented?
- If you chose a round table setup: Are there enough tables? Are there too many of them? Are they too spread out? Are they too crowded? Does each have the right number of chairs?
- If you chose a theater-style setup: What can you do to prevent the back rows from filling first, with late arrivals causing distractions by coming to sit at the front rows? For example, you could start by setting up only the front rows, and set up new rows when they fill up.

Audiovisual Aids

This section covers premeeting work on the following audiovisual aids:

- PowerPoint or overhead apparatus
- Flip charts
- White board
- Microphones

PowerPoint Apparatus, Overhead, or Slide Projector

- Have you ensured that the computer, the projector, and the screen are properly set up, clearly focused and sufficiently tested?
- If presenters are bringing their own equipment, have you ensured that all cables are compatible, and that you have sufficient time for teardown and setup be-

tween presenters? (This disruption can be avoided by asking all presenters to e-mail their presentations to the logistics master, who can set them up, in the correct order, prior to the meeting.)

▲ Does the overhead projector obstruct the view of any attendees?

▲ Is the screen located in a place where everyone can see it? (You may need to walk to different parts of the room to check how visible it is.)

▲ Do you or the speaker have a contingency plan in case the apparatus does not function at the start, or fails halfway through? This could be done by having a backup flip chart presentation, or by using the printed copy of the presentation to guide the group through the discussion.

▲ Do you have additional lightbulbs for the overhead projector?

▲ Do you have extension cords or power boards?

Flip Charts

▲ Are there as many flip charts as you ordered?

▲ Are flip charts placed where everyone can see them?

▲ Do they have enough blank sheets of paper on each easel?

▲ Are the easels stable? (If they are wobbly, warn those who will use them, to prevent injuries.)

▲ Will people be able to flip the paper without it falling over? (If not, you may need to improvise, e.g., use masking tape to form a barrier preventing the paper from falling over. But do test your improvised arrangement. You don't want it to collapse in the middle of the meeting. Incidentally, given the low cost of flip charts, have you considered buying your own reliable one?)

▲ Did you ask those who have premade flip chart presentations to come early, so they can mount their presentations on the flip chart before the meeting begins?

▲ If several flip chart presentations are to be made, were they mounted on the flip chart in the right order? Is it easy to tell where each presentation begins and ends? (You may need to attach color paper clips to the first page of each presentation.)

▲ Are there enough felt pens of different colors? Have you checked each one of them to ensure that it is not dry?

White Board

- Is the white board visible from each part of the room?
- Is the white board clean?
- Are fresh erasable felt pens available?
- Is there an eraser?

Microphones

- Have the microphones been set up in the right places?
- Have you tested each microphone?
- Does someone know how to adjust the volume controls?
- Who is available to solve problems (such as deafening squealing)?
- Can you turn off the sound system altogether if it is nonworkable?

Catering Arrangements

- When are refreshments, beverages, and meals scheduled to be provided?
- You should check with the caterer on the day of the meeting to confirm any arrangements. Confirm that catering will be provided at least ten minutes before a scheduled break. Ask the caterer to let you know when they are set up, and to alert you well in advance if there is a problem.
- Did you let caterers know where to set up the refreshments (inside or outside the room) and whether they are free to enter the room while the meeting is in session?
- Were sufficient quantities of the required food and beverages brought in? How quickly can additional supplies be provided, if needed?
- Is the food fresh? If not, can anything be done about it besides complaining?
- Are the coffee and tea you ordered hot? Were the decaffeinated and herbal varieties brought in, and are they clearly marked?
- Are the sodas or juices cold? If not, can anything be done about it?
- Were sugar, artificial sweeteners, milk, and cream brought in for hot beverages? Are the milk and cream clearly marked?

- Were cups, glasses, plates, cutlery, and napkins brought in?
- Have members with special dietary requirements been accommodated?

PRESENTER'S CHECKLIST

Here is the checklist for a presenter on the day of the meeting:

- Arrive early and get yourself ready for the presentation.
- Work with the logistics master to set up and test audiovisual aids you require.
- If the audiovisual aid (e.g., PowerPoint apparatus) does not work or cannot be set up for maximum effectiveness, you may need a contingency plan, such as preparing a flip chart outline of your key points, or guiding the members through a printed point-format summary of your presentation. You may also want to have transparencies of your slides with you, so you can use an overhead projector as an alternative.
- Test the microphone (if one is used) and get comfortable with it. Don't try to be a hero and speak without one if the meeting room is large, the acoustics are poor, or there are members who are hard of hearing.
- Confirm how much time you have for the presentation, how much time for questions, and when you will begin speaking. Ask whether someone will time you or you will time yourself.
- Give your introduction details to the person who will introduce you. To avoid any nasty surprises (many people don't know how to properly introduce a speaker), write the introduction yourself. See Chapter 9 for a sample introduction under invitation master's checklist.

GREETING MASTER'S CHECKLIST

The greeting master may be the meeting facilitator, but this task may be delegated to one of your members. Why not have a different greeting master at every meeting? Here is the greeting master's checklist:

- Arrive early and get yourself set up for the meeting, so you are free to greet others.
- Greet people coming to the meeting, especially invited speakers, consultants, and guests.

▲ Explain the seating arrangements. Give guests your group's welcome package. For a sample, see Chapter 9 under invitation master's checklist.

▲ Give guests meeting materials and find out if they have any questions about the meeting.

▲ Usher guests and newcomers to the refreshment table and introduce them to members.

▲ Welcome guest presenters or advisers and introduce them to the meeting facilitator and to the person who will introduce them to the group.

Minute Taker's Checklist

Here is a checklist for the minute taker for the day of the meeting:

▲ Arrive early and sit close to the meeting facilitator, so you can pass him or her notes if you have trouble capturing the decisions made or the key discussion points.

▲ Sit in a place where you can see and hear every attendee. Some members mumble, and you need to see them to capture what they are saying.

▲ Ensure that you have a list of all attendees, with all the names spelled correctly, so you can record who was at the meeting.

▲ If possible, have a laptop computer, so you can record key points instantly.

▲ Obtain copies of any presentations, so you can follow along.

▲ Have a template for the meeting (based on the agenda and the decision-making options that were identified prior to the meeting), so you can record key points next to the respective agenda items. For a sample template see Chapter 9, under minute taker's checklist.

ELEVEN

Launching a Meeting

Having defined what a good meeting looks, sounds, and feels like (Chapter 8), having planned it (Chapter 9), and having prepared for launch (Chapter 10), you now must launch the meeting.

The effect of a smooth launch is to:

- Establish a positive, purposeful, and collaborative tone for the meeting.
- Break the ice.
- Have everyone on board, as committed, disciplined, confident, and informed participants.
- Establish clarity about the meeting's purpose and other parameters.
- Increase the likelihood of collaboration and teamwork.
- Entrench the principles of fairness, equality, and common sense.
- Reduce the likelihood of counterproductive behaviors and minimize their impacts on the meeting.
- Reduce interpersonal tensions and focus the meeting on issues.

This chapter gives you a smorgasbord of tools and scripts to launch a meeting. Keep in mind that not all of these tools will always be needed. Choose the ones that are relevant to your meeting. Specifically, the following activities to launch the meeting are described:

▲ Facilitating an on-time start

▲ Opening remarks

▲ Explaining the parameters of the meeting

▲ Establishing support for the agenda

▲ A warm-up activity

Facilitating an On-Time Start

Meeting time is costly, and every minute should be treated as a precious commodity. With this in mind, it is important to start the meeting at the scheduled time. This goal can be accomplished by a range of activities, some of which are outlined in Chapter 9 (see timing master's checklists).

Here are the steps to be taken on the day of the meeting to facilitate an on-time start:

1. Assuming most members are there, alert the members that the meeting is about to begin. Do so a few minutes before the scheduled start time: "Can I have everyone's attention please? We will start the meeting in two minutes, so please take your coffee or refreshment and go to your seat. Thank you."
2. You can be creative and get their attention by gently blowing a train whistle a few minutes before the start time, and then making the above announcement. This will help you start the meeting on a lighthearted note.
3. You can approach groups of members informally and ask them to take their seats, or you can send someone else to do it for you: "Can someone go to the hall and ask people to come in, please? We need to start this meeting."
4. If too many members are absent at the scheduled start time, you may need to do one or more of the following things:

   ▲ Let members know of the problem and ask their permission to start the meeting late: "Can I have everyone's attention please? It is 9 A.M., and we normally like to start on time. However, as you'll notice, many people are still not here, and I am told that there is a traffic jam on highway 15. Is it OK to wait for ten minutes?"

- ▲ While they are waiting, you can ask them to start thinking about one or two key agenda items and jot down a few notes about them: "While we are waiting, can you please review agenda items 6 and 7, and think about your responses to the following questions: ____?"

5. If it is clear that the meeting will be impractical to hold (e.g., a major snowstorm), you may need to reschedule it. If you do this, make a concerted effort to notify those who may be on their way. Call their offices or cell phones, so they stop struggling to make it to the meeting.
6. If it is reasonable to expect that absent members will arrive soon, you can start the meeting now by dealing with agenda items that do not require everyone's presence.
7. Avoid the mistake of just waiting and not giving an explanation for the delayed start. Those who arrived on time deserve to have the meeting started on time, or, at the very least, to be given an explanation.

OPENING REMARKS

In your opening remarks for the meeting, you may do the following:

- ▲ Welcome everyone to the meeting.
- ▲ Remind them of the overall mandate and where the group is in relation to it.
- ▲ Briefly state the nature and purpose of the meeting and what it is intended to achieve.
- ▲ Comment on the significance of the meeting.
- ▲ Briefly introduce guest speakers, advisers, and observers. Alternatively you can invite the greeting master or other members to make such introductions.

Sample Script: Opening Remarks

"Can I have everyone's attention please? It is now 2 o'clock and we need to get the meeting started. Good afternoon, everyone, and welcome to the monthly meeting of the information technology department of Idaho Telephone Company. My name is Denise Jang, and I am the assistant manager of the department.

"As you know, we have a tradition of rotating the chair among different members, so each one of us can be on the hot seat once in a while. It gives our manager Judi a break, and makes us develop leadership and facilitation skills. Today it is my turn to chair the meeting.

"It is also our tradition to state the mandate and the mission of our department at the start of the meeting, so here goes: 'The mandate of the information technology department is to develop innovative solutions to address our company's information technology needs, in order to enhance our company's competitive edge in the marketplace, help our employees work smarter instead of harder, and generally improve the efficiency and effectiveness of our operations.' We need to keep thinking about this mandate as we go through our meeting.

"So far this year we have advanced our mandate through the following initiatives: ____. For the remainder of this year, our focus as a department is on advancing our mandate by pursuing the following initiatives: ____.

"The purpose of this meeting is to hear and discuss progress reports from our various project leaders and to reach consensus on a few issues. Some of these issues are complex and difficult, and we need everyone's cooperation, support, and active listening so we can resolve them and make good decisions for the company.

"Before I explain the agenda for this meeting, I would like to ask our greeting master, Jack, to introduce a few special guests."

Explaining the Parameters of the Meeting

After the opening remarks, the facilitator should explain the parameters of the meeting, including some or all of the following:

- ▲ The time frame for the meeting.
- ▲ The participation protocol for the meeting, including, for example, how people are recognized to speak and how fairness is maintained. This is also the time to encourage members to speak concisely and explain if and how guests may participate.
- ▲ The desired climate and tone for the meeting and how members can help maintain them.

- Any logistical details that the members need to be aware of (catering, location of washrooms).
- Establishing how members can give feedback on the meeting.

Sample Script: Establishing Meeting Parameters

Here is a sample script to establish meeting parameters (continued from the above script):

"Thank you, Jack, for the introductions, and welcome to all our advisers and guests. Next I need to remind everyone of a few parameters for this meeting.

"First, the timing: As indicated on the agenda, we are scheduled to end this meeting by 5:00 P.M., or sooner if we are efficient. We cannot end later than 5, because people have other commitments to attend to.

"I am assuming that everyone has made the commitment to be here for the full duration of the meeting. We need you here, in body and in spirit, so we can benefit from your knowledge and ideas. In case you haven't already done so, please reach over to your cell phone and turn it off. Has everyone done it? Thank you.

"There will be a ten-minute refreshment break at 3:30 P.M., and you can follow up on any messages at that time."

The following text, to establish participation protocol, may be needed in a larger meeting, a smaller meeting where the members are working together for the first time, or a contentious meeting, where there is a risk of discussions becoming disorderly and chaotic.

"We need to establish a few participation guidelines, in order to give everyone a fair and equal opportunity to speak and to maintain good decorum. Here they are:

"First, we generally speak by raising hands and waiting for our turn to speak. Those of you who barge in will have to forgive me if I say 'Hands up please!!'

"Second, in order to give as many people as possible a chance to speak, we should make our comments concise and to the point. So please don't be offended if I show you a 'circle the field' sign or point to the hourglass as a gentle reminder to wrap up.

"Third, if you want to speak more than once on the same issue, I may need to ask you to wait while I check if there are any first-time speakers on it.

"I will follow these guidelines in a flexible manner, and I will need your support to run a good meeting.

"Feel free to complain in case I miss something or you notice a problem with the way the meeting is run or you think we're rushing through with a bad decision. You can use the squeaky toy animals to complain. They are there to remind you that 'suffering is optional.'

"Does anyone have any questions on the guidelines for the meeting? Can I count on your support? Thank you."

The following text may be needed when launching a contentious meeting:

"Before we get going with the agenda, we need to talk about the climate and tone for this meeting.

"As you know, the issues that we are scheduled to deal with are complex and sensitive and have created some conflict and difficulties for us in the past. Having said that, I am confident that we can work together and deal with these issues effectively and make good decisions for the organization.

"To achieve good results, our discussions will need to be hard on the issues, but soft on the people. We will need to treat each individual with respect and give him or her the same courtesy that we expect when we speak. If by chance your comments become personal, I will have to say something like: 'Please keep your comments to the issues, not the people.'

"My next comment is about listening. I hope each one of us keeps an open mind. Yes, we will need to speak, but, even more so, we will need to listen fully and give one another the benefit of the doubt. It was said that we were given two ears and one mouth, and that we should be using them in that proportion: listen at least twice as much as we speak.

"A wise person told me that diversity of opinions is something we should celebrate. If someone has a vastly different opinion than ours, we should not try to argue against it right away. Instead, we should learn from it, because it may represent another important piece of the truth. By building the bigger truth together, we stand to make decisions that are better, more credible, and more durable.

"Can I count on you to help me maintain a positive, respectful, and collaborative climate at this meeting? Thank you. I appreciate your support."

The following comments may be needed if guests or observers are at the meeting:

"For our guests and observers, you received our visitors welcome package. In it we say that we welcome guest comments just before the meeting ends. Despite this general guideline, if you see us doing something that you think is absolutely foolish, feel free to pass a note to me through Jack, our host who greeted you when you came in."

The following comments relate to the logistics of the meeting:

"As to the logistics of this meeting: There are complimentary phones for local calls only just outside the room. The washrooms are down the corridor to your right.

"Refreshments are in the back of the room. If you need to refresh your coffee or tea cup while the meeting is in progress, feel free to do so quietly, as long as not all of you do it at once."

The following text will remind members to give feedback on the meeting:

"In front of each of you there is a sheet marked "meeting feedback." As we go through the meeting, please make note of any observations about the meeting, positive or negative. At the end of our meetings we allow ten minutes for members to comment on what they liked about the meeting, and how future meetings can be improved. In addition, your feedback sheets will be collected and will be used when planning future meetings.

"Of course, your feedback is welcome anytime, and there are about 300 working days in a year to give it. If you see a problem with the decisions we make or how the discussions go, you can also let me know during a refreshment break or after the meeting."

Sample Meeting Feedback Sheet

Long Range Planning Committee, Visions Corporation Inc.

Meeting Feedback Sheet

Meeting date: April 19, 2002

1. On a scale of 0 (couldn't be worse) to 5 (couldn't be better), rate the meeting:

Assessment category	*Rating (0 to 5)*	*Assessment category*	*Rating (0 to 5)*
Appropriate agenda?		Did people listen?	
Courtesy and respect shown?		Fairness maintained?	
Good use of time?		Everyone pulled weight?	
Creativity and innovation?		Was it varied and fun?	
Quality decisions made?		Room and logistics OK?	

2. Specifically, what went well and should be repeated next time?

3. What did not go well and should be avoided next time? Any suggestions on how to do it?

4. What else can be done to improve the quality of our meetings?

5. Do you have new ideas that will keep our future meetings fresh and exciting to attend?

6. Your name (optional): ________________ Phone: ________________ E-mail: ________________

(If we know who you are, we can follow up with you for clarification of your ideas, and we can also acknowledge you if we use any of your suggestions)

Thank you for participating in this meeting and for taking the time to share your feedback

Establishing Support for the Agenda

An important part of launching the meeting is establishing the "road map for the journey," or the agenda for the meeting. By establishing support for the meeting's agenda, the facilitator ensures that everyone is "on-board" and understands:

- ▲ The meeting's overall destination (overall outcomes)
- ▲ Each segment of the journey (agenda items)
- ▲ The stops made along the route (breaks or interim milestones)

A good agenda would not be possible without substantial planning work done before the meeting. Review the agenda master's checklist in Chapter 9 for tips on designing agendas.

In order to establish support for the agenda, you may need to do the following:

- ▲ Briefly review the main agenda segments and how long they are estimated to take.
- ▲ Ask members if they have any questions or concerns about the proposed agenda.
- ▲ See if members' concerns or requests can be addressed.
- ▲ Resolve disputes about the agenda.
- ▲ Obtain commitment for the agenda in its original or modified form.

Sample Script: Mapping Out the Agenda

"Next we need to map out the agenda, which was developed with your input. We will start with a brief icebreaker. We will then continue with progress reports and decisions that need to be made as a result of these reports. Decision-making options are shown in your meeting packages. This should take us until the 3:30 break.

"After our break we will discuss several new and exciting initiatives and decide whether and how they should be pursued. This should take us until 4:50 P.M. In the last ten minutes we will welcome closing comments and feedback from members and guests.

"Are there any questions or concerns about the agenda?"

Next, the facilitator will do the following:

- ▲ If there are no concerns about the agenda, assume that there is support for it and proceed: "There appear to be no concerns about the agenda as presented, so I'll assume it has your support. Let's carry on with item 1."
- ▲ If there are questions, answer them or delegate them to someone else.

▲ If there are concerns about the agenda, facilitate decisions on whether or not it should be changed (see next section).

Dealing with Requests to Change the Agenda

If there is a request to change the agenda and it seems to make sense (e.g., a request to change the sequence of agenda items, or a request to allocate more time to a certain agenda item and less to another, or a request to add another break), do the following:

1. Ask: "Is this change acceptable to everyone?"
2. In the absence of any concerns about the suggested change, go ahead and make it.
3. If there are concerns about the proposed change, find out what they are and act accordingly. For example, "You prefer to finish earlier instead of taking another break. Well, how about if we leave the agenda the way it is for now, see how the meeting unfolds, and make the decision about another break later? Is this acceptable? Thank you. Let's continue."
4. If the request would have a substantial impact on the agenda (e.g., a request to add a time-consuming item that may not be ripe for discussion or decision making), it's OK to discourage it. For example, "Ron, our time is limited, and I don't see how we can accommodate this item, especially since it has not been studied like the other items on today's agenda. Would you mind proposing it at a future meeting and prepare a report on it in advance?"
5. If the member persists with an unreasonable request, ask the group what it wants to do:

▲ Ask: "What do other people think? Should this item be added?"

▲ Give them a chance to respond briefly and proceed accordingly: "Ron, based on the group's feedback, we will not deal with this item today."

▲ If needed, you could go as far as taking a show of hands on the suggested change: "Let me take a show of hands. Would you please raise your hand if you think this item should be added to the agenda? Thank you. Would you please raise your hand if you think it should not be added? Thank you. The item will not be added. Let's move on."

Note: Some members may hesitate to raise their hands to say no, for fear of hurting someone's feelings. You need to clarify that it is OK for members to say no and that no one should be offended if their requests are not accommodated.

Mistakes to Avoid

A common mistake that facilitators make when establishing agendas is making all agenda-related decisions unilaterally (by the facilitator) and without even asking the group what it wants to do. This makes no sense. It is their time as well as yours. They deserve the courtesy to at least be asked about changes to the agenda, even when in many corporate settings you, as the group's manager, have the ultimate say.

Another common mistake is capitulating to strong-minded or persistent members and making whatever changes they want. This practice makes a meeting a free-for-all and amounts to the tyranny of the minority. If you face it, try the above scripts. Democracy is powerful; the members get to make the decision, and you gain support by giving them the clout they deserve.

A WARM-UP ACTIVITY

A plane's engine needs to be warmed up before an actual launch. A meeting can also benefit from a brief warm-up activity. Warm-up activities:

- Get everyone involved right at the start of the meeting.
- Establish an expectation of an inclusive meeting (which you must live up to later).
- Add an inspiring or a fun dimension at the start of the meeting.
- Help to set the tone for the meeting.
- Relieve tensions at the start of a contentious meeting.
- Get participants to take themselves a little less seriously.
- Break down barriers among participants.

One type of warm-up is an opening prayer or spiritual thought: "We usually open our meetings with a word of wisdom. Cherry, it's your turn today. Go ahead." Note: If a prayer is used to open the meeting, make sure it is appropriate. It may need to be nondenominational, not favoring one religion or ethnic group over another.

Icebreakers are another type of warm-up:

- "We usually open our meetings with a warm-up activity, to give everyone an opportunity to network and break the ice. So here goes: Your assignment for the next five minutes is to meet as many new people as you can and tell them about your dream vacation spot: Assuming that money and time were not an obstacle, where might you be right now?"

- "Could everyone please spend three minutes and jot down the three best things about our department and the three most ridiculous things about our department. Afterwards we'll get you to share them."
- "We haven't seen one another for a full three months. Shall we go around the room and hear from each individual what success or horror story has happened in your area? No more than one minute per person, please. Dawn, go ahead."

The comfort gauge can be used at the start of a contentious meeting, where there is plenty of suspicion and distrust at the beginning:

> *"Before we discuss the issues, we need to do something to break the ice and get us off to a good start. I am sensitive to the fact that some of you may not be very optimistic about this meeting. We need to talk about your level of optimism and why it is where it is.*
>
> *"I want you to rate your optimism on a scale of minus five to plus five. Zero means you think this meeting will make no difference whatsoever and things will stay exactly the same. Minus one to minus five means things will get worse. Plus one to plus five means this meeting will make a difference and things will get better and stay that way. In a moment I will ask you to think about your personal level of optimism as it stands now and write it down.*
>
> *"Once you've done it, I will ask if anyone wants to comment on their numbers, on a purely voluntary basis, and we can talk about why your optimism level is where it is. Anyone who does not want to share their observations can keep them private.*
>
> *"At the end of the meeting, I will ask you to repeat the same exercise, and we'll see if the meeting has made a difference in your optimism level.*
>
> *"Does anyone have any questions? If not, go ahead and rate your optimism level."*

After five minutes, facilitate a discussion of their optimism levels and the reasons for them. Give them a reasonable opportunity to share their ratings, but be open to the possibility they may not be ready to do so yet. If this is the case, move on and try again later.

You may end the above discussion by introducing another tool:

> *"Let me share with you my own optimism level. You may be surprised to hear me say that, in my view, this meeting will make absolutely no difference, unless . . . (pause for a couple of seconds) unless two things happen:*
>
> *"The first thing that must happen is systemic changes. We need to make changes to how we work and communicate with one another, and we need to work together to reduce the potential for conflict. We need to make sure that roles and responsibilities are very clearly defined and that lines of reporting and accountability are respected.*
>
> *"The second thing that needs to happen if this meeting is to make any difference is that each of you must make a personal commitment to change how you do things.*
>
> *"So here is a table of personal commitments for you to consider. The table has two columns: the things you'll stop doing and the things you'll start doing as a result of this meeting. You'll notice the table is empty. As we go through this meeting, I would pause from time to time and ask you to add items to both columns of this table. This will become your list of personal affirmations to review from time to time after this meeting ends."*

As a result of our discussion today, I will STOP doing the following things:	**As a result of our discussion today, I will START doing the following things:**
Making assumptions before hearing all the facts. Listening selectively.	Giving other people the benefit of the doubt and hearing them out. Slowing myself down and listening to all sides of a story.

Note: The above list includes sample affirmations that members could write down. The actual affirmations will vary from one person to another.

- As the meeting progresses, you can pause from time to time and say: "How about if we pause for a moment and revisit our personal table of affirmations. Is there anything you want to add to the STOP column and the START column as a result of our discussion so far? Please take a moment to think about it and add items to your lists."
- After they revisit the table of affirmations you may ask if members want to discuss what they wrote down: "Does anyone want to talk about the affirmations you wrote down? It's OK if you say no, but I thought it might be helpful if we heard from at least some of you. Anyone?"
- At the end of the meeting, you could ask them to rate their optimism levels again, and see if, in their minds, the meeting has made a difference.

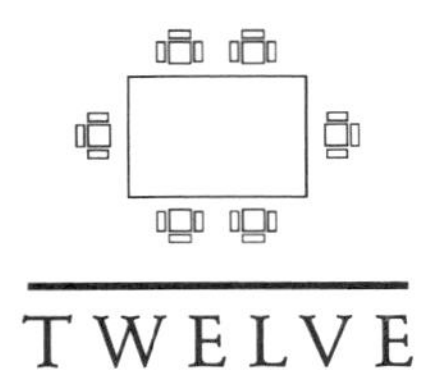

TWELVE

STEERING A MEETING TO ITS DESTINATION

After launching the meeting (Chapter 11), it's time to steer it towards its destination. If the journey is successful, members will share information, generate ideas, solve problems, build consensus, make good collective decisions, and advance the group's mandate.

As you steer a meeting to its destination, you need to share the stewardship of the meeting with your members, manage the overall agenda, and manage time, issues, and people, creating the right balance among them. With this in mind, your tasks as you steer the meeting to its destination include:

- *Time Management*. Monitor the clock and ensure that time is well spent.
- *Issues Management*. Ensure that issues are covered effectively and lead the group to making responsible, credible, and durable decisions that will work well for the organization and its stakeholders.
- *People Management*. Engage all members in the discussions and respond to signals they send your way, so as many of them as possible will arrive at the same destination together, as willing, active, and enthusiastic partners.

Creating the right balance among time, issues, and people management requires care, tact, and common sense. It demands listening and paying attention to the clock, the agenda, and the people present. Without the right balance, you may encounter the following problems:

- You could pay too much attention to the agenda and the clock and, by doing so, leave people behind. They may be frustrated by your frequent and aggressive interventions to enforce time limits and follow the agenda in the strictest manner. They may arrive at the same destination, but not as active, willing, and enthusiastic partners.
- You could pay too much attention to what individuals want. Doing so, you may end up accommodating each person's desires, being too nice, and hesitating to intervene if someone rambles or digresses from the agenda. You may end up appeasing a few persistent members at the expense of the group as a whole. Very little will get done.

In this chapter, the following aspects of steering a meeting are covered:

- Sharing the stewardship
- Managing the overall agenda
- Managing time in a meeting
- Managing issues in a meeting
- Managing people in a meeting

Sharing the Stewardship

Compare the following journeys to the dynamics that you observe in your meetings:

- *A Train Ride*. One person steers the train. The passengers sit back and enjoy the ride, as passive spectators. If they notice a problem, they trust the engineer to address it, and if she or he doesn't, they keep quiet. They don't dare to ask whether the engineer may not be paying attention or may even be asleep at the wheel. They don't want to risk making anyone angry with them and are afraid of "rocking the boat." Does this journey resemble what you see in your meetings? How many passive spectators do you have?
- *A Canoe Ride*. Yes, one person does the overall steering, blows the whistle, and moves the rudder, so the canoe will reach its destination. But each passenger has

a paddle and must row. If even one rider does not row, the canoe goes in circles. Each person is an active contributor, and no one is a passive spectator. Does this journey resemble what you see in your meetings? How many active and enthusiastic contributors do you have?

In traditional corporate settings, the primary responsibility for steering a meeting to its destination rests on the shoulders of the meeting facilitator. If things go well, the facilitator gets all the credit. If things go poorly, the facilitator gets all the blame.

This chapter does not negate the significance of the role of the meeting facilitator. However, it suggests that many benefits can be realized if leaders can learn to let go, delegate duties, and share the burden of stewardship with team members. If you, as the officially designated facilitator, share the responsibility for steering the meeting, more of your members will:

- ▲ Be prepared to step in and chair a meeting in your absence
- ▲ Give you feedback on your facilitation style
- ▲ Express concerns and suggest ways of addressing them
- ▲ Take lead roles on agenda items by making presentations and facilitating discussions
- ▲ Make helpful suggestions to break deadlocks
- ▲ Find creative solutions to seemingly insurmountable problems
- ▲ Be conscientious about the use of time
- ▲ Be prepared to question the quality of proposals or decisions
- ▲ Join you in demanding excellence from others
- ▲ Act as team players and help you in building a team
- ▲ Pull their weight at the meeting (see Chapter 13), knowing that "a chain is only as strong as its weakest link"

Here are some of the benefits of sharing responsibility (see Chapter 8) and involving members in planning and steering your meetings:

- ▲ Meetings become more efficient, inclusive, collaborative, dynamic, engaging, and fun.

- Counterproductive behaviors, such as rambling, digressions, hidden agendas, distracting side conversations, and others are not tolerated. Members give themselves permission to complain about such behaviors if the facilitator does not do so. Interventions by members are considered a duty and not something to apologize or feel guilty about.
- The leader's sense of isolation is diminished, if not eliminated. As a manager, you may have had the sense that "it is very lonely at the top," when people give you no credit for good things and are quick to criticize you when things go wrong. The reality will be very different when members share the responsibility for the success of your meetings.
- Team members are more enthusiastic about their work and deliver better results. They come to meetings prepared and participate in the group's work because they truly want to, not because they are told to be there, nor because they get paid for it.
- The quality of the consensus reached is boosted and the group is more likely to earn the respect of management and other stakeholders. The group's decisions are more durable because more perspectives are taken into account before they are made.
- The likelihood of nasty surprises and things falling apart is reduced when all members act as your eyes and ears and give you "heads up" warnings about potential problems.
- Members develop leadership skills and the organization is less dependent on the expertise of just a few. This is good for succession planning.

Managing the Overall Agenda

Once the meeting is launched (see Chapter 11), it should progress in a logical order (for agenda ideas see Chapter 9 for ROI, timing, and agenda masters' checklists). Your group does not have lock into one standard agenda or another, as long as the sequence is sensible and facilitates progress. Here are two possible progressions to consider: (1) starting with the past (progress reports), then moving to the present (incomplete issues), and then to the future (new issues), or (2) starting with simple agenda items, to build momentum, and then taking on more challenging and complex issues. This section elaborates on typical steps in managing the flow of the agenda:

- Clearing obstacles to progress
- Reviewing minutes and follow-up on action items (the past)
- Hearing and discussing reports (the past and the present)
- Unfinished business (the past and the present)
- New issues for problem solving and consensus building (the future)
- Dealing with consent agendas
- Changing the agenda in midstream
- Giving progress summaries on the agenda
- Breaking the continuity of a meeting

Clearing Obstacles to Progress

Often events that occur before a meeting have the potential of undermining progress at the meeting itself. For example:

- A team member is angry with another for making insulting comments before the meeting. There is tension between the two.
- A team member believes that he was treated unfairly by the manager, but instead of talking about it, he sits back resentfully and does not participate actively in the meeting.
- Some members believe the consensus-building process is futile and meaningless, that management has already decided what it wants to do, and that the group's recommendations will be ignored. There is tension in the air at the start of the meeting.
- Several nasty e-mails have been exchanged among a few people, but each member of the team was sent copies of those e-mails. The group is in the middle of an "e-mail war."

If your journey is to have a smooth start, you need to clear any obstacles in front of your vehicle. Similarly, if your meeting is to have a smooth start, you need to clear obstacles to consensus building before attempting to move forward. There are two ways of clearing obstacles to progress:

- Obstacles can be cleared before the meeting, through mediation or direct communication with key individuals. This will be the case if only a few individuals are involved in the dispute (as in the first two examples above). See Chapter 2 (the facilitator as a mediator) for examples of interventions between meetings.

- Alternatively, obstacles can be addressed early in the meeting itself. This will apply if the dispute affects the entire group (as in the third and fourth examples above).

Here is an example of clearing obstacles to progress at the start of the meeting:

> *"Before we start with our agenda, we need to clear the air about a few outstanding issues. There have been some exchanges of unpleasant e-mails that were copied to each one of us. Some of you have accused management of being less than sincere, and expressed doubts about the integrity of our consensus-building process.*
>
> *"We need to talk about what is causing the suspicion and mistrust, and clear the air before we carry on with our business. I suggest we allow half an hour for this discussion. Is this acceptable? Thank you.*
>
> *"Can we start with you, John? What is your version of events and what makes you believe that ____?"*

John explains, and key points are recorded on a flip chart. Then other members are asked the same question: "What about you, Helen, what's your version of events?" As the discussion unfolds, members may realize that tensions were partly caused by misunderstandings. The discussion should lead the group to:

- Determine which are the real problems and which are only perceived problems
- Identify systemic problems and communication breakdowns
- Rebuild mutual trust and respect
- Rebuild confidence in the integrity of the consensus-building process
- Regain the ability to work together, as a cohesive and collaborative team
- Remove obstacles to consensus building
- Clear the air and be better ready for the rest of the meeting

Reviewing Minutes and Follow-Up

Before moving on to new issues, the group should review what was done at the previous meeting and any follow-up on previous decisions. These objectives are achieved by a review of the minutes of the previous meeting (see Chapter 15 for sample minutes). This item is usually the first on the agenda and should not consume a great deal of time. Its main benefit is placing the present meeting in the broader context of the past and the future. The review of the minutes should lead to the following outcomes:

- ▲ Reviewing what was done at the last meeting.
- ▲ Checking the accuracy of the minutes, making corrections where needed, and then verifying them as being correct. This task will consume little or no time if the minutes were recorded accurately in the first place, and if draft minutes were circulated and reviewed by members, and all corrections were sent back to the minute taker prior to the meeting.
- ▲ Reporting on follow-up on decisions made at the last meeting.
- ▲ Pointing to any "loose ends" left at the last meeting, e.g., items that were postponed or parked due to a lack of time, or items that were referred to a subgroup for further study before decision making.

Sample Script: Reviewing Minutes and Follow-Up

Here is a script for addressing this agenda item:

"The first item on the agenda is the minutes and follow-up on the last meeting. The main things we did at the last meeting were: ____, ____, and ____.

"Things we were unable to complete at the last meeting were as follows:

- ▲ The discussion of HR policies was postponed to this meeting, under item 8.
- ▲ The staff orientation package was sent to all departments for comment and we are waiting for their responses. It will be scheduled on next month's agenda.

"The minutes of the last meeting were circulated to everyone by e-mail. Thank you for sending in your corrections. They were integrated into a revised copy, which you received. Assuming there are no further corrections, the minutes will be verified as being an accurate summary of what we did at the last meeting. Are there any errors in the minutes? (Pause). Thank you. The minutes are approved.

"We need to check about follow-up on decisions made at the last meeting.

"Rebecca, you agreed to ____. How did it go?"

Rebecca may indicate she has a separate report later on the agenda.

"Another follow-up item was ____, which was delegated to Stan. Any update, Stan?"

Continue with other follow-up reports.

"This concludes a review of the minutes and follow-up. We'll move to the next agenda item, which is ____."

As the minutes are reviewed, some members may want to revisit a decision that was made at the last meeting. Check the section on revisiting previous decisions under managing issues in meetings.

Hearing and Discussing Reports

Following the review of the minutes, reports can be presented by individuals or subgroups. Where needed, actions can be taken on recommendations contained in a report. Chapter 9 includes guidelines for report writers. Here are a few suggestions for the presenter of a report:

▲ Prepare a written report and include it in the premeeting package, instead of giving an "off-the-cuff" report verbally at the meeting. This is especially important if the issues are complex or the report recommends action to be taken by the group.

▲ The practice of bringing a written report to a meeting without advance circulation is unfair and should be avoided. Members cannot be expected to make informed decisions on reports they have just received.

▲ Avoid reading the report aloud, word for word, since this is likely to be a waste of time (given that everyone received the report and should have read it).

▲ Avoid editorializing on your report and telling long stories. Just give them the key facts: "My progress report was included in the package. The main highlights are as follows: ____."

There are two types of reports: (1) reports for information only and (2) reports for discussion and decision making.

Reports for Information Only

Reports that are only for information can be handled as follows:

1. The member presents the report.
2. Other members ask questions.
3. If, as a result of the questions asked after a report, an idea surfaces that is worth pursuing and discussing in some detail, the following can be done:
   - ▲ If the discussion will not consume time at the expense of other issues, it can take place immediately.
   - ▲ If the discussion will take time, it should be added to the group's "parking lot" and discussed either later in the meeting (after prescheduled agenda items have been dealt with), or at a future meeting, as follows: "Thank you, Tony, for this idea. It seems like it will take some time to discuss it, and we have a busy agenda. I suggest we park it for now, and pick it again later, when our agenda is concluded, or at the next meeting."
   - ▲ An exception to the above approach can be made if the group decides that the discussion is urgent and should not be postponed.
4. Having considered a report, the group moves on to the next one.

Sample Script: A Report for Information Only

"I am proud to report the following achievements:

- ▲ First, our department has had a month with no lost workdays due to accidents.
- ▲ Second, the number of customer complaints about quality dropped from ten to five.
- ▲ Third, the number of customer compliments on quality of service rose from two to ten.

"We are definitely making progress, and I would like to explain briefly what we have done to be so successful in the areas of safety, quality control, and customer service:

"First, in the area of safety, we have ____.

"Second, in the area of quality control we have ____

"Third, in the area of customer service we have ____

"Does anyone have any questions on my report?"

Take questions.

"Any more questions? Thank you. This concludes my report."

Reports for Discussion and Decision Making

If the report is for discussion and decision making, the progression should be as follows:

1. A member presents the report and explains the history, the research done, and the conclusions reached.
2. The member then presents and explains the recommended decisions, which should be clearly identifiable in the report (bolded or boxed).
3. If several decision-making options are presented, there should be a comparison of benefits and drawbacks among them.
4. The group asks questions about the report.
5. The group discusses the proposals and reaches consensus on the outcome. The chosen course of action may be as proposed in the report, or the group may come up with a better option. If so, the report writer should take it in stride and not be offended by the fact that his or her solutions were not accepted. Nothing should be taken personally. The first priority is to make the best decision for the organization.
6. The group identifies action items and implementation duties to follow up on the decisions: Who will do what and by when?
7. The group's consensus and action items are recorded in the minutes.

Note: Follow-up duties should be assigned to the people best suited for them, and not necessarily to the first person who volunteers. Efforts should be made to delegate follow-up duties to newer or less experienced members, to help them develop their skills and confidence levels. Here is an example:

> *"We need to decide who will follow up on this report. This seems like a job that some of the newer members could get involved in. How about you, Sam, can we ask you to do it? You're not sure you can do it? Well, I wouldn't have suggested it if I didn't think you could. How about taking it on, and seeing Bruce after the meeting for some help? Thanks, that's great."*

Sample Script: A Report with a Recommendation

"The human resources committee has considered sexual harassment policies for the company. Today I will present new policies recommended for approval. My report was included in your packages, and I would like to highlight the four main parts:

▲ First, the background that prompted us to address this issue

▲ Second, the research that the committee did

▲ Third, the conclusions we reached, and

▲ Fourth, the proposed new policies on sexual harassment

"I will need about five minutes for each part. I will take questions after the first two parts and after the next two parts. The total amount of time for my presentation, including questions, is thirty minutes. Afterwards, we will discuss what should be done with the proposed new policies.

"Let me start with some background on external and internal circumstances that led us to develop these new policies (a PowerPoint slide, consistent with the precirculated handout package, is reviewed).

"Having given you the background for our work, let me proceed to the second part of my report: The research that we did. (Give key points on the research.)

"I have now covered the background for our work and the research that we did. Are there any questions about the first two parts of the report? (Take questions for up to five minutes.)

"The third part of our report includes the conclusions we reached. They are as follows: _____.

"The fourth part of our report includes the policies recommended in light of our conclusions. The policies are in your report. Here are the main ones: _____.

Are there any questions on the conclusions and the recommended policies?"

After the question period, the group discusses the proposed policies and may make the following decisions:

▲ The group can decide to approve the policies as presented.

▲ The group can ask the committee to modify the policies to address certain concerns, and bring the recommended policies back at a future meeting.

▲ Some individuals may want to nitpick and improve the detailed wording of the document at the meeting itself. In larger meetings with more than ten people, such an effort can be a colossal waste of time. It is usually best to focus on general principles and key concerns only, and leave it to the committee to work out the detailed wording. Here is a sample script for you:

"Thank you, Gloria, for the suggested changes. I was just wondering: Given our busy agenda, would it be better if we focus only on the main principles behind the policies, and leave it to the committee to work out the detailed wording? Brad, would you take Gloria's suggestions to the committee? Thank you."

- The group can postpone the decision on the policies until the next meeting, giving members more time to digest the presentation, or giving the committee more time to modify the policies to address concerns and suggestions made at the meeting.

Sample Script: A Follow-Up Report by a Committee

"At the last management meeting there was a proposal to hold an open house for the public to take a look at our plan to build a new cement plant. Some of you expressed a concern about potential negative reactions to this idea by our municipal council.

"I was asked to contact the municipal administration and see what we might do to avoid any conflict. Their suggestions are included in my report. I will highlight them and take any questions. After I do this, we can discuss whether we still want to pursue the open house idea, and, if so, under what conditions."

Unfinished Business

After the review of the minutes and any reports, the group can address any unfinished business. This typically includes issues or decisions that were postponed from an earlier meeting for one or more of the following reasons:

- A meeting ran late and there was no time to conclude all prescheduled issues.
- An issue was a last-minute addition to the agenda and the members did not want to be rushed into making a decision on it.
- Members were bogged down on an issue, were unable to make progress on it, and chose to park it while making progress on other issues.

▲ The discussion of an issue became too emotional and personal and members needed "time out" to think about it without the pressure to make a decision right away.

When Should Unfinished Business Be Considered?

Under traditional agendas, groups schedule unfinished business between reports and new business, and it usually makes sense to do this. However, the group should not become a slave to its traditions. Items of unfinished business should be scheduled where it makes the most sense to do so. Here are examples of departures from the traditional agendas:

▲ An unfinished business item may logically fit after (not before) a new business item.

▲ An unfinished business item may be less urgent than a new business item. The group should give itself permission to consider the more urgent item earlier.

▲ An unfinished business item may become irrelevant. The group should not force itself to retain it and should feel free to drop it from the agenda. Remember, "Suffering is optional."

Sample Script: Unfinished Business

"Next we have unfinished business. The first item is a proposal to purchase new office furniture, which was postponed at the last meeting due to a lack of time. The proposal is that we purchase five workstations with matching chairs, to replace the old furniture on the first floor. Is there any discussion on this proposal?" (Members comment.)

After some discussion: "Are we ready to make a decision on this proposal? Thank you. The proposal is that we purchase five workstations with matching chairs to replace the old furniture on the first floor. Are we in agreement to approve this purchase and send it to the purchasing department for processing? Any lingering concerns? (Pause.) Thank you. The proposal has been approved.

"Tom, would you please contact the purchasing department and ask them to let us know when we can expect the furniture to be here? Jackie, please record the decision and the follow-up in the minutes. Thank you."

New Issues for Consensus Building

Having reviewed the minutes, heard reports, and dealt with unfinished business ("the past"), your group is ready to consider new business ("the present and the future"). New business should include opportunities to discuss and solve problems and build consensus on new issues. New issues can make a meeting meaningful and engaging. They can create opportunities for members to be proactive and discuss new and interesting initiatives.

See the section on managing issues in a meeting later in this chapter for examples of problem solving and consensus building on new issues.

Dealing with Consent Agendas

As indicated in Chapter 9 (see agenda master's checklist), it is sometimes helpful to combine all routine and noncontroversial decisions under one agenda item called "consent agenda." A consent agenda allows for such items to be decided quickly. Here is a script for dealing with consent agenda:

> *"Next we have agenda item 5, the consent agenda. Under this item we have grouped several noncontentious decisions and expenses, as shown in the package that you received before the meeting. We can make the decision on all of these items and expenses as a group, without bringing each one of them for discussion separately, unless any of you believes certain items need separate discussion.*
>
> *"So let me ask: Are there any items in the consent agenda that require any discussion?"*

Individual members may indicate that certain items on the consent agenda need some discussion before a final decision on them is made.

> *"Items 5.7 and 5.9 were pulled out of the consent agenda for a separate discussion. Are we in agreement on the remaining decisions on the consent calendar? Any objection or concern about*

approving these expenses? Hearing no objection, all items and expenses on the consent agenda, excluding 5.7 and 5.9, have been approved.

"We'll now have a separate discussion on item 5.7. Richard, you asked to pull it out from the consent agenda. What are your concerns or comments?"

Next, you'll need to address items 5.7 and 5.9 and facilitate decisions on them.

Changing the Agenda in Midstream

Once the agenda has been accepted at the start of the meeting (see Chapter 11 on launching a meeting), the expectation is that the group will follow it in the approved sequence and remain on track and on time. However, as you steer the meeting to its destination, you may encounter circumstances or obstacles that may compel you to change the route. For example:

- ▲ An urgent issue surfaces and requires immediate attention.
- ▲ A member receives an urgent message requiring him to leave, and the item that he is supposed to handle is not scheduled until much later on the agenda. The agenda may need to be changed to accommodate this member (unless "urgent messages" are a recurring phenomenon for this member and the group is getting annoyed).
- ▲ A guest speaker or expert has not arrived in time for their scheduled presentation. You can move other items forward and deal with them while you're waiting.
- ▲ An adviser has arrived on time for their agenda item, but your meeting is running late. Yes, you can ask the adviser to wait, but in fairness to her or him, you may need to halt the discussion, have the discussion with the adviser, and return to the halted issue later.
- ▲ It becomes apparent that, in order to deal effectively with one issue, another issue that is scheduled later on the agenda must be dealt with first.

Here are a few things to consider about changes to the agenda in midstream:

- ▲ Before deciding to change the agenda, consider the impact of the proposed change on other agenda items, e.g., by changing the order on the agenda, subsequent agenda items may be pushed to the end and there may be less time available for them. Another impact could be cutting short a speech by a highly paid guest speaker.

- ▲ The decision to change the agenda should generally be made in consultation with the group (democracy). The decision should not be made unilaterally by the facilitator (monarchy), nor should it be made at the insistence of one persistent member (a free-for-all, or anarchy).

Note: The need to change the agenda will be minimized through good planning, i.e.:

- ▲ A full analysis of issues will help you establish a logical sequence. You will be able to group together related issues and put them in the proper order. This will reduce the need to change the agenda sequence in midstream.
- ▲ Establish that members are expected to arrive on time and be there for the full duration of the meeting, and that they should arrange to have their messages taken and addressed by someone else. This will help you create continuity at the meeting and reduce the need to change the agenda to accommodate departing members.
- ▲ Realistic time estimates will increase the likelihood that your group will be able to address each issue within the allocated time.

Sample Script: Skipping Less Urgent Items

"Before we continue, we need to make a decision about the agenda. We had a really good discussion on the previous issue and we managed to solve a very significant problem. However, it took us a bit longer than we expected. Looking at the remainder of our agenda, it seems like items 9 and 10 are urgent. Can we postpone items 7 and 8 to the next meeting, and deal only with items 9 and 10 today? Thanks. Let's proceed with agenda item 9, which is _____."

Sample Script: An Urgent Message

Sam: "I have just received a message that my wife's car broke down. She is okay, but I can stay for no more than thirty minutes.

Can I make my presentation on agenda item 8 now, take a few questions, and then leave?"

Don (facilitator): "Sam, it's very nice of you to offer to stay longer, but you don't have to. We can postpone item 8 to the next meeting. On the other hand, I know you've been looking forward to making this presentation, and I'm sure everyone will agree to change the agenda and let you do it now. What do you prefer to do?"

Sample Script: The Agenda Sequence Does Not Make Sense

"It seems like this decision is dependent on what we do with agenda item 10. Is this OK with everyone if deal with item 10 now, and then come back to item 4? Thank you."

Sample Script: Disagreement About the Proposed Agenda Change

Jon: "I was just called to another meeting, and I have to leave in fifteen minutes. Let's switch to item 7, so I can make my presentation and leave."

Phil: "I have a concern about this. Our guest speaker is waiting at the reception area, and he needs to leave for another meeting in thirty minutes also. It's unfair to ask him to wait and be late to his next meeting. Jon, didn't we agree to block off the time for this meeting and let our staff know we are not available for messages?"

Joan (facilitator): "What does the group want to do? Do you want to switch the agenda and hear Jon now, or do you prefer to stick to the original plan and hear our guest speaker? It looks like you want to stay with the original plan.

"Sorry, Jon. We'll have to hear your presentation at the next meeting, and that's too bad, because we've been looking forward to it. Can you ask the other group whether you can be late for their meeting? In any event, can we count on you to make sure this does not happen again? We need you to make the commitment to be here for the full duration of our meetings."

Giving Progress Summaries on the Agenda

If an agenda has more than one item, it is helpful to make overall progress summaries on the entire agenda from time to time. Logical times to make an overall progress summary on the agenda are after a major agenda item is concluded, or after a break. A progress summary on the agenda should include:

- A look backward: stating what was done so far
- A look forward: stating what remains to be done and how much time is left for it

Example: Progress Summary

Here is an example of a progress summary on the full agenda: "Welcome back from the break. Before we continue, let me take a moment and review where we are on the agenda."

A look backward: What was done so far? "So far we've covered items 1 to 4. We managed to come up with some great ideas on how to improve our e-commerce results, and made some decisions on several new products. In my assessment, the benefits of this meeting so far have been substantial. Congratulations on your great work. Let's keep up the momentum."

A look forward: What remains to be done? "We still have two items to address: Item 5 deals with customer complaints, and item 6 deals with telecommuting issues. It is now 3:30. We are fifteen minutes ahead of schedule and should be able to end the meeting before 4:30. Does anyone have any questions before we continue? (Take questions.) Thank you. Let's proceed to item number 5 on customer complaints."

Breaking the Continuity of a Meeting

Having a logical progression for a meeting (starting with a review of minutes, continuing with reports, and then unfinished and new business) is important. In general the agenda should be used as a road map, and should provide the structure that enables the group to be productive and reach its destination.

Having a road map does not mean that the journey must be completed in one stretch. The rowers on your canoe may be tired and in need of a break, to rest, recharge their batteries, and get ready for the next segment of the journey. If you insist on a nonstop journey, they will lose their effectiveness. Some will stop rowing, and others may just jump overboard.

Similarly, the agenda should not be followed so rigidly that it leaves people behind. Your group should be flexible and have a physical or mental break from time to time. Having completed a substantial agenda item, your members need and deserve a break from the continuity of the meeting before sinking their teeth into the next substantive issue. Without downtime, some of them may be operating at a saturation level, and some may even begin to daydream.

The benefits of breaking the continuity of a meeting include:

- Giving the members opportunities to rejuvenate, rest their brains, and get ready for the next substantive issue
- Rewarding the members for good progress
- Adding surprises and variety to the meeting
- Making the meeting more fun
- Making the meeting more varied, engaging, and interesting
- Creating opportunities to celebrate successes
- Making members look forward to the next meeting, because they enjoyed this one so much

Sample Script: A Refreshment Break

"Congratulations. We've just concluded several important agenda items and made some great decisions. You deserve a break and a reward. Randy arranged for some tasty surprise refreshments for us, and he guarantees that all the calories were taken out of them. Enjoy. Let's resume in fifteen minutes."

Sample Script: A Brief Funny Anecdote

"Before we move to the next agenda item, we need some downtime. Mike has a couple of anecdotes and he promises that they will be brief, funny, and . . . appropriate."

Sample Script: A Mind Bender

"Our next agenda item is _____. This is a challenging issue, and it will likely require some creative thinking. We will need to let go of past traditions and become more visionary. To get us into the creative mode, I have a mind-bending puzzle for you:

"Here (on a flip chart or a white board) is a string of letters: speineavepnlpeltetsers Your assignment, should you choose to accept it, is to delete seven letters from this string, and then tell us what you are left with. A hint: what you'll be left with is very sweet."

After a few minutes ask members to stop, and check how many have the answer, which is: pineapples. This answer is reached by removing the letters that spell "seven letters," and not seven letters, as most people assume. Reaching this answer requires members to let go of instinctive assumptions and to allow themselves to go beyond their normal thinking patterns.

This mind-bending exercise is fun, departs from the formality of the meeting, provides some downtime, and makes people think.

Sample Script: The Sisters and the Orange

The next script draws on an example from the book *Getting to Yes*, by Roger Fisher and William Ury (Penguin Books, 1983):

"Before moving to the next agenda item, I have a puzzle for you. It comes from the book *Getting to Yes*. How many have read this book? Well, if you did, please don't say anything.

"In their book, the authors, Fisher and Ury, relate the story of a father who had to arbitrate between his two daughters who were fighting over one orange. Imagine yourself in the role of the father. You have the decision-making power. Each daughter wants the entire orange. What would be a wise decision?"

Here are the typical answers that you are likely to receive when you ask this question:

- ▲ Cut the orange and give one half to each sister.
- ▲ Have the orange yourself.
- ▲ Flip a coin and give the orange to the sister who wins.
- ▲ Find another orange and give each sister one orange.

Is any of these options as smart as it can be? No.

The story ends like this: The father, taking the first route, cuts the orange and gives each sister one half of it. What do the sisters do? One of them peels her half of the orange, eats the inside, and throws the peel away. The other sister peels her half of the orange, throws the inside away, and uses the peel to bake a cake.

So, was it a smart decision? Clearly not, since both sisters could have had everything they wanted. Why did they not get everything they wanted? Because they did not ask each other, "What do you want the orange for?"

This story can be used for fun and to break the continuity of the meeting, but it also offers valuable lessons to meeting attendees:

- ▲ It provokes people to consider their thinking habits. It challenges them to avoid jumping to conclusions and trying to solve a problem before knowing exactly what the problem is. Instead of arguing and offering rebuttals or alternative solutions, they should listen and ask "why" and "how" questions. How needed are these lessons in your meetings?
- ▲ It suggests that a "compromise" is not always the best outcome. Compromise means people need to give up something and cannot get all they want and legitimately deserve. By listening, members can identify common ground and diverging interests and reach holistic solutions. More people can get much more than they think they can by speaking less, and by listening and asking more probing questions.

Another way of learning from this story is this: If one member has solution A and another has a seemingly conflicting solution B, one of a few things can be done:

- ▲ A vote can be taken. The solution that gets more votes wins and the other solution loses. This is the win-lose approach.

- ▲ The group works together to find solution C (a win-win solution), which would integrate the advantages of both A and B and remove the risks of both. Finding solution C requires more listening and consensus building.

Sample Script: How Well Do You Listen?

Tell your members this story once only and ask them to pay attention to every detail:

"You are driving a bus from downtown New York City to Queens. Five passengers board the bus at the first stop. Ten more passengers board the bus at the next stop, and one of them is a blind man. Upon entering the bus, the blind man screams that he must be seated. The other passengers are puzzled because the bus is half empty, but then they realize that the man can't see this and help him out. Two minutes later the bus breaks down in the middle of a bridge. People begin to complain and two of them get into a fistfight. Five police officers board the bus and arrest the culprits. Question: What is the name of the driver of the bus?"

The answer: Your name, since you are the driver of the bus.

The lessons?

- ▲ *On the Listener's Side*. Listen to every detail of the story, including the first and the last word. Ask questions to clarify a speaker's message. Ask people to communicate only what matters and avoid cluttering key messages with irrelevant data.
- ▲ *On the Communicator's Side.* Make it easy for others to listen by communicating simply and concisely, emphasizing key points, and giving them only the information they need. It helps if you state your key message up front: Give them the "punch line" first !

Sample Script: Mild Aerobic Exercise

Another way of breaking the continuity and providing downtime in a meeting is by physical movement, such as a walk around the block or even mild aerobics or stretching exercises:

"We've been sitting and working hard for a while. As you know, Dave is a fitness instructor and has prepared a mild aerobic exercise for us. If you prefer not to participate, you can go ahead and do something else. Of course, if you do that, Dave will cry for five days, but he will eventually get over it and forgive you. Dave, take it away. You have ten minutes."

Example: Celebrating Successes

Finally, a good way to break the tedium of a meeting and provide downtime is by recognizing special contributions and achievements. See Chapter 13 in the section on celebrating successes for examples of doing this.

MANAGING TIME IN A MEETING

Successful time management in a meeting means that, as you steer a meeting to its destination, you pay close attention to the clock and ensure that:

- Time is well spent. Meetings are expensive, and every minute should deliver value.
- Each issue is allocated time in accordance with its value. You need to avoid spending 90 percent of the time on issues that make little or no difference.
- Measured and sustained progress is made from the start of the meeting until the end. You need to avoid the "rush hour syndrome," whereby twenty minutes before the meeting ends members realize they have yet to conclude half the agenda. They rush things through and risk making bad decisions.

This section gives you time management tools for meetings:

- Giving periodic timing updates
- Closing the discussion on an agenda item
- Extending the time for an agenda item
- Encouraging efficient participation by individuals

Giving Periodic Timing Updates

To keep the meeting on time, members need to be given periodic timing reports. Such reports heighten awareness of time constraints, encourage members to stay focused on the agenda, and reduce the likelihood of rambling, repetition, digressions, and backtracking.

Sample Script: Setting a Time Target

10:15: "Before we go further, I am watching the clock and the number of issues which are left on the agenda, and I am wondering: How much time do we need for this issue? Would fifteen minutes be enough? Thank you. We'll end the discussion at 10:30 and move on to the personnel report."

10:27: "We have three minutes left for this issue. Let's bring closure to it. Are we in agreement that the best route to go is route A? Thank you. Roger, would you please follow up by ____? Thank you. Let's move on to the personnel report."

Sample Script: Lunch Time Is Approaching

"It is now 11:30 and we have thirty minutes before lunch. We have three items to discuss before lunch and they are: ____, ____ and ____. Shall we try to cover each one of them in about ten minutes? Thank you."

Sample Script: We Are Really Efficient

"It is 2:30, and we seem to be twenty minutes ahead of schedule. Congratulations! We are making great progress. Shall we take a short break, or shall we keep up the momentum and continue? I was told that it's not a crime to end a meeting early, and we need to avoid the prediction that 'work will expand to fill the available time.'"

If your group is ahead of schedule, you can also choose to insert a downtime activity (see earlier subsection on breaking the continuity of a meeting).

> Caution: Don't rest on your laurels and don't let the good momentum subside. Too many groups note that they are ahead, slow down, and end their meetings late.

Closing the Discussion on an Agenda Item

You will need to bring closure to an issue if any of the following occur:

- ▲ The time allocated for the agenda item has ended.
- ▲ The discussion appears to subside.
- ▲ The discussion has become repetitive and no new information surfaces.

Your overall goal should be to bring a smooth and natural closure to an issue. Abrupt closure is risky and can lead to bad decisions being forced through in a hurry. To achieve a gradual and natural closure on issues, you should:

- ▲ Ensure the scope of the agenda is reasonable (not too many issues scheduled).
- ▲ Establish a timed agenda (see Chapter 9 under agenda master's checklist).
- ▲ Keep the meeting moving at a good pace.
- ▲ Let members know in advance how much time is allocated to an issue before the discussion on it begins (see section on managing issues in a meeting).
- ▲ Give members periodic progress reports on how much time is left for an issue (see previous subsection).
- ▲ Give members periodic summaries of progress and consensus reached, and ask whether they are ready to make a decision.
- ▲ Encourage members to be focused and discourage repetition, rambling, and digressions.
- ▲ The decision to close the discussion should be made by the group, and not be forced by the group's facilitator (autocratic decision making) or by a few members who are getting impatient. (In formal meetings such members "call for the question," incorrectly believing that they have the power to unilaterally close the discussion.) Below are a few examples that show how a group decision to end the discussion can be made.

Example: Preapproved Timed Agenda

As recommended in this book, the group can agree to a timed agenda, allocating time to issues. In such cases, the facilitator will need to indicate that time has run out and lead to closure; "The time for this issue is coming to an end, and we need to make a decision."

Example: Listening for Repetition

If a timed agenda was not approved, the facilitator or any member can listen and determine whether the discussion is becoming repetitive, and, if so, say something like this:

"We seem to be hearing the same arguments. Does anyone have any new information to add, and, if not, shall we close the discussion on this issue, make our decisions, and move on to the next? We have plenty to do, and we need to keep things moving."

Example: Using Summaries of Progress to Close Discussion

You can use a progress summary to close discussion, as follows:

- ▲ Indicate the need to reach closure and move on.
- ▲ Summarize what was discussed about this issue (but keep it concise and accurate).
- ▲ Articulate what you understand the group's consensus to be.
- ▲ Ask if your summary is accurate and, if it is not, change it.
- ▲ State the proposed course of action and ask if it is acceptable to the members.
- ▲ Ask the minute taker to record the consensus in the minutes.
- ▲ Move on to the next issue.

Here is a sample script to support the above sequence:

"Our time is running out, and we need to move on to the next issue in five minutes. Let me summarize what I believe we agree on and see if I have it right. What I think we agree on is: _____. Does it sound right? Any concern? If not, let's have this consensus recorded in the minutes and move on. Next we have agenda item 8, which is _____."

Extending the Time for an Agenda Item

You need to create a balance in your meetings between the need for structure and the need for flexibility. Yes, there is merit to estimating how much time a major issue will require, and then watching the clock and ensuring that time allocations are respected. But there may also be a need to facilitate a decision to extend the time for an issue.

Before allowing an extension of the time on an issue, consider the following:

- ▲ The group should keep in mind that the extra time given to one issue will be taken away from other issues.
- ▲ The decision to extend the time should be made in consultation with the group (democracy). It should not be a unilateral decision by the facilitator (monarchy), nor should it be made at the insistence of one member (a free-for-all, or anarchy, or "the tyranny of the minority").
- ▲ If the issue is very far from closure and a substantial extension is needed, it may be better to postpone the item until later in the same meeting, after all high-priority items have been dealt with. Alternatively, the item can be postponed to a future meeting.

Sample Script: Extending the Time (Informally)

"Looking at my watch, I see that we have five minutes left for this issue, but the discussion does not seem to be near closure. Shall we allow a ten-minute extension, or would it better to park this issue until later in the meeting, after we've covered all essential items, that is items 3 to 7? What do you think?"

Sample Script: Extending the Time (Show of Hands)

"Aaron would like us to continue this discussion on this issue by thirty minutes, but I need to check whether this would work for the group. An extension means we will be late for other issues and less time will be available for them. Is it acceptable to extend the time by thirty minutes?

"I see that some members are objecting to this. Let's find out why."

Have a brief discussion (not thirty minutes long . . .) on whether an extension is a good idea. If Aaron persists with his request, you may need to take a show of hands:

"Let me take a show of hands. Raise your hands if you want to extend the time by thirty minutes. Thank you. Raise your hands if you prefer to park the issue until later (or postpone it to the next meeting). Thank you. Based on this show of hands, we will postpone the remainder of this discussion to the next meeting. Let's move on to the next issue, which is _____."

Encouraging Efficient Participation by Individuals

The previous subsection explained how to manage time on a per-issue basis. This subsection explains how to limit time that is taken up by each individual. Given the frequent tendency to ramble, repeat arguments, dominate, digress, or backtrack in meetings, you can end up with 90 percent of the time being consumed by 10 percent of the people. The quality of the discussions and the decisions will deteriorate. Your efforts to encourage efficient participation by individuals may include both preventive work and interventions at the meeting.

Preventive Work

Focused and efficient participation by individual members can be encouraged at the planning and launching stages of the meeting (see Chapters 9 and 11 for details). For example:

- The notice of the meeting can specify a few participation guidelines: "As a reminder, our meeting protocol is to participate by raising hands, not voices. We keep our comments concise and focused, create equal opportunities for members to speak, and avoid domination, repetition, digressions, and backtracking."
- In the opening script for launching the meeting (see Chapter 11), members can be asked to speak concisely, listen to what's being said, and avoid digressions, backtracking, repetition, and domination.

- In large or formal groups it is sometimes customary to agree at the start of a meeting to formal time limits on speaking. For example, each person may speak up to two times on each issue, each time up to three minutes, with first-time speakers getting priority over second-time speakers. However, such speaking limits introduce an element of formality. If used too rigidly, this formality can constrain creativity and prevent the free flow of discussions.

Interventions at the Meeting

As the meeting progresses, the facilitator (or any member) may need to intervene, encourage efficient participation, and prevent repetition, digressions, backtracking, or domination.

Sample Script: Establishing Speaking Limits (Informally)

"Next on our agenda we have the issue of Internet surfing for private use during working hours. I know many of you will have something to say about this issue. Given that we only have half an hour for this item, I suggest that each person be allowed to speak once, and keep their comments no more than about two minutes. I would also ask you to listen to other people, and if your point was made by someone else, just say 'ditto' and avoid repeating it. Do these guidelines sound reasonable?"

Sample Script: Stopping Rambling

A verbal intervention: "Brent, our time is running short. Can you please wrap up?"

Another verbal intervention (if the first one does not work): "Thank you Brent. You are making the point that ____. We need to move on. Judy, you're next. Go ahead."

Nonverbal interventions (let members know in advance that you'll use them if needed):

- Establish eye contact with the rambler and point to your watch.

- ▲ Move your hand in a circle, showing it's time to "circle the field."
- ▲ Show a picture of a landing airplane.
- ▲ Point to a cue card that says "Conclusion please."
- ▲ Have green (one minute left), amber (thirty seconds left), and red (time's up) lights.

Sample Script: Stopping Backtracking or Digressions

A preventive approach: "To help us stay on track and move ahead, could everyone please pay attention to the discussion and make sure that your point is relevant to what's being discussed? Sometimes we wait in line to speak, and by the time our turn comes, our point is no longer relevant to the current discussion."

A remedial approach: "Phil, excuse my interruption, but how is your comment related to agenda item 6, which is ____?" or, "Cathy, we already covered the issue of ____ and we are on to the issue of ____. Can we please stay on track?"

A nonverbal approach: Wave a cue card saying "On track?" or a picture showing a train off the rails.

Sample Script: Preventing Domination

"Thank you, Jack and Jill, for your input. Does anyone who has not spoken have something to add? How about you, Ruth, how does it look from the perspective of a project assistant? Can you help us out?"

Or:

"We've heard from Jack and Jill. How about if each member takes a minute to jot down on a piece of paper where you stand on the issue right now? Afterwards, we can go around the table and hear briefly from everyone."

MANAGING ISSUES IN A MEETING

Now that you have learned to manage time in your meetings, your next goal is to manage issues effectively. Your goal should be to make sure that issues receive proper coverage and that quality decisions are made. This section offers you tools to manage issues in a meeting:

- ▲ Mapping out an agenda item
- ▲ Giving progress summaries on agenda items
- ▲ The steps for solving a problem
- ▲ The steps for handling a proposal
- ▲ Taking informal and formal votes
- ▲ Changing the wording of a proposal or document
- ▲ Delaying, delegating, parking, or dropping an agenda item
- ▲ Revisiting a previously made decision
- ▲ Dealing with a deadlock
- ▲ Using special discussion activities
- ▲ Using flip charts to record consensus

Mapping Out an Agenda Item

Just as it is necessary to map out the overall meeting agenda (see Chapter 11 on launching a meeting), it is helpful to map out each agenda item and describe how it is set to unfold. Mapping out an agenda item increases the likelihood that you will be able to steer the meeting to the right destination and arrive there on time. In your "mapping out" statement, you may cover some or all of the following details:

- ▲ Why is this agenda item important?
- ▲ How is this item related to the group's mandate?
- ▲ Is the item for information only?
- ▲ Is it for discussion and exchange of views?
- ▲ Is it for consensus building and decision making?
- ▲ What key issues and concerns need to be addressed?

- ▲ What questions need to be answered?
- ▲ What decisions need to be made?
- ▲ What are the criteria that the decisions must meet?
- ▲ How will the discussion on the item unfold?
- ▲ Who will report on it?
- ▲ Who will lead the discussion?
- ▲ What is the time available for this item?

Sample Script: Mapping Out the Process for Progress Reports

"Next we have agenda item 3, progress reports by members. The purpose is to give us an appreciation and an understanding of what other departments are doing. We have a total of fifteen minutes for this item. Each member will be given a total of two minutes to report on events in their department. Once all reports have been presented we will take questions on them. Please listen to presenters and jot down any questions while they speak. We'll start with the system security department. Randy, go ahead."

Sample Script: Mapping Out an Informal Discussion with No Decisions Expected

"Next we have agenda item 8, the decision to hire a new systems analyst. Tina, our department manager, has the final say on this decision, but wants our input on the five candidates we've met.

"We have half an hour for this item. Do you prefer to talk about one candidate at a time, or do you want unstructured discussion? OK. We'll have an unstructured discussion. Who would like to go first? How about you, Stephanie? Any thoughts on the candidates we've met and which came across well or not so well to you?"

Sample Script: Mapping Out Discussion of Three Options for Decision Making

"Next we have agenda item 10, about rearranging our office space. This issue has been difficult for some of us, since it affects our personal space at work. As we agreed, we'll allow one hour to this discussion, and we'll end it by noon.

"We have three options, which were sent to you for review before the meeting. Ruth, the chair of the subcommittee who prepared the options, will start the discussion by making a ten-minute presentation. Please do not interrupt her, but write any comments and questions down and save them until after she speaks.

"At the end of Ruth's presentation we will assess the three options. Ideally, when we finish our discussion, we will reach consensus on what the best option is. Keep in mind that we are not limited to these three options, and we can invent a new one. Does anyone have any questions about how the discussion will unfold? Is everyone comfortable with it? OK, Ruth, go ahead."

Giving Progress Summaries on Agenda Items

If an issue is complex and time-consuming, it is helpful to articulate periodic progress summaries on it. A progress summary may contain the following ingredients:

1. A review of what was done on the issue, which would include a summary of agreements reached so far and an acknowledgment of the group's progress on this issue
2. A summary of what remains to be done
3. A summary of areas on which agreement has not been reached
4. A list of areas that are yet to be covered
5. A list of the decisions that are yet to be made
6. A confirmation that the above summaries are accurate
7. A reminder of how much time is left for this issue
8. An assessment of the remaining work on this issue:
   - ▲ How much of it can be completed at this meeting

- What areas may need to wait for another meeting
- What areas require more study before a final decision

Periodic progress summaries can help you achieve the following outcomes:

- Focus the discussion on key themes.
- Keep the meeting on track and moving ahead.
- Acknowledge successes.
- Tie up any loose ends and clarify the decisions that were made.
- Help the minute taker record an accurate summary of the meeting.
- Minimize repetition, i.e., points that were covered are included in a summary, making it clear they do not need to be repeated. Here is an example of a subsequent intervention: "Thank you, Ralph. The issue of customer impact has already been addressed and the consensus was recorded on the flip chart. We need to look at issues we have not addressed yet, and right now we're on the issue of _____."
- Lead to a natural and gradual closure on the issue.

A progress summary on an issue should be:

- Concise, brief, and to the point.
- Logical and well organized.
- Complete, i.e., include all significant and relevant points.
- Focused on the relevant portions of the discussion, while removing insignificant data.
- Accurate and consistent with the intent and spirit of the discussion that preceded it (it should not be the facilitator's interpretation of what was done or agreed to).
- Objective and focused on bottom-line issues.
- Purposeful and geared towards decision making.
- Worded in the affirmative, which means converting comments about what should be avoided into what needs to be accomplished. For example, instead of saying, "The consensus is that we have low morale and no one really cares," say, "The consensus seems to be that more should be done to boost morale and increase the commitment levels of staff members to their jobs."

Example: An Interim Progress Summary on a Divisive Issue

"We've had quite a discussion, but we are definitely making progress. Before we go further, let's review the key points made so far. I will start where I think we have common ground, and move on to the areas of concern.

"First, the common ground: It seems like we agree this project is generally a good one and that we should probably pursue it, if and when our concerns are addressed. Is this a correct statement of consensus? Any opposition to it? Thank you. Let's record this as an area of consensus.

"Next we need to review the areas of concern.

"First, some of you are concerned that we may be moving too fast and that we may be pushed to make quick decisions without a full evaluation of long-term impacts of this project on the company. It was suggested by several of you that we should take our time and be more measured and deliberate with this project.

"Second, there is a question about the budgetary impacts of this project on other initiatives, and whether those impacts need to be addressed before we proceed.

"Third, there are questions about the collaboration with other organizations, and a concern about the lack of a firm commitment from them to this project.

"Is this an accurate summary of your concerns? Did I miss anything?"

Take additional concerns from the group and refine the consensus. Lead discussions of specific concerns. Then make another summary statement and lead to closure:

"OK, so where do we go from here? Shall we postpone the decision on this project until the next meeting? Shall we start a committee to look at the concerns and report back to us with a recommendation at the next meeting? What do you think?"

Here is a flip chart that reflects the above interim summary:

Areas of agreement	Concerns
Project = a good idea Pursue after concerns addressed	Speed of decision making Impacts on other initiatives Partner commitment seems uncertain

Example: Converting Frustrations into Affirmative Requests

The following example shows you how interim progress summaries can turn disputes and tensions into opportunities.

Susan, an impartial facilitator, is asked to lead a meeting where members of a team are to discuss the working relationships with their manager. The group's manager, Rob, decides to give the group privacy, but asks Susan to summarize the feedback and plan a subsequent meeting with him in attendance.

The discussion at the meeting is intense, honest, and blunt. Several accusations are leveled at Rob. For example:

- "Rob never listens to us."
- "He ignores our input."
- "He make his decisions in isolation."
- "He doesn't seem to care about or have any idea of the impacts of his decisions on us and our customers."
- "Rob micromanages us. He tells us not only what to do, but also how to do it. He has trouble letting go, has no clue how to delegate, and doesn't seem to have much trust and confidence in our professional judgment."
- "Rob doesn't stand up for our group in senior management meetings. He seems to go where the wind blows and is afraid of rocking the boat."

After an hour of the group "venting" its frustrations, Susan summarizes the discussion in concise point-format. She avoids negative language (what Rob does not do or does poorly) and instead uses affirmative language (what Rob should be doing), as follows:

"Thank you for your openness and honesty throughout this discussion. Before we go any further, I need to summarize what I think I heard you say. In my summary I will focus on what you want Rob to do, as opposed to what you want him to stop doing. When I finish, you can tell me whether I missed anything. Does this sound reasonable to you? Thank you. Here goes:

"In your comments you raised several concerns about Rob's management style. You made the following suggestions:

- Advance notice of changes: You would appreciate it if Rob gave you advance notice of upcoming decisions.
- Listening and consultation: You would like Rob to listen to you more and take your input into account before he makes decisions that affect you and the customers.
- Delegation: When it comes to areas in which you are experts, you would prefer it if Rob only told you what needs to be done, and then left it to you to figure out how to get it done. You want him to let go and give you room to put your skills to work.
- Representation: You would like Rob to represent your group's interests to senior management in an assertive, confident, and unapologetic manner. You want him to be proactive and establish his own direction, rather than wait for his boss or colleagues to take the lead.

"Is this an accurate and complete summary what you want from Rob? Did I miss anything?"

Susan then listens to the group's responses. She enhances and refines the summary based on the group's suggestions and requests, and she records key points on a flip chart. Again, she converts complaints and accusations into affirmative statements.

Having done this, Susan realizes that the group has been focusing only on Rob's shortcomings, without any mention of his redeeming qualities. She decides to pursue this issue proactively, even though it is outside her original mandate:

"OK, we have fifteen minutes left before ending this meeting. We appear to have made plenty of progress. However, I am missing one important piece of the puzzle. I believe our summary will be more balanced and complete if we go beyond what Rob does wrong and how he should change his management style. What I am missing is an acknowledgment of the positive things about Rob.

"Would you be amenable to talking about what you appreciate about Rob as a manager? After all, you are still working for him, and you generally seem to enjoy your work, right?

"So are there any things you appreciate about Rob's management style and want him to continue doing?"

After fifteen minutes, Susan has several notes of appreciation to add to the summary: She says:

"Let me summarize what I think you appreciate about Rob's management style and what you want him to continue doing:

▲ Openness to feedback: You seem to appreciate Rob's willingness to hear your feedback and his commitment to improving his working relationship with you. This was evident to you by the fact that he scheduled this meeting, hired an impartial facilitator, and chose not to attend, so you could be free to express your concerns.

▲ Rob has a clear sense of purpose and vision for the department.

▲ Rob is consistent and reliable. He is always there for you when you need him.

▲ You appreciate Rob's sense of humor and the fact that he knows how to lighten things up.

"Did I miss anything? If not, I want to suggest a follow-up plan and check if it would be acceptable to you. Here goes:

1. By Wednesday I will prepare a written summary of this meeting and send it to three of you for review.
2. I will call the three readers on Friday for any feedback on the report.
3. I will make any needed corrections to the report.
4. I will arrange to meet Rob and discuss the report with him.
5. My meeting with Rob will likely lead to a follow-up meeting with both you and Rob in attendance. You can then talk about specifics.

"What do you think? Does this plan sound reasonable to you? Thank you. Does anyone have any closing comments before we end this meeting?

"One last thing from me before we close the meeting: I want to say how much I appreciated and enjoyed working with you. I

> thought we had a very productive discussion. I am confident, and I hope you are also, that working relationships in your department will get better and better. Thank you, and have a great day."

The Steps for Solving a Problem

If an issue is complex or controversial, your group should resist the temptation to leap to "solution-mode." Trying to solve a problem without defining it fully and precisely is equivalent to prescribing a cure without knowing what the ailment is: You might end up prescribing major surgery when an aspirin will do.

Rushing to solution-mode prematurely has the following risks:

- ▲ Bad and costly decisions may be made. If all you did was to relieve the symptom, the real problem will be reincarnated later and may come back to haunt your group.
- ▲ Legitimate concerns may be ignored and may not be integrated into the solution. You may end up with majorities overpowering minorities, win-lose solutions emerging, and an adversarial climate developing.
- ▲ Dissatisfied members are unlikely to be active and enthusiastic partners in the important implementation stage. They may even undermine the implementation, overtly or covertly.

Instead of leaping to solution-mode, your group should take a more deliberate and measured approach to problem solving. The approach should be: "Let's find out first what the problem is; that is the real problem, and not just the surface issue."

The six steps in a systematic and deliberate problem-solving process are:

1. Defining and exploring the problem
2. Establishing the criteria that the solutions must meet
3. Brainstorming for solutions (no evaluation yet, just a free flow of ideas)
4. Assessing each idea to determine whether it meets the established criteria
5. Choosing the best idea (which may combine elements from several ideas)
6. Establishing the implementation plan and assigning follow-up duties to members

See Chapter 1 for more details on this six-step approach to problem solving. The remainder of this section includes:

- An example of using an evolutionary approach to problem solving
- A case study that illustrates that premature solutions can be very costly

An Evolutionary Approach to Problem Solving

When addressing a complex issue, an evolutionary approach should be used, to avoid leaping prematurely to solution-mode. The level of discussion on such an issue should reflect its developmental stage (see Chapter 1 for a discussion of the evolution of issues), i.e.:

- *Conception Stage.* The issue is brand-new and has just emerged at a meeting. The group recognizes that this is a complex issue requiring an evolutionary approach and places it in its "parking lot," so it is not lost.
- *Birth.* After preliminary research, the issue is placed on a future meeting agenda. It is discussed in general terms. No decisions are forced at the birth stage. The group only explores the problem to be solved and the related issues.
- *Adolescent Stage.* People begin to form opinions on how the issue should be addressed. Given the contentious nature of the issue, members are fighting and arguing over it. The adolescent issue is opened for discussion of all views, but without contemplating closure. The discussion is intended to collect all pieces of the truth and then to take some time to think about them. With no threat of closure, members listen better and work collaboratively towards win-win solutions.
- *Mature Stage.* The adolescent fighting is over. Decision-making options are prepared and evaluated by the group against objective criteria. In the mature stage the group is likely to make mature and durable decisions, usually by consensus and with little or no opposition.

Sample Script: Conception Stage Issue

"Thank you, Roger, for raising this issue. It certainly seems to fit within our mandate. Given that this is a new issue, can we park it for now in our idea list or "parking lot"? We have a busy agenda, and this idea looks like it might take some time and could also benefit from some research and analysis."

Note: Members should be made familiar with the concept of a "parking lot." Agenda planners should review parking lot issues on a regular basis and look for opportunities to include them on future agendas, after the needed research on them is done.

Sample Script: Birth of the Issue

A month later: "Next on our agenda we have a new issue that Roger raised a month ago. It suggests doing shift work instead of the usual 9 to 5 workday for everyone. We will start by hearing from Roger, who prepared a report for us. We will then discuss the idea and decide how to pursue it further. Just a reminder that, since this is a new issue, we will only do brainstorming. We won't be making any decisions today."

The discussion unfolds as follows:

- ▲ Roger presents his analysis and answers questions.
- ▲ Members discuss the idea and decide that shift work deserves consideration (given the needs of customers to be served outside the 9 to 5 time frame, and given that the competition is already doing this). However, they are nervous about how such a major change will affect their work and personal lives.
- ▲ A subcommittee is formed and is asked to take the group's concerns and suggest ways of addressing them.

Sample Script: Adolescent Stage

Three months later: "Next we have the issue of shift work, and we have one hour to discuss it. We started talking about this issue three months ago. It has proven to be contentious, and some of you have been concerned about how it will affect your job and private life.

"I want to start by reassuring you that we are not in a rush to make this decision. We want to take your input into account before finalizing anything. Management will likely want to take action within six months. This gives us time to develop consensus on the route to take, keeping in mind that the status quo is not an option.

"With this in mind, I suggest we discuss the different aspects of this issue over the next three meetings, with a goal of agreeing on a recommendation at our July meeting. Does this sound reasonable? Thanks.

"For today, I suggest we focus on the problems with the current work arrangement, and how these problems may affect productivity, efficiency, and customer service. Does this sound reasonable to you? OK. Let's start.

"Why don't we take the next few minutes for thinking and note taking. Please jot down a few ideas on how things look from your perspective. To what extent does the current 9 to 5 schedule work and to what extent does it not work? Let's take five minutes for thinking and writing."

Note: With the threat of an imminent decision averted and with the reassurance that their input will be taken into account, members will be more likely to think and speak rationally and move the issue from adolescence to maturity. They will also be prepared to listen to different views with an open mind.

The remainder of the discussion could unfold as follows:

▲ After five minutes of thinking and writing, ask members to share their thoughts with the person sitting next to them. This activity (which could be scheduled to take five to ten minutes) will further break the ice and promote teamwork and collaboration.

▲ After the small group discussions, solicit comments from members. Record key points and repetitive themes on a flip chart.

▲ After the discussion (thirty minutes or so), summarize the main points made and come to a decision on what the next steps should be. For example, a subcommittee could be appointed to summarize the consensus on the problem and its impact, recommend criteria that any solution must meet, and identify a few options for decision making. It will send its report to the members and present it at the next meeting.

Sample Script: Maturity

A few months later: "Next on our agenda we have the issue of shift work. We have one hour for it. The good news is that we have made great progress and that the subcommittee has some very interesting options for us to discuss today.

"Our job today is to analyze three options. We should be able to decide which is the best option to present to management. The option we end up choosing should maximize the benefits of change while minimizing the negative impacts on staff. We may also opt to present all three options, ranking them as our number 1, 2 and 3, or we could even invent a better option here today.

"We'll start with the subcommittee's presentation. Jonathan, go ahead."

Here is how the discussion could unfold:

- ▲ The subcommittee makes its presentation of the three options.
- ▲ The subcommittee takes clarifying questions on the various options.
- ▲ The three options are posted on separate flip charts on the walls. The members are given one "sticky note" each. They are asked to walk around the room, speak to other members about the different options, and then vote for their favorite one by placing their sticky on it.
- ▲ Alternatively, members could be given three stickies each: one blue (signifying the preferred option), one green (signifying second best), and one yellow (signifying third place). When tabulating the votes, a weighted voting system could be used: Blue gets three points, green two points, and yellow one point.
- ▲ After fifteen minutes, the meeting is resumed and the result of the vote is reviewed and discussed. The group can still opt for a recommendation that is different than the one that received the most points. A mature group recognizes the validity of new input and always looks for ways to enhance the quality of its decisions.

CASE STUDY:

Premature Solutions Can Be Very Costly

This case study illustrates how rushing to solution-mode can constrain the discussions and lead to shortsighted decisions. Such an outcome is very likely when there is more to the issue than meets the eye.

The Departure Point: A Hiring Proposal

A proposal is presented to a management group, to approve the hiring of five new computer programmers and the purchase of five computer workstations. The reasons given include the following:

- Programmers are behind in their work.
- Customers are complaining about lateness and poor service.
- There is a need to expand services and serve customers for longer hours.

The remainder of the case study describes the discussion progressing along two possible routes, with substantially different results.

Route 1: Start with the Solution

Under route 1, the discussion progresses as follows:

- Members are uneasy about the large expense, but they are somehow locked into discussing the hiring proposal and nothing else. The discussion is too structured and does not give them flexibility to explore the problem further or discuss other solutions.
- A few hours later, members are tired and ready to go home. They approve a modified proposal: "To hire six new computer programmers and purchase six computer workstations. The annual budgetary increase, including salary, equipment, furniture, and maintenance costs should not exceed $450,000."

Route 2: Start with the Problem

Under route 2, the group sets aside the proposal and begins the discussion by exploring the problem. This is done by the facilitator saying something like: "Thank you, Murray, for this proposal. I suggest we park it for now and not lock ourselves into discussing one solution right away. We need to start our discussion by finding out first what is the problem we are trying to solve. This problem may be more complicated than we see right now."

The group follows by asking probing questions. Members discover several things that were not apparent when the discussion began:

- Tensions among programmers and their manager are reducing the staff's efficiency.
- Some programmers operate in isolation ("loose cannons"), and not as team members.
- There may indeed be a need for more staff, but the shortage is not in computer skills, but in people skills and customer service skills. Looking for people who only have computer programming skills will not address the real problem.
- Customers complain more about how they are treated on the phone than about lateness.

After this informal discussion, the problem is clear, and a few options to solve it emerge. The discussion is concluded with the approval of the following processes:

- Having an analysis by an HR consultant of all tasks currently being performed by the computer department.
- Realigning priorities within the department, so all essential work can be completed expeditiously, and nonessential work can be dropped or rescheduled.
- Reviewing the mandate and work practices within the computer department, to make it more customer-responsive and more consistent with market realities.
- Starting a team-building effort within the department, mediated by an external facilitator.
- Once the department has been "reformed," examining the need to hire new staff and purchase new equipment.

The following is a comparison between routes 1 and 2:

Route 1 (solution first)	*Route 2 (problem first)*
Delivers a shortsighted result that addresses the symptoms of the problem (backlog of work) but does not solve the root causes (the internal climate in the computer department).	Addresses the underlying problem, not only the symptoms. Reflects more creativity and visionary and holistic thinking.
Is expensive, and the returns on this investment ($450,000) are questionable.	Is likely to be less costly, and delivers high returns on investment: a more efficient and collaborative computer department.
The rigidity and the poor focus of the	The flexibility and the logical focus of

discussion leads to a waste of time and is bound to be harder on the members.	the discussion save time at the meeting. Members leave the meeting confident and comfortable with the progress they made.
Why is route 1 so unprofitable? Because it starts with a solution. The cart is before the horse.	Why is route 2 so profitable? Because it starts with a full analysis of the problem. The horse is before the cart, where it belongs.

The Steps for Handling a Proposal

A proposal is essentially a solution to a problem, and it can be developed in one of two ways. (1) The proposal can be developed outside the meeting. A designated individual or subgroup analyzes a given problem, conducts necessary research, and identifies decision-making options. An analysis of these options is then presented to the group in a written report. (2) Or, as an alternative, a proposal can be developed at the meeting itself. Members explore a problem to be solved, identify several options for decision making, compare advantages and disadvantages, and then choose the best option.

Once a proposal is ready, it requires some or all of the following five steps:

1. The proposal is articulated in concise and clear terms.
   - ▲ Ideally, the proposal should be in writing, so each member can read and refer to it. It can be included in a report or displayed on a flip chart or overhead transparency. The purpose of insisting on written proposals is to ensure clarity.
   - ▲ All ambiguities should be removed before a decision on the proposal is made.
2. The proposal is opened for discussion. Some members may speak in favor of it, some may speak against it, and others may express mixed feelings about it.
3. The wording of the proposal may be changed before members agree to support it (see the section after next on changing the wording of a proposal).
4. When the discussion ends, the members are asked whether they support the proposed course of action (see section on taking informal or formal votes).
5. If the group agrees to the proposal, follow-up duties are assigned.

Sample Script: A Research-Driven Proposal

In this script, it is assumed that a proposal has been prepared before the meeting, and is presented to the members for consideration and approval:

"The report by the human resources committee recommends that we approve the staff orientation program. The proposed program was included in the premeeting package. Is there any discussion on the document?"

Next, members discuss the proposed orientation program. Some components of the program are changed, some are deleted, and new components are added to the program as a result of the discussion. When the discussion seems to have ended the leader says:

"Are there any more comments on the proposed orientation program, as changed? Is it acceptable to the group? Any lingering doubts? If not, we'll record in the minutes that the program has been approved, with the noted changes. Thank you, everyone, and a special thanks to Donna, Rick, and Jonathan for preparing the document.

"Before we move on, we need to decide on follow-up steps for the program. Donna, would you finalize the program and package it for circulation to all departments in the company? Would you also prepare a covering memo to explain the package? Thank you. Should Donna mention in her memo names of individuals who will be available to answer any questions about the program? How about Rick? Jonathan? Thanks."

Sample Script: A Consensus-Driven Decision

In the following script it is assumed that no proposal was prepared prior to the meeting, and that consensus was recorded on a flip chart while the issue was discussed:

"Based on the informal discussion we've had on the issue of shared office space, I put down a few notes on the flip chart. Let me see if I can read my own handwriting. The consensus of the group seems to be as follows:

- It is not cost-effective for us to move to new premises, even though we expect substantial growth in staff.
- We should hire a telecommuting consultant to advise us on how we can use alternative work methods to alleviate the pressures on our office space.
- Karen should solicit cost proposals from three telecommuting consultants and invite them to present their proposals to us at our next meeting.

> "Is this an accurate summary of our consensus? Did I miss anything? Is there any further discussion on it? Thank you. Matt, would you please record the consensus in the minutes? Thank you, everyone. Let's move on to the next issue on the agenda."

Taking Informal or Formal Votes

The previous section described the steps for handling a proposal. Assuming a shared decision-making process, the decision on a proposal is made by the group, by an informal or formal voting process.

Informal Votes

If the group is reasonably harmonious, it will rarely be necessary to call for a show of hands. Under these conditions, informal votes can be taken, using the following steps:

1. Articulating the proposed course of action.
2. Asking whether this course of action is acceptable to the group.
3. If there is no concern or objection, the proposal is deemed to have been approved.
4. If there are remaining concerns, they are addressed by facilitating a decision to:
   - ▲ Improve the wording of the proposal before approving it.
   - ▲ Postpone the proposal to a future meeting.
   - ▲ Delegate the proposal to a subgroup for implementation, with instructions to address lingering concerns.
   - ▲ Refer the proposal to a subgroup for research and analysis that will be reported in a future meeting.

Formal Votes

Unanimity on a proposed course of action is not always possible to achieve. In such instances it may be necessary to "bite the bullet" and resolve the impasse by taking a formal vote on the proposal, by a show of hands or secret ballot.

As explained in Chapter 5 on rules of engagement, a formal vote is usually majority-based. If more members vote in favor of a proposal than against it, it is approved. If the number of votes in favor of a proposal equals or is less than the number of votes against it, the proposal is defeated.

Sample Script: Should Music Be Allowed at Work?

"We've been discussing whether playing music at low volumes on the job is appropriate for our company, and we do not appear to have unanimity on which way we should go. Management expects a recommendation from us today, so I'll need to take a show of hands. Please raise your hand if you think allowing music at low volumes on the job is a good idea. I am counting six hands. Raise your hand if you think it's a bad idea. I am counting four hands. We'll report to management that, by a vote of six to four, we believe it is acceptable to play music at low volumes on the job."

Sample Script: Should This Behavior Be Tolerated?

"It is time for us to make some tough decisions on the termination of the employment of one of our managers for inappropriate behavior that occurred twice. Some of you believe the problem is serious and that we cannot afford to give him another chance, and others are prepared to give him the benefit of one more chance.

"In fairness to the manager in question, we cannot wait any longer. We need to make the decision today. In the absence of unanimity, I will take a show of hands. Please raise your hand if you are in favor of terminating the employment of ____. I am counting three hands. Raise your hand if you are against it. I am counting two hands. By a vote of three to two, we have agreed to terminate the employment of ____."

Sample Script: Which Firm Shall We Choose?

"Does anyone have anything new to add to this discussion? If not, we will proceed to closure. The decision we need to make is which of the three consulting firms to hire for this project. We listed the selection criteria, interviewed the consultants, and evaluated all three firms. Firm A has more experience. Firm B is new but has great people and good references. Firm C costs less than the other two firms.

"Based on the discussion, we don't have unanimity on which firm to choose, but time for this project is running out and we need to move on. I will go around the room and ask each one of you which firm you prefer, A, B, or C. Ron? Susan? Bev? etc. Thank you. We have three for firm A, six for B, and two for C. Based on this, we will go with firm B. Can we depend on everyone to support this decision and work with Firm B, even if your first choice was A or C? Thank you."

Sample Script: A Secret Ballot

If a private vote will enable the members to vote more honestly and without fear of consequences, you can facilitate a vote by secret ballot. The steps for a vote by a secret ballot are as follows:

- Articulate the proposed decision.
- Circulate ballots, one per member (unless the group has a weighted system of voting or proxies are allowed).
- Ask members to mark their ballots clearly, fold them, and hand them back.
- Have the ballots counted, possibly by an independent party.
- Announce the result and have it recorded in the minutes.
- Ask the members whether they agree to have the ballots destroyed.

"We will now vote on the employee of the month award. We have three candidates: Mel Jones, Tammy Dixon, and Chris Stein. Since this is a very personal decision, I think a private vote by secret ballot would be appropriate. Am I right? Thank you.

"Ruth, would you please circulate one ballot per person? Would everyone please wait and don't mark your ballot until I explain the voting process?"

When Ruth finishes distributing the ballots, say this:

"Thank you, Ruth. On your ballots you'll see the three names with a box next to each one of them. Please mark only one box on your ballot. Then fold it and hand it to Charles, our human resources adviser."

After a minute or so, say:

"Has everyone handed in their ballots? If you haven't, please raise your ballot, so Charles can collect it. Thank you. Charles, you can go ahead and count the ballots."

When the results are known, say this:

"Thank you, Charles. Here are the results of the vote on the employee of the month: ____"

Some groups announce the actual count results, e.g., "Mel Jones received two votes, Tammy Dixon received three votes, and Chris Stein received six votes. Chris Stein is the employee of the month." Other groups may be concerned about the possibility of embarrassing the nonwinners, and prefer to only announce the winner but not the exact numbers of votes.

Changing the Wording of a Proposal or Document

A proposal or a document that is to be approved by the group should be clear, concise, and complete before a final decision on it is made. If members are uncomfortable with a proposal or a document, they can suggest changes to address their concerns. Wording changes can help achieve the following goals:

- Greater clarity
- Removing ambiguities
- Adding parts that are not covered in the original proposal
- Deleting parts that are not acceptable to the group
- Integrating legitimate needs stated or implied by members (see the following sample script)

There are two types of changes to a proposal or a document: (1) housekeeping changes, which can be made quickly and with no discussion, and (2) substantive changes, which should be opened for discussion.

The actual decision to change the wording of a proposal or a document should be made with the involvement of the group. It should not be made unilaterally by the leader nor should it be imposed by a few vocal members. Including the group in the decision to change the proposal is especially important if the proposed change is contentious.

The decision to change the proposal can be made informally or formally:

- ▲ Informally, by asking if the members agree to the change. This would typically apply to a noncontroversial change: "Given this new information, is it OK to change the amount from $5,000 to $5,500?" (Pause.) "Thank you, the change will be made."
- ▲ Formally, by getting a sense of how many are in favor of the change and how many are not. This approach would typically apply to a controversial change: "Jack is suggesting that we change the proposal by switching from five to ten workstations. This is a substantial change to the proposal, and the group should discuss it. Are there any comments about the suggested change?"

At the end of the discussion, consensus may emerge about the suggested change. However, there will be times when you will need to take a show of hands to resolve a disagreement about a proposed change. For example, "Let me take a show of hands. Raise your hands if you are in favor of adding five workstations. Thank you. How many are against it? Thank you. It seems like most of you don't want to add five workstations."

The following ideas will help you make the amending process simpler, smoother, more logical, and less time-consuming:

- ▲ Save time at the meeting by reducing the likelihood of housekeeping amendments. Arrange for all proposals to be reviewed by a good writer, to address grammatical and typing errors, awkward and confusing sentences, inappropriate language, weak and ambiguous words, etc.
- ▲ Capitalize on the skills of your "nitpickers" by involving them in writing documents and proposals.
- ▲ If a proposal or a document under discussion is so poorly worded that it takes too much meeting time to improve, it should be sent to a "wordsmith" or a committee to work on. The refined document can be presented later at the same meeting, or at a subsequent meeting (if the decision on the proposal can wait).
- ▲ The group should be wary of excessive nit-picking and attempts to make the wording of a proposal perfect when its intent is clear. The risk of trying for perfection is that members may lose precious time that should be spent on the core proposal. Here is a script to use if the discussion focuses on minor changes instead of the core proposal:

"Can I make an observation? It seems to me we're getting bogged down in small details and doing the work of a wordsmith. It is laudable that we want to make the document perfect, but we need to be focusing on the core proposal itself and the principles behind it. I think we should get back on track. Why don't we leave the detail work for someone to work on and present to us after the coffee break? In the meantime, I suggest we focus on core questions behind this issue, like ____."

The following are three examples of the process for modifying a proposal or a document.

Sample Script: Integrating Legitimate Needs Stated by an Opponent

With more critics than creators, many good initiatives are torpedoed because members are too busy criticizing them, and/or leaders or proponents are too busy defending them. When faced with opposition to a proposal, discussion leaders should:

- ▲ Avoid being defensive.
- ▲ Treat the objections as legitimate "pieces of the truth" that need to be explored.
- ▲ Listen and ask probing questions about the objections. For example, the leader can ask questions like these: "What do you mean by ____?" "What specifically concerns you?" "What impacts are you worried about?" "What would we lose if we gave up the existing system?" "What threats does the new system present?"
- ▲ Listen and convert complaints and criticisms into affirmative needs.
- ▲ Make an effort to integrate legitimate needs by changing the wording of the proposal.

Here is a script that illustrates how to convert objections into affirmative needs and integrate them into a proposal:

Facilitator: "The proposal is that we go into a new decentralized organizational structure, with local locations having greater autonomy. The detailed proposal was circulated to you before the meeting. Is there any discussion on this proposal?"

Mary: "This is not comfortable at all. It really makes me feel nervous."

Facilitator: "What about this proposal makes you feel nervous?"

Mary: "It feels like we're losing all control and accountability. Local managers will be like loose cannons and will not work as team players. We will never be able to regain control once we give it away. I know there are some theoretical advantages for greater local autonomy, but I just cannot support this proposal. It's way too risky. We're much better off with the existing system."

Facilitator: "Thanks, Mary. Let me see if I understand your concerns. For this new system to work, you would need more accountability and better reporting built into it. It also sounds like you want to make sure local managers act responsibly and support the central office. Finally, it seems that, for you to be comfortable with this proposal, you need to see the central office having the authority to intervene if a local manager is not working as a team member. Does this cover your concerns?"

Mary: "Yes, exactly. How did you do that?"

Facilitator: "How did I do what?"

Mary: "What I said was a series of complaints and criticisms. But you managed to turn them into something positive and useful. That was very effective."

Facilitator: "Thank you, Mary. It's nice to be appreciated. Ron, how can the proposal be changed to retain the advantages of greater local autonomy, while maintaining the levels of accountability that the current system has?"

Ron: "Let me think about that over coffee break. Mary, would you join me and help me with this change while we are out on a break?"

After the break:

Ron: "Mary and I worked out new wording for the proposal that has enough autonomy and enough accountability. Here are the changes: _____."

Facilitator: "Are these changes acceptable to the group? Are there any concerns about them? OK, the changes will be made. Good work, Ron and Mary. Are there any other comments about the proposed new organizational structure?"

Note: The facilitator was able to turn the objections into legitimate affirmative needs, and was able to turn Mary from a critic into a creator.

Sample Script: Processing Changes to a Position Document

The script below shows how a significant document can be discussed, amended, and approved. The process being followed consists of the following steps:

1. A general discussion of the goals and principles behind the document
2. A page-by-page review and improvements to the wording of the document
3. A final approval of the amended document

The scenario is as follows: A native Indian community sets out to approve an important document. The document states the principles to follow when negotiating agreements with government agencies. The group retains a consultant to review its needs and prepare a draft document for consideration, amendment, and approval at a one-day community workshop.

The document is precirculated to the members of the community, who are asked to review it and prepare to discuss it at the community workshop. Here is how the community workshop unfolds:

Facilitator: "Good morning, everyone, and welcome to this meeting. We have an important document to discuss, improve, and approve today. This document will help us negotiate with government agencies and shape the future of our community.

"Before I explain the agenda for this meeting, I would like to invite our elder John to share with us an opening prayer. Please stand."

After the prayer:

"Thank you, elder John, for those inspiring thoughts. Let's keep these thoughts in our minds as we carry on with this meeting. Let me start by explaining the agenda for the day.

"We will start with a one-hour presentation by our consultant, Richard Wise, who prepared the document. Richard made a special effort to make the document simple, nontechnical, and reader-friendly. We assume you reviewed the document and that you will be able to discuss it today.

"Richard will explain what guided him as he prepared the document for us. His presentation will be broken into three parts, and there will be question periods between the parts. You will have many opportunities to get involved. It will not be a straight lecture.

"After the presentation, which should end at 10:15, we will take a fifteen-minute break, at which time we encourage you to talk to people you have not met and discuss your impressions of the proposed new document.

"After the break, we will break into small groups at your round tables and discuss the document for thirty minutes. There will be specific instructions for you at that time.

"After the small group discussions we will go through the document together, discuss it, change it, and then approve it. We expect to finish by 4 P.M., with a lunch break from noon to 1 P.M.

"Are there any questions about the day? Thank you. Let's work together to make it a very beneficial day and a turning point for our community. Let me start by introducing our adviser, Richard Wise, to make his presentation of the proposed new document."

The presentation is made and questions are addressed. A refreshment break follows. After the break, the small group discussions proceed at the round tables, with each group being asked to consider different questions about the document (see Appendix 2 for an example of structuring and facilitating small group discussions). Afterwards, the discussion in the full group resumes:

Facilitator: "Thank you for your work in small groups. We will now go through the document page by page, discussing the content and suggesting changes as needed. In the interests of time, please concentrate more on substantive changes and less on housekeeping changes.

"Starting with page 1: The main sections are ____ and ____. They cover the subjects of ____. Highlights are: ____. Are there any comments?"

A member suggests a change to strengthen and clarify a paragraph on page 1.

Facilitator: "There is a suggestion to change the word ____ in the third paragraph to ____, in order to articulate a clearer, stronger and more confident message. If the change is made the third paragraph will read as follows: ____ (emphasize the change). Is this change acceptable to the group? Any concern about it? Thank you, the change will be made. Are there any further concerns about page 1?"

A member suggests inserting a new paragraph at the start of section 2.

Facilitator: "There is a suggestion to insert a new paragraph at the start of section 2, expressing our belief in the principle that ____. Shall we leave it to our consultant Richard to draft this new paragraph and present it to us after lunch? Thank you. Richard, do you need any clarification on the intent of the extra paragraph?"

Richard clarifies his understanding and the group is comfortable with it.

Facilitator: "Are there any more concerns about page 1 of the document? If not, let's move on to page 2, which covers the following sections: ____, ____ and ____. The subjects are ____. The highlights are: ____. Are there any comments about page 2?"

A member suggests a change to the third paragraph.

Facilitator: "There is a suggestion to change the third paragraph, fourth line, by replacing the word ____ with ____, so the sentence will reads as follows: ____. Is this change acceptable? I see some members are concerned about it. Let's find out what the concerns are: Steve . . . (Steve comments). Susan . . . (Susan comments). Are there any more comments about the suggested change from ____ to ____? Does anyone have an alternative wording that will address everyone's concerns?"

If a third alternative is found, articulate it and see if it is acceptable. If an acceptable third alternative is not found:

Facilitator: "A third alternative is not evident, so I suggest we take a show of hands. Raise your hands if you are in favor of the original wording, which is ____. Thank you. Raise your hands if you are in favor of the proposed new wording, which is ____. Thank you. The current wording will remain unchanged. Are there any more comments about page 2?

"If not, we are now at our lunch break, and we've made great progress. We'll resume at 1 P.M. and continue with the remainder of the document. Please make it a working lunch and continue to discuss your thoughts about the new document. See if you can break bread with people you haven't met before. See you back here at 1 o'clock."

After the lunch break, the process continues:

- ▲ Richard presents the new paragraph for page 1. The group agrees to insert it.
- ▲ Someone comes up with a better alternative for the change that was not approved before the break. The alternative wording is discussed and approved.
- ▲ The remaining pages are discussed and more changes are made.

When the group concludes the discussion, the facilitator says: "We have now concluded the discussion of the document. Is it fair to say that it has your support and can be presented to the government as your statement of principles? Let me take a show of hands. Those in favor of the document please raise your hands. Thank you. Any opposed? Thank you. It seems like a unanimous vote to me. Congratulations everyone. We can now negotiate with government agencies as a united community."

Note: Given the inclusive and thorough process, the above approach typically leads to a unanimous endorsement of a document, despite the odd disagreement over some of its sections.

Sample Script: The Gradual Buildup of a Proposal

The following sample script shows you how the amending process of a proposal can be handled. It starts with a proposal and several suggested changes to it. The suggested changes are then treated as different decisions that need to be made. At the end of the process, the consensus is consolidated and the decision is finalized. With this approach the change process has the semblance of building something from its components, instead of tearing it apart (as the usual amending process often does).

Shirley (facilitator): "The next agenda item is a suggestion that our company get involved in charitable activities. The specific proposal is to donate $1,000 to the United Way campaign this year. Does anyone have any comments on this proposal?"

Suzanne: "I think we should be more generous and donate $2,000."

Rick: "Why the United Way? Why not the Salvation Army? They do great community work, especially around the holiday season."

Ron: "I think we should also encourage each employee to donate through payroll deductions."

After further discussion, the facilitator proceeds as follows:

Shirley: "I've been making notes on the flip chart. Based on our discussion, it seems to me we need to make four decisions:

- ▲ First, whether donating money to a charitable cause is a good idea.
- ▲ Second, if we say yes to the first question, how much we should donate altogether this first time: $1,000? $2,000?
- ▲ Third, we need to decide which organization we want to donate to: the United Way, the Salvation Army, another organization, or maybe a few of them.
- ▲ Fourth, we need to decide whether employees should be encouraged to donate through payroll deductions.

"Does this cover the scope of what we need to decide? Thank you. Let's discuss these decisions one at a time, starting with the first question: Should we donate any money to charitable causes? Remember, we're not talking about the amount or to whom, just whether this is a good idea at all. Any comments?"

After further discussion, the facilitator says this:

Shirley: "Any new comments on whether donating to charitable causes is a good idea? Well, based on our discussion, it is safe to say that you think donating money to charitable organizations is a good idea and that our company should pursue it.

"Let's continue with the second decision: How much money altogether should we donate to charity this time? Remember, we are not talking about whom to give it to yet. Just the total amount. Any comments?"

Sometime later:

Shirley: "Based on our discussion, it appears like everyone is comfortable donating a grand total of $5,000." (Surprise!!) "Let's continue with the third decision: Which organizations should we donate to, and how much?"

Sometime later:

Shirley: "Let me summarize our consensus so far: We agreed to donate a total of $5,000 to the United Way Campaign, out of which $2,000 will be a designated donation to the Salvation Army and $3,000 to the United Way general fund. Chuck, please record our consensus in the minutes.

"I am looking at my watch, and we're out of time on this agenda item. The question of whether employees should be encouraged to donate through payroll deductions will take more time than we have today. We'll need to deal with it at the next meeting, under unfinished business."

Analysis of the Above Script

The above approach differs from the often wasteful amending process, whereby any proposed word changes are discussed in isolation and in no logical sequence, and whereby amendments often preempt the discussion on the core proposal.

For illustration purposes, imagine what a waste of time it would have been if the group argued endlessly about the amount to be donated if a majority of them didn't want the company to get involved in charitable activities at all.

The facilitator should feel free to establish the logical sequence of subdecisions, and start with the one that needs to be made first. If the outcome on this decision is negative, the other components of the proposal will likely not be pursued.

Delaying, Delegating, Parking, or Dropping an Agenda Item

As you steer the meeting to its destination, it may become apparent that spending time on an issue or forcing closure on a proposal would be unwise. You can then facilitate a decision to delay, delegate, park, or drop the agenda item.

Here are some of the mistakes made when dealing with inappropriate agenda items:

1. Members do not question the inclusion of inappropriate agenda items (see Chapter 9 on agenda master's checklist).
2. Inappropriate items are added at the last minute and consume time early in the meeting, at the expense of other important items that need full consideration.

3. The group capitulates to persistent members who demand the inclusion of inappropriate agenda items. The facilitator doesn't know how to say no. Members either don't notice the problem or hesitate to complain.
4. The facilitator starts a time-consuming argument with a member as to the appropriateness of an agenda item, instead of letting the group decide whether to include it or exclude it from the agenda.

Here are the main options for dealing with inappropriate agenda items at the meeting:

1. *Delay it.* The group can decide to postpone the item to later in the same meeting or to a future meeting. This option will be useful if:
   - ▲ The group is bogged down and is not making any progress. Disengaging from the issue will give members time to come up with creative ideas to break the deadlock.
   - ▲ It is late, and there is no time to give the item the full consideration it needs.
   - ▲ Tempers are flaring, and there is a need for a cooling-off period.
2. *Delegate it.* The group can decide to refer the item to a member or a subgroup for study, to fill information gaps and do some necessary research and analysis. The group can also decide that the item does not need interactive discussion and can be delegated to a person or subgroup for decision and implementation.
3. *Park it.* The group can decide to place the item in the "parking lot." The parking lot is reviewed from time to time by the agenda designer, and items are pulled from it and placed on the agenda. This would apply to a new idea that surfaces as a result of the discussion.
4. *Drop it.* The group can decide to drop the item from the agenda, because it's an off-mandate item or the item is not urgent and is not a current priority for the organization.

Sample Script: A Late Addition to the Agenda

Establishing support for the agenda is done at the launching stage of the meeting (see Chapter 11). At that stage, requests to add items to the agenda can be addressed. If a member proposes a late addition to the agenda, and the late item seems inappropriate, you can say something like this:

"Reg, our practice is that new items are only added if they are urgent or not time-consuming. The one you're suggesting seems to be a substantial item that can and should wait until a future meeting."

If Reg persists and claims that the item is urgent, you can ask for a show of hands:

"Let me take a show of hands and see what the group wants to do. Please raise your hand if you think this item should be postponed to a future meeting. Thank you. Please raise your hand if you think it should be added to this meeting's agenda. Thank you. Reg, based on this vote the item will be postponed to the next meeting."

Sample Script: It's Just Too Hot

"It seems like the issue is just too difficult to reach closure on. It feels like we could use a cooling-off period. Would it be OK to postpone this discussion until the next meeting, when we've had some time to think about it?"

Sample Script: Not Enough Information

"There appear to be too many unanswered questions here. Under these conditions it would not be smart for us to make a decision that we may regret later. I suggest we send this issue back to the consultant, with instructions to address a few key questions. Is this an acceptable way to go with this issue? Thanks. Let's identify the questions that we need the consultant to address: _____."

Sample Script: An Item of Questionable Value

"I was just wondering: Isn't this the type of administrative decision that we can delegate to _____? I am not sure why we're discussing it, when we have other issues that need our attention.

Can we let go of this issue and move on? Can I also suggest that in the future we avoid scheduling items like this one on the agenda in the first place?"

Caution: Avoiding the Responsibility to Make Decisions

Some groups overuse the above four options as an avoidance mechanism, in order to shy away from making tough decisions. In such instances the above four options will not be appropriate. The appropriate option will be for the group to tackle the tough issues and make the difficult decisions, as controversial as they may be.

Revisiting a Previously Made Decision

From time to time a member will want to bring back an issue that was dealt with at a previous meeting or earlier at the same meeting. Here are a few principles for revisiting a previously made decision:

- ▲ A proposal that was not approved may be brought back before the group at a subsequent meeting. Circumstances may have changed and the outcome may be different this time.
- ▲ A proposal that was approved but was not implemented, or one which is possible to reverse or modify, can be revisited at a subsequent meeting. As a result of revisiting the decision, the group may end up modifying or reversing it.
- ▲ If the group believes revisiting a previous decision is a waste of time or is not appropriate for another reason, it can refuse to spend the time revisiting it.
- ▲ If a member wants to revisit a decision at the same meeting when it was made, there must be a compelling reason to do so, i.e., new information surfaced and it could lead to a different outcome. Here too the group has the option of refusing to revisit the decision.

Sample Script: Revisiting a Previously Defeated Proposal

Al (a persistent advocate): "We should really take a second look at our decision not to allow any more overtime. I have new information that proves this is a good idea."

Gina (another member): "I don't think we should revisit the decision. We've looked at this issue five times in the past year, and the reasons against more overtime are quite clear and compelling. We have more pressing issues to focus on today, and we should not spend time on revisiting the overtime issue."

Charlie (facilitator): "Perhaps Al can briefly tell us what his new information is, and the group can then decide whether to revisit the decision or not."

Al explains briefly.

Charlie: "What does the group want to do? Do you want to revisit the decision? No? Sorry, Al, but they don't want to do it. We'll move on to the next agenda item."

If the group seems divided on whether or not to revisit the issue, a formal vote can be taken:

Charlie: "Let me take a show of hands on whether the overtime issue will be revisited. Please raise your hand if you think it should be revisited. Thank you. Please raise your hand if you think we should not revisit the overtime issue. Thank you. There is a majority who wants to revisit this issue. We'll schedule the revisiting on the new business portion of our agenda."

Dealing with a Deadlock

From time to time your group will find itself unable to make progress on an issue. Here are some of the warning signs (red flags) indicating that your group is bogged down:

- The same members dominate the discussion.
- Many members are holding back or are busy doing something else.
- The same arguments are being heard, and no one seems to change his or her position.
- The discussion goes in circles and lacks focus or direction.
- Members press their views, interrupt others, and are not listening.
- The time allocated for an issue has long passed, and the group is headed to "rush hour," i.e., leaving many important decisions to the last fifteen minutes of the meeting.

▲ The discussion is monotonous and boring.

If the group is bogged down, it should stop what it's doing and start doing something different. There is no sense squandering even more time on a process that is not working. Here are a few scripts that can help you break a deadlock in a meeting:

Sample Script: Dealing with Easier Issues First

It is natural to be drawn to the most difficult issue first. But the size of such an issue may be too intimidating early in the discussion. It may be better to start a list of issues and start with decisions that are easier to make:

"It seems to me we're trying to answer the biggest and most difficult question first. Can we try a different approach? How about if we start a list of all the questions we need to address, and then begin by answering a few easier questions and building some momentum. I have a feeling that when we get to the bigger issue, it will not look quite as big as it does now. Does this sound like a reasonable way to go? Good. Let me start a list of all the questions that we need to address in connection with this issue."

Sample Script: Dealing with the Right Issues

Sometimes a group is bogged down because it is focused on the wrong issue, or looking at the right issue from the wrong angle.

"I'm not sure we're focusing on the right issue now. We are talking about our internal structure and asking who will get along better with whom. As a result of this, we are getting stuck in power struggles. What we should be asking is: How can our structure serve our customers better? Our customers are the ultimate boss. If we look at things from their perspective, other things will fall into place."

Sample Script: A Summary of Progress (or Lack Thereof)

"I am looking at my watch and the amount of progress we've made on this issue. I am also looking at the remainder of our agenda. Perhaps I can summarize the points on which we agree and where we still need to make progress, and then we can decide what to do.

"First, the areas of agreement. We seem to agree on two points: _____ and _____.

"On the other hand, we seem stuck in the following areas: _____, _____, and _____.

"Here is a suggestion: Would it be OK to have Tim, Judy, and Cathy look at these issues and report back to us at the next meeting? Thank you. Let's move on to the next item on the agenda, which is _____."

Note: When choosing the members of the subgroup to resolve outstanding issues, consider a combination of some vocal members and some quiet but insightful ones.

Sample Script: Advocating the Opposite Position

"I am hearing two opposing views on this issue. Time is running out, and we can't seem to make much progress. I have a suggestion to get us beyond our current thinking and listen better. Here it is:

"Would each one of you please team up with a person who has an opposing view? I'll wait until you've done that. (Pause.)

"Now here is your assignment, and you have no choice but to accept it. Take the person you chose for a twenty-minute brisk walk outside. While you walk, see if you can articulate, with passion, the view of your partner, which is opposite to yours. After you do this, your partner will tell you whether she or he has been heard and understood by you. Then reverse roles and your partner will do the same. Any questions? Thanks. See you in twenty minutes."

Note: When members come back, they are likely to have realized how little listening they did while the meeting was in progress. This humbling experience may compel them to listen to differing views and learn from them. Creative ideas may become more abundant, and the deadlock may become easier to resolve.

Sample Script: Some Solitary Thinking

"We seem to be going around in circles and hearing the same arguments, and the time for this issue is slowly but surely running out. Here is a suggestion: For the next three minutes would each of you take a piece of paper and jot down your thoughts on this issue. No talking, just thinking.

"After three minutes of silence I will call on some of you, especially those who have not spoken on this issue, to give us advice on how we can move forward."

Caucusing with Subgroups

As an impartial facilitator, you may end up mediating a meeting between two groups that have difficulties working together. The meeting between the two groups may become deadlocked if members are uncomfortable disclosing important information, for fear of compromising their negotiating positions.

A useful tool to consider in such meetings is holding separate meetings, or "caucuses," with each group. During the caucus meetings, members of both groups will feel freer and more open to disclosing and discussing their bottom-line issues and "hidden agendas." You can then gather the relevant information and determine the direction of the joint meeting when the two groups resume joint discussions.

For sample scripts on caucusing options see Chapter 17 on contentious meetings.

Using Special Discussion Activities

Various chapters in this book refer to special discussion activities that you can use to replace the traditional "everyone sits around the same circle and talks." Special discussion activities can achieve these benefits:

- ▲ Introduce variety to a meeting
- ▲ Engage more members in consensus building
- ▲ Include more perspectives in the discussion
- ▲ Lead to better collective decisions
- ▲ Enable members to interact and work with one another

Typical special discussion activities include:

- ▲ Discussions in small breakout groups, followed by reports to the bigger group
- ▲ Setting up flip chart sheets on the walls around the room and asking members to work on them to set priorities and build consensus

It is not always appropriate to have special discussion activities. Here are two examples of mistakes made with special discussion activities:

1. A speaker asked his audience three times within a thirty-minute presentation to break into small groups and explore obscurely defined topics. Each of the three small group discussions was two minutes long, hardly enough time for people to say hello. Needless to say, the exercise was meaningless and achieved nothing. A more effective way to engage the audience would have been through a question period. Sometimes it is best to keep things simple. Don't try something just because someone else did or it seems like a fun thing to do. Think it through from the audience's perspective. Will it work for them?
2. In a meeting of a professional association, with a large number of guests in attendance, the president asked everyone to break into small groups and discuss what the association could do to attract more members. Several guests were uncomfortable being drawn into the internal affairs of the association, but found it very awkward to tune out or remove themselves from the discussions. The small group discussions and the topic selection were definitely not appropriate in this setting.

Here are a few tips to consider for special discussion activities:

- ▲ Be sensitive to the group.
- ▲ Determine whether the activity is appropriate and whether it is the best use of time.

▲ If in doubt about the proposed activity, ask the group at the start whether they think it will work.

▲ Have a contingency plan, in case they refuse to go for the special activity or it fails.

▲ Give them enough time for the activity, to make it meaningful.

▲ Give them clear instructions and state the precise questions to consider. See the following sample script.

Sample Script: Breaking into Discussion Groups

"Here is how I suggest we address these three issues. I suggest we break into three small discussion groups, with each group giving detailed attention to one of the three issues. We'll allow twenty minutes for the discussion in small groups. At the end of the small group discussions, we will hear from each group and discuss the issues further in the full group. Does this sound like a reasonable approach? Thanks.

"We'll set up the three small groups in a moment. But before we do that, here are a few requests: Please select an individual in your group to take notes on your group's flip chart. Second, please make a special effort to involve everyone in the discussion, at least once. I will walk around the room once you start and see if you need any help. I will also wave timing alert signs: ten minutes left, five minutes left, two minutes left, and time is up. Are there any questions?

"Let's set up the small groups. Please start counting one, two, three, and then again. (Members count off.) OK, would all the members with number one go to this corner of the room? Here is the envelope with your question. Would all the twos go to this corner? Here is your envelope. And would all the threes go to this corner? Here is your envelope.

"Is everyone set and ready to go? OK, twenty minutes. Go."

Using Flip Charts to Record Consensus

Various sections in this chapter refer to recording consensus on a flip chart. The benefits of using this technique are:

- ▲ Members see the main discussion points.
- ▲ The discussion is focused along key themes shown on the flip chart.
- ▲ Repetition is reduced, i.e., if a member returns to a previous point, the facilitator can say, "As you can see, this point is already on the flip chart."
- ▲ It helps the facilitator summarize the discussion in a concise point-format.
- ▲ It helps the group identify areas of agreement and disagreement.
- ▲ It helps facilitate closure on issues.
- ▲ It helps the minute taker take accurate summaries and does not require them to record every word said at the meeting.

Here are a few practical tips when recording the consensus on a flip chart:

- ▲ Record only key words, not long sentences. For example, convert "We are really doing a bad job at communicating with our customers and letting them know what's happening" into a concise note such as "Improve customer communication." (Note the reframing of the complaint into an affirmative need.)
- ▲ Write legibly and quickly.
- ▲ Use abbreviations and signs, so you can write fast and don't slow down the discussion. For example, instead of "improve customer communication," write "cust. comm." and draw an arrow pointing up next to it.
- ▲ If the same point is repeated, put a mark next to it, indicating it was mentioned again.
- ▲ Record the items in separate columns if they correspond to different categories. For example, have a separate column for risks and one for opportunities.
- ▲ Place the flip chart on the side that will enable you to write on it without turning your back to the group. (If you are right-handed, put the easel on your left side. If you are left-handed, put the easel on your right side.)
- ▲ You may want to delegate the task of recording consensus on a flip chart to another member, so you can focus on the group. If you do this, you should pick someone who has legible handwriting and can write fast, and also listens well and can reframe issues appropriately. Ask the individual chosen not to write word for word, but only key points. You may want to direct what should be recorded. For example, "Chuck, please record 'improve customer service.'"

Managing People in a Meeting

Having learned how to manage time and issues in the two previous sections, you now need tools to manage people and bring out the best in them during a meeting.

The people management tools given in this section are intended to help you address the following challenges:

- ▲ Drawing out the best in your members
- ▲ Capitalizing on members' knowledge and expertise
- ▲ Engaging members through all the senses
- ▲ Responding to verbal and nonverbal signals

Drawing Out the Best in Your Members

As you manage people in a meeting, one of your goals should be to draw out the best in each one of them. To achieve this goal you need to make it your business to get to know as many of your meeting participants as possible.

One way of getting to know your members is through an orientation process. See Chapter 4 for more details on how to select, orient, and nurture your team. In order to draw out the best in them during meetings, you need to ask each of them questions like the following:

- ▲ What do you like about our meetings?
- ▲ What do you dislike about our meetings?
- ▲ What do you need to perform to your best ability in meetings?
- ▲ What will cause you to perform to your worst in meetings?
- ▲ What will make your meeting experience richer and more satisfying?
- ▲ What will cause you to look forward to meetings, instead of looking for reasons to avoid them?
- ▲ What areas of your expertise would you like us to capitalize on in a meeting?
- ▲ Are there subjects or times when you prefer to sit back and listen?
- ▲ What meeting skills would you like to develop, e.g., presentation skills, facilitation skills?
- ▲ Is there anything about my facilitation style that works for you?
- ▲ Is there anything about my facilitation style that does not work for you?
- ▲ Are there individuals whose behaviors make your meeting experience positive? How?

▲ Are there individuals whose behaviors make your meeting experience negative? How?

Take the answers to the above questions into account when you plan your next meeting.

Capitalizing on Members' Knowledge and Expertise

There is no sense having talented people sit through a meeting without the organization benefiting from their knowledge, skills, expertise, special talents, and unique and creative ideas. Unfortunately, far too often this is the reality, and the quality of the discussions and the consensus suffers because of it.

One tool that will help you capitalize on what members have to offer at a meeting is an inventory list, matching member skills with agenda items. An example of such a matrix was given in Chapter 2. Here it is again:

	Jack	Bonnie	Ruth	Derek	Steve	Ron	Phyllis
Agenda item 1	S	M	O	M	S	S	P
Agenda item 2	M	S	M	O	S	M	S
Agenda item 3	O	P	S	S	O	M	S
Agenda item 4	S	O	S	S	P	S	O

▲ *S* means *substantial knowledge and expertise*. You must hear from this member during the discussion on this issue.

▲ *M* means *marginal knowledge* and little interest by this member on this issue. You may call on him on her for an impartial observation.

▲ *P* means *potential interest* in this topic. It may be productive to delegate a low-risk assignment to such members, so they "get their feet wet."

▲ *O* means *out of the box*. This member is a potential source of fresh ideas on this topic, and has a reputation for unique and "off-the-wall" ideas.

As the discussion on an issue progresses, review your list and ask questions like:

▲ Who should we hear from and haven't yet?

▲ Who has a potentially useful outside (nonexpert) perspective to offer?

▲ Who can offer a fresh idea to break the deadlock we're in?

Balance the need for a free-flowing discussion with the need to bring different perspectives into it. Invite quiet members to speak, even if they're not raising their hands. For example:

- ▲ To an *S* member: "Sophie, we haven't heard from you, and you have lots of expertise in this area. What do you think?"
- ▲ To an *O* member: "Goldie, we need a rescue. Do you have a fresh idea to take us beyond this deadlock?"

Engaging the Members Through All the Senses

It is truly a challenge to gain and hold the attention of a group of people for the full duration of a meeting. As the meeting progresses, the facilitator should monitor the members and see that as many of them as possible are engaged in the discussions. Chapter 8 explains how to plan a meeting to be "multisensory" (see the section "Variety and a Light Touch).

Responding to Verbal and Nonverbal Signals

A key role for you as a meeting facilitator is to always be tuned in to the mood and the needs of your group. You need to listen to the participants and maintain eye contact with them, and respond effectively to their stated and unstated (implied) needs. This means you must always examine the verbal and nonverbal signals that members may be sending your way.

This section describes typical signals to watch for during a meeting and offers options for responding to them. It is divided into two categories: (1) responding to personal signals and (2) responding to collective signals.

Responding to Personal Signals

If you observe or hear this signal:	*You may need to respond like this:*
Mona is sighing with frustration, or rolling her eyes, or exchanging a cynical look with Judy when Stan is speaking.	"Just a minute, Stan. Mona, I can see you are disagreeing with Stan. Can you please hear him out first and then speak?" Or: "Stan, some members seem ready to move on. We need you to wrap up." Or: Speak to Mona and Judy after the

	meeting about the need to treat other members with respect.
Gina seems unusually quiet. She may be upset or distracted by something.	"Gina, is everything OK? It's unusual to not have you participate actively. Is there a problem we should know about?" Or: Approach Gina at the break or after the meeting and find out what the problem is. It may have nothing to do with the meeting, but she would appreciate your sensitivity.
Tom seems delighted with something you or someone else said.	"Tom, I can see you are pleased. Any comments?"
Phil is looking nervously at his watch.	"Is there a problem, Phil? How are you doing for time?"
An unexpected thing just happened. Mark, who was holding stubbornly to his opinion until now, suddenly acknowledges that he has been missing an important point. He then makes a major concession.	"This is just great, Mark. Thank you so much for the concession. It helps a lot. It must have been hard for you to make it when your department was affected by it so much."
Russ had worked very hard on an idea, which was then turned down by your boss. He is very discouraged. He tells you he is thinking of quitting the group.	Ask one of the members of the group to publicly acknowledge Russ's special contributions at the next meeting. Give him a gift in appreciation of his efforts. It may or may not compel him to stay, but he will appreciate working with your group.
Fred has just given a great presentation and you are very proud.	If it is appropriate, state your sentiment at the meeting. To be on the safe side (in case some members may not have liked what Fred had to say), save your compliment for after the meeting: "Fred, your presentation was outstanding. I was very proud of you."
Jenny raises her voice, her tone is harsh and hostile, and she is verbally abusive.	"Jenny, can we soften the tone of the discussion? I understand your

If you observe or hear this signal:	*You may need to respond like this:*
	frustration, but can we keep things civil?"
Just before the break, Reg says, "I find this remark offensive" and leaves the room angry.	Find him, ask him what he found offensive, and see whether it can be addressed after the break.
Kelly's idea was scoffed upon by Drew, a very vocal and opinionated member. Kelly is visibly upset and close to tears.	Call a break. Comfort Kelly and reassure her that her idea will be discussed. Ask Drew to soften his criticism of new ideas. The fact that he has been a member for a long time does not make his input any more valid than Kelly's input.
Rob approaches you during the break: "There is a major problem with this group. There are several members who won't say a thing. On the other hand, there are other members who think they own this organization."	Start the meeting by saying, "I am wondering if we might discuss an issue with our group's dynamics before we continue. Can we take a couple of minutes to do this? It seems to me, and others have made the same observation, that some members speak and participate more than others. The impact is that we miss the insights of newer and quieter members. What can we do to even the playing field, so we can hear from quieter members also?" Or start saying no to dominant members: "We need to hear from those who have not spoken." Or call upon quiet members: "Shirley, what do you think? Can you help us out with this issue?"
David starts a side conversation with Vicky. She is trying to concentrate on the meeting but is too polite to say no.	You may need to interrupt whoever is speaking and intervene: "David, is there a problem?" Once the problem is addressed, you can carry on. Or you can talk to David after the meeting: "David, I noticed that during

	the meeting you were talking to Vicky. She went along with you, but I sensed that she might have preferred to focus on the meeting. You may want to ask her for feedback." Or you can talk to Vicky: "Vicky, I noticed David was speaking to you and I sensed that you wanted to say no but didn't. Do you want any ideas on how to say no, graciously but firmly?" ("David, if you don't mind I am trying to concentrate.")
Emily has just expressed a strong opinion. You know that Jackie has information that will shed a more objective light on the issue.	"Thank you, Emily. Jackie, can you help us out with this issue?"
Jake says: "But George and his department feel very strongly that this should not be done. Our department is very much in support of his position." You look at George and see him shaking his head with apparent disbelief.	"Thank you, Jake. I'll let George speak for himself. George, where do you and your department stand on this issue?"
Linda's facial expression tells you that you managed to baffle and confuse her. She is an astute woman, so you must have done really poorly by managing to confuse her . . .	"I lost you, Linda, didn't I? Where did I confuse you? Do you want me to start over?"
Shawn speaks with a soft voice, and others are trying very hard to hear him.	"Shawn, we need you to raise your voice, or you may want to stand or go to a microphone to be heard." If this does not work because of the poor acoustics of the room, reassure everyone that you will briefly recap Shawn's point when he finishes speaking: "Here is the gist of what Shawn was saying: _____. Am I right, Shawn?"

If you observe or hear this signal:	*You may need to respond like this:*
Members can't read what's on the flip chart or the overhead projector.	Take the corrective action needed. This may mean having a contingency plan. Why not just talk to them and not worry about the bells and whistles of the audiovisual aids?
Don, anxious to speak, raises his hand and does not put it down. It's distracting for others. Plus, he is not likely to be listening to what Rita is saying right now.	"Just a second, Rita. Don, I saw your hand and I added your name to the speakers' lineup. You can put it down now and focus on what Rita is saying. Thanks. Rita, go ahead."
Rochelle has a rebuttal for every comment and is dominating the discussion.	"Thank you Rochelle. We need to hear from some of the members who have not spoken." Or: "Rochelle, do you want to hear my answer to this question? If you don't, that's fine with me. But there is no sense in my giving it if you won't hear it. If you do want to hear me, I need you to slow down a bit and avoid forming your rebuttal while I'm speaking. Is this a reasonable request?" Or you might need stronger medicine: "Rochelle, I was just wondering: Is it within the realm of possibility that you will change your mind on this issue?"
Paul seems really nervous before a presentation. He is fidgeting, pacing, and sweating. When you speak to him, he sounds breathless and incoherent.	"Are you a bit nervous, Paul? It's a very important presentation for you, isn't it? Well, if it's any help, I think you can relax. It's clear to me that you've worked very hard on this presentation. I know you'll do just great. Here, have a glass of water. Now, is there anything I can help you with? Just in case you need it, here is a piece of advice someone gave me: When you give your presentation, pretend you are having

	one-on-one conversations with your best friends. It works for me."
After a heavy lunch, Chuck has fallen asleep.	"How about if we stood up and stretched for a moment? Lets resume in two or three minutes." Or introduce a discussion activity that will get everyone involved, like having discussions in small breakout groups, with everyone standing up. Or send everyone for a walk, or conduct mild aerobic exercise, or just pick up the pace of the meeting.
Terry seems really stressed and uncomfortable.	"It seems that we haven't had a washroom break for a while. Why don't we break for five minutes?"
Moe puts on his coat and goes back to his chair.	"Is it cold in here? Can someone please put up the heat?"
Fay's comment makes it evident she missed important points that were either stated earlier in the meeting, or were covered in a premeeting document that everyone was expected to review before the meeting.	Take note of it and talk to Fay after the meeting: "Fay, can I give you some feedback on the last meeting? I did not want to embarrass you in front of other people, but some of the questions that you were raising were covered in the reports that everyone was given before the meeting. Can I ask you to take the time to review the premeeting package next time?"
Eleanor makes a presentation that comes across as flat and incoherent. Her visual and vocal animation are nonexistent.	Talk to her after the meeting: "Eleanor, can I give you feedback on your presentation at the last meeting? Thank you. Based on how you answered this question, I sense that you agree there was room for improvement. Would you consider taking a presentation skills course or joining your local toastmasters or international training in communications club?

If you observe or hear this signal:	*You may need to respond like this:*
	Great. I am very pleased about that. In the meantime, do you want to hear my specific suggestions for your presentation to the management committee next week?"
Susan makes a religious slur at the meeting, not realizing that Abe may be sensitive to it.	"Susan, I have a feeling some members may be sensitive to the word '_____.' I know you didn't mean any harm, but I thought I should mention it to you."
During a lull in the meeting, Amos tells a condescending joke about women. He thinks it's funny, and everyone seems to be taking it as good fun, but you are not sure.	Talk to Amos after the meeting: "Amos, I have to talk to you about telling jokes about women in meetings. I know everyone laughs along with you, but with some jokes you never know what some people may be thinking. Not everyone may be laughing. Having fun is a great way to lighten up our meetings, and I encourage it. But can you choose your jokes more carefully next time?"
Pressed by others to make changes to her work routine, Kim says: "OK, I will change, but only if you change a few things on your side, like: _____."	"Kim, I don't know how productive it is to mix the two issues. Can we make one decision at a time, each one on its own merits, without making one change conditional on the other?"

Responding to Collective Signals

If you observe or hear this signal:	*You may need to respond like this:*
A lack of acknowledgment: Members are too busy talking and making their own points, but no one acknowledges	Acknowledge what people say, build on it, and reinforce their concepts. Use their own words and attribute ideas to

the validity of what other people are saying.	them. For example, "As Liz was saying a minute ago, we need to _____ in order to achieve _____." Or: "How would this solution address Neal's concern about _____?" Or: "This seems to work very well with Pat's argument that _____." Or: "As you were saying earlier, Russ, we need to _____. It seems like Cathy's idea will help achieve this goal."
The meeting is dominated by two vocal members. Other people are exchanging looks that indicate frustration.	"Shall we hear from members who have not spoken? How about you, Peter?" (assuming Peter has shown frustration)
There is tension in the room and you can't tell what is causing it.	"Is everything OK? Is there a problem? I am getting a sense of discomfort from the group, and I'm not sure what it's about. Can someone help me out?" If this does not help, you may want to call a break. Individuals may approach you in person and give you the feedback you need. Or you can approach individuals yourself and ask them what they think the problem is.
The group has just tackled a major obstacle and reached an important milestone at the meeting.	"Congratulations, everyone. You've done some great work here. Why not give yourselves a big round of applause. You deserve a reward, so here are some special chocolates for you."
The meeting started on the adversarial note, but, as the end of the meeting approaches, you are sensing a subtle shift to a more collaborative mood.	"Before we close the meeting, I would like to acknowledge something. Two hours ago we started this meeting with plenty of anxiety and animosity. What I am sensing now is much more confidence and comfort and perhaps even an optimistic mood. I don't think I can use the words 'happy ever after' to describe our mood right now, but we have certainly made progress. Let's keep up the good work."

If you observe or hear this signal:	*You may need to respond like this:*
Members are really disappointed with a setback that the group encountered with a major stakeholder. They have been working hard on this assignment and feel very disheartened and upset.	"I need to say something about this setback. First, I am just as disappointed as all of you with this turn of events. We've worked long and hard on this project, and it hurts to have this outcome. At the same time, we should not lose sight of the fact that we have created an excellent proposal, and that we have shown ourselves to be a very cohesive team. On those counts, every one of us has reason to be very proud. I suggest that, in the immediate term, it's OK to just let it hurt for a while. But in the longer term we need to learn our lessons from this experience and plan to do better next time. So let's hold our heads high and look forward to the next challenge. What do you think?"
The discussion becomes emotional and stoops to personal levels. Everyone talks at once and levels personal accusations against other people. The mood is ugly.	"Can we stop this? I know the issues are difficult, but we have human beings here, and they deserve better treatment than this. Can we stick to the issues, but be soft on people?"
You are not sure how the group is doing and you want to check this out.	Try asking these questions from time to time: "How are we doing?" "Are we making progress?" "Is anyone suffering yet? Remember what we said earlier: Suffering is optional." "We seem stuck. What do you think we should do?"

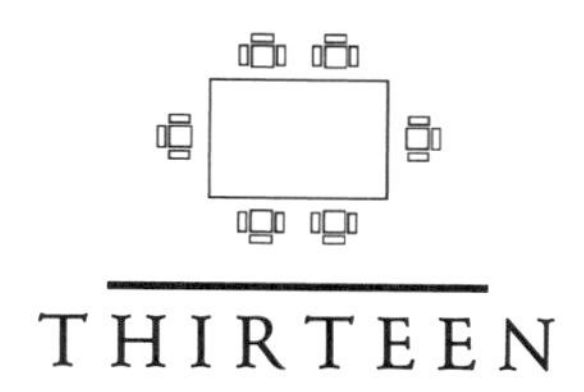

THIRTEEN

Pulling Your Weight in a Meeting

With the meeting being steered confidently to its destination, and with time, issues, and people being well managed (see Chapter 12), the leadership tasks have been addressed. However, looking beyond the leadership aspects, there are many other roles and activities that individual members get involved in during a meeting.

This chapter offers tools for meeting participants, so they can pull their weight and contribute to the meeting's success. With these tools, each individual should be able to participate as an active and motivated team player. A meeting then resembles a canoe ride, with every crew member rowing and making a difference. Specifically, this chapter offers tips and ideas to meeting participants on these topics:

- Staying alert
- Exercising due diligence
- Lining up to speak
- Communicating
- Listening

- Asking questions
- Thinking
- Making presentations
- Answering questions
- Converting negativity into affirmative needs
- Giving and receiving feedback
- Celebrating successes
- Off-line interactions and consensus building
- Helping out
- Managing your hot buttons
- Asserting yourself without getting angry
- Turning failures into learning opportunities
- Taking minutes

STAYING ALERT

To pull your weight, you need to be alert and involved throughout the meeting. Consider the canoe analogy: If a crew member is asleep or daydreaming, other members have more work to do. The canoe may end up going in circles and making little or no progress.

To stay alert and involved at the meeting, consider the following tips:

- Get a good night's sleep the night before the meeting.
- Avoid a heavy meal before a meeting.
- It is best to avoid any alcohol before or during a business meeting.
- Avoid drinking too much coffee or soft drinks. Try instead the natural juices and the healthier herbal or green tea or water.
- If there is catering at the meeting, don't eat too much and avoid sampling every cake during the breaks. Try instead fresh vegetables or fruit, which may be less flavorful but are less demanding on your digestive system.
- Make suggestions to the facilitator before the meeting on how to make it interesting, engaging, and fun. For example, "Tom, I have a couple of short funny

stories that are appropriate for our group. Let me know if and when you need them at the meeting. I will not be offended if you ignore me altogether, but I thought I'd offer some levity if we need some."

If the discussion is boring or you have trouble keeping awake, consider the following tips:

- Feel free to stand and move around if you need to, but let the facilitator and the members know in advance that you might need to do this to stay focused and alert.
- Suggest ways of breaking the monotony of the discussion. For example, "Can I make a suggestion? I don't know about everyone else, but I am at a saturation point. Can we take a ten-minute break? Can we ask our budding fitness instructor Jean to help us sharpen our stretching skills?" or "May I say something? It feels like our progress has been slow and tiring. Can we change the pace by breaking into small groups and having stand-up meetings, with each small group discussing one of the four aspects of this issue?"

If an agenda item is of no relevance or interest to you, consider the following tips:

- Try listening to the discussion anyway, and see if you can learn something from it, or if you can offer an "outsider's perspective" on it.
- If you know in advance of the meeting that you will not have anything useful to contribute on certain agenda items, see if the agenda can be arranged so all items requiring your participation will be scheduled in one stretch. This will enable you to arrive before they start and leave when they end.
- If the above is not possible and you have something else to do, see if you can excuse yourself from the meeting when it comes to such items.
- Alternatively, you can stay in the room and attend to other tasks without distracting other members. To do so, it is best to physically remove yourself from the group and go to the back of the room.
- If you remove yourself from the discussion, let the group know you're doing this: "Sam, I hope it's OK to excuse myself for the next two items. I don't have anything to contribute on them. I'll rejoin everyone when we get to item 6."

Exercising Due Diligence

Pulling your weight in a meeting means you should show due diligence and assist the group in making responsible, credible, and durable collective decisions. You need to exercise due diligence, scrutinize proposed courses of action, and be prepared to ask tough questions, even at the risk of disapproval by others. To make it easier for you to interject and make strong points, replace your strong statements with pointed rhetorical questions (see below).

Here are a few tips for exercising due diligence in a meeting, using a questioning style:

1. Examine and scrutinize proposals and do not hesitate to point to weaknesses in them:

   - "Can I say something? I can see the strengths in this proposal. The solution is simple, and it is also customer-friendly. At the same time, I am concerned about costs. Can we really afford it? Will we get enough of a return on investment? Will other important priorities suffer because less money will be available for them?"
   - "Before we move ahead, may I say something? I feel I wouldn't be doing my job if I didn't play devil's advocate with you. The proposal is to deal with one customer who cheated us by requiring everyone else to follow very cumbersome procedures. Have we thought about the 99 percent of our customers who are decent? Might we be sending some of them to the competition with these complicated procedures? Are we trying to kill a fly with a sledgehammer? Instead, should we consider some tightening of procedures, without punishing good customers for being loyal to us?"

2. If you are criticizing a proposal, you should also be prepared to propose an improvement or a better alternative. It is much easier to be a critic than a creator:

   - "I like this idea, but I see one problem with it: ______. Here is a suggestion on changing the approach to address this problem: ______. I believe this change will retain the strength of the idea while preventing this problem from occurring. What do you think?"

3. Don't hesitate to say something that appears to go against the grain, even if some of your colleagues are traditional thinkers. Don't let the proverbial "We've already tried it" or "This won't happen around here" deflate your enthusiasm and creativity. A meeting is not a popularity contest. It is a process to achieve the best results for the organization. All perspectives should be considered before a decision is made, especially if its impacts are substantial. Here are two scripts for you:

   - "Before we give up on this idea, I am wondering whether we are letting perceived obstacles stop us from making progress. I know this idea is unusual, but the problem we are facing is also unusual. Can we look more carefully at the merits of the idea, see if it can be changed to address any concerns, and make it more palatable to senior management?"

- "Can I ask a question? Is it necessarily true that if an idea failed in the past it is bound to fail today? Could it be that the organization just wasn't ready for it then, and it may be ready for it now? Could it be that it's not the idea that was problematic, but the way it was packaged and introduced?"

4. Similarly, feel free to interject if a new member's question, concern, or "off the wall" idea has been trivialized and dismissed too quickly by a long-standing member. Try this:

   - "Before we let go of this idea, I was wondering if Sylvia might explain it to us a bit more. I hear Amy's concern, but I also think Sylvia's idea has some interesting aspects. Sylvia, can you explain what you meant by _____? And how would your idea work given the concern that Amy raised?"

5. Encourage other members to speak up and add their perspectives to the discussion, especially those who tell you during the break, "I'd never say it to Jack's face, but this proposal is really bad. Here is why. . . ." Ask them, "Is there a reason why you won't say that at the meeting?" If you can't persuade them to do so, ask if it's OK for you to share their concern without pointing to them as the originators: "Do you mind if I talk about this when the meeting resumes? I won't mention that it came from you, but I think this point needs to be made." When the meeting resumes, you can do one of a few things:

   - Introduce the other member's concern: "Before we move on, I need to bring up a concern that came up in conversations at the break. Here it is: _____."

   - You could comment on the process: "Can I share a concern about our meetings? I am getting a sense that our discussions are so intense that some people are intimidated and don't say important things at the meeting; things that could possibly help us break deadlocks and make better decisions. I am wondering what we need to do to make it safe and comfortable for people to speak up at meetings."

   - If you are not comfortable making the above statement at the meeting, you can discuss it with the facilitator at the break or after the meeting.

6. Feel free to raise questions and concerns about the use of time at the meeting:

   - "I hate to do this, but I have to ask some pointed questions: Is our time spent in the most productive way right now? Are we making meaningful progress? Is our company getting a good return on investment on this meeting? It feels to me like we're discussing small details when we should be focusing instead on the big picture, talking about things like: _____. Am I the only one feeling this way?"

7. Do not hesitate to suggest that a decision seems rushed and that it should be delayed:

   ▲ "Before we close off on this decision, I was just wondering: Aren't we moving a little too fast on it? Have we examined all the facts, have we answered all the questions, and are we satisfied with the answers? I for one have some questions that have not been fully addressed. For example: _____. Can we postpone closure until the committee answers these and perhaps other questions that members may have?"

8. If you become aware that some other members have not prepared for the meeting and have not reviewed their meeting packages, do something about it. For example:

   ▲ Speak at the meeting: "May I raise a concern? I couldn't help but notice that some of us opened our meeting packages just before the meeting. I don't think we can make responsible decisions unless everyone prepares for the meeting. I have two suggestions: First, I suggest we postpone the decisions on _____ and _____ to the next meeting. Second, I suggest each one of us work hard to make our reports more concise and readable, so it is easier for everyone to review them before a meeting. Am I making any sense?"

   ▲ Speak to the facilitator after the meeting: "Rob, I have a hard time when I see people opening their meeting packages at the meeting itself. I also have a problem when I receive important reports late or at the meeting itself, without enough time to review them. I think our company deserves a more responsible decision-making process. Do you agree with me, and, if so, do you want some of my ideas on how we could prevent these problems in the future?"

9. If you are concerned that members are relying too much on trust and do not pay as much attention to key points as they should, you can intervene:

   ▲ Raise the concern directly: "Can I raise a concern? I sometimes get the impression that we rely too much on trust, to the extent that we become a bit lazy and don't scrutinize reports as much as we should. Yes, it is flattering to me when you trust me so much, but it also makes me feel nervous. As experienced as I may be, I am perfectly capable of making mistakes. I would rather you asked me tough questions about my reports. Is this a reasonable request?"

   ▲ Try a lighthearted approach: "Before I present my report, I have a question: How many of you read every word in my report and understand it completely? Great. Well then, how many of you discovered two very significant typing errors that I deliberately put in on pages 1 and 4? I only see two hands. Well, there is a message here: We can't take things for granted and we can't assume that reports are accurate. I think we need to pay more attention to them, so we can make informed decisions. Now that I've gotten your attention, here are the two typos: _____"

Lining Up to Speak

Pulling your weight in a meeting needs to be done in an orderly and coordinated fashion. It is difficult to concentrate in a meeting when everyone speaks at the same time. For a meeting to proceed smoothly and avoid chaotic discussions, participation protocol needs to be in place. A part of pulling your weight in a meeting may mean being patient and waiting for your turn to speak, and listening to others while you wait. Under such a protocol:

- Members line up to speak.
- Members are given equal opportunities to speak.

This section covers the following aspects of speakers' lineups:

- Protocol in a small and informal meeting (seven or fewer participants)
- Protocol in a larger meeting (eight or more participants)
- Allowing exceptions to the speakers' lineup
- An unusual approach: The roaming rock

Protocol in a Small and Informal Meeting

In a small and informal meeting (seven or fewer participants), taking a list of those who want to speak and establishing a speakers' lineup may be too rigid and formal. It may have a stifling effect and may constrain the discussion. In such a meeting a free-flowing discussion should be allowed, as long as:

- Members are conscientious about not dominating.
- Members allow one another to finish speaking before they respond.
- Members keep their comments concise and to the point and avoid rambling.
- The facilitator or any member intervenes from time to time and invites members who have been quiet to share their perspectives. For example, "I wonder what

you think about this idea, Bernie. You have done some work in this area. Can you help us out?" or "Shall we go around the room and hear a brief statement from each member on where they stand on this issue? If you have nothing to add, say 'pass.' How about starting with you, Josh? What's your view on this issue?"

Keep in mind that even in a small meeting there may be a need to be more formal. For example:

- ▲ In a municipal council, which meets in the presence of the general public, council members should wait for the mayor's acknowledgment before they speak: "Next on my list I have councilors Jones and Richards. Councilor Jones, go ahead."
- ▲ If the issues in a small meeting are contentious and emotional, a speakers' lineup will help the facilitator deal with interruptions and emotional outbursts: "Just a minute. It seems like we need some formality. Let me take a speakers' list: Who wants to speak? Alana, Joe, Petra. Thanks. Alana, you go first."

Protocol in a Larger Meeting

In a larger meeting (eight or more participants), the lack of a participation protocol and a speakers' lineup can lead to chaotic and dominated discussions. Here are a few suggestions to manage the speakers' lineup in a larger meeting:

- ▲ Members should give an indication to the facilitator that they want to speak. They can do this by raising their hands, or by lining up at a microphone. They should generally avoid "barging in" with their voices, especially when other members are waiting for their turns to speak.
- ▲ If more than one member wants to speak, the facilitator (or a member designated as "lineup manager") keeps track of the speakers' lineup and the number of times each person has spoken. The facilitator or "lineup manager" indicates who speaks next.
- ▲ A person who has not spoken on an issue is generally given priority over a person who has. This guideline is intended to create balance and prevent domination.
- ▲ To increase the likelihood of this protocol being followed, it should be articulated by the facilitator during the launching of the meeting (see Chapter 11):

> *"I know many of you will want to speak at this meeting. To ensure fairness and equality, we need a few participation guidelines. Here they are:*

"Please raise your hands if you want to speak, so I can keep a speakers' lineup.

"Please don't be offended if I say 'Hands up, please' if you happen to barge in with your voice.

"If you want to speak a second time on the same issue, you will need to wait until first-time speakers on the issue have spoken. The intent is to give people equal opportunities to speak.

"Please keep your comments concise and to the point. Given the large number of members here, please keep your comments under three minutes every time.

"Does anyone have any questions about these guidelines?"

Here are two scripts to manage the speakers' lineup as the meeting progresses:

- Three members raise their hands at the same time: "Is there any discussion on this issue? I see three hands. Gina will go first, then Dave, and then Chris."
- A member wants to speak for the second time: "Fiona, you'll need to wait a moment. I am looking for first-time speakers. Does anyone want to speak on this issue for the first time?"

Allowing Exceptions to the Speakers' Lineup

Speakers' lineups have their limitations and imperfections. Here are a few problems that are created if they are enforced too rigidly:

1. By the time someone's turn to speak has come, his or her view may have already been presented by someone else. The discussion could become repetitive.
2. By the time someone's turn to speak has come, the group is on to a different subtopic. The member's comment would amount to "backtracking."
3. A member whose comment was misinterpreted would have to wait anxiously until all first-time speakers have spoken before clarifying it. She or he may not be listening anymore.
4. A member who is the sixth on the lineup may have a comment that will make the comments by speakers 2 to 5 unnecessary and could save time. A rigid lineup will not allow for this to happen.
5. A member who has a concern about a nonsubstantive issue would not be able to make it until his or her turn comes. By then it may be too late. For example:

▲ A member may have a difficulty hearing someone with a soft voice. Should he or she have to wait in line to express this concern?

▲ A member notices that the flip chart is about to collapse.

▲ A member notices that a guest speaker for whom everyone has been waiting has just arrived.

▲ A member notices that the meeting is off track and the discussion is poorly focused, wasteful, and not relevant to the issues at hand. If she or he has to wait in line, precious time may be wasted.

To address the above imperfections in a speakers' lineup, your group needs to decide how to make exceptions. Several qualifiers may need to be added to the participation guidelines. As an example, here is what the facilitator could say:

> *"We will follow the speakers' lineup in a flexible manner. Here are a few requests and some exceptions to the rule:*
>
> *"First, the requests. Please listen to the discussion and consider the following:*
>
> *"If, by the time your turn comes, your point has been made by someone else, consider not repeating it. Just say: 'My point has been made by ____.' This will help us avoid repetition and save time.*
>
> *"If, by the time your turn comes, your comment no longer appears relevant or the group is on to a different topic, consider not making your point, unless you have new information to offer. This will help us make progress and avoid backtracking.*
>
> *"Alternatively you can say something like: 'I'm on to a different point. Are we through with the point we're discussing now? Do we need to bring closure to it? If so, I will wait.'*
>
> *"And now, the exceptions to the rule:*
>
> *"First exception: If your comments were misinterpreted and this is having a negative impact on the discussion, you can wave a red flag or give us another signal to bypass the normal lineup. But do it only if absolutely necessary. If you do it, please do not take too long to make your point, and don't abuse this privilege.*
>
> *"Second exception: If you have an urgent comment to make, like being unable to hear someone, or if you see a major flaw with our discussion, you can wave a red flag or give us another signal*

> *to bypass the normal lineup. But do it only if your reason is compelling. We need to be fair to those who are waiting to speak."*

If members abuse the above exceptions and bypass the speakers' lineup for less than legitimate reasons, the facilitator or any member can intervene:

> *"I am having a bit of frustration when members bypass the speakers' lineup to give a rebuttal. In fairness to those who are waiting for their turns to speak, we cannot turn this into a back-and-forth debate between two of us, to the exclusion of other people."*

An Unusual Approach: The Roaming Rock

In some native Indian groups, members place a rock in the center of the discussion table. Another variation is to have a roaming microphone (battery operated) instead of a rock. The roaming rock or the microphone can be used instead of a speakers' lineup, as follows:

▲ When a member wants to speak, she takes the rock.

▲ When the member finishes speaking, she puts the rock back at the center of the table, or passes it on to someone else.

▲ After a person finishes speaking, the group sits in silence for a few seconds, giving everyone time to absorb what was said.

▲ After the short lull, another member takes the rock and speaks.

The roaming rock system has the following advantages:

▲ Members listen and do not interrupt, because they can only speak when holding the rock.

▲ Discussions are measured and deliberate.

▲ People are forced to slow down and think.

▲ Mutual understanding, respect, and support rise.

▲ The discussion is less likely to become dominated. Members who have spoken will be very conscientious about "hogging the rock" and speaking too often.

▲ Members tend to be more focused as they speak.

Conversely, the roaming rock system has the following disadvantages:

▲ Progress can be very slow.

▲ It is difficult to stop a member who is rambling, digressing, or backtracking.

To benefit from the advantages and overcome the disadvantages of the roaming rock system, there should be a way for the facilitator or other members to interject if the discussion is going off the rails or if another problem occurs. Here are a few suggestions to help achieve this goal:

▲ The facilitator and the members are given tools for use if there is a problem, such as red flags to wave or squeaky toy animals to press.

▲ Alternatively, the facilitator and the members may be given cue cards saying, in large-size print: "On track?" or "Focus please," or "Time to move on." When they wave the sign, the speaker can make the necessary adjustment or ask the complainer to explain the concern.

COMMUNICATING

To pull your weight in a meeting, you will sometimes need to speak up. Consider the following suggestions:

▲ Speak clearly and audibly. Look for signs of members having trouble hearing. Look for signs of members not following what you say. If you need to stand to project better, do so. If the meeting is held in a large room, you may need to use a microphone, or go to a place from which you can be better heard. If you're not sure whether you can be heard, ask, "Can everyone hear me?" Make your voice consistent and avoid dropping your volume or swallowing the tail end of a sentence or word.

▲ When you finish speaking, check whether you were heard and understood. Ask "Did I make sense?" or use a lighthearted approach: "Did I manage to confuse anyone?"

▲ Make your voice expressive and interesting and avoid monotony. Vary your vocal intonation, volume, and pace, and add vocal emphasis to key words and sentences. Pause periodically to breathe and give the listeners a chance to do the same. Make eye contact with the listeners as you speak. The occasional smile and appropriate facial expressions will make your visual presence more compelling.

- ▲ Be aware of your body language, and avoid sending the wrong message by gestures like the following: pointing an accusatory finger at someone else; waving your fist; folding your arms in front of you, appearing defensive; or leaning back and appearing detached from the meeting.
- ▲ Stay on track. Focus on the current issues and avoid digressions and backtracking. Keep your comments concise and to the point. Avoid rambling and repeating yourself. If a short reply will suffice, give it and stop. Focus your comments on issues, not on individuals or personalities.
- ▲ Avoid blaming and accusing others. Be accountable and remember, when you point a finger at someone else, there are three fingers pointing right back at you.
- ▲ Avoid lengthy preambles to justify the points that you have not even made yet. Just give them the goods. Keep it simple and precise. Give them your key point up front and don't keep them in suspense. Unlike a joke, where you save the punch line to the end, here you need to give them the punch line first.
- ▲ Avoid apologizing for your point of view before you even tell them what it is (e.g., "I really don't want to hurt anyone's feelings or make it sound like I don't appreciate the wonderful work that was done here. I don't even know if I have enough information to say this, but ____"). Speak with confidence and give your perspective the stature and respect it deserves. Speak from the heart and make your message compelling.
- ▲ For longer statements, try a "sandwich" approach: First, tell them what you'll tell them (a brief and concise opening statement); second, tell them (elaborate on your opening statement, using concise point-format, and giving examples in support of your points); and third, tell them what you told them (reinforce or repeat your opening statement). Here is an example of a well-focused statement:
  - ▲ "I have two major concerns about this proposal: A financial concern and an ethical one. Let me start with the financial concern (elaborate and give an example). Having covered the financial side, here is the ethical concern (elaborate). And so again, I have financial and ethical concerns about this proposal, and I do not believe we should approve it. My preferred alternative is ____."
- ▲ Think before you speak, and avoid impulsive off-the-cuff reactions that may be too defensive or emotional. Impulsive reactions may be misinterpreted or misunderstood, and you may regret them later.

- ▲ To avoid impulsive reactions, learn to slow yourself down. One way of doing this is to force yourself to jot down your key points before saying anything. Build your "sandwich" first (see above example). Speak only when you have a clear sense of direction, and when you know what to say and what not to say.
- ▲ Before you speak, pay attention to what others are saying. If your point was already made, avoid repeating it. If the group has moved on to a different topic, avoid backtracking, unless absolutely necessary.
- ▲ Give others room to speak and avoid domination. If someone interrupts you, avoid talking at the same time and competing for air time, since neither of you will be listening. Just stop and say, "May I finish?" Resume speaking when the other person agrees to be quiet and hear you out. You can suggest that she or he make notes of her or his response while you speak.

LISTENING

When you aren't speaking, you shouldn't remain idle. You still need to pull your weight by listening to others. Far too often, and especially in meetings, we are too busy talking to pay attention to what others are saying. The result is that we repeat ourselves, misinterpret what others are saying, and miss opportunities to make informed and intelligent decisions for the organization. Here are a few tips to help you listen better in meetings:

- ▲ Listen to learn. Assume each person has something new and exciting to teach you, regardless of their experience, age, gender, or other factors. Give speakers your full and undivided attention.
- ▲ Have a pen and paper handy and make notes of key points that a speaker is making, even if you don't like the argument or the individual. Just note each point and listen to the next. If you focus too much on your rebuttal, you will be distracted and miss the things on which you and the speaker fully agree. Consider your response only when you fully understand the other person.
- ▲ To confirm that what you heard is indeed what the other person said and meant, try paraphrasing it. This will be especially useful if the issues are controversial or if the other person rambles. Here is an example: "Let me see if I understand. I think I hear you say that _____. Did I get it right?"
- ▲ Force yourself to ask probing questions to learn more about the speaker's perspective:

- "Tell me more. What do you mean by _____?"
- "How do you envision this process unfolding? Have you taken into account the fact that our senior management has been very conservative in its approach?"
- "I need to understand something: What did I do or say that gave you the impression that I _____?
- "Why is this problem so significant? Can you explain to me what impact it is having and on whom?"
- "Do you have any thoughts on why _____ is doing it? What is he looking to achieve?"
- "What exactly are you trying to accomplish by this proposal?"
- "What exactly are you concerned about? Is it about _____, or _____?"

▲ Listen to the message, and try not to be distracted by the delivery. Most people are not perfect communicators. Their important messages may be diluted by low and monotonous voices, no facial expression, poor sentence structure, or rambling. The fact that they are not perfect communicators (who is?) should not detract from the value of their messages.

▲ In addition to listening to what people say, pay attention to their vocal expressions, facial expressions, and body language:

- A low volume may mean a person is getting defensive.
- A loud voice may mean a person is angry or aggressive. It may also mean he or she is excited about something.
- A sigh may indicate frustration.
- A smile may mean someone approves of what you are saying. It may also mean he or she thinks it is funny or ridiculous.
- A frown may mean a person is confused or that he or she disagrees with you.
- Finger pointing may mean you are being warned or blamed for something. It may also mean the speaker is being emphatic.
- Leaning back may be taken to show cynicism and contempt, or it may mean a person is tired and wants to change positions.

▲ You can respond to body language in the following ways:

- If you can tell the reason for the body language, you can take corrective action: "I apologize. I should have explained what the abbreviation XYZ means."

- If you don't know how to interpret the body language, you can ask a question: "Is there a problem with what I said?" or "Am I going too fast?"

▲ Recognize the enemies of listening and avoid them:

- Avoid selective listening, i.e., hearing only what validates and confirms your views and filtering out data that conflicts with them. You need to hear the full message.
- Avoid impulsive dismissal of new or off-the-wall ideas before examining their merits. An unconventional idea may be exactly what's needed to break a deadlock in a meeting. Always keep an open mind.
- Avoid "tuning out" when someone you don't like starts talking. Give others credit and the full benefit of the doubt, regardless of how unsophisticated and misguided you may think they are. Assume they have a new point to make. Who knows, this new attitude of yours could become a self-fulfilling prophecy, and they may indeed say something you did not expect them to.
- Avoid listening with the sole purpose of rebuttal.
- Avoid instinctive "yes, but" statements. The fact that you say the "but" with passion makes the "yes" sound insignificant. Instead try this: "Yes, I hear you, and this is what I think I hear: ____. Am I right? Thank you. Here is another piece of the puzzle that we need to consider." By showing that you truly heard the other person, you could compel him or her to give you the same courtesy and listen to your view.
- Never act like an arrogant and conceited "know-it-all." Always be humble, open, and ready to be surprised and learn something new. If this is your demeanor, people will find you more accessible and easier to work with. You will find yourself learning from anyone, starting with the newest member of your team and going as far as the taxi driver who brought you to the meeting.

▲ If something can be done to help you listen better, ask for it. For example:

If this is making it difficult for you to listen and concentrate:	Say something like this:
Rob speaks softly or is fading away at the end of a sentence.	"Rob, do you mind speaking up?" or "Rob, can you keep your voice consistent? You tend to fade away at the end of sentences, and I don't want to miss what you are saying."

If this is making it difficult for you to listen and concentrate:	Say something like this:
Ed is speaking too fast.	"Ed, I need you to slow down and pause between sentences. I am having a hard time catching up to you."
Sue has given a long and confusing answer to a simple question.	"Sue, I was hoping for a simple yes or no. Can you help me out by giving me a short and direct answer?"
The discussion has been moving too fast, and you could use a concise refresher of the key points that were covered.	"Ruth, can you possibly review the main points we agreed to so far? We've been going at the speed of light and I must say I am lost."
Phil is using technical jargon that you don't understand.	"Phil, I am a novice in this field and I don't understand all the technical terms. Can I ask you to explain technical terms and abbreviations before you use them? For example, what do you mean by _____?" Or: "I have a favor to ask of anyone getting ready to give us a technical presentation. Could you possibly prepare a list of technical terms and abbreviations, with plain language explanations of what they mean?"
Everyone talks at the same time. Interruptions are rampant and you have trouble following what people are saying.	"Can we please have only one person speaking at a time? I am finding it hard to concentrate." Or: "Can we please let people finish what they're saying? I am trying to make sense of the discussion, and there are too many loose ends because of the interruptions. Tom, can you finish your thought on _____?"
Linda is making an argument, but you are having difficulty understanding how it is connected to the issue at hand.	"Linda, I am having trouble connecting what you're saying to the core issue of _____. Can you help me out?"

If this is making it difficult for you to listen and concentrate:	Say something like this:
You are distracted by outside noise and are having trouble hearing.	"Sam, can I interrupt you? I am being distracted by outside noise and I can't hear you well. Can someone close the door, please?"
The person sitting next to you keeps asking questions or sharing remarks with you. You would rather focus on the meeting.	"Dan, I am trying to concentrate. . . ." Or: Bring your finger to your nose to motion Dan to be silent and to focus on the discussion. Or: "Dan, you should say this to the entire group."

ASKING QUESTIONS

Questioning is a powerful way of pulling your weight in a meeting. Questioning is a communication and listening tool. You can use questioning to achieve the following goals:

1. Use questions to probe and obtain clarification and additional information (see previous section).
2. Use questions to raise concerns about a proposal or an argument.
   - ▲ "I was just wondering about this proposal: Did the committee think about the impact this project will have on ____?"
   - ▲ "May I ask a question? I'm not sure I follow your logic. How does ____ lead you to conclude ____?"
   - ▲ "Am I missing something here? How will this proposal solve the problem of ____, which was the reason for customer complaints? Are we treating the symptom or the cause?"
3. Use questions to get the group's attention before making a statement.
   - ▲ "Can I have everyone's attention please?"
   - ▲ "Can I ask a question?"

- "May I make an observation about the way the discussion has gone so far?"
- "Can I get you to listen to my full explanation, without interruption?"
- "May I finish?"

4. Use questions to check how open another person is to hearing you out.

   - "Do you want to hear my answer?"
   - "Will anything I say or do change your mind?"
   - "Are you open to the possibility I might say something you don't already know?"
   - "Do you have any leeway to move from your position?"
   - "I'm just wondering: Might there be a third solution that is better than both yours and mine, and, if so, are you really interested in finding it?"
   - "Are we hearing each other out? If not, would it better to agree to disagree for now, end this meeting, and think about it some more on our own?"

5. Use questions to test and build openness to a new idea, or to get people to examine fixed attitudes or positions.

   - "Can we test a completely different way to solving this problem?"
   - "Can I tempt you with an off-the-wall idea?"
   - "Can we try looking first at the benefits of this restructuring plan, and only then analyze the potential negative impacts and how they might be managed?"
   - "OK, I can see that this idea will not fly here in its present shape. But could we pull the good elements from it and see if we could use them in some way?"
   - "Can I clarify something? I'm not suggesting that we become best friends with this organization and forget all the past animosities. All I am doing is raising a simple question: Is it within the realm of possibility that we could learn to get along, given our common interest and given that we share the same premises?"
   - "I was just wondering: Is it possible that Christine's behavior is made worse by how she is treated by other people?"

- ▲ "Are you open to the possibility that, with the right guidance and accountability in place, Don could be a constructive and effective member to add to our team?"
- ▲ "Here is a thought for you: Could it be that Jack has a legitimate concern that we should consider, but the manner in which he presents it makes it difficult for us to listen to him and evaluate what he is saying with an open mind?"
- ▲ "Could it be that Bob is behaving like this not because he is a mean-spirited person, but because no one has ever given him honest and direct feedback on what he does and how it affects other people?"
- ▲ "Can I be a devil's advocate for a moment?"

6. Use questions to convert a critic into a creator.
   - ▲ "What needs to be done to make the process fair and equitable?"
   - ▲ "How could the proposal be modified to be more realistic financially?"
   - ▲ "What can we do to address your concern about _____?"
   - ▲ "Is there a way we can shift the discussion from blaming and accusing to working together and finding solutions?"
7. Use questions to give feedback and subtly request corrective action.
   - ▲ "Are you aware of the fact that you are doing _____?"
   - ▲ "Are you aware of the impact of your approach on _____?"
   - ▲ "Is there a reason why you are raising your voice right now?"
8. Use questions to force yourself and others to slow down, listen, and think.
   - ▲ "Can we please slow down for a moment? It seems like we're on a fast train with no brakes. I need time to breathe and digest this information."
   - ▲ "Wouldn't it better if we postponed this issue until the next meeting, to give us a cooling-off period and more time to come up with new solutions?"
9. Use questions to make your communication style engaging and interactive.

Instead of this statement:	**Try this question or series of questions:**
"We have to do this or else we'll be in trouble."	"Have we thought about the consequences of doing this? Doesn't it

	make more sense to do _____ and have the benefit of _____, instead of _____?"
"I think this initiative will reduce our customer service levels, and here is why: _____."	"I was wondering: How will this initiative affect customer service levels? I have a feeling that it would make them worse, because _____. Am I making sense?"

Here are a few cautions when asking questions:

- Avoid lengthy preambles or excessive apologies before or after asking the question. Get to the point, make your question brief, and then stop.
- Never assume your question is dumb. If you are asking it, there is a good chance others may also be wondering about it. It may be that they need to be reminded of an important point they are missing. They will be grateful for your initiative.
- Soften your questions and avoid an accusatory tone or implying an individual is stupid or malicious. Focus on issues and behaviors, not people. For example:

Instead of this hard question:	**Try this softer approach:**
"This statement is offensive, insensitive and defamatory. How dare you talk to me like that?"	"I must say I am finding this statement hard to take. Can I ask you to not use this language? We agreed earlier to talk about issues, not people. Can we please maintain courtesy and respect?"
"Can't you see what you're doing to our customers by _____?"	"I am trying to understand what you are trying to achieve with this new procedure. Can you explain it to me? Specifically, I don't understand how it jives with our policy of good customer service. Am I missing something?"
"Why do you badmouth me behind my back?"	"Can I raise an issue with you? It came to my attention that you've been raising concerns about the way I work. I have two questions for you: First, is there something I'm doing that makes

Instead of this hard question:	Try this softer approach:
	it difficult for you to give me this feedback directly? Second, what exactly are you concerned about? I would really like to know."

THINKING

There is often far too much talking and far too little thinking in a meeting. How can people form an intelligent opinion about issues when they don't have opportunities to think? A meeting should be slowed down from time to time, allowing members to consider what has been said and where they should go next. Here are a few ideas to stimulate thinking during a meeting:

▲ When speaking, members need to ask more thought-provoking questions and make fewer rambling statements. See previous section about asking questions.

▲ Speakers should make their presentations intellectually stimulating and interactive (see next section about making presentations in a meeting). While a presentation is made, members should be invited to consider how it applies to their own situations. For example, "In my presentation, I will cover eight keys to working better as a team. After I explain each one of them, I will ask you to think for a minute or so and write your thoughts about how our own team is doing. At the end of my presentation, which should take no more than twenty minutes, I will ask you to comment on what you came up with."

▲ If needed, a member can suggest a thinking break: "Can we slow down a bit? We've been moving very quickly, and I am not comfortable rushing to make a decision so fast. Can we have five minutes for solitary thinking, to consider this issue without saying a word to anyone else, and just jot down our ideas on paper? Would this be productive?"

▲ Introduce thought-provoking puzzles and games to get people to think creatively. For examples, see Chapter 12.

MAKING PRESENTATIONS

Participants may also pull their weight by making presentations in a meeting. Prepared presentations by in-house speakers or outside experts can help the group to achieve the following:

▲ Broaden the group's knowledge base and expertise.

▲ Introduce outside perspectives, which can help generate new ideas.

▲ Serve as a catalyst for the group to take a second look at good ideas that were rejected in the past. Strangely, the same idea that was unsuccessfully introduced by a member of the group may sound much more compelling when it comes from an outside expert.

▲ Introduce variety and change the pace of the meeting.

A presenter should offer the most current and most relevant information, and should always customize it to the needs of the group. Here are two thoughts to consider:

▲ As an in-house speaker, you should avoid being casual about the presentation. Just because everyone knows you doesn't mean they deserve less than your best.

▲ If you are an outside speaker, it should not matter how much you are getting paid, whether you are getting paid at all, whether you were treated badly by the person who invited you, or whether you had an unpleasant day. Your listeners still deserve your very best every time.

For tips on *preparing* an effective presentation, see the presenters' checklists in Chapters 9 and 10. Here are a few tips for *delivering* the presentation:

1. If you are an outside speaker, be professional and objective. Avoid sounding like you're telling the group what it must do, especially if your presentation touches on contentious issues. To emphasize your objectivity, you can open your presentation by saying:

    "Before I start my presentation, I should say that I am sensitive to the fact that the issues addressed in my presentation have been controversial for you.

    "As a professional, it is my job to give you my best advice, based on an objective assessment of your circumstances and my experience with other clients. At the same time, I am an outsider to your organization, and it is up to you, as my clients, to decide what to do with my advice. Just so you know, I make it my practice to leave my ego at home, and I do not get offended if a client chooses to ignore my advice. Having said all of that, let me start with my presentation."

2. Arrive early, test any audiovisual equipment you'll need and confirm additional details.
3. If your presentation is not scheduled until later in the meeting, ask the group to arrange a break before your presentation, so you can set up and test any equipment and get ready for the presentation.
4. Insist on having a question and discussion period, or intersperse question periods between the major parts of the presentation.
5. Be sensitive to the audience and ask them to signal to you if your technical terms confuse them. Consider giving them:
   - ▲ Cue cards to wave at you saying "slow down," "plain language, please."
   - ▲ Squeaky toy animals, to help them complain if they have difficulties following your presentation.
6. Check from time to time whether they are still with you. For example:
   - ▲ "How are we doing so far?"
   - ▲ "Have I left anyone behind?"
   - ▲ "How many of you don't know the term ____? OK, ____ means ____."
   - ▲ "This is a technical topic, and there is no such thing as a stupid question. Someone told me the only stupid question is the one you don't ask. Are there any questions so far?"
7. Check whether they are restless and ready for you to move on to another part of your presentation. This may happen if you:
   - ▲ Dwell on an insignificant part of the presentation too long.
   - ▲ Take a long time to get to the most interesting and relevant parts.
   - ▲ Ramble, editorialize, apologize, or rationalize.
   - ▲ Try to please everyone and answer questions as you go along.
   - ▲ Lock into a series of follow-up questions with one or two individuals.
8. Be sensitive to the group's time constraints. Even if they are not complaining, say, "How are we doing for time? I was scheduled to speak for only half an hour. It's great to have your interest, but I don't want to overstay my welcome." Or, "I was told that, as a presenter, it is better to leave the audience before they leave you. So let me summarize and then close my presentation, so you can get on with the rest of your meeting."
9. If you're an outside speaker, let them know in advance of your fee. To be on the safe side, have things documented and signed. If you bill them by the hour and

they invite you to attend the full meeting, you need to establish in advance what time you will and will not bill them for. You don't want the glow and fond memories you leave behind to vanish when they receive your bill.

Answering Questions

As a meeting participant, you may be in a position to pull your weight by responding effectively to questions. The time to do so will be after:

- Making a formal presentation
- Discussing a report you prepared
- Proposing that a certain decision be made
- Speaking or making a suggestion during the discussions

Here are some "don'ts" to keep in mind when answering a question:

- Don't miss the point of the question or answer a different one altogether.
- Avoid making your answer long and rambling.
- Don't interpret a probing question as an attack on your integrity or a personal insult.
- Don't listen to only half of the question and interrupt the questioner prematurely.
- Don't feel compelled to answer every question or fake it when you don't have an answer. There is nothing wrong with saying, "I don't have an answer for you."
- Avoid being "cute" or "funny" or responding with a condescending off-the-cuff comeback.
- Don't fail to capitalize on the knowledge of other people who are present and can give better answers than you. Avoid treating such people as threats.
- Avoid being drawn into speculating on events that are beyond your control.
- Avoid being drawn into making broad generalizations. If asked, "What do you think about politicians?" avoid saying, "I think all politicians are overpaid." Instead say, "I make it my habit not to generalize. Do you have a more specific question for me?"
- Don't answer a tough question too quickly, only to realize five minutes later that you missed the most significant point, or that you said something you shouldn't have.

- ▲ Avoid locking into follow-up questions and debate with one or two very interested or persistent persons, to the exclusion of other people who have questions and are waiting patiently. Sooner or later, you will run out of time and leave them behind.
- ▲ Avoid showing with your body language how much you disapprove of the question or the person asking it: a frown, raised eyebrows, looking away, an audible sigh, winking and smiling to one of your fans, etc.
- ▲ Don't show your disapproval and impatience with your choice of words or a condescending tone that implies "How can you ask a stupid question like that?" or "You mean you don't know that our company ____?"

Here are a few tips to consider as you answer questions or manage a question period after a presentation:

- ▲ Encourage questioners to be brief and concise: "I can see many of you have questions, and I also know we only have fifteen minutes for this discussion. Can I ask you to make your questions concise and to the point, so we can accommodate as many people as possible? Thanks. Who has a question?"
- ▲ Make your answer direct, concise, brief, and well organized. For example, "My answer is that this is a good idea, for two main reasons: quality and cost. On the quality, ____. On the cost, ____. So, for quality and cost considerations, I think doing ____ is a good idea."
- ▲ If you don't have an answer or can't give it, here are a few options for you:

If this is the case:	**Try this approach:**
You don't know the answer, and the issue is marginal or irrelevant to the discussion.	"I don't know the answer. This is not my area of expertise. Are there any other questions?" Or: "I don't have an answer for you, but you can talk to Shawn during the break. He is the expert in this area. Are there any other questions about my areas of expertise?"
You know the answer, but it is not appropriate for you to give it, e.g., it covers confidential issues.	"As you can appreciate, exact profit figures are not something I can discuss in an open forum. What I can discuss

	are the areas of _____ and _____. Do you have any questions about them?"
You can give an answer, but Terry has more complete information.	"Terry, can you help us out with this question?"
You have the answer in your files back in the office, and the questioner is the only one who is interested in it.	"I don't have the information here, but I will be glad to give it to you when I'm back at the office. Would you please give me your phone number or e-mail address after the meeting?"
You have the answer in your files back in the office, and everyone will appreciate having it.	"I am sorry. I should have had these numbers here today, but I don't. I will send them to everyone by e-mail once I'm back in my office.

- Honesty is the best policy. Don't hesitate to give bad news that the questioner may not expect or want to hear. Be prepared to admit flaws or imperfections. For example:
  - "I sense that some of you may not like my answer, but I have to give you the information directly and honestly. The fact is that _____."
  - "I wish I could have given you happier news, but there is no sense making things look pretty when they are not. The fact is _____."
  - "I have no trouble acknowledging that this proposal has a few flaws, some of which you pointed to. At the same time, in the overall balance, I believe this proposal presents the smallest risk and the largest opportunity for us."
- Maintain an open and accessible demeanor and make it easy for members to ask you questions, as tough as they may be. Legitimize and validate concerns instead of trivializing them or feeling threatened by them. The less sensitive or defensive you are and the less you take things personally, the more productive the discussion will be. Remain confident, calm, and reassuring, and your credibility and stature will be boosted. For example, you may say:
  - "I welcome any questions, as tough and as challenging as they may be. I know the issues I spoke about are difficult, and this makes it essential for me to listen and fully understand your concerns."
  - "There is no need to apologize for asking this question. On the contrary, given the impact of this decision on your daily work routines, and given that you spend one third of your life at work, it is more than legitimate for you to raise

concerns about changes like this one. As to your question, here are a few thoughts ____. Am I helping?"

- Slow yourself down. Before answering the question, take the time to understand what the questioner is really asking. She or he may not be communicating coherently and clearly, and the issue may be too technical for them. Help them out by listening and clarifying what information they need. For example:
  - "I'm not sure I understand. What do you mean by ____?"
  - "Let me see if I understand. Are you asking me about ____?"
- Have a pen and paper handy, and jot down the key points that the questioner is raising while she or he is speaking, especially in the case of a multifaceted question. When she or he finishes (uninterrupted by you), you can say: "You are asking several questions. They are about finances, human resources, and information technology aspects of this proposal. Let me address them one at a time. First, the financial impacts. . . . (etc.)"
- If you are not sure you answered the question, you may need to check:
  - "Did I answer your question?"
  - "Did I make sense?"
  - "Am I helping?"
- If you are managing a question period and everyone is asking questions at once, you may need to say something like: "Can we have only one person speaking at a time? I will take questions from Mary, then Stan, and then Jerry. Mary, go ahead."
- If you are a presenter and a questioner is focusing on one part of your presentation and has many follow-up questions, you may need to interject and move on to other areas and engage other people in the discussion: "Bev, I have to move on to other people who have questions, and we need to cover other aspects of my presentation, including, for example, the area of technical support. Does anyone have questions about that part of the presentation?"
- You may want to be proactive and preempt some questions, by integrating them into your prepared presentation. For example, "In preparing my presentation, my first thought was to give you a lecture. But then I realized it would be more productive to list some of the questions you might have on this topic and then answer them one by one. Based on my discussion with Roberta prior to the meeting, I was able to identify five key questions that appear to be most relevant to your group. They are: (read them from a PowerPoint slide or a flip chart). Let me go through them one by one. We will then have a general question period."

- ▲ If a question is not really a question, but an argument, don't feel compelled to respond. It is fine to just say, "Thank you for your comment. Are there any more questions?" People are entitled to their opinions, and you don't have a monopoly on the truth. Responding to every argument and trying to prove you are right may present you as closed-minded and defensive, and may discourage further questions or dissenting views.

A Problem: The Silence Is Deafening

Consider this difficulty. After your brilliant presentation at a meeting, no one seems to have any questions. Yet you know there probably are some. The silence is deafening. What can you do? The answer to this question depends on the reason for the silence.

1. It is possible that the members were fully engaged by your presentation. Your asking for questions might have come as a complete surprise to them and caught them off-guard. To prevent this problem in the future you can do the following:

   - ▲ Alert them early in the presentation that there will be a question period: "At the end of my presentation, about twenty minutes from now, there will be a ten-minute question period. I will look forward to hearing your questions then. You have an outline of my presentation in front of you. As I go through it you can jot down any questions for a later discussion."

   - ▲ Remind them that the question period is coming: "I have five more minutes in the presentation. Hopefully you've been writing down a few questions, because the time for questions is coming very soon."

   - ▲ Have a few typical questions ready, just in case members might be slow in raising their hands: "Are there any questions? Wow, no questions. Well, to be on the safe side, let me tell you about a question that I am often asked. By the time I've answered it, you may have some of your own questions. The question is this: _____"

2. Another possible reason for the lack of questions is that your presentation was so perfect that it left no question unanswered. If so, it's OK to quit while you're ahead. But don't quit too fast. First, do the following:

   - ▲ Ask again: "Any questions at all? Did things make sense to you? Do you need anything clarified? (Pause long enough.) OK, I suppose there is no crime in ending a few minutes early and giving you more time for the rest of the meeting. It's been a pleasure speaking to you, and I want to thank you for the invitation. Have a great day."

- ▲ If appropriate, poke fun at the situation: "Please don't all speak at once," or, "Wow, I didn't know I was capable of leaving no question unanswered!"

3. The lack of questions may be due to your presentation being irrelevant to the listeners. It could also be that you bored them so much that half of them are asleep and the other half are daydreaming. Wait briefly to see if there are any questions, then thank them and stop. But do ask the facilitator to give you feedback on your presentation afterwards.

CONVERTING NEGATIVITY INTO AFFIRMATIVE NEEDS

In order to make progress in a meeting, the focus of the discussion needs to be affirmative, even when the departure point is negative. Each participant should pull his or her weight to help the group to shift from complaints and criticisms to a more constructive approach.

Reframing is a tool to convert negative statements into affirmative ones. To reframe a negative statement, you need to identify the legitimate interest or need that underlies the statement, and shift your group and your meetings from the left column to the right one in the following list:

Shift from this:	**To this:**
A negative focus: talking about what you don't have or what you want to avoid.	An affirmative focus: talking about what you need and what you want to achieve.
A personal focus (accusations and searching for someone to blame).	A collective focus: identifying communication breakdowns and systemic gaps that need to be bridged.
Adversarial arguments: "It's you against me."	Collaborative discussions: "You and me against the problem," Or: "All of us working together to have a better team and make better collective decisions for the organization."
Complaints (what someone is not getting).	Legitimate needs and requests (what the group or an individual is entitled to).

Helplessness, waste of time and energy, aimless and unproductive discussions.	Proactivity, empowerment, and a sense of purpose, confidence, and focus.
Destructive tensions and anxieties that strain the group and make its members operate at a fraction of their potential.	Negative energies are rechanneled and used for making better decisions and building a better organization.

Here are a few examples of how negative statements can be reframed into affirmative ones:

A negative statement in a meeting:	The affirmative needs:	A reframing response:
"I have no idea why this meeting was called. It's a colossal waste of time and money."	Clarity of purpose Good use of time A sense of pride and accomplishment	"You want us to have a clearer definition of why meetings are called, so you know why you're here and what difference you are supposed to be making, and so time is spent more productively. Thanks for your feedback."
"The biggest problem with this proposal is that it costs too much and the returns on investment are questionable."	Better management of expenses A better return on investment	"You are suggesting that we need this project to be more cost-effective and profitable. Can you see places where this proposal can be changed to reduce costs and increase the returns on investment?"
"The biggest problem we have is that it doesn't matter what we do here. All our good work goes to waste once it hits the desk of the CEO. He	A meaningful and inclusive process The ability to make a difference Being taken seriously Respect and recognition	"I hear you. I can see how much of a difference it would make if you knew that our CEO had a good appreciation of our work

A negative statement in a meeting:	The affirmative needs:	A reframing response:
always torpedoes our recommendations. It's extremely upsetting and demoralizing."	of the value of the team's work by the CEO	and respect for what we do. Perhaps we can look at two questions: First, what can we do to communicate more effectively with our CEO? Second, is there something we can do to anticipate any potential objections that the CEO may have to our ideas?"
"Our meetings are boring and put everyone to sleep. Our guest speakers don't amount to anything."	Have interesting meetings that keep you awake and alert Have informative guest speakers	"I hear you. You want our meetings to be more interesting and engaging, and you're suggesting that we should be more selective about who we invite to speak to us. How would you like to work with Ruth and present a few ideas on how we might achieve these goals?"
"This idea sounds great in theory, but it just won't fly. We tried it before and the people who undermined it are still around."	Being realistic and spending time only on ideas that have a chance of being implemented Working better with stakeholders that stopped decisions from being implemented in the past	"Thanks. You want to make sure that we only spend time on ideas that have a reasonable chance of being supported by influential people in this organization. "There are a few questions we could ask: First, does this idea have merit, and is it indeed the best way to solve the problem that we identified? Second, what

		were the reasons it did not work in the past? Is it the idea itself? Or is it that stakeholders should have been given an early warning about it? Or is it that they should have been invited to comment on it and make suggestions? Or is it something else? Third, if it is indeed a good idea, how can we overcome the obstacles and make it more likely to be supported by our stakeholders? "Why don't we address these questions separately, starting with the idea itself: Is it a good one? Is it compelling enough for us? Is it the most effective way to solve the problem that we identified earlier?"
"Here we go again. You interrupted me. So what if I went a bit overtime? All this formality is stifling us and killing any creative thinking. I'm fed up. This is very upsetting."	Being treated with respect and sensitivity Creating an appropriate balance between the need to move forward and the need to be flexible and hear from different people	"I'm really sorry, Beth. I had no idea how much my interruptions upset you. I guess I can be a bit too rigid and formal. I obviously need to ask the group for feedback on my facilitation style. We need to decide how we can create a balance between two things. We need a degree of structure in our meetings, so we can keep

A negative statement in a meeting:	The affirmative needs:	A reframing response:
		them on track and finish our agenda on time, and we also need flexibility to enable us to speak freely and think creatively. What do you think? How can we achieve those two goals?"

GIVING AND RECEIVING FEEDBACK

In a dysfunctional meeting, feedback is held back. The lack of direct, honest, and principled feedback creates tensions, causes members to operate well below their full potential, and strains the decision-making process. When feedback is finally shared, it is typically done when things are unbearable. Under these conditions, the feedback is often given in a hostile, accusatory, destructive, and hurtful manner.

On the other hand, in a well-functioning meeting feedback is shared on a regular basis and is treated as a gift and as something to learn from. Members greet complaints with the same enthusiasm they greet the compliments. They use feedback to build relationships and enhance the quality of the discussions and the decisions. In healthy team settings, some feedback is exchanged during a meeting, and some is shared during breaks or between meetings.

Chapter 4 includes tips for the team leader on giving feedback and on taking it from team members. The same principles apply to meeting participants pulling their weight by giving feedback or taking it from others. As a reminder, good feedback is:

- ▲ Principle-based
- ▲ Specific
- ▲ Accountable and not accusatory
- ▲ Constructive, focusing not only on the problem, but also identifying possible solutions

- Measured, given after confirming that the recipient is prepared to hear it
- Interactive, given not as a lecture, but as a series of questions
- Objective, focused on issues and behaviors, but soft on people and personalities
- Given regularly, instead of being a rare occurrence
- Balanced by positive feedback and celebration of successes (see next section)

Giving Feedback: Making It Easier for Others to Receive

Feedback that is hard to receive:	Feedback that is easier to receive:
"You ramble too much."	"May I interject? I am getting anxious about our time and have another meeting to go to. Jack, can you please make your point faster?"
"These comments are very offensive. How can you be so rude and insensitive?"	"Can we slow things down a bit? I am finding the tone of this discussion and the language used very hard to take. Can you please soften the tone of this discussion? It would make it easier for me to listen to you."

Receiving Feedback: Making It Easier for Others to Give It to You

Here are some examples of statements that make it difficult for others to give you feedback:

- "Yes, I hear you. But you are failing to understand a few very important things here. For example, _____."
- "That's not true at all. I respect Bob a lot."
- "Who's complaining about me? I demand to know. How dare they speak behind my back? They should be ashamed of themselves."

- "You're not so perfect yourself. Here are a few pieces of dirt I have on you."
- "Yeah, yeah, yeah. I heard that stuff before. Thank you very much. Anything else? OK, Bye. What a jerk."

Now here are some statements that will make it easier for others to give you feedback:

- "Thank you. I had no idea I was doing this. I appreciate your feedback and it's very helpful to me. Would you please give me feedback again if you see me doing something that doesn't work?"
- "You got my attention. Can you tell me more?"
- "Can you be more specific? What do you mean when you say ____? I want to understand."
- "You're saying that I come across as aloof and uncaring. What specifically do I do that gives you this impression? And what would you see me doing to come across differently?"
- "Do you have any suggestions for me? If you don't have any now, can you think about it and talk to me later?"
- "Sean, I really want to discuss this feedback with you, but I don't want to interfere with the flow of this meeting. Can we meet tomorrow to discuss it?"

CELEBRATING SUCCESSES

People are often quick to criticize, but are very sparing with positive feedback. Groups need to celebrate successes publicly, and a meeting is a good place to do it. Recognition and expressions of appreciation should become a habit. The abundance of positive feedback will reward and perpetuate positive behavior. It will make it easier to give people critical feedback. Positive feedback can acknowledge either a work-related achievement or unique contribution, or a personal achievement or special event outside work. The individual leading the celebration of a success can be the meeting facilitator, or preferably another meeting participant (to share the stewardship of the meeting and have more individuals pull their weight).

Example: Celebrating Work-Related Contributions

The following is an example of celebrating special contributions by team members.

Sue (facilitator): "Before we move on, we've been working hard, and we could give our brains a bit of a rest. Don, this is a good time for you to make a few special presentations."

Don: "Thank you, Sue. My job is to recognize a few individuals for special contributions. First, we need to give the 'spark of the month' award. We give this award to an individual who was able to think creatively and help us when we were truly bogged down. To receive the spark of the month award, please help me welcome our one and only Richard 'Sparky' Wade." Don leads the applause and gives Richard the award.

"Congratulations, Richard. Keep on sparking.

"We have two more awards to give: The mentor of the year, or the member who helped newcomers in the most substantial way, and 'the rock of the year,' the person who came to every meeting on time, stayed here for the full duration every time, and contributed well. I will present these two awards later in the meeting."

Example: Celebrating an Outside Achievement

The following example shows you how the success of a member outside the office can be celebrated in a meeting.

Facilitator: "Before we move on, I would ask Roger to help us celebrate something."

Roger: "Today I have a very pleasant duty to perform. Stella, please come forward. Thank you. Today, we need to recognize Stella for a special achievement. As some of you know, Stella was recently recognized by the Association of Professional Engineers as the Engineer of the Year, for her innovative and pioneering work on our project.

"Stella, not to be outdone by your professional organization, we have two special awards to give you. First, I will give you this certificate of appreciation from the company. And, second, there a special gift for you from our CEO. It is a two-week cruise for two from Singapore to Australia, first class, with all expenses paid.

"Let's acknowledge and thank Stella for her special work and for making all of us very proud." (A round of applause and a standing ovation follows.)

> To which Stella will hopefully not respond by saying, "I do not deserve this" (as many people do, essentially implying that the giver of the award has poor judgment and has no idea what she or he is talking about), nor will she say: "It's simple justice and long overdue." Instead, she might say something more profound and meaningful like this:
>
> "Thank you so much, Roger. This is quite a surprise. It is very heartwarming, flattering, and humbling to be acknowledged so publicly and so generously for my work. Yes, I am very proud of this achievement. But even more so, I am proud of the work itself, and the fact that all of us have been able to do it together, as a cohesive and wonderful team. We have been able to put our company in the forefront, as a pioneer and a leader in this field, so this recognition is just as much yours as it is mine.
>
> "I want to thank all of you for always challenging me to think creatively and follow up on my sometimes crazy ideas. And just in case you wondered, I have a good idea of whom I will take on the cruise with me. The bad news is: It will not be one of you. Thank you again for all your support."

OFF-LINE INTERACTIONS AND CONSENSUS BUILDING

Pulling your weight should not occur only while a meeting is in progress. The consensus-building process should be ongoing. Information gathered when a meeting is not in progress (off-line) is just as important as information gathered at the meeting itself. Off-line interactions and consensus building can occur:

- ▲ Just before the meeting begins
- ▲ During the meeting itself
- ▲ During refreshment breaks
- ▲ Immediately after the meeting
- ▲ Between meetings

Here are a few examples of off-line interactions:

- ▲ At a premeeting social, with refreshments or a sit-down meal, members can do some "social catching up," but can also chat informally about issues scheduled for the meeting, and can give the facilitator or others useful information, such as:

- "Charlie is really mad about ____. I just thought you might want to know."
- "Cindy called to say she'll miss the meeting because of a family emergency. She asked whether her report could be postponed until the next meeting."
- "There was a new and major development on agenda item 6. Here it is ____. I thought I'd give you a heads-up warning on it."

- During the meeting, you can schedule structured off-line discussions and consensus-building activities. For example, "Based on our discussion so far, there are four main questions for us to address. They are: ____, ____, ____, and ____. To give each one of you an opportunity to participate more fully, I suggest that for the next twenty minutes we work in small groups of three, with each group dealing with one of the four questions. At the end of twenty minutes we will resume the discussion."

- In addition to sipping coffee or juice during refreshment breaks, members should be encouraged to approach the facilitator and give him or her feedback or information that they were unable to give at the meeting. Members can be encouraged to share information off-line, as in the following examples:
  - At the start of the meeting, you can say: "Before we get the meeting going, I need to ask each one of you for a favor: If there is an idea or a piece of feedback that you don't get to share while the meeting is in progress, please don't lose it. Put it down on paper and pass it on to me or discuss it with me at the break or after the meeting. We don't want to lose your good ideas. Can I count on you to share them?"
  - Just before a break, you can say: "Before we go on our refreshment break, would you please come and see me if there is something I need to know, or something that was missed at the meeting so far? OK, it's break time. Ten minutes. We'll resume at 10:41."

- As soon as a meeting ends, people typically rush to their next commitments. But this should be the time when some debriefing and winding-down may be beneficial. Here are two options:

1. Just before the meeting ends say: "Just before we close the meeting, I would like to remind you to complete the feedback sheets and pass them on to me. Also, I will stay around for at least ten minutes, so please feel free to stay and give me some of your feedback informally."

2. A postmeeting social event can be scheduled (instead of or in addition to the one scheduled just prior to the meeting). This postmeeting event can be used for informal exchange of views and feedback.

- After the meeting, members should be given opportunities to share feedback and suggestions. For example:
  - There could be a suggestion box placed in a prominent location. There should be token (or substantial) prizes given for "the suggestion of the month."
  - The group's leader should have an open door policy, and so should other team members. The notion should be, "If there is a problem, let's talk about it now, rather than hang on to it until the next meeting."

Off-line interactions should be viewed as more than just social events. They are vital opportunities to build a team and develop consensus, and can deliver the following benefits:

- Allow the members and the leader to remain connected, "take the pulse of the group" more frequently, and stay in touch and in tune with others.
- Enable the group and its leader to gather intelligence relevant to a meeting and to continually capitalize on the knowledge, expertise, and skills of all members.
- Give the facilitator and the members advance warnings of potential trouble, so they can respond to it proactively.
- Make the consensus-building process more gradual, continuous, and progressive.
- Allow the group to correct errors that were not captured during the interactive discussions during meetings.
- Give quieter members more opportunities to have their input considered off-line.
- Give members opportunities to get to know one another as human beings. This can reduce the likelihood of adversarial relationships developing among them. When people know one another socially, they are more likely to try to understand counterproductive behaviors without automatically attributing malice to individuals.
- Reduce the likelihood of side conversations during meetings (social chats) and increase the likelihood that members will be focused on the business of the group.

A Word of Caution

Some people view off-line information-gathering and consensus-building activities with suspicion and distrust. They see such efforts as undermining the collective expression of the group's consensus in a meeting. Here are a few ideas on how to avoid such perceptions:

- ▲ The purpose of off-line interactions should be explained to the group. Members should discuss any questions or concerns they may have about using off-line interactions to help conduct the business of the group.
- ▲ Significant decisions should not be made off-line. They should be brought to the group for interactive discussions in a face-to-face meeting.
- ▲ If actions that affect the entire group were taken as a result of off-line discussions, the group should be kept informed about them.

Helping Out

As the meeting progresses to its destination, there may be a few technical glitches along the way. Members should be prepared to pull their weight and help address such difficulties and minimize their disruptive impacts on the meeting. Many glitches can be prevented through good planning and premeeting work (see Chapters 9 and 10). Still, even with the best and most thorough planning, the odd glitches are unavoidable. Here are a few examples:

The unexpected event:	**What needs to be done:**
The mysterious words "no connection" appear on the PowerPoint screen (they are not a part of the presentation). The speaker appears upset and nervous.	An experienced PowerPoint presenter should help out. Possibly click the mouse or check the connections.
Smoke comes out of the projector. It's a short circuit or a burned-out lightbulb. The speaker pokes fun at it and says, "I didn't know my presentation was so hot."	Someone needs to figure out the safest way to prevent a fire or unplug the equipment without being jolted. Someone else needs to see if a window can be opened to prevent the smoke detector and water sprinklers from going off.
A presenter does not know how to focus the projector on the screen.	Help him or her fix it or come up with a contingency plan: "Why don't you just talk to us? The bells and whistles

The unexpected event:	What needs to be done:
	are nice, but we don't have to have them. The content is what we need."
A flip chart takes its revenge and collapses on top of the person flipping it. (This is not funny; it's dangerous.)	Help the person recover and see if he or she is OK. Reset the flip chart or get a replacement.
The guest speaker knocks the water jug over his notes. It clearly was not a part of his plan.	Bring a few napkins and help clear the mess; hopefully the speaker can manage with the wet notes. (You can't fix that. You may be a superperson, but there is a limit to what you can do.)
A presenter just lost her train of thought and says: "I am completely lost. Where was I?"	Remind her where she was. No one has a perfect memory. We're all human.
A floor microphone is set up for a person who is five feet tall. A man who is six-foot-six-inches tall can't figure out how to adjust the height of the stand. He finally gets frustrated and picks up the entire stand in the air.	He solved his own problem, albeit he worked harder and not smarter. Someone needs to explain to the group how to adjust the height of the stand. It's really quite simple.

MANAGING YOUR HOT BUTTONS

People may push your "hot buttons" from time to time in a meeting. Most times they will do so inadvertently and with no malice. They may not know that these are your hot buttons. On rare occasions they will do so maliciously, with the intent of provoking and manipulating you, and causing you to lose your confidence.

To pull your weight effectively in a meeting, you need to recognize and manage your hot buttons. The hot buttons could be:

- *A Slur*. Someone uses a sexist, racial, or religious slur that offends you or someone you care about.
- *Dishonesty*. Someone tells a blatant lie at the meeting. You're the only one who knows this.

- *Manipulation*. Someone is trying to "sweet talk" you into doing something you don't want to do, e.g., offer you a favor or a concession in exchange for something else.
- *Talking Behind Your Back*. Someone spreads rumors about you behind your back.
- *Being Misrepresented*. Someone misquotes you or exaggerates what you told him or her in private: "Goldie doesn't like our manager one bit."
- *Being Ignored*. A colleague turns his back to you when speaking to the rest of the group.
- *Backtracking*. Someone agreed to a significant change at a previous meeting, but denies it or looks for a way out. You feel betrayed.

Your instinctive reactions to these "hot buttons" being pushed could include one or more of the following:

- You lose your confidence and perform at a fraction of your potential.
- You feel incompetent, worthless, and useless, forgetting all the good things you've ever done.
- You feel confused and lost, and lose your energy, stamina, and enthusiasm for the rest of the day or even longer.
- You feel hurt or guilty, and blush or apologize nonstop.
- You feel your heart rate go up, and start to speak really fast.
- You lose your temper, or you give the silent treatment to the individual who made you mad.

Instead, you should use one of the following alternatives:

1. Slow yourself down. Imagine a red sign flashing this message: "Stop, look, and choose a different response; one you'll be proud of in the long run."
2. Have your own cue cards (to slow down and manage your frustration), saying things like:
   - Slow down!
   - Breathe!
   - Drink water!
   - Smile at yourself.

- You look really funny when you get angry.
- Things could be a lot worse. Just imagine . . .

3. Ask yourself questions like the following:
   - "Is there a legitimate reason why this person would behave like this?
   - Am I overreacting? Why? Am I reading more into this than I should?
   - Did I do something to earn this treatment?
   - Am I losing my focus? Am I about to react in a way that I will regret later? What reaction will I be proud of later?
   - Is there a creative way of responding and pleasantly surprising everyone?
   - What would the person I respect the most want me to do right now?
4. Remind yourself of your proudest achievements. Make a list of them if needed.
5. You may want to act like a self-cleaning oven. Let go of the hurt and carry on without drawing attention to your personal discomfort. As you get busy, the discomfort may gradually dissipate (time is a great healer), and you will likely get a more objective look at what happened.
6. Add an item to your IOU list, and plan to follow up privately with the individual or the facilitator after the meeting.
7. Write your thoughts down. Writing can help rechannel your frustration into a positive direction, refocus your energy on the things that matter, and rebuild your confidence.
8. Look for feedback from someone you respect. Avoid looking for feedback from those who will automatically take your side or vice versa.
9. When you regain your composure, assert yourself from a position of strength, without getting angry (see next section for examples).

Asserting Yourself Without Getting Angry

As a meeting participant, you may need to assert yourself if:

- You were not heard or understood.
- You were interrupted.

- ▲ Your idea was dismissed too quickly.
- ▲ You perceive a problem with the way the meeting is run.
- ▲ One of your hot buttons is being pushed (see previous section).

Being assertive is not synonymous with being aggressive, unpleasant, angry, or defensive. In fact, it is quite possible to assert yourself while remain calm and confident and without having to raise your voice. Here are a few general tips for asserting yourself in a meeting:

- ▲ If you are to assert yourself while remaining calm, you'll need to recognize and manage your hot buttons (see previous section).
- ▲ You cannot always depend on someone else, like the meeting facilitator, to stand up for you and intervene on your behalf. Some facilitators will, but many won't. Remember that suffering is optional and take responsibility for your own experience at the meeting.
- ▲ You may feel nervous about asserting yourself. Typical symptoms of nervousness include sweaty palms, pounding heart, and shaking knees. But do it anyway; you'll find that it gets easier and more natural with practice.
- ▲ Keep in mind that if you perceive a behavior to be counterproductive, there is a good chance that others feel the same way. Your reward for asserting yourself will likely come in the form of expressions of thanks after the meeting, such as, "Thank you so much for speaking up. I was feeling exactly the same way. I learned a lot from what you did and how you did it."
- ▲ If your intervention does not work, don't give up too fast. It's possible that the group was not ready for it and members were taken by surprise. Try again another time and change your approach. Old habits may be hard to break, but not impossible.
- ▲ Don't overdo it and don't make yourself a nuisance. There are times when it is best to let certain things continue. Choose the areas in which to intervene immediately and those that you could follow up on after the meeting or at a future meeting.
- ▲ You may want to suggest a fifteen-minute discussion just before the end of a meeting, when members will share feedback on how the meeting went. (This is known as a "bouquets and brickbats" session. Bouquets are compliments, and brickbats are ideas for improvement.)

Assuming you choose to intervene and assert yourself, you need to do so without getting angry. Remain calm, confident, and respectful of others:

- ▲ Focus on the behavior and not on the person.
- ▲ Focus on broadly accepted principles: fairness, equality, respect, and common sense.
- ▲ Focus on the need for the group to make good decisions and how this goal could be better served by the change you are suggesting.
- ▲ Focus on the need to pursue the mandate of the group in the most effective way.
- ▲ Avoid blaming and accusing others; just demand a better system of running a meeting.
- ▲ Soften your intervention by asking a question instead of giving an order. Instead of saying, "Be quiet and let me finish!" try, "May I finish, please?"

A Five-Step Recipe for an Effective Intervention

1. Get their attention.
2. State an observation about something that doesn't work.
3. State the impact of the event or the behavior you observe.
4. Suggest an alternative and explain its benefits.
5. Look for a commitment or feedback

Here is an example:

1. Get their attention: "Can I say something, please? Thank you."
2. State the observation: "It seems to me that this is a complex issue which has many aspects, but we're not dealing with it in a logical order."
3. State the impact: "The impact is that we may spend our time on side issues without focusing on important ones."
4. Suggest an alternative: "My suggestion is that we brainstorm for a few minutes, list the main issues, prioritize them, and then deal with them in order of importance."
5. Look for a commitment: "Does this sound like a reasonable way to go?"

Your actual intervention will not always need to be as elaborate as in the above five-step process. It may be enough to do it in one or two steps. Often you will achieve more with a short statement.

Techniques to Get Their Attention

Here are a few techniques to stop the chaos and get the group's attention:

- ▲ Ask for the space to speak: "May I say something?" Then stop and wait for them to be quiet. If at first you don't succeed, try again. Don't be shy, and if you need to raise your voice the next time, do it without being harsh or unpleasant.
- ▲ Make an audible noise, e.g., blow a whistle or press on a squeaky toy animal. When they notice you and are quiet, start to speak.
- ▲ Give a visual signal, like waving a cue card saying in large print: "Are we on track?"
- ▲ Do something unexpected that will get their attention. Use your imagination.
- ▲ Use the "pregnant pause" technique. Raise your voice and ask half a question: "Can I . . . ," then pause until they are quiet, and then give the second half of the sentence (or the full sentence): ". . . say something?"
- ▲ If you have an unusual idea and want their undivided attention, try a soft approach. For example, "I have a new idea. It may be a good idea, or it may be a bad one. I don't know. But I want you to hear me out and then tell me what you think. Here goes ____," or, "Can I tempt you to consider an idea that is completely outside the box? OK, I will, but I need you to hear me out."

Note: The above preambles are softly assertive and are hard to brush aside. They will likely get their attention and entice them to hear you out.

Here are a few scripts for you to assert yourself without getting angry:

The problem:	**The intervention or assertion script:**
Your fresh idea was dismissed too quickly.	"Can I say something? I have a feeling I did not explain my idea as clearly as I might have. I still think it is worthwhile considering. Can I explain a couple of points that I missed the first time?" Note: This script presents you as accountable and there is no blaming or finger pointing in it. The phrase "You did not understand me" is replaced by "I did not explain well enough."

The problem:	The intervention or assertion script:
Tony is very defensive about what you say and seems to take it as a personal criticism.	"Tony, I need you to hear me out. This has nothing to do with you personally. It has to do with our policies and procedures. As tough as it may be, we need to be able to discuss these things rationally."
Digressions from the agenda	"Where are we on the agenda?" or "Didn't we already make that decision?"
Off-mandate discussion	"I was just wondering: How is this agenda item connected to our mandate, which is _____? Isn't this something that _____ should be doing, not our group?"
Repetition	"Can I make an observation? I think we are beginning to sound repetitive. I am concerned that we might be losing precious time. Are we ready to make a decision on this issue and move on?"
A bad decision	"I can see everyone is ready to make a decision on this issue and move on. I agree that efficiency is important. At the same time, I think there are some gaps in this proposal and we should not rush it through. For example: _____. Can we postpone the decision until the next meeting, when we've had time to think about these gaps?"
You are criticized harshly. The other person yells and waves fingers at you. You feel like a little kid, being put down by a parent or a teacher.	"Jim, I have two things to say: First, I appreciate your feedback, and, I want to see what I can learn from it. The second thing is that it would make it easier for me to hear you if we could lower the volume and soften the tone of this conversation. Is this a reasonable thing to ask you to do? Thank you. Now,

	can you explain what you meant by _____?"
The meeting is bogged down on an issue.	"Can I make an observation? We've been working on this issue for an hour now, and we seem stuck. If we continue, we may lose time on other important issues, or we may hit the meeting's rush hour. May I suggest that we deal with other, easier issues now, and then come back to this one later, hopefully with some fresh ideas?"
One of your hot buttons is being pushed (see previous section).	*A racial or sexist slur*: "_____, (name), I have to say this. You may think this reference to women is funny, but I find it hard to take. I would appreciate you not doing it again." *Dishonesty*: Speak to the individual privately after the meeting: "_____ (name), I didn't want to embarrass you at the meeting, but I have a problem with how you represented things. You said _____, and I remember _____. Am I missing something?" *Manipulation*: You could say: "Thanks, but no thanks." If the attempt to manipulate happens in front of other people in a meeting, it may be best to not even dignify it with a comment. But maintain your integrity and refuse to go along with what the person wants you to do. *Talking behind your back*: Speak to the individual in person: "_____ (name), I understand that you've been saying _____ about me. Is this true? If so, is there a reason why you don't say it directly to me? Is there something I can do to make it easier for you to do this?" *Being misrepresented*: "_____ (name), can

The problem:	The intervention or assertion script:
	I ask for a favor? I understand you've been telling people that I feel a certain way about other people. I would really prefer to speak for myself and tell people directly. This way there will be less of a chance of any misunderstandings." *Being ignored*: "_____ (name), can you turn your back so I can see you? It's hard for me to understand when I don't see your face." *Backtracking*: "Am I missing something, _____ (name)? I am looking at the minutes of the last meeting and see very clearly an agreement by you to do _____. Now I am hearing something else from you. I thought we agreed not to backtrack. What is happening here?"

Example: Can One Person Make a Difference?

Rudy, a businessman, went to a meeting of a professional association to hear a well-known guest speaker. The event coordinator started the meeting by saying: "Before we hear the guest speaker, I suggest we break into small groups, talk about the speaker's topic for twenty minutes, then present our observations to the bigger group, and then have a coffee break. After the coffee break, in about an hour from now, we will hear the guest speaker."

Rudy was unhappy. He came to the meeting to hear the guest speaker, and he felt cheated by what he saw as a "divide and conquer" approach. He hesitated to interject, because he was new to the group. But then his hand magically rose and he said, "May I make a suggestion? I understand the plan that you explained, but for me it won't work. I came to this meeting to hear the guest speaker, and I would prefer it if we started with her presentation. However, being new to this group, I would not want to impose my wishes on everyone. I am wondering what other people here prefer to do."

Much to Rudy's surprise, most attendees preferred his plan to that of the event coordinator. The plan for the meeting was changed. Thankfully, the event coordinator did not take Rudy's suggestion as a personal attack (as some facilitators might). He even thanked him for it.

The message? Any participant, as new and as inexperienced as he or she may be, can and ought to make a difference in a meeting. Here are a few lessons to learn from this example:

- As a member, you need to give yourself permission to intervene. Don't be your own worst enemy by trivializing your concern and giving up before you even try.
- As a meeting facilitator, you need to be receptive to suggestions. Acknowledge that you don't have a monopoly on ideas on how to structure a meeting, and make it OK for participants to make suggestions. Park your ego outside and be prepared to listen and learn from others.
- Note one key strength of Rudy's approach: He did not expect the meeting to necessarily go his way. He invited input from other members regarding his idea. It's a democratic approach, whereby the group makes the decisions. It is not anarchy, where one strong-minded member makes the decisions, nor is it monarchy, where the facilitator makes them.

Turning Failures into Learning Opportunities

A meeting participant is bound to make the odd mistake. As human beings we are not perfect and, despite our good intentions, we are capable of "dropping the ball." Small mistakes may not be problematic, but big and embarrassing ones are more difficult to deal with.

The fact that you made a mistake is less significant than how you deal with it. You can deal with a mistake in a way that makes things worse, or you can turn the failure into a learning opportunity. The notion should be that "we only have successes around here." Indeed, after you pay the price for a mistake and recover from it, you can celebrate this failure and use it to:

- Learn from it and improve the way you work.
- Reinforce communication and procedures, so others are less likely to repeat the same mistake in the future.
- Be grateful that things did not turn out any worse than they did.

Here are a few tips for dealing with a mistake you made:

- Before you start blaming and tormenting yourself and apologizing to the entire world, find out exactly what caused the mistake. It may have been your fault, but it may also have been the result of a systemic problem (see below).
- If someone immediately assigns blame to you and demands an apology, you can say, "I will have no difficulty apologizing, as long as I know what I am apologizing for. Right now I don't know enough about the problem to give you an intelligent answer. Can I find out exactly what happened and get back to you?"
- If it was indeed your fault, leave your ego at home and do not hesitate to say, "I'm sorry." It takes confidence to admit you made a mistake. The key is to learn from your mistakes and move on. As long as your overall performance is exemplary and as long as mistakes such as this one are the exception and not a repeated pattern, you are doing fine.
- Take corrective action to remedy the consequences of your errors.
- Ask yourself: "What caused me to make this error, and what can I do to avoid repeating it? Should I have listened better? Should I have paid more attention to my e-mails?"
- Ask whether there are systemic problems within the organization that make people prone to making such mistakes, e.g., a lack of checks and balances, a lack of accountability, poor listening, a lack of feedback, or poorly defined policies and procedures.
- Avoid carrying the guilt and blaming yourself forever, unless you really enjoy "beating yourself up." At some point you need to forgive yourself and move on.
- Who is to blame is relatively unimportant, and that's why apologizing should not be an issue. The key is to move beyond assigning blame to a person, and shift the focus to a systemic problem. A mistake can be used as an opportunity to strengthen policies and to bridge systemic gaps that create risk for the organization.
- If your group has a history of always looking for the guilty party to blame, try saying this: "I can see that finding out exactly who is responsible for a failure may be significant to some of you. At the same time, usually it is not only one

individual that's to blame, but also the system, the relationships, the policies, and the procedures. Yes, assigning blame has its benefits, but we should be investing more energy in bridging the systemic gaps, so we can prevent these failures from happening in the future."

Example: An Unrealistic Policy

Gretchen, a new member of a group, approved a small expenditure without consulting the group. She did it in the interest of expediency. At the next meeting she was harshly criticized for not bringing the expense to the group for approval, as required by its policies.

Gretchen promptly apologized for the violation of the policy (which she did not know about): "I sincerely apologize for my mistake. I didn't know about the policy, but that's no excuse. I should have made it my business to find out about it."

But then Gretchen raised a few questions: "How realistic is this policy? Does it serve the organization well? What if an important opportunity would be lost unless someone could make a decision quickly and give the financial commitment to back it up?"

As a result of this feedback, the group reviewed its policy and changed it to be more realistic and flexible. Accountability was retained, but leeway and discretion were added. As a result, each member was given limited discretionary spending powers, while being required to report on expenditures at the next meeting.

Example: A Fatal Accident

A fatal workplace accident occurred in a mine, and the driver of a large truck was killed. The accident was studied and the findings were presented at the next safety committee meeting.

At first, the finger of blame pointed to the driver. By all accounts, he drove recklessly under the influence of alcohol. He also did not wear a safety belt, as required by company policy. Then the finger of blame pointed to the supervisor: Why did he allow this to happen?

After further examination, the committee shifted from assigning blame to examining systemic gaps that allowed the accident to happen. The following significant facts were discovered:

- ▲ Drivers were trusted to let the supervisor know if they had too much to drink.
- ▲ Safety manuals were outdated, confusing, and hard to read.
- ▲ Several drivers were illiterate and could not read the safety manuals.
- ▲ Supervisors were demoralized because unionized workers recently received a pay increase and they didn't. This might have had a negative impact on due diligence. There is no excuse for sloppiness, but people do not perform their best when they are unhappy.

As a result of this analysis, the committee realized that, with the existing systemic problems, the company was lucky that much worse accidents did not happen. Several initiatives were taken to bridge the systemic gaps and correct the significant deficiencies in the company's safety procedures. Among other things:

- ▲ The safety manual was updated and made easier to read. It was also made more readily available to mine workers, drivers, and supervisors.
- ▲ Driver training and safety awareness programs were enhanced.
- ▲ A special program was initiated to teach illiterate drivers safety procedures and make sure they understood them.
- ▲ Negotiations about pay and benefit improvements were started with supervisors.

TAKING MINUTES

Minutes, or meeting summaries, are important documents. They can serve the group by:

- ▲ Recording the decisions made and any action items: who will do what and by when?
- ▲ Capturing the essence of the discussion that took place at the meeting, i.e., the key points that led the group to its consensus.

Minutes should be:

▲ Action-oriented: Focused primarily on what was done and the decisions made at the meeting, and not on every word uttered by every member

▲ Objective: Focused on the group's actions and not on individual actions or statements

▲ Concise and reader-friendly

This section focuses on what the minute taker should do at the meeting itself. See Chapter 9 for the minute taker's planning checklist and Chapter 15 for sample minutes of a meeting.

The minute taker should not require shorthand training nor should an audiotape recorder be needed, since the minutes should not include every word that was said at the meeting. If the same point was made five times, it only needs to be recorded once.

The minute-taking task can be made so easy that any participant can do it. In fact, you may want to rotate the minute-taking task among members, so each individual can learn to listen and capture the essence of what took place in a meeting.

It is not unusual for the meeting facilitator to take minutes. In fact, taking minutes can be a way for the facilitator to focus the meeting and reduce repetition. For example:

▲ At the start of the meeting: "As we go through our discussions, I will record highlights on the flip chart. From time to time I will review progress. I will use the flip charts to compile the minutes. I will try to write fast, and I will record only the key words, so I don't slow down the meeting."

▲ Capturing a key point: "Hold it for a second, Evelyn, I need to record the point you just raised on the flip chart."

▲ Subtly pointing to repetition: "Thank you, Warren. Your point about the impact of outside noise on productivity is already on the flip chart. Does anyone have any new points to add?"

If you are asked to take minutes but are not facilitating the meeting, consider these tips:

1. Position yourself next to the meeting facilitator, so that you can easily hear him or her articulating the consensus and the action items. You can also get him or

her to slow the meeting down and help you record accurate and concise minutes. (Note: There is no need to apologize for doing this. If the meeting is moving too fast for you, chances are it is moving too fast for other people. They will be grateful for your initiative.)

2. Establish with the meeting facilitator what is the acceptable way for you to intervene and ask for help if it is difficult to capture the essential points in the discussion, i.e., whether it is OK for you to speak up and ask for help. For example:

   ▲ If the group leaves too many "loose ends," you can say: "Before we continue, can someone tell me what happened to the discussion about the customer appreciation day? Did we make a decision about it?"

   ▲ If confusing technical terms and abbreviations are used, you can say: "I am having trouble following the discussion and taking the minutes with these technical terms. Can someone help me out? What does _____ mean?"

3. Establish whether it's OK for you to write your own summaries and confirm them with the group. For example, "Here is what I have in the minutes so far: The key points that were made are: _____, _____ and _____. The agreement is that we do four things: _____, _____, _____, and _____. The areas that are left for us to work on are: _____, _____ and _____. Did I get it right?"

4. Establish whether it is preferable for you to not speak up, but instead pass the facilitator notes requesting help.

5. Establish whether it's OK to have cue cards (S.O.S. cards) to show the facilitator when you need help. For example:

   ▲ "Summarize key points"

   ▲ "Repeat proposed decision"

   ▲ "Point-form summary would help"

   ▲ "Facilitate a decision on the change"

   ▲ "Slow them down"

   ▲ "Clarify technical terms"

See Chapter 9 for the minute taker's planning checklist, and use a template to record the discussion and the consensus reached by the group.

FOURTEEN

Landing a Meeting

Now that the meeting has been steered to its destination (Chapter 12) with everyone pulling their weight (Chapter 13), it is now time to land the meeting. Often facilitators make the landing sudden and abrupt: "OK, we're done. Bye." A smooth landing is preferable.

This chapter outlines steps that will help make the landing of your meeting more measured and gradual. Keep in mind that not all steps will be needed in all meetings, and you can delete or add items to the list. In any event, it is suggested that you allocate time for the closing portion of the meeting, from five minutes for a short meeting to thirty minutes for a long one.

Here are the main steps to consider when landing a meeting:

- Alert everyone that the meeting is in its last stages.
- Review the progress made at the meeting.
- Establish follow-up actions that will be taken after the meeting.
- Establish the next meeting date.
- Acknowledge special contributions to the success of the meeting.
- Take feedback on how the meeting went (see Chapter 11 for a sample feedback sheet).

- Invite members to stay for a postmeeting social event, if one is scheduled.
- Make announcements and ask if others have any.
- Share a closing thought or delegate this task to someone else.
- Thank the participants for their contribution.
- End the meeting.

Sample Script: Landing a Meeting

3:30 P.M.: The closing portion is coming

"We are now on the last item before the closing portion of the meeting. As a reminder, we are scheduled to end the meeting by 4 P.M. and we need about fifteen minutes for the closing portion."

3:45 P.M.: Summary of progress and follow-up actions

"We are now at the closing portion of the meeting. We need to do a few things between now and 4 o'clock:

- First, I will summarize our consensus and establish any follow-up duties.
- Second, we'll give details about the next meeting.
- Third, we'll acknowledge special contributions to the success of this meeting.
- Fourth, we'll invite you to share any feedback about the meeting.
- Fifth, there will be a few announcements.
- Finally, we will have an inspirational closing thought.
- We will then end the meeting, at which time you can stay for networking and special refreshments, courtesy of Paula and Ed.

"Let me start with a review of what we've accomplished today:

"The purpose of this meeting was to establish roles and responsibilities for each one of us for the coming six months, as we work together to develop corporate standards for our new e-commerce activities. We started with proposed policies and organizational structure, which were prepared by Jerry and Tamara in cooperation with Futures Unlimited HR Consulting.

"We agreed to approve parts A, C, and D of the document with the following changes: ____.

"Parts B and E were referred back to Jerry and Tamara, who will look at how our concerns can be taken into account. If needed, Jerry and Tamara will consult further with Futures Unlimited, and the total budget for this extra consultation will not exceed $1,000.

"Jerry and Tamara, will you be able to send us a written report by November 28th? This is a week before our next meeting, which is set for December 5th. Thank you.

"Did I miss anything in my summary of the meeting? Are there any questions or concerns or anything that needs to be added, deleted, or changed? Thank you.

"Rick agreed to prepare minutes of our meeting. He will send a draft copy to each one of you as an e-mail attachment by Friday morning. Please review the summary and send Rick any corrections by Monday at 4 P.M., so he can correct and file them and send you a revised copy.

"Rick has passed you a sheet with your names on it. Please put down your phone numbers and e-mail addresses. He will compile the list and send it to everyone along with the minutes."

Place and time of next meeting

"As I mentioned, the date of the next meeting has been set for December 5th. The timing will be from 1 to 4 P.M. We will let you know of the location for the meeting when we send you the agenda and meeting package.

"In the next meeting, we will address parts B and E of the structure document along with the report by Jerry and Tamara. We will then begin to discuss the actual standards project. It will undoubtedly be an interesting discussion. Don't let anyone tell you that standards are boring.

"An agenda and documents for the meeting will be sent to you by December 1st. Please make sure to read them and prepare for the meeting. Let me know if you have any questions or concerns.

"As I said many times, I have an open door policy. I promise to take your feedback, good or bad, as a gift and as something to learn from. There are 365 days in a year, and our communication does not have to happen only during meetings."

3:50 P.M. Acknowledging special contributions

"We have four more things to do before we close the meeting: special acknowledgments, feedback on the meeting, announcements, and a closing thought.

"The first acknowledgment is that, in my estimation, we have made remarkable progress today, and we should be proud of it. We had some bumps on the road, and we dealt with them in an honest, direct, and highly effective manner. I believe we've shown ourselves to be a cohesive team, and this bodes very well for our project and for the company.

"So feel free to reach over to your neighbor now and give him or her a gentle pat on the back. Nothing else, now . . . just a gentle pat on the back. Or shake their hand if you prefer. Congratulations again.

"Here are two specific acknowledgments:

"First, special thanks to you, Jerry and Tamara, for your report, and please pass on our collective thanks to the consultants. You've laid out the groundwork for us and given us a sense of focus and direction. You were open and receptive to our feedback and questions on your report, and you were not in any way defensive to the changes that we made. I have a small token of appreciation for each one of you: a box of smoked Pacific salmon, which I know you both like.

"Let's thank Tamara and Jerry for a job well done. (Lead a round of applause.)

"Second, we have the star award, for the person who made a very significant contribution at this meeting. For this time only, I get to make this decision. In future meetings, you will vote on who should get this award. But for today, the recipient of the star award, is the individual who challenged us to think beyond the obvious. And the winner is (drum roll) Maureen. Here is your award, Maureen, a star-shaped clock for your desk. Please keep up the good work!!"

3:52 P.M. Feedback on the meeting

"Next we need to discuss your feedback on the meeting. Please take a moment and complete the feedback sheets. We'll hear some of your comments in a couple of minutes."

After a few minutes:

"Does anyone need more time? If you do, raise your hand. Thank you, let's take a few seconds to wrap it up.

"OK. Does anyone want to comment on the meeting now? What did you appreciate, what did not work, and what can we do better next time?"

A few minutes later:

"Thank you for your feedback. Please pass the feedback sheets to me. I will review them fully after the meeting. And, as I said earlier, your feedback is welcome anytime."

3:57 P.M. Announcements

"I have one announcement: Our company's Christmas party is on December 10th.You and your spouse or significant other are invited, but you need to RSVP by December 3rd.

"Are there any other announcements¿"

Closing Thought or Prayer

"Just before we close, Stacey has an inspirational thought for us."

Note: If a prayer is used to close the meeting, make sure it is appropriate. It may need to be nondenominational, not favoring one religion or ethnic group over another.

4:00 P.M. Closing

"Thank you very much for coming to this meeting. See you on December 5th."

Notes:

▲ Door prizes: In some groups it is customary to have door prize draws before the meeting ends. Usually this is done in larger meetings, sometimes with the goal of enticing members to stay until the meeting ends. It's a bit manipulative, but it works. But don't let it be the only reason for staying. Make the meeting pleasant, engaging, and efficient.

▲ Comfort or optimism gauge: If your group used an optimism meter at the start of the meeting (see Chapter 11), it may be productive to check the optimism level just before the meeting ends: "Before we close the meeting, I would ask you to think again about your personal levels of optimism and comfort with our decision-making process, as you did at the start of the meeting. Use a scale of minus 5 to plus 5 and rate your optimism level now. When you finish, we'll compare your rating now to the rating at the start of the meeting. We can then talk about whether this meeting has made a difference."

FIFTEEN

POSTMEETING ACTIVITIES

So you've had your meeting. Is your work done? Of course not. The follow-up and the consensus-building activities continue between meetings. There are several things that need to be done to maintain the momentum and capitalize on the progress made at the meeting. This chapter covers the following activities after a meeting:

- ▲ Preparing and circulating the minutes
- ▲ Taking follow-up actions
- ▲ Analyzing the meeting
- ▲ Using meeting assessment checklists: the six Ws

PREPARING AND CIRCULATING THE MINUTES

Minutes, or meeting summaries, are important documents. Depending on the organization, minutes can help achieve the following purposes:

- ▲ Documenting the consensus reached and what led to it
- ▲ Creating a historical record of the activities of the group
- ▲ Reminding members who were present of what was done and agreed to at the meeting

- ▲ Informing members who were absent of progress made at the meeting
- ▲ Reminding members of agreements and promises they made at the meeting and hence serving as a follow-up tool
- ▲ Informing outside parties (e.g., your boss, other departments, and internal and external stakeholders) of developments that affect them
- ▲ In the case of a public body (e.g., a municipal council, a school board, a legislative assembly, etc.), creating a public record of the decisions of the group, which can then be made available to citizens (subject to applicable freedom of information and protection of privacy legislation)

The following data should be recorded in the minutes:

- ▲ Background details about the meeting, i.e., the name of the group, the date, the place, the purpose, the attendance, and other details about the meeting.
- ▲ The decisions that were made and a summary of the thought process that led to them.
- ▲ Action items (e.g., who will do what and by when?). With this information, minutes can be used as a way of reminding members of commitments they made. The facilitator can highlight the follow-up duties assigned on each member's copy of the minutes, using a highlighting pen or another method.
- ▲ In more formal bodies, such as boards of directors and governmental bodies, details on parliamentary procedure used are recorded. For guidelines on what to record and what not to record in such meetings (motions, amendments, etc.), consult your favorite book on rules of order. You'll find my views on this subject in Chapters 7 and 8 of *The Complete Handbook of Business Meetings* (AMACOM, 2000).

Minutes should be:

- ▲ Action-oriented, i.e., focused primarily on what was done and what was decided at the meeting, and not on every word uttered by every member.
- ▲ Objective, i.e., the focus should be more on the group's action and less on what individuals said or did.
- ▲ Concise, well organized, and reader-friendly.
- ▲ Accurate, i.e., the minutes should be a record of what was done, and not a record of what someone wished had been done. The minutes should not be "doctored" by the chair if she thinks a decision made at the meeting was inappropriate.

The Case Against Verbatim Minutes

Some organizations have the bad habit of recording verbatim (word-for-word) minutes. If you want to change this counterproductive practice, you need some arguments against such minutes and in favor of simpler and more concise minutes. Here are a few arguments you can make:

- With verbatim minutes, the focus becomes personal (what people said) rather than collective (what the group did).
- With verbatim minutes, a member may end up arguing, "I did not say this," and another will respond, "Yes, you did, and I can prove it. Let's listen to the tape." After listening to the tape, the response may be, "Well, maybe I did say it, but I didn't mean to. . . ." Chaos prevails, and precious meeting time is wasted on these arguments.
- Verbatim minutes tend to be lengthy and repetitive, and contain plenty of useless and irrelevant information. Members, who are often busy people (with jobs, volunteer work, and family life), tend to ignore such minutes, since they are tedious, take too long to read, and provide limited value.
- Verbatim minutes take a long time to prepare. The minute-taking task becomes onerous. The minute taker may require shorthand training and an actual audiotape of the meeting.
- With each word being recorded, members can become uneasy about saying things at the meeting, for fear of being embarrassed and having their own words come back to haunt them. Verbatim minutes can become an impediment to creativity, spontaneity, and full participation in meetings.

Steps to Follow After the Meeting

1. Draft minutes should be prepared and sent to the group's members for review:
   - For sample minutes, see further in this chapter.
   - The first draft should have the title "draft minutes" on every page.
   - A deadline should be given for pointing out any errors in the minutes.
   - A cover sheet may be included, highlighting action items. For example:

Individual:	Responsible for action items:
Joanne	3 and 5 solo, 4 jointly with Rose
Joseph	1
Rose	2 solo, 4 jointly with Joanne
Peter	6

2. Feedback from members should be integrated into the minutes. The corrected minutes should then be:

▲ Entitled "revised minutes" with the date of revision on every page (to distinguish them from the draft minutes).

▲ Sent to the members, together with the package for the next meeting, so they can prepare for it. The summary of action items can serve as a reminder to follow up on promises made at the meeting.

3. If there are disagreements about the content of the minutes, these steps should be taken to correct the minutes:

▲ In most corporate settings, it makes sense to allow the group's leader to make this type of decision. It should not consume any time at the next meeting. However, if the disagreement is divisive, it may be smart to involve the group in resolving it, even when the group's leader has the authority to make this type of decision.

▲ In formal groups, the minutes are typically brought to the next meeting for approval by the group. In this case corrections are made by the group before the minutes are approved. Disputes can be resolved by a formal vote: "Raise your hands if you believe the correction should be made. Thank you. Raise your hands if you think it should not be made. Thank you. The correction will be made (or will not be made)."

▲ Some minute takers keep an audiotape of a meeting, to definitively address any disagreements. This should not be necessary for most groups.

4. Disagreements about minutes can be minimized through good preventive work, i.e.:

▲ Keep the minutes brief and concise. Stay focused on the decisions and the main points made in the discussion, and avoid word-for-word minutes.

▲ Remain as objective as possible and try to avoid attributing comments to individuals. Instead of, "Ray said that _____, and Joanne said _____," try,

"The main points made in the discussion were: ____, ____ and ____," without mentioning who said what (unless this is absolutely essential or required by your group's policies).

- ▲ At the meeting, decisions and action items should be articulated clearly before moving on to the next agenda item. The minute taker can also repeat the decisions and the action items and ask for confirmation of accuracy before moving on. Members can indicate any inaccuracies right there and then. Clarity at the meeting is the best preventive medicine.
- ▲ The minutes should be prepared and reviewed shortly after the meeting, when the events are recent and the minute taker's memory is fresh.
- ▲ The minute taker and the group's leader should review the minutes before sending them out, to ensure they are accurate and free of grammatical or typographical errors. Pay attention to small details.

Next is a sample of minutes for you to consider. You can use your word processing skills to improve the layout to suit your group's needs, or you can invent an entirely different layout.

Example: Minutes

Minutes of the IT Committee of XYZ Corporation,
February 23, 2010

Place:	Red Rose Room, People Friendly Hotel, New York City
Date and Time:	February 23, 2010, 2:00 to 4:15 P.M.
Attendance:	Derek Lee (facilitator), Information Systems Division Theresa Green, Human Resources Division Monica Rothberg, Accounting Division Fred Ferguson, Customer Services Division
Purpose:	1. To choose a company for information technology training 2. To review emerging IT trends

1. IT Training

Discussion and decisions:

Derek presented a summary of the pros and cons of three companies (see attachment). The following main points were made in the discussion:

- Company A has a lot of experience, but is also the most expensive bidder. Staff members are busy, and it may or may not be possible for them to meet our time constraints.
- Company B is new, but has excellent staff. It seems eager to get the business, but has no track record to speak of.
- Company C is the lowest bidder, but not all of their references check out. Some are OK, but some of their clients indicated that trainers were ineffective.

The committee was generally in favor of Company B, and decided that:

- Reference checks on its principals are needed.
- If the references check out, discussions need to take place on how XYZ's training needs will be met. The focus should be on customization of the training to XYZ's needs.

Action items:

Theresa to check Company B's references and let everyone know the results by e-mail by February 28, 2010.

If references check out, Derek and Fred will arrange a meeting with Company B, and will report back to the Committee for a final decision at the March 10 meeting.

If references do not check out or if the discussions with Company B are not successful, Derek may schedule a teleconference call to discuss what to do next.

2. Emerging IT Trends

Discussion and decisions:

Monica reported on IT industry trends that affect accounting practices, namely: ____.

Theresa reported on a conference on telecommuting. Her main points were: ____.

The committee decided that the above trends should be addressed at the next meeting. Theresa will discuss how telecommuting can be used to make XYZ Corporation better positioned for growth over the next ten years.

Action items:

Theresa to prepare a report on telecommuting and its applicability to XYZ by March 5th, so it can be circulated to committee members prior to the March 10th meeting.

TAKING FOLLOW-UP ACTIONS

There are two types of follow-up actions that need to be taken after a meeting:

1. Follow-up on decisions made at the meeting.
2. Giving feedback ("bouquets and brickbats") to meeting participants.

Follow-Up on Decisions Made at the Meeting

Without follow-up on the decisions made in a meeting, you could find yourself with plenty of reasons and excuses ("I had an emergency," "I forgot," "I had other priorities," "I had no cooperation from suppliers"), but very few results. Here are a few tips to ensure follow-up on the decisions made in a meeting:

1. As soon as a decision is made, action items and deadlines should be immediately confirmed with each person at the meeting. For example:

   "Before we move ahead, let me just confirm follow-up duties, so we can record them in the minutes.

   "Bonnie, you will contact Accounts Receivable about this issue and let me know of the outcome by Monday, right? Thanks, Bonnie.

   "Jack, you will do research on the Internet, check with at least three colleagues from your professional association about emerging trends in this field, and prepare a written report by Monday March 25th. OK? And you will make the report concise and reader-friendly, for those of us who are novices in the field, right? Thank you, Jack.

   "Phil, did you record all of this in the minutes? Thanks, Phil. Let's move on."

2. All decisions and action items should be recorded clearly in the minutes of the meeting (see previous section in this chapter):

   ▲ The action items should be highlighted (e.g., by bolding, or by being placed in a separate column).

- ▲ There should be a clear indication of who is to do what and by when.
- ▲ The minutes should be sent to the members as soon as possible after the meeting, along with a memo requesting that they review any action items assigned to them and let you (the meeting facilitator or the group's leader) know immediately of any potential difficulties in meeting a deadline.

3. You may need to personalize the copy of the minutes that each individual receives, to draw the reader's attention to his or her action items. For example:

- ▲ Use a highlighting pen and point out the action items that the individual is responsible for.
- ▲ Attach a sticky note or a personal memo, saying something like: "Randy, please note your action items: 4, 7, and 10."
- ▲ Use a reader-friendly column format to clearly note in the minutes who is assigned to the action item.
- ▲ Alternatively, a cover page can be added to the minutes, tabulating who is responsible for what (see previous section on minutes for an example).

4. Each member should generally be depended on to keep any promises and commitments she or he made. She or he should:

- ▲ Give the group's leader and others progress updates on a timely basis.
- ▲ Advise the leader immediately of any difficulties in completing assigned duties.

5. It may be wise for the group's leader to check with each individual on progress, especially on critical items, e.g., "Drew, I just thought I'd check on how you're doing with your research on public relations trends. Are you making progress? Do you need any help? It's quite important to get the report out to the group no later than next Tuesday. Can we count on you to meet this deadline? Thank you. Please let me know if you need any help."
6. Some people argue against checking with individuals on progress. They suggest that this would amount to "baby-sitting," and that people should be counted on to deliver results, without any reminders. Indeed, with high-performance and "low-maintenance" individuals, the above reminders may not be needed. However, the fact remains that some of your members may be "high-maintenance" individuals and may need the "baby-sitting" to deliver the results the group needs. You need to be practical. Assuming people are going to always be reliable may be too big a risk for you to take.

7. If it becomes apparent that an individual is not going to complete an action item, corrective action may be needed. Options to consider include:

   - Give the job to someone else.
   - Extend the deadline for the assignment.
   - Drop this item from the next meeting agenda.

8. If an individual who followed up on an action item will miss the next meeting, this should not relieve him or her from completing the assignment. The member should be expected to pass on the report to the meeting facilitator or someone else, so it can be presented at the meeting.

Giving "Bouquets and Brickbats" to Members (IOU List)

As the meeting progresses, the group's leader and other members should keep a list of IOUs, or feedback that could not be communicated at the meeting itself, but still needs to be given. For example, you may need to do the following after the meeting:

1. Compliment and thank individuals privately for a job well done at the meeting. Do it even if they were already acknowledged publicly. The extra reinforcement will boost their enthusiasm and commitment to the group.

   - "Donna, I did not get to tell you this in person at the meeting, but that presentation was really well done. You told me before the meeting how nervous you felt about speaking in public, but I have to tell you that you came across as a very confident and effective presenter. If you had any nervousness, it sure did not show. Congratulations, and thanks for doing it."

2. Apologize to individuals whom you may have offended inadvertently. For example:

   - "Sara, I really apologize for interrupting you at the meeting. I hope you understand. I was trying to move the meeting along, while working hard to be as sensitive as possible to individuals. It's tough to find the right balance between making progress and inclusiveness, especially when time is tight and issues are controversial. But I did want to apologize to you."
   - "Shawn, thank you for complaining about being ignored by me on the speakers' lineup. My peripheral vision was blocked, and I need to do something about it next time. I will do my best not to do this again. But just in case I do, would you please pass me an 'urgent note' or make some noise? Thanks.

I can give you a squeaky toy animal if it will make it easier for you to complain."

- ▲ "Tina, I realized after the meeting that I should have listened to you more carefully, and that you were making some new and very valid points. My apologies if I got too defensive in the heat of the discussion. I will do my best to slow down and avoid impulsive reactions to what you say."
- ▲ As an alternative, you could send the individual you offended a personal apology note.
- ▲ In some instances you could add a touch of finesse by making a tangible "peace offering." Send the individual a token gift or flowers, or be creative and send him or her an IOU note. The envelope will say IOU, and the inside will have a promissory note saying something like "lunch at a restaurant of your choice."

3. Give individuals feedback that was not possible to give at the meeting. For example:

- ▲ To a late arrival: "Vanessa, is there a reason why you were late the last couple of meetings? We really needed you for the discussion at the start of the meeting. Can we count on you to make every effort to be there on time in future meetings?"
- ▲ To a side talker: "Michael, can I give you some feedback about the last few meetings? Thank you. You may not have been aware of it, but the conversations you were having with Amy were distracting to several people. In fact, I have a sense that Amy might have preferred to focus on the meeting and had a hard time saying no to you. We need everyone to be focused on the meeting. Can I get you to handle any private communication before the meeting begins?"
- ▲ To someone who was harsh: "Ben, I need to give you some feedback about your participation at the meeting. Is this a good time? Thanks. I am sure you didn't mean any harm, but your tone of voice and some of the words you were using were hard for some people to take. I know you feel very strongly about these issues, and that's great. But can I get you to soften your tone and your choice of words? I think it will make it easier for everyone to listen to what you have to say. What do you think?"
- ▲ To an astute but quiet member: "Irene, I was just wondering: Is there something we can do to make it easier for you to speak up in meetings? I value your expertise, and I think there is a lot that we could learn from you. What do you think?"

ANALYZING THE MEETING

Each meeting has its strengths and weaknesses. Your group should assess its meetings and look for ways to improve them. The purpose of your postmeeting assessment should be:

- To find out what worked at the last meeting, and plan to repeat it
- To find out what did not work at the last meeting, and plan to avoid it
- To look for new things that can be done to make future meetings fresh and exciting to attend

Here are a few ways of evaluating your meetings:

- Chapter 8 includes the ten key ingredients of a successful meeting. You can use the various sections in Chapter 8 to assess a meeting you had, determine which of the ten ingredients were present and which were absent, and plan your next meeting accordingly.
- Ask members to complete feedback sheets (given to them at the start of the meeting) as the meeting progresses and remind them to give them to you before leaving. See sample feedback sheet in Chapter 11.
- Just before the meeting ends, remind members to complete their feedback sheets and turn them in.
- If you don't have feedback forms, ask members to put their ideas in a suggestion box or just write them down and give them to you.
- Ask them to write their names on the feedback sheets, so you can follow up with them and clarify what they meant, if needed, and so you can give them credit for their ideas.
- At the landing stage of the meeting (see Chapter 14), invite members to briefly comment on the meeting's "bouquets" (what went well) and "brickbats" (what did not go so well).
- You can use the assessment checklists given later in the chapter for a postmeeting analysis.
- Suggestions that are implemented should be publicly acknowledged and token awards should be given for them. This will encourage members to continue giving feedback.

USING MEETING ASSESSMENT CHECKLISTS: THE SIX WS

This section includes checklists to help you prevent problems encountered in a meeting from recurring at the next one. Unlike Chapter 8, which presents an affirmative vision for a meeting, the checklists below are problem-driven. Specifically, the six Ws of a meeting are considered (note: "HOW" is one of the six Ws, but, unlike the other five Ws, the W is at the end):

- The WHYs and WHATs of a meeting (group's mandate, meeting's purpose, agenda)
- The WHENs of a meeting (schedule, time management, efficiency)
- The WHOs of a meeting (participants)
- The HOWs of a meeting (participation protocol, discussion activities)
- The WHEREs of a meeting (location, room, environment, logistics)

For each of the six Ws, the checklist gives you:

- A list of questions to ask about a meeting you had
- Typical problems that may have occurred
- What can be done to prevent such problems from occurring in the future

Questions to Ask About the WHYs and WHATs of a Meeting

- Was the group's mandate clear to everyone?
- Was the purpose of the meeting clear to everyone?
- Was the agenda followed?
- Were the intended outcomes of the meeting achieved?
- Did the meeting advance the group's mandate sufficiently?
- Was the meeting worth holding? Did it deliver a good return on investment?

To avoid this WHY or WHAT problem in the future:	You may need to do this:
The discussion proved the group's mandate is outdated and meaningless	It is time to renegotiate your group's mandate with your boss and make it

To avoid this WHY or WHAT problem in the future:	You may need to do this:
and that no one is serious about it. Members attended because they had to be there. (After all, it's their job, and they should be obedient, right?)	more meaningful. Once you've done this, you need to explain the revised mandate to your group and get their commitment for it. (They should be at meetings because they want to, and not because they have to.)
Members didn't know why the meeting was called and had no idea why they were there.	Stop calling meetings on a moment's notice. Determine what needs to be achieved at the meeting, and decide who should be there and for what purpose. Let everyone know of the meeting's purpose well in advance. Develop clear agendas.
There were many digressions from the agenda, and the meeting did not achieve its purpose.	State the purpose when you launch the next meeting and explain the main results that need to be achieved. Keep the meeting on track and prevent digressions: "Right now we are on item 8, the proposed PR campaign. We need to stay on track."
Only 10 percent of the meeting time was spent on issues that were significant to the group's mandate. The rest of the time was spent on small issues that could have been dealt with outside the meeting. Some members like to micromanage, and others feel helpless to stop them.	Be selective with your agenda items. Include only items that will deliver the greatest return on investment and will advance the group's mandate in the most substantial way. Other items should be dropped, delayed, or delegated. Members should be encouraged to ask questions like: "Is our time spent in the most meaningful way right now?" or "Does this issue really need to take up our time?" or "Are we micromanaging now?"
An agenda item was not ripe for discussion and decision making. Important data was missing and much-needed research had not been done.	Delay such items until they are ripe for discussion and decision making. Make it OK to say no. An agenda should not be a free-for-all.

Progress on an agenda item was nonexistent.	Clarify the decision-making options on agenda items, so members know where they could go with it.

Questions to Ask About the WHENs of a Meeting

- Was the meeting scheduled at an appropriate and convenient time?
- Was the meeting duration appropriate?
- Did the meeting start on time and end on time (or early)?
- Was the right amount of time allocated to each issue?
- Did members speak briefly, concisely, and clearly?
- Was time evenly divided among the members?

To avoid this WHEN problem in the future:	You may need to do this:
The meeting started late.	As a first step, schedule the meeting at a reasonable hour. Second, state the opening time in the notice of the meeting and indicate your intention to start exactly on time. Third, you can schedule networking and refreshment time before the meeting. Fourth, you can establish creative penalties for latecomers and fun rewards for those who consistently arrive on time.
Some members could not concentrate because the meeting was held at mealtime, and no food was provided. Stomachs were rumbling.	If you hold a meeting at mealtime, feed them or remind them to bring a brown bag.
The meeting ended late. Members ended up missing the start of their next meetings.	Establish a closing time in the meeting's notice and repeat it at the start of the meeting. Manage time so each issue receives proper attention and measured progress is made. Watch the clock and

To avoid this WHEN problem in the future:	You may need to do this:
	give members timing progress reports: "We have one hour left before we close and we have the following issues to address ____."
Members complained that the meeting was too long or that they were tired of sitting.	Make the meeting shorter, or schedule breaks, or plan activities that allow people to move around, e.g., run a part of the meeting standing up, or have members walk around the room and put sticky notes on flip charts to set priorities, or schedule exercise breaks. (Remember, the human mind will absorb only as much as the human seat will endure.)
You hit rush hour, e.g., fifteen minutes before the meeting ended you realized that half the agenda was not completed. You rushed important items through, making some bad decisions in a hurry.	Avoid scheduling too many items on the agenda. Allocate sufficient time to major agenda items. At the start of the meeting get members to agree to a timed agenda. Keep an eye on the clock and give members periodic progress reports: "We have ten minutes left for this issue and then we need to move on to the discussion on ____."
Some members rambled and took too long to make their points.	Ask members to make their comments concise, clear, and brief. Give ramblers feedback before the next meeting or send them to communication courses. In a large or formal meeting, you may want to establish time limits on speakers.
The meeting was dominated by a few members: 90 percent of the time was consumed by 10 percent of the people. Important perspectives were excluded from the decision-making process.	Say this at the start of the meeting: "We need to make sure we give everyone equal opportunities to speak. With that in mind, please make room for other people to speak. From time to

	time I will ask: Does anyone who has not spoken want to speak?"
Your guest presenter took an hour and a half to speak and no one knew how to stop him.	Establish your expectations with each speaker in advance, i.e., the topic and the issues you need them to address, and how much time they will have. Establish how the two of you will work together to ensure that time limits are respected.

Questions to Ask About the WHOs of a Meeting

- ▲ Were the right people present at the meeting?
- ▲ Was everyone there for the full duration of the meeting, in body and in spirit?
- ▲ Did members work well together?

To avoid this WHO problem in the future:	You may need to do this:
Several of the members who attended did not need to be there or were only needed for a part of the meeting. On the other hand, key decision makers who were badly needed were absent.	Plan your invitation list more carefully and ensure that key individuals are there. Conversely, ask whether everyone really needs to be there, and, if so, which agenda items are relevant to them. Consider inviting some people only to a part of the meeting, when they can make a contribution. Run a tight ship, so when they come, the meeting will be ready for them.
Several members missed the meeting without notifying you.	First let them know they were missed. Next find out why they were absent. The reason may have been: ▲ The timing of the meeting (inconvenient?) ▲ The quality of the meeting (boring?) ▲ Competing demands on their time

To avoid this WHO problem in the future:	You may need to do this:
	▲ Low commitment level to your group's work Address the cause of their absence without getting angry. Ask them to let you know in advance if they will miss a meeting, so you can plan accordingly.
Some members appeared to be daydreaming or busy doing something unrelated to the meeting.	Ask whether they needed to be at the meeting. If not, don't invite them next time. If they are needed, find ways of engaging them in the discussion, e.g., give them lead roles on agenda items, or ask for their comments: "Geoff, you have expertise in this area. Can you help us out?" He will never daydream again.
Cell phones rang and people walked in and handed messages to attendees, which meant some of them had to leave the meeting or come in and out.	Ask members to arrange for their messages to be taken by someone else, so they can be at the meeting from start to finish, in body and in spirit. At the start of the meeting, say: "Would everyone please raise their right hand, reach over to their cell phones, and turn them off." Make exceptions only for absolute emergencies.
A member did not read the meeting package. You know this because you saw him open the package just before the meeting, or his questions clearly indicated a lack of preparation.	Talk to him after the meeting and find out what the problem was. If the reports were too long or too technical and confusing, ask report writers to make them more concise, use plain language, and include executive summaries and definitions of terms and abbreviations. On the other hand, if the lack of preparation is because the member does not make your meetings a priority, ask for a renewed commitment. If he or she

	is not prepared to give it, you may need to bite the bullet and ask the member to leave the group.
An invited consultant was there for the full duration of the meeting, but was invited to speak only at the end. You have just received his bill, and he charged you for the full meeting.	Establish expectations and billing arrangements with advisers in advance. You may need to invite them to come at designated times and not for the full meeting.
Richard seemed really defensive, and rolled his eyes every time Joan spoke. The discussions were tense.	It's time to invite the two for a heart-to-heart talk about the tension between them. You may need to mediate this dispute.
It became apparent that Randy violated confidentiality guidelines and revealed the details of a confidential decision. He was quoted in the newspaper about it.	Review and update your confidentiality guidelines, send relevant excerpts to the members as a reminder, and have a private talk with Randy. Disciplinary action may be needed if he violated them knowingly or this is not the first time.
A member seemed close to tears or even cried at the meeting, and no one knew how to deal with it.	Find out why the member cried and whether it had anything to do with the meeting itself. If so, see what can be done about it.

Questions to Ask About the HOWs of a Meeting

- Was participation protocol followed?
- Was the meeting varied, interesting, and engaging?

To avoid this HOW problem in the future:	You need to do this:
Members interrupted one another and were not listening. As a result, nothing was achieved, and people were angry. Some are ready to quit.	Establish that members speak by raising hands, not voices, and that interruptions are to be generally avoided. Encourage members to listen

To avoid this HOW problem in the future:	You need to do this:
	to others fully prior to forming their rebuttals.
One member spoke rudely, made personal accusations, and was verbally abusive.	Have a private discussion with the offending member and see if she or he is prepared to offer an apology. Alternatively, discuss the problem in your opening comments at the next meeting: Ask members to focus on issues, not people. Indicate your intention to intervene if they don't respect this guideline.
There were too many distracting side conversations.	Find out why: ▲ If the meeting was boring, make the next one interesting. ▲ If reports were confusing, get members to ask their questions up front, so they don't have to distract their neighbors with their questions. ▲ If members are used to having side conversations, suggest at the start of the next meeting to have only one meeting at a time.
The meeting was boring, and a few people even fell asleep.	Introduce some variety to the meeting (see Chapter 8 for ideas). Give each member a lead role at the next meeting. And pick up the pace, please!

Questions to Ask About the WHEREs of a Meeting

- ▲ Was the meeting location appropriate?
- ▲ Was the size of the meeting room appropriate?
- ▲ Did the room setup allow the necessary amount of interaction?
- ▲ Was the room appealing and pleasant?
- ▲ Did the air conditioning or heating work?
- ▲ Were the food and beverages tasty, and of the right quantity and quality?

- ▲ Were audiovisual aids properly set up, and did they work?
- ▲ Did audiovisual aids help or did they overformalize the discussions?

To deal with problems about WHERE issues, you may need to do one or more of the following:

- ▲ Find a new meeting location and make sure all your needs can be met. Insist on professionalism and attention to detail. Your group deserves it.
- ▲ Inspect the room and the logistical arrangements in person a few days before the meeting. Inspect it again on the day of the meeting.
- ▲ Learn to ask probing questions when you negotiate with meeting planners and catering departments. Never assume anything, and don't rely on blanket reassurances like, "Everything will be fine. . . ." Make it your business to confirm arrangements and test and retest equipment.
- ▲ Consider delegating logistical duties to a logistics master or an outside professional, to free you to focus on the substantive aspects of the meeting.
- ▲ Book the meeting room for at least half an hour before the meeting is set to begin, so you can arrive early and prepare the meeting for a smooth launch (see Chapters 10 and 11).

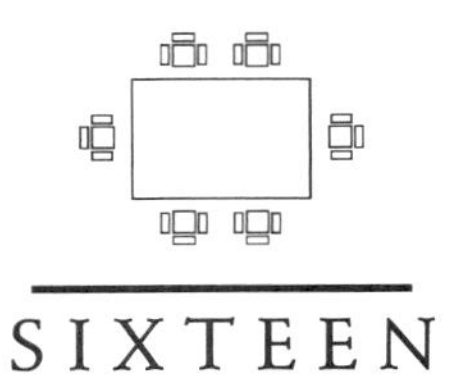

SIXTEEN

Virtual Meetings

Virtual meetings are consensus-building methods other than face-to-face meetings, where everyone is present in the same room and can see and hear everyone else. Virtual meetings include consensus building by correspondence, teleconference calls, videoconferencing, and electronic meetings.

This chapter focuses on some of the practical aspects of virtual meetings. No attempt is made to give you an up-to-date summary of technologies for teleconferencing, videoconferencing, or electronic meetings. Technology in these areas evolves quickly, and what is state-of-the-art today may be obsolete tomorrow. Specifically, this chapter covers the following topics:

- Advantages of virtual meetings
- Disadvantages of virtual meetings
- General tips for virtual meetings
- Building consensus by correspondence
- Building consensus by teleconference calls

- Building consensus by videoconferences
- Building consensus by electronic meetings

Advantages of Virtual Meetings

- Usually less costly than face-to-face meetings. There are no travel, accommodation, or meeting room costs involved.
- Less disruptive. Members can participate from the comfort of their own offices or homes. If it is not practical to start a virtual meeting on time, members can work on other things while they are waiting in their own offices or homes.
- Tend to be more efficient, focused, and businesslike than face-to-face meetings. Members are less likely to digress, ramble, or be casual about the meeting.
- Are ideal for simple decisions that need to be made between face-to-face meetings. A face-to-face meeting becomes something to look forward to, since it is focused on more substantive issues.
- Members tend to listen more intently and are less likely to be distracted or intimidated by facial expressions or body language of others.
- Members have more opportunities to develop and showcase their writing and thinking skills than in a face-to-face meeting (where most of the communication is spoken). You may discover members of your team have talents you didn't know about.

Disadvantages of Virtual Meetings

- It is difficult, if not impossible, to respond to facial and vocal expressions. Members may be listening or reading the words, but may miss the ideas and the passion behind them. Therefore the decisions may not be as holistic as they need to be.
- It is difficult, if not impossible, to detect an emotional reaction to the discussion and respond to it with a supportive statement, without seeing the individual who may need this support.
- It is easy to tune out in a virtual meeting, without anyone knowing that you are doing it.
- Virtual meetings do not engage people on a human or social level to the extent that face-to-face meetings do. The business may indeed be done efficiently, but

without the social and human interaction, there is no real opportunity to build cohesion, teamwork, synergy, and loyalty to the organization.

- It is more challenging to maintain privacy and confidentiality in a virtual meeting, e.g., an e-mail exchange or an electronic meeting may offer less protection of information. Therefore people may be less comfortable discussing sensitive issues.

GENERAL TIPS FOR VIRTUAL MEETINGS

Your group should have guidelines for virtual meetings in place. Such guidelines should address questions like the following:

- What types of decisions can be made only in a face-to-face meeting?
- What types of decisions can be made in a virtual meeting?
- Which kinds of virtual meetings is the group comfortable with?
- What skills do members need to participate effectively in virtual meetings?

When to Use Virtual Meetings

The group should use virtual meetings whenever:

- Information needs to be exchanged and discussed by the full group between face-to-face meetings.
- An urgent decision needs to be made by the group, and it is not practical or justifiable to disrupt schedules and hold a special face-to-face meeting.
- Subcommittees that were given research tasks may meet by teleconference call or build consensus by e-mail exchanges or electronic meetings.

When Not to Use Virtual Meetings

Virtual meetings should not be used to address issues that are complex or controversial, or require interactive discussions for any other reason.

Retaining Face-to-Face Meetings

The group should not abolish face-to-face meetings altogether, but can have fewer of them, and focus them only on:

- Contentious or complex issues, where the discussions could get emotional
- Substantive issues that require fully interactive discussions, which rely on facial and vocal expressions
- Team-building activities, which require members to physically be together, e.g.: analyzing case studies in small groups, solving work-related puzzles together using their hands, etc.

CASE STUDY:

An E-Mail Battle

Roger had a disagreement with Susan. He decided the best way to argue his case was to send a nasty e-mail to Susan. But he didn't stop there. He copied the e-mail to all team members. Not to be outdone, Susan responded in kind. Other members jumped into the fray, and a full-fledged e-mail battle ensued.

Is this an effective way to resolve a dispute? Not likely. Disputes like this should be addressed in face-to-face interactive discussions. In an e-mail battle the human touch is lost. Without direct interactions there are no opportunities to take into account facial and vocal expressions, or verify what an individual meant by a certain word. Misunderstandings are bound to develop a life of their own. The conflict is worsened, and common sense is lost.

Building Consensus by Correspondence

One form of a virtual meeting is building consensus by exchanging e-mails, faxes, interoffice mail, or regular mail. The objectives of such a process should be the same as those of a face-to-face meeting:

- To benefit from the knowledge, expertise, and skills of all participants
- To identify areas of agreement
- To identify areas of disagreement, or ones that require more work

Here are the steps that could be taken to build consensus by correspondence:

1. A discussion leader is designated to facilitate the consensus-building process.
2. The discussion leader prepares a document that defines the issues to be addressed and the questions to be answered by the group.

3. The document is sent to members by a chosen method (e-mail, fax, courier, or mail), along with a covering memo that requests immediate confirmation that the material was received and whether the deadline can be met. The memo also requests immediate confirmation that the questions are sufficiently clear, and, if not, the areas in which clarity is needed. Finally, the memo also asks for a response to the questions in the document by a given deadline.
4. Shortly after sending the document, the discussion leader may need to review preliminary feedback from members, revise the document, and resend it to the members. The leader should also contact members who did not confirm receipt of the document and find out what the problem is.
5. Close to the response deadline, the discussion leader may need to remind members to send their submissions on schedule.
6. Following the response deadline, the discussion leader reviews the members' submissions and may contact them for clarification. The discussion leader summarizes the comments, and outlines the areas of agreement and the areas of disagreement that require further work.
7. The discussion leader sends a summary of the consensus and requests that members point out any corrections that should be made to the summary, and suggest how the areas of disagreement should be addressed.
8. The discussion leader reviews the comments from the second round, revises the summary, and sends it to the members for input, and the consensus continues to build.
9. At some point, a face-to-face meeting is held, to confirm the consensus and to address unresolved issues.

Example: An Introductory Letter from a Discussion Leader

At the request of your boss, you are to build consensus on enhancing safety procedures in the branch offices of your company. You want to include all seventy branch office managers in your consensus-building efforts. Here is a sample introductory letter for you to consider:

Dear Branch Manager:

My name is Ron Weinstein, and I was asked by our vice president of operations to facilitate a consensus-building process, involving each one of you, on ways of enhancing safety in all branch offices of the company. Safety is important to all of us, and we need to standardize our approach. Therefore this consensus-building effort is very significant, and I need your help with it.

The purpose of this letter is to start the consensus-building process. Please consider the safety aspects in your branch and let me know:

- What your existing safety procedures are
- Whether you think they are adequate
- What can be done to improve them
- Whether you have any unique ideas to share with other branch offices
- What support and expertise you need from the head office in this area

Enclosed is a questionnaire for you to complete. Please send it back to me by March 31, 2002, so that I can summarize all responses. Please review the questionnaire and contact me at 333-333-3333 or by e-mail at safetycomesfirst@xyz.org if you have any questions about it.

For your information, here is how I see this consensus-building process unfolding:

1. *Summary.* I will review your completed questionnaires and prepare a summary by April 7, indicating the areas of agreement and areas of disagreement. I will send you the summary and ask for your feedback on it.
2. *Revision.* Based on your comments I will revise the summary and send it to you again.
3. *Teleconferences.* By the last week in April, I will arrange teleconference calls with groups of six of you, to discuss the summary.
4. *Advisory Committee.* Early in May, I will organize a face-to-face meeting of an advisory committee that will include some of you, to look at the issue of safety further and propose specific improvements to our procedures.

As you can see, it's a long-term process, and your support is essential to make it work. Thank you in advance for your input, and I am looking forward to working with you to enhance safety across our operations.

Best regards,

Ron Weinstein

BUILDING CONSENSUS BY TELECONFERENCE CALLS

Teleconference calls are very useful if a group's decision needs to be made quickly, or the group's leader or a member needs input on an emergent issue. Teleconference calls should be planned carefully and executed with utmost care, to ensure their limitations do not block the group from making progress.

General Tips for Teleconference Calls

- ▲ Teleconference calls are best suited for small groups, with no more than six to eight members. In the absence of visual feedback, they can be challenging to manage and are therefore not effective with larger groups. (An electronic meeting or building consensus by correspondence will likely work better for larger groups.)
- ▲ Teleconferences that last longer than an hour tend to lose their effectiveness. It may be best to limit the scope of the discussion to two or three clearly defined questions and, if needed, schedule another teleconference call at a later date.
- ▲ Teleconference calls that involve operator assistance can be costly. If your group is small, you may be able to connect everyone without operator assistance.
- ▲ Instead of using a phone, you can get connected by voice through the Internet. In this case:
  - ▲ You can use technology for interactive presentations, whereby everyone dissects charts and diagrams that are transmitted online.
  - ▲ If the meeting is between two or three people, it is relatively easy to add a visual dimension to the interaction by having a video camera installed at each location.

Planning Teleconference Calls

To ensure that discussions are productive and well focused, the teleconference leader should plan it with attention to detail:

- ▲ Identify the key questions to be addressed (ideally no more than three or four of them).
- ▲ Budget time for each question, let members know in advance of time constraints, and prepare to manage time with absolute precision.

- For each question, establish the main options to consider, so members can decide which one they prefer. For example, if the options are A and B, send members an analysis of the pros and cons of each option in advance of the teleconference call.
- Send the agenda, the time frame, and a concise summary of the issues and decision-making options to all participants for review prior to the teleconference.
- Emphasize the importance of being fully prepared for the teleconference call.

Here are a few technical tips to consider for a teleconference call:

- Find out where each participant will be and ask them to wait at the phone at the scheduled teleconference time.
- Emphasize that if they receive a call from anyone other than yourself or the operator, they must end that call quickly. You don't want the operator to get a busy signal or be switched over to voicemail.
- Ask the operator for your teleconference number and for instructions on dealing with these potential challenges:

1. How do you reinitiate the teleconference call if it is terminated prematurely?
2. How do you reinstate a member who was dropped from the teleconference call?
3. What number should a member call to get reconnected to the call (in case she or he was dropped from it and you did not notice)?

Participant Dos and Don'ts for Teleconference Calls

Pure teleconference calls employ only vocal communication. Therefore, as a participant, you must do the following:

- Rely heavily on your listening skills.
- Identify yourself before speaking.
- Communicate clearly and project your voice.
- If you tend to speak too fast, slow down a bit.
- If you speak too slowly, pick up the pace.
- Make your voice animated and expressive.
- Keep your voice consistent and avoid the common habit of dropping your volume at the end of a sentence. People can't read your lips or see your eyes or facial expression. You must enunciate clearly and emphasize key words or concepts.

- Confirm from time to time whether you have been heard and understood.
- Respect a speakers' lineup, as monitored by the facilitator.
- If there is no speakers' lineup and it is needed, suggest that it be used.
- Be supersensitive to others and resist the temptation to dominate with your voice.

Sample Script: Launching a Teleconference Call

Here is a sample script for opening a teleconference call:

"Good afternoon, everyone. Thank you for making yourselves available for this teleconference call. Let me start by confirming everyone is here:

"Ruth, are you with us? Harry? Tina? Tom? Ron, are you with us? Thank you.

"Before we get going, please write down the toll-free number and our customer number. You'll need to call this number if you get dropped from this teleconference call: Here are the numbers ____.

"The purpose of this call is ____. The key questions for us to answer are: ____, ____, and ____. Did everyone review the discussion document with the analysis of the issues scheduled for the discussion today? Thank you.

"We have one hour for this teleconference call, and we'll need to be very efficient and precise. I will monitor the clock closely and see if we can stay within fifteen to twenty minutes for each one of the three questions.

"I have a few requests for you: Please speak straight into the phone, keep your voice clear, audible, and consistent, and keep your comments concise and focused. I will need you to identify yourself before you speak, and, if more than one of you want to speak, I will take a speakers' lineup.

"Does anyone have any questions? Thank you.

"Let's get on then with the first issue on the agenda, which is: ____. As shown in your package, the options to choose from are A, B, and C, and the list of pros and cons were given. The question is which of the three is the best option, or is there a fourth option that is better than all three?

"Ron, do you want to start the discussion?"

Tips for Managing the Teleconference Call

1. Keep idle chatter to a bare minimum.
2. Keep a dynamic pace, to engage the members and keep them interested. Boredom may cause members to tune out or even find a mysterious way of being disconnected from the teleconference call.
3. Intervene decisively if someone's voice is dropping or if there is another problem:
   - ▲ "Sean, we need you to raise your voice."
   - ▲ "Paula, we missed the last part of your sentence."
   - ▲ "Can you please identify yourself?"
   - ▲ "Can you please wait for acknowledgment before speaking? I am keeping a speakers' lineup."
   - ▲ "Susan, are you there? Good. I thought we might have lost you. Any comment from you?"
4. Time is too tight to squander. As the teleconference call continues, interject whenever needed to keep it on track and on time:
   - ▲ "We have two more issues to discuss. They are: _____ and _____. We have thirty-five minutes left. This gives us fifteen minutes per issue and five minutes for the wrap-up."
   - ▲ "We have five more minutes before we move on to the next issue."
   - ▲ "Ralph, time is running out. We need you to make your point faster."
   - ▲ "Debby, we need to move on. You are making the point that _____. Does anyone have a new comment?"
   - ▲ "Edith, we already made this decision. Right now we are on to the issue of _____. We need to stay on track and keep moving ahead."
   - ▲ "Randy, you may not know, but this idea was considered last week, and it is not a viable option for us. We have to stay within certain parameters."
   - ▲ "We have five minutes left before we all turn into pumpkins, and we seem to have finished the agenda. How are we doing? Does it feel like we made progress? Have we missed anything? If not, let's talk about follow-up."

BUILDING CONSENSUS BY VIDEOCONFERENCES

Videoconferences are similar to teleconference calls, in that members participate from several locations. They differ in that members can also see one another. In the ideal setting, video recording and display apparatus is set up in each location, so members can see and hear members in other locations.

The advantage of videoconferences over teleconference calls is that members can make eye contact with one another and respond to facial expressions and body language. Videoconferencing technology is advancing rapidly. Therefore no attempt is made in this book to describe detailed technical procedures, which may be relevant when written but are likely to be outdated by the time they are read.

The guidelines for running a videoconference are no different than for a face-to-face meeting (see Chapters 9 to 14), but the facilitator and the members need to consider the following:

- ▲ The facilitator and the members need to be sensitive to those who participate from satellite locations and make extra efforts to not leave them behind.
- ▲ If the apparatus is complex, have a technical expert on hand to set up, manage, and operate the equipment, and ensure that any technical glitches are quickly overcome and do not slow down the meeting. This will free members to focus on the issues at hand without losing precious time to technological battles.

BUILDING CONSENSUS BY ELECTRONIC MEETINGS

Electronic meetings are interactive discussions conducted over the Internet. Technology and software in this area are moving rapidly and providing increasingly creative opportunities for interactive discussions and consensus building. For example:

- ▲ Interactive discussions with audio and video dimensions added. Members can hear and see one another, and can also interact by typing on computer keyboards.
- ▲ Silent interactive discussions on given topics, with everyone typing and reading what others are typing simultaneously. A great deal of information is exchanged very quickly. The constraining rule of "one person speaks at a time" is not needed, and the amount of information used to build consensus increases dramatically.

Here are two specific scenarios to consider:

1. Online presentations and conferences
2. Chat room discussions and consensus building

Online Presentations and Conferences

There is no need to have a face-to-face meeting to hear a presentation by a remotely located member or supplier. There is also no need to pay travel expenses for a subject matter expert to make a presentation at a face-to-face meeting. Instead, she can:

- Make a PowerPoint presentation online from her location
- Respond to questions from members who are viewing it on a shared video screen (in a meeting) or their own computer screens

More and more organizations conduct educational conferences on the Internet. This eliminates the need to travel long distances to hear reputable speakers. Conference participants can remain in the comfort of their own homes or offices, sign on to a conference, choose the presentation they like, listen to the speaker live, and send in their questions while the presentation is ongoing.

Chat Room Discussions and Consensus Building

Interactive discussions can be facilitated in a secure private chat room. Technology allows visual aids, such as electronic white boards and PowerPoint slides, to be presented, analyzed, and modified online by the various participants. Everyone sees any proposed changes and is able to comment on them or make their own changes. If the software used is advanced and members use it effectively, the discussions can be highly interactive, and the quality can be superior to a face-to-face meeting.

The risk with electronic meetings is that they can become a "free-for-all" and achieve very little. To avoid this, a basic structure should be introduced to the discussions. Here is an example of a procedure for such a meeting:

- The facilitator explains the purpose of the electronic meeting, outlines the agenda, and establishes the timing, i.e., how much time is allocated to key agenda items, and when the electronic meeting is scheduled to end.

▲ Members may comment on or express concerns about the agenda online, and the agenda may be modified to accommodate their suggestions.

▲ The facilitator introduces the first agenda item, briefly explains the background for it, and states the key questions to be addressed in the online discussion.

▲ Members are given a time limit to comment simultaneously on each question. Everyone can read what everyone is typing and can respond to it immediately.

▲ At a given time the facilitator halts the discussion and summarizes the key points made and the areas of agreement and disagreement.

▲ Members are given a limited time to comment on the facilitator's summary.

▲ At the end of this response period, the facilitator amends the summary and confirms that it is acceptable to the members.

▲ If unanimity is impossible to achieve, three options may be considered:

1. The facilitator can ask the group if it wants to extend the discussion, and, if so, for how long. This can build a greater level of support for the decision.
2. The decision can be delayed.
3. A formal vote can be taken, with the facilitator typing the exact wording of the proposal. Participants identify themselves (using secure codes) and whether they vote in favor, against, or abstaining. The facilitator tallies the vote and announces the result.

▲ The facilitator proceeds to the next agenda item and deals with it in a similar manner.

When compared to face-to-face meetings or teleconferences and videoconferences, the above process has several advantages:

▲ Much more information is exchanged and many more ideas are likely to emerge, given the absence of the constraining "one person speaks at a time" rule (which applies in face-to-face meetings, teleconference calls, and videoconferences).

▲ Since people read much faster than they speak, the collective thought process and consensus building can move quickly.

▲ Undistracted by facial or vocal expressions, members do much more thinking than they would in a face-to-face meeting, teleconference call, or videoconference.

▲ Quieter members, who are less likely to speak up in a face-to-face meeting, are more likely to "speak" here. In fact, they may prove to be more expressive in writing than the vocally dominant members. The group has a better chance of benefiting from everyone's insights and ideas.

- There is no need to monitor a speakers' lineup and admonish members for barging in or interrupting others. In an electronic meeting everyone can "speak" at the same time and everyone sees what other people are thinking.
- In a real meeting side conversations would likely be distracting and annoying to other members. In electronic meetings the software allows a member to "whisper" online, i.e., send a private note to another member. There is no need for a facilitator to intervene and say: "Can we have only one meeting at a time, please?" In fact, "a whisper" can be productive and helpful.

Cautions for Electronic Meetings

- Online interactive activities should only take place if every member can type on a computer keyboard at a reasonable speed, and knows how to use the applicable software. Here are two options to upgrade member skills: (1) Members should be encouraged to take typing courses, and (2) Internet tutors (fresh out of school) should be engaged to coach long-standing members. The members will benefit from the tutoring, and the tutors will benefit from the depth of business experience of the people they coach. It will be a small investment with win-win outcomes.
- New technologies should not be like "a new toy" or "the flavor of the month." People should not become so obsessed with them that they forget their intended uses: to assist in the interaction, save time and resources, and enhance the consensus-building process. Technology should not become the exclusive domain of technical wizards. Everyone must be comfortable with it before it can truly make a difference.
- When facilitating online discussions, be mindful of security of information, especially when sensitive issues are discussed. It may be better to discuss such issues in a face-to-face meeting. If a sensitive issue is to be discussed online at all, chat rooms should be private and secure, and encrypted message protocols should be used (consult your Internet expert about this).

SEVENTEEN

Contentious Meetings as Opportunities

Inevitably, your group will encounter controversies with respect to issues or changes under consideration. Controversy as such is not bad, and differences of opinion should not be a cause for panic. In fact, the premise of this chapter is that controversy and internal disputes can be converted from problems into opportunities.

This chapter discusses the challenges of planning and facilitating contentious meetings. Specific subjects are:

- ▲ Identifying the causes of controversies
- ▲ Identifying the costs of poorly managed controversies
- ▲ Identifying the benefits of well managed controversies
- ▲ Reducing the occurrence of controversies
- ▲ Detecting controversies at an early stage
- ▲ Preventive and proactive planning for contentious meetings

- Issue management tools for contentious meetings
- Process management tools for contentious meetings

Identifying the Causes of Controversies

Reasons for controversies fit within two main categories: substantive controversies and process-related controversies.

Substantive Controversies

A meeting can become controversial due to differences of opinion on substantive issues. The intensity of the controversy is usually proportionate to the impact of the group's decisions on its members and stakeholders. Here are a few examples of substantive controversies:

- Should a major purchase or initiative be made when its benefits are disputed?
- Are proposed cutbacks in staffing or service levels justified?
- Should the services of a key staff member or adviser be terminated?

Differences of opinion on issues are natural. Unanimity on everything is not realistic, nor is it desirable. Indeed, if everyone thought the same way every time, there would be no individual initiative or creativity. This would make for a very dull and uninspiring organization.

Several barriers stand in the way of resolving differences of opinion effectively:

- Leaders panic and believe their power and control are being threatened by dissenting opinions. They react by trying to stifle, dominate, or placate dissenting members. They hesitate to let go of absolute control and are not used to addressing differences of opinion in an open, honest, direct, and principled manner.
- Dissenting members are entrenched in hard positions and are busy arguing for their points of view. They show no desire to listen and find common ground.
- The group discusses solutions before fully exploring the problem.
- The group spends more time on side issues than on the main issues at the core of the controversy.

- ▲ Some members are driven by narrow interests and make no effort to focus on the organization's mandate and the stakeholders it is intended to serve.
- ▲ There is a focus on individuals and personalities instead of issues.

Process-Related Controversies

A meeting can become tense or controversial due to process-related issues. For example:

1. The organization may be operating with a top-down management style. Managers make significant decisions without advance warning and without consulting members or stakeholders. People may not disagree with the decision itself, but may object to the manner in which it was made.
   - ▲ *Example*. Senior management decides to cut down the budget of a department without consulting its manager or staff. The department manager announces the cuts at the next staff meeting. The meeting becomes chaotic and emotional. Fear, distrust, and resentment develop. Morale is lowered, and productivity and customer service levels decline. The savings that the budget cuts were anticipated to generate do not materialize, because the company loses staff and customers.
   - ▲ *Solution*. The outcome would have been different if the department manager was given the parameters of the problem (competitive pressures and tighter profit margins) and was asked to consult his staff and identify ways of solving the problem. The directive of "cut your budget now" should have been replaced by: "We need your help in solving a problem that affects all of us." The staff meeting to discuss this problem would have likely been much more productive. Staff members would have become partners in a problem-solving process.
2. The team has an unclear, outdated, or unrealistic mandate, or a lack of commitment to it. Members do not understand why they are at a meeting and what difference they are supposed to be making. As a result they focus on small issues. Personal conflicts balloon out of proportion, and the group and its meetings become dysfunctional.
3. The team has unclear roles and responsibilities and confusing lines of reporting and accountability.
   - ▲ *Example: The Loose Cannon*. A member works independently and negotiates a contract with an outside party, with no regard for other team members and

without considering the impact of his actions on the group's work. At the next meeting the group is faced with the fact that a binding contract was signed. Accusations fly, and the meeting runs out of control. The source of the problem is a lack of clear definition of a member's duty to work as a team member.

4. Knowingly or inadvertently, a team member may violate one of the group's ethical guidelines. Other members become resentful, but don't give feedback. The tension at a subsequent meeting is substantial. Progress is undermined by issues that are hidden beneath the surface

   ▲ *Example.* A member reveals confidential information to an outside party or violates conflict of interest guidelines (see Chapter 5).

5. The majority may overpower the minority. Decisions are made in a rush, and several members and their legitimate concerns are ignored or stifled. The dissenting members are resentful and hold back in future meetings, or take their revenge by undermining the group's work, or wait patiently until they become the majority.
6. There are problems with the manner in which feedback is delivered. A member delivers valid criticism to another, but gives it in a harsh and insulting manner. The other member takes it as a personal attack. At the next meeting the two make no eye contact and ignore each other. Progress grinds to a halt.
7. The group reacts to crises by searching for guilty persons, instead of identifying systemic problems that caused them.
8. Communications break down, leading to rumors, unfounded fears, loss of trust, personal animosities, and nasty power struggles.
9. There are no procedures to prevent, detect, and resolve disputes.

Assignment: Examine a Controversy You Recently Faced

Consider a controversy that surfaced in a recent meeting, and answer the following questions:

▲ Was the controversy substantive, i.e.; caused by differences of opinion on an issue?

- ▲ What process-related issues worsened the controversy?
- ▲ Were the issues blown out of proportion due to communications breakdown?
- ▲ What could have been done to prevent the controversy in the first place?
- ▲ What could have been done to reduce the negative impacts of the controversy?
- ▲ Did the controversy leave a long-lasting negative residue?
- ▲ Did the controversy damage relationships beyond repair?
- ▲ Can the controversy be turned into a learning opportunity, and, if so, how?

Assignment: Examine Your Attitude Towards Controversy

Consider your attitude and expectations when you encounter conflict and controversy:

- ▲ Do you panic?
- ▲ Do you fear that you might lose control?
- ▲ Do you hope that the controversy will somehow go away?
- ▲ Do you tend to deny the existence of the controversy?
- ▲ Do you trivialize the importance of the issues raised?
- ▲ Do you underestimate the power and influence of dissenting members?
- ▲ Do you overestimate the power and influence of dissenting members?
- ▲ Do you look for tools to overpower dissenting or disruptive members?
- ▲ Do you plot "back-room" strategies that will lead to certain outcomes?

IDENTIFYING THE COSTS OF POORLY MANAGED CONTROVERSIES

Having identified the reasons for controversies, you need to consider the prices you pay if they are poorly managed:

- ▲ *Wasted Efforts*. Small but contentious issues receive more attention than they deserve, at the expense of more significant issues. It can become a case of "the lower the stake the larger the argument." A group may spend hours arguing about a small expense, while quickly "rubber stamping" a very large one.

- ▲ *Emotional Impacts on People.* Members are focused on fighting each other, instead of building a strong and thriving organization.
- ▲ *Reduced Commitment Levels.* Members become demoralized and disappointed with the group or the organization. Some may operate at a fraction of their potential. Others may start finding creative excuses to miss meetings. Others may leave. With the group's reputation for bad meetings, it may be difficult to replace members who leave.
- ▲ *Undermined Decisions.* Some members may accept the group's decisions reluctantly, while others may undermine them passively or even fight them. Companies and government agencies have found their pet projects blocked by civil disobedience or by lawsuits because of their ineffectiveness at dealing with contentious issues.

Identifying the Benefits of Well-Managed Controversies

Many facilitators heading to a tough meeting do not consider positive outcomes. More often they are preoccupied with trying to survive the meeting, prevent disruptions, and control the members. These are defensively driven goals, and do not show confidence on the part of the facilitator.

Given the potential impacts of a contentious meeting, you need an affirmative focus, going beyond what you want to prevent, and looking at what you can achieve. Yes, you want to manage the risks, but your more important goal should be to maximize the opportunities. There are two types of benefits you can pursue: substantive benefits and process-related benefits.

Substantive Benefits

If the controversy is substantive, plan and manage the meeting to achieve the following benefits:

- ▲ Having a full discussion on the issues at hand, with all sides being heard and understood
- ▲ Making responsible and credible decisions that will endure the test of time
- ▲ Bringing closure to tough issues and freeing the group to focus on other priorities

Process-Related Benefits

If the controversy is process-related, plan and manage the meeting to achieve the following benefits:

- Decreasing tensions and getting members to work as a team. They don't have to become each other's best friends, but should learn to work together, as enthusiastic partners (appreciating what others have to offer) and not as "reluctant neighbors."
- Increasing trust and respect among the members of the group.
- Resolving process-related issues. For example:
  - Reinforcing the group's mandate and increasing the members' commitment to it
  - Clarifying roles and responsibilities of members
  - Strengthening the lines of communications and accountability: who reports to whom, and who tells whom what to do
  - Establishing ways of reducing the likelihood of disputes
  - Establishing methods of resolving disputes
  - Establishing guidelines on giving and taking feedback
- Documenting the lessons learned from the controversy for:
  - Future reference by other teams
  - Presentation as a case study at your professional association's next conference

REDUCING THE OCCURRENCE OF CONTROVERSIES

As a leader, your goal should be to reduce the occurrence of controversies or prevent them from escalating out of control. The best way to achieve this is by building a solid foundation for your team's consensus-building efforts (see Part I, Chapters 1 to 7). The following ingredients are essential to reducing the occurrence of controversies, minimizing their destructive effects, and increasing your capacity to turn them from problems into opportunities:

- A shared understanding of participatory decision-making principles (see Chapter 1)
- A team leader who is firm, fair, honest, respectful, inclusive, and focused (see Chapter 2)
- A team mandate that is clear, current, compelling, and realistic to achieve (see Chapter 3)

- A well-laid-out workplan and schedules for your group's work, supported by the necessary financial, logistical, and human resources (see Chapter 3)
- The right members for your team, with the best combination of knowledge, skills, expertise, confidence, humility, commitment levels, creativity, and positive attitudes (see Chapter 4)
- Clear rules of engagement that cover accountability in decision making, conflict of interest and confidentiality guidelines, and parameters of formal voting (see Chapter 5)
- A team culture and ethics document, outlining the group's values, how it does business, how it resolves conflict, and how its members work together (see Chapter 6)
- Mutually enhancing relationships with internal stakeholders (your boss, management team, and board of directors, as well as colleagues and support staff) and external stakeholders (customers, suppliers, and the community; see Chapter 7)

Here are examples of how the potential for a controversy can be reduced:

This controversy:	**Can be prevented by:**
Decisions are made without consulting subordinates, causing tensions and low morale.	Embracing a "bottoms-up" approach to corporate decision making, whereby input from staff members is actively solicited before decisions that affect them are made (Chapters 1 and 2).
Personal clashes occur when different people pull in different directions.	Establishing a clear, meaningful, and compelling mandate (Chapter 3).
A team member makes commitments to suppliers without checking with the group first. The leader and other group members are angry.	Establishing roles and responsibilities, lines of accountability, and culture and ethics for the team (Chapters 5 and 6).
Feedback is held back, and this creates tensions and undermines progress.	Teaching members to give feedback in a way that makes it easier for others to receive it, and to receive feedback in a way that makes it easier for others to give it (see Chapter 13).

This controversy:	Can be prevented by:
Too many important decisions are made by narrow majorities, leaving disenfranchised and demoralized minorities behind.	Slowing things down and avoiding a rush to decision making. Structuring discussions of contentious issues so all sides are heard, and so the group makes decisions that are holistic, credible, and durable (see Chapters 5 and 12).
A committee's recommendation is torpedoed by senior management. Committee members are upset and vent their anger at the next meeting.	Upwards management: Staying in touch with your boss and senior management, keeping them updated and consulted, earning their respect by doing excellent work, and intervening to ensure that your team is taken seriously (Chapter 7).
Community groups undermine your project by civil disobedience or court action. Community meetings are chaotic.	Consulting the community before finalizing your decisions, and, whenever possible and appropriate, taking their concerns into account (Chapter 7).
Two members resent each other because of an interaction that occurred outside the meeting. The meeting goes nowhere because of the tension.	Mediating disputes before the meeting (Chapters 2 and 4).

DETECTING CONTROVERSIES AT AN EARLY STAGE

Leaders often ignore emerging controversies, with the hope that they will somehow go away. Indeed, sometimes things do take care of themselves and no intervention is needed. However, many times conflict becomes worse if left unattended. A lack of intervention may create a fragmented team and make your meetings dysfunctional. The appearance of peace and calm can be deceiving. Here are a few tips for detecting controversies at an early stage:

- Never ignore or trivialize a rumor or a "red flag" indicating a problem. Make it your business to find out what is happening, or you may be stuck with nasty surprises.
- Be prepared to address emerging problems proactively, well before they become unmanageable.

- ▲ Make it easy for team members to approach you with any concerns. For example, "As a reminder before we close this meeting: I need you to let me know of any concerns you have. Please give me advance warning about potential difficulties. We need to be proactive and solve problems before they become unmanageable."
- ▲ Ask your boss to give you advance warning of any emerging problems at senior management levels that could affect your team's work.
- ▲ Let your group's internal and external stakeholders know that you welcome any feedback or words of caution from them.
- ▲ Give other people "heads up" warnings of potential controversies. They will likely return the favor. For example, say this to your boss: "Tim, I was just wondering: Are you aware of the fact that ____? You're not? Well, here is what I heard: ____. I thought I'd let you know, so you're not taken by surprise."

Preventive and Proactive Planning for Contentious Meetings

When preparing for a contentious meeting, your efforts should be two-tiered:

- ▲ Preventive planning: To reduce the destructive effects of the controversy on the meeting.
- ▲ Proactive planning: To maximize the opportunities and benefits from this meeting.

Please review Chapter 9 for a complete coverage of planning tools for meetings. This section gives you planning tools that are unique for contentious meetings:

- ▲ Deciding who will chair
- ▲ Establishing the direction
- ▲ Preparing the agenda
- ▲ Establishing the protocol
- ▲ Facilitating agreement on the agenda and protocol
- ▲ Resolving potential problems proactively before the meeting

Deciding Who Will Chair

The more divisive the issues are, the more important it is that the facilitator be neutral and avoid taking sides. This may be difficult if, as a team leader, you have been closely involved with the issues. Yes, you may have read Chapter 2 on the various hats of the facilitator. But if the issues are difficult, your group may be better served by an impartial facilitator.

You can look for an impartial facilitator within the organization, or you can look for an externally hired professional. For further analysis of the advantages and disadvantages of bringing in an external facilitator, see the section on "the external facilitator" in Chapter 2. Regardless of who chairs the meeting, here are a few tips to consider:

- Consult the group about who should the chair the meeting. Give the members the options, with advantages and disadvantages, and ask for their input. You would not want to put an external person in the awkward position of having to justify why she or he should chair the meeting. Try this: "In the next meeting we are dealing with a few contentious issues. Normally I am the one who chairs meetings. But in this case, since all of us are involved in the issues, we could probably benefit from having an outsider chair the meeting. Here are a few possibilities: We could ask Charlie from HR, or we could invite Lynn from Facilitation Solutions. You've met both of them. What do you think? Should we look for an impartial chair? If so, who would be best: Charlie, Lynn, or someone else?"
- The chosen facilitator should be involved in planning the contentious meeting (see further).
- The selected individual should be highly skilled and be able to wear as many of the facilitator's hats as possible (see Chapter 2).

Establishing the Direction

The first step in planning the contentious meeting is to define the direction for it. To do this, you will need to identify the core problem, the main reasons for the controversy, the possible solutions, and the potential benefits of the meeting. Here are a few of the questions to ask:

- What are the substantive issues to be resolved?
- How are these issues affecting the group's mandate?
- What are the sticking points and how significant are they?
- What side issues may be muddying the water?
- What process-related issues complicate things (e.g., low trust levels, top-down management style, a confusing mandate)?

- What are the possible solutions to the core problems?
- What are the pros and cons of each of the potential solutions?
- What benefits could this meeting provide?

To establish the answers to the above questions, you can do the following:

- Review background material.
- Research the issues.
- Interview all sides to the controversy. You may hear conflicting accounts, so listen with a degree of skepticism. Some individuals may try to convince you they are right and everyone else is wrong. You'll need to clarify that all you're doing is collecting information, and that your effectiveness will be compromised if you take sides.
- Interview outside individuals who know the group or have worked with it.

A CASE STUDY:

A Divided Board of Directors

Murray, a professional meeting facilitator, was hired by a board of directors. His given assignment was to conduct one of his usual board development workshops. The person who hired him could not provide any details on why the workshop was held. He suggested a standard workshop would be fine, and that no customization was needed. Based on this, Murray could have treated the session as noncontentious. But . . .

Murray asked if he could interview the various board members. After an initial reluctance, the list of names and phone numbers was given to him. He then asked that board members be advised that he would be calling to interview them, and this was done. The interviews offered a range of responses:

- Some board members denied the existence of any problem: "We are a great board, and we are doing a wonderful job. You want proof? Just look at our bottom line. Yes, it would be fun to have a workshop, but I doubt it would change anything."
- Two board members (members B and C) were unhappy with their meetings. They resented the fact that member D was dominating, promoting his own "pet projects," and not looking after the interests of the organization as a whole.

- Member D thought the board was narrow-minded and had no tolerance for new ideas. He was offended by the fact that members B and C were exchanging dirty looks every time he spoke at a meeting. Their "insulting" behavior was causing him to be even more persistent.
- Member E suggested senior staff were not accountable to the board and were getting too involved in the board's policy-setting efforts. She also suggested some staff members were hostile towards her.

Murray realized the problem went beyond the board and into its relationship with the staff. He expanded the scope of his interviews and asked to speak to senior staff members. The results were as follows:

- The CEO said he thought member D was trying to micromanage the staff and tell them what to do. Affected staff were getting confused and could not tell who their boss was.
- One of the vice presidents said she thought the board's chairperson did not show enough leadership and was unable to control his wayward members. She apparently expressed this sentiment to other staff members and to some customers.

As he was analyzing the magnitude of the problem, Murray couldn't help but ask himself: Why did they not volunteer this information to me? His lesson was this: Never assume people are telling you everything you need to know. Probe, ask for more information, and always be a curious learner.

Murray's analysis led him to conclude that:

- There was no clear distinction established between organizational interests and narrow interests. This deficiency was leading member D to promote his own pet projects and not pay as much attention to the broader interests of the organization.
- Board members kept feedback to themselves or shared it within their own cliques. They ended up giving the feedback anyway, through facial expressions and body language.
- Some board members were possibly micromanaging the staff.
- The distinctions between board and staff authority were blurred.
- Staff members were possibly crossing the line when criticizing the board as they did.

Murray then defined the direction and potential benefits of the board workshop:

- Reinforcing the board's mandate and clarifying the difference between an organizational interest and a narrow interest, with examples resembling the board's circumstances

- Clarifying board member roles and responsibilities
- Getting board members to share feedback directly and work as a cohesive team
- Establishing accountability: Who reports to whom and who tells whom what to do?
- Improving communications among board members
- Clarifying the board's relationship with senior management

Instead of having one workshop, Murray suggested three separate sessions:

- One session with the board only
- One session with senior staff only
- One joint session with both the board and senior staff together

Preparing the Agenda

After you establish an affirmative and beneficial direction for a contentious meeting, you need to design the agenda for it. See Chapter 9 for general ideas on agenda design, e.g., how to frame issues, allocate time, and establish discussion activities.

Here are a few tips that will be particularly useful when preparing the agenda for a contentious meeting:

- ▲ Define the questions to be addressed clearly and concisely.
- ▲ Make the agenda realistic. If many issues could be covered, list all the issues that could be addressed, and make it abundantly clear that this is more of a "wish list" than a firm agenda.
- ▲ Prioritize and clarify which issues are essential to cover, which ones would be nice to cover, and which ones will be covered only if time is available.
- ▲ Give as many members as possible assignments for the meeting. For example, vocal members from various sides to a dispute could be asked to prepare presentations. You can even be gutsy and suggest that opposing sides work together to prepare a joint presentation. Let the reconciliation begin before the meeting.
- ▲ Circulate the agenda to the members for review and feedback well before the meeting.

- Independent research may be needed to help settle a dispute. If such research has been done, include the results as an attachment to the agenda.

Establishing the Protocol

The more contentious the issues, the more essential it will be to establish a participation protocol and etiquette for the meeting. Here are the participation guidelines to consider:

- Speak only after being acknowledged by the facilitator.
- Listen and allow people to finish what they are saying. Interruptions are discouraged.
- Keep your comments focused on the issues at hand and avoid digressions.
- Make your comments concise and to the point and avoid rambling and repetition.
- Stay focused on the issues and avoid personal accusations.
- Keep your language clean.
- Avoid domination. First-time speakers get priority over second-time speakers.
- The facilitator may intervene if the protocol and etiquette are violated, and a member is also entitled to complain if the protocol and etiquette are violated.
- The facilitator, or the group collectively, decides how strictly these guidelines will be followed.

Facilitating Agreement on the Meeting Agenda and Protocol

Having established the meeting's direction, potential benefits, agenda, and protocol, you need to facilitate agreement on them. A suggested memo to help achieve participant support for the parameters of the contentious meeting appears below. The goals of premeeting communication are as follows:

- To include the members in the planning process
- To create a sense of focus and purpose for the meeting
- To set high expectations for the meeting

- To convert members from critics into creators
- To allay fears and reduce anxiety about the meeting
- To boost members' confidence in the facilitator's leadership style
- To help convert the meeting from a potential "war zone" into a "construction zone"

Example: Premeeting Memo

Dear members,

First, I want to thank each of you for speaking to me by phone about the October 23rd meeting. The feedback from everyone has been very helpful in planning the meeting. It will undoubtedly help me run a productive and beneficial meeting. We have some tough issues to deal with, and I will need your support to make sure we do so effectively.

As I explained in my conversations with you, my role as facilitator will be to lead the meeting in a fair and inclusive manner. I will have to remain neutral, but I will take the liberty of raising tough questions if others are not doing it.

At the meeting we will need to hear the different perspectives and put together all the "pieces of the truth." We will need to work together to bring closure to divisive issues, and help the company get back on track and maintain its competitive edge in the marketplace. I know the stakes are high and some of you are anxious about the meeting, but I am confident we can make it productive and create win-win solutions to the problems we face.

Based on your input, I have identified a few key problems, possible solutions, and what benefits we can expect from this meeting (see enclosed summary). I have also put together a preliminary agenda for your consideration (see enclosure). Please don't let the large list of items overwhelm you. It is more of a wish list than a firm agenda. We will cover as much of it as possible, but our first priority will be to have quality discussions.

Finally, I prepared a set of participation guidelines for the meeting, to help us achieve the following goals: to give every individual an equal opportunity to speak, and to have a well-organized discussion.

Please review the enclosed documents and call me at 888-888-8888 or send me an e-mail at letsmakepeace@facilitator.com with any suggestions and concerns. This is your meeting, and you need to be comfortable with the agenda and the guidelines for it.

Thank you for your support. I am looking forward to working with you on October 23rd.

Resolving Potential Problems Proactively Before the Meeting

As you prepare for the contentious meeting, you will become aware of potential trouble that could make the meeting even more difficult to manage. For example:

- Two members had a nasty argument and are not talking to each other.
- Several members are highly skeptical of the meeting, believe they will be ignored, and are getting organized to disrupt it and fight for their cause.
- You are holding a community consultation meeting on a sensitive issue. As you prepare, you discover some senior staff members of the sponsoring organization treat the meeting as a necessary evil and have no intention of taking the community input seriously. You are worried the community may find out about this and the meeting will become chaotic.

To convert the above problems into opportunities, you need to be proactive and initiate contact with individuals. Your goal should be to:

- Learn more about them and their views and concerns
- Understand and support them without necessarily agreeing with their views
- Redirect their potential negativity into constructive channels
- If possible, adjust the meeting agenda to address legitimate concerns you learn about

Sample Script: A Mediation

Two members had a loud argument and are not talking to each other. You are concerned about the destructive effect this could have on the meeting, so you ask both of them to meet you (possibly after you've had private discussions with each one of them):

"Thank you, Jill and Ray. As I mentioned on the phone, the purpose of this meeting is to see whether we can resolve the issues between you, so all of us can come to the next meeting without any baggage, ready to work together. The stakes are high at the meeting and we cannot afford to allow personal tensions to make us ineffective.

"My suggestion is that each one of you state what you think the problem is and what has annoyed you. The other person and I will ask a few clarifying questions. I will list the concerns on the white board. Once both of you are comfortable that you've been heard and understood, we will see what we can do to get back on track. Please keep your comments to the issues and avoid personal accusations. See if you can use the word 'I' more than 'you.' Does this sound reasonable? OK, who would like to start?"

For a more detailed approach to mediation see the section in Chapter 2 on the facilitator as a mediator.

Sample Script: Clarifying Expectations

You are getting ready to facilitate an interdepartmental meeting, when you become aware that representatives from one department feel threatened by one of the proposals. They believe they will be ignored, and are getting ready to be disruptive and fight for their position at the meeting. You set up a meeting with the department manager:

"Thank you, Ruth. My purpose in meeting you is twofold:

"First, I want to hear about any concerns you may have about the next interdepartmental meeting, and see if and how they can be addressed.

"Second, I want to explain to you how I intend to run the meeting and see whether I can count on your support.

"I know you only have twenty minutes, so we need to move quickly. Let's start with your concerns. I understand your department is worried about proposal A. Can you tell me more about that?"

Here are the potential outcomes of this discussion:

- ▲ You could clarify that proposal A is preliminary and open to amendment.
- ▲ You could ask Ruth to work with her department to propose an alternative that will address its concerns without diluting the proposal. Given this opportunity, Ruth will likely be a more constructive participant at the meeting. She and her colleagues will come to meeting to build, not to destroy.
- ▲ You could explain how you intend to run the meeting and ensure everyone is treated fairly and equally. You could then ask if Ruth has any questions or concerns about how the meeting will be run. As a result of this discussion, Ruth will likely be more comfortable attending the meeting.

Sample Script: A Briefing with Senior Staff

You are planning a community consultation meeting on a sensitive issue. You discover that some senior managers in your company treat the meeting as a necessary evil and have no intention of taking the community input seriously. You are worried about the integrity of the consultation process and about the potential fallout if the community finds out about the attitudes of the managers. The community meeting could become chaotic.

You arrange a meeting with the managers and say this:

"Thank you for coming to this meeting. I called it to discuss a concern I have about the upcoming public consultation meeting. I want to make sure all of us have the same understanding of what we are trying to achieve at this consultation meeting. We have about thirty minutes now, so we'll need to be focused and clear.

"Let me start by asking you a question: How many of you believe this consultation meeting is just a necessary evil, and wish we didn't have to go through this exercise? Thank you for being honest. I appreciate that. Here is where I stand on this issue:

"I know that, in part, the company is holding this consultation meeting because we are required to do so by government regulators before we can get this project going. However, I also believe we can look for some benefits from this meeting. I believe the community can offer us useful advice that will help us make better decisions about this project. More than that, I believe it is crucial for all of us to go to this meeting with a genuine commitment to listen and learn, and without prejudging the quality of the public input in any way. Now that's my piece. Am I making any sense?"

Next, you could invite them to share their perspectives on the public consultation meeting and its purpose. At some point, you may need to clarify the following point:

"I need to make sure we are consistent in what we believe in and in how we communicate to the community. There is nothing worse than the public embarrassment when people accuse you of a tokenism process and quote one of your senior executives to confirm it. We need to assume that every word that we say to anyone, including our closest colleagues, will be quoted on the evening news. This means there is no such thing as 'speaking off the record.' Your words must always match your beliefs.

"So, when I say public input is valuable and must be treated as such, I am not just being a naïve optimist. I am also being practical. Can I count on your support?"

Note: If needed, you can tell them the story of two forestry executives who were sharing condescending remarks privately ("off the record") about environmental groups, without realizing the person riding the elevator with them was a newspaper reporter whose tape recorder happened to be turned on. At the end of the elevator ride, he asked them whether they would elaborate on their comments.

Example: Flowers and Chocolates

Lou was about to chair a contentious meeting of his regional managers. One of the managers, Joyce, had always been very critical of Lou and disrupted his meetings. This time Lou decided to think creatively, avoid defensiveness, and treat Joyce as though she was a reasonable person, even though he had every reason not to. He even wrote her a personal note before the meeting, pledging to listen to her feedback with an open mind, and promising to treat her criticism as though she were giving him flowers and chocolates.

Much to Lou's amazement, Joyce approached him at the start of the meeting with a bouquet of flowers and a box of chocolates. She said, "Your note was most refreshing. It was the last thing I expected you to do. I hope we can work in the future better than we did in the past."

ISSUE MANAGEMENT TOOLS FOR CONTENTIOUS MEETINGS

Having prepared for the contentious meeting (see previous section), you need to manage it. This section gives you tools to manage the issues and resolve differences of opinion. The next section gives you tools to manage the interaction. Please review Chapters 12 (steering a meeting to its destination) and 13 (pulling your weight in a meeting) for more tools.

This section includes the following:

- The essential ingredients of a consensus-building process
- How to map out a contentious agenda item
- How to facilitate consensus building on a contentious issue
- What to do if unanimous support for a decision cannot be achieved
- Taking a sober second look at a proposed agreement before finalizing it

The Essential Ingredients of a Consensus-Building Process

The following are some of the essential ingredients of a process for managing issues and resolving differences of opinion in a contentious meeting:

- Members listen more than they speak.
- There is trust and respect among members.
- Members maintain a high commitment level to the group's mandate and avoid being distracted by side issues.
- The climate is collaborative and is focused on issues, not on individuals: "It is not you against me, but you and me against the problem."

▲ Differences of opinion are celebrated. The objective is not to defeat the opposite view, but to create solutions that build on the strengths of all opinions offered.

The ideas in the previous section (proactive planning) should help you introduce the above ingredients to your meeting. You then need to reinforce these ingredients as the meeting progresses.

How to Map Out a Contentious Agenda Item

In order to create a focus for the discussions on a contentious issue, you need to map it out. In your opening statement you need to:

▲ State what the issue is.

▲ Briefly highlight essential background information.

▲ Explain how the item will be discussed.

▲ Outline the key questions to be addressed.

▲ If needed, set time limits on the discussion.

Here is an example of a "mapping out" statement:

Sample Script: Mapping Out Statement

"The next issue is our reporting and accountability in our organization. It has been a difficult issue for many of you, and we need to resolve it today. To start the discussion, we will hear a five-minute presentation by Joe, who is in favor of ____, and then a five-minute summary by Terry, who is in a favor of a very different view, which is ____. Then we will ask them questions, and then we'll discuss the following key questions:

1. What are we looking to achieve by clear reporting and accountability?
2. How can we balance the need for freedom to do certain things with the need to keep our operations consistent and to keep our senior executives informed?
3. In which areas should field managers be free to act without consultation?

4. What budgetary limits and discretionary powers should field managers have?

"We have one hour for this discussion.

"Does anyone have any questions before we start?

"OK, Joe, go ahead with your summary."

How to Facilitate Consensus Building on a Contentious Issue

The following steps can be used to build consensus on a contentious issue:

▲ All points of view on the issue are heard.

▲ The main points raised in the discussion are recorded on a flip chart or another visual aid, or the facilitator can summarize them from time to time.

▲ The areas of agreement are recorded separately.

▲ The disputed areas are recorded separately.

▲ When all views have been presented, the facilitator summarizes the areas of agreement and confirms them.

▲ Next the facilitator states the areas of disagreement and facilitates a decision on how they should be dealt with (see next subsection).

For examples, see the section on managing issues in a meeting, in Chapter 12.

What to Do if Unanimous Support for a Decision Cannot Be Achieved

If a proposed course of action emerges, but unanimous agreement on it is impossible to achieve, it can be addressed in one of three ways:

1. By a formal vote: "It seems like the choice is between two options, A or B, and that it is impossible to find a C option without diluting the outcome. We need to make a decision today, and we cannot wait any longer. Unless anyone can think of a different way, the only method I can think of is to settle this issue by a show of hands. Would you please raise your hands if you are in favor of option A? Thank you. How about option B? Thank you. Option B seems to be the preferred option by a majority of you. Let's move on to the next issue."

2. By delaying the decision until a future meeting and thereby allowing a cooling-off period.
3. By delaying the decision until expert advice on contentious areas is obtained. In this case, the group should agree on the following parameters:
   - ▲ Which expert should be selected? Who is trusted by all sides to this issue?
   - ▲ What questions should the expert address?
   - ▲ What budget should be established?
   - ▲ Who should pay the expert's fee?

Taking a Sober Second Look

If an agreement is reached quickly, it is sometimes better to delay a final commitment on it. The reasons for taking a second look are as follows:

- ▲ People may have second thoughts after the meeting.
- ▲ Members may realize they missed important points.
- ▲ Members may realize later that the organizations they represent will never accept this agreement (i.e., they made a commitment while feeling "warm and fuzzy," without realizing the real-life impacts of this agreement).
- ▲ The agreement may look great in theory, but may fail at the implementation stage. It may be smart and responsible to "test" the agreement and "experiment" with it before finalizing it.

Here are two sample scripts that will help you slow down the rush to make promises that members may find difficult to keep.

Sample Script: A Sober Second Thought at the Meeting Itself

"We are getting close to the end of this meeting, and we have made remarkable progress on a set of very difficult issues. Before we finalize our agreement, we need to make sure that we are truly comfortable with it. I suggest we do this:

"I will repeat the main points of the proposed agreement. Then I will ask you to think about it by yourself for about ten minutes and ask a few soul-searching questions I'll give you in a moment, without talking to anyone else.

"I know some of you may be thinking: After all this work, why is he taking a risk that we could erase all our progress? Why is he not letting us pop open the champagne? I appreciate that sentiment, but I am thinking about many agreements that were made without a sober second look, and were never implemented. I think it would be better for us to be safe than sorry. So is it OK to do this, to be doubly sure the agreement will work for all sides?

"Thank you. Here are the main points of the proposed agreement: ____.

"Here again are the questions to consider on your own for ten minutes:

- Will this agreement really stick?
- Will it work for the people (or department) I represent?
- Which parts am I truly comfortable with?
- Are there parts I am not sure about?
- Did we miss anything?

"Let's talk again in ten minutes."

Sample Script: Testing the Idea After the Meeting

"Can I make a suggestion before we finalize this agreement? It seems to me we covered quite a lot of new ground today and resolved some tough issues, and that's great. At the same time, we need to be practical and think about the departments we represent and what they might think about this agreement. So instead of finalizing this agreement today, would it better to go back, discuss it with your staff, test some of the ideas, and meet again next week to finalize the agreement, potentially with some changes?"

PROCESS MANAGEMENT TOOLS FOR CONTENTIOUS MEETINGS

In addition to managing the issues and building consensus, you need tools to manage the interaction between members. This section offers you the following guidelines and tools:

- Activities just before a contentious meeting
- An opening script for a contentious meeting
- Clearing obstacles to consensus building
- Dealing with counterproductive behaviors
- Disengaging from the discussions and taking time out
- Closing a contentious meeting

Activities Just Before a Contentious Meeting

See Chapter 10 for tips on preparing to launch a meeting. The following are tips that are unique to contentious meetings:

- Make sure all logistical details are handled. The last thing you want is to increase the already high level of anxiety by a stuffy or cold meeting room, microphones that don't work, or wobbly flip charts.
- It is probably best to delegate the logistical details to someone else, so you can focus on the people present and on building rapport with them.
- In a contentious meeting you may be better off with simple visual aids or with none at all. Elaborate presentations tend to turn the meeting into a lecture, when members would much rather have an interactive discussion. Fancy PowerPoint presentations can give the impression of finality and a predetermined agenda, and can stifle discussions. Try flip charts instead. Keep formal presentation time to a bare minimum.
- Arrive early and make yourself available to members who have concerns or questions about the meeting. Keep your "antenna" up and pay attention to potential trouble. Be prepared to be proactive, and see if you can address any concerns before the meeting begins.
- Invite members to talk to you before the meeting about any questions or concerns they may have. Your rewards will be those precious "heads up" warnings, helping you avoid nasty surprises at the meeting.
- Be calm, reassuring, supportive, understanding, and approachable. Anxious members will appreciate the appearance of a confident and trustworthy leader at the front of the room.

The Opening Script for a Contentious Meeting

In your opening script for the contentious meeting you can:

- Establish a positive, constructive, and principled tone for the meeting.
- Reinforce the organization's mandate and the values in which everyone believes.
- Explain the agenda and time frame for the meeting.
- Explain the protocol and etiquette for participating in the meeting.

Example: Someone to Watch Out For

This example shows how preventive and proactive planning and a good opening script can work well in a contentious meeting:

Roberta was asked by her boss to facilitate an interdepartmental meeting. As she was getting ready, she was warned to watch out for Fred, an outspoken and dominant member who disrupted past attempts to reconcile differences between the departments.

Roberta thanked her boss for the warning, but proceeded to treat all participants, including Fred, as reasonable people. She contacted Fred and other key participants prior to the meeting, to establish the agenda and participation guidelines. She clarified that her role would be to run the meeting in a fair and impartial manner and ensure that everyone get equal opportunities to be heard. This approach was acceptable to everyone, including Fred. It also established trust for Roberta and respect for her role as an impartial facilitator.

In her opening remarks, Rebecca welcomed the members and explained the agenda. She then included the following comments:

"I am mindful of the fact that the issues to be discussed today are not easy and have created tensions between the two departments for a while. At the same time, I am confident we can work together to address the issues constructively and make this meeting an opportunity and a turning point for the company and for all departments. Does this sound like a desirable goal to you? How many of you think we can make progress today? Any skeptics? Thank you. It's nice to see a good degree of both optimism and skepticism. We need both.

"As I indicated to you before the meeting, my role today is to ensure that everyone is treated fairly and that all views have a chance of being heard. If and when our discussions get heated, and they probably will, I may need to intervene and say something like: 'Can we please let people finish speaking?' or 'Can we please focus on the issues, not the people?' or 'Does anyone who has not spoken have something to add?' I am assuming this is acceptable to you.

"I brought along this train whistle to help me get your attention, just in case I need to. Here is how it sounds (blow the whistle). Does anyone have any questions or concerns? Thank you. I am looking forward to working with you to achieve positive outcomes at this meeting."

As a result of her proactive approach, the meeting ran smoothly. Some interdepartmental issues were resolved, and others were identified as needing more work. Everyone, including Fred, participated in a reasonable and principled manner. The fact that Roberta treated all members as reasonable people became a self-fulfilling prophecy.

Clearing Obstacles to Consensus Building

People are likely to feel tense at the start of a contentious meeting. These tensions may distract them and get in the way of building consensus. It may be helpful to clear the obstacles to consensus building before talking about the substantive decisions that need to be made. Here are a few tools to achieve this goal:

Sample Script: The Comfort Gauge

The comfort gauge is a tool for discussing and possibly clearing obstacles to consensus building. To start this discussion you need to prepare and circulate copies of a chart like the one below. You can start the discussion by saying this:

"Before we start with the first agenda item for this meeting, I was thinking that some of you may be a bit tense because of the difficult issues we have to address today. I think it would be useful to check your level of comfort right now and to talk about it briefly.

To do this, I have given each one of you a sheet with a table on it. I will ask you to write down two numbers in the middle column.

"The first number should show your level of comfort and trust level with this meeting: On a scale of minus 5 to plus 5, how comfortable are you with this meeting? Minus 5 is very uncomfortable, and plus 5 is very comfortable.

"The second question is about your level of optimism that we can make progress today. On a scale of minus 5 to plus 5, how confident and optimistic are you that we can resolve the issues that are facing us? Minus five is very pessimistic. Plus 5 is highly optimistic.

"Please think about it and write the two numbers down now."

Levels of comfort, confidence, and optimism	At the start of the meeting	At the end of the meeting
Comfort level (−5 to +5)		
Confidence and optimism level (−5 to +5)		

"Did everyone finish writing down their numbers? Who needs more time? If you do, raise your hand. Thank you. Now, you don't have to talk about what you wrote. You can keep it private. But I would like to at least give you an opportunity to talk about your ratings. If you want, tell us what you wrote and why. Keep in mind: there is no right or wrong. Anyone?"

The benefits of the comfort gauge are as follows:

- It relieves tension at the start of the meeting.
- It can lighten things up. People can poke fun, smile at themselves, and realize things are not all that bad.
- It can cause members to see the human side of people whom they have been accusing and blaming for difficulties.
- It can clarify misunderstandings.
- It makes members aware of the obstacles to consensus building, so they can work together to bypass them and make the meeting productive.

- ▲ It helps the group to measure progress: Before the meeting ends, ask members to rate their levels of comfort and optimism in the right-hand column. Then facilitate a discussion on what they wrote. Hopefully the ratings moved higher!
- ▲ If progress is made, this tool boosts the group's comfort, optimism, and confidence, and develops a sense of cohesion and teamwork.

Sample Script: Addressing "Hidden Agendas"

Members often accuse, blame, and say things behind people's backs, but never say these things in a meeting. It may be beneficial to bring forward such allegations and "hidden agendas" proactively. If not, they can become a source of tension and anxiety and an obstacle to listening. They can undermine progress and reduce levels of trust and openness.

Here is a sample script to help you address hidden agendas:

"Before we go ahead, there are a few issues that have come up between meetings. These issues are not a part of our formal agenda, but they are definitely underneath the surface. They can have a negative impact on the quality of our discussions and on the levels of trust we have for one another. Therefore we need to discuss them and put them to rest now.

"One allegation that was made is that nothing we say here will make a difference and that management has already made up its mind on how to proceed. This is a serious allegation, and I pursued it with my boss. He clarified that management is firmly behind us. I need to hear whether anyone still has a question or concern about this. Is there something that leads you to believe there is a predetermined agenda? If so, what is it? Any comment?"

At this stage solicit their comments. Then continue to another "hidden agenda" issue. Another approach is to list all the issues up front and then deal with all of them together.

Note 1: If members have a real difficulty entering this discussion, it's possibly because they are surprised by your openness and candor. If this is the case, you may want to ease them into the discussion more gradually. For example:

- "Can you please think about this question privately for two minutes? Then you can talk to the person sitting next to you about it."

Note 2: Make it easy for members to participate frankly and openly and don't treat their comments defensively. Just ask clarifying questions:

- "Can you be more specific?"
- "What do you mean when you say ____?"
- "I need to understand: How do you conclude from ____ that there is a predetermined agenda?"

Note 3: Keep in mind that if allegations were made, there is a reason for them:

- There may indeed be a predetermined agenda, i.e., despite your boss's reassurance, management's actions indicate there is one. In this case you may need to follow up again with your boss.
- There may not be a hidden agenda, but there is perception of one. In this case, management needs to work to regain everyone's trust.

Dealing with Counterproductive Behaviors

In the heat of the discussion of a contentious issue, members may not pay attention to meeting protocol and etiquette. You should never assume they are doing so out of malice. At the same time, you need to intervene and restore civility, order, and respect.

Here are a few sample interventions for you:

Sample Script: Interruptions

"Rick, can we let Tina finish speaking? I know the issue of ____ is very annoying and upsetting for you, but she is talking about another point altogether. Can you please hold your response until she is finished?"

Sample Scripts: Everyone Is Speaking at Once

One response may be to let them do this for a while, and, at the first opening, say this:

"Can I make an observation? It seems clear that we are hitting the sensitive issue right now. Based on what I heard, the main sticking points are the following: _____, _____, and _____. Shall we deal with them one at a time? And can we speak one at a time? Thank you. Let's start with the first point, which is _____. Mary, I sense that this one is really important to you. Can you comment?"

If chaos is a repetitive phenomenon and is affecting the productivity of the meeting, you may need to intervene more aggressively:

"Can we have only one person speaking at a time? I know the issues are difficult and many of you have things to say. But it's very hard to figure out what you're saying when everyone is talking at once. So can I take a speakers' list? OK. The subject is _____, and the question is: _____. Who would like to speak? I have Chuck, Leslie, and Bobbi. Chuck, go ahead."

Yet another option is to have a silent meeting, with everyone seated at workstations, and with all comments displayed simultaneously on one big video screen in the front of the room. This way everyone can "talk" at once. Members can even use the software to whisper to their neighbors without having a negative impact on the meeting. See Chapter 16 for more on virtual meetings.

Sample Scripts: Verbal Abuse and Disrespect

A member is abusive and levels personal accusations: "You are incompetent and have no idea what you're doing" or "You don't care about the company and the customers. All you care about is your fat monthly paycheck." You need to intervene decisively and stop the abuse. For example:

- "Can we please focus on the issues, not the people?"
- "Can we stop this? I know things are difficult, but we have to remember that the people we work with are human beings, and this language is hurtful. So please, let's keep the language

clean and focus on the issues, and let's not say things we will regret later. We belong to the same organization, and after this meeting we need to work together. Can I have your support?" (Your intervention will likely not need to be this long, and you can choose only a part of this script.)

Don't insist on the offender making an apology. You may not get one, and you don't want to stall the meeting arguing about the need to have someone apologize. But do follow up with the individual afterwards:

"Ron, I have to say that speaking as you did to Wes came across as harsh and unfair. I think it would mean a lot to him if you apologize to him in person. It's up to you to make this decision, but I think it would help. We are all human beings and deserve to be treated with respect."

You may need to follow up in person with the offended individual:

"Tina, I am really sorry you had to go through this. The personal accusations against you were definitely uncalled for. I thought you handled them with dignity and style, and I will work with others to make sure this doesn't happen again."

Sample Script: Threats

Here's a sample script for dealing with threats, such as "You'd better give us ____, or you can forget about our support for ____":

"Can we stay on the issue we are dealing with now? I don't know how productive it is to link it to other issues and try to trade one promise for another. But, Chris, something about this proposal does seem to annoy you. Am I right? If so, what is it? We need to make the decision as fair as possible."

Disengaging from the Discussions and Taking Time Out

Taking time out from the discussions is necessary under the following conditions:

- Discussions are too heated or too emotional, and a time out will provide a cooling-off period.

- There has been too much talking and not enough thinking or listening.
- Someone seems to be holding back, and you are not sure why.
- Someone seems disruptive, and you are not sure why.

Here are a few options to consider:

1. *A Break*. "It seems to me we could use a cooling-off period. How about if we take a twenty-minute break? You'll find some cold juices and soda. But before you go, here is a suggestion: If you feel like some fresh air, why don't you go for a walk with someone who has the opposing view, and try to articulate passionately his or her point of view, just for the fun of it? Then ask your partner to tell you whether they have been heard and understood. Some of you complained about not being listened to, and this exercise should show all of us to what degree we listen to other points of view. OK, we'll resume twenty minutes from now. It is 10:22. Be back at 10:42." (Pick an odd time, for the fun of it.)
2. *Quiet Thinking Time*. "We've been doing a lot of talking, and it looks like it's time to stop talking and start some solitary thinking. For the next five minutes, please think on your own, and without talking to anyone else, about the following question: _____. Please write down your thoughts, and we will discuss them when you finish. It's quiet time for the next five minutes."
3. *A Private Caucus*. This could occur at the initiative of the facilitator: "We seem to be stuck right now. I wonder if we might try something to break the deadlock. I have a feeling that a separate meeting with some of you might help me understand your perspective better. I could have a caucus with Sam, Mike, and Rita, and then caucus with Ken, Rebecca, and Sean. How about it? Sam, Mike and Rita, would you please join me in the room next door. The rest of you can take a break."

   A caucus can also be held at the initiative of a member or a group of members. The facilitator can suggest this possibility at the start of the meeting: "There may be times when you do not feel comfortable speaking about something, and could use me as an impartial sounding board privately. If this is the case, just ask to meet me separately. We will have to take a break to accommodate you, or you can ask for a caucus with me after the meeting."

During a caucus meeting, you can find out about the issue that the subgroup hesitates to speak about in the presence of the other subgroup. The subgroup may be concerned about revealing a significant piece of information, for fear it might undermine its position. The new information that you gain might help you steer the full group to resolving the dispute.

Closing a Contentious Meeting

Chapter 14 on landing a meeting includes a detailed closing script for a meeting. Here are a few points that are unique to closing a contentious meeting:

1. Summarize progress and highlight the areas in which consensus was reached and the areas in which work remains to be done.
2. Establish the next steps, which may include:
   - ▲ Communicating the consensus to outside stakeholders and receiving their endorsement.
   - ▲ Testing the agreement and determining the degree to which it works in the field.
   - ▲ Having research done or obtaining expert advice on unresolved issues, for reporting back at a later meeting.
   - ▲ Establishing a follow-up meeting to reexamine the areas of agreement and work on unresolved issues.
3. If you used the comfort gauge (see earlier in this section), use it again in the closing stages of the meeting. Get members to rate their comfort and optimism levels and compare them to what they wrote at the start of the meeting. Hopefully the numbers are higher at the end of the meeting.
4. Compliment the group on working together and dealing with the issues effectively: "In closing, I would like to thank you for your active and constructive participation in this meeting. We had some tough issues to address, and we dealt with them in a dignified, civil, and principled manner. We have reached some agreement, and there is still some work to be done. I believe this meeting will be remembered as a turning point in the relationship between our departments. Today we began to resolve some long-standing issues and started a process of healing and reconciliation. It was my pleasure working with you today, and I am looking forward to our meeting in June."

EIGHTEEN

TROUBLESHOOTING GUIDE

This chapter is your troubleshooting guide for meetings. It gives you ideas on how to diagnose and cure the most common meeting ailments and how to prevent them. It consolidates many of the interventions given in Chapters 8 to 17 into condensed and easy to use tables. Specifically, this chapter covers the following topics:

- Diagnosing meeting ailments
- Principles for curing meeting ailments
- Curing facilitation ailments
- Curing agenda ailments
- Curing time management ailments
- Curing commitment-level ailments
- Curing protocol and etiquette ailments
- Curing discussion-quality ailments
- Curing logistics ailments
- Benefiting from incurable meeting ailments

DIAGNOSING MEETING AILMENTS

A meeting ailment is a problem that occurs in a meeting and that may have a negative impact on the use of time, the quality of the discussions, and the decisions made, or on the people involved. Examples of meeting ailments are:

- ▲ A meeting is dominated by a few members, to the exclusion of others.
- ▲ A member digresses from the agenda.
- ▲ A member is verbally abusive towards others.

As in medicine, there are two types of cures to a meeting ailment:

- ▲ A *preventive* cure means preventing the ailment with premeeting work.
- ▲ A *remedial* cure means dealing with the ailment if and when it occurs in a meeting.

Before jumping in with both feet and attempting to cure a meeting ailment, it is important to diagnose it and ask questions like the following:

- ▲ Is it indeed an ailment? Is it having a negative impact on the use of time, the quality of the discussion, and the people at the meeting?
- ▲ If it is an ailment, how serious is it? How large is the negative impact on the meeting?
- ▲ Is it a problem that will resolve itself in time, without external intervention?
- ▲ Will the intervention cause more harm than the ailment itself?
- ▲ If an intervention is needed, how strong should it be?

Trying to cure a meeting ailment without diagnosing it is risky. It amounts to a doctor:

- ▲ Sending someone to a hospital when he or she is not sick.
- ▲ Prescribing drugs when the problem is temporary and will disappear by itself.
- ▲ Prescribing something that will solve the problem but will have significant side effects, sometimes worse than the problem itself.

▲ Prescribing major surgery when an aspirin will do.

▲ Avoiding intervention because it may inflict short-term pain. Hesitation may cause the problem to get worse and require a much stronger intervention later.

Here are a few examples of counterproductive interventions and alternative ones:

The Ailment	A Counterproductive Intervention	An Alternative Intervention
A member digresses from the agenda by telling a short lighthearted story. No one is complaining. In fact, people seem to welcome the comic relief.	An intervention in the form of "Can we please stick to the agenda?" would be rigid and constraining. In fact, it would likely cause more harm than the digression itself.	Stop being a nitpicker. Smile at yourself and carry on. In other words: Relax, let go, and don't tamper with success.
A member is being disruptive, uncooperative, and verbally abusive.	Your inclination may be to say, "Behave or I'll ask you to leave," knowing that other members will cheer you on. But as right as all of you may seem to be, the threat may worsen the situation. If the member refuses to leave, your authority will be undermined. Trying to follow up on your threat and physically remove him would be risky.	Try the "carrot" (an invitation to participate constructively) before you wave the "stick" (the threat of removal from the meeting): "Harry, in fairness, we need to give other people a chance to be heard, just like you. Can I also ask you to please focus on issues, and soften your tone and word selection? Other people may find them hard to take."
It is clear that a member did not read the premeeting reports.	You might scold the member publicly and remind her how important it is to prepare for meetings. You might be 100% right, but doing this in front of everyone may be embarrassing.	A postmeeting intervention may achieve the same result without embarrassing the individual in front of everyone. Talk to her after the meeting.
An aggressive member gets his way every time, and no one has the courage to give him feedback. Many people think he is beyond hope and are afraid of his temper.	You might act on the same fear and avoid intervention. The quality of discussions and the decisions will continue to suffer, and the members will be unhappy with your leadership.	You must intervene now. If you wait, the ailment will become worse and will require stronger medicine. Relationships may be damaged beyond repair. You may lose key team members.
In one meeting a facilitator was distracted by two members who were having a side conversation.	Instinctively, the facilitator turned to the two and asked them to be quiet: "Can we have only one meeting here?" Later the fa-	The facilitator should have checked first what the problem was (diagnosis before intervention). He would have discovered it was not

The Ailment	A Counterproductive Intervention	An Alternative Intervention
	cilitator found out that one of the two members was physically handicapped and the other was trying to help her address a discomfort she was having. The facilitator's intervention, though well meant, was seen as harsh and insensitive.	a meeting ailment and left the two members alone or even offered some help.

PRINCIPLES FOR CURING MEETING AILMENTS

Having diagnosed a meeting ailment accurately (see previous section), you need to consider the most effective way of curing it. Here are a few general principles to consider:

- Before intervening to cure the ailment, determine how much of a negative impact it is having, whether an intervention will help or cause more harm than the ailment itself, and what is the best time to intervene.
- Consider whether the cure should be remedial (what can be done to cure the ailment right now) or preventive (what can be done to prevent the ailment in future meetings) or both. Preventive cures are generally preferable to remedial ones, but you will not be able to anticipate every ailment (even people who exercise regularly and eat healthy food will encounter the occasional flu).
- Your departure point should be to assume each member will act as a reasonable person if treated as such consistently. Never assume that people act out of malice. Instead look for misunderstandings and communication breakdowns as the causes for meeting ailments.
- If you intervene verbally to cure a meeting ailment, make your statement simple, brief, clear, focused, and principled. Avoid long and convoluted lectures. Just tell them what the difficulty is, what impact the behavior is having, and what corrective actions you are asking them to take: "Ken, can we speak by raising hands, not voices? Other people are waiting for their turns to speak. Betty, you're next."
- Use affirmative language. Tell them what you want them to do, instead of what you want them to stop doing. Instead of "Don't interrupt," say, "Can we please let Robin finish?"

- Soften your interventions by framing them as questions instead of orders. Instead of "Get to the point already," try, "Can you please get to the point? We are running short on time."
- Use the word "I" less and the word "we" more. Instead of saying, "I won't allow you to digress from the agenda," say, "Can we please stay on track?" Instead of "I can't tolerate this language," try "Can we please use appropriate language?"
- Balance the rights of the individual with the rights of the group. Effective meeting management is not about being nice and always accommodating everyone. It is about being principled. By being too nice to one person, you may be not so nice to many others who are getting frustrated and expect some leadership from you.
- What you say is just as important as how you say it. You may need to soften your tone of voice and facial expression. Conversely, you may need to sound less tentative and more confident, definitive, and unapologetic. Use the "iron hand in a velvet glove." It is entirely possible to be gracious and firm at the same time.
- Nonverbal cures can be just effective as verbal ones. For example, if there is a side conversation, you could get everyone to stop talking and wait. The silence will likely compel the side talkers to refocus on the meeting.
- Use the "carrot" approach first, and "wave the stick" only when absolutely necessary. Give a disruptive member every opportunity and incentive to participate constructively. In all likelihood, you will not need to resort to threats.
- What should you do if, despite your "carrot" approach, an individual refuses to cooperate?
    - Don't fall into the trap of capitulating to the member.
    - Similarly, don't try to overpower an individual on your own.
    - The "ultimate stick" should be to ask the group what it wants to do by taking a vote: "Let me check what other people want. How many people want to revisit this decision? How many think we shouldn't? We have a majority that does not want to revisit the issue. We need to move on."
- The above approach relies on the group to help you. Democracy is your most powerful tool:
    - It keeps you calm, cool, and collected: Instead of losing your temper or feeling threatened, you just take a show of hands. It's easy, but very potent.
    - It isolates disruptive behavior.
    - It avoids dominance by the minority.

- It shows respect for the majority.
- It engages members in decision making.
- It converts members from passive spectators ("who will win this battle, the facilitator or this stubborn member?") to active partners in decision making ("I get to decide how this meeting will be run").
- It puts the group in charge of its meetings.

▲ The facilitator should not have a monopoly on interventions. Following the principles of shared responsibility and the motto of "suffering is optional," individual members should feel free to intervene and help cure a meeting ailment. For example, "Excuse me. I'm having trouble concentrating when three people speak at once. Can we start a lineup and let people finish speaking?"

CURING FACILITATION AILMENTS

Many ailments occur when a meeting is led by a facilitator who:

▲ Prepares inadequately for the meeting, or does not prepare at all

▲ Does not understand the organization's mandate or fails to reinforce it

▲ Is autocratic and imposes decisions on the group

▲ Is too passive and hesitates to intervene if there is a problem

▲ Hesitates to bring closure to issues

▲ Conversely, is always in a rush to close discussions and move on

▲ Unnecessarily interrupts speakers

▲ Dominates discussions and rebuts every statement made

▲ Lectures or scolds members and tells them what's good or bad for them

▲ Is too accommodating to individuals at the expense of the group as a whole

▲ Fails to clarify proposals and agenda items

▲ Frames consensus incorrectly, sometimes appearing to suit his or her own bias

▲ Starts and ends meetings late

Typical root causes for facilitation ailments are:

▲ A lack of clarity of the facilitator's role. Some see it as a position of power, authority, and control. Others believe the facilitator must always be pleasant and accommodating.

- A lack of good role models in the facilitator's position.
- Acceptance of poor facilitation as a fact of life, and a lack of initiative by members to do something about it, i.e., members are passive, choose to suffer under an ineffective facilitator, and don't dare do anything about it.

Preventive Cures for Facilitation Ailments

The following steps should be considered to prevent facilitation ailments:

- A facilitator should be chosen primarily for the ability to lead, chair meetings, and build consensus, not because of popularity or technical expertise. The classic mistake is to promote an excellent engineer with no people skills and no leadership training to a manager's position. It's unfair to both the individual and the group.
- There should be a facilitator's orientation manual and a mandatory training program, to ensure the individual can wear as many of the facilitator's hats as possible (see Chapter 2).
- There should be a member's orientation manual and training program, to emphasize the notion of shared responsibility, and legitimize members' rights and the obligation to complain if there is a problem in a meeting.
- Members should be given opportunities to give direct feedback to the facilitator. For example, just before a meeting ends, members can be asked to comment on what went well at the meeting and what could be done to improve future meetings.
- In the absence of the above, members should give themselves permission to intervene and address a meeting ailment. An intervention by a member does not have to be harsh or defensive. It can be gracious and firm. You don't have to start an aggressive revolution, just a quiet and subtle evolutionary process to improve the productivity of your meetings.

Remedial Cures for Facilitation Ailments

Here are a few examples of interventions by members to cure facilitation ailments:

If the facilitator does this:	You can do or say this:
The facilitator comes to meetings unprepared.	Say this at the break: "Cindy, can we talk? Thanks. I am having a hard time.

If the facilitator does this:	You can do or say this:
	I need to have a sense of focus and leadership from you at our meetings, and I am not getting it. Can I give you examples of what you could do to help me?’
The facilitator does not understand the organization’s mandate or fails to reinforce it.	Say this: “Dave, I am getting confused. What exactly is our group mandated to do, and how is what we’re doing right now related to it? Would it be reasonable to ask you to repeat our mandate from time to time, or at least to state it once at the start of a meeting?”
The facilitator is autocratic and imposes decisions on the group.	“Lil, can I say something before we move on? I accept that as a manager you are entitled to make decisions. But it seems to me that when a decision affects each of us, there is some value to at least hearing us out before you make the decision. Am I making sense?”
The facilitator is passive and hesitant to facilitate closure on an issue.	“Brad, aren’t we ready to make a decision on this issue? I have another meeting to go to and I am worried that, at the current rate, we will run late and I won’t be able to get to my other meeting on time.”
The facilitator is always in a rush to move to the next issue.	“I hate to do this to you, Elliott, but this fast pace doesn’t feel right. I realize there is a need for us to make progress. But I think we need to slow down just a bit, or else we could make decisions and regret them later on.”
The facilitator unnecessarily interrupts a member.	“Excuse me, Mike, I was trying to follow what Josh was saying. Can I hear him out?”

The facilitator dominates discussions and rebuts every statement made.	"Bob, is there a way we can hear from all of us first, and give priority to those who have not spoken? I appreciate that you have a lot to say about this issue. But it seems to me we could also benefit from other points of view."
The facilitator lectures or scolds the group.	Say this during a break: "Richard, you said you would welcome our feedback anytime. Can I give you some now? Thanks. I didn't want to say anything at the meeting itself, but your comments about ____ were a bit hard to take. They came across as top-down, a bit like a 'sermon from the mount.' I know you didn't mean it, but it came across that way to me. I just thought I'd let you know."
The facilitator is too accommodating to individuals, at the expense of the group as a whole.	Say this during a break: "Helen, can I give you some feedback on the meeting? Thanks. Here goes. It's very nice that you want to accommodate people at the meeting. At the same time, when you accommodate one person too much, the rest of us may be getting impatient and ready to move on. Do you want my suggestions on how to keep a diplomatic style and move the meeting along at the same time?"
The facilitator fails to clarify proposals and agenda items.	"Shawn, I am confused. Do you mind explaining where we are on the agenda and what proposal we are discussing?"
The facilitator frames consensus incorrectly, sometimes appearing to suit his or her own bias.	"Just a minute, Phil. I'm not sure that's what we agreed on. I seem to remember that we agreed on ____, not ____. Am I right? Can we check with other people before we move on?"

If the facilitator does this:	You can do or say this:
The facilitator starts and ends meetings late.	Say this during a break: "Chris, I am having a hard time when I make an effort to arrive on time and we start late. Also, it is hard for me to make commitments after the meeting when I don't know whether we'll end on time. Can we get our meetings started and ended on time? Can we discuss this issue with the group, so we can get a better commitment from everyone?"

CURING AGENDA AILMENTS

The Ailment	Remedial Intervention	Preventive Intervention
Inappropriate Agenda Item "This issue is outside our mandate."	As soon as you find out, facilitate a decision to delete the item from the agenda, and save the time for mandate-related issues.	Refuse to include issues that do not relate to the group's mandate. No more "free-for-all" agendas!
Wrong Priorities Low-priority items are scheduled early and are given too much time. High-priority items are scheduled later, and could be squeezed out of this meeting.	At the start of the meeting change the sequence of agenda items. Allocate time to issues in proportion to their significance.	Prioritize items when designing agendas. Establish a logical sequence, dealing first with urgent items. Allocate time proportionately to the significance of items. 90% of the time should produce 90% (not 10%) of the results.
Reactive Agenda Your group spends most of its meeting time on reactive agenda components, doing the things it must do, but none of the things that would be fun to do. Meetings are boring and uninspiring.	Collect ideas from members on what issues they would enjoy discussing. This will help make the agenda more meaningful and meetings more enticing to attend. Put one of these proactive agenda items on this meeting's agenda.	Establish a schedule of proactive agenda items, based on a long-range plan. Or create an idea file with interesting issues that should be dealt with when there is time. Schedule at least one fresh and enticing item on each meeting agenda.
Confusing Agenda Item It is not clear what an agenda item means, and how it will be dealt with.	Before starting the discussion on an agenda item, map it out. Explain	Give a clear indication on the agenda (or on an attachment to the agenda) as

	whether the item is for information only or for discussion and decision making, how the discussion of this item will unfold, and how much time has been allocated for it.	to the nature of each item (for information? for decision making?), the options for decision making, and how much time has been allocated for it.
No Agenda You called a meeting hastily, without a precirculated agenda.	Start by clearly explaining the purpose of the meeting, the need for its urgency, and what it is intended to achieve.	Never do this again (or at least make last-minute meetings the exception and not the norm), since this practice is very annoying and unsettling.
Crowded Agenda There are too many items on the agenda, which means you will inevitably hit "rush hour" (15 minutes left to finish half the agenda).	Deal with high-priority items first. Postpone some items, delegate some items, and drop nonessential items altogether.	When planning the meeting, scrutinize agenda items, estimate how much time they will require, and ensure that the scope of the meeting is realistic. Feel free to say no to items that can wait or do not belong on the group's agenda.
Surprise Agenda Item Last-minute additions to the agenda and nasty surprises hijack the focus of the meeting.	The group, collectively (possibly by a show of hands), can refuse to address last-minute additions to the agenda, or demand the reason for their urgency. In any event, last-minute additions should not be discussed until all prescheduled items have been concluded, unless the group believes such late items are urgent and should be considered sooner.	Entrench the notion that last-minute additions to the agenda should be the exception and not the norm. Also establish that, as a general rule, prescheduled items are discussed first.

Curing Time Management Ailments

The Ailment	Remedial Intervention	Preventive Intervention
A Presenter Goes Overtime A guest speaker goes overtime. Other agenda items could suffer as a result of this.	Interject: "Excuse my interruption, Professor Jones. How much more time do you need?"	Establish time limits with your guest speakers before the meeting, and let them know how you will indicate to them that time is running out.

The Ailment	Remedial Intervention	Preventive Intervention
Never-Ending Statements A member doesn't seem to know when and how to stop talking.	"Jack, we need to move on. Your point that we need to ______ has been made. Judy, you're next." Or: "I hate to do this, Jack, but I'm having trouble following you. Tell me this: If you had to make your point in one sentence, what would it be?" Or: Have a cue card saying: "Time to land," or make eye contact with the member and move your hand in a circle, like a plane circling the field, or point to your watch.	Say this in your opening script: "We have lots to cover today, and we need to be focused and efficient. Would you please keep your comments to the point? Thank you. Please don't get mad at me if I remind you of time constraints when needed. I need your help to keep us moving."
Late Start People are slow to settle down in their spots. Some have not arrived. Will the meeting start on time?	A few minutes before the scheduled start time, ask members to take their coffee and take their seats. If not everyone is there, you can start the meeting on time and start with less significant agenda items. If it is not practical to start on time, ask those who are there if it's OK to wait, or give them an assignment to get busy with on their own.	Make sure the start time is reasonable. In the notice of the meeting announce a social and networking time just before the meeting, and state your intention to start exactly on time. Try a fine and reward system, whereby latecomers would pay a small fee for a charitable cause or a year-end party, and consistent attendees would receive token awards at the year-end party.
Late Ending The meeting continues past the established closing time. Some leave. Others stay (resentfully), but their subsequent commitments suffer.	You should have alerted members to the fact that the closing time was approaching, and should have facilitated a smooth landing (see Chapter 14). If the meeting is about to go overtime, the facilitator or a member can intervene: "In fairness to everyone, we agreed to end this meeting at 4, and people have made other commitments. Let's close the meeting now, and continue with the remainder of the agenda at the next meeting."	Establish a realistic agenda for the meeting and allocate time for major items. Start the meeting on time, and give members periodic progress statements on time: "We have 15 minutes before we move on to agenda item 6," or: "We have 10 minutes before closing time. Let's summarize and talk about follow-up."

No Ending Time Scheduled	"In fairness to those of you who have other plans, we need to set a closing time for this meeting. Is 10:30 OK with you?"	Estimate an ending time, have it printed on the agenda, and communicate it to the members before the meeting. Remind everyone of the proposed closing time at the start of the meeting, and see if they are comfortable with it.
Early Ending The meeting is about to end early.	It is not a crime to end a meeting early. You can break the good news to the members, and quit while you're ahead.	If your estimate of the required time was too generous, budget more realistically next time. Conversely, if you rushed things through, check if the quality of the decisions suffered. You may need to be more measured and deliberate and slow things down a bit next time.
Late for a Scheduled Item The time scheduled for an agenda item has ended, but another 15 minutes are needed to facilitate a natural closure on it.	Halt the discussion and facilitate a decision on whether to extend the time for this agenda item. It should be clear that the 15-minute extension will be at the expense of the remaining items.	Allocate time realistically, monitor the clock as you go along, and give members progress statements on how much time is left for the current agenda item.

Curing Commitment-Level Ailments

The Ailment	Remedial Intervention	Preventive Intervention
No Preparation A member opens the envelope containing the meeting package and starts reading the reports for the first time at the meeting itself.	If too many members are doing this, an informed decision cannot be made. Suggest a reading break. Some agenda items may be too important and may require advance thinking by all. It may be best to postpone them to a future meeting.	Say this at the meeting: "Based on our discussions, it seems that some members have read the material more carefully than others. Can I ask everyone to please prepare next time, so all of us can be more focused and efficient?" Another option: Speak to repeat offenders during breaks or between meetings: "Paul, I really need you to be better prepared for meetings. I know you're

The Ailment	Remedial Intervention	Preventive Intervention
		a busy person, but our discussions suffer when people don't read reports prior to meetings. Can I count on your support next time?"
Quiet Members A member shows no interest in the discussions (she or he is not participating and seems preoccupied with another task).	If someone has nothing to contribute, see if they can be excused from the meeting. Otherwise, find ways to involve them in the discussions. For example: "Joan, can you help us out with this issue?" If a member is only interested in some agenda items but not in others, she or he can be invited to the relevant portions of the meeting only.	Have private discussions with quiet members and give them feedback on their participation in meetings. For example: "Joan, do you have a moment? I have a question for you. At our last meeting, you seemed preoccupied. Is there something I should know about?"
Coffee Break Debates No one says much during the meeting, and a significant proposal is approved quickly and without questioning. But then there is a coffee break, and the real discussion begins, with the consensus being that "that was a very stupid decision."	If it is apparent that a bad decision was indeed made, have it revisited when the meeting resumes.	At the next meeting, emphasize in your opening comments the importance of speaking up before (not after) decisions are finalized. Clarify that "there is no such thing as a stupid question, except, perhaps, the question you don't ask."
Broken Promises A member never gets things done on time and always offers good reasons for not completing assignments.	Reassign tasks to more reliable members, unless you are convinced that this member will get it done. Express your disappointment: "I must say I am disappointed. I would have hoped you would at least give an advance notice that you are having difficulties meeting the deadline."	When a task is given, confirm it verbally, record it in the minutes, and follow up after the meeting by phone, to check about progress. Send this member to a time and priority management training program.
Tardiness and Early Departures Rick arrives late and seems anxious to leave.	Ask Rick what the problem is, and whether he can focus on this meeting. If it is not possible for him to do this and he is there only in body but not in spirit, he may as well not be there at all.	Be selective when you choose team members. Clarify that you expect them to be in meetings from start to finish, in body and in spirit. You may need to contact members like Rick before a meeting to confirm their attendance, or

		check if there is a problem you can help them with.
Absences Rachel is absent from a meeting without notifying you.	If she is responsible for an agenda item, it may need to be postponed to a future meeting or reassigned to someone else.	Contact Rachel, tell her she was missed, find out why she was absent, and see what can be done to prevent it in the future. Ask members to alert you in advance if they will miss a meeting. Run meetings that no one will want to miss.
Same Volunteers Always You ask for volunteers to carry out a certain assignment, and always get the same people.	Don't look for volunteers at random, but say: "Cathy, could we interest you in doing this? We need to share the workload and get everyone to develop more experience. What do you think?"	Create an inventory of the skills and expertise that each member has to offer. Also list the skills they want to develop. Assign tasks based on this list and not based on who volunteers first.
Falling Asleep Members are falling asleep, especially in the afternoon or after a heavy meal.	Ask them to stand up and stretch, or send them for a walk around the block. Facilitate parts of the meeting standing up. Pick up the pace of the meeting. Try mild aerobic exercise (stretching).	Plan the next meeting to be shorter, better focused, more interesting and engaging, and more fun. Plan some activities that will get people to move around. Avoid hot and heavy meals. Alcohol is definitely out.

Curing Protocol and Etiquette Ailments

The next table describes protocol and etiquette ailments and the remedial cures for them. Preventive cures are not included because they are the same for all of them:

- Establish the participation protocol and etiquette (see Chapter 8).
- Reinforce them with your opening comments for the meeting.
- If needed, speak to those who don't observe them prior to a meeting.

The Ailment	Remedial Intervention
Chaos Everyone is talking at the same time.	"Can we have only one person speaking at a time?" Or: "Can I have everyone's attention? It's great that so many of you want to speak. Let me start a speakers' lineup, so we can take

The Ailment	Remedial Intervention
	turns. Who wants to speak? OK, we'll start with Joe, then Ruth, then Abe. Joe, go ahead."
The Hanging Hand Gerry raises his hand and does not put it down.	"Gerry, I saw your hand and added your name to the speakers' lineup. You can put it down now. It's distracting for other people."
The Frown, Sigh, or Dirty Look Nancy seems annoyed. She frowns, sighs, or exchanges cynical looks with Donna every time Paul speaks.	Ask: "Just a moment, Paul. Nancy, if you have a comment on what Paul is saying, could you please make it when your turn comes? Thank you. Paul, please continue." Or: "Just a moment, Paul. Can I ask everyone to please give those who speak the same respect and attention that we want when we speak? Thank you. Paul, please continue."
Barging In Jack barges in when Joan's turn to speak has come.	"Excuse me, Jack, but it's Joan's turn now. Do you want me to add your name to the list? OK. Joan, go ahead."
Domination The discussion is dominated by two outspoken members.	If the two are very knowledgeable and make a substantial contribution, and no one seems to be bothered by the domination, you can let it continue, at least for now. At some point you may need to intervene: "Can we hear from members who have not spoken? How about you, Tom? You had unique experience in this area. Can you help us out?"
Interruptions Tom interrupts Jenny.	"Tom, can you let Jenny finish? If you want to respond, would you please write your points down so you don't forget them, and tell us later what they are? Thank you. Jenny, go ahead."
Side Conversation Graham and Leslie whisper or conduct a side conversation while Josh is speaking.	Your cure will depend on the reason for the side conversation. For example, you could ask Josh to pause and then wait silently for a few seconds until Graham and Leslie stop. The discussion can then continue without the distraction. You could interject: "Josh, can you hold it for a minute? Graham and Leslie, is there a problem?" If the side conversation is clearly counterproductive and distracting, you could say: "Graham and Leslie, this is distracting. Can we have only one meeting at a time?"
Digression Ron talks about an issue that is not related to the agenda, or goes back to an issue that was concluded.	"Ron, how is this related to the proposal to renew the lease for our building? It isn't? Then could you save your comments for later

	in the meeting? We have a busy agenda and we need to stay on track." Or: "Ron, we already dealt with this issue. We need to move on."
Verbal Abuse Fiona questions Neal's integrity and credibility.	"Fiona, can we keep the discussion on the issues, not the people? I know the issues are difficult, but we need to soften the tone of our comments, to make it easier for people to hear us out."
Insensitivity Chad uses a term that is insulting to one culture, or tells an off-color joke.	"Chad, may I make a comment? I know you didn't mean any harm, but I have a feeling that some people may find this joke offensive. We need to be careful with the words we choose and the jokes we tell."
Patronizing Rob, a long-standing member, says: "Come on, guys, don't you realize that _____? This idea is plain stupid, and it is just not going to happen. Let's be serious now."	"Can we slow down, Rob? I can see how strongly you feel about this. At the same time, we need to listen and evaluate new ideas carefully, and avoid dismissing them too quickly. Sally, do you want to elaborate on your idea? What did you mean by _____?"
Hidden Agenda Larry's participation puzzles you. There appears to be something he is not saying.	"I must say I am puzzled by the twists and turns at this meeting, and I am wondering whether certain things have been left unsaid. Am I right? Can someone help me out? Larry, am I missing anything?" Or: Approach Larry at the next break for some feedback.

Curing Discussion-Quality Ailments

The ailment	Remedial Intervention	Preventive Intervention
Predictability Discussions are predictable, reflecting no imagination, creativity, or visionary thinking. The enemies of creative thinking are there in force: "We've tried it and it didn't work." "I can give you at least five reasons why it won't work." "We're doing very well, so why tamper with success?"	Be brave and dare to introduce novel ideas. Challenge members to switch from the weak position of a critic to the stronger position of a creator: "Can I make an observation? It seems to me that for every new idea we are quick to identify reasons why it wouldn't work. Someone told me it is much easier to be a critic than a creator. Can we change our mind-set, let go of the past, and start thinking as creators? Here is an unusual	Add fresh and creative minds to your team, to balance the voices of experience (who are needed for continuity). Initiate private discussions with members about the quality of the group's decisions. Persistence will work, so don't give up too quickly on your efforts to convert them from critics into creators. Follow up with advocates of the status quo after meetings and see if you can inspire a change in attitude.

The ailment	Remedial Intervention	Preventive Intervention
	idea that was mentioned earlier. Susan suggested that ______. Did we dismiss this idea too quickly? Does the fact that things work so well now mean we can rest on our laurels? Can we afford to not consider changes to get us ready for the next decade?" Note: The above intervention is not framed as a lecture, but as a series of thought-provoking questions.	For example, "George, can I give you some feedback? Thanks. Here is what I observe: It is clear that you know our history very well. You are always able to give us words of caution based on the past. At the same time, we need to look beyond the past and into the future. Circumstances change, and the fact that something didn't work in the past does not automatically mean it won't work now. Am I making any sense?"
Late Reports Several reports and support documents are received late, giving the members no time to review them, and making it difficult for them to make informed decisions.	If the related agenda item cannot wait, call a break and give the members time to read the report. If the agenda item can wait, suggest it be postponed to the next meeting.	Ask report writers to manage their time and priorities, so the above practice is avoided or minimized. Ask members to support report writers by giving them needed data on schedule.
Poorly Written Reports Reports and support documents are poorly written, confusing, fragmented, disorganized, and full of unexplained technical terms and abbreviations.	Ask the presenter to answer clarification questions from members before starting the discussions of the issues at hand.	Coach report writers or have them take technical writing or business writing courses. Better yet, why not schedule such a course in-house for all team members? Technical writing is a very valuable skill. Insist that reports be clear, concise, to the point, and well organized, with short paragraphs and concise point-format summaries, and with key points highlighted and easy to find. If needed, ask for a table of contents, a page numbering system, an executive summary, and a central list of technical terms and abbreviations.
Premature Solutions A member proposes a solution prematurely, before the problem has been fully explored.	"Jerry, thank you for your idea. I'll record it for now, but can we wait before we discuss it? I am sensing that we need more time to de-	Before opening a complex issue for discussion, explain how the process will unfold: defining the problem; identifying criteria for solu-

	fine the problem before discussing solutions."	tions; brainstorming for solutions; evaluating each solution; selecting the best solution; and deciding on implementation and follow-up.
Premature Closure A decision is being rushed through, and it almost seems futile to raise a concern in the face of the "steamroller effect."	"Can we slow down just a bit? I know our time is running short and everyone is excited about this new idea. At the same time, I have a few concerns about it, and I think rushing it through would be risky. Can I tell you what my concerns are?"	When the discussion on a complex issue begins, explain the risks of rushing to closure on a fresh idea that was not fully examined. Explain the benefit of a "sober second look" before finalizing a decision.
Repetition The discussion is repetitive. Everything that needs to be said has been said.	"Does anyone have anything new to add, and, if not, shall we bring closure to this issue? We have a busy agenda and we need to move on."	At the beginning of the meeting encourage members to be efficient and avoid repetition.
Narrow Interests Promoted Chuck promotes the interests of his own department and ignores the interests of the full organization.	"Chuck, I need to remind you that our job as a corporate committee is to look after the interests of the full organization. Our rules of engagement clearly say that the interests of individual departments come second."	Develop a member orientation package that includes the rules of engagement for the team (see Chapter 5). Organize training programs for new members, to establish their roles and responsibilities. Have refresher programs for experienced members.
Hesitancy to Criticize Members hesitate to question and scrutinize proposals ("Criticism is not a nice thing to do").	"I sense some hesitancy to criticize or ask questions, when this is exactly what we need to do. Please, there is no such thing as a stupid question, and criticizing an idea is OK. No one should take criticism as a personal attack."	In your opening remarks, emphasize that questioning and scrutiny of ideas is part of exercising due diligence. Teach members to give criticism in a way that makes it easy to receive, i.e., make it principled, objective, supportive, and hard on issues but soft on people.
Objection to a New Policy Earl articulates very clearly what is wrong with a proposed new policy.	Get Earl to shift from opposing to proposing: "Earl, are there any changes you could propose to address your concerns? If you don't have any now, would you think about it at the	Involve potential critics in developing new proposals. Ensure that new proposals are presented as preliminary, and clarify that ideas for improvement are welcome.

The ailment	Remedial Intervention	Preventive Intervention
	break and bring some ideas when we restart the meeting?"	Avoid elaborate PowerPoint outlines or fancy-looking documents that give the impression of finality and discourage suggestions to change them. How could anyone dare to mess up something that it so well laid out?
No Positive Reinforcement Members are quick to criticize others, but are very sparing with accolades ("No news is good news, and good news is no news").	Start recognizing special contributions and celebrating successes: "Thank you, Gene, for preparing such a detailed and comprehensive report. How about showing our appreciation to Gene with a round of applause?"	Develop a program to celebrate member achievements and group successes. Recognize task-related milestones or non-task-related events (birthday? a new offspring?)
Nit-Picking Members nitpick at words, propose small changes, and shift the focus of discussion away from the main issues.	"Cliff, can I make a comment? It's great that you want the words to be exactly right. I am concerned, however, that we are spending a lot of time on wording changes, and missing the discussion of the principles at the core of this proposal. Can I get your proposed amendments after the meeting?"	Talk to nitpickers between meetings and offer them feedback. It may also be productive to involve them as devil's advocates by having them help prepare proposals and documents. Use their wordsmithing skills to benefit the group.
Technical Jargon A presenter uses technical jargon and abbreviations and members appear confused.	Interrupt the presenter: "Excuse me, Brian, but do you mind explaining what the term ______ means? It's a new term for several of us."	Ask presenters before the meeting to use plain language whenever possible and not make assumptions about the members' level of knowledge and experience. Ask them to provide lists of technical terms and abbreviations. Ask them to make it abundantly clear to members that it is OK to ask for clarifications when needed. Finally, ask them to pay attention to facial expressions that signal confusion. Give members cue cards to use if they are confused: "Too technical," "Confusion here," "Plain language, please."

What Exactly Are We Agreeing to Do? The proposal under consideration has not been clearly stated.	"Before we finalize the agreement on this proposal, we need to clarify what the proposal is. Let me read it to you again: ______. Is it clear to everyone? Do you need me to clarify anything?"	Ask the presenter of a proposal to submit it in writing and include it in the package of documents that is sent to everyone before the meeting.
Apparent Hesitancy Members seem tentative about their support of a proposal. They don't seem to oppose it, but something is missing. Pushing this proposal through would be irresponsible.	Remember that silence does not mean agreement. Say something like this: "Is there a problem with this proposal? I am sensing some discomfort about it, but no one is saying anything. Your silence is deafening. Can you help me out? I don't think we should rush this proposal through unless you are comfortable with the outcome." Or: "I am not sensing a full commitment to this idea. Shall we take a ten-minute break, and would you please talk to other people about what may be missing in this proposal? We'll resume in ten minutes."	Ensure that proposals are clear and balanced and address as many concerns as possible. Encourage members to propose amendments to improve the quality of decisions, or ask that a decision be delayed if it is premature to make it.
Aimless Statements A member speaks with no clear focus, or starts with a long preamble before getting to the point.	Try one of these interventions: "I am having trouble following. Where exactly are you going with this?" Or: "What exactly is your point?"	Coach members or send them to communication training programs, so they learn to speak concisely and clearly. Teach members to use the "sandwich" approach: (1) Tell them what you'll tell them: "I am against this idea, and I'll tell you why." (2) Tell them, i.e., elaborate on your reasons in concise point-format: "My first reason is _____. Second, _____, and finally ______." (3) Tell them what you told them: "Therefore, I don't think this is a good idea."
Aimless Overall Discussion Several ideas and issues are raised, but in a random order, and with no focus.	"So far we've raised several points in the discussion: First , second ______, and	Map out each agenda item before the discussion begins. Outline the questions

The ailment	Remedial Intervention	Preventive Intervention
	third ______. Shall we address these points in some detail, one at a time? How about starting with ______?"	that need to be addressed, the key decisions that need to be made, and the time allocated for the item.
A Deadlock There are three distinct proposals, with no apparent agreement on which one is best. The discussion is not going anywhere.	Here are a few options for you: ▲ Skip to an easier topic and return to this one later. ▲ Select three members, one strongly supporting option A, one supporting B, and one C. Ask them to work together during a break or after the meeting and come up with a fourth option that would be better than all three. ▲ If there is no time to wait, it may be OK to take a show of hands and determine which of the three proposals has the highest level of support. It may also be OK to delegate the final decision making to the group's leader.	Prior research of issues may reveal some interesting solutions that will address more concerns and needs and will therefore attract broader support.
No Follow-Up Established A proposal is approved, but implementation duties are not assigned.	"Before moving to the next item, we need to establish who will do what and by when. Jackie, would you do ______? Thank you. Richard, would you take care of ______? Thank you."	At the beginning of the meeting indicate that, after making a decision, the group may also need to decide on how it will be implemented. Ask them to remind you to do that if you forget.
A Small Setback A small setback or failure in one area causes the group to negate progress made in other areas.	Acknowledge the setback and its impact, while reminding the members of the broader perspective, including successes and achievements: "The road to success is full of bumps." For example, you can say this: "Can I say something? I have a feeling that you are allowing this one setback to erase all the progress we've	Establish the following notion with the group at its formation stage or before a meeting: "There are no failures around here, except the failure to learn from mistakes and move on."

	made. Can I suggest that we remind ourselves of all the good things that happened over the past year, like ____? In the balance of things, we've done very well. Let's not forget that."	

Curing Logistics Ailments

The Ailment	Remedial Intervention	Preventive Intervention
Poor Audibility Members say, "Can't hear you" or point to their ears, indicating they need more volume.	Speak up, and ask others to do the same. You may ask speakers to stand up or come to the front and face the group. In large groups or large rooms insist on the use of microphones. Try this: "Andy, can you please speak up? People are having trouble hearing you." Or wave a cue card saying, "Volume, please."	Arrange a room with good acoustics and with no noise distractions (loud fan, a disco next door). Consider microphones.
Nonfunctioning AV Equipment The light bulb in the overhead projector is burned out, there is no electricity in the outlet, or there is no overhead screen.	Try fixing it. If you can't, see if you can carry on without it, or skip to another item while a technician works on it. You can't afford to lose precious time to logistical difficulties.	Remember Murphy's Law: "If anything can go wrong it will, at the worst possible time." Arrive early and test every piece of equipment.
Catering Glitches The refreshments or meal are late, or the wrong food arrives (remember those dietary requirements?), or not enough food, or too much of it.	Ask your logistics master to take corrective action. Advise the members of the problem. You may want to accept the imperfection, or you may continue with the meeting until the problem is addressed to your satisfaction.	Have your logistics master communicate your group's expectations to the caterers clearly and fully. It is wise to ask them to confirm their understanding of your needs, possibly in a written contract.
Visual Distractions Members are distracted by those who enter or leave the room or get up to grab a coffee, or by the sun shining in their faces.	Do what is needed to eliminate the distractions. e.g., move the facilitator's location away from the refreshment table and the entry and exit doors. Close the curtain to block the sun.	Anticipate problems and take corrective action before the meeting begins.

The Ailment	Remedial Intervention	Preventive Intervention
Restlessness Members appear restless or physically uncomfortable.	Ask what the problem is and address it. If they have been sitting too long, call a break. If the room is too hot or too cold, take corrective action.	Plan enough breaks. Make sure the room temperature and ventilation are comfortable before the meeting begins.
Room Too Large or Too Small	Check if another room is available (in the same hotel or at another location close by). If this is impossible, ask members to assist you in making the best of an imperfect situation. If the situation is entirely unworkable; suggest rescheduling the meeting.	Estimate the number of people who will likely come and select the appropriate room size. Have a contingency plan in case of an unexpectedly high turnout.

BENEFITING FROM INCURABLE MEETING AILMENTS

There will be times when you will not be able to cure a meeting ailment or when an intervention will not be appropriate. In such cases, you will just have to accept the ailment and learn to live with it. Just as there is no such thing as a perfect body, there is no such thing as a perfect meeting.

Whenever you are unable to intervene and make the meeting perfect, you need to remind yourself of the serenity prayer: "Lord, give me the courage to change the things that I can, the humility to accept the things that I cannot change, and the wisdom to know the difference between the two."

Being stuck with the ailment, you could choose to get frustrated with it and suffer. But why suffer? Why not find some benefits in this ailment and convert it from a problem to an opportunity? After all, suffering is optional. . . .

Here are a few examples of the opportunities that incurable meeting ailments present:

The incurable ailment:	The opportunities that it presents:
The meeting is adversarial, emotional, and chaotic. Members are arguing and	▲ They are letting off steam and relieving tensions. As soon as they

being verbally abusive with one another. When you try to intervene, they start yelling at you.

have finished doing that, they will likely be better able to listen to one another and work as a team.

- ▲ When the chaos ends, people may see the human side of others. They may "look at themselves in the mirror," realize how hurtful and unreasonable they have been, and soften their approach. They may even realize they were taking themselves too seriously, and that things are not so bad after all.
- ▲ True, they are not exactly being polite, but they are probably much more honest than usual, and saying things they have been holding back from each other (or saying behind people's backs). It is easier to resolve issues that are out in the open.
- ▲ As a facilitator, you can use the opportunity to observe them, listen, take notes of key concerns, and identify any systemic weaknesses that have made this dispute happen, e.g., a lack of procedures for exchanging feedback on a regular basis, or a lack of trust. When they have finished venting, you can summarize the discussion objectively and work to solve these systemic problems.
- ▲ As bad and ugly as it may look, the heated discussion is certainly not boring, and no one is likely to fall asleep as they might in more civilized meetings. The heated interaction will at least have some entertainment value. It could provide material for a skit at year-end fun night (provided issues have

The incurable ailment:	The opportunities that it presents:
	been settled and people can look back and poke fun at themselves).
An invited expert (or your CEO) rambles and takes a long time to answer questions. Your group needs the information, and you cannot possibly train him to communicate concisely in the middle of a meeting.	▲ You can learn to listen better and convert rambling statements into concise summaries. At the end of a five-minute statement you could say this in one minute: "Let me confirm the three key points that I think you are making. They are _____, _____, and _____. Am I right?" The speaker and everyone else will be astonished and learn from your ability to listen. ▲ You can recognize the need to organize a hands-on workshop on speaking and listening skills, with videotaping used to give your members direct feedback. They will learn and have fun while doing it. If you're brave, you can invite your CEO to sit in, at least as an observer. ▲ You can learn the importance of conveying your expectations and time constraints to invited speakers in advance of a meeting: "Our agenda is busy. We have thirty minutes for your presentation, and we need you to be concise, especially when you answer questions."
The air conditioning fan is too noisy, but without it the meeting will be too stuffy. Or there is a revival meeting next door, and no other meeting room is available.	▲ You and your members can learn to project your voices and listen closely to what others are saying. ▲ You and your members can learn to pay attention to facial expression, lip movement, and hand movement. ▲ Perhaps you can try running the meeting without anyone saying anything, but communicating only in writing or with facial expressions

<table>
<tr><td></td><td>and hand gestures. Sound impossible? At least try it and see what you learn from the experience.
▲ You can learn to be more careful when you choose a meeting room next time.
▲ You can try getting a discount on the meeting room cost because no one told you about the noise problems.</td></tr>
<tr><td>The agenda has proven to be too ambitious. One item required much more time than you anticipated. However, the discussion was very positive and necessary, and everyone felt good about it.</td><td>▲ You can be grateful for the progress that was made. (The cup is half full, not half empty.)
▲ You can learn to relax and stop being a fanatic about time.
▲ You can learn to allocate time more realistically when you plan your next meeting.
▲ Perhaps the issues that were not completed could benefit from a delay.</td></tr>
<tr><td>Carl gets mad at you and leaves the meeting, threatening never to come back. Before leaving, he promises to retaliate by ruining your reputation and undermining the work of your team.</td><td>▲ This may be the final push for you to sign up for the conflict resolution course you've been putting off, or take the time to read Chapter 17, to help you manage controversies more effectively.
▲ Perhaps Carl needs a break from the team, and vice versa. The separation may force everyone to think about the relationships among team members and about how meetings are run.
▲ Your team may end up rallying behind you, but you should learn to resist being seduced by flattery and see if the dispute with Carl can be resolved.
▲ Carl may discover he overestimated his influence and ability to inflict damage. He may very well come</td></tr>
</table>

The incurable ailment:	The opportunities that it presents:
	back and apologize, but you will have an opportunity to insist he follow the same rules as everyone else. ▲ Perhaps Carl was reacting to your efforts to even the playing field and not let him get his way every time (as he did in the past). If your efforts cause him to leave your team permanently, it may not be a bad thing. You need team players. The fact that a person is an expert in a given field is not enough of a reason to keep him or her on your team.
Jerry, whose input is crucial to an important agenda item, has not shown up for the meeting with no reason for his absence.	▲ You can skip his agenda item and allow more time for other items. Otherwise you can plan to end the meeting early. Members will likely thank you for that. ▲ You can try to deal with the issue in Jerry's absence, and may discover that his input is not all that essential after all. No one is indispensable. In his absence you may end up with a creative solution that his presence might have prevented.
The coffee is too cold or too weak, the juices are too warm, and the herbal tea and Diet Coke that were requested did not arrive. Lunch is not here and members are hungry. Some stomachs are rumbling.	▲ You and your team can learn to survive in less than perfect conditions. You can learn to enjoy cold coffee, or joke about it, or realize that you drink too much of it. You may discover that orange juice is much tastier and healthier than Diet Coke. ▲ You can learn to appreciate the fact that when you complain about poor service you usually get an apology and some form of compensation.

	▲ You can have fun brainstorming and figuring out how much worse things could have been.
Despite your constant reminders, people still come late to meetings, don't prepare for them, and come mainly to network and socialize with their colleagues.	▲ You can be grateful that they are at least coming to meetings. ▲ You can capitalize on the fact that they like to interact with one another and make the discussions and consensus-building activities more interactive, knowing that they will not hesitate to jump in and participate fully. ▲ You can schedule social and networking time immediately before the meeting, to entice them to arrive on time. ▲ You can learn to loosen up and relax and adapt your style to suit the group.

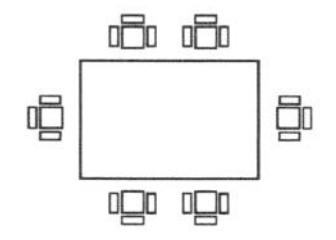

Appendixes

Case Studies

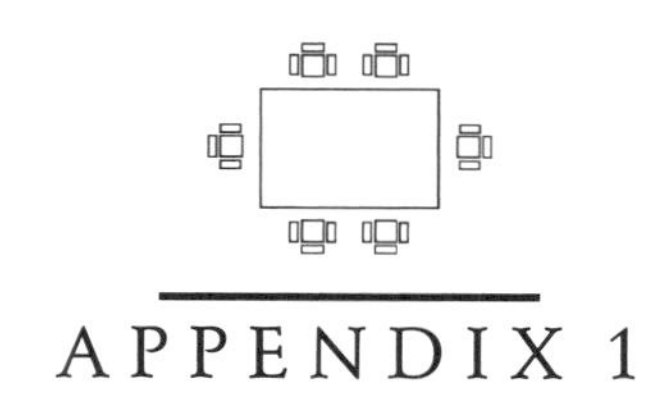

APPENDIX 1

The Auto Rental Company

This appendix is an illustration of how to launch a complex and challenging consensus-building process. It outlines some of the steps that need to be taken to build the foundation for shared decision making. It shows how some of the tools discussed in Chapters 1 to 7 can be used.

The Background

You are one of the most trusted and respected individuals in a national car rental company. Your CEO asks you to help him address major systemic problems that affect the company's profitability and threaten its future viability.

The company consists of hundreds of car rental outlets nationwide. Some of the outlets are owned by the company and some are semiautonomous franchises managed by independent operators. All outlets are given a degree of latitude, but are supposed to follow basic standards, maintain financial performance, and remain accountable to the company's head office.

In reality, however, corporate standards have not been enforced and local managers have been given free rein over the operation of their outlets. Local managers have come to resent the national office and see it as a necessary evil. They consider the profits sent to the head office as "taxation without representation." They believe standards are outdated or do not address unique local circumstances.

As a result of this free-for-all situation, the following problems have emerged:

- ▲ Customer service levels have been vastly different from location to location.
- ▲ Customer complaints have been on the rise, leading to embarrassing media coverage.
- ▲ The company's reputation has been suffering.
- ▲ The competition has been gaining ground and the company's profit levels have been declining.
- ▲ Staff morale has been low. With a highly competitive labor market, the company has been losing valuable staff, and this has led to disruptions and lack of continuity at local operations.
- ▲ Human resources practices have varied from location to location. The number of complaints about sexual harassment has been increasing. The company has been the target of costly lawsuits for wrongful dismissals alleged to have occurred in its local car rental outlets.

The company's management has made various attempts to intervene and enforce its standards. However, local managers, who have been accustomed to free rein, have resisted these interventions, for fear that their power bases and clout were about to be taken away from them. They recognize that there is a problem, but they don't trust the company's executive committee to solve them.

What makes matters worse is the fact that your CEO and his senior officers are not working as a team. Several vice presidents have built close alliances with vociferous franchise managers, and could undermine any proposed changes that might threaten local power bases. Others believe the CEO's management style is too autocratic.

The CEO is well aware he has the authority to shut down or force a takeover of noncomplying local operations, but he is concerned about the potential disruption and other negative impacts of such a move. He is also intrigued by your inclusive consensus-building approach. He can see that it can produce better long-term results. He is prepared to give your approach a chance.

Specifically, your CEO asks you to complete a "quick and dirty" consultation program with local managers within one month, and prepare a solution to what he calls "gross insubordination and corporate malaise." You suspect he did not consult his management team about your assignment. You may also need to negotiate a broader mandate, because the issues are complex and tricky. Settling on a one-month "quick and dirty" consultation program will set it up for failure.

How should you launch this program? There is more than one way of doing it. This appendix proposes one approach to kick-starting your consensus- and relationship-building efforts. It includes five steps:

1. Communicating to the CEO
2. Communicating to the executive committee
3. Defining the parameters of the consultation program
4. Communicating to local managers
5. Planning to sustain the momentum

Step 1: Communicating to the CEO

Following is a sample script of what you might say to your CEO in response to his request that you plan and facilitate this consultation program.

Sample Script: Responding to the CEO's Request

"Thank you, Jeff, for your request. This is a complex and exciting process, and I am flattered to be asked to lead it. I fully agree with you: We need greater consistency throughout the system, more accountability, and better fiscal results. We also need to regain our competitive edge, and be better positioned to respond to emerging trends.

"I need to think about the project and assess how I can make things work. You want quick results from this process, and I can see why you cannot afford to wait. I think we need to balance your need for expediency with the need to achieve quality outcomes that will endure. Can I meet you once I've thought about this? I need to discuss my overall mandate, budget, schedules, and other parameters, and I may need to negotiate the scope and time frame for this assignment. When can we meet? Next Tuesday? Would 10 to 11 A.M. be OK? Thank you.

"Before you go, I have two favors to ask of you.

"My first request is for permission to speak to each member of the executive committee privately. My second request is to make a presentation to all of you at your April 22nd executive committee meeting.

"Why am I asking this? Because I want to make sure the committee is united in its support of this project. We cannot afford to have any senior executives sitting on the sideline as critics. I believe it is crucial to have all of them as active and enthusiastic partners in this project. This may seem like an ambitious goal right now, but I am optimistic that we can achieve it.

"Can I have your permission to send them a brief memo about what I am doing, in preparation for a presentation of my proposed approach at the April 22nd executive meeting? Do you want to see the memo before I send it out? How about if I show it to you when we meet next Tuesday? In the meantime, can I ask your secretary Gina to book 45 minutes on the executive committee's agenda? I know it's a lot of time to ask for, but this is really important. There is a lot at stake here."

STEP 2: COMMUNICATING TO THE EXECUTIVE COMMITTEE

To introduce yourself and the consultation program to the executive committee, you may write a memo such as the following.

Example: Memo to the Executive Committee

Dear executive committee member:
Jeff [the CEO] has asked me to initiate and facilitate a consultation program with the managers of our local operations. This initiative is intended to get everyone working together to overcome current difficulties and achieve a few outcomes:

- ▲ Make sure the company is able to compete effectively, deliver first-class service to our customers, and be better positioned to respond to emerging industry trends.
- ▲ Standardize our operations across the country and build greater consistency throughout the system, so a customer walking into a New York City office will receive the same level of service as one walking into our office in Honolulu.

- ▲ Improve relationships between local managers and the company's head office, and develop mutual understanding, respect, teamwork, collaboration, and shared ethics and values throughout the company. Given the competitive pressures that we face, it is imperative to have all components of the company working together, as one big cohesive team.
- ▲ Establish the best way to balance the needs for local accountability to the head office with the need for managers to have leeway and freedom to respond to local circumstances.

It's a big job, and I need your full support in making it successful. Here are the things I need from you:

1. I need to be reassured that you are solidly in support of this effort. I have a complicated assignment ahead of me, and I need to know I am backed by a strong and united executive committee. I recognize there may be differences of opinion among you about this project. I need to know what your concerns are now, before I start speaking to local managers. I cannot afford to have any senior executive being any less than a full partner in this process.
2. I need your input and advice on this assignment. To this end, I would like to set up a thirty-minute appointment with you sometime in the next ten days. We should meet in person, but, if you prefer, we can speak on the phone. We can discuss questions like:

- ▲ What is your view of the situation?
- ▲ What do you think is the best way of dealing with it?
- ▲ How should I be approaching local managers?
- ▲ What can I do to work well with them?
- ▲ What are the things I should do and the things I should avoid?

3. I have asked Jeff for an opportunity to make a presentation to the executive committee at your April 22nd meeting. By then I will have spoken to each senior executive, and will have a preliminary proposal on how the consultation program should unfold. I hope to have a full discussion, and I am looking forward to receiving your feedback.

Please contact me at ____ if you have any questions, concerns, or suggestions. I am looking forward to working in partnership with you on this important assignment.

STEP 3: DEFINING THE PARAMETERS OF THE CONSULTATION PROGRAM

After interviewing the senior executives, you could propose the following parameters of the consultation program at the executive committee meeting:

Proposed Mandate

To plan and facilitate a company-wide consensus-building effort, with the goals of gathering feedback and advice from local managers on how to:

- Standardize operations
- Create the right balance between local autonomy and accountability to the national office
- Deliver consistent customer service across the company
- Make the company competitive
- Prepare the company for the challenges ahead
- Integrate input from local operations into corporate change initiatives

Expected Returns on Investment (ROI)

- Benefit from the knowledge and expertise available in local operations.
- Develop a pool of successful ideas that have been used in local operations.
- Enhance the quality of decisions made on the national and local levels.
- Enhance customer service levels and thereby increase customer loyalty.
- Boost staff morale, motivation, loyalty, and teamwork across the company.
- Position the company to introduce and implement needed changes.
- Make the relationships between the national office and local operations more harmonious, so everyone can work together, as a cohesive team, to make the company more competitive.

Potential Activities to Achieve This ROI

1. Consulting with local managers—by phone, fax, e-mail, or visits to local operations—to identify areas of potential change, such as:

- ▲ Standardization and consistency across the system
- ▲ Reporting and accountability of local operations to the national office
- ▲ Quality management and control
- ▲ Fiscal management
- ▲ Human resource management

2. Setting up regional forums with all local managers within a geographic region in attendance
3. Getting customer feedback via questionnaires, focus groups, and other methods
4. Establishing a committee of key local managers, to advise the executive committee on the implementation of changes on an ongoing basis
5. Regular reporting to the executive committee by the leaders of the consultation program

Resources Needed

- ▲ Office space and equipment
- ▲ Administrative support
- ▲ Budget for staff, advisers, meeting rooms, and travel
- ▲ External facilitators for regional forums
- ▲ Consultants in management, marketing, customer service, quality, and human resources

Note: Clearly, this is not the "quick and dirty" one-month consultation program that your CEO requested. You'll need to negotiate your mandate, scope of work, budgets, and other parameters, so the consultation program is meaningful and delivers value to the company.

Step 4: Communicating to Local Managers

Having secured the support of the executive committee, you need to introduce yourself and the consultation program to the managers of local operations. Here is an example of a letter you might send to a representative group of local managers.

Example: Announcement Letter

Dear Patricia:

My name is Jeremy Prescott and I was asked to facilitate a consultation process between the national office of our company and local operations. The purpose of this program is to establish what can be done to make our company more competitive and make our operations more consistent across the nation. Our big challenge will be to find the right balance between local autonomy and accountability to the national office.

I am aware of the fact that things have been less than harmonious between some local operations and the national office. Misunderstandings and communication breakdowns appear to have built some anxiety and tensions across the company. I believe the best thing we can do for our customers and staff is to learn from past grievances and forge ahead.

To start this dialogue, I need some feedback from you. In the next day or two I will call to set up a telephone interview with you. The purpose of this interview will be to discuss a few aspects of the relationship between the national office and your local operation. For example, I'd like to ask you:

▲ In what ways does this relationship work for you? Do you receive the support you need?

▲ In what ways does the relationship not work? What are the areas of tensions?

▲ In what ways could the relationship work better and provide more value to your operation and the company as a whole?

▲ What changes could be made to achieve accountability and an overall consistency in our local operations while allowing an appropriate degree of local autonomy?

▲ How should changes be facilitated to retain the strengths of the system and minimize disruptions to local operations and customer service?

Please feel free to contact me at ____. Thank you for your support. I am looking forward to speaking to you soon and to working with you to make this consultation program beneficial.

Step 5: Planning to Sustain the Momentum

Kick-starting the consultation program is only the start of your journey. You will need to sustain the momentum gained at the start of the process. Make sure everyone is on board for the duration and arrives at the same destination together, as active and enthusiastic partners. "Everyone" includes senior executives, local managers, staff, customers, and suppliers. To sustain the momentum, you need to:

- Continually build and maintain the relationships with your boss and the executive committee.
- Keep local managers informed and involved.
- Engage other stakeholders in discussions: staff, customers, and suppliers.
- Resolve disputes that you will undoubtedly encounter.
- Remain optimistic and confident, despite the many setbacks you may suffer.
- Be a realistic visionary. Have your head in the sky, but feet firmly on the ground.
- Learn to wear the many hats of a facilitator (see Chapter 2).

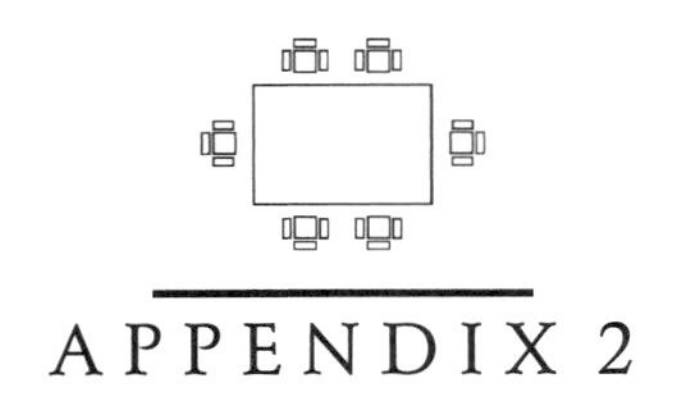

APPENDIX 2

The Public Park Policy

This appendix includes a case study of an actual stakeholder consultation program that I planned and facilitated. Some of the exact details have been altered, to protect the identity of individuals, but the essential ingredients of the process have been retained.

The Assignment

A government agency was preparing to establish a ten-year plan for designating and maintaining public parks in the area under its jurisdiction. I was engaged to plan and facilitate a stakeholder consultation program, intended to integrate stakeholder input into the ten-year plan.

The first component of the consultation program was a one-day stakeholder forum. Attendees in the forum were to include stakeholders from government, affected industries (forestry, agriculture, and mining), environmental groups, and academic institutions. The agency gave me a list of about 100 organizations to contact, with the hope that about sixty representatives would attend.

I was given the following directions:

- The agency wanted most of the one-day forum to be dedicated to interactive discussions and consensus building. Formal presentations were to be kept to a minimum.

▲ The interactive discussions were to be in small breakout groups of no more than ten people each, with each group being led by a professional facilitator. I was to locate and hire six such facilitators.

▲ The agency wanted two of its managers and one external expert to make short presentations.

▲ I was to clarify to everyone that the consensus built during the forum would be of an advisory and nonbinding nature, since the agency could not relinquish control of its mandate to stakeholders.

▲ If those present at the forum were interested in follow-up discussions after the one-day forum, an advisory stakeholder committee could be formed, and the agency was prepared to fund three of its meetings.

As I was planning the one-day forum, I faced several challenges:

1. There were tensions between business stakeholders and environmental activists. Business was concerned that industrial opportunities could be curtailed by expanded parks. Environmental activists wanted to create more parks and had been involved in ugly clashes with industry in the past. Would people want to be in the same room with one another?
2. Several stakeholders were skeptical of the government agency's motives and doubted its sincerity in initiating this consultation program. Some saw the entire process as a gesture of tokenism and did not think their input would be taken seriously.
3. It was a challenge to find effective facilitators who would lead the potentially emotional discussions effectively and make the forum beneficial.

In the remainder of this appendix I discuss some of the activities I was involved in and the tools I used to address the above challenges. Specific areas include:

▲ Communicating with agency staff

▲ Communicating with stakeholders

▲ Communicating with the facilitator team

▲ Liaison with invited speakers

▲ Liaison with the conference facility

▲ The agenda for the forum

▲ Dealing with the possibility of external disruptions

▲ The opening of the forum

- ▲ The small group discussions
- ▲ Follow-up on the forum
- ▲ Feedback on the forum
- ▲ Lessons learned from the forum

COMMUNICATING WITH AGENCY STAFF

Given the potential for conflict, it was important for me to work with the agency's senior staff and make sure we had the same understanding of the goals of the forum and everyone's roles in it. My intention was to ascertain that everyone was committed to listening and learning from the forum.

I found out that some managers were skeptical about the process and had little or no respect for some of the participants. They thought the forum was going to be a waste of time and were "tagging along" reluctantly. I wanted them to participate as confident, proactive, and willing partners.

I opened my first meeting with the agency staff with a statement like this:

> *"Thank you for coming to this meeting. I am looking forward to working with you to ensure we have a successful and productive stakeholder forum. The purpose of our meeting today is to discuss the parameters of the forum and your individual roles in it. We set aside two hours for this discussion. I am assuming everyone has planned to be here for the full meeting. Am I right? Thank you.*
>
> *"The first thing we need to articulate clearly is the purpose of the forum. As I see it, the purpose is to enable the agency to learn from stakeholder input, integrate the lessons into the ten-year park plan, and thereby make the plan more realistic, fair, and responsive to stakeholder needs.*
>
> *"I understand that past meetings with stakeholders were not always very productive, and that the goal I just stated may sound like an overly optimistic fantasy, but in my view it is attainable.*
>
> *"My commitment as the overall facilitator of the forum is to do my best to make the discussions civil, dignified, well focused, and productive. I think we can make this happen, despite the*

tough issues we need to deal with, despite some negative interactions in the past, and despite some distrust that may be out there.

"But I can't do it alone. I need your full support as the sponsoring agency. Before we go any further, I need to know whether any of you have any hesitation or concerns about the forum. I need you to tell me if you are skeptical about it and whether you are uncomfortable with some of the stakeholders. Feel free to tell me if you think I am a naïve optimist. I've been told that before. Whatever it is, I need to hear you now, so I can respond to your concerns. Who wants to start?"

The results of the above meeting and subsequent meetings with the agency's staff were as follows:

- ▲ We agreed that the agency would take stakeholder input seriously, integrate legitimate and realistic requests into the park plan, and explain why certain requests were not accepted.
- ▲ We established that stakeholders must be treated with genuine respect and must be given the benefit of the doubt, regardless of past adversarial interactions.
- ▲ We agreed on the agenda for the forum.
- ▲ We clarified each person's roles and responsibilities at the forum.
- ▲ We established who would be the agency's spokespersons to media reporters and what they should and should not say.
- ▲ We clarified that agency staff attending the forum would participate with the primary intention to listen and learn from stakeholders, and with the secondary intention of offering clarifications, on an as-needed basis.

A Mistake to Learn from: An Elaborate Discussion Paper

Before I was hired, the agency prepared a discussion paper entitled "Park Management in the 21st Century." The purpose of the document was to help frame the discussions at the forum. In it the agency outlined the challenges ahead, the issues, and some of the options it was considering.

There was one problem with the discussion paper. It looked so perfect that it gave the impression of finality. It was printed on glossy paper and was laid out very professionally, using elaborate graphics and desktop publishing. A person receiving it might hesitate to scribble, make notes on it, or give red marks to areas of concerns. Doing so would ruin the perfect appearance of the document.

To avoid the appearance of finality and to give readers license to critique the document, it would have been better to:

▲ Make the document look less professional and more tentative.

▲ Indicate clearly on each page that this was a draft document and that it was OK to critique and mark it with a red pen, highlighting pen, or any other method.

COMMUNICATING WITH STAKEHOLDERS

To start the communications with stakeholders, I arranged for letters to be sent to each of the 100 organizations and individuals, similar to the following:

> *Dear Mr. Jones,*
>
> *I was recently asked by the Parks Agency to plan and facilitate a one-day forum entitled "Park Management in the 21st Century." The forum will take place on November 10, 2002. The location is yet to be established. The purpose of the forum is to involve stakeholders such as you in discussions and consensus building on future park management policies.*
>
> *Please confirm in writing or by phone whether your organization will be represented at the forum and, if so, by whom. To enable us to have a productive discussion, we need to limit the number of participants in the forum to about sixty. I need to receive your response by October 7, 2002.*
>
> *Thank you for considering this request. I am looking forward to hearing back from you.*

Learning from a Mistake: Excluding a Stakeholder

A few days after the letters went sent, an executive from the government agency called me with a crisis. It turned out that the list of stakeholders I was given excluded one environmental group. The reason for the exclusion was that, based on past experience, the group was seen as potentially disruptive and unruly. The excluded group was told about the forum by another environmental group (news travels quickly), and contacted the agency to find out why it was excluded. Dissatisfied with the response, the excluded group contacted the media and the elected officials to complain.

Before giving my advice to the agency, I asked a few questions:

- Are this group and its mandate affected by the subjects to be discussed at the forum?
- Is it legitimate for the group's interests to be represented at the forum?
- Does the group have a unique perspective to offer?
- If the group participates constructively, will there still be a problem in having it at the forum?

Based on the answers to these questions, my advice was to invite the group to the forum. I spoke to the group's representative prior to the forum about the agenda and participation guidelines for the event. He proved to be a constructive and helpful participant at the forum. Yes, he had plenty to say, but he did not dominate, and other stakeholders were given equal opportunities to contribute.

Further Communications with Stakeholders

The response to the first letter was better than expected. We had seventy people plus eight agency representatives to accommodate. This meant we had to have seven small groups instead of six. I had to find one more professional facilitator for the small group discussions. The agency agreed to increase the budget for the forum and pay for the extra facilitator's fee and the extra catering.

With the participant list in place, I scheduled interviews with fifteen representatives of the various sectors involved: industrial, governmental, community groups, and academia. I made sure to contact individuals that the agency indicated were very outspoken. Most interviews were conducted by phone, but some were face-to-face. The process was time-consuming but was also an important effort in building collaboration and establishing a joint sense purpose at the forum.

Specific outcomes of the interviews were as follows:

- I learned more about each interviewee's unique perspectives on park policies and the impacts that changes might have on their interests. As might be expected, I discovered that some of the tensions among stakeholders were based on incorrect assumptions and misunderstandings.

- I dealt with concerns or questions about the forum. Some of the concerns were about potential meeting disruptions. I promised to do my best to make the meeting focused and efficient, but also fair and inclusive. Some participants wondered whether the agency was sincerely interested in their input, and expressed frustration with being ignored in the past. I clarified that I could not make promises for the agency, but that the intent expressed to me appeared to be genuine. I encouraged them to set the past aside and participate constructively in the forum.
- I explained the forum's agenda and took suggestions on it, and I addressed questions about my facilitation style. I told them it was OK to complain if something was not going well at the forum. Finally, I asked them to help me make the forum a success.

COMMUNICATING WITH THE FACILITATOR TEAM

As indicated earlier, small group discussions at the forum were led by professional facilitators. The intent of having professional facilitators was to make sure the discussions were well focused and efficient, and also fair and inclusive. I hired seven facilitators based on the following criteria:

- Impartiality
- Ability to lead group discussions and facilitate consensus building
- Ability to be firm and prevent domination by outspoken individuals
- Ability to deal with conflict
- Ability to listen and summarize consensus

Once we agreed on a facilitator's fee, I sent each one of them the proposed agenda, the agency's discussion paper, and other relevant documents. I scheduled a briefing of the facilitators' team to discuss expectations and desired outcomes. One facilitator was unable to attend the briefing, and I arranged to meet her separately.

The roles of the small group facilitators were as follows:

- To assist the small groups in identifying areas of agreement and disagreement
- To choose an individual who would report to the forum on behalf of the small group (unless the small group preferred the facilitator to report back to the forum on its behalf)

▲ To listen to the presentation made to the forum by the small group's representative, and comment if the small group's consensus was misrepresented or if anything was missed

Liaison with Invited Speakers

There were four formal presentations to be made at the forum:

1. Opening remarks by the agency's CEO. He welcomed the participants, explained the purpose of the forum, and emphasized the agency's commitment to listen and learn. He then introduced me to lead the forum.
2. A presentation by a senior agency executive, explaining the options outlined in the agency's discussion paper and answering questions. He agreed to keep his comments to twenty minutes and then take questions for another fifteen minutes. He asked me to moderate his question period.
3. A presentation by an external expert on stakeholder involvement in government decision making. We agreed on a fifteen-minute duration for her presentation, with a fifteen-minute question period. She preferred to handle the question period herself.
4. A presentation by the CEO of the agency just before the day ended, to give the agency's response to the consensus that emerged and indicate how the agency would follow up on the forum. He indicated that ten minutes would be sufficient for his presentation. He did not need to have a question period.

In communicating with each speaker, I did the following:

▲ Established the focus of the presentation and what could be done to make it relevant to the group.

▲ Offered guidance and feedback on the presentation's content. The purpose of this feedback was to help speakers gear their presentations to the group's needs.

▲ Established audiovisual requirements.

▲ Explained time limits and how I would indicate how much time they had left. I had signs showing "five minutes left" in green, "two minutes left" in amber, "question period" in blue, and "time is up" in red.

▲ Obtained information about speakers' qualifications, so I could introduce them to the group.

LIAISON WITH THE CONFERENCE FACILITY

We were fortunate to have conference center staff who were professional and who attended to our smallest requirements. Here are a few of the logistical details that had to be taken care of:

- The meeting room had to be large enough to accommodate up to 100 people, seated at round tables. I wanted to create a sense of community, which a theater-style room setup would not have done.
- I needed a facilitator table, a speaker's podium, seven flip charts (one for each small group), fresh felt pens, and an overhead projector and screen.
- I needed four microphones:
  - One microphone exclusively for the facilitator, to lead the discussions and moderate the question periods after one of the formal presentations. (Sharing a microphone with the presenters would have been awkward.)
  - One microphone for the presenters.
  - Two floor microphones, to enable small group representatives to present their consensus.
- I needed small breakout rooms. It would have been nice to have seven of them (one for each small group, so they could have complete privacy and not be distracted by other small groups). However, this would have been too expensive, plus there were only three extra rooms available. I took them. Three groups had complete privacy. The other four groups were placed in the four corners of the large room, as far away from each other as possible. It worked.
- As for catering, I asked for coffee and tea in the morning and during breaks, and a vegetable and sandwich lunch. In hindsight, I should have ordered juices and fruit for the afternoon.
- I asked that a separate lunch be provided for the facilitators in one of the small breakout rooms, where we had a facilitators' debriefing from 12 to 12:30 (to exchange feedback about the morning and get ready for the small group discussions in the afternoon).
- I asked that background music be turned off.
- Signs were set to direct people to the forum, and it was also announced on the video display.

- A registration table was set up, offering a list of participants and packages that included a welcoming letter, the forum's agenda, and a list of the members of the small groups (e.g., the list for Group A had ten participant names and the name of its facilitator). At the door, each participant was told which group she or he was in; otherwise they would have needed to scan all seven lists for their names.

The Agenda for the Forum

7:45 A.M.: Registration, refreshments
8:30: Welcoming remarks (Agency CEO)
8:45: Forum guidelines (Facilitator)
9:00: "Challenges and opportunities in park management" (Discussion paper explained)
9:20: Question period
9:35: Small group discussions (seven groups, different topics given to each group)
10:30: Refreshment break
10:45: Presentations of small group consensus:
Five-minute presentations by each group representative.
Small group facilitator or members comment about errors or omissions.
Follow-up discussion by the full forum.
Noon: Working lunch: Mix and discuss the consensus with people you have not met.
(Facilitator team meets in a separate room for a debriefing on how the small group sessions in the morning went, and what adjustments need to be made in the afternoon sessions)
1:00 P.M.: Summary of morning results, questions, and comments
1:30: "Stakeholder involvement and government decision making" (Keynote presentation)
1:45: Question period
2:00: Small group discussions (same seven groups, a different set of topics)
3:00: Refreshment break
3:15: Presentations of small group consensus:
Five-minute presentations by each group representative.
Small group facilitator or members comment about errors or omissions.
Follow-up discussion by the full forum.
4:15: Where do we go from here? (Agency CEO)
4:30: Adjournment

DEALING WITH THE POSSIBILITY OF EXTERNAL DISRUPTIONS

A few days before the forum there was a controversy involving mining activities that were taking place inside a potential new park. Environmental groups, including some that were scheduled to participate at the forum, were angry with the park agency and were speaking to the media. The agency became concerned that all our preparation would go to waste. There were also fears that public demonstrations would be organized and the forum would be disrupted.

The questions I was asked to consider were:

- What can be done to ensure constructive participation by environmental groups?
- What precautions should be taken to protect the forum from external disruptions?
- Should security guards be hired to prevent outside people from disrupting the forum?

My approach was as follows:

- I contacted participants from environmental groups, confirmed their participation in the forum, and reminded them of the starting time. All confirmed that they would be there.
- I decided against hiring security guards, since I thought this would be "overkill." I saw the presence of security guards as being contrary to the climate of openness and collaboration that was created for the forum. The potential benefit of having security guards would have been offset by the negative message it would have sent.
- To prevent the "mass invasion by protesters" that everyone was afraid of, we placed the registration desk in front of one entrance door and locked the other doors to the room. We also alerted the conference center management of the possibility of a disruption, and they were ready to provide staff to assist us if and when needed.

In the end there were no public demonstrations. All participants showed up on time and participated constructively. Our preventive work appeared to have paid off, or maybe it was luck.

The Opening of the Forum

At 8:25 A.M., I alerted participants that the forum would begin at 8:30, and invited them to get a refill of coffee (probably not a good idea) and take their seats.

At 8:30, the agency's CEO gave his opening remarks.

At 8:45, I was getting ready to map out the day, when someone brought to my attention that all the industry people were seated at the same table, as were all the environmental activists. I suppose they were acting on the premise that there is strength in numbers. However, I was concerned this would lead to entrenchment and division, when the goal was collaboration.

In hindsight, we might have prevented or lessened this problem in one of several ways:

- ▲ Preassigned seating, whereby different sectors would be represented at each table
- ▲ Encouraging people (at registration time) to sit next to people they have not met
- ▲ Putting up an overhead transparency saying something like this: "In the interest of making this a learning day, you are encouraged to mix and mingle. Why not start by sitting at a table with people from outside your industry or sector? Feel free to change tables as the day progresses if you want to meet other people." I ended up adding that statement to my opening script for the forum.

My opening statement covered the following topics:

1. Protocol:
   - ▲ Speak from the microphone, so you can be heard and so we can keep a lineup.
   - ▲ Keep your comments focused and to the point.
   - ▲ Help us achieve balance by not dominating the discussion.
   - ▲ Suffering is optional: It's OK to complain if the meeting is not going well.
2. Climate and consensus-building guidelines:
   - ▲ Listen with an open mind and give others the benefit of the doubt.
   - ▲ Shift from win-lose arguments (I am right and you are wrong) to win-win consensus building (each one of us has a different piece of the truth, and if we listen, we will build the bigger truth from which good consensus will emerge).

My words came back to haunt me half an hour later, when I did a poor job of paraphrasing what someone said. A few participants leapt to their feet and kept me honest. I thanked them for practicing the "suffering is optional" motto, and asked them to keep it up.

THE SMALL GROUP DISCUSSIONS

Overall, the small group discussions were very productive and got people involved in interactive consensus building. Some of the exchanges were heated, but people also listened and learned from what others said. People appreciated the balance between formal presentations and the informal small group sessions.

Here are some of the things we did to increase the productivity of the small group discussions:

- ▲ The names of the participants were preassigned, with the intention of creating balance and mixing the various sectors: industry, environmental groups, government, and academia.
- ▲ There was one representative from the sponsoring government agency in each group. We emphasized that their role was to listen and offer clarifications, but not to take strong advocacy positions or dominate the discussions.
- ▲ My assistant and I stopped by each group several times and monitored the flow of the discussions. I shared feedback with the facilitators during the lunch break debriefing. They in turn gave me feedback on how I ran the plenary discussions.
- ▲ I had timing signs ready and used them to give small group facilitators signals of how much time was left in the discussion: "twenty minutes left," "ten minutes left," "five minutes left," and "time is up." The facilitator would let the participants know how much time was left. It was hard for some groups to end the discussions, but the timing signals helped bring closure.
- ▲ There were three different topics for the small groups in the morning and three other topics in the afternoon. Limiting the coverage to three topics each time meant there was enough variety but not too much of it. Here is an example of how the topics were divided: Topic 1 was given to small groups 1 and 2; topic 2 was the subject of discussion in small groups 3 and 4; and topic 3 was assigned to small groups 5, 6, and 7.

The small group discussions were not without problems. In one group there was a rambling member and the facilitator was ineffective at asking him to wrap up. In another group one member was impatient and kept on making cutting remarks and interrupting others.

My general approach was to let the facilitator deal with such problems. After all, that's what they were paid to do. I had to remind myself of the phrase, "If you hire a chef, stay out of the kitchen."

Nonetheless, there were occasions when the impact of a disruption was too substantial and the small group facilitator was unable to deal with it. In those instances I intervened. For example:

- When I observed a group dominated by one member, I said, "Can I briefly interject before I go to the next group? We need to get as many people involved in this discussion as possible, and time is short. Based on what I see, I think we need to pick up the pace. Thank you. I'll get going now."
- On one occasion I knelt next to a participant who was behaving rudely and said quietly to him, "We need to let people finish what they are saying." He did not take it too kindly. When the facilitator turned to him for a comment, he said, "I was just told to shut up." Had I done the right thing? I don't know. But the discussion in that small group did become more civil. The facilitator told me later that she and her group were helpless in dealing with this man and that they had appreciated my intervention.

The small group consensus was then presented to the full forum. Some presentations were more effective than others. Here are a few things to note:

- Some small groups chose one of their members to present the report, while others asked the facilitator to do it. In either case, the presenter needed time to compile the data and come up with a coherent summary. In some small groups that was quite an undertaking, and the quality of the presentation was not high. In others, where the facilitator made the effort to produce interim summaries of consensus and areas of differences, the job was a lot easier.
- Some presenters used a flip chart to make their presentations, and others used their own summary notes. The flip chart approach was much more interesting and easier to follow. It also made my job of summarizing the day easier. In hindsight, I should have encouraged everyone to use this approach.
- At the end of each small group presentation I asked for input from its facilitator and members. Was the report an accurate and fair representation of the discussion? If not, what was inaccurate and what was missing? Asking this question proved to be important, since some presentations were inaccurate or incomplete.

- The fact that the same topic was covered by at least two small groups helped compensate for the imperfections in the reports.
- The virtually unanimous complaint was that there wasn't enough time to reach consensus and prepare summaries. There were several lessons to learn about allocating and managing time. It should be noted that the above complaints did not dampen the enthusiasm and positive overall feedback on the day.

FOLLOW UP ON THE FORUM

In the closing portion of the forum, the agency's CEO made a commitment to follow up on the forum. As a result, the following things were done:

- I was asked to prepare a summary of the consensus and circulate it to the participants for comment.
- I revised the summary to reflect participant feedback. Note: I had to be very careful not to allow participants to alter history. The summary was to be a record of what happened, and not what someone wished had happened. I did, however, write a special section to record dissenting opinions, and they were referred to as "personal comments" and not as group consensus. This approach proved to strike a good balance between the desires of the whole group and those of individuals or subgroups.
- The agency formed a committee of stakeholders to work on the ten-year plan further. Twelve members were chosen by the agency. They included representatives from all sectors affected by the agency's proposed policies as well as individuals with unique expertise (university faculty and practitioners in related fields).

FEEDBACK ON THE FORUM

Here is the feedback form I used for the forum:

"Park Management in the 21st Century" Stakeholder Forum

Evaluation Form

Your name (optional): ____________________

Small Group Number: ____________________

1. Plenary sessions:
   Rate the forum on a scale of 0 (poor) to 10 (excellent):
   a. Morning presentations: _____

b. Afternoon keynote address: _____
c. Productivity of plenary sessions: _____
d. Forum facilitator effectiveness: _____

Further comments on plenary discussions:

2. Small group discussions:
   Rate the small group sessions on a scale of 0 (poor) to 10 (excellent):
   a. Productivity: _____
   b. Quality of discussions: _____
   c. Balanced participation: _____
   d. Facilitator effectiveness: _____

   Further comments on small group discussions:

3. Overall ratings:
   Overall ratings of the day on a scale of 0 (poor) to 10 (excellent):
   a. Overall effectiveness: _____
   b. Pre-forum communications: _____
   c. Quality of discussions: _____
   d. Climate and tone: _____
   e. Facilities and room setup: _____

   Further overall comments:

Here are a few notes about the feedback sheet:

- The participant's name was optional. If they gave it, it made it possible to follow up with them and get clarifications of their input.
- The place to put the rating is on the right-hand side and not the left-hand side. This is logical, since people read from left to right.
- To get quality feedback, I pointed to the feedback sheet at the start of the meeting, highlighted the questions to be addressed, and asked members to jot down comments as the forum progressed. I also reminded participants of the feedback sheets at opportune times, e.g., just before lunch.

Here is some of the feedback participants gave on the forum:

- On the positive side, people thought it was a productive day and felt they had a decent opportunity to be heard. They noted that they learned a few things, got to know some of their "foes" as human beings, and were encouraged by the sponsoring agency's attitude.
- Several participants wanted more discussions like this and were pleased with the intent to form a stakeholder committee. They wanted to be kept informed of any future developments. They also wanted the opportunity to comment on the revised plan before it was finalized.
- Some participants complained about the fact that stakeholder committee participants were going to be selected by the sponsoring agency. They thought a more democratic approach should have been followed.

LESSONS LEARNED FROM THE FORUM

It was a humbling and educational experience to plan and facilitate the forum. In hindsight it resembled a journey with many twists and turns, culminating in a one-day event. The lessons I learned are as follows:

- *The Importance of Planning.* Given the complexity of the task, the sensitive nature of the issues, and the large number of people involved, every small detail had to be considered, from room setup to negotiations with stakeholders.
- *To Panic or Not to Panic.* There were several occasions when my client and I could have reacted with panic to a potential problem. It was important to resist reacting like this. It was more effective to assess the potential for trouble and determine the most effective way of dealing with it. Heavy-handed tactics (such as security guards) were clearly inappropriate.
- *Humility.* As experienced as I was as a facilitator, I had to "park my ego at the door" and be prepared to listen and learn from all participants. Had I acted arrogantly or had I been defensive to feedback, I would have lost my effectiveness and credibility.
- *The Importance of Relationship Building.* Yes, I had to attend to logistical details. But the most important and most enjoyable part of my task was relationship building with agency staff, stakeholders, facilitators, presenters, and conference facility staff. It felt like I was assembling an elaborate quilt, with diverse perspectives and personalities, and bringing everyone together to work as one big team towards a common goal. It's a powerful, exciting, educational, and very satisfying experience. I highly recommend it.

Index

About the Author

Eli Mina, M.Sc., P.R.P., is a professional meeting facilitator, management consultant, and seminar leader, who runs a unique consulting and training practice out of Vancouver, Canada. Since 1984, Eli has served his clients by chairing contentious meetings, mediating organizational disputes, and demystifying and humanizing the rules of order for meetings. Eli's clients come from business and industry, government, school districts, credit unions, regulatory bodies, and the nonprofit sector.

Eli is the author of *The Complete Handbook of Business Meetings* (AMACOM, 2000), and he has published many articles in business, professional and trade magazines. He has a master's degree in engineering, completed a conflict resolution certificate program, and holds the designations of a Professional Registered Parliamentarian (PRP) and Certified Professional Parliamentarian (CPP).

Contact information for speaking engagements and consulting assignments:

Phone: 604-730-0377
Fax: 604-732-4135
E-mail: eli@elimina.com
Web site: www.elimina.com